Indiana in the Civil War Era

1850-1880

———— • ————

THE HISTORY OF INDIANA

VOL. III

Published in observance of the sesquicentennial of Indiana's statehood in 1966 by the Indiana Historical Society and the Indiana Historical Bureau with the aid of a grant from Lilly Endowment, Inc.

INDIANA
IN THE
CIVIL WAR
ERA
1850-1880

by Emma Lou Thornbrough

INDIANA HISTORICAL SOCIETY
Indianapolis 1989

Reprinted 1977, 1989

The paper used in this publication meets the minimum requirements of American National Standard for Information Sciences—Permanence of Paper for Printed Library Materials, ANSI Z39. 48-1984.

∞

ISBN 0-253-37020-5 cloth
ISBN 0-87195-050-2 paper

PREFACE

The present work is Volume III of a projected five-volume history of Indiana to be published by the Indiana Historical Society and the Indiana Historical Bureau. It deals with the era of the Civil War and Reconstruction, extending from 1850 to 1880. Inevitably there will be some chronological overlapping between the volumes of the history, and I have reached agreements with the authors of those immediately preceding and following mine as to the treatment of certain overlapping subjects. For example, the second Indiana Constitutional Convention, which met during the winter of 1850-1851, will be dealt with in Volume II, while in the first chapter of this volume I deal with certain developments prior to 1850—the status of the Negro, the antislavery movement, and temperance—in order to provide a background for the political history of the 1850's.

The writing of this book raised serious problems of selection and proportion. I have sought—although I may not have succeeded—to avoid writing a book which is a mere compilation of names, facts, and dates. I have tried to present a balanced account, with attention to political, economic, social, and cultural developments. Some readers may feel that a disproportionate amount of space is given to political history, but the period is one in which political developments were of unusual significance.

I have tried to utilize such scholarly writing as has already been done and also to examine basic source materials—published and unpublished—for all major topics. On some subjects much research has already been done but on others nothing of a scholarly nature has been written and it was necessary for me to do basic research and to write my account almost entirely from primary sources. Other scholars have done thorough and painstaking work on political history prior to 1865, but little has been done on the politics of the post Civil War years. Although the period covered by this book is one in which significant economic changes occurred, relatively little research has been done on economic developments. Excellent books dealing with some of the cultural developments of the period have already been published by the Indiana Historical Society and Indiana Historical Bureau. In this book I have not attempted to duplicate the works of Wilbur D. Peat and Arthur W. Shumaker in the fields of architecture and literature. Limitations of time and space have compelled me to treat in cursory fashion some topics which deserve more thorough treatment. I hope that the initial work which I have done will inspire others to make further studies on these subjects.

A number of persons have been of help to me in the preparation of this volume. I am indebted to Alan T. Nolan, who read the first five chapters of my manuscript. He was especially helpful in sharing his great knowledge of military matters with me and in making suggestions which I tried to incorporate into Chapter V. Needless to say any errors in the account of Indiana's part in the Civil War were made by the author (who has no claim to being a military historian) rather than by Mr. Nolan. Donald F. Carmony and Clifton J. Phillips, who are writing volumes II and IV of this series, also made helpful suggestions. Most of the research for the book was done at the Indiana State Library. The entire staff of that institution and especially Hazel Hopper and the other members of the Indiana Division were most helpful, as was Caroline Dunn of the Indiana Historical Society Library. I was fortunate to have the services of a superior typist, Margaret Martin. I owe an especial debt of gratitude to Dorothy Riker and my sister, Gayle Thornbrough, for their meticulous care in editing the manuscript and seeing it through the press. Part of the research for the book was made possible by a Faculty Fellowship from Butler University.

May, 1965   E. L. T.

CONTENTS

ILLUSTRATIONS

MAP

CHAPTER I
ATTITUDES AND ISSUES AT MIDCENTURY

AT THE MIDDLE of the nineteenth century Indiana was still a rural, agricultural state but she was no longer a frontier state. In 1850 she was the seventh state in the nation in population. The overwhelming majority of her inhabitants lived on farms and made their living from the land. In 1850 only 4.5 per cent of the population was in cities of more than 2,500. Madison and North Madison, with a combined population of a little more than 9,000, was the largest city in the state, but the combined population of New Albany and Jeffersonville, which were contiguous to each other, was slightly more than 10,000. Indianapolis, the capital city, located in the center of the state, had slightly over 8,000 inhabitants. The largest concentration of population was still in the towns along the Ohio River, but by 1850 the rate of immigration in the southern part of the state was declining.[1] Most newcomers settled in the central part, where farmlands were superior to those in the southern part where many counties were hilly and less fertile. Indiana was growing so rapidly that an English visitor in 1853 commented: "Towns and cities spring up in this wonderful country like Jonah's gourd. . . ."[2]

But in spite of rapid increase in population many people moving westward, especially European immigrants, by-passed Indiana and settled in the states to the north and west. This, it was believed, was due to ignorance of the opportunities which Indiana had to offer. In 1851 Governor Wright complained that there was "less known abroad, this

[1] See below, pp. 536 ff., for a more complete discussion of population.

[2] *A Friendly Mission. John Candler's Letters from America, 1853-1854* (Indiana Historical Society *Publications*, XVI, No. 1, Indianapolis 1951), p. 44.

day of Indiana, in her great elements of wealth, than any other State in the Union of her age and position." Indianans generally were optimistic over the prospects of their state at midcentury. The worst rigors of the pioneer period were past, and the future looked full of promise. "We have no past," declared a publication launched during the fifties. "No crumbling monuments rear their frowning heads and bid us pause. We are looking forward, not backward, and we feel the fresh life and bounding pulse of youth." "No Western State, we think," rhapsodized one paper, "has more towns that are advancing with greater rapidity than those of Indiana. Railroads and Plankroads, an industrious and growing population, and enterprise and energy, in every pursuit, are developing with astonishing progress her whole Agricultural area and building up at every point demanded by present or prospective Commerce cities which shall be the centre of Manufactures and the heart into which shall pour the flowing and returning arteries of Trade."[3]

Confidence in the superiority of the form of government and institutions of the United States reinforced optimism over the prospects of Indiana. National pride was strengthened by the contrast between conditions in the United States and Europe, which had recently been convulsed by revolutions. "The general prosperity of our beloved country, is a just source of pride and congratulation to every American citizen," Governor Paris C. Dunning asserted with satisfaction in his message to the state legislature in December, 1849. "Whilst some of the oldest governments of the world are tottering to their fall, by the revolutionary spirit of their citizens, our Republican institutions—simple, yet sublime in their structure —based in the affections—identified with the interests—incorporated with the feelings—and sustained by the will of a free and intelligent people—are diffusing over their citizens

---

[3] Indiana State Board of Agriculture, *Annual Report,* 1851, p. 255; *Indiana School Journal* (Indianapolis), I (January, 1856), 3; Madison *Weekly Courier,* November 26, 1851.

the benign influences of domestic quiet, wholesome laws, and the preservation of their civil and religious rights and privileges."[4]

Devotion to the Union was strong in Indiana, and as growing sectional bitterness between North and South created increasing tensions, Indiana leaders and newspapers repeatedly reaffirmed this devotion. During the crisis which led to the Compromise of 1850 the overriding issue in Indiana was the maintenance of the bonds of Union, even if it meant accepting provisions which were unpalatable. Governor Joseph A. Wright, who was undoubtedly the most popular political figure of the fifties and whose utterances probably reflected prevailing opinion as well as did any man's, was especially emphatic in asserting Indiana's devotion to the Union and in denouncing sectionalism. Wright was responsible for the inscription engraved on the block of Indiana limestone which was placed in the Washington Monument in the nation's capital: "Indiana knows no North, no South, nothing but the Union." In his message to the state legislature which met after the adoption of the Compromise, Wright urged Indianans to reject the "ultra-ism" of extremists of both North and South. "Indiana," he repeated, "takes her stand in the ranks, not of *Southern destiny,* nor yet of *Northern destiny.* She plants herself on the basis of the Constitution; and takes her stand in the ranks of American destiny." With his pleas for avoidance of sectionalism Wright sometimes pointed to the growing strength of the West and emphasized that Indiana and her neighbors had a peculiar responsibility in strengthening the forces of Union by acting as a balance between Northeast and South. In an address at Indiana Asbury College in 1850, in which he spoke of the need to inculcate a love for the Union, he said: "The time has now arrived when the influence of the West, in her conservative spirit, should be felt in the settlement of all our national questions."[5]

[4] Indiana *Senate Journal,* 1849-1850, p. 15.

[5] *Ibid.,* 1850-1851, pp. 29, 31; Joseph A. Wright, *An Address Delivered at*

Along with national pride and love for the Union, Indianans also showed evidence of a feeling of western sectionalism. Historically the state had strong ties with the South. Most of the early settlers had come from the South, and economic ties with that region were close. The bonds between Indiana and the East were less strong. Backwoods Indiana tended to look with suspicion and resentment upon the more sophisticated and cultivated and industrial East. These feelings were intensified by the patronizing attitude which Easterners adopted toward Indiana. Yankees enjoyed poking fun at Hoosiers and emphasizing their general backwardness. Evidence of resentment against eastern attitudes abounds in newspaper comments and political speeches. There was a widespread feeling that eastern interests were dominant in Congress and that the West fared badly. A "Convention for the Protection of Western Interests," made up of businessmen and politicians from western states, met in Evansville in 1850 to ask Congressional aid for a number of projects. Resolutions adopted by the convention complained that "Western interests are very little cared for in our National Legislature."[6]

§   §

In politics Indiana was normally a Democratic state, and the Jeffersonian-Jacksonian tradition was strong. Speeches by

the Installation of Rev. L. W. Berry, D. D., as President of Indiana Asbury University, July 16, 1850 (Indianapolis, 1850), p. 15. A convention of delegates from several western states which met in Evansville in 1850 to seek ways of securing aid from Congress for projects of interest to the West, affirmed devotion to the Union. "At all times and under all circumstances," it declared, "our people have been conservative—so far from being either 'secessionists' or 'disunionists'—they have but 'one country, one constitution, one destiny.' Our attachment to the North and to the South is equal." Proceedings of the Convention for the Protection of Western Interests. Held at Evansville, Thursday, November 19, 1850 (Evansville, Ind., 1850), p. 12.

6 Proceedings of the Convention for the Protection of Western Interests, p. 10. Even Ohioans sometimes looked down upon their neighbors to the West. An Ohio newspaper in an editorial declared that the reason that the Republican party fared worse in Indiana than in any other state in the North in 1856 was due to the high degree of illiteracy and ignorance among Hoosiers. Columbus (Ohio) Independent, quoted in Richard Lyle Power,

politicians were full of references to "democracy" and "republicanism" and "equality," and the principles of limited government and devotion to *laissez-faire*. And in fact, the role of government in the lives of the people of the period was very limited. Much of the simplicity of the pioneer era persisted. One English visitor to the United States in the 1850's wrote that he found in reality very little of the "equality" and "democracy" in the United States of which Americans liked to boast, but in Indianapolis he found a greater degree of consistency with these ideals than any other place. Governor Wright, whose annual salary was only $1,500, was a poor man who had put aside opportunities to make money in order to devote himself to public service. His manners and attitudes were those of a "consistent Republican." He did his own marketing and did not consider it a degradation to carry a market basket.[7]

What was praised as "republican simplicity" was sometimes merely a euphemism for niggardliness on the part of the legislators. In his last message to the Assembly in 1857 Wright urged an increase in the salary of the governor, saying it was impossible for the chief executive of the state to perform his necessary functions unless he had a private income. His successor renewed the plea for an increase in the governor's salary but emphasized more strongly the need for more funds for the Supreme Court, which was badly in arrears in its work, with more than nine hundred undecided cases on its docket. Supreme Court judges were required by law to be present in the state capital only sixty days a year, and this was as much time as they could afford to spend on their judicial duties because of their inadequate pay.[8] More striking evidence of

Planting Corn Belt Culture (Indiana Historical Society *Publications*, XVII, Indianapolis, 1953), pp. 83-84. *Yankee Notions,* a periodical which first appeared in New York in 1852, took special delight in lampooning Hoosiers. *Ibid.,* p. 85.

7 Hon. Amelia M. Murray, *Letters from the United States, Cuba and Canada* (two volumes in one, New York, 1856), pp. 323-324.

8 Indiana *Senate Journal,* 1857, p. 69; 1859, p. 17. Governor Ashbel P.

unwillingness to appropriate money was the state of education. In spite of provisions in the 1816 Constitution which declared it the duty of the General Assembly to provide for schools "wherein tuition shall be gratis, and equally open to all," Indiana lagged behind most other northern states in the establishment of free public schools. The high rate of illiteracy was a source of embarrassment, but support for a system of public schools maintained out of taxation was only beginning to gain general acceptance in 1850.

The reluctance of lawmakers to spend money for public services was partly a reaction against lavish expenditures of public money on the ill-fated internal improvements program during the 1830's. It was also a carry-over from the pioneer period in which every one was compelled to fend for himself without aid or hindrance from government. This, combined with a spirit of lawlessness, which was another legacy of the pioneer era, led to a curious effort to maintain law and order through private efforts. Examples of vigilance committees and mob law were common. They were even given legal sanction by a law of 1852 which authorized the formation of companies "for the detection and apprehension of horse thieves and other felons." Under the law companies of private individuals were allowed to organize and were given the rights and privileges of constables in arresting criminals and recovering stolen property. The law, not surprisingly, appears to have led to an increase in mob activity. In various parts of the state there were secret societies which usurped the prerogatives of regulating the morals of communities and so intimidated the local law enforcement officials that they were afraid to restrain them.[9]

In 1859 Governor Ashbel P. Willard reported that many associations had been formed under the Horse Thief Law and had arrested and punished individuals without bringing

Willard, Wright's successor, also urged an appropriation for a library for the use of the Supreme Court.

[9] *Revised Statutes of Indiana,* 1852, I, 318-320; Indiana *Senate Journal,* 1855, p. 34.

them to trial in regular courts of justice. He insisted that all accused persons should be tried in regular courts and asserted that there would be no necessity for such associations if sufficient funds were appropriated to pay sheriffs and police officers.[10] Efforts to repeal the Horse Thief Associations Law were shunted aside. One senator insisted that in his county there was an association which included "some of our best citizens, who believe they have been enabled to render great service to the community in the protection of their property, in the manner allowed by this law." Members who advocated repeal spoke of the "cruelties, murders and unrelenting inhumanities perpetrated under this act." Others admitted that outrages had occurred but insisted that they were not the result of the law.[11]

Associations authorized by the 1852 law were most numerous in the sparsely settled counties in the North, but they were found in all parts of the state. By 1859 there were thirty-eight companies of Regulators in the extreme north. When their activities came under attack, they published a pamphlet in their defense. It insisted that these organizations were necessary in order to shield young people from criminal influences. "If we would have good society, good governments and loyal subjects," asserted the pamphlet, "we should look to the influences that are surrounding the young. And when the arm of the law signally fails to rescue them from the power of these vampires, by tacitly indulging them to roam unmolested, devasting every principle of morality inculcated by parental teaching, there is a law prominently inscribed upon the title page of every man's declaration of rights, an inherent law, a law of his nature, which under such circumstances it becomes his imperitive [sic] duty to obey for the safety and welfare of himself and family." To Noble County, which

10 *Ibid.,* 1859, p. 15. Willard said: "While this class of officers are unpaid, we may expect that an indignant people, who have been outraged by criminals, will disregard the law, and punish without authority those whom [sic] they believe have done wrong."

11 Indiana General Assembly, *Brevier Legislative Reports,* II (1859), 161.

was sparsely settled and a refuge for outlaws, the organization of Regulators was said to have been a "star of hope,— the omen of better days to Northern Indiana."

It was customary for the Regulators to arrest suspected criminals and bring them before a committee where they were examined and urged to confess and give information about their associates. "In some instances, where good advice and gentle means failed to accomplish the desired effect, a more rigid course of treatment was resorted to." In 1858 one group, the Noble County Invincibles, apprehended an alleged murderer. After "a full and fair investigation" they determined that he was guilty and ordered him to be hanged. On the day of the hanging a vast crowd assembled at Ligonier to witness the event. About the same time Regulators held a grand parade at the Old Settlers meeting at Kendallville. Some three hundred men on horseback "moved down in majestic strength," carrying banners. One of them contained a picture of a captured criminal and the words, *"No expense to the county."*[12]

If the state and local governments performed few services, the role of the general government was even more limited. Prevailing philosophy, especially in the Democratic party, emphasized states' rights. Governor Wright sometimes spoke of the Union as a confederacy. He deplored the "vast machinery of the national Government" and especially the increased expenditure of money by Congress.[13] He insisted that

[12] *History of the Regulators of Northern Indiana,* Published by Order of the Central Committee (Indianapolis, 1859), pp. 17, 18, 21, 63. For accounts of other associations organized under the law, see *Constitution and By-Laws of the Newton and Spring Valley Horse Thief Detecting Company* (Indianapolis, 1854); B. J. Griswold, *Pictorial History of Fort Wayne, Indiana* (2 volumes, Chicago, 1917), I, 440; *History of Vanderburgh County, Indiana* (Madison, Wisconsin, 1889), p. 86. Associations of this sort continued to exist for many years. In 1877 a convention of the Wabash Association of Horse Thief Detective Companies met. It included fifty companies in northwestern Indiana and eastern Illinois. Indianapolis *Daily Sentinel,* August 15, 1877. See Chapter VI, pages 270-273, for later instances of mob rule.

[13] *An Address delivered by Gov. Joseph A. Wright, on the 6th Day of October, 1853, at Livonia, Washington County, Indiana, to the District Agri-*

the hopes of the Union rested upon "the adoption of that system of legislation that throws the several States and Territories of the Union more and more upon their own resources, and confines the action of the General Government within the limits defined by the Constitution."[14] Senator Jesse D. Bright, the most powerful Indiana figure in national politics during the fifties, was an equally strict constructionist, who never failed to denounce any sign of usurpation of states' rights by the Federal government or any tendency toward strengthening that government.[15]

Both Wright's and Bright's actions were consistent with their philosophy. But many other politicians of the period, while professing devotion to states' rights and limited government, at the same time sought Federal aid for a variety of projects. Wright complained that "in our day, it seems that he who takes the greatest interest in obtaining the expenditure of millions by the general government, even for local objects, is to be regarded as the successful statesman, and the most worthy of popular applause."[16]

The aforementioned Convention for the Protection of Western Interests which met at Evansville in 1850 was called primarily to seek Federal aid for western development. Judge John Law, an Indiana Democrat, was chairman of the committee which drew up resolutions asking Congress for grants from the public domain "to aid in the prosecution and construction of all legitimate objects of Western internal improvement, national in their character." The resolutions declared that it was the duty of Congress to donate public

cultural *Society, Composed of the Counties of Washington and Orange* (Indianapolis, 1854). See also Wright's message to the legislature in 1850, where, in referring to the Compromise of 1850, he spoke of the crisis which threatened the "integrity of our confederacy of States" and "our compacts with the Great Confederacy." Indiana *Senate Journal,* 1850-1851, pp. 29-30.

14 *Ibid.,* 1855, p. 38. These remarks were made by Wright in defense of the Kansas-Nebraska Act.

15 Charles B. Murphy, *The Political Career of Jesse D. Bright* (Indiana Historical Society *Publications,* X, No. 3, Indianapolis, 1931), p. 114.

16 *Address delivered by Gov. Joseph A. Wright . . . at Livonia,* p. 14.

lands to aid a geological survey of the entire United States, its duty to aid in the establishment of a national school of mines, agriculture, metallurgy, and chemistry, and even its duty to begin experiments on the capacity of steam boilers in order to ascertain the causes of explosions on steamboats.[17]

The Indiana legislature repeatedly asked Congress for appropriations for the completion of a harbor at Michigan City. Federal aid was also requested for improving the navigation of the Ohio River and for a canal around the falls of the Ohio. Interest in railroads led to efforts to secure Federal aid for their construction. At a National Railroad Convention in St. Louis in 1849 Richard W. Thompson, a prominent Indiana Whig, sponsored a resolution which declared that it was the duty of the general government to provide for the building of a railroad from the Mississippi to the Pacific Ocean. The leading Whig newspaper in Indiana expressed the view that a transcontinental railroad should be built by private enterprise, but that it should be aided by government land grants. The Indiana legislature in 1852 asked Congress for a land grant to aid in the construction of a railroad from Anderson, Indiana, to Springfield, Illinois, and thence to Hannibal, Missouri.[18]

§   §   §

Material progress and the demands of a rapidly expanding economy absorbed much of the energy and interests of Indianans at midcentury. Newspapers probably devoted more attention to railroads and their prospects than any other single subject. The novelty of the telegraph was also a source of wonder and amazement, and plank roads in some quarters were being advocated as even more important to the future of Indiana than railroads. But the people were by no means entirely materialistic. To the Puritan East Indiana seemed a

---

[17] See note 5 above; *Proceedings of the Convention for the Protection of Western Interests,* pp. 3-4.

[18] Indiana *General Laws,* 1849-1850, pp. 241, 243; *Special and Local Laws, 1852,* p. 183; *General Laws,* 1853, p. 146; 1861, p. 187; Indianapolis *Indiana State Journal,* November 12, December 3, 1849.

land of infidelity—perhaps because only two Congregational churches were reported in the state in the 1850 census. Episcopalians were not much more numerous than Congregationalists. The Methodist and Baptist denominations were by far the most numerous in the state, but there was a substantial number of Presbyterians, who probably exerted an influence out of proportion to their numbers. Members of the recently founded Disciples of Christ or Christian Church were fourth in number. Quakers were less numerous but were influential in certain parts of the state.[19]

Religion and the Bible were certainly powerful influences in shaping attitudes. Men in public life made frequent references to God and invoked Biblical authority. Governor Wright was a Methodist and very active in the affairs of that denomination. When he entertained foreign visitors, he took them to church on Sunday morning. One visitor, a Hungarian who accompanied Louis Kossuth on his visit to the United States, went with Wright to the Methodist Church. "I saw that Methodism is the form of Protestantism that best suits the people of the West," he wrote. "No glittering formalities, no working on the imagination, not much of reasoning; but powerful accents and appeals to conscience, with frequent references to the Scriptures, interwoven with frequent warnings, pointing to heaven and hell. The audience seemed deeply moved; they sang unmusically, but prayed earnestly. I could not doubt the deep religious conviction of the people." In the afternoon Wright took his visitor on a tour of the Indianapolis Sunday schools. The Governer spoke to each group on the importance of religion as the basis of the social order.[20]

Another visitor, an Englishman, who was taken to the Episcopal Church, felt that observance of the Sabbath was carried to extremes. "The Sunday is kept at Indianapolis, with

19 Power, *Planting Corn Belt Culture*, p. 83; U. S. Bureau of the Census, *Seventh Census of the United States*, 1850, pp. 800-805. See below, pp. 597 ff., for a more detailed account of religion.

20 Francis and Theresa Pulszky, *White, Red, Black: Sketches of American Society in the United States* (2 volumes, New York, 1853), II, 11, 12.

Presbyterian strictness," he found. "No trains start, letters do not go, nor are they received, so that a father, mother, husband, or wife may be in extremity and have no means of communicating their farewells or last wishes if Sunday intervenes. Surely this is making man subordinate to the Sabbath —not the Sabbath to man."[21]

A reference to God was written into the preamble of the new State Constitution of 1851. A group of citizens, while declaring their "hostility to all profane alliances between Church and State," asked that the preamble contain an acknowledgment of "the gracious Providence of God in bestowing upon us the great manifold blessings of a Christian civilization." In the debates in the convention one delegate said it was regrettable that neither the Constitution of the United States nor that of Indiana contained a "direct recognition of that Great and Glorious God, who plants a nation and plucks it up at his pleasure." Other delegates, while protesting their devotion to religion, questioned the propriety of including a reference to God and religion. In the end the convention voted to include in the preamble the words: "We the people of the State of Indiana, grateful to Almighty God for the free exercise of the right to choose our own form of government. . . ." But it is worth noticing that in spite of the prevailing orthodoxy the convention contained two men who were well known as religious freethinkers—Robert Dale Owen and John Pettit. The latter was notorious for his attacks on religion. Both men were elected to the United States House of Representatives in spite of their unorthodox views, and Pettit was elected to the United States Senate.[22]

§   §   §   §

Religious beliefs were influential in shaping public attitudes toward certain of the great questions of the day. The churches

[21] Murray, *Letters from the United States,* p. 322.

[22] *Debates and Proceedings of the Convention for the Revision of the Constitution of the State of Indiana, 1850* (2 volumes, Indianapolis, 1850), I, 852. For the debate on the question see *ibid.,* I, 852-857. Pettit was elected

were deeply involved in the controversy over slavery and the related question of the status of the Negro in American society, and Biblical authority was frequently invoked in the debate over these questions. Religion and the churches were also involved in the temperance question. Since slavery and temperance came to overshadow all other political issues in the fifties, it is appropriate to explore at some length the earlier history of both issues in Indiana.

It has frequently been said that Indianans were more tolerant of slavery and less aroused by the antislavery movement than were people in most northern states. George W. Julian, the most outspoken and influential foe of slavery among political leaders in Indiana, spoke of the state as "an outlying province of the empire of slavery,"[23] but this characterization was not entirely accurate. During the territorial period in Indiana there had been a proslavery element which had successfully contravened the prohibition against slavery in the Ordinance of 1787. But antislavery forces were dominant in the convention which framed the Constitution of 1816. The constitution not only prohibited slavery and involuntary servitude but declared that "no alteration of this Constitution shall ever take place so as to introduce slavery or involuntary servitude." The constitution was interpreted by the Indiana Supreme Court as having extinguished slavery completely. By 1820 vestiges of slavery had virtually disappeared.[24]

It is probably more accurate to describe the dominant attitude in Indiana as neither proslavery nor antislavery but as anti-Negro. There were few persons who wanted to see slavery introduced into the state, but there was widespread

to the United States Senate to fill the vacancy caused by the death of James Whitcomb and served from January 11, 1853, to March 3, 1855.

[23] George W. Julian, *Political Recollections 1840-1872* (Chicago, 1884), p. 115.

[24] For a fuller account of slavery in the territorial period and the Convention of 1816, see Emma Lou Thornbrough, *The Negro in Indiana. A Study of a Minority* (*Indiana Historical Collections*, XXXVII, Indianapolis, 1957), Chapter I.

and intense race prejudice and fear of the competition of Negro labor—due in part to the fact that a large part of the population of Indiana came from the nonslaveholding class of southern whites. The result was a proscriptive code designed to keep the small Negro population in an inferior position and to prevent the settlement of Negroes from the slave states. The severity of the Black Laws, which were copied in large part from the codes of southern states, was remarkable in view of the small size of the Negro population, which at no time before the Civil War constituted more than 1 per cent of the total population.[25]

Both the constitutions of 1816 and 1851 limited the right to vote to white men. Legislation adopted by the territorial legislature and retained in force until 1865 prohibited Negroes from giving testimony in court in a case in which a white man was a party. Intermarriages between white persons and Negroes were forbidden under extreme penalties. These laws defined as "Negro" any person with one eighth or more of Negro blood. Such public schools as there were were exclusively for white children. The Indiana Supreme Court ruled in 1850 that Negro children could not attend public schools even if they paid their own tuition.[26]

Not content with imposing these disabilities upon residents of the state, Indiana lawmakers also sought to prevent more Negroes from moving into the state. There was fear, especially in the counties along the Ohio River, of an influx of superannuated slaves who had been emancipated by their masters and sent to free soil. A law adopted in 1831 required that Negroes who came into the state must post bond, which would be forfeited if they became public charges or were convicted of a crime.[27]

The Constitutional Convention of 1850-1851 debated at length the question of the status of the Negro. The sugges-

[25] Thornbrough, *Negro in Indiana*, p. 44.
[26] *Ibid.*, pp. 21, 119-126, 162-166 and *passim.*
[27] *Ibid.*, pp. 57-59.

tion of one youthful delegate, Schuyler Colfax, that a proposal to give Negroes the right to vote be submitted to a
referendum was brushed aside without receiving serious consideration. Several delegates indulged in extreme expressions
of racism and belief in white supremacy. There was sentiment
in favor of denying Negroes the right to acquire real estate
in the state. This proposal was not adopted but an article was
incorporated in the finished constitution which prohibited
Negroes from coming into the state to settle and which encouraged the colonization of those already resident in the
state. This was Article XIII, which was submitted to the
voters separately and which was ratified by a larger margin
than the main body of the constitution.[28]

The extreme manifestations of racism in the laws of Indiana
undoubtedly reflected prevailing prejudices, but they do not
give a complete picture. It is doubtless true that a majority of the population was convinced of the innate inferiority
of Negroes and was determined that they should be kept forever in a degraded condition. But there was a minority who
opposed the Black Laws and worked actively for their repeal
and also tried in other ways to improve the condition of the
Negro population. Most conspicuous among this group were
the Quakers, especially those in the eastern counties—Wayne,
Randolph, and Henry. Many of them had come to Indiana
from the South, especially North Carolina, because of their
opposition to slavery. Frequently Quaker pioneers were accompanied by their emancipated slaves. Later, fugitive slaves
and other Negroes moving into the state were likely to head
toward Quaker communities, and settlements of Negroes were
often found near Quaker neighborhoods. The Committees of
the Concerns of People of Color of the various Friends meetings assisted Negroes who came into the state and tried to
rescue free Negroes who were sometimes kidnaped from Indiana soil and carried away to be sold into slavery. These
committees helped Negroes find employment and took an in-

28 *Ibid.,* pp. 64-69.

terest in promoting their spiritual welfare and in helping them establish schools.[29]

There were some activities on behalf of the Negro population by other religious groups, but they were less important. However, many Christians who looked upon Negroes as hopelessly inferior creatures, unfit to associate as equals with white men, found it difficult to reconcile slavery with Christian teachings. To these people the idea of emancipating slaves and colonizing them in Africa offered an ideal solution to a difficult problem. The United States could thus rid itself of a population generally regarded as undesirable, and at the same time the emancipated Negroes from America could serve as agents to carry Christianity to African heathen. The American Colonization Society, founded in 1817, included many distinguished Americans among its members. At first it received widespread support throughout the North and upper South by men who genuinely hoped for the ultimate extinction of slavery. The Indiana Colonization Society was organized in Indianapolis in 1829 as an auxiliary to the national society. Its first president, Jesse L. Holman, was succeeded by Judge Isaac Blackford, who held the office for many years. Other well-known men noted for their support of philanthropic enterprises also supported the movement. But from the beginning, support of colonization was linked with the movement to prevent Negroes from settling in the state and with the hope of persuading those already resident in the state to leave and move to Africa. Most of the financial aid of the colonization society came from the churches. In the early period Presbyterians were most generous in supporting it. The first financial contribution to the American Colonization Society from Indiana was made in 1828 by the Kingston Presbyterian Church in Decatur County, a church which was later to be strongly antislavery. While serving as a minister in Lawrenceburg

[29] Thornbrough, *Negro in Indiana,* pp. 33-37, 49-51, 100-102, 167-169. Quakers who were active in helping slaves to escape to free soil made up part of the so-called Underground Railroad in Indiana. Best known of these was Levi Coffin, who had come from North Carolina to Newport in Wayne County. *Ibid.,* p. 43.

Henry Ward Beecher was an active colonizationist. Methodists and Baptists also gave support. Some Quakers were interested in colonization, although from the beginning most members of that denomination opposed the expatriation of Negroes as unrighteous.[30]

The Indiana Colonization Society languished after a few years and became inactive in 1838, but it was revived in 1845. During this second period of its existence it was closely linked with racist doctrines and with political activity. Many politicians embraced colonization as the solution to the problems of slavery and race relations—perhaps because this enabled them to occupy a position in which they simultaneously expressed their abhorrence of slavery and their belief in white supremacy. Almost every session of the Indiana legislature passed a resolution in favor of colonization. In his message to the General Assembly in 1850 Governor Wright pointed out that both southern and northern states were adopting increasingly harsh measures toward free Negroes and urged that Indiana take her stand "in this great struggle for the separation of the black man from the white," as the only means of ameliorating the condition of the unfortunate Negro. Even during the Civil War, as a United States senator, chosen as a member of the Union party, Wright continued to insist that the redemption and regeneration of the American Negro depended upon colonization.[31]

[30] *Ibid.,* pp. 73-77; Marion C. Miller, The Antislavery Movement in Indiana Unpublished Ph. D. thesis in History, University of Michigan, 1938), pp. 50, 57. In 1829 and 1830 the Indiana legislature petitioned Congress to use Federal funds to aid in colonization. The second petition pointed to the "evils attending the alarming increase of colored people in this State." *Ibid.,* p. 47. A report from the Committee on the Concerns of the People of Color for 1836 urged Friends to take no part in movements which tended "to promote the unrighteous work of expatriation." The report of the committee for 1839 also expressed similar sentiments. Thornbrough, *Negro in Indiana,* p. 77.

[31] *Ibid.,* pp. 82, 89-90. The Indianapolis *Indiana Free Democrat,* February 10, 1853, declared, in reply to Wright's message to the legislature in 1853 in which he again urged colonization: "We are no enemy to colonization. As a means of civilizing Africa, spreading the Christian religion . . . we hail it with joy," but not as a means of regenerating and disenthralling American

The Constitutional Convention of 1850-1851 included in the article excluding Negroes from the state a provision that fines collected for violations of the article should be used to colonize Negroes already resident in Indiana. The 1852 legislature passed a law creating a state fund for colonization which remained on the statute books until 1865. Throughout these years a state colonization agent was employed, and a campaign was carried on to persuade and assist Indiana Negroes to emigrate to Africa. As a means of reducing their total number in the state, colonization was a total failure. Negroes simply could not be persuaded to emigrate. Even though they were subjected to heavy disabilities, they were Americans who preferred to remain in the United States rather than accept expatriation. Nevertheless, some Indiana politicians continued to assert that the solution of the race problem lay in colonization.[32]

The colonization movement was based on the assumption that the United States was a white man's country where Negroes could never hope to achieve equality. Colonization propaganda stressed the degraded condition of American Negroes and their alleged inferiority and thereby appealed to race prejudice. As this became apparent, many church members who had at first supported colonization out of humanitarian motives abandoned the movement. In the 1830's many former colonizationists began to support a movement which demanded immediate emancipation of all slaves and the elevation of Negroes to a status of equality in the United States. In 1832 the American Antislavery Society was founded on these principles. It and the many state and local antislavery societies affiliated with it denounced colonization as a scheme which actually strengthened slavery and perpetuated the degradation of free Negroes.

Negroes. During the 1850's the colonization movement assumed an almost exclusively anti-Negro character. But a few antislavery men continued to support it, including Calvin Fletcher, chairman of the Free Soil Central Committee. Miller, Antislavery Movement in Indiana, p. 184.

[32] Thornbrough, *Negro in Indiana,* pp. 82-91.

The militant antislavery movement developed more slowly in Indiana than in Ohio and other parts of the North, partly because race prejudice was apparently more intense in Indiana and partly because no such program of proselyting by antislavery missionaries was carried on in Indiana as was carried on in Ohio.[33] The first antislavery society in the state appears to have been the Decatur County Anti-Slavery Society, which was organized in 1836 by a group which withdrew from the Decatur County Colonization Society. About the same time a group of nine young men at Hanover College formed a society with a constitution which affirmed the right of slaves to be free and to enjoy their freedom in America.[34]

In September, 1838, a State Anti-Slavery Society was organized at Milton, Wayne County. Its statement of purpose included the following: arousing public feeling against slavery by "appeals to the hearts and the consciences of men"; "dissemination of knowledge respecting the evils of slavery, and the duty and safety of immediate emancipation"; and the elevation of the colored population "by promoting their moral and intellectual improvement and by endeavoring to remove the prejudice" against them. The group endorsed the Free Produce movement and agreed to send petitions to Congress asking for the abolition of slavery in the District of Columbia and warning Congress to beware of the schemes of colonizationists.[35]

[33] Ohio had Black Laws similar to those enacted in Indiana, but they were repealed in 1849, and the Ohio Constitutional Convention of 1850 failed to adopt an exclusion article. Illinois, on the other hand, had Black Laws which equalled in their severity the laws of Indiana. Leon F. Litwack, *North of Slavery: The Negro in the Free States 1790-1860* (University of Chicago Press, 1961), pp. 70-74, 93. Theodore Weld, who played a conspicuous part in abolitionizing Ohio, intended to lead a campaign of antislavery proselyting in Indiana in 1836 but was prevented from doing so by a physical collapse. Gilbert H. Barnes, *The Anti-Slavery Impulse, 1830-1844* (New York, 1933), pp. 105-106.

[34] Miller, Antislavery Movement in Indiana, p. 65; Thornbrough, *Negro in Indiana*, p. 76.

[35] *Proceedings of the Indiana Convention, Assembled to Organize a State Anti-Slavery Society Held in Milton, Wayne Co., September 12th, 1838* (Cin-

Meanwhile, numerous local antislavery societies were being formed. At least thirty-four were organized. All the leading Protestant denominations played a part. Most societies were organized in churches, frequently under the leadership of a minister, but their membership was likely to be interdenominational. Leadership was drawn from men of all denominations, many of whom were laymen. There were also examples of antislavery societies made up entirely of women. The two earliest societies mentioned above were formed by Presbyterians, but the largest number of antislavery societies were in counties in which Quakers were especially numerous— Wayne, Randolph, Henry, Rush, Union, Grant, and Jay. One of the early groups was the Neels Creek Anti-Slavery Society in Jefferson County, which was organized in 1839 under the leadership of the Rev. Lewis Hicklin, a Methodist minister. Some Methodists were interested in promoting denominational antislavery societies. An example was the Wesleyan Anti-Slavery Society of Wayne County. In 1841 the Indiana State Wesleyan Anti-Slavery Society was formed. Because the Baptist organization was so decentralized it is difficult to determine to what extent Baptists were involved in antislavery activity, but some churches, such as the Lancaster church in Jefferson County, were hotbeds of abolitionism. As early as

cinnati, 1838) ; Miller, Antislavery Movement in Indiana, pp. 67-68. The Free Produce Movement was begun by Quakers as a method of weakening slavery by refusing to use the products of slave labor. The movement was endorsed by William Lloyd Garrison and by many local antislavery societies. In September, 1838, the American Free Produce Association was founded in Philadelphia with Gerrit Smith as president. In Indiana the Free Produce Movement was closely associated with the Antislavery Friends. In 1842 the Western Free Produce Association was organized by Friends in Union County. Several local organizations were formed in Indiana. Levi Coffin was prominent in the movement and operated a Free Produce store in Cincinnati for a time. The standard work on the subject is Ruth K. Nuermberger, *The Free Produce Movement: A Quaker Protest Against Slavery* (Duke University Press, 1942). See especially pp. 21, 25, 48-51. *The Protectionist* and *Free Labor Advocate* were published in Wayne County, Indiana, as organs of the Free Produce Movement. See *The Protectionist,* Prospectus [1840], p. 9; No. 5, p. 67; *Free Labor Advocate,* 10th month, 15, 1842, and below, note 40.

the 1830's two churches of the Disciples of Christ in southern Indiana — the Silver Creek and Jeffersonville churches — agreed not to have fellowship with groups which sanctioned slavery.[36]

Although the impetus to the antislavery movement was primarily from the churches, the slavery question proved to be a disruptive issue in all denominations. Churches were by no means unanimous in their support of antislavery activity, and in most denominations antislavery men appear to have constituted a radical minority. In the churches, as in politics, they were likely to be looked upon as agitators and troublemakers by conservatives.

The division between Old School and New School Presbyterians, which began in 1837, was partly over slavery, with the former representing a conservative position, while the latter urged that the church indict slavery. In 1843 the New School Presbyterian Synod adopted a resolution prepared by Stephen C. Stevens of Madison, an elder in the church and one of the leading antislavery men in the state, which declared that "emancipation is the best preparation for liberty." The New School Presbyterians of Indiana bombarded every General Assembly of the church with memorials on the subject of slavery. For example, in 1854 the presbyteries of Indianapolis, Elkhart, Madison, and Crawfordsville sent petitions asking the assembly to express opposition to the extension of slavery in the territories. When the General Assembly failed to take action, it was condemned by the Indiana Synod.[37]

36 Miller, Antislavery Movement in Indiana, pp. 69, 75; Thornbrough, *Negro in Indiana,* p. 178; Robert Oldham Fife, Alexander Campbell and the Christian Church in the Slavery Controversy (Unpublished Ph. D. thesis in History, Indiana University, 1960), p. 64. Such minor groups as the United Brethren and Universalists also took strong antislavery positions. Miller, Antislavery Movement in Indiana, p. 198.

37 Miller, *op. cit.,* pp. 113, 226. Henry Ward Beecher, while minister of the Presbyterian Church at Lawrenceburg, was the main speaker at the Fourth of July colonization meeting in that town in 1838. He declared that colonization and abolitionism were totally irreconcilable; that the two were "antipodes of each other," and that the way to get rid of the "evils" of abolitionism was

Among Methodists, who were numerically the most important denomination in Indiana, there were similar dissensions. After the editor of a leading Methodist paper, the *True Wesleyan,* withdrew from the Methodist Church because it did not exclude slaveholders from membership, an Indiana State Wesleyan Anti-Slavery Convention, meeting in Newport in 1843, resolved to secede from the Methodist Church. At a national convention in Utica, New York, that year the Wesleyan Connection of the United States was organized. Several Wesleyan congregations noted for their antislavery zeal were organized in Indiana. At the General Conference of the Methodist Episcopal Church in New York in 1844 a split occurred over the right of members of the clergy to hold slaves which resulted in the withdrawal of most southern conferences. Thereafter there was a tendency to try to avoid giving offense to those southern members who had not withdrawn. This caution was usually reflected in actions taken by the various conferences in Indiana, but not always. In the fifties many Indiana conferences voted to make voluntary slaveholding grounds for refusing church membership. Twelve memorials, bearing 1,797 signatures asking such action, were sent from Indiana to the General Conference which met in Buffalo in 1860. Only one opposing petition, from a quarterly conference in the southeastern part of the state, was received.[38]

The majority of members of the Disciples of Christ sought to avoid direct involvement in the slavery controversy. Alex-

to promote colonization. Paxton Hibben, *Henry Ward Beecher: An American Portrait* (New York, 1942), p. 74. Stephen C. Stevens came to Brookville, Indiana, as a youth in 1812. Later he moved to Vevay before taking up permanent residence in Madison. He served successively in the Indiana House of Representatives, of which he was Speaker, the Indiana Senate, and the Indiana Supreme Court. As a lawyer he defended Negroes in court on several occasions. William W. Woollen, *Biographical and Historical Sketches of Early Indiana* (Indianapolis, 1883), pp. 352-359; Thornbrough, *Negro in Indiana,* pp. 60-61.

[38] Jacob Piatt Dunn, *Indiana and Indianans: A History of Aboriginal and Territorial Indiana and the Century of Statehood* (5 volumes, Chicago and New York, 1919), I, 518; Miller, Antislavery Movement in Indiana, p. 241.

ander Campbell, founder of the Disciples, advised: "Let *political* Abolitionists and political anti-Abolitionists fight this battle themselves; and let Christians do justly, love mercy, and walk humbly with our God, and then our righteousness shall flow as a river, and our peace as the waves of the sea." But other Disciples felt that Christians had an obligation to reform society and play an active part in the crusades against slavery and intemperance. They especially deplored efforts to use the Bible as authority in support of slavery. One prominent Disciple who differed with Campbell over the position which Christians should take in the slavery controversy was Ovid Butler, one of the founders of North Western Christian University, later Butler University. Butler expressed a difference of opinion with Campbell over the obligation to support the enforcement of the Fugitive Slave Law of 1850. Christian Scriptures, said Butler, taught the universal brotherhood of man. This he considered "the radiating point of all Christian faith and Christian duty." How, he asked, could obedience to the Fugitive Slave Law be made to harmonize with this principle?[39]

Differences over how best to deal with the problem of slavery led to a schism in the Indiana Yearly Meeting of Friends. The heart of the dispute was whether or not mem-

[39] Fife, Alexander Campbell and the Christian Church in the Slavery Controversy, pp. 170-177. See the letter of Ovid Butler to Alexander Campbell on the Fugitive Slave Law, March 29, 1851, in the *Millenial Harbinger* (Bethany, Va.), Series IV, Volume I (1851), 430-434. Butler was a native of New York State. While he was a boy, his family moved to Jennings County, Indiana. In 1825 young Butler began the practice of law in Shelbyville. In 1836 he moved to Indianapolis, where he became one of the outstanding lawyers of the city, building up a lucrative practice. One of his partners for a time was Calvin Fletcher, with whom he was also associated in a number of philanthropic and political activities. In 1848 Butler abandoned the Democratic party and allied himself with the Free Soilers. He established the *Indiana Free Democrat* at Indianapolis as the Free Soil organ, and later helped to purchase the Whig *Indiana State Journal* and make it into a Republican paper with antislavery views. *Encyclopedia of Biography of Indiana,* edited by George Irving Reed (2 volumes, Chicago, 1895-1899), II, 42-43. For Butler's part in the founding of North Western Christian University, see below, Chapter XI, pages 518-519.

bers should be active in antislavery societies outside the Society of Friends. In 1841, in an effort to settle the matter, the Yearly Meeting closed meetinghouses to antislavery lectures. In spite of this action some of the more ardent antislavery members, who were most numerous around Newport in Wayne County, continued to be active in antislavery societies. In 1842 the Yearly Meeting "disqualified for usefulness" on important questions eight of the leading antislavery men. This led to an open schism, with the antislavery group withdrawing and forming the Indiana Yearly Meeting of Anti-Slavery Friends. This schismatic group, which included perhaps two thousand of the twenty-five thousand Friends in the state, carried on a vigorous denunciation of slavery and colonization. They were more active than any other group in promoting the Free Produce Movement and in trying to improve the condition of the Negro population of the state.[40]

As early as 1838, when the State Anti-Slavery Society was formed, the question arose as to the extent to which political activity should be used to promote the aims of the society. At that time it was agreed to interrogate candidates for public office as to their views on slavery, but a separate political party was deprecated. In 1839 the Neels' Creek Anti-Slavery Society resolved not to "support men at the ballot box who betray the rights and liberties of northern freemen to win the country and smile of the South," but it did not favor a separate party

[40] The schism continued into the 1850's but some measure of reunion was effected by 1857. A brief account of the schism is given in Thomas E. Drake, *Quakers and Slavery in America* (New Haven, Conn., 1950), pp. 162-165. Walter Edgerton, *A History of the Separation in Indiana Yearly Meeting of Friends* . . . (Cincinnati, 1856), is a detailed account by one of the leading members of the Anti-Slavery Friends. Anti-Slavery Friends and supporters of the Free Produce Movement were associated in the publication of certain antislavery periodicals. The first of these was *The Protectionist,* a semimonthly published during 1840-1841 at Newport in Wayne County by Arnold Buffum, a former president of the New England Anti-Slavery Society. The *Free Labor Advocate and Anti-Slavery Chronicle,* a semimonthly edited at first by Henry H. Way and Benjamin Stanton and later by B. and E. Stanton, was published at the same place from 1841 to 1848. *Jubilee,* another antislavery paper, was also published at Newport during the same period.

on grounds that it would injure the cause of abolition. Some Quakers opposed political activity in the belief that reliance should be placed on spiritual weapons rather than on the ballot, which was a "carnal weapon." However, Indiana members of the Liberty party were sufficiently organized in 1840 to choose presidential electors; they received a total of thirty votes in the November election from four counties—Dearborn, Jefferson, Jennings, and Morgan.[41]

The first state convention of the Liberty party met at Newport in 1841. In 1843 Elizur Deming of Tippecanoe County and Stephen S. Harding of Ripley County were named as candidates for governor and lieutenant governor but polled less than 2,000 votes. In 1844 Harding campaigned vigorously for James G. Birney, the Liberty candidate for President, who received about the same number of votes. Harding, a pioneer abolitionist, was a better-known figure than Deming. He left the Whig party in 1840 because it failed to include a denunciation of slavery in its platform. Harding believed that the United States Constitution was an antislavery document and that the Founding Fathers had not expected slavery to be perpetuated. During the campaign of 1844 he encountered considerable hostility. When he spoke at Versailles he was faced with an armed crowd which threatened violence. At Knightstown that same year he engaged in a famous debate with the state agent for the Colonization Society before a friendly audience composed predominantly of Quakers. Harding flayed his opponent for invoking the Bible and Christianity to support the inhumanity of slavery.[42]

41 Miller, Antislavery Movement in Indiana, pp. 68, 79-80; *The Protectionist*, Prospectus, p. 9; "The First Manumission Society," *Indiana Magazine of History*, VII (1911), 185; *Indiana Election Returns, 1816-1851 (Indiana Historical Collections*, XL, Indianapolis, 1960), p. 37. It is well known that the antislavery movement nationally was split between advocates and opponents of political action. William Lloyd Garrison was bitterly opposed to political action, as were many other New Englanders. Western antislavery men were more likely to support political action.

42 Miller, Antislavery Movement in Indiana, pp. 80, 104, 109; Etta Reeves French, "Stephen S. Harding: A Hoosier Abolitionist," *Indiana Magazine of History*, XXVII (1931), 212-221.

Stephen C. Stevens of Madison, the Liberty candidate for governor in 1846, declared that the abolition of slavery must be accomplished "over the dead bodies of both of the old political parties." By 1848 it appeared that his prophecy might be fulfilled. After the Mexican War the question of whether slavery would be permitted in the territories acquired as the result of that war was a burning issue. As was to be expected, both major parties tried to find a position on slavery extension which would offend as few people as possible. Indiana Democrats and Whigs took the stand that the proposal of David Wilmot of Pennsylvania that Congress should prohibit slavery in any territory acquired from Mexico was premature. Both parties deplored extremism on the slavery question and expressed devotion to the compromises in the Constitution. Richard W. Thompson of Terre Haute, one of the most influential Whigs in the state, expressed a typical Whig position. "Both Northern and Southern ultra groups went too far," he said. "The *ultra* feelings of neither of these parties have yet—to any great extent—reached the West," he said, with satisfaction, in 1847. "Here we occupy a *conservative* position—denouncing slavery as an evil, on the one hand, and admitting all the constitutional rights of the slave states on the other." But Thompson admitted that Congress had the right to control slavery in the territories. He thought the Wilmot Proviso premature but said he would vote for it if compelled to vote on the question. The Democratic state platform of 1848 declared:

Resolved, that the great Democratic Party of the Mississippi Valley knows no North, nor South, but like her noble rivers they comprehend both extremes, and looking to the Constitution of these United States that binds together the extremes of this Union, with its compromises, we regard every and any effort upon the part of the National Legislature (under present circumstances) to bind the future inhabitants of any portion of our territory as to their local institutions or internal affairs . . . as improper, and calculated to create local and sectional divisions and weaken the bonds and ties of this great confederacy.[43]

[43] Woollen, *Biographical and Historical Sketches,* p. 355; manuscript dated

The equivocal position of the major parties was unacceptable not only to Liberty party men but to antislavery Whigs and Democrats as well. The result was the meeting of a "Free Territory" State Convention in August, 1848, which laid the foundation for a third party and elected delegates to attend the convention in Buffalo which launched the Free Soil party. Of these delegates sixteen were former Whigs, fourteen former Democrats, and eight Liberty party men. Stephen C. Stevens of Indiana called the Buffalo convention together at its first session. In the November election of that year Martin Van Buren, the Free Soil presidential candidate, polled over eight thousand votes in Indiana. In three counties the Free Soil vote exceeded the Whig vote, and some other normally Whig counties were carried by the Democrats as the result of the defection of Whigs to the Free Soilers.[44]

After this display of strength by the new party both major parties showed a tendency to embrace Free Soil principles. Leading Whig newspapers expressed a willingness to make the Wilmot Proviso the issue in the next campaign, and the Whig state convention which met in January, 1849, went on record as favoring the abolition of slavery in the territories and in the District of Columbia. Resolutions of the Democratic state convention which met the same month declared that slavery ought not be introduced into any territory where it did not already exist and that it was the duty of Congress to prevent the introduction of slavery into New Mexico and California. In the Congressional contests in 1849, instead of nominating separate candidates, the Free Soil party submitted to the nominees of the major parties a questionnaire to ascertain their position on the question of slavery extension. Nearly

June 8, 1847, in Richard W. Thompson Papers, Indiana Division, Indiana State Library; Indianapolis *Indiana State Sentinel* (semiweekly), January 13, 1848.

44 Miller, Antislavery Movement in Indiana, pp. 139-143; Roger H. Van Bolt, "The Hoosiers and the 'Eternal Agitation', 1848-1850," *Indiana Magazine of History,* XLVIII (1952), 335-338. The three counties were Grant, Jasper, and Lake. *Indiana Election Returns, 1816-1851,* pp. 59, 60, 64, 65.

every candidate of both parties declared himself sympathetic toward the Free Soil position. In eastern Indiana, where anti-slavery attitudes were strongest, George W. Julian, an avowed abolitionist and Free Soiler, was elected to Congress as the result of a fusion with the Democrats of his district.[45] In his message to the legislature in 1849 Governor Dunning, a Democrat, while denying any desire to interfere with the con-stitutional rights of persons in the slave states, declared: "That Congress possesses this power [of prohibiting slavery in the territories] does not admit of a doubt." He added that Congress should exercise this right in order to limit the "bale-ful influence of human slavery," and requested the legislature to pass a resolution to that effect. A resolution adopted in January, 1850, asked that any law which Congress might pass organizing territory acquired from Mexico should contain a provision forever excluding slavery.[46]

In short, at the beginning of 1850, it appeared that both major parties had embraced the Free Soil principles of oppo-sition to the extension of slavery. But events of the next few months were to show that in large part this was due to political expediency. The seeming accord on the nonexten-sion of slavery was irretrievably shattered by the controversy over the adoption of the Compromise of 1850. Expressions of sympathy for Free Soil principles uttered in 1849 were to become a source of embarrassment in the fifties, especially to Democratic politicians.

§ § § § §

At the same time that antislavery forces were carrying on a crusade to convince men of the evil of slavery and the need for

[45] Van Bolt, *op. cit.*, pp. 342-346; Miller, Antislavery Movement in Indiana, pp. 145, 147. Following the election of 1848 the Indianapolis *Indiana State Journal* and the Richmond *Palladium*, both Whig papers, expressed support for the Wilmot Proviso.

[46] Indiana *House Journal*, 1849-1850, pp. 17-18; Indiana *General Laws*, 1849-1850, pp. 246-247. Democrats had a majority in the General Assembly at this session. See also William O. Lynch, "Anti-Slavery Tendencies of the Democratic Party in the Northwest, 1848-50," *Mississippi Valley Historical Review*, XI (1924-1925), 319-331.

political action to extirpate it, a crusade was being waged against strong drink. A typical subject for a student debate in the 1840's was, "Which is the greater evil, Slavery or Intemperance?"[47] Many of the same people who opposed slavery were also identified with the temperance movement. Like the antislavery movement temperance was closely associated with the churches. But while the slavery issue was likely to divide the churches there was no such division over the fight against liquor as there was between colonizationists and immediate abolitionists. The temperance movement did not arouse the antipathies which the slavery controversy engendered. It also had more the character of a fraternal movement than did the antislavery movement and thereby gained support. Like the crusade against slavery the temperance forces expected at first to rely on moral suasion to achieve their aims but later became deeply involved in political activity.

A state temperance society was launched in Indianapolis in December, 1829, a few weeks after the founding of the Indiana Colonization Society. It had the support of some of the most distinguished men in the state. The first president was Judge Jeremiah Sullivan of Jefferson County. Stephen C. Stevens was one of the vice-presidents; James M. Ray was secretary. Stephen S. Harding was a participant. In 1842, the fight against drink took a new form when the Washingtonian movement invaded the state. Members of this society, which had originated in Baltimore among a group of reformed drunkards, were required to take a pledge not to use intoxicants nor to traffic in them and "in all suitable ways to discountenance their use throughout the community."[48]

These early efforts appear to have attracted only a small and sporadic following, but the success of the Sons of Temperance, who first appeared in Indiana in 1845, was spectacu-

[47] Notes for a debate, March 2, 1846, in the Austin H. Brown Collection, Indiana Division, Indiana State Library.

[48] Dunn, *Indiana and Indianans*, II, 1032-1033, 1038-1039; *An Address Delivered to the Washingtonian Temperance Society, at Greencastle, Indiana, by John C. Chiles, December 31st, 1842* . . . (Greencastle, n.d.), p. 14.

lar. This was a secret fraternal organization founded in New York in 1842. It had all of the paraphernalia and appeal associated with secret societies—a ritual, password, regalia, and processions. The first lodge or division in Indiana was formed at Brookville in 1845. By 1848 there were 152 lodges in the state, and by 1850 it was reported that 336 charters had been granted. Influential men in most communities in the state were identified with the organization.[49]

Sons of Temperance were required to be total abstainers. Their constitution forbade members to "make, buy, sell, or use as a beverage, any spiritous or Malt Liquors, Wine or Cider." The interpretation of this prohibition led to some dissension. A question which presented much difficulty was whether sweet cider or merely hard cider was included. There were also questions as to the precise meaning of the term "use as a beverage." The Grand Division ruled that a man who drank whisky after being exposed in a storm must be expelled, declaring: "If we are to allow that members of the Order are to prescribe alcohol as an antidote against the effects of fatigue, and hunger, and cold, we may at once abandon our institution."[50] Members of the Sons of Temperance not only abstained from drink themselves, they also sought to educate the public as to the evils of alcohol and to reform drunkards. *"The drunkard is still a man,"* declared the Grand Worthy Patriarch, highest officer of the order, in an address in 1846. "And being a man, let it be urged that, so long as he

[49] *Proceedings of the Grand Division of the Sons of Temperance of the State of Indiana,* May, 1846-July, 1848, pp. 5, 9, 57, 134; *ibid.,* October, 1850, p. 13. One indication of the strength of the movement is the fact that in 1847 Senator Edward A. Hannegan, who had a reputation for being addicted to strong drink, was reported to have joined the Fountain County Lodge.

[50] *Ibid.,* 1857, pp. 119-120; April, 1849, p. 6. The Brookville Lodge voted in 1847 to expel a member for "drinking sweet cider as it ran from the press," but the Grand Division rescinded the action because at the time the member had first taken the pledge sweet cider had not been interpreted as being included. The question of sweet cider continued to present difficulties, and prohibition of its use was difficult to enforce. A member of one lodge was expelled who drank wine for therapeutic reasons.

is this side of hell's dark cavern, he may be restored to society; and that to make efforts for such restoration is the dictate of Christianity and philanthropy, and one of the leading objects of our association."[51]

Other fraternal organizations were affected by the zeal for temperance. In 1844 the Indiana Grand Lodge of the Masonic Order condemned the "intemperate use of spirits" as contrary to divine law and the rules of morality and as "grossly unmasonic." It recommended to subordinate lodges that they discountenance the use of spirituous beverages by Masons. In 1853 the Grand Lodge declared that it was "highly unmasonic" for any member of the fraternity to be engaged in the manufacture or traffic of intoxicating liquors as a beverage. It declared that it was the duty of subordinate lodges to correct evils of intemperance among their members and to expel those who did not reform after a second admonition.[52]

Temperance organizations used a variety of means to win converts and influence public opinion. There were numerous temperance publications, most of which were short-lived.[53] More spectacular were the temperance camp meetings and festivals at which speakers aroused their listeners to a high emotional pitch by depicting the evils of strong drink. A striking example was a camp meeting held near Crawfordsville in 1851. It began with a parade which included members of

51 *Ibid.,* May, 1846-July, 1848, p. 12. A women's auxiliary, the Daughters of Temperance, was formed in 1849. By 1850 it reported a total of forty-one chapters in the state. There was also a junior organization, the Cadets of Temperance. Charles E. Canup, "Temperance Movements and Legislation in Indiana," *Indiana Magazine of History,* XVI (1920), 18.

52 Dunn, *Indiana and Indianans,* II, 1040.

53 The earliest known temperance publication in Indiana was the *Temperance Advocate,* published in Greencastle by John W. Osborn as early as 1837. *Ibid.,* II, 1043. The Sons of Temperance began the publication of the *Family Visitor* in Indianapolis in 1848. It was a weekly, which included short stories, editorials, poems, and jokes, all stressing the evils of drink. This was succeeded in 1851 by the *Temperance Chart,* which was first a semimonthly, and then a weekly. It, in turn, became the *Temperance Union* in 1854. The Daughters of Temperance published the *Temperance Wreath* in Connersville in 1854, and moved it to Indianapolis the following year.

the Sons of Temperance, Daughters of Temperance, Cadets of Temperance, Washingtonians, and Odd Fellows. According to the account in the *Temperance Chart,* before the meeting began there were nine "liquor hells" in the community, but by the time the meeting ended five of them had been closed and their stocks destroyed. Early in 1852 Indianapolis was the scene of a temperance revival during the course of which several prominent citizens, including Governor Wright, formed the "Social Order of Temperance" and signed the pledge. Meetings were held every evening—in private homes, schoolhouses, the county courthouse, and in the streets. As the result of this intensive campaign it was reported that about nine hundred persons, some of whom were "the hardest cases" in the city, had signed the pledge and joined the order.[54]

More prosaic were efforts by temperance groups to exert pressure on the state legislature. In 1847, partly as the result of their efforts, a law was passed which enabled the voters in a township to prevent the licensing of liquor shops by voting against them in a popular referendum. After the enactment of the law the temperance forces sought to secure a majority of "no license" votes in each township. In 1849 at the meeting of the Grand Division of the Sons of Temperance it was reported that the "no license" ticket had prevailed in many elections, but at the 1850 meeting the tone of the report was rather pessimistic. Many friends of temperance had been defeated at the polls in local elections, especially in commercial centers. In some towns along the Ohio River, it was reported, "our friends have met with disaster and defeats,

[54] *Temperance Chart,* October 1, 1851, February 16, 1852; Indianapolis *Indiana State Journal,* April 13, 1852. During the course of the Crawfordsville meeting one liquor dealer who was persuaded to sign the pledge offered his stock "as a sacrifice to the good cause." Immediately a crowd of temperance workers gathered at his shop, rolled out casks of liquor into the street, and opened them with hatchets, with the result that "mixed liquors ran in a large stream down the gutter." After the revival in Indianapolis a temperance camp meeting was planned in the same city for the following September. Railroads offered to carry passengers at half fare in order to enable people from all over the state to attend. *Temperance Chart,* August 25, 1852.

and the pirate's flag of 'License' has been unfurled in triumph." Meanwhile, at the 1849 meeting it was decided to work to bring an end to the license system and to secure legislation which would "make the traffic in intoxicating drinks a penal offence, placing it where it deserves to be, among the catalogue of crimes." The following year it was claimed that petitions bearing over twenty thousand signatures had been presented to the General Assembly. In the work of sending petitions the Sons were joined by other groups—notably the Methodist churches, in which temperance resolutions by the hundreds were adopted during the late forties. So great was the pressure that in his message to the legislature in 1849 Governor Dunning remarked: "The Temperance cause is one which is deeply agitating the public mind." While admitting that he could not "subscribe to all the ultra views advanced by some of the advocates of this great and glorious cause," Dunning recommended legislation to arrest the vice of drunkenness, a recommendation which the lawmakers failed to follow.[55]

While the pressure from the temperance groups was powerful, there were other pressures which caused the lawmakers to hesitate. Persons with a vested interest in the manufacture and sale of alcoholic beverages, as was to be expected, resisted all restrictive legislation. The Germans, who were becoming increasingly important as a political factor, were also opposed to restrictions. Many other moderate people felt that efforts to extinguish the liquor business completely and to brand the purveyors of drink as criminals were too extreme and would not be enforceable. One such person, in a letter to the *Indiana State Sentinel,* sarcastically remarked that wine and other intoxicants had been used by Christians for two thousand years and that only recently had it been discovered that the producers and sellers of alcohol were "murderers." He declared

[55] *Proceedings . . . of the Sons of Temperance,* April, 1849, p. 6; April, 1850, p. 8; October, 1850, p. 14; Canup, "Temperance Movements," in *Indiana Magazine of History,* XVI, 19; Indiana *Senate Journal,* 1849-1850, p. 28.

that so long as there were people who wanted to consume liquors there would be persons who would cater to their wishes and that restraining legislation would be a dead letter. The surest way "to effect a decided change in regard to the use of alcoholic fluids as a beverage," he concluded, "will be 'persuasion' and *example,* not force or abuse."[56]

§ § § § § §

Some of the same persons who were waging the fight for temperance and who were seeking to release slaves from bondage were also interested in the emancipation of women from the legal disabilities imposed upon them. George W. Julian and other antislavery leaders espoused the woman's rights movement. Amanda M. Way, who instigated the woman's suffrage movement in Indiana, was an active abolitionist, and many other members of antislavery societies were identified with women's rights.[57] But the movement for the emancipation of women had relatively little popular support. Few people took it seriously and many ridiculed it or looked upon it as a dangerous manifestation of radicalism, contrary to the teachings of the Scripture. The prevailing attitude was reflected in the remarks of one of the members of the Constitutional Convention of 1850-1851, who declared that women already had "all the rights which the Bible designed them to have in this Christian land of ours." The occasion for this remark was a debate over the proposals by Robert Dale Owen to put into the new constitution guarantees of the rights of women to hold property. Opponents of Owen quoted many Biblical passages to show that he was "radically wrong." Owen's

[56] Indianapolis *Indiana State Sentinel* (triweekly), January 5, 1850.

[57] Amanda Way of Randolph County is an excellent example of one individual who was prominently identified with all the major reforms. She was not only an active suffragist but also an active antislavery worker and temperance advocate. She is reputed to have been the first woman in the United States licensed to preach by the Methodist Episcopal Church. During the Civil War she served as a nurse in military hospitals. In 1871 she moved to Kansas, where she continued her career as a preacher and reformer. Indianapolis *Star,* February 14, 1923 (clipping in Indiana Biographical Series, I, 10, Indiana Division, Indiana State Library).

efforts failed, but a group of leading women in the state gave a testimonial dinner honoring him for his work in their behalf. These same women, however, were careful to dissociate themselves from the movement which was being launched by a few feminine radicals to give women the same political rights as men. In a communication which they sent to the press in connection with the Owen dinner they declared that they deprecated "the efforts of those of our sex who desire to enter the political arena—to contend with men at the ballot box, or sit in our public councils. . . ."[58]

A more militant group of women met at Dublin in Wayne County in October, 1851, and organized a Woman's Rights Association, declaring "that unless women *demand* their rights politically, socially and financially, they will continue in the future as in the past, to be classed with negroes, criminals, insane persons, idiots and infants." The constitution adopted at this first meeting provided for annual meetings at which there should be reports on "Woman's Labor and Remuneration, Woman's Legal Condition, Woman's Social Position, and Woman's Education." Thereafter local societies were organized, and annual conventions were held regularly at which the delegates made and listened to speeches on the status of their sex and passed resolutions. One of the principal resolutions declared: "while we will make all due efforts in other ways to 'elevate woman,' the right of suffrage is, in our opinion, the basis of our enterprise, since we do not seek to place woman under man's protection, but to give her the power to protect herself." Other resolutions condemned the usages of society which barred women from entrance into

[58] *Debates and Proceedings*, I, 815-819; Indianapolis *Indiana State Sentinel* (triweekly), December 10, 1850. The efforts of Robert Dale Owen in behalf of woman's rights in the convention are well known but have frequently been misunderstood. As early as 1847 the Indiana legislature had granted married women the right to devise property and to control real estate. Indiana *General Laws*, 1846-1847, pp. 45-46, 108. In the Constitutional Convention Owen sought to supplement these rights by extending them to include personal property and to safeguard them by writing them into the constitution. Richard W. Leopold, *Robert Dale Owen, A Biography* (Cambridge, Mass., 1940), p. 273.

institutions of higher learning and into the professions, and declared that members of both sexes should be educated together, "without selection of studies or limitations of time on account of sex." It was also declared that labor should be rewarded, not according to the sex of the worker, but according to the work performed.[59]

At one convention a male speaker quoted certain Biblical passages regarding the duty of a wife to submit to her husband as a reply to some of the women's demands. Thereupon one woman answered that Paul and Peter "wrote for other times than ours," and asked whether Democratic and Whig politicians felt themselves bound by such Biblical commands as "Honor the King." After this session the leading Whig newspaper in the state spoke disapprovingly of the tendency of the women "to underrate or reject the authority of the Bible and its claim to inspiration."[60]

The climax of the woman's rights movement in the period preceding the Civil War was reached in 1859 when a petition was presented to a joint session of both houses of the state legislature. Dr. Mary F. Thomas presented the petition, bearing the signatures of more than one thousand men and women, which asked for equal political rights for women and for the abolition of all legal enactments which made a distinction on account of sex. This was the first time that a woman had spoken before the legislature. The men listened politely and referred the petition to a committee, which reported back that in the opinion of the majority it would be inexpedient to legis-

[59] Preamble and Constitution, Minutes of Woman's Rights Association of Indiana 1851-1881 (Typewritten MS, Indiana Division, Indiana State Library); Indianapolis *Indiana Free Democrat,* November 2, 1854. Conventions were held as follows: at Dublin, 1851; Richmond, 1852 and 1853; Indianapolis, 1854 and 1855; Winchester, 1856 and 1857; Richmond, 1858. From 1859 to 1867 the organization was dormant. Lucy Stone addressed some of the conventions of the 1850's. Harvey L. Carter, A Decade of Hoosier History: Indiana, 1850-1860 (Unpublished Ph. D. thesis in History, University of Wisconsin, 1938), pp. 373, 374.

[60] Indianapolis *Indiana Free Democrat,* November 26, 1854; Indianapolis *Daily Journal,* quoted *ibid.*

late on the subject.[61] The woman's rights movement had little impact upon Indiana politics, but the antislavery and temperance forces were major forces in causing a political upheaval and realignment of parties in the fifties, as will be shown in the next chapter.[62]

[61] Minutes of Woman's Rights Association, pp. 43-44; Indiana *House Journal,* 1859, pp. 157, 182, 472. Mrs. Mary F. Thomas of Richmond was a doctor of medicine and the first woman delegate to the Indiana State Medical Association as well as the first woman to address the legislature. Kate Meehan Cox, The History of Woman's Suffrage in the State of Indiana, 1816-1883 (Unpublished Master's thesis in History, Indiana University, 1927), p. 72.

[62] Some of the same persons who were interested in the antislavery and temperance movements were also interested in the peace movement. A convention of delegates from various parts of the state met in Indianapolis in June, 1851, to pass resolutions approving the objects of the World Peace Convention which was to meet at Frankfurt-am-Main in 1851. Jeremiah Sullivan was president of the convention, Stephen C. Stevens was one of the vice-presidents, and James M. Ray was secretary. Indianapolis *Indiana State Sentinel,* June 15, 1851.

CHAPTER II

POLITICAL REALIGNMENTS
IN THE FIFTIES

INDIANA POLITICS in the fifties was a serious and time-consuming business and at the same time a source of diversion and recreation. A Methodist clergyman from Great Britain who happened to be a guest of Governor Joseph A. Wright during the campaign of 1856 commented upon the extreme partisanship of the persons whom he met in Indianapolis. "Though moderate and temperate men in other matters," he remarked, "in politics they are most resolute and determined," displaying "no forebearance towards others who are forward to proclaim political convictions." They were wont to praise outrageously public men and newspapers of their party and to castigate unsparingly their opponents. "Unflinching adherence to party is principle with them," he observed, "and to forsake a party is regarded as an act of the greatest dishonour."[1]

Feelings probably ran higher in 1856 than usual, but the observations would have applied to any political campaign of the decade. Although the major political parties contained within their ranks the most diverse elements, and although intra-party feuds were many and bitter and complex, they tried to present a united front to the opposition. The newspapers from which the views of the voters were presumably shaped were almost without exception strongly partisan. Publishers and editors were nearly always closely associated with a party organization, and the financial success of many papers depended upon political subsidies.

Politicking went on almost continuously. Under the first state constitution the governor was elected for a three-year

[1] Frederick J. Jobson, *America and American Methodism* (New York, 1857), pp. 116-117.

term, which meant that presidential and gubernatorial campaigns seldom coincided. Under the new constitution governor and President were elected in the same year, but other state officers were elected every two years, and some local elections were held in the intervening years. Nominations were made far in advance of election day. Local conventions were held to draw up resolutions to instruct district and state conventions, and then meetings were held to ratify the actions of state and national conventions. Pre-election campaigns were marked by rallies, torchlight parades, barbecues, and other jollifications which formed an important part of social life. People traveled many miles to hear speakers. Railroads sometimes offered half fares for persons attending political rallies. Most of these were day-long affairs. It was the heyday of political oratory, and speaker after speaker would regale the audience for two or three hours. Sometimes there was violence when rowdies from the opposing political camp appeared to heckle or even break up meetings. One custom which tended to have a moderating effect upon the speakers and to bring an element of reason into the campaigns was the joint canvass which was often made by candidates for the higher offices—especially the governorship and Congressional seats. Opposing candidates frequently traveled together and spoke from the same platform. For example, in 1852 within less than two weeks the two candidates for governor made joint appearances in eighteen towns in southeastern Indiana.[2]

Looseness of election laws led to many irregularities on election day. The evils most constantly complained of were vote buying, the importation and "colonization" of voters, and the stuffing of the ballot box. The Constitution of 1851 (Article II, section 2) gave the right to vote to white male citizens over twenty-one who had resided in the state for six months and to white males of foreign birth who had resided

[2] Carter, Decade of Hoosier History, p. 79. For the speaking itinerary of Oliver P. Morton, gubernatorial candidate in 1856, see Logan Esarey, *A History of Indiana from its Exploration to 1922* (2 volumes, Fort Wayne, Ind., 1924). II. 647n.

in the United States for one year and in Indiana for six months and had declared their intention of becoming United States citizens. The law governing elections contained loopholes and omissions which made honest elections virtually impossible if there were persons who wished to commit fraud. The law required the voter to vote in the township or precinct in which he resided, and inspectors were required to swear that they would "not knowingly" permit an unqualified person to vote, but there was no provision for voter registration and no guarantee that election boards would be bipartisan. Voting was by ballot, but although the state furnished locked ballot boxes, the ballots were furnished by the candidates themselves or the parties. Candidates tried to have their ballots printed on a distinctive type and color of paper—a practice which made it easy to determine whether or not voters voted as they were paid to do.[3]

In every election, with monotonous regularity, both parties accused their rivals of fraud. In the contest of 1856 charges were especially bitter. The outcry, in a year in which the whole country was aroused over illegal voting in Kansas, was sufficiently loud that outgoing Governor Wright and incoming Governor Willard both asked for legislative action. Governor Wright declared that the recent elections had convinced him that, "unless some effectual means can be adopted to protect the elective franchise from corruption and desecration, our

---

3 Indiana *Revised Laws,* 1852, I, 260-267. The law provided that when a person offered to vote, the inspector was to pronounce his name "in an audible voice," and if there were no objections, to permit him to vote. Any person who offered to vote might be challenged by any qualified voter. If challenged, he was required to swear that he was twenty-one years old, had met the residence requirement, was generally known by the name under which he sought to vote, and that he had not voted at any other polling place during the present election. If during the counting two ballots were found "purposely folded together," they were to be rejected. One method of fraud was to obtain some of the distinctive paper which a candidate used for his ballots and have other names printed on it and give these ballots to the unsuspecting voter. See Indianapolis *Daily Sentinel,* May 11, 1857, for charges that this was done in the mayoralty election in Indianapolis.

institutions will soon be at the mercy of an unlicensed mob."
He also asked for penalties against betting on elections, which
he said was a growing evil. Two years later Willard referred
to the common practice of men voting in counties where they
did not reside and said that frequently election officials connived at the practice. But the legislature ignored the requests
of Wright and Willard for penalties for such practices and
also ignored a similar plea from Abram A. Hammond, the
next governor.[4]

At the beginning of the decade of the fifties the Democrats
were clearly the dominant party in the state. Only twice—in
1836 and 1840—had Indiana cast its electoral vote for a
Whig. After a brief interlude of Whig rule Democrats had
regained control of the state legislature in 1842 and of the
governorship in 1843 and had continued their hold. In 1850
all state officers were Democrats and the legislature was
under Democratic control. Both United States senators were
Democrats as were eight of the ten members of the United
States House of Representatives. Approximately two thirds
of the members of the Constitutional Convention elected in
1850 were Democrats.

Democrats were steeped in the Jeffersonian-Jacksonian tradition of strict interpretation of the Constitution, limited government, economy, a low tariff, and opposition to monopolies.[5]
While there was general agreement as to these principles,
there was much feuding within the party between factions and
personalities. During the fifties the two most important personalities were Joseph A. Wright—governor from 1849 until
1857—and Jesse D. Bright, who was elected to the United
States Senate for three terms, serving from 1845 until 1862.
Wright was certainly one of the most popular politicians in
the history of the state. His was the proverbial, but not
unusual story, of the poor boy who made good through his

[4] Indiana *Senate Journal,* 1857, p. 61; 1859, p. 18; 1861, p. 20.

[5] For a statement of principles and measures that received the support of
the Democrats, see Indianapolis *Indiana State Sentinel,* January 1, 1850.

own efforts. Wright liked to tell of his early struggles as a poor farm boy who had come to Indiana from Pennsylvania with his parents and had worked as a janitor while attending Indiana University. Part of his political appeal lay in his indentification with causes which had widespread popular support. He was interested in promoting agriculture and was a colonizationist and a friend of temperance. In religion he was a Methodist. In spite of his personal popularity, his influence in the Democratic organization was limited. "He was strong with the people, but weak with the leaders," a contemporary observed.[6]

Wright was no match with Bright as an organizer or manipulator, nor was he the ruthless fighter the Senator was. Bright was another self-made man. Born in New York, he had come to Madison as a boy and had made a fortune through his own efforts. Among his numerous holdings were lands in Kentucky worked by his slaves. In spite of limited education and some crudities of speech and manner he quickly rose to the top in Indiana politics. He was elected lieutenant governor in 1843 at the age of thirty-one, winning a larger number of votes than the candidate for governor. In 1845 he was elected to his first term in the United States Senate. For years he maintained autocratic control over the Indiana Democracy, not so much through popular support as through his ability to organize a machine loyal to himself and because he had ample financial resources. Imperious in manner, he "brooked no opposition either from friend or foe." A "foe" was one "who would not do his bidding," and in his eyes the only test of loyalty to the Democracy was loyalty to Jesse Bright. His dislike and contempt for Wright were unbounded. In the Senate he acquired power as the result of seniority and organizational ability. He became president pro tem. in 1854

6 Woollen, *Biographical and Historical Sketches,* p. 101. For a detailed treatment of Wright's early life, see Philip M. Crane, Onus with Honor: A Political History of Joseph A. Wright, 1809-1857 (Unpublished Ph. D. thesis in History, Indiana University, 1961).

and was seriously mentioned as a presidential possibility in 1856.[7]

The Whig minority in the state lacked cohesiveness and principles except insofar as they were drawn together by their common distaste for the Democracy and their admiration for Henry Clay. Whigs tended to be townspeople of substance— bankers, lawyers, and businessmen. There were likely to be differences between the Whigs of the northern and southern part of the state over such issues as internal improvements and slavery, and the result was that the party usually tried to avoid national issues and to concentrate on local questions and personalities.[8]

There were no state-wide Whig leaders with influence comparable to that of Bright, or even Wright. One of the most important men in the party was John D. Defrees, who was successively a printer, lawyer, newspaper editor, and banker. He was a native of Tennessee who had moved to Indiana by way of Ohio. After practicing law in South Bend, he moved to Indianapolis, where he published the Indianapolis *Journal,* the most influential Whig organ, from 1846 to 1854. In 1852 he was chairman of the Whig Central Committee and two years later one of the most powerful figures in the emerging Republican party.[9] In Crawfordsville was Henry S. Lane, another lawyer and banker, who had made a brilliant record in the Mexican War after serving one and a half terms in Congress in the early forties. He had spent his youth in Kentucky, where he had developed a lasting devotion to Henry

[7] Woollen, *Biographical and Historical Sketches,* p. 223; Wayne J. Van Der Weele, Jesse David Bright, Master Politician from the Old Northwest (Unpublished Ph. D. thesis in History, Indiana University, 1958), *passim.* For an account of the feud between Wright and Bright see especially *ibid.,* pp. 96-98.

[8] See, for example, the letter of Godlove S. Orth to Schuyler Colfax in J. Herman Schauinger (ed.), "The Letters of Godlove S. Orth, Hoosier Whig," *Indiana Magazine of History,* XXXIX (1943), 367-368, in which he advocated a policy of "stooping to conquer" by abandoning "high-strung Whig doctrine" and appealing to local prejudices in order to win office.

[9] Woollen, *Biographical and Historical Sketches,* pp. 485-487.

Clay. Like his hero, he was a colonizationist, opposed to agitation on slavery, but unlike Clay was an ardent temperance man.[10] Another promising young Whig was Schuyler Colfax, editor of the South Bend *Register*. He was of Yankee origin and more inclined to antislavery views than Defrees or Lane. In the Constitutional Convention of 1850-1851 he was one of a tiny handful who opposed the restrictions which the constitution imposed upon Negroes. But, somewhat ironically, he later embraced nativism and was secretly a member of the Know Nothing party.[11] Perhaps the best example of genuine Whiggery in the state was Richard W. Thompson of Terre Haute. Virginia-born and reared, he was described as a "gentleman of the old school" and one of Indiana's best orators. He was a strong advocate of government aid to railroads and even more strongly opposed to agitation against slavery. His scorn of abolitionists was unbounded, and as a member of Congress he had refused to vote for a resolution asking for the introduction of a bill to prohibit slave trade in the District of Columbia. After the eclipse of the Whig party as a national organization, Defrees, Lane, and Colfax all moved into the nascent Republican or People's party in 1854. But Thompson embraced the Know Nothing or American party as more nearly embodying true Whig principles. In 1860 he supported the Constitutional Union party and became a Republican only after the outbreak of the Civil War.[12]

[10] Woollen, *Biographical and Historical Sketches*, pp. 120-129; Walter R. Sharp, "Henry S. Lane and the Formation of the Republican Party in Indiana," *Mississippi Valley Historical Review*, VII (1920-1921), 98; James A. Woodburn, "Henry Smith Lane," *Indiana Magazine of History*, XXVII (1931), 279-287; and sketch of Lane in *Dictionary of American Biography, Authors Edition* (20 volumes and Index, New York, 1928-1936).

[11] Willard H. Smith, *Schuyler Colfax. The Changing Fortunes of A Political Idol* (*Indiana Historical Collections*, XXXIII, Indianapolis, 1952) is a scholarly, impartial biography.

[12] Charles Roll, *Colonel Dick Thompson. The Persistent Whig* (*Indiana Historical Collections*, XXX, Indianapolis, 1948) is a sympathetic political biography.

The decade of the fifties saw a political upheaval which toppled the Democrats from their long ascendancy and which saw the Whig party disappear but rise again in a sense stronger than ever as a powerful influence in the new Republican party. The slavery question was an important but by no means the only factor which precipitated this new alignment. In 1849, as noted earlier, both major parties had taken a position against the extension of slavery. This was due in part to the strength which the Free Soilers had shown in 1848 and in part to the bitterness which Democrats felt at the support which normally Democratic voters in the South had given to the slaveholder, General Zachary Taylor, in 1848. In January, 1850, a state meeting of Whigs adopted a series of resolutions in which they expressed opposition to the extension of slavery in the territories while at the same time abjuring any right to interfere with slavery in states where it existed. The *Indiana State Sentinel,* the most important Democratic paper, under the editorship of Jacob P. Chapman, took a strong antislavery position. Slavery, it declared, was a curse and "the creature of *special legislation* and a *local* and State institution, that shall not be extended into the free territories of the common domain, *where it is not.* . . . On this point the Democracy of the free states are *fixed stars,* whose light will guard and protect *free soil* for the inheritance of free men, and *free labor."* About the same time Democratic Representative Graham N. Fitch, in a speech in the House of Representatives, attacked the proslavery forces in Congress for their aggressiveness and their threats of disunion over admitting California as a free state.[13]

But developments during the next few months brought a marked change in tone in utterances by leaders of both parties. In the face of what appeared to be genuine threats of disunion during the critical 1850 session of Congress, people

[13] See Chapter I, pp. 25-28; Indianapolis *Indiana State Journal,* January 21, 1850; Indianapolis *Indiana State Sentinel,* January 5, March 9, 1850. See also Lynch, "Anti-Slavery Tendencies of the Democratic Party . . . 1848-50," *Mississippi Valley Historical Review,* XI, 319-331.

in Indiana as well as their representatives in Congress drew back in alarm and urged a spirit of compromise and conciliation toward Southerners who were aroused over the question of California and the possible exclusion of slavery from the remainder of the Mexican cession. Clearly with most Indianans devotion to the Union and the desire to avoid disruptive controversy were stronger than their desire to limit slavery expansion, which they regarded as something of an abstraction in view of the climate and geography of the territories involved.[14]

Free Soil views of the *Indiana State Sentinel* went into sudden eclipse in May, 1850, when the paper was sold to William Austin Brown, Democratic representative in Congress from the Indianapolis district. It was rumored, although indignantly denied, that Jesse Bright had contributed to the purchase in the hope of having an organ to build up support for his re-election to the Senate in 1851.[15] Bright himself served as a member of the committee of thirteen headed by Henry Clay which framed the "omnibus bill" embracing the measures which were ultimately adopted individually and known as the Compromise of 1850. The views expressed by him on the floor of the Senate probably reflected the views of most of his constituents. "Sir, I am not mistaken," he asserted, "when I declare that the sound-thinking practical men of the great and growing West of all parties, are tired

[14] Most Indianans also viewed with apprehension and distaste the views of the southern extremists. When John C. Calhoun, most intransigent of the Southerners, died during the session, one Hoosier observed: "The great southern agitator is no more, and I hope the doctrine that slavery is a divine right & political blessing will end with him. . . . I think we shall hear less hereafter about *disunion*, and in view of this desireable [*sic*] end, Mr. Calhoun can well be spared." George W. Ewing to Allen Hamilton, March 31, 1850. Allen Hamilton Papers, Indiana Division, Indiana State Library.

[15] Indianapolis *Indiana State Sentinel*, June 19, August 28, 1850. In commenting on the sale of the *Sentinel*, the *People's Friend* of Covington spoke highly of George and Jacob Chapman, the former publishers, but said, "An unfortunate penchant, recently exhibited, for free soilery, has alienated them to some considerable extent in the affections of many of the simon-pure democracy." Quoted, *ibid.*, May 25, 1850.

of this eternal agitation." He urged taking "a great middle conservative course," and after the Compromise was completed he declared: "I now endorse it, broadly, distinctly, and emphatically."[16]

It is not recorded that Bright voted for the Fugitive Slave bill, but he voted for all of the other Compromise provisions, and his colleague, James Whitcomb, voted for the entire Compromise. Five of the Indiana House members were recorded as voting against the Fugitive Slave bill. Edward McGaughey, the only Whig in the Indiana delegation, voted for the measure.[17]

Back home Governor Wright lost no opportunity to emphasize Indiana's devotion to the Union and the need for moderation. In June, when Governor Crittenden of Kentucky paid a much publicized visit to Indianapolis, Wright spoke against sectionalism, agitation, and extremism. Standing arm in arm with Crittenden, he declared he "knew no North, no South, nothing but the common brotherhood of all, working for the common good." In an address at Indiana Asbury University in July, 1850, Wright spoke in similar vein. "Let us not be alarmed at the word *compromise*," he said, and he advised his listeners to "renounce all sectional parties—sternly rebuke any and every effort to form a northern party!"[18]

Although public opinion was generally favorable to compromise, the Fugitive Slave measure was extremely objection-

[16] Roger H. Van Bolt, "The Hoosiers and the 'Eternal Agitation,' 1848-1850," *Indiana Magazine of History*, XLVIII (1952), 358; Murphy, *Jesse D. Bright*, p. 117. Richard W. Thompson, the Whig leader, had written to Bright, urging him to support the Compromise "as a peace offer upon the altar of the Union" and had strongly defended the Fugitive Slave bill. Roll, *Colonel Dick Thompson*, p. 141. See Holman Hamilton, *Prologue to Conflict. The Crisis and Compromise of 1850* (University of Kentucky Press, 1964), for a recent treatment of the Compromise.

[17] Van Bolt, "The Hoosiers and the 'Eternal Agitation,'" *Indiana Magazine of History*, XLVIII, 361; Van Der Weele, *Jesse David Bright*, p. 72; Indianapolis *Indiana State Sentinel*, September 21, 1850.

[18] *Address . . . at . . . Asbury University, July 16, 1850*, p. 16; Indianapolis *Indiana State Sentinel*, June 1, August 17, 1850; A. Dale Beeler, "The Election of 1852 in Indiana," *Indiana Magazine of History*, XI (1915), 302.

able to many. The Indiana congressmen who voted for it no doubt felt that it was the price which they had to pay for preserving the Union and the Democratic party. But many men thought the price was too high. Antislavery men not only protested the law as inhuman but announced their intention of refusing to obey it. On the Sunday after the law was adopted, the minister of the Kingston Presbyterian Church closed his sermon by saying: "To law framed of such iniquity I owe no allegiance. . . . I will act with any body of decent and serious men . . . in any mode not involving the use of deadly weapons, to nullify and defeat the operation of the law." The Indiana Methodist Conference "cordially approved" an editorial in the *Western Christian Advocate* condemning the law. The Centerville *Indiana True Democrat,* organ of the Free Soilers, branded it an "infamous" and "Heaven daring act" and declared that it "must be treated as a nullity." Numerous protest meetings were held in antislavery strongholds. A meeting of "friends of freedom" in Centerville, which was addressed by George W. Julian, repudiated "with scorn every settlement of the slavery question which is arrived at by yielding of rights on the part of the North to the supercilious demands of Southern slaveholders." The "blood hound Fugitive Slave Bill" they intended to make powerless by their "absolute refusal to obey its inhuman and diabolical provisions."[19]

Some Democratic newspapers were outspoken in their denunciation of the law. The Lafayette *Courier* cried out that there had never been enacted "a more atrocious law." W. R. Ellis of the Goshen *Democrat* called William J. Brown of the *Indiana State Sentinel* a "doughface" for voting for the bill. "The moment the policy of the bloody bill is fastened upon the Democracy of Indiana," warned the *Indiana Statesman,* "that moment we go into a minority." The Mad-

[19] Miller, Antislavery Movement in Indiana, p. 180; Indianapolis *Indiana State Sentinel,* November 5, 1850; Centerville *Indiana True Democrat,* October 11, November 8, 1850.

ison *Courier* called the law "repugnant to all the feelings of a man living in a free state."[20]

The *Sentinel* accused these papers of trying to disrupt the Democratic party and called for upholding all the Compromise measures as the "final" solution to the slavery controversy, warning that "the majority [the North] must protect the constitutional rights of the minority [the South], or the minority will lose all attachment to the Union." It was "worse than useless," the *Sentinel* insisted, to preach against slavery without providing some sort of a remedy for the evils which would stem from its abolition.[21]

The adoption of the Compromise and the fear that further agitation on slavery would disrupt the party brought an end to the trend toward an alliance between Democrats and Free Soil men which had seemed apparent in 1849. In his message to the legislature in December, 1850, Governor Wright sought to assure the South that Indiana would live up to her constitutional obligations. "Our compacts with the Great Confederacy to which we belong," he said, "have been faithfully kept in letter and in spirit." Once again he reiterated: "Indiana takes her stand in the ranks, not of *Southern destiny*, nor yet of *Northern destiny*. She plants herself on the basis of the Constitution. . . ." In the Constitutional Convention meeting in Indianapolis during the winter of 1850-1851, delegates from both parties overwhelmingly endorsed the Compromise and declared that it was the duty of all good citizens

20 Lafayette *Courier*, quoted in Indianapolis *Indiana State Journal*, October 17, 1850; Indianapolis *Indiana State Sentinel*, August 7, 1850; Indianapolis *Indiana Statesman*, quoted *ibid.*, November 21, 1850; Madison *Daily Courier*, October 23, 1850, quoted in Frank S. Baker, "Michael C. Garber, Sr., and the Early Years of the Madison, Indiana, *Daily Courier*," *Indiana Magazine of History*, XLVIII (1952), 400.

21 Indianapolis *Indiana State Sentinel*, October 19, 1850. The leading Whig paper was less warm in its endorsement of the Fugitive Slave Law than its Democratic rival. It admitted that the law was wrong and should not have been enacted, but said that so long as it was the law of the land it should be enforced. Indianapolis *Indiana State Journal*, October 21, 1850.

"to carry out, in good faith, the conditions of that compromise on the subject of domestic slavery."[22]

The Terre Haute *Journal* no doubt spoke the truth when it declared: "The negro fanaticism which prevails to such an alarming extent in many of the Northern States, has but few devotees in Indiana, and those who are tinctured with the abolition malady are in a great measure prevented from carrying their opinions into practice by the immense preponderance of public sentiment in favor of sustaining the compromises of the constitution, the laws of the land, and the rights of our southern brethren." But although those "tinctured with the abolition malady" were in a minority, they were a dedicated and vocal minority, and they continued to make the Fugitive Slave Law the prime target of their attack. In spite of the strength of the "finality" movement, in its operation the law actually had the effect of strengthening antislavery sentiment in the state.[23]

Although the number of runaway slaves was not large, the sight of one nearly always aroused sympathy. The *Indiana Free Democrat* estimated nine tenths of the residents of Indiana would at least "give a crust of bread and a cup of water to a weary fugitive. . . ." In 1852 persons heretofore indifferent as to the plight of the slave were emotionally aroused as the result of reading *Uncle Tom's Cabin*, which

[22] Indiana *Senate Journal,* 1850-1851, pp. 29-31; *Journal of the Convention of the People of the State of Indiana to Amend the Constitution, Assembled at Indianapolis, October, 1850* (Indianapolis, 1851. Reprinted by offset process by the Indiana Historical Bureau, 1936), pp. 331-332.

[23] Terre Haute *Journal* quoted in Indianapolis *Indiana State Sentinel,* November 21, 1850. A state Christian Antislavery Convention in 1851, which included representatives of Friends, Presbyterians, Baptists, and Wesleyans, declared that the law was "unconstitutional and inhuman" and called for disobedience to it by every person unwilling to "wear the chain and submit to the lash of southern despots." Indiana antislavery men attended Christian Antislavery Conventions in both Cincinnati and Chicago in 1850 at which the law was excoriated. In a speech at the Chicago convention Stephen C. Stevens made the principal address, in which he flayed Daniel Webster for his support of the measure. Miller, Antislavery Movement in Indiana, pp. 194, 196; Centerville *Indiana True Democrat,* July 3, 1851.

George W. Julian characterized as "the world's greatest missionary of freedom, and the harbinger of deliverance to the African race." In Indiana as in the other northern states the success of Mrs. Stowe's book was phenomenal. "Hundreds and hundreds sat up all night to finish it," one reader recalled. "In every family there were those waiting to pick the book up the moment it was laid down. It was in every mind and on every tongue."[24] Just when the impact of the book was at its height, a notorious episode in Indianapolis caused a wave of revulsion against the Fugitive Slave Law and convinced many people of the authenticity of the evils of the slave system portrayed by Mrs. Stowe. The central figure in the strange case was John Freeman, a Negro who had lived in Indianapolis for about ten years and acquired a small business and won the respect of all who knew him. In 1853 a man from Missouri appeared, claiming that Freeman was his escaped slave and seeking to carry him off under the procedures provided in the 1850 law. Freeman was fortunate in having friends among influential people and received legal counsel from some of the best lawyers in the state. As the result of painstaking efforts on their part it was proved that not only was Freeman not the escaped slave of the man claiming him but that his appearance and physical characteristics were quite different from those of the slave, and that the claimant and his accomplices had perjured themselves. Freeman was saved—but he had spent nine weeks in jail, been subjected to numerous indignities, and had exhausted his savings in proving his identity! The case was followed with intense interest throughout the state and had an incalculable effect upon public opinion.[25]

[24] Indianapolis *Indiana Free Democrat,* June 9, October 6, 1853; Reminiscences of Jane Merrill Ketcham (Typewritten MS, Indiana Division, Indiana State Library), p. 90. See the speech of George W. Julian at the Free Democratic Association Convention, May 25, 1853, in which he emphasized the importance of Mrs. Stowe's book in winning antislavery converts and weakening the efforts of the politicians to suppress agitation over slavery. George W. Julian, *Speeches on Political Questions* (New York, 1872), p. 90.

[25] Thornbrough, *Negro in Indiana,* pp. 115-118; Charles H. Money, "The

Meanwhile, during the political campaign of 1852 the Democrats had tried to silence controversy over slavery by emphasizing the finality of the Compromise. As early as February, 1851, the *Indiana State Sentinel* had announced that it would not support for the presidency any man who favored the repeal of the Fugitive Slave Law, and in his message to the legislature in December, Wright had declared that Indiana would not support for office anyone who favored in any way reopening the issues which had been settled by the Compromise. In April, 1852, Indiana's entire delegation in the United States House of Representatives voted for a resolution endorsing the finality of the Compromise and deprecating further agitation about slavery. The Democratic state convention early in 1852 endorsed the finality of the Compromise and renominated the popular Wright by acclamation. Ashbel P. Willard of Floyd County was nominated for lieutenant governor. Most of the remainder of the state ticket was made up of men from the southern part of the state. It appeared that Democrats in the northern part of the state had weakened their influence by their earlier endorsement of Free Soil principles.[26]

On the national scene the Indiana delegation, under the discipline of Bright, tried to create a presidential boom for a native son, General Joseph Lane, Mexican War hero and governor of Oregon Territory. Later they threw their support to Lewis Cass. They felt no enthusiasm for Franklin Pierce who was finally nominated.[27]

Fugitive Slave Law of 1850 in Indiana," *Indiana Magazine of History,* XVII (1921), 180-198.

[26] Indianapolis *Indiana State Sentinel,* February 26, 1851; Indiana *Senate Journal,* 1851-1852, p. 26; Beeler, "Election of 1852," *Indiana Magazine of History,* XI, 307-308, 311-312; William E. Henry (comp.), *State Platforms of the Two Dominant Political Parties in Indiana, 1850-1900* (Indianapolis, 1902), pp. 5-6. See Van Der Weele, Jesse David Bright, pp. 118-119, for an account of Bright's efforts to prevent the renomination of Wright.

[27] Beeler, "Election of 1852," *Indiana Magazine of History,* XI, 318-319; Roger H. Van Bolt, "Indiana in Political Transition, 1851-1853," *ibid.,* XLIX (1953), 149-150.

There was probably some truth in the claim made by Democrats that no one wanted to accept the Whig nomination for governor and run against Wright. The man designated was an Indianapolis merchant, Nicholas McCarty, a person of some ability but no match for Wright as a campaigner. In their state platform the Whigs simply ignored the question of slavery and the Compromise. They endorsed economy in government, a tariff to encourage home industry, and Congressional appropriations in aid of internal improvements. Controversial issues were avoided by simply asserting: "We do not deem it necessary to further reiterate the distinctive principles of the Whig party, which are well known, in the success of which we believe the prosperity of the country is involved, and for the triumph of which in the approaching contest we here pledge ourselves to each other and to the country." The Indiana delegation was solidly behind the nomination of Gen. Winfield Scott as Whig candidate for President, but neither Scott's candidacy nor anything that the Whigs did appeared to arouse much popular enthusiasm during a campaign which was on the whole apathetic. Old issues like the tariff and internal improvements failed to spark any interest.[28]

No one was particularly surprised when Democrats scored decisive victories on both state and national tickets. Wright defeated McCarty by about ten thousand votes, and, except for a lone Whig, the entire Congressional delegation was Democratic, and Democrats won control of the state legisla-

---

[28] Beeler, "Election of 1852," *Indiana Magazine of History,* XI, 313; Henry (comp.), *State Platforms,* pp. 7-8. Whigs claimed that the low tariff which the Democrats had passed in 1846 was a triumph for British interests. Headlines in the Indianapolis *Indiana State Journal,* August 20, 1852, cried: ALLIANCE BETWEEN THE LOCOFOCO PARTY IN THE UNITED STATES AND ENGLAND TO BREAK DOWN AMERICAN MANUFACTURERS AND THUS SECURE THE MARKET FOR ENGLAND. In his speeches Wright expressed orthodox Democratic views on the tariff and sub-treasury, but put most of his emphasis upon the sound condition of Indiana finances and the reduction of indebtedness under Democratic rule. Beeler, "Election of 1852," *Indiana Magazine of History,* XII (1916), 37.

ture by a margin of about two to one.[29] The outcome of the election appeared to reflect weariness with the slavery issue and to be an endorsement of the Compromise of 1850. The Free Soil candidate for governor, Andrew L. Robinson, received a bare three thousand votes, while John P. Hale and George W. Julian, the Free Soil candidates for President and Vice-President, received only about seven thousand votes in Indiana.

In spite of the seemingly discouraging results, the Free Soil men felt that the time was ripe for renewed action. In January, 1853, they met to form the state Free Democratic Association, with Ovid Butler as president, for the purpose of forming local organizations and disseminating their principles. In a remarkably prescient speech at the Free Soil state convention in May, George W. Julian declared that antislavery men should rejoice at the "dispersion and ruin" of the Whig party and the "morbid growth and dropsical condition" of the Democrats as reflected in the outcome of the 1852 election. He declared that there were irreconcilable differences within the Democratic party which would soon cause factions to "fall to devouring one another," and that a new party "dedicated to liberty" must surely arise out of the ruin of the old parties. When Julian spoke, it was widely recognized that the Whig party had ceased to exist as a national organization, but there were few who would have predicted that the Democratic party, fresh from its sweeping victory, was also on the verge of disruption. And yet within a year Julian's prediction had come true.[30]

The historian can only speculate on what the history of political parties would have been if Stephen A. Douglas had not introduced the fateful bill which evolved into the measure known as the Kansas-Nebraska Act, providing for popular sovereignty in the two territories which it created and expressly repealing the Missouri Compromise. In Indiana, as

[29] Beeler, "Election of 1852," *loc. cit.*, XII, 46, 50.
[30] Julian, *Speeches on Political Questions*, pp. 85-88.

in the North generally, the proposal to repeal the 1820 measure was denounced as the betrayal of a solemn pledge. Douglas' somewhat disingenuous argument that the popular sovereignty principles which had been incorporated into the Compromise of 1850 regarding Utah and New Mexico territories had established the principles for all territories met with cries of disbelief. Persons who opposed slavery on moral grounds believed that limiting its expansion would ultimately lead to its extinction, and they feared the increased political strength for the slave power which would result from opening the two new territories to slavery. Economic considerations were also important. Free white laborers in the North wanted to keep the territories free because they wanted to be able to move West and to acquire homesteads and did not want to compete with slave labor.

At the outset, many Democratic newspapers throughout the state denounced the Kansas-Nebraska bill, but from the beginning the Indianapolis *Sentinel*, the most powerful party organ in the state, supported the measure and branded as "abolitionists" those who opposed it. "The organization of every new territory is a God send to fanatical abolitionism," it declared. "It opens a new field for slavery agitation; and enables them [agitators] to rake up the dying embers of sectional strife." In an editorial entitled "Who Are The Agitators Now?" the *Free Democrat* commented on the ironic fact that a party which had declared in its 1852 platform that it would resist any renewal of slavery agitation had itself precipitated the current furor. "The fanatical Abolitionists," it said, "will have to yield the palm . . . in the way of getting up excitement and agitation." The same paper asserted that a majority of the people and a majority of the newspapers in the state were opposed to the repeal of the Missouri Compromise.[31]

31 Indianapolis *Daily Sentinel,* quoted in Roger H. Van Bolt, "Fusion out of Confusion, 1854," *Indiana Magazine of History,* XLIX (1953), 364; Indianapolis *Indiana Free Democrat,* February 16, 1854. Even among the most "hunkerish"

In spite of popular protests, in the long run most of the Indiana delegation in Congress succumbed to the pressures imposed by the Pierce administration. Only two Democrats in the House, Daniel Mace and Andrew J. Harlan, voted against the Douglas bill. The one Indiana Whig, Samuel W. Parker, also voted against it. Both Senators Bright and Pettit favored the bill.[32] Once the measure was passed many of the Democratic papers which had opposed its adoption changed their tune, but some continued to oppose it, and it was apparent that when the Democrats assembled for their state convention on May 24, 1854, there was going to be a fight. Even before the disruptive Nebraska issue had arisen there was discontent over the autocratic rule of the Bright organization. Democrats in the northern part of the state, where population was rapidly growing, were resentful at failure to receive a larger share of state offices and patronage. Friends of Governor Wright resented the contemptuous treatment which he received from Bright. When it became apparent that the Pierce administration and the Bright forces were prepared to make support of the controversial Kansas-Nebraska bill the cardinal test of loyalty to the Democracy, a revolt was inevitable.

"Scarcely less abject is the slavery of party than that of the lash," the Indianapolis *Journal* commented on the eve of

or conservative elements in the Democratic party there was opposition to the Kansas-Nebraska Act. The *Free Democrat* mentioned Oliver P. Morton as one of the "Hunkers" who was opposed. But members of the old parties were cautious about organizing opposition, and it was the Free Soilers who took the initiative. They called a statewide Anti-Nebraska convention, which met in Indianapolis on March 15. Addresses were made at the meeting by such prominent Free Soil men as Julian and Ovid Butler. Meanwhile, local protest meetings were being held—in Noblesville, Plainfield, New Castle, Mishawaka, South Bend, and Goshen—within a period of a few days. *Ibid.*, February 23, March 2, 9, 16, 23, 1854.

32 Van Bolt, "Fusion out of Confusion," *Indiana Magazine of History*, XLIX, 363, 369; Carter, Decade of Hoosier History, p. 102; Charles Zimmerman, "The Origin and Rise of the Republican Party in Indiana from 1854 to 1860," *Indiana Magazine of History*, XIII (1917), 221-223. Democratic Representative Ebenezer M. Chamberlain of the Tenth District did not vote but was known to oppose the bill.

the convention. Bright forces were in control and prepared to use steam-roller tactics to override opposition. When the resolutions committee brought out a plank endorsing the Kansas-Nebraska Act, Henry Ellsworth of Lafayette and Alexander McDonald from Lake County offered substitute resolutions which were voted down. The Bright forces carried the day and the convention adopted resolutions endorsing the Kansas-Nebraska Act, the men who voted for it, Douglas, and the Pierce administration. In the weeks following, at district conventions, men who would not support the party platform adopted at the state convention were read out of the party.[33] Anti-Nebraska men were enraged at Bright's methods and cried out against the "packed" convention, declaring that it did not really represent the will of the Democrats in the state. Almost at once there was talk of forming a new anti-Nebraska convention.

Many of the men who were being read out of the Democratic party for their anti-Nebraska views were also disturbed over the position which the convention and the Bright men took on temperance. This contributed almost as much to the political revolt of 1854 as did the Nebraska question. As shown earlier, men of antislavery tendencies were likely also to be temperance men. During the 1852 campaign the temperance forces had been active in exerting pressure on candidates in both major parties. A circular of the State Central Temperance Committee was mailed throughout the state early in the year, announcing a "war of extermination" against liquor. Mere license or local option laws were not enough.

---

[33] Indianapolis *Daily Journal*, May 24, 26, 1854; Indianapolis *Daily Sentinel*, May 26, 1854; Van Bolt, "Fusion out of Confusion," *Indiana Magazine of History*, XLIX, 370-373. The accounts in the *Sentinel* and *Journal* make no mention of action at the state convention expelling anti-Nebraska members. There is a discrepancy between the contemporary newspaper accounts and the account in William Dudley Foulke, *Life of Oliver P. Morton* (2 volumes, Indianapolis, 1899), I, 37-39. No mention is made of Morton in the newspaper accounts. The press mentioned McDonald's efforts to introduce substitute resolutions, but Foulke says that Morton's efforts to persuade McDonald to oppose the Nebraska resolutions in the convention failed.

"Until intoxicating liquors are *outlawed* and *contraband,*" it declared, "our work is not half done." County conventions all over the state called for a Maine-type prohibition law and delegates promised that they would not vote for state legislative candidates who refused to support such legislation. The legislature of 1853 was barraged with petitions asking for a prohibition law. It responded with a measure which was by no means a Maine-type law, but which incorporated into a general law several features of local laws which had previously been in operation for various towns. It was a local option law which permitted voters of a township to decide annually whether or not to permit the sale of liquor within their borders. For townships where liquor was permitted, there were stringent licensing requirements. A few months after its enactment the state Supreme Court found the local option provision unconstitutional on the grounds that it violated the provisions of the 1851 Constitution which prohibited local laws and which required that all laws be of "general and uniform operation throughout the state." The court held that the fact that some townships could and did vote to prohibit the sale of liquor, while others did not, made it in operation a local law and not uniform in operation.[34]

After this setback the temperance forces were more convinced than ever of the necessity for a prohibition measure. The decision, declared the *Free Democrat,* showed the "folly and uselessness of half-way legislation." It predicted that the demand for a Maine-type law would become the leading issue in the next state election. Democratic and Whig temperance men agreed. In January, 1854, over one thousand persons, the largest gathering of temperance workers which had yet assembled in the state, met in convention. They included prominent philanthropists and clergymen, among whom Methodists were most conspicuous. Some of them were of abolitionist sympathies, others were colonizationists. Democrats, Whigs, and Free Soilers were all present. The conven-

[34] Centerville *Indiana True Democrat,* April 1, 1852; *Temperance Chart,* 1852, *passim;* Indiana *Laws,* 1853, pp. 87-89; Maize *v.* the State, 4 Ind. 342-347.

tion branded intemperance as "the scourge of our land—the fountain of crime, the source of untold social and political evils . . . corrupting the purity of the Elective Franchise, endangering the stability, if not the very existence of our free institutions." They then declared that no prohibition law would satisfy them which did not contain "the principles of SEIZURE CONFISCATION AND DESTRUCTION OF LIQUOR." They voted to refuse to support for the legislature any candidate who was not fully committed to these principles.[35] Some Democrats saw in the temperance convention a Whig plot to break up the Democracy. "If Whiggery and Abolitionism can throw in the temperance question as an auxiliary to aid them in electing a Whig legislature," the Indianapolis *Sentinel* said gloomily, "they will achieve a triumph by the aid of temperance Democrats, which their political principles can never command." The Madison *Courier* predicted that the state election contests would hinge on the prohibition issue. "The Whig politicians," it said, "having nothing to lose, are on the side of a prohibition law. . . . The temperance men stand with the balance of power in their hands."[36]

In spite of evidence of the growing strength of the temperance forces, the Democratic state convention adopted a plank which the temperance forces regarded as an affront. While admitting that intemperance was a great moral and social evil over which legislation was desirable, the platform flatly opposed legislation which authorized "the *searching* for, or *seizure, confiscation,* and *destruction* of private property." So offensive was this to temperance men that many of them were ready to leave the party on this issue.[37]

35 Indianapolis *Indiana Free Democrat,* December 1, 1853; *Minutes of the Proceedings of the State Temperance Convention . . . Indianapolis . . . January 11, 1854,* p. 8; Van Bolt, "Fusion out of Confusion," *Indiana Magazine of History,* XLIX, 354-355.

36 Indianapolis *Indiana State Sentinel,* March 14, 1854, quoted in Zimmerman, "Rise of the Republican Party," *Indiana Magazine of History,* XIII, 216; Madison *Courier,* April 18, 1854, quoted *ibid.*

37 Indianapolis *Daily Sentinel,* May 26, 1854; Indianapolis *Daily Journal,* May 26, 1854.

In addition to the Nebraska question and temperance, two other factors contributed significantly to the political ferment which was brewing in 1854. One of these was the increasing importance of the foreign vote as the result of Irish and German immigration in the late forties and early fifties. The other was the Know Nothing movement, which was partly a response to this immigration. As noted earlier, the rate of immigration to Indiana was smaller than to neighboring states, but by 1850 there were almost 55,000 foreign-born persons in the state, and by 1860 that number had more than doubled. From the beginning the foreign vote was largely Democratic. Democrats dominated the Constitutional Convention of 1850-1851, which granted the right to vote to aliens who had lived in the United States for one year and had declared their intention of becoming citizens. In the convention some Whig delegates had vied with the Democrats in protestations of devotion to the welfare of the foreigner, but other Whigs opposed the extension of voting rights to aliens.[38]

After the political debacle of 1852 many Whigs moved into the American party, popularly known as the Know Nothing party because members were pledged to secrecy. The growth of this nativist movement was partly a reaction against the growing political power of foreigners. It was also due to the fact that nearly all of the Irish immigrants and a majority of the German were Roman Catholics. Nativism and anti-Catholicism were given impetus in 1853 by the visit of an ex-priest, Father Alessandro Gavazzi, who came to the United States to agitate against the Catholic Church. In Indianapolis he attracted large crowds when he spoke against the power of the church of Rome and against Catholic schools and described the horrors of the Inquisition. The first Know Nothing lodge in Indiana was organized shortly thereafter,

[38] See, for example, speeches of Milton Gregg, Whig, of Jefferson County, Allen Hamilton, Whig, of Allen County, and John Pettit, Democrat, of Tippecanoe County. *Debates and Proceedings,* II, 1296, 1298-1299, 1302-1304.

in Lawrenceburg, in February, 1854. Thereafter the Know Nothing movement spread rapidly throughout the state. Its program was strongly anti-Catholic, embracing hostility to alleged papal influence in politics and education, and calling for stringent naturalization laws, restrictions on immigration, and the election of native Americans only to public office. An important reason for the growth of Know Nothingism was that it coincided with the collapse of the Whig party and offered a haven for Whigs who did not wish to affiliate with other political organizations. Some Indiana Whigs, of whom Richard W. Thompson was most prominent, were attracted to the movement, not because of its anti-foreign, anti-Catholic character, but because of its conservative character and because they regarded it as the true successor of the Whig party. By early summer of 1854 the Know Nothings were numerous enough to constitute a political force with which to reckon. The Democratic state platform took cognizance of them by condemning any organization "that would aim to disrobe any citizen, native or adopted, of his political, civil or religious liberty."[39]

The anti-Nebraska Democrats, temperance Democrats, Know Nothings, and the old Free Soil men and Whigs who had not succumbed to Know Nothingism joined in a coalition in 1854 to topple the regular Democrats. Initiative for a new political party came from the Free Soilers (now under the banner of Free Democrats) and anti-Nebraska Democrats. Divisions within the ranks of the Democrats, which Julian had predicted, gave the Free Soilers their opportunity. On the day following the state Democratic convention the Free Democrats met in convention in Indianapolis and decided not to nominate a state ticket. Instead, they called for "a cooperation of all persons who are opposed to said measure

[39] Carl Fremont Brand, "History of the Know Nothing Party in Indiana," *Indiana Magazine of History,* XVIII (1922), 53, 72-73; Roll, *Colonel Dick Thompson,* pp. 146-147; Indianapolis *Daily Sentinel,* May 26, 1854; Indianapolis *Daily Journal,* May 26, 1854.

[Kansas-Nebraska Act] with a view to its repeal." They recommended a state convention "for the purpose of combining all the opponents of said measure." Simultaneously anti-Nebraska Democrats, smarting under the treatment they had received, began to organize in protest against the "packed" convention. "Democrats Arouse! Those who aspire to be our leaders have betrayed us at the late packed convention; . . . they have attempted to bind and sell us to the slave driver of the South, and the rum seller of the North." So ran the call for a meeting in Hendricks County.[40]

At meetings throughout the state men pledged to support for Congress only men who promised to restore the Missouri Compromise and for state office only those pledged to support temperance legislation. At a meeting in Madison Michael Garber, editor of the Madison *Courier,* who had earlier defied Jesse Bright in his own town over the Fugitive Slave Law and had supported Joseph Wright, Bright's arch rival, called for a state convention. Two days later Jacob P. Chapman in the columns of the *Chanticleer* sent out a call for a state convention to meet in Indianapolis on July 13 to adopt such measures as were necessary to meet the current crisis.[41]

Whigs moved cautiously, waiting for Democrats to take the initiative, but many of them were clearly eager to co-operate. Whig newspapers had consistently attacked the Kansas-Nebraska Act and had already shown a more friendly attitude toward temperance than had much of the Democratic press. After the Democratic state convention the Indianapolis *Journal* cried: "Slavery and Liquor, niggers and 'raw nips' now

[40] Indianapolis *Chapman's Chanticleer,* June 1, 1854; Logansport *Journal,* June 24, 1854, quoted in Mildred Stoler, "Insurgent Democrats of Indiana and Illinois in 1854," *Indiana Magazine of History,* XXXIII (1937), 16; Indianapolis *Daily Journal,* June 12, 1854.

[41] Indianapolis *Chapman's Chanticleer,* June 15, 1854; Zimmerman, "Rise of the Republican Party," *Indiana Magazine of History,* XIII, 232-233. For an account of the feud between Michael Garber and Jesse D. Bright see William S. Garber, "Jesse D. Bright and Michael C. Garber," *ibid.,* XVIII (1932), 31-39; Van Der Weele, *Jesse David Bright,* pp. 99-108.

form both ends and the middle of the Democratic creed." It expressed doubt that many good men, hitherto Democrats, could support the Democratic platform and expressed the pious hope that "for the good of the country" they would follow the dictates of conscience rather than of party. Some old-line Whigs held back, but many, including Defrees of the *Journal,* Schuyler Colfax, and Godlove Orth, were eager to join in a fusion movement. Orth wrote to Colfax that "the Whigs must control that convention without seeming to do so."[42]

Both Colfax and Orth and many other Whigs who urged political fusion were also Know Nothings. On the two days before the fusion convention Know Nothings met in secret conclave in Indianapolis and drew up a state constitution and ritual and agreed upon a slate of candidates whom they would support in the convention.[43]

On July 13, the anniversary of the adoption of the Northwest Ordinance, a huge crowd assembled in Indianapolis in answer to Chapman's call. Speeches were made by men who represented the various elements composing the gathering, including Chapman and Michael Garber, both anti-Nebraska Democrats, Henry S. Lane and Schuyler Colfax, Whigs (the latter also a Know Nothing), and Stephen S. Harding, Free Soiler. They agreed to take the name People's party and adopted a platform which was skillfully drawn to please the elements in the coalition and in which virtually every plank was in stated opposition to the position which the regular Democrats had taken in their platform or published views. They called for the restoration of the Missouri Compromise and resolved to "waive all former party predilections" in seeking to place in office men who would "assert the rights of

---

[42] Indianapolis *Daily Journal,* May 25, 1854; Godlove S. Orth to Schuyler Colfax, July 4, 1854, quoted in Willard H. Smith, "Schuyler Colfax and the Political Upheaval of 1854-1855," *Mississippi Valley Historical Review,* XXVIII (1941-1942), 387.

[43] Brand, "Know Nothing Party," *Indiana Magazine of History,* XVIII, 63-64, 69.

Freedom, restore the Missouri Compromise, and refuse, under all circumstances, to tolerate the extension of Slavery into Territories secured to Freedom by that Compromise." To please the temperance forces they declared in favor of a "Judicious, Constitutional and Efficient Prohibitory Law," without giving express endorsement to the seizure and confiscation features which the temperance convention had demanded. They also condemned attacks which Democrats had made upon the Protestant clergy for interfering in politics in connection with slavery and temperance.[44]

The candidates whom they nominated for state offices were new political figures who had not held office before and who were representative of the various elements in the coalition. Only one incumbent, Daniel Mace, a Democrat who had voted against the Kansas-Nebraska Act, was nominated for Congress by the People's party. Of the other Congressional nominees, some were Democrats, some were Whigs, and nearly all of them had endorsement from the Know Nothings. The new party was a coalition held together solely by opposition to the Democracy. The Free Soilers felt that the platform was too cautious on the slavery question, and many Free Soilers were suspicious of the Know Nothing movement, which they regarded as a tool for the slave power. On the other hand, some Free Soil men were Know Nothings.[45]

The Democrats professed to be quite unperturbed by the coalition of what they referred to as the "isms." One well-known Democrat predicted that "the recent union of all the isms against us will give us a fight just sufficiently warm to be interesting." But while appearing to take the new movement lightly, the Democrats also attacked it with great bitterness as a group of "mongrels, over whom waves the black flag of abolitionism and disunion. . . ."[46]

[44] Henry (comp.), State Platforms, p. 10: Indianapolis Daily Journal, July 14, 18, 1854; Zimmerman, "Rise of the Republican Party," Indiana Magazine of History, XIII, 235.

[45] Brand, "Know Nothing Party," Indiana Magazine of History, XVIII, 65, 70-71, 77.

[46] Graham N. Fitch to William H. English, July 18, 1854, quoted in Stoler,

To many the campaign was a great moral crusade, and the Democrats committed a serious blunder in deriding the "isms" and especially in attacking the activities of Methodist ministers who were denouncing the Kansas-Nebraska Act and calling for prohibition of liquor. The attacks strengthened the impression that the campaign was indeed a contest between the forces of good and evil.[47]

The necessity of defending the Kansas-Nebraska Act put the Democrats in an awkward position since in 1848 and 1849 they had opposed the introduction of slavery into any territory and had shown a tendency to make alliances with the Free Soil movement. To charges that they were proslavery, Democrats replied that they simply believed in popular sovereignty—the right of the people of Kansas and Nebraska to manage their own affairs. They repeatedly insisted that false issues were being raised—that there was no point in getting excited about the repeal of the Missouri Compromise since there was no possibility that the people in the territories involved would ever vote in favor of legalizing slavery. "We do not believe that there is a Democrat within the State," asserted the *State Sentinel*, "who, if he were a citizen of Nebraska, or Kansas, would vote to incorporate slavery among its elements. But we view the question as one involving the constitutional right of a people to make their own laws and regulate their own domestic institutions."[48]

Democrats ridiculed the temperance plank in the People's platform. A "judicious law," one editorial declared, "is one

"Insurgent Democrats," *Indiana Magazine of History*, XXXIII, 23; Indianapolis *Democratic Platform*, July 19, 1854. The Democrats characterized the convention of the new party as made up of "chiefly young men who never had any political experience, many of whom very much resembled the young man in the *Vicar of Wakefield*, who bought the large supply of green spectacles. They were essentially verdant." *Ibid*. The *Democratic Platform* was a weekly newspaper published during the campaign.

[47] For example, see Indianapolis *Daily Sentinel*, March 28, 1854; Indianoplis *Democratic Platform*, August 2, 1854.

[48] Indianapolis *Indiana State Sentinel*, September 8, 1854, quoted in Zimmerman, "Rise of the Republican Party," *Indiana Magazine of History*, XIII, 219. See also *Democratic Platform*, August 9, 16, 23, 1854.

which will enable politicians of the new school to blow hot and cold at the same time." But to many this was no laughing matter. Probably the liquor issue weighed as heavily or more heavily than the Nebraska question with many churchgoing people. The position which the Democrats occupied with regard to temperance was evidently a source of embarrassment to Governor Wright. During the campaign, it was remarked, Wright was remarkably silent. He finally made some general statements about being in favor of the "principle" of popular sovereignty, but he said nothing on the whisky question. But Wright stayed with the Democracy, even though many of his friends left it in 1854.[49]

In a campaign in which the fusionists seemed to have the advantage on the slavery and temperance questions, Democrats made strenuous efforts to capitalize on the fact that the new party was tainted with Know Nothingism. Democratic papers devoted much space to the issue and printed alleged exposés of Know Nothing ritual, oaths, and activities. Efforts were made to link the Know Nothing and temperance issue in an appeal to the foreign voter. The proposed prohibition law, it was claimed, was intended "only to punish and disgrace poor . . . Irishmen or the poor Germans." And indeed the campaign created a dilemma for German voters. Germans were aroused over the Clayton amendment to the Kansas-Nebraska Act, which limited the right to vote to citizens, and they were apprehensive over the effect the act would have upon free labor and free land. They were inclined to side with the Democrats on the temperance and Know Nothing issues but were drawn toward the new party by the slavery question.[50]

49 *Madisonian,* quoted in *Democratic Platform,* July 26, 1854; Indianapolis *Indiana Free Democrat,* September 7, 1854.

50 *Madisonian,* quoted in *Democratic Platform,* July 26, 1854: Stoler, "Insurgent Democrats," *Indiana Magazine of History,* XXXIII, 9; Van Bolt, "Fusion out of Confusion," *ibid.,* XLIX, 360. See resolutions condemning the spread of slavery which were adopted at a meeting of Free Germans from the entire state. Indianapolis *Daily Journal,* June 3, 1854.

When the votes were in, it was apparent that the new party had won a smashing victory. They elected the entire ticket of state officers by margins of about 13,000. In the Congressional races they won nine of eleven seats. Only two old-line Democrats who had voted in favor of the Kansas-Nebraska bill were re-elected. Among the newly elected representatives was Schuyler Colfax, who was to become speaker of the United States House of Representatives and Vice-President. In the elections to the state legislature, in which temperance had been the overriding issue, the People's candidates won impressive victories, gaining control of the House, although Democrats would continue to control the Senate by two votes. The outcome of the legislative contests showed clearly the sectional character of the political realignment which was taking place. Only the counties in the extreme south remained a Democratic stronghold. The only two Democrats returned to the United States House of Representatives came from districts in the extreme south. Fusionists swept the northern two thirds of the state.[51]

The most immediate fruit of the fusion victory was the enactment of the prohibition law which the temperance forces had been demanding—a law which absolutely prohibited the manufacture and sale of whisky except for medicinal purposes—and then only with the permission of county agents.[52] During the closing days of the session a bill to charter a new state bank was also passed. A considerable amount of public opposition had developed against the existing State Bank although it had proved itself to be a sound institution. Instead of seeking a renewal of the charter, which would expire in 1858, the principal stockholders decided to seek a charter for a new institution. The bank issue was not a partisan one

---

[51] Zimmerman, "Rise of the Republican Party," *Indiana Magazine of History*, XIII, 245; Van Bolt, "Fusion out of Confusion," *ibid.*, XLIX, 387. See the map showing the sectional strength of the Fusionists in Esarey, *History of Indiana*, II, 636. The two Democratic representatives re-elected who had voted for the Kansas-Nebraska bill were William H. English and Smith Miller.

[52] Indiana *Laws*, 1855, pp. 209-223.

and had received little attention during the campaign, although behind the scenes there were efforts to elect men who would favor granting the charter. Governor Wright vetoed the bank bill, partly because the question of the bank had not been discussed during the campaign. He also recommended an investigation of the lobby which had operated to secure adoption of the charter. But the bank bill was passed over his veto.[53]

The legislators were able to submerge party differences when it came to banking, but a partisan wrangle developed between the two houses which prevented the election of a United States senator to succeed Senator John Pettit. The People's party controlled the House and had a majority of twelve in joint session, but the Democrats controlled the Senate by two votes and refused to go into joint session. As a result of the deadlock Jesse Bright alone represented Indiana in the Senate until 1857.[54]

The jubilation of the temperance forces over the 1855 law was of short duration. A test case, involving an Indianapolis saloonkeeper named Beebe, was soon before the state Supreme Court, but after hearing arguments, the court adjourned for the summer, postponing a decision until November. Impatient at the delay, the liquor forces arranged to get another case before Judge Samuel Perkins of the Supreme Court in the form of an appeal for a writ of habeas corpus to release a man named Hermann who had been arrested for breaking the law. The views of Judge Perkins, who was a partisan Democratic journalist as well as an able lawyer, were well known. In the columns of the Richmond *Jeffersonian* he had criticized Wright for signing the bill, declaring that it might be enforced in Indiana, "but it could not be in any despotism in Europe without producing revolution." Perkins at once released Hermann on the grounds that the prohibition law was unconstitutional. News of the decision

[53] See below, Chapter X, pages 424-428, for a fuller discussion of the bank question.

[54] Zimmerman, "Rise of the Republican Party," *Indiana Magazine of History,* XIII, 244-245, 247-248.

was telegraphed throughout the state, and the saloons were back in business. At the November term, in language very much like that which he had used in the Hermann case, Perkins wrote an opinion in the Beebe case in which the Supreme Court declared the law unconstitutional. He held that the law was so absolutely destructive of property rights of manufacturers, sellers, and consumers of liquor as to be unconstitutional. "What . . .," he asked, "is the right of property worth, stripped of the right of producing and using?" Liquor and distilleries were property, and the legislature could not by a general law "annihilate the entire property in liquors in the state."[55]

After this decision the temperance question ceased to be important for several years. The platform of the People's party in 1856 contained a temperance plank almost identical with the one adopted in 1854 but it was ignored. By 1856 the new party was making strenuous efforts to cultivate the German vote, and as a consequence support of temperance waned.

In 1856 the Democrats were still committed to the Kansas-Nebraska Act and Jesse Bright, although both had become liabilities in the eyes of many party members. Kansas had become the overriding political issue. In 1854 Democrats had defended the Kansas-Nebraska Act as truly democratic in principle—giving the people of the territories the right to manage their own affairs without outside interference. They insisted that they did not want or expect slavery to be established in the territories. But two years later it was obvious that an abnormal situation was developing in Kansas which was making a mockery of popular sovereignty. Newspapers

---

[55] Thomas A. Goodwin, *Seventy-six Years' Tussle with the Traffic: Being a Condensation of the Laws Relating to the Liquor Traffic in Indiana from 1807 to 1883* . . . (Indianapolis, 1883), pp. 18-19; Emma Lou Thornbrough, "Judge Perkins, the Indiana Supreme Court, and the Civil War," *Indiana Magazine of History*, LX (1964), 81; Beebe *v.* the State, 6 Ind. 501-556 (1855). Perkins' opinion in the Hermann case is printed in 8 Ind. Appendix.

were full of the accounts of disorders perpetrated by "border ruffians" and of the desperate efforts of the proslavery elements to thwart the will of the free soil majority.

Interest in Kansas was heightened by the number of persons from Indiana moving to the territory, and the whole Kansas issue was dramatized by the extraordinary course of James H. Lane, who had gone from Lawrenceburg, Indiana, to Kansas. Lane, a Democrat, had been elected lieutenant governor of Indiana in 1849, and in 1852 had been elected to Congress, where he had voted in favor of the Kansas-Nebraska bill. In 1855 he moved to Kansas, and once there became active in the effort to insure that Kansas would become a free state, broke with the Pierce administration, and became a Republican. Early in 1856 he was back in Indiana, eloquently presenting the free soil cause in Kansas. In February he participated in a meeting in Indianapolis called by the Free Democratic Association to organize a committee "to raise money, purchase arms, and equip men to go immediately to Kansas." The committee included such eminently respectable and influential men as Calvin Fletcher, Ovid Butler, and Henry S. Lane.[56]

---

[56] Wendell Holmes Stephenson, "The Transitional Period in the Career of General James H. Lane," *Indiana Magazine of History,* XXV (1929), 75-91 *passim;* Zimmerman, "Rise of the Republican Party," *ibid.,* XIII, 249. In a letter to the Indianapolis *Daily Journal,* February 28, 1856, Judge John W. Wright of Logansport, a member of the committee, wrote: "If a contest with arms comes off in Kansas hundreds of Hoosiers will be there, and money can be furnished to any amount, and after it is over every aider and abettor to the ruffians . . . will be shipped South and delivered over to their masters." Quoted in *ibid.,* XIII, 255. Calvin Fletcher was the leading Indianapolis banker at this time, a Methodist, an ardent antislavery man, and a philanthropist. His voluminous diaries included many details about Indianapolis life in this period. Frequent entries throughout 1856 show concern about Kansas and Fletcher's interest in raising funds for the Kansas Aid Society. (Typewritten transcript of the Calvin Fletcher Diary, Indiana Historical Society Library.) Indiana ranked third among all the states in the number of settlers contributed to Kansas during the 1850's. William O. Lynch, "Population Movements in Relation to the Struggle for Kansas," *Studies in American History Inscribed to James Albert Woodburn* (Bloomington, 1926), pp. 383-404.

At their state convention the Democrats had no choice but to endorse the "principle" of the Kansas-Nebraska law. They also opposed the "principle" of the recent prohibition law, condemned the Know Nothings, and endorsed Jesse Bright for the presidency. For their candidate for governor, the man who would really be their standard bearer in the state campaign, they nominated an attractive and effective campaigner, youthful Ashbel P. Willard. Born in New York and educated at Hamilton College, Willard was a New Albany lawyer who had become the acknowledged leader of the Democrats in the state House of Representatives in 1850 at the age of thirty. Two years later he had been elected lieutenant governor. He was a party man, apparently without deep convictions, but possessed of such charm and oratorical ability that many who disliked his politics were nevertheless captivated by him.[57]

At the state convention an effort to unseat Bright as party leader failed. In consequence the Indiana delegation at the national convention was under his control. When it became apparent that Bright himself had no chance of winning the nomination, he swung the Indiana delegation to James Buchanan, even though a number of them wanted to support Douglas and Bright had appeared to give some assurance to Douglas that he would support him. Bright's action in swinging Indiana to Buchanan was considered influential in bringing a large part of the Ohio delegation and part of the New York delegation to Buchanan's support, thereby contributing to his nomination and the failure of Douglas to get the prize.[58]

The opposition to the Democrats continued to use the name of People's party throughout 1856 even though they sent delegates to the Republican national convention. The

[57] Henry (comp.), *State Platforms*, pp. 11-12; Woollen, *Biographical and Historical Sketches*, pp. 104-112.

[58] "Indiana in the Douglas-Buchanan Contest of 1856," *Indiana Magazine of History*, XXX (1934), 119-132; Van Der Weele, *Jesse David Bright*, pp. 168-180.

party remained a loose and not entirely harmonious coalition, in which the influence of the old Whig element was on the increase, while the influence of the Free Soilers and anti-Nebraska Democrats and Know Nothings declined. Nevertheless, a few old Whigs joined the ranks of the Democrats because they did not wish to associate with a party which in their eyes was a sectional party.[59]

In the opening address at the state People's convention Henry S. Lane spoke of Kansas but insisted that opposition to the extension of slavery was not abolitionism. James H. Lane was also on the platform and spoke in vivid terms of the situation in Kansas. The party platform opposed the extension of slavery, called for the immediate admission of Kansas as a free state, endorsed a five-year period as a requirement for naturalization, and declared that the right of suffrage should not precede naturalization.[60]

Whig influence was dominant in the convention and in the party organization. Of the state central committee of sixteen, only two were former Democrats. John Defrees became state chairman, replacing Michael Garber, former Democrat. Of the nine nominees for state offices only three were former Democrats. But the nomination for the governorship went to thirty-two-year-old Oliver P. Morton of Wayne County, who had been a Democrat until 1854. At a time when many Democrats had shown free soil tendencies, Morton had opposed the Wilmot Proviso as unnecessary and because he thought agitation over slavery harmful to the Democratic party. He had accepted the finality of the Compromise of 1850 and campaigned actively for Franklin Pierce in 1852. Like many other Democrats, he was disturbed over the Kan-

[59] See, for example, a letter of William S. Holman, a Democrat, to Allen Hamilton, a Fort Wayne banker and former Whig, who became a Democrat during the realignment of the 1850's. "I am glad," wrote Holman, that "you refuse any connection with the fanatical party which ignoring reason & common sense seizes a single idea & becomes blind to everything else." Holman to Hamilton, May 9, 1856, in Allen Hamilton Papers.

[60] Henry (comp.), *State Platforms*, p. 13.

sas-Nebraska bill but apparently his opposition to it was at first less clear-cut and unwavering than is indicated in Foulke's biography of him. At various times he was reported as being opposed to and then in favor of the bill—perhaps because he was eager to be the Democratic nominee for Congress from his district. But at least by the closing weeks of the 1854 campaign he was actively campaigning for the People's party and against the Kansas-Nebraska Act. By 1856 Morton was sufficiently identified with the Republican party that he served as a member of the resolutions committee of the preliminary convention which met in Pittsburgh in February to make plans for the first national nominating convention.[61]

The motion to send delegates from the People's convention to the national Republican convention brought protests from some of the Know Nothings, but one Know Nothing delegate said that Know Nothingism could wait—Kansas could not— and urged the sending of delegates. The delegation which went to Philadelphia was weighted heavily in favor of the conservative Whig element, but it contained a few of the reform element who had sparked the movement in 1854. Henry S. Lane presided at the state convention and in his opening address extolled the virtues of Henry Clay, asserting that if Clay were alive in 1856 he would be a Republican.[62]

George W. Julian was a member of the Indiana delegation and had served as chairman of the committee on organization at the preliminary Pittsburgh meeting. Julian was

[61] Mildred C. Stoler, "The Democratic Element in the New Republican Party in Indiana," *Indiana Magazine of History*, XXXVI (1940), 187-189; Van Bolt, "The Rise of the Republican Party in Indiana, 1855-1856," *ibid.*, LI, 207. Indianapolis *Indiana Free Democrat,* November 2, 1854, declared that Morton's "efficient services during the canvass have deservedly made him a favorite of the people," but earlier the same paper had reported that Morton had followed a wavering and inconsistent course, at times appearing to endorse, at times to oppose the Kansas-Nebraska bill. See *ibid.,* March 2, April 27, August 24, September 14, November 2, 1854, and *Chapman's Chanticleer,* July 27, 1854.

[62] Zimmerman, "Rise of the Republican Party," *Indiana Magazine of History,* XIII, 258-259; Van Bolt, "Rise of the Republican Party, *ibid.,* LI, 208-209.

eager to campaign actively for John C. Frémont, the Republican presidential nominee, and supported the platform adopted at Philadelphia, but he and other old Free Soilers were dissatisfied with the state platform adopted by the People's party and with the state candidates. One Free Soiler spoke bitterly of the state convention as "a poor miserable truckling concern without either soul or body," which had ignored antislavery principles out of deference to Know Nothings and "old fossil Whigs," but hoped to win office with the aid of antislavery votes, provided they were "not compelled to take more antislavery than they might safely take of *arsenic.*" Julian himself said that the proceedings of the convention "must have been disgusting to any looker-on having the antislavery cause at heart." His disgust was ostensibly due to the influence which he alleged that the Know Nothings exercised but was also no doubt due in part to the nomination of Morton with whom he had already clashed in Wayne County politics and whom he despised as a mere opportunist.[63]

In July, the Know Nothings held a state convention, but only about one fourth of the counties in the state were represented, most Know Nothings by that time having openly cast their lot with the People's-Republican movement. The convention adopted a platform and endorsed the candidacy of Millard Fillmore. The Know Nothings conducted an active campaign in the southern part of the state in behalf of Fillmore but abandoned the northern part of the state to the Republicans and Democrats. They had become a sectional party within the state, made up almost entirely of a few irreconcilable Whigs from the southern counties. Richard W. Thompson bore the burden of the speaking campaign. He stumped the state, comparing Fillmore to Henry Clay, as

[63] Grace Julian Clarke (ed.), "A Letter of Daniel Worth to George W. Julian and Other Documents," *Indiana Magazine of History,* XXVI (1930), 153-154; Julian, *Political Recollections,* pp. 147-157. Morton had played an active part in preventing the Democrats of Wayne County from endorsing Julian as a fusion candidate for re-election to Congress in 1851. Grace Julian Clarke, *George W. Julian (Indiana Historical Collections,* XI, Indianapolis, 1923), pp. 118-119.

"the great embodiment of the conservative national element of the country," and denouncing Republicans as "Abolitionists, disunionists, and incendiaries." For the most part, Know Nothings supported the People's candidates for state offices, but in the extreme south some Know Nothing newspapers repudiated the state ticket and platform, and at New Albany there was some violence between Republicans and Know Nothings. In this area Democrats tried to make an alliance with the Know Nothings to weaken the chances of the People's party.[64]

Between the Democrats and the People's-Republican party the campaign was conducted with an intensity probably unequalled in any earlier contest. Throughout the campaign the two youthful gubernatorial candidates made joint appearances. Willard was already well known and extremely popular, and the campaign for the first time brought Morton to the attention of people all over the state. At the state level there was no powerful issue such as temperance had been in 1854, with the result that national questions received the most attention. Developments in regard to Kansas, which were given extended coverage in the newspapers, took priority over local events. In Indianapolis, Republicans staged a parade in which one wagon carried men representing "border ruffians," a second a tableau representing Brooks's attack on Sumner, and a third, young ladies dressed in the newly fashionable hoop skirts—in honor of "our Jessie," Frémont's beautiful wife. Democrats tried to counteract the effect of the Kansas issue by appeals to race prejudice, charging that the Republicans were abolitionists and amalgamationists, bent on giving full social and political equality to Negroes. Girls in white dresses paraded with banners bearing the plea, "Fathers, save us from nigger husbands!"[65]

64 Charles Roll, "Richard W. Thompson, A Political Conservative in the Fifties," *Indiana Magazine of History*, XXVII (1931), 191; Brand, "Know Nothing Party," *ibid.*, XVIII, 275-276, 281-283. In the southern part of the state Thompson was accused of being in the pay of the Democrats.

65 Indianapolis *Daily Sentinel*, July 16, 1856; Van Bolt, "Rise of the Republican Party," *Indiana Magazine of History*, LI, 213.

In the balloting the People's party failed to make as impressive a showing as in 1854, and the Democrats were generally successful. In the October elections Willard defeated Morton by a little less than 6,000 votes and carried the rest of the Democratic state ticket to victory with him. In the presidential election in November, Buchanan carried the state with 118,672 votes to 94,376 for Frémont and 22,836 for Fillmore. The Know Nothing ticket had no important effect on the outcome, the combined vote of Frémont and Fillmore being less than that of Buchanan. In the Congressional races Democrats won four new seats and retained the two they had, while the People's party candidates were successful in five districts. As in 1854 the election showed a distinct sectional cleavage within the state. The Democrats carried the counties in the southern half of the state, while the Republicans carried the northern half. There was some evidence that Germans were turning to the Republicans. The German vote was credited with carrying Marion County for the People's party. Democrats showed greater strength in Indiana than in any of the other states of the Old Northwest. Buchanan carried Illinois, but the Republican state ticket was victorious there, while Republicans made a clean sweep in Ohio, Michigan, and Wisconsin.[66]

Both before and after the election there were charges of large-scale importation of illegal voters by both parties. Democrats, who were in power, were accused of assessing officeholders in order to raise funds to "colonize" voters in the state. Republicans made elaborate preparations to detect and challenge fraudulent voters. They were especially appre-

[66] Esarey, *History of Indiana,* II, map, p. 646, and table, pp. 648-649; Stoler, "Democratic Element," *Indiana Magazine of History,* XXXVI, 190; Van Bolt, "Rise of the Republican Party," *ibid.,* LI, 216; Carter, Decade of Hoosier History, pp. 116, 123; Brand, "Know Nothing Party," *Indiana Magazine of History,* XVIII, 289-291. Calvin Fletcher commented upon the "many changes" among German voters in 1856. He felt that the "better class" of Germans were with the Republicans but that the Irish and "Ignorant slave state men" were solidly against the Republicans. Calvin Fletcher Diary, October 3, 14, 1856.

hensive over the Irish, who were always loyal to the Democrats and who had a propensity for selling their votes and
for voting more than once. Prejudice against Roman Catholics
increased the suspicion of the political activity of the Irish.
At both the October and November elections, Calvin Fletcher,
Indianapolis banker who was an earnest Methodist and active
Republican, secured two copies of the "Catholic Bible" to use
at his polling place when Irish voters were challenged, since
he thought this might deter them from perjuring themselves.[67]

After the election it was charged that as many as five thousand illegal votes—mostly Irish—had been cast for the Democrats. On the other hand, Democrats attributed the election
of Republicans at the local level in several counties to ballots
cast by voters brought in from other counties—"vagabonds
who would sell their votes and their country for the paltry
sum of five dollars and five days board." Some substance was
given these charges by a trial in the circuit court in Fountain
County which resulted in the invalidation of the election of
the Republican candidate for county treasurer on the grounds
of illegal votes. Investigations by a legislative committee also
purported to show that prominent Republicans in Wayne and
Henry counties, Republican strongholds, had raised money to
send voters into Rush County to elect a Republican to the
state legislature, but the Republican members of the committee
strongly dissented from the report.[68]

[67] Indianapolis *Daily Senteniel*, October 21, 1856; Fletcher Diary, October
14, November 4, 1856. The entries in the diary throughout September and
October show the elaborate preparations which the Republicans were making
to get out the vote and to detect fraud. Fletcher also confided in his diary that
some Republicans were suggesting a "counter importation" of voters to
offset the frauds which they suspected the Democrats of planning. He said
he would not participate in "counter wrongs." After the election he con-
fessed that the Republicans had imported voters in some parts of the state.
"This was decidedly wrong—& God has frowned on the attempt." *Ibid.*,
September 18, 25, October 1, 16, 1856.

[68] *Ibid.*, October 16, 1856; Allan Nevins, *Ordeal of the Union* (2 volumes,
New York, 1947), I, 185; *Opinion of Hon. Wm. P. Bryant, Judge of the
Eighth Judicial Circuit, in the case of Lighty Vs. French: A Special Pro-
ceeding to Contest an Election, in the Fountain Circuit Court* (Indianapolis,

Democrats won control of the state House of Representatives in 1856, but the People's party were in a position to control the Senate by one vote through the support of two Know Nothings elected in 1854. The 1857 legislative session was marked by even more intensely partisan obstructionism than the previous session. Two United States senators were to be elected. Bright was finishing his second term and expected to be elected for a third, while there remained a second vacancy as the result of the failure of the 1855 session to agree upon a candidate. Apparently Wright had some hopes of going to the Senate after completing his term as governor, but he was thwarted in this. Instead, an arrangement was consummated under which the Democratic caucus supported Bright and Graham N. Fitch for the Senate, with the understanding that Bright would support Wright for an appointment—possibly a Cabinet post—in the Buchanan administration. In 1855 the Democrats had refused to go into joint session; in 1857 the tables were turned. Acting on recommendations of the Republican editorial convention and a Republican state convention, Republican senators refused to vote to go into a joint session to elect United States senators. Nevertheless, the Democrats, who had an over-all majority in the legislature, proceeded to re-elect Bright and to elect Graham Fitch for a four-year term. The People's party claimed that the election was invalid because the Senate had not voted to go into joint session and a quorum of both houses was not present. Both Bright and Fitch were, however, eventually seated by vote of the United States Senate, more than a year after presenting their credentials.[69]

1857); *Majority and Minority Report of the Committee on Elections on the Election Frauds in Rush Co., including Evidence in the Case; Made by the Order of the General Assembly, at the Session of 1857* (Indianapolis, 1857).

[69] Brand, "Know Nothing Party," *Indiana Magazine of History,* XVIII, 284, 293; Zimmerman, "Rise of the Republican Party, *ibid.,* XIII, 350; Van Der Weele, Jesse David Bright, pp. 197, 210-211; *Proceedings, including Speeches, Opinions and Votes in the Senate of the United States, by which the Right of the Hon. Jesse D. Bright and the Hon. Graham N. Fitch to their Seats as Senators U. S. From the State of Indiana was Confirmed* (Washington, D. C., 1858).

As the result of the deadlock between the two parties, necessary revenue and appropriation measures were not adopted
before the session came to an end. Governor Willard, abetted
by the *State Sentinel,* insisted that it was futile to call a special
session so long as the Republicans controlled the Senate. Republicans continued to blame the Democrats for blocking
necessary legislation. Regardless of where responsibility lay,
the state faced a financial crisis. Willard was confronted with
the problem of whether the state would be compelled to de-
fault on its interest payments because of failure of the legislature to act. Joseph E. McDonald, the attorney general,
advised him that the contract made by the state with the
bondholders was, in fact, a perpetual appropriation and that
no specific appropriation was necessary to pay the interest.
Willard borrowed the necessary money and paid the interest,
but because the faith of the state was not pledged for the
support of the benevolent institutions of the state, he thought
he could not spend money in the treasury to maintain them
without a specific appropriation. In consequence, the state
hospital for the insane and the institute for the blind were
closed for a few months.[70]

In his message to the 1857 legislature outgoing Governor
Wright had expressed his belief that the results of the recent
presidential election had been a victory for "that policy which
leaves the people of the several States and Territories of the
Union, to depend more and more upon their own rights and
their own resources, and confines the action of the Federal
Government within the clearly defined limits of the Constitu-

[70] Indianapolis *Daily Sentinel,* May 18, 1857; William Henry Smith, *The
History of the State of Indiana from the Earliest Explorations by the French
to the Present Time* (2 volumes, Indianapolis, 1903), I, 404-406; Zimmerman,
"Rise of the Republican Party," *Indiana Magazine of History,* XIII, 351-352.
After 1846, when arrangements had been made with the bondholders for the settlement of the debt, state officers had paid the interest without specific legislative
authorization except in 1849, 1850, and 1851, when it had been necessary
to borrow money to pay the interest. The action of a Democratic governor,
Willard, acting on the advice of a Democratic attorney general, was a
powerful precedent for the action of Republican Oliver P. Morton at the
time of the financial crisis of 1863. See below, pp. 187-190.

tion."[71] But developments of the next few months appeared to make a mockery of his optimistic words. From Kansas there continued to come reports of violence and refusal of proslavery forces to countenance free elections. In October, 1857, the proslavery territorial government, which was regarded as having been elected by the most glaring frauds, held a convention at Lecompton and drew up a constitution protecting slavery and providing for a system of ratification which made it impossible for the voters to abolish slavery completely. President Buchanan, eager to get the Kansas question settled, gave his support to admission of the state to the Union under the Lecompton constitution, thereby bringing upon his administration charges of being proslavery and of trying to force slavery upon Kansas against the will of the people. Stephen A. Douglas, convinced that a majority of the people in Kansas wanted it to be a free state, denounced Buchanan's position as a betrayal of popular sovereignty and broke with the administration.

The Lecompton issue aroused intense interest in Indiana and threatened to split the Democratic party once more. Both Indiana senators and all of the eight Indiana Democrats in the House voted for accepting the Lecompton constitution, but the general public in Indiana supported Douglas, and thirty of the Democratic newspapers in the state condemned the "Lecompton fraud." Again in 1858, Kansas loomed as the overriding campaign issue. Most of the rank and file of the Democratic party sincerely believed in popular sovereignty, and they felt that the principle was being violated in Kansas. "Although we here at Clover Land are 700 miles from Kansas, we are well posted in regard to Kansas parties . . .," wrote a resident from Clay county. "I have not seen a Democrat here in favor of admitting Kansas with the Lecompton Constitution." A few months later another voter from the same district reported: "The anti-Lecompton fever here grows hotter every day."[72]

[71] Indiana *Senate Journal*, 1857, pp. 71-72.
[72] Van Der Weele, Jesse David Bright, pp. 220, 226-229; James M. Lucas

Closely related to the Lecompton question was that of Bright's control over the Democratic party. The Senator's support of Buchanan on the Lecompton question and his opposition to Douglas caused him to be labeled by members of his own party "a tool of the South and of Buchanan." Probably three fourths of the Democratic press in the state was anti-Lecompton and favorable to Douglas. Many county conventions endorsed the same position. But Bright was still in control at the Democratic state convention on the eighth of January, 1858. Resolutions endorsing Douglas were beaten down. Thereupon Douglas men called a mass meeting on February 22, at which they passed resolutions endorsing Douglas and affirming the right of the people of Kansas to vote on their constitution. Some district conventions also split between pro- and anti-Lecomptonites.[73]

By 1858 the opposing party had finally officially taken the name Republican, and most Republican newspapers called for a straight-out Republican convention instead of a fusion movement. There was a feeling that concessions to Know Nothings in the past had weakened the party. In consequence the state platform adopted in 1858 contained no plank which even hinted at Know Nothing principles. Two persons of foreign birth were nominated for state office. But on the question of how to handle the slavery question there were differences of

to John G. Davis, December 28, 1857, H. K. Wilson to Davis, February 26, 1858, in "Some Letters to John G. Davis, 1857-1860," *Indiana Magazine of History,* XXIV (1928), 201-204. These letters show the popular interest in the Lecompton question and the efforts of the Douglas supporters to unseat Bright. In the letter quoted above, Wilson told of a meeting at Sullivan at which a speaker "dwelt on the wrongs done to Kansas, and the course pursued towards Douglas." "He handled Bright without Gloves and showed him up as a tool of the South & of Buchanan."

73 Zimmerman, "Rise of the Republican Party," *Indiana Magazine of History,* XIII, 354, 357-358, 360, 369. Many of the county conventions which denounced the Lecompton constitution at the same time endorsed the Dred Scott decision. The Bright-dominated Democratic state convention endorsed the Democratic platform of 1856 and the Buchanan administration. The platform contained a plank accusing the Republicans of fostering "the loathsome doctrine of 'negro equality.'" It expressly endorsed the Dred Scott decision. Henry (comp.), *State Platforms,* pp. 13-15.

opinion. Local Republican conventions were as loud in their denunciation of the "Lecompton fraud" as the Democrats. Some Republicans thought that victory lay in wooing anti-Lecompton Democrats by hoisting the Democratic banner of popular sovereignty. This was, of course, utterly repugnant to the old Free Soilers, who had always taken the position that Congress had not only the power but the duty to prohibit slavery in a territory.[74]

The platform adopted at the Republican state convention contained some planks designed to win anti-Lecompton Democratic votes by endorsing popular sovereignty principles and others to placate the Free Soil element. Julian tried to persuade the convention to adopt a more strongly antislavery stand by reaffirming the platform adopted at Philadelphia by the national convention in 1856, but the convention refused to support him, apparently out of fear of alienating possible Democratic support. Oliver P. Morton, who was presiding, accused Julian of factiousness.[75]

Morton and most Republicans campaigned almost exclusively on the anti-Lecompton issue, and election results seemed to show that this was sound strategy. In the Congressional elections Republicans won seven seats, two more than in 1856. One anti-Lecompton Democrat, John G. Davis, and three regular Democrats were elected. Republicans gained control of both houses of the state legislature by narrow margins. But

[74] In a call for a convention to nominate two Supreme Court judges which was issued in the name of the Republican State Central Committee, October 5, 1857, the name Republican was apparently used officially for the first time in Indiana. Zimmerman, "Rise of the Republican Party," *Indiana Magazine of History*, XIII, 352-353; Brand, "Know Nothing Party," *ibid.*, XVIII, 297.

[75] Julian, *Political Recollections*, p. 167; Stoler, "Democratic Element," *Indiana Magazine of History*, XXXVI, 192-194; Zimmerman, "Rise of the Republican Party," *ibid.*, XIII, 364. The Republican platform promised to use "all proper and constitutional means" to prevent the extension of slavery but refused to say that Congress had a duty to exclude slavery from the territories as Julian wished. For the first time the Republican platform included a homestead plank—a proposal to grant one hundred sixty acres of land to actual settlers. Henry (comp.), *State Platforms*, p. 16.

the regular Democratic ticket of state officers was once more elected.[76]

In the 1859 session of the legislature, the Republicans in the House passed a resolution calling for the admission of Kansas with a constitution consistent with the Constitution of the United States, adopted by the majority of her people, "without regard to what shall be the opinion of her people on the subject of slavery." In the debate several members asserted that popular sovereignty was sound Republican doctrine, as it had been preached in the campaign and as they understood it. One member who bore the Republican label declared: "If Kansas came in with a constitution republican in form, he was in favor of her admission, with or without slavery." Although George W. Julian might writhe at this brand of "Republicanism," others who sincerely desired to stop the extension of slavery felt that events in Kansas were demonstrating that the unhampered operation of popular sovereignty would prevent the admission of any more slave states.[77]

By 1860 the Republicans had overthrown the supremacy of the long-entrenched Democracy and emerged as a party numerically as strong or stronger than their rival. Large numbers of Democrats had joined their ranks. Except for a small band of Know Nothing Whigs who espoused the Constitutional Union cause in 1860, former Whigs had moved en masse into the new party. Concern over slavery and temperance, issues which had a stronger emotional appeal than older questions like the tariff, was the obvious reason for the political realignment. But there were other contributing factors.

---

[76] Zimmerman, "Rise of the Republican Party," *Indiana Magazine of History*, XIII, 371; Carter, Decade of Hoosier History, p. 134. In some places, especially Indianapolis and Lafayette, Germans who had formerly voted Democratic were given credit for the Republican victory. Stoler, "Democratic Element," *Indiana Magazine of History*, XXXVI, 197.

[77] House Joint Resolution 19 was introduced by Elijah Cavins, Republican. No action was taken on the resolution in the Senate. Indiana *House Journal*, 1859, pp. 304-306; *Brevier Legislative Reports*, 1859, pp. 109-110.

One was the increased political importance of the northern part of the state, where population was growing most rapidly and where the new party showed its greatest strength. Resentment against the Bright machine, especially in the northern counties, also contributed to defections from the Democrats. Economic conditions, although they did not receive much attention in political speeches or in the press, were no doubt an ingredient in the political upheaval. In 1854 and 1855 there were numerous bank failures arising out of laxity in the administration of the Free Banking law. In 1856 there were widespread crop failures and in 1857 a general depression.

The new party—which hesitated to adopt the name Republican—was a coalition held together as much by expediency and opportunism as by principle. The reform elements—the Liberty party and Free Soil men who had first raised the call for a new party—were submerged in an organization which was dominated by men who were cautious and conservative on the slavery question.

CHAPTER III
SECESSION AND CIVIL WAR

IN 1860 REPUBLICANS were optimistic over their prospects, and the practical politicians in the party did not intend that victory should elude them because of any taint of radicalism or abolitionism or humanitarian concern for the Negro which might attach to the label Republican. So far as the choice of a presidential candidate was concerned, the Indianapolis *Journal* frankly stated, ". . . we want any man for our candidate who can win, for *success is a duty.*" An opportunity to win should not be sacrificed "to some fanciful purity of faith." The *Journal* wanted the candidate most likely to win "because it is a *duty* the Republican party owes to the cause which has created it, to stop right now the advance of slavery. . . . Unite for another four years the Executive and Judicial powers for slavery, and freedom will be by law shut up in the free states, and existing there only by sufferance. . . ."[1] Republicans regarded winning control of the state legislature almost as vital as winning the electoral votes of the state. A Republican legislature would mean the election of a Republican to the United States Senate and would provide an opportunity to redistrict the state in such a way as to guarantee Republican domination for years to come.

On the subject of slavery Republicans expressed such a diversity of views that Democrats could well ask, What is a Republican? But except for a handful of old Free Soil-Liberty men Republicans were inclined to be cautious and to try to do nothing which might alienate the most conservative old-line Whigs in southern Indiana. Some, including Oliver P.

[1] Indianapolis *Daily Journal*, March 3, 22, 1860, quoted in Kenneth M. Stampp, *Indiana Politics during the Civil War (Indiana Historical Collections,* XXXI, Indianapolis, 1949), pp. 34-35; Stoler, "Democratic Element," *Indiana Magazine of History,* XXXVI, 198-199.

Morton, suggested that the best course was to subordinate slavery to other issues. In their state platform Republicans used language which could scarcely offend any resident of a free state. In an oblique slap at the Dred Scott decision they declared their opposition to the doctrine that "the Federal Constitution carries slavery into the public Territories." In words almost identical with those used by Stephen A. Douglas in his reply to Lincoln at Freeport they declared their belief "that slavery cannot exist anywhere in this government unless by positive local law," and expressed opposition to the extension of slavery into the territories. But the convention refused to reaffirm the Philadelphia platform of 1856 which had declared that Congress had the right and duty to exclude slavery from all territories. "The Republicans have stepped off their platform of 1856," gibed the *Sentinel*. "They have not the 'pluck' to face it in another canvass. They ignore the issues they regarded as vital principles not quite four years ago." And George W. Julian and his little coterie could but agree. In other planks the platform opposed the reopening of the African slave trade, demanded the admission of Kansas as a free state, and asked for a homestead law and construction of a transcontinental railroad.[2]

The leading contenders for the gubernatorial nomination were Oliver P. Morton and Henry S. Lane. Morton had carried the burden of the 1856 campaign and had strong backing for renomination. But Lane drew support from those who insisted upon rotation and because his presence would be likely to insure the support of conservative old-line Whigs. A compromise was worked out whereby Lane was nominated for the governorship while Morton accepted the lieutenant governorship with the understanding that if Republicans gained control of the legislature, they would elect Lane to the United States Senate and Morton would automatically suc-

[2] Foulke, *Morton*, I, 64; Indianapolis *Daily Journal*, February 23, 1860; Indianapolis *Daily Sentinel*, February 27, 1860; Stampp, *Indiana Politics*, p. 29; Henry (comp.), *State Platforms*, pp. 20-21.

ceed to the governorship.[3] With a platform which was inoffensive and a ticket headed by two stalwart campaigners drawn from both the Whig and Democratic parties, the Republicans faced the campaign with confidence that they had little to fear from a possible third-party ticket of former Know Nothings.[4]

The decision of the Indiana delegation to support Lincoln for the presidential nomination was dictated in a large part by expediency. The Indiana delegates were much sought after at Chicago because they were uninstructed and because it was felt that Republicans must carry Indiana in order to elect a president. A majority of the delegates, including Defrees and Colfax, probably favored the nomination of Edward Bates of Missouri because he was regarded as more acceptable to former Whigs than any other candidate. But the overriding consideration was to head off the nomination of William H. Seward, who was regarded as too strongly antislavery to be able to carry Indiana. Both Morton and Lane agreed that Seward's nomination would mean certain defeat for Republicans in Indiana. By the time the convention met, many of the delegates were prepared to support Lincoln because the cause of Bates seemed hopeless. Lincoln as a Middle Westerner and former Whig, who was regarded as less extreme on the slavery question than Seward, would appeal to conservatives and would be more attractive to German voters than Bates, who had supported the Know Nothing cause in 1856. Behind the scenes at Chicago, Lane and Caleb B. Smith worked feverishly for Lincoln, and Defrees came to the support of Lincoln as the only way of stopping Seward. Even

[3] Foulke, *Morton*, I, 66; David Turpie, *Sketches of My Own Times* (Indianapolis, 1903), pp. 183-184; Stoler, "Democratic Element," *Indiana Magazine of History*, XXXVI, 202.

[4] The Republicans had avoided using the word "Republican" in calling the state convention in the hope of holding the support of former Know Nothings. Their nominee for attorney general, James G. Jones of Vanderburgh County, was a Know Nothing and Fillmore elector in 1856. Brand, "Know Nothing Party," *Indiana Magazine of History*, XVIII, 302.

Julian, who had really wanted Salmon P. Chase, was willing to support Lincoln wholeheartedly, although he felt that those who opposed Seward represented a "superficial and only half-developed Republicanism."[5]

Meanwhile, the Douglas supporters had finally wrested control of the Democratic party from the iron grip of Jesse Bright. In spite of Bright's strenuous efforts, including, it was rumored, the use of cold cash as well as patronage, the Bright-Buchanan forces, who also had the support of Governor Willard, were unable to dominate the January convention of the Indiana Democracy. Even before the convention it was evident that Douglas had captured the rank and file and most of the party leaders. The Indianapolis *Sentinel*, edited by J. J. Bingham, had finally declared for Douglas after nearly all the other Democratic papers in the state had declared their allegiance to him. Efforts of Bright to prevent the convention from instructing for Douglas were beaten down and the victorious insurgents staged a wild demonstration. It was evident, as one Douglas delegate put it, that "the State of Indiana [was] entirely out of Jessee's Breaches Pocket [*sic*]."[6]

While the Democratic platform deplored sectional political parties and reaffirmed the popular sovereignty plank of the 1856 Cincinnati platform, it also indirectly endorsed the Dred Scott decision by defending the Supreme Court. In an effort to placate the defeated Bright forces it spoke highly of the abilities of President Buchanan. For governor the Democrats nominated Thomas A. Hendricks, a Shelby County lawyer, who had been a member of the state legislature and the United

---

5 Stampp, *Indiana Politics*, pp. 36, 38-39, 40; Julian, *Political Recollections*, p. 177. Of the nomination of Lincoln the Indianapolis *Daily Journal*, May 29, 1860, said: "If there was a sacrifice to timidity in it, it was the sacrifice of a man for the benefit of the cause."

6 Stampp, *Indiana Politics*, pp. 18, 20-21; Van Der Weele, *Jesse David Bright*, pp. 231-235; A. M. Puett to John G. Davis, January 15, 1860, in "Some Letters to John G. Davis," *Indiana Magazine of History*, XXIV, p. 209. "I guess old *Buck* begins to think there is other men in Indiana—new men now will come up," exulted another Douglas man. Aquilla Jones to Davis, January 20, 1860, *ibid.*, p. 211.

States House of Representatives and who had served as Commissioner of the General Land Office under Pierce and Buchanan.[7] Only forty years old in 1860, Hendricks was destined to become United States senator, governor, and Vice-President.

At the Charleston convention the Indiana delegation stuck to Douglas through days of fruitless balloting. After the convention split up, they supported the nomination of Douglas on a popular sovereignty platform at Baltimore. Most Indiana Democrats were bitter against the southern Democrats for splitting the party. They privately felt that the Democratic split insured a Republican victory. "Knowing as I do that secessionists truly represent the feelings of a large majority of the Southern Democrats," wrote one disgruntled Indianan, "I rather hope that Lincoln may be elected. It may have the effect to learn them some sense."[8] On the other hand, Bright, who had gone to Charleston vowing to campaign in Indiana against Douglas should his arch foe be nominated, took satisfaction in the fact that the party split gave him an opportunity to carry out his threat by working for the Breckinridge-Lane ticket nominated by the southern Democrats.[9] This would also enable him to take revenge against Indiana Democrats for their revolt against him. Together with Graham Fitch, Bright attempted to organize a Breckinridge movement. In July they began publication of a triweekly paper in Indianapolis, the *Old Line Guard*, which was more strongly anti-Douglas than anti-Lincoln. Bright was under no illusions that Breckinridge would carry the state. His purpose was to defeat Douglas and to win back control of the Democracy in Indiana.[10]

[7] John B. Nowland, *Sketches of Prominent Citizens of 1876* . . . (Indianapolis, 1877), p. 420.

[8] Austin H. Brown to John G. Davis, May 24, 1860, in "Some Letters to John G. Davis," *Indiana Magazine of History*, XXIV, 211.

[9] See Van Der Weele, *Jesse David Bright*, pp. 240-250, for an account of Bright's strenuous efforts to prevent the nomination of Douglas.

[10] *Ibid.*, pp. 250-261; Reinhard H. Luthin, "Indiana and Lincoln's Rise to the Presidency," *Indiana Magazine of History*, XXXVIII (1942), 401-402.

While the regular Democrats were faced with the defection of Breckinridge supporters, Republicans were confronted with the possibility of losing votes to John Bell of Tennessee, the candidate of the Constitutional Union party, which in Indiana was made up of the remnants of the Know Nothing party and which inherited the Know Nothing organization. Richard W. Thompson was the most influential supporter of the Constitutional Union movement, which had as its object "to remove the subject of slavery from the arena of party politics and to leave it to the independent control of the states in which it exists and to the unbiased action of the judiciary." Although the Bell men held a state convention in August, they did not nominate a separate state ticket. There were some efforts by Douglas men in southern Indiana to combine with the Constitutional Union men, but they met with little success. For the most part, Bell men appear to have supported the Republican state ticket. Thompson issued a circular urging support of Lane for governor because he was "an old Whig educated in the faith taught by Henry Clay."[11]

Although Thompson expected to vote for Bell, he was not alarmed at the prospect of the election of Lincoln, the former Whig with whom he had served in Congress. There is no better evidence of the belief in Lincoln's conservatism at this time than the attitude of the Constitutional Union men toward him. William K. Edwards, next to Thompson the most influential Bell man in the state, wrote following Lincoln's nomination: "The result of the Chicago Convention on their candidate and platform was more moderate than was apprehended or anticipated. It is quite a come-down from 1856 . . . Lincoln however to my mind is so much better than Seward and Co., that I have no opposition to him." Thompson wrote Lincoln congratulating him upon his nomination out of his personal regard and also, he said, because he regarded the nomination "as an important step toward conservatism" upon the part

11 Roll, "Richard W. Thompson," *Indiana Magazine of History*, XXVII, 195, 203; Brand, "Know Nothing Party," *ibid.*, XVIII, 304; Luthin, "Indiana and Lincoln's Rise," *ibid.*, XXXVIII, 404.

of those who comprised the Chicago convention. In a speech on behalf of Bell in August, Thompson denounced both Breckinridge and Douglas as sectional candidates and spoke highly of Lincoln. On the eve of the election, probably because he recognized the hopelessness of the Bell cause, Thompson issued a statement "To the Conservative Men of Indiana," in which he declared that if Lincoln was elected, he was confident that there would be no change in the status of slavery during the next few years.[12]

The New Albany *Tribune,* a Know Nothing paper, urged the election of Lincoln on the grounds that while he was opposed to the extension of slavery into the territories he was also opposed to Negro equality and in favor of the enforcement of the Fugitive Slave Law. This statement reflected very well the image of Lincoln and the Republican party which the Republican leaders sought to impress upon the voters during the campaign. Although Republican campaigners preferred to talk about questions other than slavery, they sought forcibly to impress upon the public that they were not abolitionists, that they did not intend to interfere with slavery in the states. Most of all they tried to counteract Democratic charges that they were "Nigger Lovers" by insisting that their opposition to the extension of slavery was not due to any especial humanitarian interest in the welfare of the slave. At the outset of his campaign Henry S. Lane asserted that Republicans intended to abide by all the compromises in the Constitution on slavery, "and if the most extreme Southerner in Carolina would be here, he would ask no more than this." He declared that he supported the Fugitive Slave Act of 1850 (although he preferred the act of 1793) and that he would have voted for it had he been a member of Congress. "Do you," he asked his audience, "discover any Abolitionism in that?"[13]

13 Luthin, "Indiana and Lincoln's Rise," *ibid.,* XXXVIII, 405; Roll, "Richard W. Thompson," *ibid.,* XXVII, 200-201, 203; Roll, *Colonel Dick Thompson,* p. 159.

13 New Albany *Tribune,* June 11, 1860, quoted in Brand, "Know Nothing

Morton, who was quite as active in the campaign as Lane, emphasized the slavery issue more strongly than did Lane and was somewhat less cautious. While denying that the government had any right to interfere with slavery in the states, he skillfully and forcibly presented the arguments for the right of Congress to prohibit slavery from the territories, thereby by implication refuting the opinion of the Supreme Court in the Dred Scott case. He emphasized that the exclusion of slavery from the territories was in the interest of the nation as a whole, while the admission of slavery benefited only a small minority. "We believe," he said,

that slavery is a moral, social, and political evil, that [it] is a curse to many people, a foe to progress, an enemy of education and intelligence, and an element of social and political weakness. . . .

But there are other considerations of a more personal and selfish character. If we do not exclude slavery from the territories, it will exclude us. . . . The introduction of slavery into a territory prevents you and your children from going there as effectually as would a legislative act. It erects a barrier to your emigration which you will never surmount.[14]

This last argument was frequently used by Republicans as refutation of the Democratic charge that they were the especial friends of the Negro. In fact, they averred, Democrats actually favored Negroes over whites because they were willing to let Negro slaves be taken into the territories. "Just how they [Democrats] manage to infer a disposition to favor Negro equalization with whites from anything Republicans believe or ever have done, nobody can tell, they least of all," protested the Indianapolis *Journal*. "Republicans oppose the extension of slavery into the territories because it compels the white laborer to work beside the Negro, and degrades labor into the occupation of a menial." It was ridiculous to bring the charge of " 'nigger equality' against a party, the

Party," *Indiana Magazine of History*, XVIII, 304; Indianapolis *Daily Sentinel*, February 29, 1860.

14 Foulke, *Morton*, I, 81.

first cardinal principle of whose creed is, exclusion of Niggers from the Territories."[15]

These protestations in no way quieted the Democrats, who were eager to capitalize on race feeling. "The equality of the Negro with the white man, universal suffrage, extending to Negroes as well as to white men," declared Douglas, "is the grand central theme of the Republican organization." Other lesser Democrats belabored the theme, warning that Republican victory would mean an influx of Negroes into Indiana to compete with white workers. Without the slightest foundation for their assertions they insisted that Republicans were also plotting Negro suffrage and the "amalgamation" of the races. To these charges Republicans responded with considerable glee that it was the Democrats who deserved the amalgamationist label since the only part of the country in which miscegenation was widely practiced was in the slave states, where most masters were members of the Democratic party. Democrats also sought to entangle the race issue with the Know Nothing issue by insisting that Republicans were more favorably disposed toward Negroes than to white foreigners.[16] Republicans, on the other hand, made more strenuous efforts in 1860 than before to win the German voters who heretofore had been traditionally Democratic and who had been suspicious of the Republicans because of their ties with the Know Nothings. Republicans appealed to national headquarters for money for German speakers and German news-

[15] Indianapolis *Daily Journal,* September 15, 27, October 1, 1860.

[16] Indianapolis *Daily Sentinel,* May 5, September 1, 1860; Emma Lou Thornbrough, "The Race Issue in Indiana Politics during the Civil War," *Indiana Magazine of History,* XLVII (1951), 168 and *passim.* In a typical piece of Democratic campaign oratory David Turpie, the candidate for lieutenant governor, cried: "Let us say that this government was made by white men, for white men, purely upon a white basis, for the security, advantage, and happiness of ourselves and our posterity, and that its deep foundation shall never be disturbed by the claims of the Negro, either free or slave." Indianapolis *Daily Sentinel,* June 21, 1860. The ticket for state offices which had been nominated in January continued to have the support of both factions of the Democratic party.

papers, since it was possible that victory might depend on the German vote. Carl Schurz was brought into the state to speak in the towns where Germans were numerous. Efforts to win the German press were successful. Papers at Evansville and Fort Wayne which had formerly been Democratic supported Lincoln. In fact, of eight German papers in the state, only the Indianapolis *Volksblatt* supported Douglas. In the election Allen County was in the Democratic column, but other counties with a large German element went Republican.[17]

Although neither of the gubernatorial candidates said much about slavery in their joint debates, their efforts to inject other issues into the campaign failed to arouse enthusiasm. Both parties were committed to support homestead legislation, but on this issue the Republicans had an advantage since Hendricks' past record on this was somewhat inconsistent and Buchanan had vetoed a homestead bill. Democrats vigorously attacked the tariff plank in the Republican national platform, warning that a Republican victory would mean a high tariff detrimental to the interests of the farmer and laborer. Lane and the Republicans took an equivocal position on the tariff since opinion in favor of protection was by no means unanimous.[18]

The campaign which the Republicans conducted was marked by more spectacles, better organized political clubs, and probably by the expenditure of more money than any previous campaign. The Lincoln "Rail Maulers" and "Wide Awakes" were uniformed groups who participated in all parades and rallies. Since Indiana was a critical state, many outside speakers stumped within her borders for both parties. Douglas himself visited the state for the Democrats, while Salmon P. Chase, Cassius M. Clay, Frank Blair, and Thomas Corwin,

---

[17] Stampp, *Indiana Politics,* p. 48; Stoler, "Democratic Element," *Indiana Magazine of History,* XXXVI, 204-205; Carter, Decade of Hoosier History, p. 69; Luthin, "Indiana and Lincoln's Rise," *Indiana Magazine of History,* XXXVIII, 398-400.

[18] Stampp, *Indiana Politics,* pp. 43-44.

as well as Schurz, appeared for the Republicans. The Indianapolis *Sentinel* reported that Seward had been requested to avoid the state during the campaign. In response to pleas from Caleb B. Smith, David Davis appealed to Thurlow Weed to send money to Indiana.

I hope the National Committee will do all they can for the State. The whole money they asked (& more if it can be raised) should be sent at once. *Men work better with money in hand.*

The first order of German speakers are needed in Indiana. . . .

I believe in God's Providence in this Election, but at the same time we should keep our powder dry.

Defrees also appealed to Weed for money to prevent the Bell men from voting the Democratic ticket for state offices. "To injure our prospects in November, I am afraid a majority of the Bell men will vote against us in our state in October . . .," he wrote. "We need money very much."[19] Republican alarm over the defection of Bell supporters to the Democrats appears to have been unfounded. Also, in spite of Bright's desire for revenge there did not appear much of a possibility that the Breckenridge vote would go to the Republican state ticket.[20]

The October state elections showed a substantial victory for Lane and Morton and the Republican legislative candidates. Republicans again won seven of the Congressional seats while Democrats retained control of the four seats they had won in 1858—all of them in districts in the southern part of the state. In spite of frantic last minute efforts of the Democrats to reverse the Republican trend, Lincoln carried the state in November, winning a clear majority over his

---

19 *Ibid.,* 45-46; Indianapolis *Daily Sentinel,* August 29, 1860; Luthin "Indiana and Lincoln's Rise," *Indiana Magazine of History,* XXXVIII, 398-399. The money which was sent—$2,000—went to pay the expenses of Carl Schurz and other speakers and to assist the German newspapers.

20 William S. Holman of Aurora predicted that the Breckinridge men in his district would support the Democratic state ticket. Holman to Allen Hamilton, September 4, 1860, Hamilton Papers.

three opponents. For the first time since 1840 the Democrats had failed to win the electoral votes of Indiana.[21]

§ §

During the last stages of the campaign the Democrats had adopted alarmist tactics, warning that a victory by the sectional Republican party would inaugurate "a strife which must end either in civil war for the mastery or a peaceful division of the Union"—and ruin for the economic interests of the Northwest. When the Republicans triumphed in the state election, the *Sentinel* cried: "The 'irrepressible conflict' of Seward and Lincoln has commenced. No human foresight can see the end." To predictions of this sort the Republican press replied that Lincoln's policies would be calculated to "restore and strengthen kind and fraternal feelings between all the patriotic citizens of the several states." On the eve of the election, the Indianapolis *Journal* scoffed that the threats of secession in the southern press were mere election-year bluff. "One single year of Lincoln's administration," it confidently asserted, would expose the hollowness of the secession threat so effectually "that it will never be heard of again."[22]

When events in the South proved the Democrats the truer prophets, there was a tendency for them to place the blame for secession squarely on the Republicans. When South Carolina announced in December, 1860, that she was severing her bands with the Union and as her sister states prepared to join her, the almost universal response of both Democrats and

21 Democrats William H. English and John G. Davis did not seek re-election to Congress. The following Democrats were elected: John Law, James A. Cravens, William S. Holman, Daniel W. Voorhees. Republicans elected to Congress were: William McKee Dunn, Albert G. Porter, Schuyler Colfax, George W. Julian, Albert S. White, William Mitchell, John P. C. Shanks. Lane and the other state officers were elected by a margin of about 10,000 votes. The official tabulation for the presidential candidates was as follows: Lincoln, 139,033; Douglas, 115,509; Breckinridge, 12,294; Bell, 5,306. Stampp, *Indiana Politics,* pp. 47n, 48n; Carter, Decade of Hoosier History, pp. 147-148.

22 Indianapolis *Daily Sentinel,* October 9, 10, 1860, quoted in Stampp, *Indiana Politics,* pp. 46-47; Indianapolis *Daily Journal,* September 7, October 16, 1860, quoted, *ibid.*

Republicans at first was to call for compromise and to shrink back in alarm from the prospect of the use of force. Many moderate Republicans, including Governor-elect Lane, appeared to be ready to abandon the Chicago platform in the interests of a compromise which would preserve the Union.

The Democratic press frequently sounded like an echo of the press of the secessionist states in placing the blame for the crisis on Republican leaders, endorsement of Helper's *Impending Crisis,* failure to enforce the Fugitive Slave Law, and especially the personal liberty laws of the North. The Indianapolis *Sentinel* declared that the North had been rife with treason ever since the antislavery agitation had begun. Republican leaders Sumner, Wade, Giddings, and Wilson had shown the South the way to treason. "Whatever may be the result of the secession movements at the South," it asserted, "nothing is clearer than the fact that the Black Republicans of the North have led the way to nullification, and disunion in these [personal liberty] laws." Judge E. M. Huntington, in a charge to the grand jury in the United States District Court for Indiana, instructed the members to uphold all Federal laws and praised Indiana for its record in enforcement of these laws. In reply the jury declared that "Northern irritations and insults," especially failure to enforce the Fugitive Slave Law, were the immediate causes for disunion. It denounced antislavery agitation and called for "faithful execution of the sacred covenants of the Constitution." Privately more moderate Democrats, while placing some blame on the Republicans, also held Northern Democrats of the Buchanan-Bright variety partially responsible for deluding the South as to the true state of opinion in the North. They also felt that Buchanan's vacillation contributed strength to the secessionists.[23]

The Indianapolis *Journal* placed the blame for the crisis on northern Democrats, accusing them of inflaming southern

[23] Indianapolis *Daily Sentinel,* December 4, 5, 7, 10, 1860; William S. Holman to Allen Hamilton, November 18 and December 28, 1860, Hamilton Papers.

fears by their campaign propaganda that Republicans were Abolitionists and advocates of Negro equality. But even though the *Journal* denied the right of a state to secede, it questioned the use of force, declaring that the "main question" was not "the constitutionality of secession, but the blood and horror of coercion." It urged the repeal of personal liberty laws, settlement of the slavery question in the territories by popular sovereignty, and the restoration of the Missouri Compromise line. The Centerville *True Republican,* Julian's paper, denounced the editorial policy of the *Journal* as one of surrender and declared that *"Free States Must Not Be Bullied."*[24]

In his message to the legislature which convened in January, outgoing Governor Hammond (a former Whig turned Democrat) blamed the crisis on the North and especially the northern clergy for their antislavery agitation and their insistence upon judging all questions from the "moral point of view." As the result of the election of a northern president by a northern party, he averred, "the instinct of self-preservation is now causing in the South that character of action which threatens to shake the fabric of our government to its center."[25]

Incoming Governor Lane, who had been reported as having suggested that the North might be willing to accept the exten-

[24] Indianapolis *Daily Journal,* November 19, 29, 1860; Centerville *Indiana True Republican,* December 6, 1860; January 31, February 7, 1861; Stampp, *Indiana Politics,* pp. 51-52.

[25] Indiana *Senate Journal,* 1861, pp. 27-28. Governor Willard had become ill during the campaign of 1860 and died on October 4, the first Indiana governor to die in office. Abram A. Hammond, his successor, was a native of Vermont who had come to Indiana as a child. He lived at various places in the state and was a resident of Terre Haute when nominated for lieutenant governor. Hammond was a well-known lawyer who had been a Whig but had transferred to the Democratic party after the disastrous campaign of 1852. In 1856 the candidate chosen for the lieutenant governorship by the Democratic convention, John C. Walker, was discovered to be too young to be eligible, and the State Central Committee named Hammond in his place. Woollen, *Biographical and Historical Sketches,* pp. 113-115.

sion of the Missouri Compromise line to the Pacific, struck a conciliatory note in his message to the legislature. He sought to allay southern fears by emphasizing that the South had been deluded as to the true nature and objects of the Republican party. He denied that the Republicans had any intention of making war upon "the interests and institutions of the Southern people." Pointing with pride to the fact that Indiana had not enacted any personal liberty laws, he called for the repeal of all "State legislation . . . contrary to the letter or spirit of the Constitution and intended to defeat the execution of any of the laws of Congress."[26]

The General Assembly, which met in January, 1861, was flooded with petitions and resolutions from Union meetings which called for a policy of conciliation and abandonment of any party platforms which stood in the way of compromise. But the Republican majority, while moving cautiously, prevented the adoption of any resolution which endorsed compromise or concessions. A joint resolution was adopted which recognized the right of states to control their own "domestic institutions" and which disclaimed any intention of violating the Constitution or interfering with laws passed under the Constitution, but which pledged support to the present or incoming administration for all measures for the preservation of the Union.[27]

Throughout the state Union meetings were called, principally by Democrats, but frequently with the support of Republicans, at which conciliatory resolutions were passed. At Indianapolis a state Union convention was held on February 22, at which Democrats, Republicans, and Constitutional Unionists were present. Robert Dale Owen served as chairman of the committee on resolutions, which urged that merely opening the territories to slavery would not strengthen the institution of slavery.[28]

26 Indiana *Senate Journal,* 1861, pp. 54-57.
27 Stampp, *Indiana Politics,* pp. 62-63; Indiana *Laws,* 1861, pp. 188-189.
28 Indianapolis *Daily Sentinel,* February 23, 1861.

Economic considerations played an important part in shaping attitudes toward the secession crises. A business slump strengthened the movement for compromise. Farmers and merchants in the southern part of the state, which traditionally had close economic ties with the South, were appalled at the thought of war. "In view of the geographical position of the State of Indiana . . ., her commercial, agricultural, mechanical and manufacturing interests being . . . interwoven and fostered chiefly by the South," declared a meeting at Salem, Washington County, "a separation therefrom would be fatal to the prosperity, glory, and wealth of our beloved State." While deprecating the calamity of disunion the meeting declared that if separation came, "the line of separation must run north of us." The New Albany *Ledger* pointed out that if the West allied itself with the South, she would retain the use of the rivers which were the natural outlets for her commerce, while alliance with the Northeast meant dependence upon railroads. Public meetings in several of the river counties expressed the view that their true interests lay with the South. In the southern part of the state the position which Kentucky would take in the crisis was regarded as of crucial importance. There was widespread fear that she would secede and cast her lot with the Confederacy, making the Ohio River the boundary between two hostile nations. The Madison *Courier,* a Republican newspaper, proposed a joint meeting of the Indiana and Kentucky legislatures to try to find some settlement of the problem. The New Albany *Ledger* expressed the hope that Indiana and Kentucky could serve as mediators and peacemakers between North and South. But other spokesmen from southern Indiana were ready to support a firm position by the Federal government. Indiana, declared Democratic Representative W. S. Holman in Congress, would "concede and concede and concede, and compromise and compromise and compromise," to preserve the blessings of Union, but "never consent, by her voice, by her acts, or by her silence that this Union shall be destroyed." Holman took a firm stand against the abandonment of Federal property in the South. "I would feed our soldiers at Fort Sumter," he said, "and leave the result with Providence."[29]

While most leaders were urging compromise or were vacillating between a policy of concession and firmness, one figure emerged who unequivocally demanded an end to concessions, no compromise with treason, and the use of force if necessary to preserve the Union. Oliver P. Morton's first opportunity to express his views came at a victory celebration of the Lincoln Rail Maulers on November 22. In a speech in which he adopted a position similar to the one which Lincoln was to take, Morton declared that coercion was nothing more than the enforcement of law and that the President of the United States had no choice but to see that the law was enforced. "We are a nation, one and indivisible . . .," he declared. "And especially must we of the inland states cling to the national idea," or face the prospect of being cut off from access to the outer world. "Shall we now surrender the nation without a struggle and let the Union go with merely a few hard words? . . . If it was worth a bloody struggle to establish this nation, it is worth one to preserve it."[30]

Although Democrats were highly critical, Morton's speech had a tremendous effect on opinion, not only in Indiana but throughout the Old Northwest, and contributed to a stiffening in the attitudes of the Indianapolis *Journal* and Republicans generally. After Lane was elected to the Senate and Morton succeeded him as governor in accordance with the agreement made before the election, Morton did not echo the

[29] *History of Lawrence, Orange and Washington Counties Indiana* (Chicago, 1884), pp. 797-798; Kenenth M. Stampp, "Kentucky's Influence upon Indiana in the Crisis of 1861," *Indiana Magazine of History*, XXXIX (1943), 264-266; Israel George Blake, *The Holmans of Veraestau* (Oxford, Ohio, 1943), pp. 94, 96. "We who have no cause of quarrel, should hold ourselves in a position where we can act, if need be, as arbiters and peacemakers between the contending factions. . . . And no two states are . . . better prepared to assume this important office than Indiana and Kentucky." New Albany *Weekly Ledger*, November 21, 1860.

[30] Foulke, *Morton*, I, 87-93.

conciliatory note which Lane had struck. On the first occasion when he made a public address after taking office, he said bluntly that he was there "to denounce treason and uphold the cause of the Union." He warned against encouraging the southern secessionists by giving the impression that the North was divided and undecided and called upon all men, regardless of party affiliation, to support the Union.[31]

Because public opinion in Indiana demanded it and the legislature authorized it, Morton appointed delegates to the national peace conference which met in February in response to a call from Virginia. In a letter to Lincoln, Morton expressed the view that it was wise to send delegates to the convention—"to take hold of it and control it," rather than "to stand by and suffer the consequences of its action when we have had no share in moulding it." But he was careful to select only Republicans and to obtain from them in advance pledges that they would reject any new guarantees to slavery. Morton had no hopes that anything would be accomplished at the peace conference and freely expressed the opinion that war was inevitable and that the public must be prepared for it. When Lincoln, during the first weeks of his administration, appeared to be pursuing the same course of inactivity followed by Buchanan, Morton became impatient. He made a special trip to Washington in March to assure Lincoln that Indiana would support a vigorous policy and to tender him six thousand troops for the enforcement of the laws. Earlier he had been making inquiries of the War Department about arms for Indiana, and some companies of the state militia had already tendered their services.[32]

Although Morton was ready to fight, public opinion had not yet generally crystallized in favor of the use of force, and Democrats continued to insist that Republicans were fomenting the crisis for their own purposes and that the true interests

31 Foulke, *Morton*, I, 102-104.

32 Robert Gray Gunderson, *Old Gentlemen's Convention: The Washington Peace Conference of 1861* (Madison, Wisconsin, 1961), pp. 33-34, 36; Stampp, *Indiana Politics*, pp. 63-64, 67-70; Foulke, *Morton*, I, 104-106, 113-114.

of Indiana lay with the South. "The people of Indiana do not intend to engage in a crusade against the South for party purposes," the Indianapolis *Sentinel* declared after Morton's visit to Washington, ". . . to advance the schemes of the abolitionists and the protectionists of New England and Pennsylvania." The *Jacksonian* of Rush County advocated recognition of the Confederate States as an accomplished fact—as the only alternative to bloody war. It expressed hope that in time seceding states would return to the Union. A meeting in Greencastle on April 10, 1861, which was addressed by Daniel W. Voorhees, adopted a series of resolutions condemning Republicans for creating the present crisis, for not accepting the Crittenden Compromise, for adopting a "sectional" tariff, and for "appointing notorious and avowed Abolitionists to high places of honor and trust under the new Administration." The meeting resolved to take as a motto: "Not one dollar, and not one man from Indiana with which to subjugate the South and inaugurate civil war!"[33]

§ § §

On April 13, 1861, headlines in the Indianapolis *Sentinel* proclaimed:

THE IRREPRESSIBLE CONFLICT INAUGURATED
CIVIL STRIFE COMMENCED IN CHARLESTON HARBOR
THE ABOLITION WAR OF SEWARD, LINCOLN
AND COMPANY

"The Abolition and disunion administration have attempted the coercion of the Confederate States. Such are the first fruits of Republicanism—the end no one can foresee."

News of the attack upon Fort Sumter had an electrifying effect upon a people hitherto hesitant and vacillating. Never had there been such excitement. News of the attack came on Saturday. In Indianapolis and other towns throughout the state men forgot their business and flocked to the newspaper offices to wait for news. A mass meeting which filled two

[33] Indianapolis *Daily Sentinel,* April 11, 15, 1861; *History of Rush County, Indiana* (Chicago, 1888), pp. 451-452.

halls and spilled over into the streets assembled that night in the state capital. Morton and other leaders of both parties addressed the throng, which endorsed resolutions supporting Lincoln's administration and declared, "We unite as one man to repel all treasonable assaults upon the Government, its property and citizens in every department of the Union— peaceably, if we can, forcibly, if we must." The next day from pulpits of all denominations many preachers called upon their congregations to rally to the support of their country.[34]

On the same day that Lincoln issued his call for 75,000 volunteers Morton had already tendered him 10,000. As soon as Morton was informed that Indiana's quota would be six regiments (4,683 men), he issued a call for volunteers and appointed Lew Wallace, who had served in the Mexican War, adjutant general. In the days following, the war excitement grew until it was reported that it appeared that the population of Indiana was ready to go en masse, if need be, to defend Washington, D.C. Volunteers poured into Indianapolis. "Soldiers, or good men willing to be converted into soldiers for the emergency, seem to spring up out of the ground, eager to protect the flag and conquer a peace," reported the Democratic Sentinel. Crowds welcomed the volunteers as they arrived and thronged about the State House, where they marched to take the oath of office. Many companies had their own flags and brass bands or fife and drums, and almost a holiday atmosphere, mingled with a feeling of solemnity, prevailed. The greatest fear of the volunteers was that they would arrive too late to be accepted. Within a week 12,000 troops had been tendered.[35]

34 Indianapolis *Daily Sentinel,* April 15, 1861; Stampp, *Indiana Politics,* p. 71; John H. Holliday, *Indianapolis and the Civil War* (Indiana Historical Society *Publications,* IV, No. 9, Indianapolis, 1911), pp. 548-549; Joseph A. Parsons, Jr., "Indiana and the Call for Volunteers, April, 1861," *Indiana Magazine of History,* LIV (1958), 7-8. In Terre Haute, which had always been regarded as a center of pro-Southern sympathies and where opposition to abolitionism was especially strong, the largest and most enthusiastic meeting in the town's history was held. Roll, *Colonel Dick Thompson,* p. 170.

35 Indianapolis *Daily Sentinel,* April 20, 23, 1861; Stampp, *Indiana Politics,*

Newspapers which had been urging compromise changed their tune and accepted the necessity for resort to force, although in some cases reluctantly. The New Albany *Ledger* became a war paper. The Indianapolis *Sentinel,* while insisting upon its right to criticize the policies of the Republican party, declared that it would be found to be "as loyal as the most patriotic Republican in maintaining the honor and advancing the prosperity of Indiana and the Union." At first the *Sentinel,* echoing the cry made earlier by its Republican rival, the *Journal,* asked, *"Of What Value Will an Union be that needs links of bayonets and bullets to hold it together!"* But by the end of April it was endorsing the position of Stephen A. Douglas, who was crying, "the most stupendous and unanimous preparation for war is the shortest way to peace," and was calling for legislation to hurry the war effort.[36]

Some Democratic newspapers like the Paoli *Eagle* declared that they were ready to repel any attempt by the South to invade the North but were "opposed to war being made upon the Southern States by the North." After Fort Sumter, the Logansport *Pharos* declared: "While we are in favor of a peaceable separation from such States as do not desire to remain in the Union, patriotism seems to demand that our capital should be protected against threatened assaults from whatever quarter they may come, and the force placed in the hands of the government to meet any exigency that may arise." But Democratic leaders emphatically denied that they would refuse to support the government in the preservation of the Union. During the early months of the war, volunteers were especially numerous from the southern and western counties which were normally Democratic strongholds. "Party lines are completely obliterated," a correspondent from Petersburg in the southern part of the state wrote to Morton, "and

pp. 71-72; Holliday, *Indianapolis and the Civil War,* p. 549; Parsons, "Indiana and the Call for Volunteers," *Indiana Magazine of History,* LIV, 9-13.

[36] Stampp, "Kentucky's Influence," *Indiana Magazine of History,* XXXIX, 267; Indianapolis *Daily Sentinel,* April 15, 16, 30, 1861.

the people are rallying as one man to the support of the administration."[37]

Partisanship was subordinated to patriotism in the special session of the legislature which Morton called to meet on April 24. The prevailing spirit was in sharp contrast to that at the regular session a few weeks earlier, when much of the time had been consumed in fruitless partisan debates over the impending crisis and Democratic efforts to embarrass the Republican majority. "We have passed from the field of argument to the solemn fact of war," Morton declared, and called upon the legislators to "rise above these paltry considerations" of party and to "inaugurate the era when there shall be but one party, and that for our country." Members responded to his plea. Most of the men who had earlier been insistent upon compromise now spoke firmly of the necessity to support the war. Resolutions were unanimously adopted declaring that Indiana was united for the defense of the government and ready to supply men and money. Measures were passed giving Morton ample authority to borrow and spend funds for purchase of arms and maintenance of troops. Other laws were passed concerning the state militia.[38]

Once hostilities were begun, the state clamored for action. The formerly timorous Indianapolis *Journal* was soon criticizing the Lincoln administration for its seeming indecision and want of energy. "Anything," it cried, "is pardonable now but inaction." The *Journal* declared: "The Country clamors for energy, decision and determination."[39] And no one embodied those qualities more strikingly than did the Indiana governor. In the military crisis Morton revealed himself as an organi-

[37] *History of Lawrence, Orange and Washington Counties Indiana*, p. 512; Logansport *Pharos*, quoted in Indianapolis *Daily Sentinel*, April 20, 1861; Stampp, *Indiana Politics*, p. 73n; letter from the office of the Adjutant General, Indianapolis, August 21, 1861, to Allen Hamilton, Hamilton Papers.

[38] Indiana *Senate Journal*, special session, 1861, p. 23; Stampp, *Indiana Politics*, pp. 61-67, 75-76.

[39] Indianapolis *Daily Journal*, April 23, 1861, quoted in Winfred A. Harbison, "Lincoln and Indiana Republicans, 1861-1862," *Indiana Magazine of History*, XXXIII (1937), 282.

zational genius, a veritable dynamo, and full of determination. Although the war which was beginning ultimately resulted in a vast expansion of Federal powers and a diminution in the role of the states, much of the war effort, particularly in the early stages, was borne directly by the states. The role of the war governors was of crucial importance, and no governor played his role more valiantly or effectively than did Morton.

The task of raising troops devolved directly upon the states, and Morton proved himself a vigorous and effective recruiter. In fact, in the first burst of enthusiasm for the war, more troops from Indiana volunteered than the Federal government was ready to handle. Washington was even less prepared to furnish the arms and other supplies which the troops needed. The problem of supplying the men in the local recruiting camps was left up to the states. Morton and the other state governors, with the sanction of the War Department, undertook to purchase the necessary arms and equipment in the open market. Although state action of this sort probably expedited the supplying of troops in the early stages of the war, it led to some unfortunate results. The competing efforts of state agents and agents of the War Department inevitably led to soaring prices and excessive profits for contractors and speculators. Morton, on his own authority, and without any legislative action, also undertook to furnish bullets to the troops from an arsenal operated by the state.[40]

In connection with the raising and equipping of troops Morton became embroiled in a number of altercations with Federal officials over what he regarded as unnecessary red tape and failure of the Federal government to pay sufficient attention to the needs of Indiana. He was also impatient with the military efforts of the Union and did not hesitate to urge his views on how the war should be conducted upon Lincoln, the War Department, and Gen. George B. McClellan. Of especial concern to Indiana was the situation in Kentucky, where the state government at first attempted to

[40] See below, Chapter IV, pages 165-167, for a fuller discussion.

pursue a policy of neutrality, excluding both Union and Confederate troops from the state. Counties in southern Indiana were frightened at the prospect that Kentucky would secede and thus bring the boundary of the Confederacy to the Ohio River. Lincoln's policy of seeming inaction, which was based on advice from Union men in Kentucky to wait for the Confederates to strike the first blow, was viewed with scorn and impatience by the active Morton. The latter sought to interfere personally in Kentucky's affairs and, along with the governors of Illinois and Ohio, urged the occupation of strategic points in Kentucky by Union forces. Both Generals Winfield Scott and George B. McClellan were opposed to such action. Scott observed that Kentucky Unionists had advised against such a course and suggested that "probably the danger can be better estimated at home than by friends abroad." Morton continued to criticize the War Department for ignoring Kentucky in spite of rebuffs. When rebel forces invaded Kentucky, Morton and the Indiana newspapers blamed Lincoln and the administration for indifference to the needs of the West. "It [the Lincoln administration] has been blind and deaf," declared the Indianapolis *Journal,* "and if it were fighting in no better cause than its own wisdom and energy it ought to be defeated." Morton expressed his disapproval to Lincoln himself, reminding the President that the Federal government was dependent upon the states for its armies, and expressing the opinion that "the hands of the men who labor without ceasing to sustain the Government should be held up and not deposed by indifference to their recommendations or demands." After Confederate troops invaded Kentucky, bringing an end to her effort to remain neutral, Morton and his supporters thought he was vindicated. He continued to issue warnings and advise the Lincoln administration on military strategy. He tried, with some success, to have Indiana troops transferred from West Virginia to Kentucky. To Morton and to the people of Indiana, Kentucky became the most important theater of the war. The Indianapolis *Journal* urged that fifty thousand troops be transferred to that state from the East. So conspicuous was Morton's concern over Kentucky and his interference in her affairs that it was sometimes said by both his admirers and his critics that he was governor of both Indiana and Kentucky.[41]

The criticism of Lincoln's Kentucky policy was but one of numerous examples of conflicts between the state and Federal government over military strategy. There were also clashes between Morton and Federal authorities over recruitment policies, the disposition of Indiana regiments, military purchases, care of sick and wounded soldiers, and other matters. Morton was especially fearful lest Indiana troops not get as much recognition as those of other states and that Indiana should be discriminated against in the number of military officers in the higher echelons.

In relations with the Federal government Morton clearly regarded himself as spokesman for Indiana and the most zealous champion of her interests, although other men from the state held offices of responsibility in the administration. Under Lincoln, for the first time, Indiana had a member in the Cabinet—Caleb B. Smith, who had been appointed Secretary of the Interior in fulfillment of a bargain made at the Chicago convention and in recognition of Indiana's contribution to Lincoln's election. But Lincoln seems to have had little enthusiasm for Smith, and Smith exerted no significant influence.[42] Late in 1862 he resigned from the Cabinet to

41 Stampp, "Kentucky's Influence," *Indiana Magazine of History*, XXXIX, 271-272, 274-276; Stampp, *Indiana Politics*, pp. 112-115; Harbison, "Lincoln and Indiana Republicans," *Indiana Magazine of History*, XXXIII, 287.

42 James G. Randall, *From Springfield to Gettysburg* (Volume I of *Lincoln the President*, New York, 1945), pp. 268-269. Caleb B. Smith was a native of Boston, Massachusetts, who spent his boyhood in Cincinnati and moved as a young man to Connersville, Indiana, where he practiced law. He served as a Whig member of the state legislature in the 1830's and as a member of the United States House of Representatives during the 1840's. While in Congress he became a friend of Lincoln's. During the 1850's he returned to Cincinnati where he devoted himself to railroad affairs, becoming president of the Cincinnati and Chicago line. In 1859 he returned to Indianapolis and became active in the Republican party. He was appointed to the Cabinet

accept the position of Federal Judge for the District of Indiana, a position more suited to his tastes. John P. Usher of Terre Haute was appointed as his successor and served throughout the remainder of Lincoln's first term, although Lincoln was not satisfied with his administration of the department.[43] Hugh McCulloch, an Indiana banker, was made Comptroller of the Currency in 1863, and was appointed Secretary of the Treasury early in 1865. McCulloch played an important part in the establishment of the national banking system, but neither he nor any other figure from Indiana wielded influence comparable to that of Morton.[44]

§ § § §

In spite of the enthusiasm with which the men of Indiana rushed to arms, it was apparent that the people of the state were by no means in agreement as to what they were fighting for. While soldiers fought and died in the field, a debate as

over the protests of Julian. He died in 1863 soon after being appointed district judge. Louis J. Bailey, "Caleb Blood Smith," *Indiana Magazine of History,* XXIX (1933), 213-239.

[43] James G. Randall and Richard N. Current, *Last Full Measure* (volume IV of *Lincoln the President,* New York, 1955), p. 278. Elmo R. Richardson and Alan W. Farley, *John Palmer Usher, Lincoln's Secretary of the Interior* (University of Kansas Press, 1960) is a recent biography. Usher was a native of New York state who moved to Terre Haute in 1840 and began the practice of law. He frequently rode circuit and in this way became acquainted with Lincoln. He served as a member of the state legislature in 1850-1851 and was an unsuccessful candidate for Congress on the Republican ticket in 1856. After the war he moved to Lawrence, Kansas, where he served as chief counsel for the Union Pacific Railroad.

[44] McCulloch was a native of Maine who had attended Bowdoin College and been admitted to the bar in Boston before settling in Fort Wayne, Indiana, in 1833. In 1835 he became cashier and manager of the Fort Wayne branch of the State Bank of Indiana, and from 1856 to 1863 he was president of the Fort Wayne branch of the Bank of the State of Indiana. McCulloch gained a nationwide reputation because this was one of the few banks which remained solvent throughout the period of the panic of 1857. In 1863 he was appointed Comptroller of the Currency on the recommendation of Salmon P. Chase. This meant that he was largely responsible for putting the new national banking system into operation. Hugh McCulloch, in *Dictionary of American Biography.* For a fuller account of McCulloch as banker and Secretary of the Treasury, see Chapter VI, pages 253, 254, and Chapter X, pages 427-428, 433.

to war aims went on at home. After the attack on Fort Sumter there was almost universal support of war to preserve the Union, but there was much concern lest the war be turned into a crusade to "subjugate" the South and to abolish slavery. At the special 1861 session of the legislature both houses resolved that in fighting the war Indiana did not intend that her men or money should ever be employed "in any aggression upon the institution of slavery or any other constitutional right belonging to any of the states." Public opinion in Indiana overwhelmingly supported the Crittenden resolution adopted by Congress in July, 1861, which affirmed that the war was fought "to defend and maintain the *supremacy* of the Constitution, and to preserve the Union with all the dignity, equality, and rights of the several states unimpaired; and that as soon as these objects are accomplished the war ought to cease." More succinctly stated the object was frequently said to be "the Constitution as it is, the government as it was."[45]

Democrats continued to deplore both secession and abolitionism and to blame both for causing the war. "There are two facts, supreme and everlasting, which will dominate and shape the civil strife which now distracts the nation," the Indianapolis *Sentinel* declared in July, 1861. "The first is, that the Union must and will be preserved; the second, that it can never be preserved by an anti-slavery policy. Secession and abolition must go down together." Opposition to abolitionism was linked to Negrophobia. The *Sentinel* emphatically denied that Democrats opposed abolitionism out of sympathy for the South. "The future of the North as well as the South, and the future of the white race on this continent, are concerned in emancipation," it declared. "The rebellion is only a question of to-day. It can be put down. Emancipation is a question for all time. The deed once done, it can not be undone. The South once converted into a St. Domingo, it must remain so until a war of races shall exterminate the

45 Stampp, *Indiana Politics*, pp. 81-82.

blacks." This theme was repeated in countless editorials, political speeches, and resolutions of political meetings. The Logansport *Pharos* recommended that no column move upon the enemy unless it carried a banner emblazoned with the words: "Non-Interference by Congress with Domestic Institutions of the Slave States." In the winter of 1861-1862 Democratic conventions in county after county adopted resolutions which condemned efforts to convert the war into a crusade against slavery and deplored suggestions that slaves be armed to help in suppressing rebellion.[46]

During the first year of the war Democrats found little to criticize in Lincoln's handling of the slavery question. In October, 1861, the *Sentinel* expressed gratification that the administration had remained free of the abolitionist influences of the Garrisons and Beechers, "who think that emancipation should be the only object of the war, and desire it to be prosecuted solely for the benefit of the Negro." Democrats praised Lincoln for removing Gen. John C. Frémont and rescinding his orders emancipating the slaves of rebels in Missouri. But Lincoln's proposals for a program of compensated emancipation were severely condemned.[47]

Conservative Republicans, who predominated in Indiana, approached the question of slavery cautiously, fearful that

[46] Indianapolis *Daily Sentinel,* July 19, December 3, 1861; Logansport *Journal,* August 31, 1861. For examples of resolutions adopted in Daviess, Decatur, Elkhart, Fountain, Fulton, Jennings, Morgan, Parke, Rush, Sullivan, Tipton, Vigo, and Washington counties see Indianapolis *Daily Sentinel,* November 21, December 10, 11, 25, 27, 1861, and January 1, 3, 6, 1862. A Democratic convention in Decatur County adopted the following: "Resolved: That we are opposed to the emancipation of the slaves in the Southern States, either by the action of Congress or that of the military power, *upon any pretext whatever;* that the consequences of emancipation would necessarily be the Africanization of the South, . . . the inauguration of a desolating servile war and filling the Northern States with a debased Negro Population, corrupting the morals of our people, increasing our public burdens and cheapening and degrading labor." *Ibid.,* December 27, 1861.

[47] *Ibid.,* October 17, 24, December 10, 1861; Thornbrough, "Race Issue in Indiana Politics," *Indiana Magazine of History,* XLVII, 170-171.

any attack on the institution might have unfortunate repercussions in the border states and among the voters in Indiana.
In December, 1861, the Indianapolis *Journal* warned that the
question of the disposal of the slaves of rebels was likely to
be disruptive and might drive loyal slave states to secession.
It urged that the question of what to do with slaves should
be postponed until the war was over. And yet the *Journal*
recognized that the war must inevitably lead to the weakening of slavery and freedom of many slaves since wherever
Union armies penetrated, slaves would be sure to run away.
Among Republicans there continued to be much sympathy
for the idea of colonization as the solution of the slave question. Albert G. Porter, Republican member of the United
States House of Representatives, advocated using money
derived from the confiscation of rebel property to colonize
members of a race which "from the prejudices of caste and
aversions of color, must always be an alien and degraded
one." Republican Senator Henry S. Lane also favored colonization, while former Governor Joseph A. Wright, whom, as
will be discussed later, Morton had appointed to the Senate
to succeed Bright, declared that any confiscation scheme must
include a plan for colonization.[48]

On the other hand, from the beginning of the war, Julian's
organ, the Centerville *True Republican,* insisted that since
slavery was the cause of the war, there could be no permanent
peace except "through the *extirpation* of its grand cause,
throughout the length and breadth of the Union," and that
"now" was the time "for effecting the good work." On the
floor of the House Julian declared that "mere suppression of
this rebellion" would be a hollow victory "if slavery shall be
spared to canker the heart of the nation anew, and repeat its
diabolical deeds." By December, 1861, Schuyler Colfax was
advocating the confiscation of slaves along with other property

---

48 Indianapolis *Daily Journal,* December 10, 12, 1861; Thornbrough, "Race
Issue in Indiana Politics," *Indiana Magazine of History,* XLVII, 175-176.

in the Confederate states since slavery was a source of strength to the rebel cause.[49]

As it became apparent that the rebellion would not quickly be crushed, many thoughtful people who had at first opposed interference with slavery in the states recognized slavery as a source of military strength to the South and began to urge its abolition as a military measure. In July, 1862, Robert Dale Owen, a lifelong Democrat, urged a general program of emancipation as the quickest way of bringing an end to the exhausting war. But Owen's proposal was as yet too advanced for the Indianapolis *Journal*. While admitting that "this radical policy" advocated by Owen was gaining in favor, the *Journal* warned "except as a last resort, as the only possible means of preserving the government, we cannot see that Mr. Owen's policy will not produce as many difficulties as it will remove." As for Horace Greeley's "Prayer for Twenty Millions," which the noted editor presented to Lincoln a few weeks later, the *Journal* expressed the opinion that Greeley's proposal "would weaken the union . . . and strengthen rebellion."[50]

The debate on the relationship of slavery to the war was an important theme in the political campaign of 1862, and opposition to emancipation undoubtedly played an important part in the outcome of the elections that year.

§ § § § §

At the beginning of the war Morton had repeatedly called for an end to partisan politics and subordination of mere party loyalties to the saving of the Union. But although the people of the state continued to support the military effort with remarkable zeal, partisanship instead of disappearing was actually intensified during the war years.

During the first months of the war Morton made conspicuous efforts to bring both Democrats and Republicans into a

[49] Centerville *Indiana True Republican,* May 16, 23, 30, 1861; *Congressional Globe,* 37 Congress, 2 session, Appendix, pp. 184-186; Smith, *Schuyler Colfax,* pp. 166-167.

[50] Indianapolis *Daily Journal,* August 11, 25, 1862.

Union organization dedicated only to the successful prosecution of the war. He gave numerous military appointments to Democrats, and a few prominent Democrats accepted his invitation to renounce party designations for the duration and join the Union movement.[51]

The expulsion of Jesse Bright from the United States Senate in February, 1862, gave Morton an opportunity to strengthen the Union movement by appointing a War Democrat to succeed him. After the election of 1860, Bright, while retaining his seat in the Senate, had virtually abandoned Indiana and taken up residence on his farm in Kentucky. Indiana Democrats were bitter against him because of his support of Breckinridge and his part in the defeat of Douglas. In May, 1861, the Indiana Senate passed a resolution, introduced by a Democrat, asking for an inquiry as to whether Bright was still a resident of Indiana and whether his continued presence in the Senate was "inconsistent with public interests and public safety." The Indiana House of Representatives by a vote of 82 to 2 passed a resolution which declared that if any United States Senator or Representative was disinclined to support such measures as were necessary to put down the rebellion, he should resign. Nothing came of either resolution, but a few months later a letter which Bright had written in March, 1861, came to light and proved to be his undoing. The letter, written as a letter of introduction on behalf of a friend of Bright's, was addressed to: "His Excellency, Jefferson Davis, President of the Confederation of States." In the United States Senate it was used as grounds for a move to expel the long-time senator from Indiana. In his defense Bright pointed out that the letter had been written before hostilities had begun, at a time when other persons in government circles were communicating with Davis. He insisted that the title used to designate Davis was a mere

51 Among the Democrats who espoused the Union movement in politics were Ebenezer Dumont, William S. Holman, Martin M. Ray, and Allen Hamilton. The New Albany *Ledger* was the most important Democratic newspaper to support the movement. Stampp, *Indiana Politics*, p. 95.

formality and in no way proved any disloyalty on his part. Nevertheless, the Senate voted to expel him from membership. As Bright's successor Morton named former Governor Wright who had just returned to Indiana after serving as minister to Prussia, but only after secretly extracting assurances from him that he favored unconditional prosecution of the war, that he would not oppose confiscation of rebel property, including property in slaves, and that he would not support the ticket and platform adopted by the Democratic state convention in January, 1862. The appointment of Bright's long-time arch foe as his successor was a fine piece of irony and a brilliant political maneuver.[52]

Although a substantial minority of Democrats appeared to support the Union movement in politics during the first part of the war, many denounced Wright as a turncoat for accepting the appointment and charged that Morton's nonpartisanship was in reality a device for weakening the Democratic party and building up the Republican. On the other hand, Julian and the radical wing of the Republicans were critical of Morton's Union movement, considering it a surrender to the Democrats. Republicans also were aware that Morton was using every opportunity to build a political organization loyal to him alone. The feud between Morton and Julian continued, and the Governor tried to undermine the Congressman in his own district. Michael Garber of the Madison *Courier* and John R. Cravens, president of the state senate, were other Republicans who were at odds with Morton. Those who opposed the Governor were likely to find the doors of political preferment closed.[53]

Although Democrats were ready to accept the necessity of fighting to preserve the Union, they were fearful that the

[52] Van Der Weele, Jesse David Bright, pp. 268-270, 272, 274-289; Calvin Fletcher Diary, February 15, 16, 24, 1862; Stampp, *Indiana Politics,* pp. 97-98. The Fletcher Diary shows that Fletcher recommended the appointment of Wright to Morton and helped compose the questionnaire which Morton submitted to Wright before appointing him.

[53] Stampp, *Indiana Politics,* pp. 83-85.

Governor Oliver P. Morton

Eleventh Indiana Volunteers Swearing to Remember Buena Vista,
Indianapolis, May, 1861
By James F. Gookins

Bounty Jumpers' Parade at Indianapolis, 1864

war would be used by the Republicans to bring about other results distasteful to them. They were also alarmed and critical over some of the methods employed by the Lincoln administration. Their protests over the way in which the war was being conducted were labeled by the Republicans as evidence that they did not support the Union and favored the South. The most important cause for the intense bitterness of politics during the war years was the tendency which Republicans had to claim for themselves a monopoly on loyalty and to equate what Democrats regarded as legitimate criticism with disloyalty.

At the outbreak of the war the Indianapolis *Journal* had accused the editor of the Indianapolis *Sentinel* of sympathizing with treason. To this the *Sentinel* had replied that it had the welfare of the country as much at heart as Lincoln or Morton and was as deeply interested in the perpetuation of the Union. At the same time it affirmed its right to criticize the party in power and declared that it would not be intimidated by threats of violence or charges of treason. Some patriotic groups insisted upon seizing men whose loyalty they suspected and compelling them to take oaths of allegiance, and in August, 1861, J. J. Bingham, editor of the *Sentinel,* was forced by a mob to go to the office of the mayor of Indianapolis and swear his allegiance. This was but one of many such incidents which became increasingly common as the war wore on.[54]

The dilemma in which Democrats found themselves was well expressed in a letter written by a member of the Indiana Senate to Allen Hamilton, one of the Democrats who had endorsed Morton's plea for a Union organization.

I can not trust myself to talk much on politics as I don't want to find fault and can't see much to approve. . . .
. . . Some crazy Republicans here in this county don't like to tolerate free speech and I regret to see the *Journal* of Indianapolis encourage

[54] Indianapolis *Daily Sentinel,* April 15, 1861; Stampp, *Indiana Politics,* p. 73; Robert S. Harper, *Lincoln and the Press* (New York, 1951), p. 327.

a mob spirit. I am afraid that an attempt will yet be made to put down free speech by mob violence.

I hope that Democrats in all parts of the State will be temperate and discreet in criticising the acts of the administration. Yet we should not consent that good Loyal union men should be mobbed for a free expression of their abhorrence and disaprobation [sic] of the acts of Gov. Morton or Pres. Lincoln. There are no traitors in Indiana. I can not believe that any man in Indiana desires the destruction of this government. Yet there are many that think the policy now being pursued by the administration will lead to that result and claim the right to give expression to that opinion.[55]

The platforms adopted by Indiana Democrats in January, 1862, blamed the Republicans for rejecting compromises which might have preserved the Union without a war. While expressing themselves as unalterably attached to the Constitution and the Union, the Democrats declared that the war should not be waged for the purpose of subjugation or conquest or for interfering with the institutions of the states. The "twin heresies" of "Northern sectionalism and Southern secession" were both condemned as well as proposals for emancipation. Interference with freedom of the press and suspension of the writ of habeas corpus were also denounced.[56]

The Republican-Union convention meeting in April adopted a very short platform which carefully ignored all issues which might create dissension. It pledged support of the war to "put down a wicked and causeless rebellion" and to preserve the Union. The Indiana volunteers were praised and were promised that while they were subduing "armed traitors in the field," the voters at home would "condemn at the ballot box all those in our midst who are not unconditionally for the Union." A slate of candidates on which Republicans and Democrats were equally represented was nominated. In an address before the convention Morton renewed his plea for the abandonment of party politics until the war was won, but

---

[55] Smith Jones, Jonesville, to Allen Hamilton, July 26, 1861, Hamilton Papers.

[56] Henry (comp.), *State Platforms*, pp. 21-23.

in the same speech dramatically announced that treasonable societies existed in the state and hinted that Democrats were implicated. A few weeks later a Federal grand jury meeting in Indianapolis appeared to give some substance to Morton's innuendoes. Empaneled by a politically minded marshal, the jury was composed entirely of Republicans and was aided by Morton in summoning witnesses. In its report it declared that there was evidence that there was in the state a "secret and oath bound organization," probably treasonable in nature, with a membership of fifteen thousand. But the extreme secrecy of the movement made it impossible to obtain concrete evidence as to its activities. The report was printed and circulated as a campaign document. Democrats insisted that it was a fabrication, based on nothing except wild rumor, and that it was deliberately concocted for use against them in the campaign.[57]

Efforts of Republicans to win political victory by branding their opponents as disloyal failed in 1862. Military reversals and policies of the Lincoln administration which were objectionable weighed more heavily with the voters than unsubstantiated charges of secret conspiracies. The result was a sweeping Democratic victory.

In the spring of 1862 the military situation was encouraging to the Republicans. There were hopes that the collapse of the Confederacy was imminent. Forts Henry and Donelson had fallen to Union forces, and McClellan was expected to take Richmond. In April the War Department stopped recruiting, thus creating the impression that no more men would be needed. But in June urgent appeals were sent out for more volunteers. In July Congress passed legislation to draft state militia if necessary to fill state quotas. In October, a few days before the election in Indiana, it was necessary to

---

57 *Ibid.*, p. 24; Stampp, *Indiana Politics,* pp. 136-137, 151; Frank L. Klement, *The Copperheads in the Middle West* (Chicago, 1960), pp. 148-149. See below, Chapter V, for a fuller account of wartime secret societies and disloyal activities.

resort to a draft to raise three thousand men whom the War Department claimed Indiana owed. Meanwhile, part of the Indiana militia had been alerted over a raid by guerrillas from Kentucky against Newburgh. This was an insignificant episode in the war, but it created great excitement, especially because some Newburgh residents were accused of being accomplices of the Kentuckians. Much more serious was the Confederate invasion of Kentucky under Kirby Smith which began in late summer. There was panic lest Kentucky be conquered and Indiana itself be invaded. Thousands of untrained recruits were rushed from Indiana to Kentucky, and many of them were slaughtered at Richmond and Perryville. Morton was severely criticized for allowing green troops to be sent into murderous combat.[58]

In addition to military defeats and the seemingly endless calls for manpower, increasing dissatisfaction with the Lincoln administration over other matters helped bring Democratic victory. Democratic politicians and the Democratic press inveighed against an increase in the tariff, which they claimed was passed to benefit the East at the expense of the West, against greenbacks or legal tender notes issued by the government, and against higher taxes. But arbitrary arrests and suspension of the writ of habeas corpus aroused more violent opposition. In Congress Representative Daniel Voorhees joined other Democrats of the Middle West in a published "Address," which assailed the Lincoln administration for "despotism" after arbitrary arrests in Maryland and Kentucky. In August, 1862, an order from Secretary of War Edwin M. Stanton authorized the arrest of persons who were found to be giving aid and comfort to the enemy, discouraging enlistments, or who gave evidence of disloyalty by speech, writing, or action. In September a wave of arrests by military officers in Indiana created a perfect storm of opposition—

<hr>

[58] Barbara Anne Feigel, Civil War in the Western Ohio Valley as Viewed from Evansville, Indiana (Unpublished Master's thesis in History, Indiana University, 1957), pp. 41-47; Stampp, *Indiana Politics*, pp. 150-151. See below, Chapter IV, for a fuller account of the military events.

especially because several of the men arrested were Democratic candidates for office. These arrests seemed to confirm
Democratic charges that Republicans were subverting constitutional guarantees and were using intimidation to prevent
a Democratic victory.[59]

Finally, Negrophobia, always a potent force in Hoosier
political psychology, was aroused as never before by the
Emancipation Proclamation, issued a few weeks before the
election. Democrats saw in the Proclamation a betrayal of
past pledges by Lincoln and the Republicans and an invitation
to servile insurrection. In Congress Voorhees charged that
Lincoln had succumbed to pressure from Horace Greeley,
"that political harlot, who appeared in a praying attitude in
behalf of twenty millions of people." The Indianapolis
Sentinel branded the Proclamation as "a confession of weakness—an acknowledgement that twenty millions of white people, with every advantage on their side, can not conquer six
millions of whites." It predicted that the results of emancipation would be disastrous and called upon the people of
Indiana to repudiate it at the ballot box.[60]

Moderate Republicans had little to say. Undoubtedly they
were fearful of the effects on the coming election. After being
twitted by the *Sentinel* for its failure to comment, the Indianapolis *Journal* somewhat lamely endorsed the proclamation
as a means of weakening the rebellion. Other Republican
papers defended it in similar language. In a speech in Washington, D.C., Morton defended the proclamation as "a
stratagem of war."[61]

Only the radical Republicans hailed the proclamation with
enthusiasm, and they were not numerous. The Centerville

[59] Stampp, *Indiana Politics,* pp. 132, 141; Klement, *Copperheads in the
Middle West,* p. 18; Gilbert R. Tredway, Indiana against the Administration, 1861-1865 (Unpublished Ph. D. thesis in History, Indiana University, 1962),
pp. 31-33. See below, Chapter V, for a fuller account of arbitrary arrests.

[60] Frank Smith Bogardus, "Daniel W. Voorhees," *Indiana Magazine of History,* XXVII (1931), 98; Indianapolis *Daily Sentinel,* September 24, 1862.

[61] Indianapolis *Daily Journal,* September 27, October 10, 1862.

Indiana True Republican, which as late as September 11 had been criticizing "the vain, the insane effort of the administration and its agents, the leading generals in the field, to save *Slavery,*" abruptly changed its tune. An editorial in the Logansport *Journal* supported Lincoln's proclamation as the most important document since the Declaration of Independence. "If slavery dies," it declared,

its death will not be upon the head of the President; nor can the North be held responsible if its perishes in this struggle. The President is justified in using all the power—moral and physical—which the people of this Government have placed in his hands, to suppress the rebellion and maintain the integrity of the Union. . . . The destruction of slavery, if destroyed at all, will be chargable to those alone who have made it necessary for the sake of preserving that more priceless and invaluable inheritance—Constitutional Liberty.

Julian, who had been urging emancipation for months, felt that Lincoln had finally awakened to the realities of what the war was about.[62]

On October 14 Democrats won a clear victory at the polls. The Democratic slate for state officers was elected by a margin of more than nine thousand. Seven of the eleven Congressional districts were won by Democrats, and both houses of the General Assembly would be controlled by Democrats by substantial margins.[63] Similar results occurred in Ohio and Illinois. It was obvious that efforts to win Democrats to

[62] Centerville *Indiana True Republican,* September 11, 25, 1862; Logansport *Journal,* September 27, 1862; Julian, *Political Recollections,* pp. 222-223; Thornbrough, "Race Issue in Indiana Politics," *Indiana Magazine of History,* XLVII, 177-178.

[63] Thornbrough, "Race Issue in Indiana Politics," *ibid.,* XLVII, pp. 178-179; Stampp, *Indiana Politics,* p. 156; Klement, *Copperheads in the Middle West,* p. 37. Ebenezer Dumont, a Democrat turned Union Republican, was victorious in the sixth district. Other Republicans elected to Congress were George W. Julian, Schuyler Colfax, and Godlove S. Orth. One of the Democrats re-elected to the House of Representatives was Daniel W. Voorhees of Terre Haute who was to become one of the most popular and one of the most controversial figures in the political history of Indiana. Voorhees was born in Ohio but was brought to Fountain County, Indiana, while an infant. In 1849 he was graduated from

support the Union Republican cause had failed. Far from quieting party conflict the war appeared to have intensified it. The bitterness of the campaign of 1862 was a prelude to deeper and more disruptive partisanship in the months to follow.

Indiana Asbury University in Greencastle and began the study of law in the office of Henry S. Lane in Crawfordsville. In 1852 he entered the law office of former Senator Edward A. Hannegan. Voorhees soon gained a reputation as a trial lawyer and orator. His tall figure and striking appearance won for him the sobriquet of "Tall Sycamore of the Wabash." One of his most notable court-room efforts was in behalf of John E. Cook, who was arrested along with John Brown at the time of the raid on Harper's Ferry in 1859. Cook was a brother-in-law of Governor Willard, and Voorhees undertook his defense at Willard's request. The effort was in vain and Cook was condemned to die for his part in the raid. Voorhees was defeated in his first campaign for Congress in 1856. In 1857 he moved to Terre Haute. He was a member of the House of Representatives from 1861 to 1866. See Chapters V, VI, and VII for details of his later political career. Biographical sketches of Voorhees may be found in Frank S. Bogardus, "Daniel W. Voorhees," *Indiana Magazine of History*, XXVII, pp. 91-103; Henry D. Jordan, "Daniel Wolsey Voorhees," *Mississippi Valley Historical Review*, VI (1919-1920), pp. 532-555; Leonard Kenworthy, *The Tall Sycamore of the Wabash. Daniel Wolsey Voorhees* (Boston, 1936).

CHAPTER IV
MILITARY CONTRIBUTION

FROM THE FIRST CALL for volunteers after the attack on Fort Sumter until the end of the war the people of Indiana furnished manpower for the Union armies on a scale scarcely matched by any other state. The size of Indiana's military contribution indicates strong support for the Union and casts doubt on the tradition that there was widespread sympathy for the Confederate cause in the state. According to Fox's *Regimental Losses in the Civil War,* which is generally regarded as the most authoritative work on the subject, under one system of computing the percentage of men of military age who served in the Union army, Delaware ranked first; under a second system Kansas ranked first. But under either system Indiana ranked second among all the states. According to Fox, if all men are included who enlisted in the armed forces, regardless of the length of time for which they enlisted, and also men who paid commutation instead of actually enlisting, in Delaware 74.8 per cent of men of military age served; in Indiana, 74.3 per cent. Under a system which excluded white men who enlisted for terms of less than three years or who paid commutation and which also excluded Negroes, Kansas ranked first—furnishing 59.4 per cent of men of military age—while Indiana ranked second with 57 per cent.[1]

After the attack on Fort Sumter eagerness to enlist brought thousands of volunteers into Indianapolis within a few days. In less than a week, according to W. H. H. Terrell, more than twelve thousand men had tendered their services—nearly three times the quota fixed for Indiana in Lincoln's call for volunteers. Hundreds of men who were unable to join com-

[1] William F. Fox, *Regimental Losses in the American Civil War 1861-1865* (Albany, New York, 1889), pp. 535-536.

panies in their home communities came individually to the place of rendezvous, clamoring for admission.[2] Six regiments of three-month volunteers were accepted at once—the Sixth through the Eleventh. The numbering of the new regiments began with the Sixth out of deference to the memory of the five regiments organized during the Mexican War. The Eleventh, whose members called themselves the Indiana Zouaves, was, in reality, the first regiment to be organized and the first to march. Made up for the most part of private military companies who had organized and started drilling before the war, it was one of the most colorful of the Indiana regiments. On the day they assembled to receive their banners, their commander, Lew Wallace, made them kneel and swear that they would never desert their regimental colors and that they would avenge the disgrace visited upon Indiana by the alleged cowardice of her troops at Buena Vista.[3]

Out of the other men clamoring for acceptance after the first six regiments were accepted, Morton on his own authority organized five more regiments for twelve months' service for the defense of the state or of the United States, if they should be needed. In June nearly all of the men in these were mustered into the service of the United States as the Thirteenth, Fourteenth, Fifteenth, and Seventeenth regiments, when the Secretary of War issued a call for volunteers to enlist for three years. In July the Twelfth and Sixteenth regiments were accepted into the service of the United States. When their brief term of enlistment of three months expired in July,

2 W. H. H. Terrell, *Indiana in the War of the Rebellion. Report of the Adjutant General* (Reprint of Volume I of the Eight-Volume Report published in 1869, Indiana Historical Society, 1960), pp. 7-8. Hereafter the reprint will be cited as *Indiana in the War of the Rebellion*, the original as *Report of the Adjutant General*. For an account of the response to the call for volunteers, see also Parsons, "Indiana and the Call for Volunteers, April, 1861," *Indiana Magazine of History*, LIV, 10-15.

3 [Catharine Merrill], *The Soldier of Indiana in the War for the Union* (2 volumes, Indianapolis, 1866, 1869), I, 61; David Stevenson and Theodore T. Scribner, *Indiana's Roll of Honor* (2 volumes, Indianapolis, 1864, 1866), I, 89-93.

the original volunteers in the first six regiments were urged to re-enlist for three years, and most of them did so. Altogether during the first year of the war infantry regiments numbered from the Sixth through the Fifty-Ninth were organized plus three regiments of cavalry and twelve batteries of artillery. Among them were regiments recruited primarily on the basis of nationality. The first of these was the Thirty-Second or First German regiment, made up of Germans from all over the state. It was organized in Indianapolis, largely through the exertions of August Willich, who had been an officer in the German revolution of 1848. The Thirty-Fifth regiment, commanded by Col. John Walker of LaPorte, was made up of Irishmen whose bright green caps were their distinguishing insignia. In 1862 this regiment was consolidated with the Sixty-First or Second Irish regiment.[4]

Even though it was apparent after the first battle of Manassas that the rebellion was not going to be crushed within a few months, volunteers continued to respond enthusiastically to every call for troops. Motives behind the eagerness to enlist were varied. Hopes for adventure and excitement and social pressures played a part. One officer, in a moment of disillusionment, commented that "nine tenths of them [volunteers] enlisted just because somebody else was going, and the other tenth was ashamed to stay home." Another observer remarked that the troops who enlisted during the first months regarded the war as a sort of "plaything" and departed laughing and screaming. But devotion to the Union and seriousness of purpose were strong, even though they were sometimes concealed by buffoonery. In October, 1861, the Adjutant General of the United States, on a visit to Indianapolis reported that Indiana had raised and equipped a larger number of troops in proportion to her population than any other state.[5]

4 Terrell, *Indiana in the War of the Rebellion,* pp. 14, 16-18, 20; W. H. H. Terrell, *Report of the Adjutant General of Indiana* (8 volumes, Indianapolis, 1869), II, 321, 352.

5 Albert T. Volwiler (ed.), "Letters from A Civil War Officer," *Mississippi*

One of the most urgent needs at the beginning of the war was for officers to command the raw recruits. But there were few men with military training or experience. For twenty-five years before the war there had been no regularly organized militia, so there were not even militia officers to appoint to commands. In the entire state there was only a handful of West Point graduates. Among them was Thomas A. Morris, who had had a successful career as engineer and railroad president prior to the war. Morton first appointed him Quartermaster General for the state. Shortly thereafter he was commissioned the first brigadier general from Indiana, but he resigned after a few months in the field. Another graduate of West Point was Joseph J. Reynolds, who had been a classmate of Ulysses S. Grant at the Military Academy and who had taught there for several years following his graduation. At the beginning of the war he was engaged in business in Lafayette. He at once tendered his services to Morton and was appointed colonel of the Tenth Regiment. The fact that he was appointed by the Governor even though he had not voted for him in 1860 was cited by Morton's friends as evidence of the sincerity of the Governor's claim that it was a "no party" war. Milo H. Hascall, of Goshen, who had a career as lawyer and railroad promotor before being commissioned colonel of the Seventeenth Indiana, was another West Point graduate.

Robert Milroy had graduated from Norwich Academy in Vermont with a degree in military science and engineering. He had been a captain in the Mexican War before taking up the practice of law. He was appointed colonel of the Ninth Indiana. Several other officers had seen service in the Mexican War. Lew Wallace, son of former Governor David Wallace, whom Morton appointed Adjutant General immediately after Fort Sumter, had served in that war although he had not taken part in any serious engagement. He soon resigned as

Valley Historical Review, XIV (1927-1928), 510; Fletcher Diary, September 5, 1861; *Soldier of Indiana*, I, 142.

Adjutant General to command the Eleventh Indiana. Nathan Kimball, colonel of the Fourteenth Indiana, who was practicing medicine in Loogootee when the Civil War began, had been a captain in the earlier war. Alvin P. Hovey, a former member of the Indiana Supreme Court, who was appointed colonel of the Twenty-Fourth, had enlisted in the Mexican War but had never actually taken part in a battle. Ebenezer Dumont, Mahlon D. Manson, and James W. McMillan, colonels of the Seventh, Tenth, and Twenty-First regiments respectively, were also veterans of the Mexican War.

Jefferson C. Davis, whom many consider the most able military commander Indiana contributed to the Civil War, had enlisted in the Mexican War as a mere boy and had attained a lieutenancy in an artillery regiment. He had remained in the army and was in command of a battery of the Union garrison at Fort Sumter. After the call for volunteers he returned to Indiana as a mustering officer but was transferred to active service in the field in August, 1861, as colonel of the Twenty-Second Indiana.[6]

All of the veterans of the Mexican War mentioned above were among the Indiana officers who made the most conspicuous records during the Civil War. With the exception of Davis all were civilians at the beginning of the war. There were other less well-known officers who had had experience in the Mexican War, but the vast majority of Indiana officers were men whose earlier education and experience were quite divorced from military affairs. Such knowledge of strategy and tactics and military organization as they had was acquired after the war started.

In the selection and promotion of officers, as in other aspects of Indiana's military effort, the Governor had great power. The authority to commission all regimental and company

---

[6] Terrell, *Indiana in the War of the Rebellion*, pp. 6, 12-13, 106n., 107; *Soldier of Indiana*, I, 25-26, 28; *Roll of Honor*, II, 493; biographical sketches of these officers in *Dictionary of American Biography*. Reynolds was colonel of the Tenth Regiment for three months; Manson became colonel when members re-enlisted for three years.

officers belonged to him. Frequently regimental commands were given as rewards for recruiting efforts. Men who had never dreamed of playing a military role were called upon by the energetic Morton and urged to recruit and take commands. One example was Conrad Baker, who in 1861 was a middle-aged Evansville lawyer, with no knowledge of military affairs. Morton persuaded him to raise and command a cavalry regiment which served in Missouri in the first months of the war. He was later brought back to Indiana to serve as Provost Marshal. Another example was Benjamin Harrison, who had been elected Reporter of the Indiana Supreme Court in 1860 and who hesitated to volunteer during the first year of the war because he felt that he could not afford to make the financial sacrifice involved in military service. During the dark days of the summer of 1862, at Morton's urging, he agreed to raise a regiment, the Seventieth, of which he took command.[7]

Both Baker and Harrison were prominent Republicans. Many other officers commissioned by Morton were men who had formerly been active Democrats, but who, like Morton himself, had become Republicans during the fifties. Two well-known examples were Alvin P. Hovey and Solomon Meredith, the colonel of the Nineteenth Indiana. Lew Wallace had been a Democrat, but according to his own account, had decided to sever his ties with that party during the secession crisis, a short time before Morton offered him the appointment of Adjutant General. Ebenezer Dumont of Vevay, colonel of the Indiana Seventh, was an active Democrat at the beginning of the war. He became identified with the Union party and was elected to Congress on the Union ticket in 1862 after being forced to resign his commission because of ill health. Nathan Kimball was another Democrat who joined the Union party movement.[8]

[7] Terrell, *Indiana in the War of the Rebellion,* p. 106; *Soldier of Indiana,* I, 159-160; Harry J. Sievers, S. J., *Benjamin Harrison. Hoosier Warrior, 1833-1865* (Chicago, 1952), pp. 167, 178-183.

[8] Lew Wallace, *Lew Wallace. An Autobiography* (2 volumes, New York,

Inevitably, in view of the powers which the Governor wielded, military appointments and promotions became linked with politics. During the first part of the war Morton made a point of giving numerous appointments to Democrats, but after a few months Democrats were accusing him of discriminating against them. Conversely, the Governor's Republican friends encouraged him to use his powers to strengthen his own party and objected when he commissioned Democrats. Morton was constantly under pressure from congressmen and local politicians to give recognition to men from their districts—sometimes as payments for political debts. A certain captain in the Nineteenth Regiment "is from my district and [you] cannot deal falsely with him," a Kendallville banker, who was a pillar of the Republican party, told Morton. There was some bickering between Morton and members of the Indiana delegation in Congress over promotions in the higher echelons. "I do not know who they are and have not been consulted," Morton protested to Lincoln over certain recommendations for brigadier generalships. "I have had much more to do with the officers than any member of Congress, and have had much more responsibility in connection with the organization than any of them, and believe I should at least have the chance of being heard before any action is taken." Lincoln promptly asked Morton to make his recommendations.[9]

Advancement was likely to be difficult for persons who did not have Morton's blessing. Walter Q. Gresham, for example, was a Republican, who had been elected to the state legislature in 1860, but he did not get along well with Morton. When he applied for a commission, he was refused. He was compelled to enlist as a private but was elected captain by members of his company and soon after was commissioned a colonel. In many cases companies were allowed to elect their

1906), I, 258-261; *Soldier of Indiana,* I, 25-26, 28; II, 135; Stampp, *Indiana Politics,* pp. 95-96, 156n.

[9] Stampp, *op. cit.,* pp. 89-91; Alan T. Nolan, *The Iron Brigade. A Military History* (New York, 1961), p. 59; Smith, *History of Indiana,* II, 47.

own officers. As vacancies occurred in companies and regiments Morton tried to promote men from the units in which the vacancies occurred.[10]

During the winter of 1861-1862 cold weather and reports that troops in the field were suffering from lack of adequate clothing caused enlistments to lag somewhat, but Union victories in the West during the spring of 1862 brought a revival of enthusiasm. There was general optimism that the war would not last much longer, and men were eager to have a part in giving a death blow to the rebellion. In April the War Department stopped recruiting, apparently out of the belief that Union armies were large enough to finish the war. But in June this policy was suddenly reversed and calls for additional troops were sent out. Morton, who had protested the earlier cessation of enlistments, went to work with his usual vigor to raise the troops, expressing the hope that this would be the last call. But in July there was another call, and by this time the early eagerness to volunteer had waned. News of military reverses plus reluctance of farmers to enter service during the summer made the task of raising quotas more difficult. Morton himself was eager to see active service and sought permission to assume a military command, but Lincoln refused, feeling that he was needed more as governor. By this time Morton was urging upon Lincoln the necessity of conscription legislation as a means of spurring enlistments.[11] On July 17 Congress authorized the President to call out the militia of the various states for nine months and to draft members if necessary. Steps were taken at once in every township in Indiana for the enrollment of men subject to the draft. There was a considerable amount of popular resentment over the prospect of compulsory military service,

[10] Walter Quintin Gresham, in *Dictionary of American Biography;* Terrell, *Indiana in the War of the Rebellion,* pp. 108, 111.

[11] Terrell, *Indiana in the War of the Rebellion,* pp. 21-22; Stampp, *Indiana Politics,* pp. 142-143; Foulke, *Morton,* I, 181-184; *The War of the Rebellion: A Compilation of the Official Records of the Union and Confederate Armies* (4 series, 70 volumes, Washington, D. C., 1880-1901), 3 Series, II, 212-213.

and a system of passes had to be used to prevent persons from leaving the state to escape enrollment. Some of the resentment arose because it was felt that the draft was conducted in a partisan manner, with Morton attempting to insure that all draft officials be Republicans who were personally loyal to him. Some disorders occurred during the enrollment and subsequent drawings of names of prospective draftees. The most serious incident occurred in Blackford County, where a mob destroyed the enrollment lists and the draft box. Prospects of conscription acted as an incentive to volunteering, and by October only about 3,000 of the total of more than 42,000 men assessed upon Indiana by the various calls of the summer of 1862 remained unfilled. This number was then drafted, but a subsequent accounting indicated that the draft had in reality been unnecessary and that the number of volunteers had exceeded the quota.[12]

In March, 1863, Congress passed an enrollment act which transferred the responsibility for raising troops directly to the Federal government under the Provost Marshal General. It provided for the appointment of a provost marshal in each Congressional district to take charge of the enrollment and enlistment of troops. Necessary troops were to be drafted when quotas were not filled by volunteers. Men who were drafted were permitted to hire substitutes to take their place or to pay $300 as commutation money for their services. The last provision was immediately attacked as unjust. The Indianapolis *Sentinel* branded it as "an aristocratic provision that should not find favor in a Democratic government," and declared that "its tendency must be . . . to excite the poor against the rich." Another paper objected that it was wrong "for a *democratic* government, which knows of no distinction among its citizens, while fighting for the perpetuity of *democratic* institutions to indulge in *class* legislation." Morton also regarded the provision as unjust and demoralizing and

12 Terrell, *Indiana in the War of the Rebellion*, pp. 49-53; Stampp, *Indiana Politics*, p. 156.

protested vigorously to the President and Secretary of War over it. The commutation provision was repealed by Congress in July, 1864, except for a provision which allowed conscientious objectors to pay the sum of money in lieu of military service.[13]

Machinery for the enrollment of all men eligible for military service who were not already in service was put into operation as soon as the 1863 act was passed. Col. Conrad Baker, who had been serving with the First Indiana Cavalry Volunteers, was appointed Provost Marshal General for Indiana. In a number of places there were manifestations of opposition to the draft and efforts to resist or escape enrollment. Some enrollment officers were accused of partisanship in performance of their duties. In Randolph County, for example, angry neighbors tore down the fences on the farm of the local enrollment officer and threw some of his crops to his hogs. In Putnam County there were reports that an armed mob had attacked the house of the enrollment commissioner in an effort to steal the enrollment books. Arrests of persons charged with resisting enrollment were made in several counties, including Boone, Johnson, Fulton, and Monroe. A group from the last-mentioned county was found guilty in Federal court of obstructing enrollment. In one township where trouble had been expected things were quiet because

[13] Indianapolis *Daily Sentinel*, March 5, 1863; Aurora *Commercial*, March 5, 1863, quoted in Stampp, *Indiana Politics*, p. 203; Foulke, *Morton*, I, 200-202; Terrell, *Indiana in the War of the Rebellion*, pp. 62-63, 65. A provision in the Indiana constitution exempted conscientious objectors from military service but required that they pay an equivalent for such exemption. In the enrollment of 1862 under the militia draft law there were 3,169 men who registered as conscientious objectors. Of these who were drafted the state required a payment of $200, but later the Secretary of War ruled that the money could not be collected under the law of 1862. Under the conscription law of 1863 there was no express provision concerning conscientious objectors, but it was presumed that they would pay the $300 commutation. The act was amended to provide that members of religious denominations which had conscientious scruples against bearing arms were to be drafted but might be assigned to non-combat duty—in hospitals or in the care of freedmen—or might pay $300. *Ibid.*, pp. 54-55, 60.

men subject to enrollment had simply "gone visiting" on enrollment day, taking their wives and children with them, and leaving only the old men to be enumerated. In Sullivan County, a Democratic stronghold, the most serious trouble occurred.[14]

The importance of the conscription legislation was the stimulus which it gave to voluntary enlistments and to the fact that it compelled townships where recruiting lagged to do their share in filling quotas. In the popular mind a stigma was attached to being drafted, and the number of enlistments always increased sharply when a draft threatened. Local governments went to extreme lengths to prevent the necessity of drafting, and Morton and the other state officials also indulged in vigorous recruiting campaigns to raise quotas from volunteers.

Conditions in 1864 created an especially acute need for manpower. The year opened with prospects of large-scale and decisive military campaigns at a time when the three-year enlistments of many troops who had volunteered during the first months of the war would come to an end. Powerful efforts were made to persuade these men to re-enlist. One inducement was the granting of thirty-day furloughs just prior to the expiration of the original term of enlistment to men who re-enlisted. Many local governments also offered bounties. At least three fourths of the men who had volunteered in 1861 and who were still in service in 1864 re-enlisted. As the result of voluntary enlistments and re-enlistments it was possible to fill repeated calls for troops without resort to the draft from the time of the militia draft of October, 1862, until the autumn of 1864. At the latter time about half of a call for 25,000 men was filled by conscription. The final call for troops in December, 1864, was filled almost

14 Terrell, *Indiana in the War of the Rebellion,* pp. 57, 67; Indianapolis *Daily Sentinel,* June 15, 16, 17, 18, 24, 29, 1863, January 7, 1864. For an account of the disorders in Sullivan County, see below, p. 201.

entirely by volunteers, only about 2,400 of 22,582 troops being draftees.[15]

Meanwhile, in the spring of 1864, in order to free as large a number of soldiers as possible for active fighting, a group of special volunteers, known as the One Hundred Days' troops, had been raised to perform limited service behind the lines. Morton and Governor John Brough of Ohio were largely responsible for the plan to raise the troops, who were recruited from all of the states in the Middle West. The men who volunteered were not exempt from the draft nor did they receive a bounty from the Federal government. Over seven thousand men from Indiana enlisted. They were sent to Alabama and Tennessee, where their principal duties were guarding supply depots and communications. Most had returned to Indiana by August, but in the short time they served they made a valuable contribution during the crucial period when Sherman was advancing toward Atlanta.[16]

There were several weaknesses and abuses in the system of raising troops, especially in the emphasis upon voluntary enlistment. One of the most obvious was the necessity for persuading men to re-enlist after the term for which they volunteered had expired. Another weakness was that there was no system of automatic replacements in regiments whose ranks were depleted. Each regiment was responsible for recruiting to fill its own ranks. As a result much valuable time and manpower were consumed in furloughing troops as an inducement to them to re-enlist and in using them as recruiting officers. Another problem was that it was usually much easier to recruit volunteers to serve in new regiments than it was to persuade them to enlist in older regiments whose numbers had been depleted. Military authorities felt that a more effective army was created by incorporating new

[15] Terrell, *Indiana in the War of the Rebellion,* pp. 37, 59. See *ibid.,* pp. 38-39, for a table showing the numbers who re-enlisted from each of the veteran organizations. See Nolan, *Iron Brigade,* pp. 267-270, for a good account of the problems of "veteranizing."

[16] Terrell, *Indiana in the War of the Rebellion,* pp. 43-48.

recruits into regiments where they would serve along side veterans. But for various reasons volunteers usually preferred new regiments. In older regiments new men had no chance of receiving commissions since offices were already filled, and chances for raw recruits to receive promotions in such regiments were slight. One advantage in the draft was that it made possible the assignment of new men to older regiments. Moreover, the creation of new regiments increased the military patronage of the governor by giving him added opportunities to dispense commissions. Those drafted in 1864 were incorporated in groups of one hundred to five hundred into regiments already in the field and performed well in the final campaigns of the war.[17]

Excessive zeal to encourage voluntary enlistments led to abuses of the bounty system. Beginning in July, 1861, the Federal government offered bounties to three-year volunteers as a method of spurring enlistments. In 1863 a bounty of $400, to be paid in installments, was offered to all veterans who would re-enlist for three years. Beginning in October, 1863, bounties of $300 were offered to new recruits who would enlist in old organizations, and shortly thereafter the same sum was offered to recruits enlisting in any regiment, old or new. Under the Federal system of bounties men who enlisted

17 Terrell, *Indiana in the Rebellion*, pp. 59, 65. A typical example of the task of raising recruits to fill an old regiment is related in *The 1864 Diary of Lt. Col. Jefferson K. Scott, 59th Indiana Volunteer Infantry* (Transcribed from the original and with an introduction by Col. H. Engerud, U.S.A., Retired. Published jointly by the Monroe County Civil War Centennial Commission and Monroe County Historical Society, Bloomington, 1962). Scott, a resident of Martinsville, was a member of a regiment whose term of enlistment had almost expired at the beginning of 1864. Scott succeeded in persuading 190 veterans to re-enlist, and they in turn returned home on furlough to recruit. In Martinsville Scott recounts that he put up posters "telling the Union loving people of the village that I could furnish accommodations for a few of the most loyal for 3 years unless sooner discharged." But he met with a discouraging response. He found the people "rather too good Union to go to war; they prefer to remain at home." He finally returned to active service in April, having recruited about 230 men for his own and other regiments. *Ibid.*, pp. 4, 5, 8, 9, 12, 15.

after October, 1863, fared better than those who enlisted earlier. The special session of the Indiana legislature in 1865 petitioned Congress to equalize bounties, and in 1866 legislation was passed which authorized additional bounties for men who had enlisted during the early part of the war.[18]

Inequities arising from the bounties paid by the United States were minor compared to those resulting from efforts of local governments. Bounties were originally regarded as a method by which local governments might help to compensate volunteers for their loss of normal income, but they came to be regarded almost exclusively as inducements for enlistment. Bounties which enabled some townships to fill their quotas with volunteers worked a hardship on others and encouraged the practice of bounty jumping. Since the law permitted volunteers to enlist from any township in the state, men naturally chose to enlist from those offering the highest bounties. The result was that men who lived in the townships which paid large bounties did not have to volunteer since quotas were filled by persons from outside, while poor townships which could not afford to pay bounties were drained of their man power but were not credited with having filled their quotas. As calls for soldiers continued competition between townships increased. Some localities offered as much as $500 to new recruits during the last part of the war. This caused bitterness on the part of men who had volunteered earlier without receiving any such inducements.[19]

Desire to escape the ignominy of the draft played a large part in converting public opinion to the use of Negro troops to fill military quotas. During the early part of the war suggestions by antislavery men that Negroes be armed were regarded as outrageous by both Democrats and conservative Republicans. "Is it possible," exclaimed the Indianapolis *Sentinel,*

18 Terrell, *Indiana in the War of the Rebellion,* pp. 75-77.
19 *Ibid.,* pp. 81-82. Terrell, *Report of the Adjutant General of Indiana,* I, Appendix, Document No. 8, pp. 75-88 shows the amounts paid by townships in the various counties as bounties.

"that the people of the North, the descendants of a proud and imperious race, will permit the Negro to be armed and placed by his [*sic*] side in maintaining a white man's government?" In his speech before the Democratic state convention in January, 1862, Thomas A. Hendricks asked: "What General would go into battle trusting to black regiments for his strength? and what regiment, made up of the proud men of Indiana, would stand in a battle, where they must lean for support upon armed negroes?" Caleb Smith, Indiana's representative in Lincoln's cabinet, declared that white soldiers from Indiana would resent serving in an army which included colored troops.[20]

Most of the protests were over proposals to use slaves in the Union army since the number of Negroes in the free states was small. But in January, 1863, after Governor John Andrews of Massachusetts received authority from the Federal government to raise a regiment of colored troops, recruitment of northern Negroes began. Some Indiana Negroes who had earlier tendered their services to Morton and been refused enlisted in the Massachusetts Fifty-Fourth, which included men from every state and also Canada. The Indianapolis *Sentinel* sneered at the recruitment of the colored regiment as a device for enabling white men of Massachusetts to escape military service, but before many months opinion in Indiana had shifted to support of the recruitment of Negroes. In November, 1863, when Morton determined to use Negro troops to fill Indiana's quota, the Indianapolis *Journal* commented that now the Negro was regarded "as excellent material for the army, and indeed no white soldier can now be found who would not sooner see a Negro with one arm off, than to have one off himself." During the political campaign of 1864 Republicans praised the record of Negro troops and twitted the Democratic advocates of white su-

20 Indianapolis *Daily Sentinel,* January 9, July 17, 1862, quoted in Thornbrough, *Negro in Indiana,* pp. 193-194.

premacy over their eagerness to use Negro troops so as to avoid being drafted themselves.[21]

Once the decision to use Negro troops had been made the Indiana authorities pushed a vigorous campaign of enlisting them to fill Indiana's quotas, and recruiting officers from other states were forbidden to operate in Indiana. Although the Federal government did not offer a bounty to Negro troops until June, 1864, several Indiana localities offered bounties. As it became increasingly difficult to find volunteers, efforts were made to persuade slaves from Kentucky to run away and enlist. Many of the Negroes enrolled at New Albany were recruited from Kentucky by brokers. A very high percentage of the adult Negroes in Indiana appear to have served in the Union Army, although some of them were credited to other states. On the other hand, some Negroes from Kentucky were credited to Indiana. Most Indiana Negroes were enrolled in the Twenty-Eighth Regiment, United States Colored Troops, which was organized in Indianapolis.[22]

Local governments were more concerned with filling their quotas than with recruiting troops who would actually fight. The result was sometimes the enlistment and payment of bounties to dubious characters who volunteered only to collect their bounties and then to desert. Criminals and even deserters from the Confederate army were sometimes enlisted. Closely related to the system of paying bounties to volunteers was the system of paying substitutes for persons who were drafted. Brokers who specialized in recruiting substitutes and in helping townships to fill their quotas did a flourishing business, sometimes in collusion with recruiting officers. During the later part of the war brokers regularly advertised in the newspapers with offers to furnish townships or individuals with volunteers or substitutes. Some advertisements said that

21 Indianapolis *Daily Journal,* November 17, 1863, quoted in Thornbrough, *Negro in Indiana,* pp. 194-196.

22 *Ibid.,* pp. 196-200. See *ibid.,* p. 199 for other regiments in which Indiana Negroes served.

substitutes or certificates of exemption could be furnished almost as cheaply for a three-year period as for one year. The following notice was typical:

CITIZENS OF INDIANAPOLIS
AND MARION COUNTY
TAKE NOTICE

If you want A Good Sound Man to Represent You in the field, you can get him at a Reasonable Price, by applying at our Office, Northwest Corner, Opposite Union Depot.[23]

It is not surprising that appeals of this sort led to bounty jumping. Desertions by volunteers recruited by such advertisements were frequent enough to constitute a serious problem. One officer reported that of 389 enlistments more than two hundred deserted almost as soon as they received their bounties. Military officers made vigorous efforts to stop these practices by arresting bounty jumpers and making examples of them in order to deter others. In November, 1864, a band of one hundred and fifty offenders, wearing placards proclaiming their crime, were paraded through the streets of Indianapolis. About the same time four men who were regarded as the worst examples of bounty jumpers—who had enlisted and deserted repeatedly—were sentenced by a court martial to be shot. One of them, a youth of only nineteen, was given a reprieve by President Lincoln, but the others were executed. In Lafayette a bounty broker was arrested along with a group of bounty jumpers. He was described as "a well-dressed chap, of a fine personal appearance, wearing a charming mustache" and dressed in "fine linen and glossy broadcloth."[24]

[23] Terrell, *Indiana in the War of the Rebellion*, pp. 85-87; Stampp, *Indiana Politics*, pp. 214-215; Indianapolis *Daily Sentinel*, November 18, 29, 1864; Indianapolis *Daily Journal*, August 6, 1864.

[24] Terrell, *Indiana in the War of the Rebellion*, pp. 86-87; Indianapolis *Daily Sentinel*, November 17, 1864; Lafayette *Journal*, quoted *ibid.*, November 29, 1864; James Barnett, "The Bounty Jumpers of Indiana," *Civil War History*, IV, No. 4 (December, 1958), 432-433.

Bounty jumpers were men who enlisted merely for the purpose of collecting their money and who deserted without actually seeing service. In addition there were other men who were deserters in the usual sense of the term—soldiers who ran away from their military posts or who failed to return after a furlough. It is estimated that about ten thousand men from Indiana regiments deserted during the course of the war. Among people accustomed to a large amount of personal freedom desertion did not seem to be a serious offense. Soldiers at first tended to look upon military service as little different from any other occupation. "To desert was simply to 'knock off work.' " When deserters appeared in their home communities they were likely to be treated as if they had merely quit a job. Sheer homesickness frequently caused soldiers to desert. One young man ran away to his home to be married and was seized as a deserter on his wedding night. In some places efforts by the military authorities to arrest deserters were obstructed by civilians. It was frequently asserted that Democrats who were critical of the conduct of the war encouraged soldiers to desert and interfered with attempts to arrest them, but the Indianapolis *Sentinel* editorially condemned interference with arrests.[25]

In addition to the men who served in the Union army a substantial number served in the Indiana Legion, the militia organization of the state. The Legion, which was organized under the militia law of May, 1861, was created for the purpose of quelling internal disorders and repelling attacks from outside the state. It was made up entirely of volunteers. There was no provision in the law giving the governor the power to compel service. Nearly all of the regiments composing the Legion were organized in the counties near the Ohio River, where there was constant fear of raids by Con-

[25] Terrell, *Indiana in the War of the Rebellion,* pp. 345-348, 563; Indianapolis *Daily Sentinel,* March 21, November 9, 1863. Terrell gives the total of deserters as being 10,846 out of a grand total of 208,367—or about 5 per cent.

federate sympathizers from Kentucky. Units of the Legion were called out from time to time to put down small-scale guerilla raids and marauding expeditions from across the river and to suppress disorders arising in connection with the draft or the apprehension of deserters. Their most conspicuous services were at the time of the Kirby Smith invasion of Kentucky in 1862, when it was feared that Indiana would be invaded, and during the Hines and Morgan raids the following year. The Legion also served as a kind of recruiting and training service for the Union army. A substantial number of men who had a taste of military experience in the Legion volunteered for service in Indiana regiments.[26]

Altogether Indiana furnished one hundred twenty-nine infantry regiments to the service of the United States. In addition she furnished thirteen cavalry regiments and three companies of cavalry, one regiment of heavy artillery, and twenty-six batteries of light artillery. According to official records the total number of troops contributed by the state was 196,363. This included 193,748 white men who served in the army, 1,078 who served as sailors and marines, and 1,537 colored troops.[27]

§ §

From June 3, 1861, when they first saw action at Philippi in Virginia, until May 13, 1865, when they took part in the last battle of the war at Palmetto Ranche in Texas, Indiana troops participated in three hundred and eight military engagements. They were found in every army and fought in seventeen states, but by far the largest amount of activity by Indiana soldiers took place in the region between the Mississippi River and the Appalachian Mountains. In view of the fact that there were well over one hundred regiments from

[26] Terrell, *Indiana in the War of the Rebellion*, pp. 135-171.

[27] Frederick H. Dyer, *A Compendium of the War of the Rebellion* (With an introduction by Bell Irwin Wiley. 3 volumes, New York and London, 1959), I, 11, 37; Fox, *Regimental Losses*, p. 532. Terrell gives the number of infantry regiments as 129 and the number of troops furnished by Indiana as 208,367. Terrell, *Indiana in the War of the Rebellion*, pp. 133-34.

the state and that they took part in such a large number of campaigns and battles it is obviously impossible to give here more than a bare sketch of the principal ones.[28]

Within a few weeks after the first call for volunteers Indiana men were on the battlefield. Most of the original three-month volunteers were sent to western Virginia to drive the rebels out of the part of the state which opposed secession and to hold it for the Union. The troops entrained at Indianapolis amid scenes of wild enthusiasm and traveled across Ohio to the accompaniment of the cheers of crowds who assembled at every stop. Five of the first regiments were organized into a brigade commanded by Gen. Thomas A. Morris. In Virginia they were soon engaged in the first fighting of the war after the attack on Fort Sumter. The Eleventh meanwhile had been sent to Evansville in anticipation of possible Confederate raids from Kentucky. But when it appeared that there was no imminent danger from that quarter, they were sent to Cumberland, Maryland. From that point they staged a dramatic raid on Romney, Virginia, marching forty-six miles in less than twenty-four hours, and by their daring helped to wipe out the stain of the memory of Buena Vista.[29]

[28] Terrell, *Indiana in the War of the Rebellion,* pp. 567-577. The only infantry divisions which served in the East throughout the war were the Seventh, Thirteenth, Fourteenth, Nineteenth, and Twentieth. In addition, the following infantry regiments which were organized in the closing months of the war served exclusively in the East: One Hundred Forty-Fourth, One Hundred Forty-Fifth, One Hundred Forty-Sixth, One Hundred Forty-Seventh, One Hundred Fiftieth, One Hundred Fifty-Second, One Hundred Fifty-Fourth, One Hundred Fifty-Fifth, and One Hundred Fifty-Sixth. The right wing of the Third Cavalry (Forty-Fifth Regiment) also served exclusively in the East as did the Sixteenth and Seventeenth Light Artillery batteries.

In spite of the small number of Indiana regiments in the East, Indiana troops participated in a larger number of engagements in Virginia than in any other state—90 in all. The second largest number of engagements in which Indiana troops fought was in Tennessee—51 in all; the third largest in Georgia —41 in all. Of course, some of these engagements were small skirmishes.

[29] *Soldier of Indiana,* I, 29-30, 46, 49; *Roll of Honor,* I, 39-61; Terrell, *Report of the Adjutant General,* II, 31-32; Kenneth P. Williams, *Lincoln Finds*

The regiments which were transferred to the service of the United States in response to Lincoln's call of May 3 for three-year troops were also soon in battle. The Thirteenth left Indianapolis on July 4 to join McClellan's army in Virginia and were at once under heavy fire. Seven men were killed in their first battle—just one week after leaving home. The Fourteenth and Fifteenth were also soon on their way to the East, where they took part in the Cheat Mountain campaign in September.[30]

The Thirteenth and Fourteenth remained in the East as a part of a brigade which also included the Seventh Indiana, under the command of Col. Nathan Kimball. In the spring of 1862 they were engaged in the battles fought during Stonewall Jackson's brilliant foray into the Shenandoah Valley. Kimball had an important part in defeating Jackson at the battle of Winchester Heights and in driving the enemy out of Front Royal. The Thirteenth and Fourteenth also took part in the Peninsular campaign under McClellan, where they were assigned to outlying picket duty, spending twenty days and nights in the open in almost constant contact with the enemy. The Twentieth, which was to prove itself as one of the most heroic Indiana regiments, was also present on the Peninsula and took part in most of the battles, suffering heavy casualties. Earlier it had witnessed the battle between the "Monitor" and "Merrimac" off Fort Monroe.[31]

At the Second Battle of Bull Run in August, 1862, the Twentieth again fought bravely and suffered heavily. In this battle the Ninteenth Indiana first took part in a significant

A General: A Military Study of the Civil War (5 volumes, New York, 1949-1959), I, 71.

[30] *Soldier of Indiana*, I, 74, 82-88; *Roll of Honor*, I, 154-204; Terrell, *Report of the Adjutant General*, II, 110, 120, 130. The Fifteenth Indiana was transferred to Kentucky in November, 1861, and remained in the West for the duration of the war.

[31] *Soldier of Indiana*, I, 445-464, 502-503, 507, 525, 540, 572-573; Terrell, *Report of the Adjutant General*, II, 110, 120, 191; Robert Underwood Johnson and Clarence Clough Buel (eds.), *Battles and Leaders of the Civil War* (4 volumes, New York, 1887), II, 299.

action. It was a part of the famed Iron Brigade, which was to become the most celebrated infantry unit in the Union army and the only brigade made up entirely of regiments from the West which fought in the East.[32] At Antietam, on September 17, 1862, scene of the most sanguinary single day of the war, the Nineteenth was one of five regiments from Indiana. Of 215 men in the regiment 106 were casualties on that bloody day. The Fourteenth Indiana went into the battle with 320 men and came out with only 140. Kimball's brigade, of which it was a part, earned the name of the "Gibraltar Brigade" at Antietam. The Twenty-Seventh Indiana also suffered heavily and earned special commendation for its part in the battle. At Fredericksburg and Chancellorsville the Seventh, Fourteenth, Nineteenth, Twentieth, and Twenty-Seventh all fought and suffered heavy losses. At Fredericksburg Kimball was seriously wounded.[33]

The same five regiments fought at Gettysburg, where most of them sustained their heaviest losses. Seventy per cent of the men in the Nineteenth were casualties on the first day of fighting, but there was no retreat except in response to orders from officers. Gen. Sol Meredith, who had been advanced from colonel of the Nineteenth to command of the Iron Brigade, was wounded. The Twentieth suffered losses of about one third its numbers, and its colonel, John Wheeler, was killed.[34]

32 Terrell, *Report of the Adjutant General,* II, 192; *Soldier of Indiana,* I, 590-592; Nolan, *Iron Brigade,* pp. 99-112; Fox, *Regimental Losses,* pp. 343-344.

33 Nolan, *Iron Brigade,* pp. 137-142, 177-188; *Soldier of Indiana,* II, 32-40, 56-70, 92-93; Fox, *Regimental Losses,* pp. 342-344, 346, 432. Fox gives the casualties of the Nineteenth at Antietam as 13 killed, 59 wounded. The Fourteenth Indiana suffered a loss of 30 killed and 150 wounded, the Twenty-Seventh Indiana had 18 killed and 191 wounded, but *not a single member of either regiment was reported as captured or missing.* The number of dead was substantially increased as some men died subsequently of wounds. The total killed in action or mortally wounded for the Fourteenth was 49, for the Twenty-Seventh, 41.

34 Nolan, *Iron Brigade,* pp. 233-259; *Soldier of Indiana,* II, 122-123; Terrell, *Report of the Adjutant General,* II, 47, 121-122, 176-177, 192, 268-269; Fox, *Regimental Losses,* pp. 342-344, 346, 439-440.

Meanwhile, the bulk of the troops from Indiana were in the theater of the war west of the mountains. In August, 1861, all of the regiments which had not yet been sent East were rushed to Missouri to reinforce Gen. John C. Frémont in a campaign to clear that state of Confederate forces and save it for the Union. Among them were the Twenty-Second and Twenty-Fourth regiments, commanded respectively by Col. Jefferson C. Davis and Col. Alvin P. Hovey, two of the most notable figures whom Indiana contributed to the war. Col. Conrad Baker, in command of the First Indiana Cavalry, also saw action in Missouri.[35] Most of the activity in that state consisted of skirmishes and guerilla operations. In 1862 Davis was given command of a division which met the Confederates at Pea Ridge in Arkansas in March of that year. Although Union losses were heavier than those sustained by the enemy, the Confederates withdrew to the Arkansas River after the battle and active resistance in the Ozark area ceased. After Pea Ridge Davis and his troops were sent down the Mississippi to join the Union forces before Corinth, Mississippi.[36]

During the fall and winter of 1861-1862 large numbers of troops from Indiana were sent into Kentucky, an area about which there was particular concern because of its proximity. During the first months of the war, when Kentucky was attempting to play the role of a neutral, Morton tried without success to persuade Federal authorities to send troops to occupy strategic points in the state. Instead Lincoln, to Morton's great disgust, insisted upon following a policy of "watchful waiting," which resulted in the Confederates making the first move. Kentucky's neutrality was abruptly ended in September, 1861, when Confederates seized Bowling Green and

35 Soldier in Indiana, I, 156-159. The Indiana regiments in Missouri included the Eighth, Eleventh, Eighteenth, Twenty-Second, Twenty-Third, Twenty-Fourth, Twenty-Fifth, Twenty-Sixth, and part of the Twenty-Eighth.

36 Ibid., pp. 206-210; Roll of Honor, I, 480-482, 494; Terrell, Report of the Adjutant General, II, 218, 278; Battles and Leaders of the Civil War, I, 324; Compendium of the War of the Rebellion, II, 675, 800-801.

Columbus. Thereafter General Grant occupied Paducah, and Union forces were poured into the state. At Morton's insistence some of the Indiana regiments which had been sent East were brought back to Kentucky.[37]

These regiments, which included the Eleventh, commanded by Lew Wallace, moved with Grant as he began his advance southward toward Fort Henry in February, 1862. After Fort Henry fell to the Union forces, Grant began to move toward Fort Donelson. In this campaign for the first time large numbers of Indiana men participated and for the first time tasted the horrors of war. One of the soldiers in the Eleventh, which was sent from Fort Henry after the assault on Fort Donelson began, recorded in his diary: "General [Lew] Wallace rode down the line and said, 'You have been wanting a fight—you have got it. Hell's before you.' " "It is very cold and we have but few rations and are suffering severely," the same soldier wrote, but added that the troops felt confident of success. The march of Wallace from Fort Henry to Donelson with reinforcements was credited with an important part in turning the tide in favor of a Union victory. He was rewarded by promotion to the rank of major general —the first officer from Indiana to attain that rank in the war.[38]

Hundreds of Indiana men were among the 1,500 dead and wounded Union troops at Fort Donelson. Some of the wounded died of the severe cold, and the bodies of the dead were found frozen to the earth. "The wounded in the field were so numerous that but few could be taken care of," wrote one participant, "and their cries and groans during that awful night I shall never forget." Many Indiana families were in mourning after the battle, but the fall of Fort Donelson was

---

[37] Stampp, *Indiana Politics,* pp. 113-116; Terrell, *Indiana in the War of the Rebellion,* pp. 274-283.

[38] *Soldier in Indiana,* I, 288-290; Williams, *Lincoln Finds A General,* III, 239, 246. For a recent account and evaluation of Wallace's role at Fort Donelson see James A. Treichel, "Lew Wallace at Fort Donelson," *Indiana Magazine of History,* LIX (1963), 3-18.

also a glorious victory. Nearly fifteen thousand Confederate prisoners were taken, many of whom were sent to Camp Morton in Indianapolis. There was widespread optimism that the war had entered upon its final phase and that Union victory was imminent.[39]

The losses at Fort Donelson were but a prelude to the terrible carnage at Shiloh, April 6-7, 1862, the bloodiest single battle in the West. Fourteen Indiana regiments fought at Shiloh. In the first day's battle the Twenty-Fifth, Thirty-First, and Forty-Fourth regiments and the Sixth Battery took part from the opening to the close. Among the many acts of bravery that day the conduct of Col. James C. Veatch of the Twenty-Fifth Indiana, who commanded a brigade, was outstanding. Two horses were shot under him, and he himself was wounded, but he refused to leave the field. The Thirty-Second (the German Regiment) under August Willich, although new to combat, displayed great coolness under demoralizing conditions. The only Indiana troops in the army commanded by Gen. Don Carlos Buell who took part in the first day's fighting at Shiloh were the Thirty-Sixth Indiana, under William Grose, who was advanced to brigade commander the next day. One of the puzzling features of the battle, and one which has led to continued controversy among military historians, was the failure of Lew Wallace and the troops he commanded to arrive earlier at the scene of battle. Because of confusion over orders he consumed a whole day in moving his troops a short distance, and arrived after the first day's fighting was over. Once his veteran troops were in action they helped turn a defeat into a bloody victory, but after Shiloh, Wallace was never again given a battlefield command. Out of the total Union losses of over thirteen thousand at Shiloh almost a tenth were Indiana men. Of the Indiana regiments the Ninth, Thirty-First and Forty-Fourth had the greatest number of casualties.[40]

[39] Williams, *Lincoln Finds A General*, III, 247; *Soldier of Indiana*, I, 294-315; *Roll of Honor*, I, 589-594.

[40] Terrell, *Report of the Adjutant General*, II, 250, 309, 322, 361, 439; *Soldier*

RECRUITING
OFFICE.

BOUNTY LAND AND BOUNTY MONEY!!

The undersigned is Commissioned by Governor Morton to enlist a Company in the Fourth Congressional District, for the 68th Regiment, and to muster recruits into the service of the United States. Pay to commence as soon as names are enrolled.

All communications addressed as below, will be promptly responded to.

LIEUT. MARSHALL P. HAYDEN,
Rising Sun, Ohio County, Ind,

July 21, 1862.

PATRIOTS YOUR COUNTRY NEEDS YOU!

THE UNION FOREVER!

Wanted--25 Men

To fill the ranks of the "INDIANA SNAKE KILLERS," in Colonel Scribner's Regiment at Camp Noble, New Albany.

Enquire of

JOHN SEXTON, Captain,
JOHN CURRY, 1st Lieutenant,
G. W. WINDELL, 2d Lieut.

Camp Noble, Aug. 30th, 1861.

Morgan's Raiders at Salem, July 10, 1863
By C. S. Haskins

The Boys in Blue—A Soldiers' Reunion at Indianapolis, 1876
By H. C. Chandler

During the spring of 1862, while Grant was advancing into the heart of the Confederacy by way of the Tennessee and Cumberland rivers, other forces under the command of Maj. Gen. John Pope were moving down the Mississippi. Five of the Indiana regiments which had spent the preceding winter in Kentucky were sent to join Pope in the vicinity of New Madrid. Indiana troops took part in the capture of Island No. 10, which the Confederates abandoned almost without a struggle after it had been shelled by gunboats. After the surrender at that point gunboats worked their way down the river, forcing the abandonment of Fort Pillow and Fort Randolph and opening the way for the capture of Memphis. Troops of the Forty-Sixth Indiana were the first Union soldiers to enter that city, on June 8 or 9, 1862, and other Indiana regiments occupied the city for a time after its surrender. Col. Graham N. Fitch of the Forty-Sixth was in charge of the government of the city after the surrender. Meanwhile the Twenty-First Indiana, the only Indiana regiment to participate in the campaigns along the eastern shore of Maryland and Virginia under Gen. Benjamin F. Butler in 1861, had accompanied him to New Orleans and were among the first troops to enter the Crescent City.[41]

In spite of Union successes in the West during the first part of 1862 the threat of a Confederate thrust into Kentucky had not been entirely eliminated. In part to relieve pressure from Union armies in other areas, in part in the hope of encouraging secessionists in Kentucky, Gen. Braxton Bragg began an advance northward which brought him into Kentucky in the late summer of 1862. At the same time Gen. Kirby Smith moved northward from Knoxville. In Kentucky the Confederates

of Indiana, I, 360-384; Williams, Lincoln Finds A General, III, 379-385; Fox, Regimental Losses, pp. 341, 348, 428. For a recent treatment of Lew Wallace's role at Shiloh, see Harold Lew Wallace, "Lew Wallace's March to Shiloh Revisited," Indiana Magazine of History, LIX (1963), 19-30. The total Union losses at Shiloh were 13,298, including 1,614 killed. Indiana losses were 1,277, including 179 killed.

41 Soldier of Indiana, I, 346-351, 414-419, 550-551; Roll of Honor, II, 380; Terrell, Report of the Adjutant General, II, 208-209, 461, 471.

met Union troops which were part of the Army of the Ohio commanded by Buell. The Confederate advance threw the border counties of Indiana and Ohio into consternation and led Governor Morton to make frantic efforts to send reinforcements into Kentucky. Gen. Lew Wallace was given a leave of absence to engage in recruiting. In August these new recruits began to move into Kentucky without any training and frequently without such equipment as tents, knapsacks, and canteens. Within a short time there were twenty Indiana regiments in Kentucky. The nature of the operation of putting the men into the field was described by the Indianapolis *Journal,* which proudly proclaimed on August 21: "Today Indiana will have in Kentucky nearly *fourteen thousand men of the new levy.* . . . We don't believe the promptness has been equalled in any emergency by any State in the Union. . . . The Rebels had cut off our army at Cumberland Gap, and were advancing with alarming speed. Men *must* be thrown in to resist them, or the war would be transferred to our own border. Governer Morton determined that the men should be sent," even though the task of equipping and transporting them seemed insurmountable. "Everything," declared the *Journal,* "had to be done that was necessary to change men just out of their shops and off of their farms into soldiers and put them into the field." The results were what might have been expected. In a series of four battles near Richmond, Kentucky, at the end of August, Kirby Smith fell upon some of the raw troops, who had been in service an average of ten to twenty days, and slaughtered them. After the battle, Gen. Mahlon D. Manson, who commanded one of the brigades which suffered most heavily, said: "Taking into consideration the rawness of the troops, there has been no battle during the war where more bravery was displayed by officers and men . . .," but people back home were appalled. Morton was criticized severely as well as praised for his part in sending inexperienced men into such danger.[42]

42 *Soldier of Indiana,* I, 605-612, II, 3-5; Terrell, *Report of the Adjutant General,* II, 98, 143; Foulke, *Morton,* I, 186-192; Stampp, *Indiana Politics,* p.

Meanwhile Bragg was advancing into Kentucky, avoiding the battle which Buell had expected to fight with him in Tennessee. John Morgan's cavalry preceded him. At Munfordville, Kentucky, Col. John T. Wilder of the Seventeenth Indiana was in command of a garrison of raw troops, but he stubbornly refused to surrender to Bragg until he was convinced that the enemy had overwhelmingly superior numbers.[43] As the Confederates continued their advance both Louisville and Cincinnati expected to be attacked. Morton declared martial law in the border counties of Indiana. Both civilians and soldiers were demoralized. Some placed the blame for the critical state of affairs upon General Buell. His lethargy and failure to take decisive action were felt to have allowed Bragg to escape. The Indianapolis *Journal* hysterically declared that Buell deserved to be shot. Morton had been highly critical of Buell for a long time, and at this juncture he also became embroiled in a quarrel with Gen. William Nelson, whom Buell had placed in command of the forces opposing Kirby Smith. Nelson offended Morton by objecting to the Governor's interference in the affairs of the Indiana regiments in Kentucky and by placing the blame for the defeat at Richmond upon General Manson. Nelson accused Morton and Gen. Jefferson C. Davis, with whom he was also feuding, of plotting against him. Matters reached a climax in Louisville, where Morton had rushed following the disaster at Richmond. During an encounter at the Galt House, Davis, who was in Morton's company, shot and killed Nelson. Morton was in no way responsible, but there was a tendency in some quarters to

153. In the same period of time and in response to the same danger Ohio sent eight regiments, while Illinois sent only one. *Soldier of Indiana*, II, 5. At the battle at Richmond the Twelfth Indiana suffered 25 killed, 148 wounded, and 608 missing, while the Sixteenth Indiana suffered 25 killed, 120 wounded, and 395 missing. Fox, *Regimental Losses*, p. 431.

43 Williams, *Lincoln Finds A General*, IV, 62-64; *Battles and Leaders of the Civil War*, III, 41; Terrell, *Report of the Adjutant General*, II, 155, 619; *Soldier of Indiana*, I, 602-604. At Munfordville the Sixty-Seventh Indiana suffered 11 killed, 32 wounded, and 888 missing or captured. Fox, *Regimental Losses*, p. 431.

link him with the killing, which occurred a short time before
the elections of 1862 and may have been a factor in the
Democratic victory.[44]

A few days after the shooting the armies of Bragg and
Buell faced each other at Perryville. Once again Indiana
regiments suffered heavy casualties, due in part to the rawness of the troops. Neither side could claim a clear victory,
but after the battle Bragg withdrew from Kentucky. The
heavy casualties at Perryville further incensed Morton against
Buell. "The butchery of our troops at Perryville was terrible," the Governor told Lincoln in a lengthy telegram in
which he blamed Union losses on lack of foresight. "Nothing," he warned, "but success, speedy and decided, will save
our cause from utter destruction. In the Northwest distrust
and despair are seizing upon the hearts of the people." Morton was gratified when shortly thereafter Buell was replaced
by Gen. William Rosecrans.[45]

After Perryville Bragg took up headquarters at Murfreesboro, Tennessee. Nearby at Stone River for three days—
from December 31 through January 2—there was fought a
battle which engaged one of the largest aggregations of Indiana troops in the entire war—twenty-six regiments and five
batteries. Indiana's losses were commensurately high—2,500

[44] Stampp, *Indiana Politics*, p. 154; Williams, *Lincoln Finds A General*, IV,
52; Foulke, *Morton*, I, 192-195; John Fitch, *Annals of the Army of the Cumberland* . . . (Philadelphia, 1863), pp. 169-170; General James B. Fry, "Killed
by A Brother Soldier," *Battles and Leaders of the Civil War*, III, 60-61n. Davis
surrendered to military authorities after the shooting and was placed under
arrest, but he was subsequently released without ever being brought to trial.
He was presumably released with the expectation that he would be tried in
a civil court, but this did not occur. Buell was highly critical of the release
of Davis. General Don Carlos Buell, "East Tennessee and Campaign of
Perryville," *ibid.*, pp. 43-44.

[45] Foulke, *Morton*, I, 195-198; Terrell, *Report of the Adjutant General*, II,
218-219, 380; *Soldier of Indiana*, I, 614-624. The anti-Buell bias of the last
account is obvious. At Perryville (or Chaplin Hills as it is sometimes called)
the Twenty-Second Indiana suffered losses of 57 killed or mortally wounded
out of 303 troops engaged. The Thirty-Eighth Indiana also suffered its
heaviest losses at Perryville. Fox, *Regimental Losses*, pp. 345, 351.

out of total Union losses of a little more than eleven thousand. The heavy losses were due in part to lack of training and experience, but the men were learning to be soldiers. A young private in a letter to his family in which he described the battle spoke of how an army was being forged under fire out of the raw recruits who had left Indiana the previous summer. "Our regiments are all very small since the battle," he wrote, "many were wounded, and many are sick. . . . Only half of the men who leave home are fit for service. The officers resign and go home and the privates die. A regiment of five hundred men, well drilled, which has had all the poor men sifted out by service, is worth two new regiments of a thousand men each."[46]

During 1863 the most important military campaign in the West was the long and complicated and frequently frustrating one against Vicksburg. By reason of its natural setting plus the fact that it was elaborately entrenched the city constituted a formidable obstacle and was probably Grant's greatest challenge. During the winter of 1862-1863 large numbers of Indiana troops were engaged in futile efforts to approach the city from the bayous of the Yazoo region. The slowness and seemingly hopelessness of the campaign caused impatience. In April the Indianapolis *Journal* pronounced Grant a complete failure. "Grant is getting along at Vicksburg with such rapidity," it commented sarcastically, "that, in the course of fifteen or twenty years, he will be ready to send

[46] Terrell, *Report of the Adjutant General*, II, 130, 309-310, 370, 390, III, 77; *Roll of Honor*, II, 352-353; *Battles and Leaders of the Civil War*, III, 619, 626-627; *Soldier of Indiana*, II, 168-171; letter of Darwin Thomas of the Eighty-Sixth Indiana, quoted *ibid.*, pp. 174-175. The Indiana regiments which suffered the heaviest losses at Stone River were as follows:

Fifteenth Indiana	38 killed	143 wounded	7 missing
Thirty-Ninth Indiana	31 killed	118 wounded	231 missing
Thirty-Seventh Indiana	27 killed	115 wounded	8 missing
Thirtieth Indiana	31 killed	110 wounded	72 missing

Other Indiana regiments which suffered heavy losses at Stone River were the Ninth, Twenty-Second, Thirty-First, Thirty-Second, and Thirty-Eighth. Fox, *Regimental Losses*, pp. 435, 341, 345, 348, 349, 351.

up a gunboat to find out whether the enemy hasn't died of old age."[47]

Just a few days earlier Grant had begun a new approach—concentrating his troops at Milliken's Bend, then crossing the river and approaching the city from below. In this phase of the struggle, at the battles of Port Gibson, Champion Hills, and Black River Bridge, large numbers of Indiana troops were engaged. At Port Gibson the Forty-Ninth Indiana won commendation for charging a battery alone and capturing it. At Champion Hills, one of the most important battles in the campaign, Indiana troops commanded by Gen. Alvin P. Hovey were conspicuous. Hovey's division bore the brunt of the battle and suffered losses of nearly one third but captured seven hundred men. In the advance from Bruinsburg, where the troops crossed the Mississippi, to Black River Bridge, Hovey's division suffered greater losses than any other division but also took a larger number of prisoners.[48]

The third phase of the Vicksburg campaign began May 19, when the city had been completely invested. The actual seige began after two unsuccessful assaults. During one of these the Eighth Indiana was the first to succeed in planting its colors on the enemy's battlement, but they were later repulsed. From May 19 to July 4 the Union armies were engaged in the trenches and in erecting fortifications, gradually pushing closer and closer to the city. Some troops were under almost constant fire—especially from rifle sharpshooters. Typical

[47] Indianapolis *Daily Journal,* April 5, 1863, quoted in *Soldier of Indiana,* II, 293.

[48] *Soldier of Indiana,* II, 301-304, 313-338; Terrell, *Report of the Adjutant General,* II, 84, 241, 471; Williams, *Lincoln Finds A General,* IV, 377-379. At Port Gibson the Eighteenth Indiana suffered the heaviest losses of any regiment of the Union Army, while the Sixty-Ninth Indiana suffered the third heaviest. At Champion Hill Indiana regiments suffering the heaviest losses were as follows:

Twenty-Fourth Indiana	27 killed	166 wounded	8 missing
Eleventh Indiana	28 killed	126 wounded	13 missing
Forty-Seventh Indiana	32 killed	91 wounded	17 missing

Fox, *Regimental Losses,* pp. 436, 437.

was the experience of the Twenty-Sixth Indiana, which spent seventeen days continuously in the trenches, firing during the day, digging at night, and sleeping only rarely. Of eight hundred men in the regiment only four hundred were still fit for duty at the end of the seige. The excessive heat of the summer sun added to their discomfort and caused some sickness. But although the seige was gruelling and hazardous, losses during the seige were relatively small—not in any way comparable to those suffered at Gettysburg, which was being fought just as Vicksburg prepared to surrender.[49]

After the fall of Vicksburg on July 4, the most important operation in the West in 1863 was the campaign around Chattanooga, a vital railroad center and link between Richmond and the southwest. In June, Rosecrans left Murfreesboro and advanced toward Chattanooga, where Bragg had taken up headquarters. As the Union forces advanced, Bragg abandoned the city. A few days later, on September 19 and 20, Rosecrans met Bragg's forces, now reinforced by troops under Gen. James Longstreet, at Chickamauga, where a battle was fought in which the rate of slaughter was comparable to that at Antietam or Gettysburg. Twenty-eight regiments of infantry and two regiments and a batallion of cavalry and eight batteries of artillery from Indiana—the second largest number of troops from a northern state—participated. Eli Lilly commanded the eighteenth artillery credited with firing the first shell on the advancing army of Bragg. Gens. J. J. Reynolds and Jeff C. Davis, John M. Brannan and A. M. McCook commanded divisions, while other Indianans, including August Willich, Charles Cruft, William Grose, John T. Wilder, George F. Dick, B. F. Scribner, and Edward A. King commanded brigades. For Indiana it was the costliest battle of the war, with over three thousand casualties.[50]

49 Terrell, *Report of the Adjutant General*, II, 56, 167, 577; *Soldier of Indiana*, II, 321-328.

50 James R. Carnahan, "Indiana at Chickamauga," in *War Papers Read before the Indiana Commandery Military Order of the Loyal Legion of the United States* (Indianapolis, 1898), pp. 86-116; Terrell, *Report of the Adjutant*

After Chickamauga the Union forces were penned up in Chattanooga, while Bragg commanded the heights around the city as well as the railroad approaches. Rosecrans was replaced by Gen. George H. Thomas, and preparations were made to send reinforcements to relieve the troops in the city. Gen. William T. Sherman advanced eastward from Memphis with forces which included several Indiana regiments. On November 23-25 another battle was fought outside of Chattanooga in which the Union won an exhilarating victory. The heights at Lookout Mountain and Missionary Ridge were successfully stormed, and the enemy was sent into retreat. Large numbers of Indiana troops were engaged, and several Indiana units could claim the honor of being the first to scale the heights and place their banners at various points. After the battle the troops were exuberant. "I told you that the Army of the Cumberland was not whipped at Chickamauga," a major of the Fortieth Indiana wrote after the battle on Missionary Ridge. "The back-bone of the Rebellion was broken last Wednesday," he exulted. In his letter he described the part which his regiment played, which was typical of many:

Stone River was a skirmish, as far as our regiment was concerned, to this affair. . . . We had to advance more than a mile, without cover of any sort, over a dead level, commanded at all points by the enemy's batteries, and for the last quarter of a mile under the fire of the infantry . . . I could see our brave boys dropping all around me as we moved forward, some killed, others desperately wounded, but the advance was not even checked. It moved on as if each man felt himself invulnerable. . . .

I have never seen anything so vicious as the artillery fire from the ridge. . . .

The [Confederate] prisoners say that our attempt to scale the height

General, II, 39, 74, 322, 690, III, 84. The Indiana regiments which suffered the heaviest losses at Chickamauga were as follows:

Eighty-Seventh Indiana	40 killed	142 wounded	8 missing
Tenth Indiana	24 killed	136 wounded	6 missing
Seventy-Fourth Indiana	22 killed	125 wounded	10 missing

The Sixth Indiana and the Thirty-Second suffered their heaviest losses for any single battle at Chickamauga. Fox, *Regimental Losses,* pp. 441, 340, 349.

was laughed at by them as absurd and impossible. They thought us insane to undertake it. After the thing was over, and I could see just what had been done, I came to pretty much the same conclusion.

Losses were heavy. The Indiana Fifteenth started up the ridge with 337 officers and men and lost 202 killed or wounded in the first forty-five minutes of battle while advancing from the line of works at the foot to the crest.[51]

While the battles around Chattanooga were being fought, other Indiana regiments comprised a part of an army commanded by Gen. Ambrose E. Burnside which was engaged in liberating the eastern part of Tennessee and securing Knoxville for the Union.[52]

Large numbers of Indiana troops accompanied Sherman in the dogged advance from Chattanooga to Atlanta. Included were forty-nine infantry regiments, seven cavalry regiments, and ten batteries of artillery. But few of these units were at full strength even at the beginning. The campaign, which lasted from May until September, 1864, was an almost continuous running battle, extending over several parallel mountain ranges. The Fifty-Eighth Indiana, which had recently re-enlisted as a veteran organization after three years' service, was now assigned to the Engineer Department and took charge of building bridges for the advancing army. Some of the rivers in the march from Chattanooga to Atlanta were bridged as many as sixteen times, frequently under enemy fire. The troops suffered much discomfort. It rained a great deal, and supply trains were unable to keep up with the advancing

[51] *Soldier of Indiana,* II, 455-479; letter of Major Henry Leaming, *ibid.,* pp. 473-476; Terrell, *Report of the Adjutant General,* II, 399, III, 146; *Battles and Leaders of the Civil War,* III, 707n. The Indiana regiments which suffered the heaviest losses at Missionary Ridge were as follows:

Fifteenth Indiana	24 killed	175 wounded	0 missing
Fortieth Indiana	20 killed	138 wounded	0 missing
One Hundredth Indiana	10 killed	102 wounded	2 missing
Sixth Indiana	13 killed	63 wounded	0 missing

Fox, *Regimental Losses,* p. 443.

[52] *Soldier of Indiana,* II, 484-489.

troops, with the result that they were on half rations part of the time. "We march sometimes night and day, and our habits are so irregular and universally fatiguing that every one feels dull and tired," a member of the Eighty-Sixth Indiana wrote. "No advance was ever made by a very large army so rapidly as this."[53]

Several sharp battles were fought with the army of Gen. Joseph E. Johnston during the advance. At Resaca on May 14 and 15 forty infantry regiments from Indiana took part as well as cavalry and artillery. The Seventieth Indiana suffered the heaviest number of casualties of any Union regiment engaged.[54] At Kenesaw Mountain terrible losses were sustained by several of the forty-eight Indiana infantry regiments which took part. Out of three hundred men the Fortieth Indiana lost 106 in thirty minutes of desperate fighting. The losses of this regiment were the heaviest of any Union regiment engaged in the battle. "If you hear anyone wondering why Sherman moves so slowly," an officer in the Seventieth wrote his wife, "you can tell them that we have not been beyond the sound of battle for a day since the 8th of May, and that our regiment has lost since that time more than one third of its number killed and wounded, besides a large number, who have fallen by the way utterly exhausted by fatigue, want of proper food and loss of sleep." One company which numbered seventy-six at the beginning of the campaign was now reduced to less than thirty. "War is simply assassination," he concluded.[55]

[53] *Soldier of Indiana*, II, 709-710, 742; Terrell, *Report of the Adjutant General*, II, 567.

[54] *Compendium of the War of the Rebellion*, II, 705; Fox, *Regimental Losses*, p. 447. The Indiana regiments which suffered the heaviest losses at Resaca were as follows:

Seventieth Indiana	29 killed	143 wounded	0 missing
Eightieth Indiana	15 killed	108 wounded	22 missing
Sixty-Third Indiana	19 killed	95 wounded	0 missing

[55] *Compendium of the War of the Rebellion*, II, 709; Terrell, *Report of the Adjutant General*, II, 352, 646; *Soldier of Indiana*, II, 719; Volwiler, "Letters from A Civil War Officer," *Mississippi Valley Historical Review*, XIV, 519-520; Fox, *Regimental Losses*, pp. 352, 452.

But in spite of losses the army advanced. "We are fighting it *now* in a way to either *annihilate* the *men* of the South, or compel the remnant to submission to the laws," wrote an officer of the Fortieth. "In spite of our losses in this army, they have been at least made up by reinforcements. . . . The South are fighting their *last men*—without resources. We can lose man for man with them, annihilate them, and have a handsome balance to our credit to commence the business of building up a nation anew out of the reliques of the old."[56]

At Peach Tree Creek Indiana soldiers helped win a smashing Union victory against the impetuous J. B. Hood, who had replaced Johnston. As Sherman's forces closed in on Atlanta, the Twenty-Second Indiana Battery claimed to have sent the first Yankee shells into the streets.[57]

After the fall of Atlanta the Union armies which had taken it were divided. Half of the Indiana regiments, now under the command of Thomas, pursued Hood back toward Tennessee and were present at his final annihilation at Nashville. The remaining Indiana regiments accompanied Sherman in his march to Savannah and northward into the Carolinas. From Atlanta to Savannah there were only skirmishes, but after the army turned north at Bentonville, a bloody battle was fought which was the last significant one in the campaign. Losses among Indiana regiments were heavy.[58]

While the bulk of Indiana troops in 1864 were engaged in the Atlanta compaign, a smaller number took part in the ill-fated Red River campaign in east Texas under the com-

[56] Henry Leaming, in *Soldier of Indiana*, II, 726.

[57] *Ibid.*, pp. 727-732. At Peach Tree Creek the Thirty-Third Indiana suffered the third highest losses of any Union regiment engaged. Fox, *Regimental Losses*, p. 453. Forty-nine infantry regiments, six cavalry regiments, and ten batteries of artillery from Indiana took part in the siege of Atlanta. *Compendium of the War of the Rebellion*, II, 715.

[58] *Soldier of Indiana*, II, 754-764, 771-784. At the battle of Nashville on December 15 and 16 twenty-seven infantry regiments, four cavalry regiments, and eleven batteries of light artillery from Indiana took part. The heaviest losses were suffered by the Fifty-First and Thirty-First regiments. *Compendium of the War of the Rebellion*, II, 876; Fox, *Regimental Losses*, p. 459.

mand of Gen. Nathaniel P. Banks. An elaborate expedition involving combined land and naval forces proved to be a fiasco.[59]

Meanwhile, four Indiana regiments in the East—the Seventh, Fourteenth, Nineteenth, and Twentieth—which had suffered severely at Gettysburg and had been largely inactive since then were with the Army of the Potomac as Grant began his advance against Richmond from the North. In the bloody battle of the Wilderness, where they were in the thick of the fighting, they suffered heavy losses, and again at Spottsylvania and Cold Harbor. They emerged from the campaign mere skeletons. Three of them had lost their regimental commanders.[60]

At the appalling battle of the Crater before Petersburg soldiers from Indiana who were members of the U. S. Twenty-Eighth Regiment, Colored, suffered heavily and won praise for their courage. The Thirteenth Indiana also sustained heavy losses before Petersburg. In the final engagements leading to the evacuation of Richmond and the surrender at Appomattox, the Twentieth Indiana had a part. By the end of the war this shattered regiment had incorporated remnants from the other three regiments which had served so gallantly in the East—the Seventh, the Fourteenth, and the Nineteenth. In other theaters of the war Indiana soldiers played a part in the final engagements, including the last battle, at Palmetto Ranche, Texas, May 13, 1865. According to some accounts the last man killed in the war was a member of the Thirty-Fourth Indiana who fell in this engagement.[61]

According to Fox's *Regimental Losses,* a total of 7,243 Indiana troops, or 4.8 per cent, were killed or mortally wounded in battle during the course of the war. A larger number died from other causes. Official records show that

[59] *Soldier of Indiana,* II, 519-534.

[60] *Ibid.,* II, 619-629; Terrell, *Report of the Adjutant General,* II, 47, 122, 177, 192-193; Fox, *Regimental Losses,* pp. 342-344.

[61] Terrell, *Report of the Adjutant General,* II, 111, 192-193; *Soldier of Indiana,* II, 669, 803; Thornbrough, *Negro in Indiana,* pp. 201-202.

17,785 died of disease—a grim comment on sanitary conditions of the age.[62] Fox includes nine Indiana regiments among the three hundred Union regiments which bore the brunt of the hardest fighting in the war and all of which lost more than 130 men killed or mortally wounded. These were the Indiana Sixth, Fourteenth, Nineteenth, Twentieth, Twenty-Seventh, Thirtieth, Thirty-Second, Thirty-Sixth, and the Fortieth. Of these the Nineteenth Indiana, of the famous Iron Brigade, suffered the heaviest losses—15.9 per cent killed or mortally wounded. The Twenty-Seventh Indiana, which fought in the East at Antietam, Chancellorsville, and Gettysburg, and also in the Atlanta campaign, suffered almost as heavily, losing 15.3 per cent. These percentages are based on the total enrollment of the regiment and include noncombatants, such as musicians, teamsters, and cooks. The percentage killed or mortally wounded would be higher if only those who were in actual combat were included.[63]

None of the more famous commanders in the war were associated with Indiana, but the state contributed a number of officers, most of whom as previously mentioned, had had little

[62] Fox, *Regimental Losses*, pp. 526-527; *Compendium of the War of the Rebellion*, I, 12. Pennsylvania suffered the highest percentage of loss of troops killed or mortally wounded of all the Union states—7.1 per cent. Fox's figures do not include sailors, colored troops, and persons who paid commutation.

[63] Fox, *Regimental Losses*, pp. 8, 10; *Compendium of the War of the Rebellion*, I, 14.

Indiana Regiments Which Suffered Losses of More Than Ten Percent Killed or Mortally Wounded

Regiment	Total Enrollment	Number Killed	Percent
6th Indiana	1,091	125	11.4
14th Indiana	1,134	150	13.2
19th Indiana	1,246	199	15.9
20th Indiana	1,403	201	14.3
27th Indiana	1,101	169	15.3
30th Indiana	1,126	137	12.1
32nd Indiana	1,283	171	13.3
36th Indiana	1,118	113	10.1
40th Indiana	1,473	148	10.0

previous military experience, who made able if less conspicuous records. Gen. Don Carlos Buell spent his boyhood in Lawrenceburg and received his appointment to the United States Military Academy from Indiana. Gen. Ambrose E. Burnside, who was born near Liberty, also received his appointment to the academy from Indiana, but neither man was a resident of the state during his military career. Three men who were residents of Indiana at the outbreak of the war attained the rank of major general. The first to receive the distinction was Lew Wallace, but, as already seen, he was never given a battlefield command after Shiloh. As military commander at Cincinnati at the time of the Kirby Smith invasion of Kentucky he fortified the city and may thus have deterred a Confederate attack upon it. He was later made military commander at Baltimore. In July, 1864, Wallace, with only about 5,800 men, marched out of Baltimore in an attempt to intercept an unexpected attack upon Washington by Jubal Early, who was advancing with an army of about 28,000. At the Battle of Monocacy Wallace was forced to retreat, but his delaying action gave time to reinforce Washington and save it from possible capture.

The second Indianan to attain the rank of major general was Robert H. Milroy, whose distinguished appearance won for him the name of the "Gray Eagle." Most of his military service was in Virginia and the eastern theater of the war. While Lee's army was advancing into Pennsylvania in 1863, Milroy's forces were taken by surprise and suffered such heavy losses that they became the subject of a military investigation. But Milroy was later exonerated of any blame. Joseph J. Reynolds, the third major general, also saw service in the eastern theater during the first part of the war. During the latter part of the conflict he was with the Army of the Cumberland. He remained in the army after the war, and during Reconstruction was in command in the military district comprising Louisiana and Texas.[64]

[64] *Report of the Adjutant General,* I, 179; sketches of Don Carlos Buell, Ambrose E. Burnside, Lewis Wallace, Robert H. Milroy, Joseph J. Reynolds,

Twenty-one Indiana officers attained the rank of major general by brevet appointments, which were in most cases given in the final stages of the war or after hostilities had ceased as recognition for wartime services. In February, 1865, Nathan Kimball, one of the most dashing officers to come out of Indiana, was brevetted major general. His part in the campaign against Jackson in the Shenandoah has already been mentioned. He also fought with distinction at Antietam, was wounded at Fredericksburg, commanded a division at the siege of Vicksburg, took part in Sherman's march to Atlanta, and served in the campaign against Hood. Another whose battle record reads like a list of the principal campaigns in the West was William Grose, a lawyer from New Castle, who first served as colonel of the Thirty-Sixth Indiana. He fought at Shiloh, Corinth, Perryville, Stone River, Chickamauga, Lookout Mountain, Missionary Ridge, in the Atlanta Campaign, and the final action against Hood. Alvin P. Hovey, after making a record on the field, especially at Shiloh and Champion Hills, was placed in command of the District of Indiana in 1864. In that capacity he was responsible for the arrest and trial of the conspirators in the treason trials in Indianapolis which are described later. Gen. Sol Meredith, who was so badly wounded at Gettysburg as to be unfit for field service thereafter, was brevetted major general during the closing stages of the war. He finished the war as commander at Paducah, Kentucky, far from the scene of conflict.[65] Jefferson C. Davis' military career was marred by his slaying of Nelson, but he was restored to duty and commanded divisions at Murfreesboro and Chickamauga and in the Atlanta campaign. He was brevetted major general on August 8, 1864.

in *Dictionary of American Biography;* Irving McKee, *"Ben-Hur" Wallace: The Life of General Lew Wallace* (Berkeley, Calif., 1957), pp. 61-74.

[65] Terrell, *Report of the Adjutant General,* I, Appendix, p. 179; II, xii; sketches of Jefferson C. Davis, Nathan Kimball, William Grose, Alvin P. Hovey, in *Dictionary of American Biography;* Nolan, *Iron Brigade,* p. 266; *Compendium of the War of the Rebellion,* I, 443.

Thirty-six Indiana men attained the rank of brigadier general. Among them were Milo S. Hascall, Mahlon D. Manson, James C. Veatch, August Willich, Ebenezer Dumont, and Walter Q. Gresham. Among the fifty-three who received brevet appointments as brigadier general were Benjamin Harrison, who was to become a candidate for governor, a United States senator, and President of the United States, and John Coburn, who was to serve two terms in the United States House of Representatives. Among the other officers mentioned above was a future cabinet member, Gresham, a future governor, Hovey, and several other men who were to hold numerous public offices in the postwar years.[66]

§ § §

The state government, and especially Morton, not only played an important part in raising troops but also in equipping them. At the beginning of the war the need for arms was acute. Before the outbreak of hostilities Morton had tried to collect such arms as there were in the state and to secure additional ones from Washington, but his efforts had produced few results. In April, 1861, the state had only a few thousand guns—most of them antiquated and out of date. The War Department and United States arsenals were not prepared to fill the needs of the rapidly expanding armies. While Morton sent repeated demands to Washington, he also sent his own agents into the field to purchase arms and other equipment. The special session of the legislature in May, 1861, passed an act "to provide for the defense of the State of Indiana, to procure first class arms, artillery, cavalry, and infantry equipments and munitions of war, making the necessary appropriations therefor, and authorizing the Governor to borrow money." The act directed the governor to procure arms for twenty thousand men and to dispatch agents to procure them. Five hundred thousand dollars were appropriated for the purpose, and the governor was authorized to borrow funds if necessary for additional purchases. Even before the

[66] Terrell, *Report of the Adjutant General*, I, Appendix, pp. 179-182.

legislature had acted, Morton had sent the Indianapolis banker, Calvin Fletcher, to the East and to Canada to investigate the purchase of arms. Later, a son, Miles J. Fletcher, was sent on a similar mission. Subsequently Robert Dale Owen, who had just returned from a mission as minister to the Kingdom of Naples, was appointed by Morton as Agent of the State, with authority to visit the eastern states and Europe to purchase arms and munitions. Until February, 1864, Owen continued in this capacity, with all purchases of arms by the state being made through him. Altogether he purchased for Indiana thirty thousand English Enfield rifles plus smaller quantities of other arms. Owen also bought some arms directly for the United States government. Most of the purchases were made through two New York houses—Schuyler, Hartley and Graham, an American firm, and Samuel Buckley and Company, an English firm. During the Confederate invasion of Kentucky in August and September, 1862, when about eight thousand Indiana troops were being rushed into service, Morton purchased arms in the open market with the Ocean Bank of New York advancing the necessary funds. For these and other arms purchased the state was ultimately reimbursed by the Federal government.[67]

In addition to purchasing arms for Indiana troops Morton established a state arsenal to manufacture ammunition. There was no express legislative provision for the arsenal but the power to establish it could be implied. It was argued that Morton had the right to set up the arsenal and spend state funds on it because the aforementioned act gave him the power to "procure" arms without specifying that they must be purchased. The arsenal began on a small scale in a blacksmith shop, with the labor at first being furnished by a detail of

[67] Parsons, "Indiana and the Call for Volunteers," *Indiana Magazine of History,* LIV, 2-3, 17; Indiana *Laws,* special session 1861, p. 13; Fletcher Diary, April 27, 28, May 1-8, 1861; Indiana *Documentary Journal,* 1863, I, Pt. 2, Doc. 1, p. 6; Report of Robert Dale Owen, Agent to Purchase Arms, *ibid.,* II, Pt. 2, Doc. 14, pp. 912-916; Terrell, *Indiana in the War of the Rebellion,* pp. 523-529.

volunteers from the Eleventh Regiment. Its activities soon expanded, and it was moved to larger quarters. Operations were under the direction of Gen. Hermann Sturm, a former officer in the German army, who had gained a knowledge of munitions in Europe. During the first months of the war the arsenal filled an acute need. Officers in the field, including Sherman, Buell, Frémont, and Grant, were eager to take all the ammunition it could make. But since no appropriation had been made by the legislature and since the arsenal had been conceived for the purpose of supplying only Indiana troops, there were no funds to finance these operations. In October, 1861, the Secretary of War and the Adjutant General of the United States visited Indianapolis, inspected the arsenal, and asked Morton to continue it. Arrangements were made to pay for buildings and materials and wages on credit until the Federal government could reimburse the state. At its height the arsenal employed seven hundred persons. Many of them were women, who worked for lower wages than men and who were well adapted to the work. Legislative investigations authorized by the 1863 session of the General Assembly reported favorably upon the arsenal and the way in which it was being conducted, but no action was taken on Morton's request that legislation be passed authorizing it and providing appropriations for its continued operation.[68]

In spite of the arrangements made with the War Department there was friction with the Federal authorities over the operation of the arsenal. The head of the Federal ordnance department favored its liquidation, and Morton sent repeated requests to the Secretary of War to keep it in operation. In 1863 a United States arsenal was opened in Indianapolis, but the state arsenal continued to operate until April, 1864. It

[68] Report of Indiana State Arsenal, Indiana *Documentary Journal,* 1863, II, Pt. 2, Doc. 13, p. 903; Report of the Military Auditing Committees for the Years 1861, 1862, 1863, and 1864, *ibid.,* 1865, II, Doc. 4, pp. 34-35, 37; Report of the Minority Committee on the Negotiation and Sale of Indiana State Bonds, *ibid.,* 1865, II, Doc. 15, pp. 528-530; Indiana *House Journal,* 1863, pp. 743-744; Terrell, *Indiana in the War of the Rebellion,* pp. 499-512.

was claimed that the state arsenal sold cartridges at a lower price than those sold by private manufacturers. Nevertheless, it operated at a profit. When its affairs were finally liquidated, it was shown that during its entire history it had made a cash profit of $74,232.[69]

During the first months of the war the state Quartermaster General had the responsibility of issuing all clothing, blankets, and other equipment to troops raised in the state. The Sixth through the Twenty-Eighth regiments and the Forty-Fifth as well as some of the cavalry and artillery units were clothed and equipped by the state. After August, 1861, an Assistant Quartermaster of the United States Army stationed in Indianapolis was in charge of the issuance of supplies. Nevertheless, Morton and the state authorities continued to take an active interest in equipping the troops. It was the policy of the Federal government not to furnish uniforms until companies were full, the men were mustered in, and their officers commissioned. But Morton considered this course too slow and tedious. He insisted that the state put the men in uniform as soon as they had enlisted and passed a physical examination. He thought that the sight of men already in uniform stimulated other men to enlist. This practice led to some difficulties in collecting reimbursement for the uniforms from the Federal government. A few volunteers who had been issued uniforms died or deserted before being mustered or they failed to pass a final medical examination. Robert Dale Owen frequently purchased such items as overcoats and blankets for Indiana troops and charged them to the United States. The solicitude for the troops shown by these purchases may have been good for morale and may have facilitated recruiting, as Morton claimed, but there were also some unfortunate results. Competition between Federal and state agents for goods which were in short supply caused prices to soar and benefited speculators. In October, 1861, the Quarter-

[69] Terrell, *Indiana in the War of the Rebellion,* pp. 512-515; Report of Military Auditing Committees, Indiana *Documentary Journal,* 1865, II, Doc. 4, p. 50.

master General of the United States asked Morton to desist from future contracting for overcoats since this increased costs without adding to the supply of overcoats.[70] For the same reason the following month the Secretary of War condemned the continued purchase of arms by the states and asked Morton to withdraw his agents, but state activities continued in spite of these pleas.

In the early months of the war the Indiana quartermaster department appears to have followed a number of loose practices in the letting of contracts and to have accepted inferior clothing. Undoubtedly this was due in part to the frantic demands for supplies and the general confusion and lack of experience. A Congressional investigating committee was later highly critical of the Quartermaster General although completely exonerating Morton of any responsibility for malfeasance. The state commissary department, which was required to feed hordes of hungry volunteers early in the war, was also the object of criticism. The Commissary General was accused of enriching himself while serving inferior rations. A legislative committee which investigated condemned the practice of adulterating coffee with ground beans and accused the Commissary General, a meat packer, of selling the state inferior products from his own establishment. The lower house

[70] Report of John H. Vajen, Quartermaster General of the State of Indiana, Indiana *Documentary Journal,* 1863, I, Pt. 2, Doc. 8, pp. 652-654; Report of Asahel Stone, Quartermaster General of the State of Indiana, *ibid.,* 1865, II, Doc. 8, pp. 204-205; Report of Robert Dale Owen, Agent to Purchase Arms, *ibid.,* 1863, II, Pt. 2, Doc. 14, pp. 922-924; Stampp, *Indiana Politics,* p. 110. See Smith, *History of Indiana,* II, 51-54, for some of the exchanges between Morton and Federal officials who objected to Morton's efforts to supply Indiana troops. Some light is thrown on the question of Federal-state relations by a letter from Asahel Stone, the state agent, to Morton from Missouri, November 25, 1862. Stone reported that members of an Indiana cavalry regiment had accepted the jackets, pants, caps, boots, and shirts which the United States furnished them, but they refused to accept the drawers because they were not woolen. Stone expressed the hope that Indiana could furnish woolen underwear. Furthermore, the Indiana troops had refused the socks which the United States furnished "because the ladies in their part of the state propose to donate them." Reports of Special Agents, Pay Agents, *et al.* Visiting Troops, Indiana *Documentary Journal,* 1863, II, Pt. 2, Doc. 24, p. 1058.

of the state legislature demanded that he be removed, and a few days later he resigned. Part of the criticism of the food was no doubt due to the fact that soldiers and public were unaccustomed to the privations created by war. In September, 1861, the United States took charge of feeding troops within the state.[71]

After troops had left the state for service in the field, concern of the state authorities for their welfare continued. The Governor cherished and deserved the name of "soldiers' friend." He exercised personal supervision over many details connected with troops, frequently visiting training camps and battlefields. One soldier recalled how the Governor came to their quarters "and talked to the boys as though they all belonged to his family." Another soldier in the Army of the Cumberland wrote to his family, "You ought to hear the shouts of the soldiers from all states whenever Governor Morton is mentioned." Members of the Governor's staff, especially his personal secretary, Col. William R. Holloway, acted as his personal emissaries in keeping the men in service aware of the solicitude of the Governor and the folks back home. After the Federal government took over the responsibility of feeding troops in the state, Asahel Stone, the state Commissary General, was sent on a roving assignment by Morton to investigate the needs of soldiers in the field. Morton and his secretaries carried on a voluminous correspondence with officers of the Indiana regiments, and the soldiers in the field were encouraged to write letters and to frame other communications such as petitions and memorials to the legislature and letters to the press, expressing their views on politics and the conduct of the war.[72]

71 Stampp, *Indiana Politics,* pp. 111-112; Terrell, *Indiana in the War of the Rebellion,* pp. 538-543; Report of John H. Vajen, Quartermaster General, Indiana *Documentary Journal,* 1863, I, Pt. 2, Doc. 8, pp. 649-675; Report of Asahel Stone, Commissary General, *ibid.,* I, Pt. 2, Doc. 12, p. 807.

72 Oscar O. Winther (ed.), *With Sherman to the Sea, The Civil War Letters, Diaries & Reminiscences of Theodore F. Upson* (Bloomington, Indiana, 1958), p. 56; *Soldier of Indiana,* II, 184; Report of Asahel Stone, Commissary General, Indiana *Documentary Journal,* 1863, I, Pt. 2, Doc. 12, p. 807. Several of Stone's

One of the most important examples of state enterprise in connection with the military effort was provision for the care of the sick and wounded. At the very beginning of the war General Wallace requested two Indianapolis physicians, John M. Kitchen and P. H. Jameson, to take charge of the sick among the volunteers assembling at Camp Morton. What was regarded by the doctors as a temporary call soon became a permanent duty when they were given charge of the medical department of all military camps in the Indianapolis area. This meant the medical care of all regular troops plus the members of the Indiana Legion and prisoners of war.[73]

Far more difficult was the work of caring for soldiers in the field. The system which Indiana developed was copied by other states, but no other state carried on as extensive work of this sort. In March, 1862, when for the first time Indiana troops suffered heavy casualties, the Indiana Sanitary Commission was created. Morton appointed the members, with William Hannaman, an Indianapolis businessman, as its director. As the war dragged on, the commission expanded into an elaborate organization of auxiliary societies, solicitors, and agents. Through voluntary contributions of both money and goods the commission supplied troops in the field and in hospitals. Appeals for support were made through public meetings and the press, and a network of local auxiliaries was organized in every county and in many townships. In 1863 and 1864 sanitary fairs were held in communities all over the state to raise money. Goods and money collected locally were forwarded to county seats and then to Indianapolis, where there was a warehouse for storing and distributing supplies. Records show that contributions included all kinds of foodstuffs, clothing, bedding, bandages, soap, whisky, wine, tobacco, writing papers, Bibles, and other books. From Indi-

letters are published in Reports of Special Agents, Indiana *Documentary Journal*, 1863, II, Pt. 2, Doc. 24. They give a good picture of his operations in distributing supplies, arranging for furloughs, etc.

[73] *Report of Hospital Surgeons, Drs. Kitchen & Jameson* (Indianapolis, 1863).

anapolis supplies were forwarded to cities closer to the battle-fields. The goods collected and the money spent by the Sanitary Commission were private, voluntary contributions, but most of the work of distribution was carried on by military agents whose salaries were paid by the state. Military agencies were maintained at such places as Louisville, Nashville, Chattanooga, New Orleans, and St. Louis.[74]

After Fort Donelson, Morton volunteered to General Halleck to take care of three hundred of the wounded at Evansville, five hundred at New Albany, and three hundred at Indianapolis. Surgeons and nurses under the direction of Dr. J. M. Kitchen went by special train to Kentucky to bring back the wounded. After Shiloh, river boats, carrying three hundred nurses and sixty doctors and sanitary supplies, plied back and forth between Indiana and Pittsburg Landing, bringing aid to the wounded and carrying hundreds of them back to hospitals in Indiana. After the battle at Stone River, surgeons and nurses traveled by steamboat up the Cumberland River to care for the wounded, and similar missions were sent out after other battles.[75]

Morton was always eager that as many of the wounded as possible should be cared for in hospitals in Indiana, but agents were also active in setting up hospitals near the front. After the battle of Perryville, an Indianan, Dr. E. W. Banks, was placed in charge of hospitals in nearby Danville, Kentucky. "Our army returning through Danville," he reported, "left

74 *Roll of Honor*, I, 25-26; Olin D. Morrison, "Indiana's Care of Her Soldiers in the Field, 1861-1865," in *Studies in American History Inscribed to James Albert Woodburn* (Bloomington, Indiana, 1926), pp. 279-280; *Proceedings of the Indiana Sanitary Convention Held in Indianapolis, Indiana, March 2, 1864* (Indianapolis, 1864), pp. 45-65; *Report of the Indiana Sanitary Commission, Made to the Governor, January 2, 1865*, in Indiana *Documentary Journal*, 1865, II, Doc. 5, pp. 69-200. At the beginning of 1865 the report of the Sanitary Commission showed that a total of $155,796.45 in cash had been collected plus goods valued at $313,605.66, making total contributions of $469,402.11. *Ibid.*, pp. 71-72. A complete inventory of cash contributions, contributions in goods, and an inventory of goods distributed is given *ibid.*, pp. 85-107, 108-113, 113-158.

75 *Ibid.*, p. 79; *Soldier of Indiana*, II, 175; Morrison, "Indiana's Care of Her Soldiers in the Field," pp. 280-283; Foulke, *Morton*, I, 165.

upon the streets four thousand sick and wounded soldiers. They were placed in churches, colleges, houses, blacksmith shops, stables, in fact, Danville was one great hospital." A few days later a heavy snow storm fell, but by that time the wounded were all housed and being cared for, although a shortage of sanitary stores was reported. Of the men hospitalized at Danville about four hundred were from Indiana, while smaller numbers of Indiana troops wounded at Perryville were cared for at Perryville and Lebanon.[76]

Some of the most heroic work in aiding soldiers in the field was done by volunteers who gave their services without pay. Especially notable was the work of George Merritt, an agent of the state Sanitary Commission, who helped in caring for the sick and wounded at Pittsburg Landing, Memphis, Helena, Nashville, and Chattanooga, and who spent two months with Sherman's armies in the march toward Atlanta. He was on hand when an ambulance carrying 1,200 wounded men of Hooker's army reached Kingston, Georgia, after traveling all day over rough roads in a scorching sun. The men were *"so tired!* oh, so tired and sore!" wrote Merritt. "The mountain of suffering seemed so big that it seemed useless to attempt to alleviate it by removing one at a time; but that was the only way. . . ." In two hours 1,200 wounded men had been unloaded, fed, and their wounds dressed. The hospital tents would house only about one half of the amputees. Most of the rest had to lie on the ground. From Kingston the worst cases were carried by rail to Chattanooga. Merritt went along, traveling, in his words, "with the biggest load of suffering ever hauled by a locomotive."[77]

None who served the Union cause displayed more fortitude than the Indiana women who served as nurses to the armies in the field. After the battle of Stone River twenty-five women, under the charge of Merritt, were sent to Nashville

[76] Reports of Special Agents, Indiana *Documentary Journal,* 1863, II, Pt. 2, Doc. 24, pp. 1167-1169.

[77] Report of the Indiana Sanitary Commission, *ibid.,* 1865, II, Doc. 5, pp. 181-182.

and nearby points to care for the wounded. Thereafter there were on an average always about fifty female nurses in the field. The men in the Sanitary Commission as well as the soldiers gave them unstinted praise. "Their delicate skill in the preparation of diets, their watchful attention to the slightest want, their words of sympathy and encouragement, have made the hospitals a home," said one report, "and in hundreds of instances, have almost lured the poor sufferer from death unto life." Especially brave and beloved was Mrs. E. E. George, who accompanied Sherman's army to Atlanta. She was "always on duty, a mother to all, and universally beloved, as an earnest useful Christian lady."[78]

In addition to caring for the sick and wounded the military agents and sanitary agents performed a variety of other services. Among them was the distribution of foods to supplement the regular army diet. From Georgia Merritt wrote asking for a supply of pickles and kraut to combat the scurvy which was prevalent among the troops. Sometimes there were delays in these operations because the army needed all available wagons to get ammunition to the front. "And as the first business is to whip the rebel," wrote Merritt, "I don't think it right to interfere with those articles coming." After Sherman entered Atlanta agents distributed nearly a thousand barrels of vegetables and fruit from warehouses in that city.[79]

Agents tried to arrange for transportation home for soldiers who were furloughed or discharged. They furnished legal aid to protect soldiers against scoundrels who sought to "fleece" them of their pay and bounties. They preserved the names of soldiers who died and kept records of the graves of those who were buried in military cemeteries and sent home memorials and keepsakes of the dead.[80]

78 *Ibid.*, p. 79; Report of Indiana Military Agencies, *ibid.*, 1865, II, Doc. 9, p. 299.

79 Report of the Indiana Sanitary Commission, *ibid.*, 1865, II, Doc. 5, pp. 183-187.

80 Report of Indiana Military Agencies, *ibid.*, 1865, II, Doc. 9, pp. 296-297. In Reports of Special Agents, *ibid.*, 1863, II, Pt. 2, Doc. 24, there are many letters from all parts of the country showing the multifarious activities of the agents.

Morton's efforts were largely responsible for alleviating somewhat the condition of Indiana troops who were held as prisoners of war in the area of Richmond during the winter of 1863. After receiving reports that the men were suffering from hunger and exposure (although their rations were about the same as those of the Confederate soldiers), Morton began negotiations with Confederate authorities which resulted in his being allowed to send food, clothing, and blankets to the prisoners.[81]

Indiana's efforts on behalf of her troops in the field won much praise—especially for Morton. "The peculiar and constant attention to the troops his state has sent out so promptly, is the prominent feature of Governor Morton's most admirable administration," reported one of the correspondents of the New York *Tribune*. "In all our armies, from Kansas to the Potomac, everywhere I have met Indiana troops, I have encountered some officer of Governor Morton going about among them. . . . Would that the same tender care could be extended to every man, from whatever state, who is fighting the battles of the republic."[82]

But laudable as were Morton's efforts they led to a considerable amount of friction with military personnel and Federal agencies. In March, 1862, for example, Morton and General Halleck became involved in a squabble over clothing for Indiana troops stationed near New Madrid, Missouri. Morton felt that the men needed additional clothing but Halleck disagreed and repeatedly refused the Governor's offers to supply the men. Morton finally succeeded in getting some supplies sent from Indianapolis. But a month later he and the general were again at odds over the Governor's insistence upon bringing five hundred sick soldiers from Nashville to Indiana for convalescence. When Halleck refused to

[81] Report of Asahel Stone, Quartermaster General, Indiana *Documentary Journal*, 1865, II, Doc. 8, pp. 205-206; Morrison, "Indiana's Care of Her Soldiers in the Field," *Studies in American History*, pp. 290-291.

[82] New York *Tribune*, December 18, 1862, quoted in *Soldier of Indiana*, II, 68.

furlough the men, Morton appealed over his head to the Secretary of War and received permission. Generals in the field were inclined to regard the policy of bringing sick soldiers home on thirty- to sixty-day furloughs as demoralizing to the service, and on several other occasions Morton went over their heads in order to bring the men home. He became embroiled with Buell over the treatment of men in the Forty-Ninth Indiana at Camp Cumberland Ford. Partly because of the unhealthful location of the camp a large percentage of the men stationed there became sick. When Buell did not act as promptly as Morton thought he should, the latter appealed to the Indiana delegation in Congress and to Lincoln himself to improve conditions in the camp and to send sick men to Lexington on furlough. As noted elsewhere Morton was partially responsible for the replacement of Buell by Rosecrans following the battle of Perryville. Buell retained a grudge against Morton. In an article written years after the war he criticized Morton's efforts to retain a "quasi authority" over Indiana troops in Kentucky and his "habitual intervention in favor of Indiana troops" under Buell's control. This interference the General attributed to the Governor's desire "to preserve his influence with the troops, the people, and the Government." The result, Buell felt, was to impair discipline and ultimately his own command.[83]

Relations between the United States Sanitary Commission and the Indiana Sanitary Commission were never cordial. The state agency was opposed to uniting with the national organization, asserting that it was best equipped to look after the welfare of Indiana men. On the other hand, spokesmen for the United States commission were critical of what they characterized as the "indiscreet zeal which was willing to recognize State lines even in its ministrations of mercy on the battlefield." They regarded Indiana's efforts as a manifestation of "that obnoxious heresy of State sovereignty, against which the

---

[83] Morrison, "Indiana's Care of Her Soldiers in the Field," *loc. cit.*, 284, 288; Buell, "East Tennessee and Campaign of Perryville," *Battles and Leaders of the Civil War*, III, 42-43.

whole war was directed." Against this "Stateish spirit the Sanitary Commission resolutely set its face at all times." Indiana's Adjutant General defended the Indiana Sanitary Commission against attacks in his official report, concluding: "There was nothing to gain by changing the State Commission to an auxiliary of the United States Commission. And there was something to lose—the home interest, the State pride, and the liberality impelled or increased by them."[84]

In addition to its activities outside the state the Indiana Sanitary Commission operated a "Soldiers' Home" in Indianapolis, a place of rest and refreshment for soldiers of all states who passed through the city. A building which could accommodate one hundred men, constructed in part out of funds from the Federal government, was opened in August, 1862. It was totally inadequate and was expanded into the largest institution of its kind in the Middle West. At the peak of the war it could lodge 1,800 men and could feed eight thousand daily.[85]

Another building which was constructed and maintained in part out of funds from the Sanitary Commission was the "Ladies' Home," located near the railroad station. It was for the benefit of the wives and mothers and children of soldiers who passed through the city. Many women and children who had little or no money and no friends in the city were lodged and fed in the home.[86]

[84] Charles J. Stillé, *History of the United States Sanitary Commission* (Philadelphia, 1886), pp. 150-151, quoted in Terrell, *Indiana in the War of the Rebellion*, pp. 419-420; *ibid.*, p. 426. For a fuller discussion of the criticism of Indiana's efforts by the United States Sanitary Commission and Indiana's defense, see *ibid.*, pp. 418-426. See also a letter from A. Stone to Governor Morton, May 17, 1862, from Pittsburg Landing, in which Stone complains of his difficulties in arranging that soldiers on the hospital boat shall be "exclusively Indianans." Reports of Special Agents, Indiana *Documentary Journal*, 1863, II, Pt. 2, Doc. 24, p. 1045.

[85] Report of the Indiana Sanitary Commission, Indiana *Documentary Journal*, 1865, II, Doc. 5, p. 80; Report of Asahel Stone, Quartermaster General, *ibid.*, 1865, II, Doc. 8, pp. 210-214; Terrell, *Indiana in the War of the Rebellion*, pp. 455-458.

[86] Terrell, *Indiana in the War of the Rebellion*, pp. 459-460; Report of the Indiana Sanitary Commission, Indiana *Documentary Journal*, 1865, II, Doc.

A problem of far greater magnitude than caring for transient soldiers and their relatives was the problem of the families who were deprived of their normal income because the head of the family was in the army. Next to the suffering of the men on the battlefield and in the hospitals the greatest hardships of the war were borne by their dependents, for whom the government made pitifully small provision. An important reason for desertion undoubtedly was that soldiers ran away from the army in order to try to provide for the needs of their families. Bounties offered by Federal and local governments were regarded as a contribution to the care of soldiers' dependents as well as inducements to enlist, but they were inadequate to meet their needs. The Federal government paid no allowances to soldiers' dependents. The Indiana legislature in the special session of 1861 authorized county commissioners and incorporated cities and towns to levy special taxes to raise money to care for the families of volunteers, but in some places the law was a dead letter. As late as December, 1864, the commissioners of Marion County, the most populous in the state, had spent no public funds even though private groups petitioned them to do so. Such public money as had been spent was appropriated by the city and township governments. In Vanderburgh County the commissioners appropriated money for the relief of soldiers' families who were "in actual need" and were bona fide residents of the county. Wives were to receive five dollars a month, with an additional two dollars for each child under ten, while orphans were to receive four dollars a month. Altogether a total of $4,566,898 was spent by local governments in the state for aid to soldiers' families, or less than one third of the amount spent for local bounties—$15,492,876. In many places the discrepancy was even greater. In Allen County, for example, over half a million dollars were spent on bounties, but only seventy thousand dollars for soldiers' families.[87]

5, pp. 80-81; Report of Asahel Stone, Quartermaster General, *ibid.*, 1865, II, Doc. 8, pp. 214-216.

87 Indianapolis *Daily Sentinel*, December 20, 21, 1864; Evansville *Times*,

Finally, as the result of the failure of the local governments to act, at Morton's insistence the 1865 session of the legislature provided a special state tax to be spent by county commissioners and township trustees for soldiers' families. Under the apportionment fixed by the state auditor on the basis of anticipated tax receipts, wives and widows were expected to receive $2.70 per month, with an additional 67 cents for each child, while motherless children would receive $1.34. It was stipulated that grants should not be made to persons who had "sufficient means for their comfortable support." This legislation, coming at the very end of the war, obviously had little effect since most soldiers returned home before it went into operation.[88]

Such assistance as soldiers' families received was for the most part in the form of private benevolence. At first most families were cared for by relatives or friends, but during the winter of 1862 organized efforts were begun. As cold weather and rising prices foreshadowed hardships, in November, Morton issued an appeal to the people of Indiana for aid. He made similar appeals in 1863 and 1864. From all over the state Morton received letters telling him of families of soldiers who were in need, but he had no funds for them and could only appeal to private benevolence. Morton recommended the formation of local citizens' committees to ascertain needs and to solicit contributions. In many communities "Soldiers' Aid Societies" were organized; in other places the local sanitary societies performed similar functions. Ministers from the various churches were especially active in seeking contributions. Some money was raised at fairs and balls, but a more common practice was to designate a certain day on which contributions were solicited. These days became gala

quoted *ibid.,* December 19, 1864; Terrell, *Indiana in the War of the Rebellion,* p. 80; Terrell, *Report of the Adjutant General,* I, Appendix, pp. 75-76, 88. The total contributions for the aid of soldiers' families made by the townships and counties of the state are listed *ibid.,* pp. 75-88.

[88] Indiana *Laws,* 1865, pp. 93-98; Terrell, *Indiana in the War of the Rebellion,* pp. 449-453.

occasions, especially for farmers, who drove through the streets in a procession, carrying gifts of food or fuel. For example, one morning in January, 1863, a procession of twenty-five wagons, loaded with wood and foodstuffs, accompanied by a band of musicians, wended its way into Richmond from the farming community of Middleboro. A few weeks later Boston Township in the same county put on a similar display. In March, 1863, a procession of Marion County farmers, preceded by an escort of soldiers and a band, paraded around the State House in Indianapolis. Thanksgiving Day was observed in many places by processions bearing contributions for soldiers' families. On Thanksgiving in 1864 all ablebodied men in Muncie went out into the woods to chop fuel for soldiers' families.[89]

It is evident that private individuals responded willingly, and even enthusiastically, to pleas for assistance. Prevailing opinion at the time seems to have been that the people of the state were generous. Many contemporary accounts attest to this, among them that of W. H. H. Terrell, Morton's devoted Adjutant General. "It is very questionable," he said, "if any nation can exhibit a more creditable proof of the remedies as well as the power, the will as well as the wealth of a people, to take from their government a burthen that it could not bear but which rested, if not lightly, at least not painfully, upon their own willing shoulders." But to a later generation it appears that government failed to assume a responsibility which it might very well have borne. And however generous private contributions may have been, they were sporadic and unsystematic, and, as one newspaper put it, they were dispensed "more like charity than a debt" owed to the families of men who were sacrificing themselves in their country's service.[90]

89 Terrell, *Indiana in the War of the Rebellion*, pp. 445-448; *History of Wayne County, Indiana* (2 volumes, Chicago, 1884), I, 683-684; Indianapolis *Daily Sentinel*, March 14, 1863, December 5, 20, 21, 30, 1864.

90 Terrell, *Indiana in the War of the Rebellion*, p. 448; Indianapolis *Daily Journal*, August 2, 1864.

CHAPTER V
DISUNION AT HOME

THE MOST SENSATIONAL and controversial aspects of the war years in Indiana arose out of claims that disloyalty to the Union cause was widespread in the state and that thousands of Indiana residents were members of secret societies which were engaged in conspiracies to aid the Confederacy. At the same time Indiana was acquiring a reputation as one of the states which responded most willingly to repeated calls for manpower to crush the rebellion. It is difficult to reconcile the tradition of people who were willing to make unlimited military sacrifices with the tradition of a state which was honeycombed with treason. A pamphlet issued by the Indiana Republican State Central Committee in 1876 declared that Governor Morton was compelled to fight two rebellions—one in the South and one in Indiana. "The history of the Greek and Roman Republics, in their worst stages of corruption, scarcely furnishes a parallel to the gigantic insurrectionary plots brought to light in the exposition of the 'Sons of Liberty,'" declared a laudatory contemporary biography of Morton. Recent scholarship, on the other hand, tends to minimize the extent of disloyalty. One scholar, who has painstakingly examined the evidence on which the tradition rests, finds it a "Republican-constructed myth," "a political apparition which appeared on the eve of elections." He scoffs at the notion that there was disloyalty on a scale sufficient to constitute a serious threat.[1]

One of the difficulties in attempting to deal with the subject is that precise definitions of "loyal" and "disloyal" are im-

---

[1] *Oliver P. Morton, of Indiana. His Life and Public Services* (Indianapolis, 1876), p. 46; William M. French, *Life, Speeches, State Papers and Public Services of Gov. Oliver P. Morton* (2d edition, Cincinnati, 1866), p. 435; Klement, *Copperheads in the Middle West*, p. 205.

possible. The words mean different things to different people. The war years were a period of unparalleled bitterness and intensity of feeling. "There were," says one of the first scholars to attempt an objective treatment of the subject, "few who could see any middle ground between intense patriotism and active disloyalty; between devotion to the union and sympathy for secession; between a 'peace democrat' and a 'hissing copperhead.' "[2] But if one accepts a recent definition of Copperheadism as "avid opposition to the Lincoln administration," and adds to it avid opposition to Governor Morton, the number of Copperheads in Indiana was large. Those who wanted to see the Union permanently divided and who were ready actively to help the Confederate cause were very few. A small group apparently became convinced, in the face of repeated military defeats for the North, that the war effort was futile and that sooner or later a permanent split was inevitable. Holding these views they felt that if disunion was inevitable, the Old Northwest should cast its lot with the South rather than New England. Others, of similar views, felt that the longer the war dragged on the greater would be the bitterness between North and South and the more remote the possibility of reconciliation. Hence these "peace men" urged an armistice. But many who were reconciled to fighting to the bitter end for a Union victory protested that they were fighting for the "Union as it was" and were vehemently opposed to the revolutionary changes which the war was bringing in its wake. While essentially loyal, some of the group lost their sense of proportion and appeared to condemn more harshly the acts of Lincoln and Morton than those of the Confederacy.

"Copperheadism" was a complex amalgam, but Copperheads as a group were conservative Democrats who felt that Republicans, both at the Federal and state level, were using the war as an excuse for furthering revolutionary aims and

[2] Mayo Fesler, "Secret Political Societies in the North during the Civil War," *Indiana Magazine of History*, XIV (1918), 184.

gaining political advantage. Much of the opposition to the Lincoln administration arose out of the alarm over what was regarded as flagrant disregard for constitutional limitations and guarantees of individual liberties. The draft, the suspension of the privilege of the writ of habeas corpus, arbitrary arrests, the use of military courts, interference with freedom of the press, emancipation by executive order, and many evidences of increasing centralization of power in Washington filled political conservatives with alarm. Economic changes and measures which accompanied the war were equally as disturbing to people steeped in the agrarianism of Thomas Jefferson and in the tariff and monetary theories of Jacksonian democracy. A protective tariff, increased taxes of all sorts, the issuance of greenbacks, the establishment of the national banking system, were all distasteful. Closely linked with opposition to these measures were traditional western sectionalism and prejudice against New England. Deprived of their southern allies in Congress, many Middle Western Democrats feared that the predominantly agrarian interests of their section of the country were now at the mercy of the industrialists of the Northeast. Finally, the fact that the war meant emancipation of the slaves and the beginning of the breakdown of racial barriers aroused the Negrophobia which was a part of the psychology of most western Democrats.

In Indiana the personality and methods of Governor Morton exacerbated the bitterness and fears of his Democratic opponents, and his disregard for constitutional processes alarmed them. They were also convinced that he was using the war to further his own personal and partisan interests. "He trafficked in the blood of the country, in its woes to advance his personal interests . . .," the leading Democratic paper charged after the war. "Not a regiment was raised during the war, not a battle was fought, not a public duty was discharged by any citizen of the state, which His Excellency did not endeavor to appropriate to his own aggrandizement."[3] Most of all, Democrats were outraged by the Republican tendency to claim for themselves a near monopoly of patriotism and to stigmatize as evidences of disloyalty what Democrats considered their legitimate right to criticize. Democrats insisted that there was a distinction between the government and its administration and that even in time of war they had a right to criticize the administration. As the war dragged on and the suffering and losses continued to mount, both Democrats and Republicans resorted to more and more extreme and irresponsible charges and methods.

§ §

The Democratic victories in the elections of 1862 were followed by an imbroglio in the next legislature which led to a breakdown in constitutional government. "The secret enemies of the Government," said a contemporary biography of Morton, gained control of the legislature by "every means, fair and foul." The 1863 legislature, according to the account,

was principally composed of men sworn to oppose, to the bitter end, the prosecution of the war, and to leave no effort unmade to divest Governor Morton of his military authority and his glory; of men who . . . had placed themselves in power for the sole purpose of thwarting the plans of the Government and encouraging the enemies of American liberty in their work of rebellion and destruction.

On the other hand, a recent study insists that "Morton had no scruples when it came to turning events to the advantage of his party, and his narrow partisanship helped to precipitate a constitutional crisis. . . ."[4]

After the Republicans were repudiated in the elections in Ohio, Indiana, and Illinois in the fall of 1862, there began to be rumors of plots on the part of the Democrats in those states to create a Northwestern Confederacy. "I am advised," Morton telegraphed the Secretary of War, "that it is the intention of the Legislature when it meets in this State to pass

---

[3] Indianapolis *Daily Herald*, January 26, 1867.

[4] French, *Oliver P. Morton*, p. 253; Klement, *Copperheads in the Middle West*, p. 25.

a joint resolution to acknowledge the Southern Confederacy and urge the Northwest to dissolve all constitutional relations with the New England States." There were rumors that secessionist sympathizers in the legislature and their allies in secret disloyal societies would attempt to seize control of the state government and the state arsenal by force. A campaign was begun to rally support for the Union cause and to thwart any treasonable designs entertained by the legislators. At Union rallies Republicans accused the opposition of disloyalty and denounced all criticism of the war effort. Resolutions adopted at many of these rallies declared that to make a distinction between government and the administration was "treasonable" and tended "to the destruction of all government."[5]

Men in military service were aroused over the reported conspiracies. Gen. Robert Milroy, Morton's close friend, threatened to return "to exterminate treason at the North." Memorials and resolutions from soldiers in the field denounced traitors at home and warned of retribution when they returned. The impulse for these resolutions appears to have come from officers friendly to Morton, but Morton had knowledge of their plans to use the troops for this purpose and gave his approval. Democrats, on the other hand, were critical of efforts by the military to intervene in civil government.[6]

[5] Terrell, *Indiana in the War of the Rebellion*, pp. 25-28; Klement, *Copperheads in the Middle West*, p. 53; Foulke, *Morton*, I, 213-214; Stampp, *Indiana Politics*, p. 172; Fletcher Diary, January 1, 11, 1863. Fletcher records a conversation with Morton during which the Governor informed him that he had evidence of a conspiracy to take Indiana out of the Union and join with the southwest slave states to make a new empire. According to Fletcher, secessionist secret societies were widespread, and, at Morton's instigation, counter societies of armed Union sympathizers were being formed in every county.

[6] Foulke, *Morton*, I, 231-235; Stampp, *Indiana Politics*, pp. 172-173, 175; Fletcher Diary, February 3, 1863. Morton told Fletcher that he had procured memorials and protests from over fifty regiments and expected to receive similar messages from all the other regiments. He asked advice from Fletcher as to how to present them to the legislature and the public.

Throughout the legislative session members of both parties were guilty of petty and irresponsible partisanship which was especially shocking when the nation was engaged in a war for survival. At the very beginning Republican senators refused to go into a joint session for the purpose of electing a United States senator and staged a bolt, threatening to disrupt the whole session. After two days they returned, and the Democratic majority elected David Turpie to fill the unexpired term of Jesse Bright and elected Thomas Hendricks for a six-year term. Meanwhile, the Democrats had refused to hear Morton's message to the legislature on the grounds that no quorum was present as the result of the Republican bolt.[7]

Democrats consumed much of this session abusing Lincoln and Morton and the conduct of the war, bewailing emancipation and the loss of constitutional liberty, and airing economic grievances. Republicans made charges of Democratic disloyalty and professed to see evidences of a conspiracy to aid the Confederacy in every Democratic move.

There were a few "peace Democrats" who introduced numerous resolutions. One of these declared that it was "manifest that peace could never be restored by the sword" and urged the restoration of the Union by compromise. Others called for an armistice. All of these resolutions were referred to the appropriate committees, but none of them ever reached the floor of either house for debate.[8] The final report of the Senate committee on Federal relations bitterly criticized the Lincoln administration and Congress for alleged despotism and condemned various measures, especially the Emancipation Proclamation. But, while condemning and denouncing "the flagrant and monstrous usurpations of the Administration," it declared that secession was "heresy" and rebels were "traitors." The preservation of the Union was declared to

---

[7] Stampp, *Indiana Politics*, pp. 168-169; Foulke, *Morton*, I, 214-217. Turpie served from January 14 to March 3, 1863.

[8] Stampp, *Indiana Politics*, p. 171; Terrell, *Indiana in the War of the Rebellion*, p. 322. These resolutions are summarized *ibid.*, pp. 308-325.

be a necessity, "and under no consideration or circumstance will we ever consent to surrender it. We must be one people, under one government and one flag."[9]

Democrats professed to be alarmed over Morton's dictatorial tendencies and introduced various measures which were designed to curtail the Governor's powers and give Democratic state officers a larger voice. The session came to an end in an impasse over a Democratic militia bill which would have divided control of the militia between the Governor and the Democratic state officers. In order to prevent action on the bill all but four of the Republican members bolted. With the Governor's approval they went to Madison, where they could easily cross the river into Kentucky if the majority tried to force them to return. They refused to return for even the final two days, and the session ended without the enactment of more legislation.[10]

In the recriminations which followed Republicans justified their action on the grounds that the militia bill was part of the treasonable conspiracy being fomented by the Democrats and that they had pursued the only possible means of killing it. Morton declared that the passage of the militia bill "would have been an act of revolution inevitably attended by civil war and a collision with the Government of the United States." There were only two alternatives, he said—either to bolt or to let the bill pass and see "the revolution consummated and civil war begun."[11]

The bill was a partisan measure, designed to curb the Governor's patronage, but it is doubtful if it violated the constitution. In any case the Republican bolt seems to have been premature. Democrats insisted that it was highly unlikely that the bill would have been acted upon since there were about one hundred bills on the calendar which would have received prior attention. Moreover, they pointed out, if it

9 Indiana *Senate Journal,* 1863, pp. 699-700.

10 Foulke, *Morton,* I, 236-239; Stampp, *Indiana Politics,* pp. 177-178.

11 Oliver P. Morton, *Speech . . . at Union State Convention . . . February 23, 1864* [Indianapolis, 1864], p. 4; Foulke, *Morton,* I, 239.

had passed, the Governor could have vetoed it, and then the Republicans could have bolted if that was the only way to prevent its adoption over his veto.[12]

As the result of the Republican withdrawal the legislative session ended without the enactment of appropriation bills. Democrats expected that Morton would be compelled to call a special session in order to secure money to run the government for the next two years, but they underestimated the Governor's resourcefulness and audacity. He did not call the legislature into special session but instead managed by a series of extra-legal methods to raise the necessary money. He justified his failure to call a special session on the grounds that "the designs and temper of the [Democratic] majority" would have made it futile. All Union men, he asserted, felt that to reconvene the Democratic legislature would have been dangerous.[13]

Democrats countered by placing the blame on the Republicans for the failure to adopt the appropriation bills and by crying that it was the Republicans who were bent on revolution. There was no more justification for the Republican bolt, declared the Indianapolis *Sentinel,* "than there was for the secession of JEFF DAVIS and company. The apology offered by the Republicans is, that minorities have the right, under the constitution, to defeat what they may deem oppressive or unjust legislation, by setting at naught the organic law of the State. If that position be correct, and the Republicans say it is, it is a complete justification and vindication of the rebellion which the Administration is exhausting the treasure and blood of the nation to suppress."[14]

12 "Facts for the People," published by the Democratic State Central Committee in Indianapolis *Daily Sentinel,* April 9, 1864.

13 Morton, *Speech . . . at Union State Convention,* p. 9. Morton met with the Union Republican members of the legislature and a few others, including Senator Henry S. Lane, Gen. Sol Meredith, and Calvin Fletcher, to consider whether to call a special session. The group voted unanimously against such action. Fletcher Diary, June 9, 1863.

14 Indianapolis *Daily Sentinel,* April 3, 1863.

Democrats tried to compel Morton to call a special session by preventing him from using funds which were already in the state treasury to pay the interest on the public debt. The state auditor, Joseph Ristine, a Democrat, acting on the advice of Attorney General Oscar B. Hord, another Democrat, refused to pay the money which was due July 1, 1863, on the grounds that no funds could be drawn from the treasury without a specific appropriation from the legislature. The Indiana Supreme Court, which was controlled by Democrats, upheld the auditor's refusal to withdraw the money from the treasury. Morton cited as precedent for his right to spend the funds the fact that during the administration of Governor Willard funds had been expended without specific authorization by the legislature. He also argued that failure to pay the interest would constitute impairment of the obligation of a contract by the state and thereby violate the Constitution of the United States.[15]

The Indianapolis *Journal* denounced the decision of the court and the "hocus-pocus of a sham law suit," but declared against a special session of the legislature because the "rebels" wanted a special session "to consummate their schemes of revolution . . . and for nothing else."[16]

There were rumors that a resort to force might be used to seize the money from the state treasury, but instead Morton turned to the New York banking firm of Winslow, Lanier & Company and made arrangements for the payment of the interest. Altogether from 1863 to 1865 the banking firm advanced $600,000. The Governor took some remarkable steps to raise the necessary money for other state expenses. He received a considerable amount of assistance from the Federal government, which assumed some of the state's mili-

---

[15] Joseph Ristine, Auditor of State *v.* the State of Indiana *ex rel.,* the Board of Commissioners of the Sinking Fund, 20 Ind. 329-345 (1863); State *ex rel.* Board of Commissioners *v.* Ristine, 20 Ind. 345-383 (1863); Letter of Morton to Mr. Winslow, April 23, 1863, in Indiana *Documentary Journal,* 1865, II, Doc. 16, pp. 542-543.

[16] Indianapolis *Daily Journal,* June 13, 1863.

indebtedness and paid $90,000 for ammunition furnished
e state arsenal. Finally, Secretary of War Stanton, in
     Morton found a kindred soul, advanced $250,000 out
_ _und which he had for the use of states threatened with
rebellion. Morton also appealed to Republican county officials
and to private individuals for money.[17]

After the Governor collected the money he dared not deposit it in the state treasury because he could not force the
Democratic treasurer to pay it out again in the absence of
authorization by the state legislature. Therefore he organized
his own bureau of finance under the direction of W. H. H.
Terrell, his military secretary, who was responsible to Morton
alone. The funds were kept in a safe in the Governor's office.
"Morton accomplished what had never before been attempted
in American history," declared William Dudley Foulke in
his laudatory biography of Indiana's wartime governor. "For
two years he carried on the government of a great state solely
by his own personal energy, raising money without taxation on

[17] Stampp, *Indiana Politics,* pp. 180-184. William R. Holloway, Morton's
secretary, wrote to Richard W. Thompson, asking him to use his influence
with men of his county to persuade the commissioners to advance Morton a
sum of money in the absence of the usual legislative appropriation. "If
this could be done," he wrote, "it would enable the State Government to
triumph." March 12, 1863, Richard W. Thompson Papers, Indiana Division,
Indiana State Library.

Many years later John Coburn gave the following version of the crisis
to William Dudley Foulke, Morton's biographer: "When with a large amount
here, in the State treasury, of public money, the proper officers of state refused
to pay the interest of the public debt then due, the object being to destroy the
credit of this State.

"I was here, in command, for a few days, of some troops, temporarily
absent from the front, and called upon Gov. Morton and told him, that I
would take my command and seize the treasury; break open the vaults and
deliver to him the money if he would appoint, or obtain in any way, a committee of respectable citizens to count the money at the time of seizure.

"He took time to consider it; and so the matter ended.

"History tells what became of that money.

"It was evident that men of desperate character were attempting to
annihilate the credit of the State. The war was at our State Capitol at that
moment." John Coburn to William Dudley Foulke, December 18, 1899, William
Dudley Foulke Collection, Indiana Division, Indiana State Library.

his own responsibility and disbursing it through bureaus organized by himself."[18]

Democrats raged against Morton. They accused him of dictatorship, comparing him to Charles I, who, too, had broken up a legislature and resorted to "illegal forced loans and benevolences." But they were powerless to stop him, and he hit back at his critics by stigmatizing them as rebel sympathizers. Probably no speech stung Morton more than one made by Judge Samuel E. Perkins of the Indiana Supreme Court in Morton's home town, Centerville, during the campaign of 1864. Perkins said that he had just learned that "the public treasure of the state was, in fact, in the breeches pocket of Governor Morton, or in his illegal bureau of finance." This, declared the judge, "was the course of all usurpers. . . . The Governor refuses to trust the representatives of the people, seizes the public treasure, and without giving any bond, spends it at will. Thus did Caesar, Cromwell and others. . . . Morton had, no doubt, done it, thinking it was right for him to usurp in time of trouble, but this was a monstrous doctrine." An article appeared in the *Journal* in response to Perkins which was probably written by Morton. "It is scandalous," it declared, "that such a diatribe, so utterly destitute of truth, should be uttered by a Supreme Court judge; and more scandalous still, that he should publish it. We wish we could believe, in charity, that these charges were made in ignorance of the truth; but they are too preposterous for belief by men of even less common sense than Judge Perkins."[19]

§ § §

Economic dislocation which accompanied the war and some of the economic measures adopted by the Republicans in Congress were sources of discontent. Closely linked with resent-

---

[18] Foulke, *Morton*, I, 253-257; Stampp, *Indiana Politics*, p. 181. Foulke entitles the chapter dealing with this phase of Morton's career, "I Am the State."

[19] Indianapolis *Daily Sentinel*, June 26, 29, 1863; Foulke, *Morton*, I, 299n.

ment over economic grievances was western sectionalism. Indiana Copperheads were convinced that the Republicans in Congress were enacting a program beneficial to the industrial interests of the Northeast. It was frequently asserted that the Republicans were deliberately using the war to carry out an economic program which would have been impossible of enactment if the representatives of the seceded states had been present in Congress. Along with economic measures went a consolidation of power in the central government which was alarming to men of the Jeffersonian tradition.[20]

The Republican Indianapolis *Journal* observed with satisfaction that "the nation wages war and prospers," while Republican banker, Calvin Fletcher, found it "astounding" and "almost incredible" that the nation should be so prosperous while the calamities of war were upon it. But Democratic Congressman Daniel Voorhees charged that it was the "contractors and plunderers and lobby thieves," who were "the loudest and most persistent for the continued prosecution of the war"—men whose motto was to make money while the poor soldier froze to death in the shoddy blankets which they supplied.[21]

For many the war meant higher wages, handsome profits, and a rise in real estate values. For others it meant a disruption of the usual way of making a living and economic hardships. For everyone war meant a sharp increase in the cost of living. Prices soared, and there was much resentment against speculators and profiteers. In November, 1862, in an appeal to Congress for higher pay for volunteers, Morton asserted that the cost of food had increased 120 per cent, and

[20] It is interesting to notice that the "Copperhead" interpretation of the war bears a striking resemblance to the "economic" interpretation of the late Charles A. Beard and other historians with economic determinist tendencies.

[21] Indianapolis *Daily Journal*, February 9, 1864, quoted in Kenneth M. Stampp, "The Impact of the Civil War upon Hoosier Society," *Indiana Magazine of History*, XXXVIII (1942), 9; Fletcher Diary, December 31, 1862; Voorhees, *Speeches*, pp. 122-123.

the cost of clothing 60 per cent since the beginning of the war.[22]

Disruption of trade with the South worked an especial hardship upon certain groups—boat builders, some merchants, and farmers who had sold the bulk of their crops to the southern market. Some contraband trade with the Confederate States continued. Goods were carried to Louisville and other river towns and then transported southward via rail or river, but this constituted only a small fraction of the prewar traffic.[23] After a time the loss of business with the South was partially compensated for when river boats were chartered by the Union government for military purposes and when wartime needs created a demand for foodstuffs. But the war meant new trade patterns. Railroad transportation became increasingly important, and although railroads performed invaluable services in the war effort, there was increasing resentment against them. Value of some railroad stocks soared as lines paid off their indebtedness with government contracts for transporting troops and military supplies. Military requirements always had priority, with the result that regular business was subjected to interruption and delay. The general public felt that they were exploited and subjected to discriminatory practices. Many of the grievances against railroads against which the Grange inveighed in the seventies were first voiced

[22] Stampp, "Impact of the Civil War," *Indiana Magazine of History,* XXXVIII, 5. The Indianapolis *Daily Sentinel,* August 17, 1864, called attention to the rise in cost of living, comparing costs under Buchanan and under Lincoln. It gave the following figures:

	under Buchanan	under Lincoln
2 pounds of coffee	$ .20	$1.40
2 pounds of sugar	.20	.70
loaf of bread	.05	.10
dozen ears of green corn	.10	.25
2 dozen eggs	.18	.30

[23] A. L. Kohlmeier, *The Old Northwest as the Keystone of the Arch of the American Federal Union* (Bloomington, Ind., 1938), pp. 214, 239-240; Terrell, *Indiana in the War of the Rebellion,* pp. 496-498; James W. Pigg, Civil War Sentiment in the Lower Wabash Valley of Indiana (Unpublished Master's thesis in History, Indiana University, 1958), pp. 23-25.

during the war years. During the 1863 legislative session there was a long discussion of alleged unfair practices. Resentment against railroads was an important ingredient in Copperheadism. The president of the Illinois Central Railroad felt that high freight rates which farmers had to pay to get their products to eastern markets contributed heavily to the unrest in the Middle West in 1862-1863. "It is not a question of loyalty," he insisted, "but . . . one of bread and butter."[24]

Rising prices worked a hardship on nearly everybody, and Democrats blamed this burden on the Republican tariff policy and taxes. In Congress Daniel Voorhees assailed the tariff as "a robbery, a direct plunder on honest labor," which forced the western farmer and workman to pay "three or four times the ordinary price for the articles which he has to buy. . . ." The increase in prices, he complained, did not go into the government treasury but went "directly into the pockets of the millionaire, the nabob, the monopolist of the manufacturing districts." Voorhees branded midwestern congressmen who voted for a protective tariff "apostates to their section," who enriched "manufacturing monopolists" by subjecting the agricultural West to "onerous and unequal burdens." James A. Cravens, congressman from a southern Indiana district, which had lost much of its normal trade with the South, privately expressed the opinion in 1861 that his section would have to choose between the free trade policy of the Southern Confederacy and the high tariff policy of the manufacturing Northeast.[25]

In his keynote address to the Democratic state convention in January, 1862, Thomas A. Hendricks turned his wrath upon the tariff and the eastern manufacturers who sought to

---

[24] Terrell, *Indiana in the War of the Rebellion,* pp. 489-490; *Brevier Legislative Reports,* VI (1863), 78-79, 153-154; Frank L. Klement, "Middle Western Copperheadism and the Genesis of the Granger Movement," *Mississippi Valley Historical Review,* XXXVIII (1951-1952), 688.

[25] Voorhees, *Speeches,* pp. 123-124; Klement, *Copperheads in the Middle West,* pp. 8-9.

make the Westerners "the 'hewers of wood and drawers of water' for the capitalists of New England and Pennsylvania." In the Copperhead legislature of 1863 the tariff was attacked in similar language, and it was asserted that New England was being enriched by the war, while the burdens of the people of Indiana were almost greater than they could bear. Resolutions adopted by the Senate in the report of the committee on Federal relations condemned the Morrill Tariff as discriminatory to the Northwest. In Sullivan County, hotbed of Copperheadism, a meeting adopted resolutions declaring that in view of high prices placed on goods by eastern speculators they would refuse to sell except when paid an adequate price and would avoid buying manufactured goods from the East. A Democratic meeting in Brown County declared: "Our interests and inclinations will demand of us a withdrawal from political association in a common government with the New England States, who have contributed so much to every innovation upon the Constitution, to our present calamity of civil war, and whose tariff legislation must ever prove oppressive to our agricultural and commercial pursuits."[26]

Closely related to dissatisfaction caused by the rise in the cost of living was depreciation of the currency. Issuance of the treasury notes popularly known as greenbacks was viewed with apprehension by some conservative Republican bankers, but the new money was especially repugnant to Jacksonian Democrats, who clung to the belief that gold alone constituted a sound currency. The Democratic press predicted "inflation, speculation, and, possibly financial ruin," as the result of the greenbacks. In two opinions Judge Samuel E. Perkins of the Indiana Supreme Court condemned the heresy of paper money although he avoided actually declaring the legal tender legislation unconstitutional on the grounds that the state court

[26] Stampp, *Indiana Politics*, p. 132; *Brevier Legislative Reports*, VI (1863), 164-165; Indiana *Senate Journal*, 1863, p. 699; Thomas J. Wolfe (ed.), *A History of Sullivan County Indiana* . . . (2 volumes, New York, 1909), I, 97; Klement, "Middle Western Copperheadism and Genesis of the Granger Movement," *Mississippi Valley Historical Review*, XXXVIII, 682-683.

should avoid ruling on the question until after it had been decided by the United States Supreme Court. In one opinion he suggested various grounds on which the legal tender legislation might be invalidated, declaring that because the money depreciated, it "operated as a fraud on the public creditors and a hardship upon the honest public servants, by depreciating and debasing the currency." He also declared that it amounted to taking private property without just compensation and operated as a forced loan to the government.[27]

Because of the rise in the value of gold which accompanied the depreciation in the value of paper, state banks were compelled to suspend specie payment. The Bank of the State of Indiana officially suspended payment in coin when Perkins ruled that although the charter required it to redeem notes in gold and silver, it could redeem in treasury notes since Congress had declared them legal tender.[28]

The establishment of the national banking system also caused dismay among Democrats, who regarded the banking legislation as reviving in another guise the "monster of privilege" which Jackson had denounced. But some wealthy Democrats welcomed the new banking system. The First National Bank of Indianapolis was directed by William H. English, a prominent member of the party.[29]

Democrats constantly attacked the increase in taxes and government expenditures and the rising national debt. "Four brief but terrible years under the present administration," thundered Voorhees, "will have consumed more than three times as much of the wealth, the labor, the taxes of the people,

[27] Fletcher Diary, February 28, December 31, 1862; Stampp, *Indiana Politics,* p. 139; Thornbrough, "Judge Perkins, the Indiana Supreme Court, and the Civil War," *Indiana Magazine of History,* LX, 90-94; Reynolds *v.* the Bank of the State of Indiana, 18 Ind. 467-475 (1862); Thayer *v.* Hedges and another, 22 Ind. 282-310, especially 286-287 (1864). Perkins' reasoning anticipated that of Chief Justice Chase in Hepburn *v.* Griswold, 8 Wallace 603 (1870), one of the legal tender cases.

[28] Reynolds *v.* the Bank of Indiana, 18 Ind. 467.

[29] Stampp, "Impact of the Civil War," *Indiana Magazine of History,* XXXVIII, 7. See below, pp. 424-439, for a more detailed account of banking.

as every other administration of the government put together, from Washington to James Buchanan!" He could see only a dismal future in which there was "no land of rest . . . for the tired taxpayer"—a future in which "cowering bankruptcy" was "as certain and as fatal . . . as the fall of Lucifer. . . ."[30]

§ § § §

Economic grievances were real, and politicians were able to exploit them, but they did not have as great an emotional and psychological impact as abolition of slavery and the fear of Negro "equality." Opposition to the Emancipation Proclamation which had helped to sweep Democrats into office in 1862 was unabated in the 1863 session of the legislature. Democratic members introduced numerous resolutions condemning Lincoln's "executive usurpation." A large part of the majority report of the Senate committee on Federal relations was devoted to the question of emancipation and embodied some of these resolutions. It called the President's proclamation "unconstitutional, unwise and calculated to do the cause of the Union incalculable injury, by dividing its friends and uniting its enemies" and demanded it be immediately withdrawn. Indiana, it declared, was "ever ready and willing to do battle for the Union and the Constitution," but it solemnly protested against the diversion of her blood and treasure for the enforcement of that or any other emancipation scheme. Uncompromising opposition was expressed to all measures which might cause Indiana to be overrun "with a worthless and degraded negro population."[31]

It was frequently asserted that a policy of emancipation weakened and divided the North in the prosecution of the war while it had the effect of uniting the South and strengthening its determination. "Wicked acts of the abolitionists have done the Union cause more harm, and done more to strengthen the

---

[30] Voorhees, *Speeches*, pp. 163-165, 171.

[31] *Brevier Legislative Reports*, VI (1863), 12, 42, 45, 112; Indiana *Senate Journal*, 1863, pp. 697-698.

Rebels than anything the Rebel chief and his Congress could possibly have done," declared one state senator. In Congress Voorhees said that the "abolition policy" had caused "the loyal enthusiasm which impelled men at first to rush to the field," to dwindle as they lost faith in the administration. The Indianapolis *Sentinel* printed numerous letters from soldiers in the field who expressed their opposition to emancipation. "We want the Union as it was . . .," wrote one member of the Army of the Potomac. "We don't want the North flooded with free niggers. We want Indiana exclusively for intelligent, free white men."[32]

Lincoln's amnesty proclamation of December, 1863, evoked more protests from anti-abolitionists because it made acquiescence in the end of slavery a condition for amnesty and peace. "It recognizes the future equality of the white and black races," lamented Democrats of the Seventh Congressional District. During the political campaign of 1864 Democrats continued to denounce emancipation, the amnesty proclamation, and the use of Negro troops and to inflame race prejudice by predicting an influx of cheap Negro labor after the war. "This is a white man's government, founded by and for white men; and . . . we never will submit to being placed upon an equality with the African race," ran a typical resolution, which condemned the amnesty proclamation as evidence that the war was now being prosecuted solely for the purpose of freeing Negroes. At a Democratic rally of the Sixth Congressional District a banner was erected in front of the speaker's stand bearing the following inscription:

> Oh, Fathers
> Oh, Brothers
> Save us from Negro
> Equality and Despotism[33]

[32] Indianapolis *Daily Sentinel*, February 25, March 5, 1863; Voorhees, *Speeches*, p. 118.

[33] Indianapolis *Daily Sentinel*, January 12, 1864; Resolutions of Brown County Democratic convention, *ibid.*, August 16, 1864; Indianapolis *Daily Journal*, September 19, 1864.

Democrats in the Indiana delegation in Congress refused to vote for the Thirteenth Amendment even though it was apparent by early 1865 that slavery was doomed. Even William S. Holman, who was no friend of slavery and who urged a vigorous prosecution of the war, opposed emancipation as a war upon the institutions of the states and refused to vote for the amendment. He asserted that slavery was already dead and hence the amendment was unnecessary and that to amend the Constitution created a dangerous precedent. Voorhees also opposed the amendment on the grounds that it was "an act of bad faith, on the part of those in power, to seize this time of patriotic sacrifice, on the part of all, to carry out and culminate a favorite partisan scheme. . . ." Further he held that the Constitution did not authorize an amendment by which a citizen was divested of acquired rights of property. In the Senate Thomas A. Hendricks was one of only six who voted against the amendment.[34]

Opposed to these men who stood adamantly against the inevitable changes in the status of the Negro population which the war brought were a variety of groups who accepted emancipation with varying degrees of enthusiasm. The Centerville *Indiana True Republican,* expressing the views of the old antislavery element in the Republican party, hailed Lincoln's proclamation of January, 1863, as the "grandest and brightest [act] of all history"—an act which would make the United States once more "the beacon light to all the oppressed of earth." Most Republican-Union men simply justified emancipation as a measure of military necessity, without regard to humanitarian considerations. "We recognize in the war power of the Constitution, the right of the President to use all the necessary and Christian means to weaken, cripple and destroy this rebellion," declared resolutions of a Union meeting in Indianapolis in January, 1863, "and we therefore ap-

---

34 Blake, *Holmans of Veraestau,* pp. 120, 124-126; Voorhees, *Speeches,* p. 178; Thornbrough, *Negro in Indiana,* p. 204.

prove of his Proclamation giving freedom to all the slaves of rebels."[35]

Military necessity was also used as justification for the arming of slaves. Some of those who favored the use of Negro troops were quite explicit in denying any intention of accepting Negroes as equals. Speaking in defense of the Emancipation Proclamation at a Union rally, Gen. Nathan Kimball denied that he was an abolitionist. He would not consent to fight by the side of a Negro, he said, "but he would take Negroes and let them fight Negroes." Another speaker at the same meeting said that Negroes should be taken for military purposes, just as mules had been. "We took colored mules, curly headed chattels are no better," he said.[36]

"I want to see the Negro armed, and make him and his rebel master fight it out . . .," wrote an officer from a camp near Murfreesboro, Tennessee. "I propose putting the negro in the war, and in so doing some will get killed. . . . What is left, give them a country somewhere in the Southern domain, and make them go to it."[37]

By the end of 1863 even conservative Republicans were insisting that since slavery was the fundamental cause of the war it must be extirpated before there could be any hope of lasting peace. Some of them began to invoke moral and humanitarian arguments. "To expect to enjoy freedom ourselves, while we condemn a whole race to abject slavery, is contrary to the lessons of history and to our own experience," declared the Indianapolis *Journal*. Oliver P. Morton, who had shown a notable lack of enthusiasm when Lincoln first announced a policy of emancipation, while continuing to defend the policy as an exercise of the war power, gradually took higher ground. Emancipation, he told the Union state convention which met in February, 1864, was "not only sanc-

---

[35] Centerville *Indiana True Republican,* January 8, 1863; Indianapolis *Daily Journal,* January 15, 1863.

[36] Indianapolis *Daily Journal,* February 13, 1863.

[37] *Ibid.,* March 2, 1863.

tioned by the laws of war and upheld by the Constitution" but was "in especial harmony with the principles of Eternal Justice and the revealed word of God." Slavery at last stood "naked before its natural enemies—Liberty, Morals, Religion and the public safety," and had fallen, "pierced by a dart from each."[38]

The day after Morton's speech the Indianapolis *Journal* in a stinging editorial denounced as "Copperheads" those who opposed the end of slavery. It ridiculed the claim that abolition by action of the Federal government was a threat to constitutional liberty. "How does 'constitutional liberty die,'" it asked, "when every day is making it more certain that the Constitution will never again allow anything but liberty under it?" For a long time the *Journal* took the position that a constitutional amendment abolishing slavery should be postponed until after the war was over, but after the Union national convention in Baltimore in June, 1864, it declared that the time had come to abolish slavery completely, once and for all—that it was a moral necessity.[39]

§ § § § §

During the first part of 1863, while normal operation of state government broke down, tensions among the civilian population and clashes between civilians and the military reached a peak. The press was full of accounts of affrays and rumors of disloyal plots to encourage desertion and resistance to the draft. In February there was much excitement when a group of soldiers were sent to Morgan County to round up deserters hiding there. Several civilians were charged with resisting efforts to arrest deserters, but only four were convicted.[40]

In several counties, including Johnson, Putnam, Boone, Fayette, Rush, Monroe, and Daviess, there were reports of

38 Indianapolis *Daily Journal,* November 24, 1863; February 24, 1864.

39 *Ibid.,* February 25, June 15, 1864.

40 *Ibid.,* February 3, 1863; Indianapolis *Daily Sentinel,* February 3, 4, 17, 19, March 2, 1863.

interference with enrollment for the draft and some instances of destruction of enrollment books. Disorders of this sort became so frequent that on June 11 Governor Morton issued a proclamation warning of the penalties involved in obstructing the draft. About this time an assistant provost marshal was shot and killed during the course of the enrollment in Rush County. A few days later Senator Hendricks made a speech in Rushville in which he urged obedience to the conscription law and expressed confidence in Conrad Baker, the provost marshal, and his assistants. In Sullivan County an enrolling officer was shot and killed from ambush. The murder was attributed to persons opposed to the draft although this was never proved. Daniel Voorhees, who had opposed conscription in Congress, went to the county and urged compliance with the law and was given credit for preventing further disorders.[41]

Sullivan and Greene counties were the scenes of numerous violent affrays ascribed to disloyal organizations. In Brown County, another Copperhead stronghold, one of the most sensational episodes occurred. In April a group of armed men, led by Louis Prosser, a Democrat who was a former member of the state legislature, invaded a Union rally. Prosser shot and killed a soldier in the crowd and was then himself killed by a Union officer. A commission appointed by Morton to investigate the incident reported many other acts of violence and intimidation of Union supporters in the county. Bands of armed men, presumably with treasonable intentions, were reported drilling.[42]

41 Indianapolis *Daily Sentinel,* June 11, 19, 1863; Terrell, *Indiana in the War of the Rebellion,* pp. 359-360; Wolfe (ed.), *Sullivan County,* I, 106; Roll, *Colonel Dick Thompson,* p. 183; Tredway, Indiana against the Administration, pp. 129-131; Pigg, Civil War Sentiment in the Lower Wabash Valley, pp. 102-105. See Voorhees, *Speeches,* pp. 103-126, for the speech of February 23, 1863, in which he attacked the proposal for conscription as an act of despotism.

42 Fesler, "Secret Political Societies," *Indiana Magazine of History,* XIV, 208-209; Tredway, Indiana against the Administration, pp. 118-122; Terrell, *Indiana in the War of the Rebellion,* pp. 351-352.

Meanwhile, politics took a more extreme form. Violence frequently flared at political rallies. In the township elections of April, 1863, there were reports of disorders and of efforts by soldiers to prevent Democrats from voting.[43] Prior to a statewide Democratic convention which met in Indianapolis on May 20 there were rumors that members of secret treasonable societies who would attend were plotting an attack upon the state arsenal and Camp Morton. Gen. Milo Hascall, who was in command of the military district of Indiana, stationed soldiers at various points in the city to protect government property and to guard against any armed uprising. On the floor of the convention Daniel Voorhees denounced the military arrest of Clement Vallandigham of Ohio, which had occurred a few days before, as an invasion of constitutional rights. Other speakers inveighed against the usurpation of power by the Federal and state officials, but no one advocated armed resistance. While Thomas A. Hendricks was speaking, a band of soldiers, armed with bayonets, entered the hall and moved toward the platform. At this point the convention hastily adjourned. During the course of the day there were numerous fights outside the convention hall, and several Democrats were arrested for carrying concealed weapons or were taken to military headquarters and questioned. Two trains leaving the city that night were stopped by soldiers, who boarded them and demanded that the departing Democrats surrender their weapons. Several hundred revolvers were seized. Other guns were thrown out of the windows of the coaches into a small creek, Pogue's Run, from which the incident came to be known as the Battle of Pogue's Run. Republicans insisted that the men who had the guns had planned an armed uprising but had been too cowardly to carry out their plot. The Democratic *Sentinel* saw in the interference of the military, evidence that Indiana was under a military despotism.[44]

[43] Indianapolis *Daily Sentinel,* April 7, 20-27, May 5, 1863.

[44] Foulke, *Morton,* I, 273-277; Stampp, *Indiana Politics,* pp. 199-201.

A few weeks later the state was thrown into a state of hysteria by Confederate raids on Indiana soil. In June a horse-stealing expedition of rebel cavalry commanded by Capt. Thomas Hines crossed the Ohio near Cannelton. Hines escaped back into Kentucky, but most of his men were killed or captured by units of the Indiana Legion. Others drowned in trying to escape.[45]

In July, rejoicing over the fall of Vicksburg and victory at Gettysburg was turned into panic at the news that Gen. John Hunt Morgan and some two thousand cavalry troops had crossed the Ohio River at Mauckport and were advancing northward. Morgan, who was acting in disobedience to orders from Bragg, apparently intended to create a diversion which would relieve pressure on Bragg's army and perhaps hoped to release Confederate prisoners and to enlist the support of Confederate sympathizers among the Indiana populace. His men seem to have been more intent on pillaging and plundering than any military objectives. They advanced first toward Corydon, where they seized a supply of fresh horses and ransacked the stores. From there they swept on to Salem. There was fear that the invading troops would advance to Indianapolis, but south of Seymour they turned eastward to Vernon and Versailles, and entered Ohio, where Morgan was captured. In the face of the threat Indiana united to resist the enemy. Any help which Morgan may have anticipated from Confederate sympathizers did not materialize. Such sympathy for the Confederate cause as may have existed in southern Indiana was dissipated by the indiscriminate looting by Morgan's men, who carried off horses and stores without regard to the political views of their victims.

The people rallied to Morton's pleas for defenders. Throughout the southern half of the state members of the Indiana Legion organized to resist. Within two days in Indianapolis there were 20,000 untrained but eager defenders.

45 Terrell, *Indiana in the War of the Rebellion*, pp. 204-208; Feigel, Civil War in the Western Ohio Valley, pp. 92-97.

Within forty-eight hours 65,000 men had gathered. In the words of W. H. H. Terrell, Morton's secretary and adjutant, this was "such a display of patriotic energy and devotion as may safely challenge a comparison with any similar exhibition in history." The fact that men from all parts of the state, without regard to politics, rushed to repel the Confederate invaders belies the tradition of widespread disloyalty and sympathy for the Confederacy. And yet Republicans gave Morton almost exclusive credit for saving the state and suggested that disloyal elements in the state were partly responsible for the decision to invade. On the other hand Democrats insisted that Republican propaganda and exaggeration regarding disloyalty had been responsible for bringing Morgan into the state.[46]

During 1863, while internal dissension was at its height, there were numerous efforts to suppress newspapers which showed Copperhead leanings. In an attempt to prevent speeches and editorials which he thought gave aid and comfort to the enemy, Gen. Ambrose E. Burnside, Commander of the Department of Ohio, issued an order in April, 1863, which stated that "the habit of declaring sympathy for the enemy" would not be tolerated. Persons who committed "acts for the benefit of our enemies" would be "tried as spies or traitors." Shortly thereafter Gen. Milo H. Hascall issued Order No. 9, declaring that all newspapers or speeches which advised resistance to conscription or to any other war measure or which endeavored "to bring the war policy of the Government into disrepute" would be considered as violating Burnside's edict. He justified suppression of criticism on the

[46] The foregoing account is based principally upon Terrell, *Indiana in the War of the Rebellion*, pp. 209-254; William E. Wilson, "Thunderbolt of the Confederacy, or King of Horse Thieves," *Indiana Magazine of History*, LIV (1958), 119-130; Foulke, *Morton*, I, 278-285; Stampp, *Indiana Politics*, pp. 205-210. A recent detailed and romanticized account is Allan Keller, *Morgan's Raid* (Indianapolis, 1961). Terrell gives the size of Morgan's forces as 2,200, basing the figure on that given in Basil W. Duke, *History of Morgan's Cavalry* (Miami, Ohio, 1867).

grounds that "the country will have to be saved or lost during the time this Administration remains in power, and therefore he who is factiously and actively opposed to the war policy of the Administration is as much opposed to his Government."[47]

The Republican press praised Hascall's order, but Democrats denounced it as an unwarranted infringement of freedom of speech and press. Several newspapers announced their intention of defying the order. For calling General Hascall a donkey and speaking in disrespectful terms of General Order No. 9, the editor of the Plymouth *Democrat* was arrested and taken to Cincinnati and arraigned before a military court. The proprietors of the paper were compelled to obtain a new editor and to post bond which would be forfeited if the order was again violated. When the editor of the Bluffton *Banner* boasted of his intention of defying the order, Hascall warned him to disavow the intention or discontinue publication altogether, but apparently no measures were actually taken against the paper. The editor of the Columbia City *News* received orders that it must "hereafter publish a loyal paper" or discontinue publication, but the editor, insisting that he had criticized Hascall's order but had not defied it, refused to retract. The South Bend *Forum* was suppressed for boasting of its intention of violating the order.[48]

More common than suppression by military orders were examples of destruction of Copperhead newspapers by mobs

[47] Klement, *Copperheads in the Middle West,* pp. 88-89; Indianapolis *Daily Sentinel,* April 30, May 4, 1863. It was as the result of incidents growing out of defiance of Burnside's order that Clement Vallandigham of Ohio was arrested by military authorities. In June, 1863, the Chicago *Times* was temporarily suppressed on orders of Burnside. Morton considered Hascall a fourth-rate man. He opposed his appointment, was critical of his order and his conduct, and was instrumental in securing his removal. See Fletcher Diary, May 17, 1863; Stampp, *Indiana Politics,* pp. 198-202.

[48] Stampp, *Indiana Politics,* pp. 198-199; *The American Annual Cyclopædia and Register of Important Events, 1861-1902* (42 volumes, D. Appleton & Company, New York, 1864-1903), 1863, p. 423, hereafter cited as *Appletons' Annual Cyclopædia;* Indianapolis *Daily Sentinel,* May 6, 16, 18, 1863, October 8, 1864.

of superpatriots. Union soldiers were frequently involved. In March, 1863, a group of Union soldiers, most of them paroled prisoners taken at Murfreesboro, who were en route from Cincinnati to St. Louis, destroyed the Richmond *Jeffersonian.* There were reports that in Indianapolis they planned to attack the offices of the *Sentinel* but were prevented by military authorities. Early in 1864, when several Indiana regiments were home on furlough, there was a wave of attacks on newspaper offices. In February a small band from the Twenty-Ninth Indiana Regiment mobbed the offices of the La Porte *Democrat,* destroyed the presses, and then departed by rail for Indianapolis. The following month a group from the Twenty-Fourth Indiana Regiment partially destroyed the offices of the Vincennes *Sun.* Another group from the same regiment made a similar attempt on the Princeton *Union Democrat* but were prevented when soldiers from the Seventeenth Indiana intervened. Other newspaper offices which were mobbed at one time or another during the war included the Terre Haute *Journal,* the Rockport *Democrat,* and the Franklin *Herald.*[49]

In the face of efforts to suppress criticism Democratic politicians became more defiant. Some of them seemed to be courting the kind of martyrdom which befell Vallandigham in Ohio. They continued to call for the preservation of the Union as it was and to accuse the party in power of subverting the Constitution. To charges that they were disloyal they cried that it was those who were willing to crush out freedom of speech and press and "who justify the despotic usurpations of a faithless administration," who were in reality disloyal. In Congress in a speech deploring the loss of constitutional

[49] Indianapolis *Daily Sentinel,* March 17, 18, April 11, 1863, February 24, March 7, 8, October 8, 1864; *Appletons' Annual Cyclopædia,* 1864, p. 393; Tredway, Indiana against the Administration, pp. 37-42. As early as October, 1861, soldiers from the Forty-Third Indiana stationed at Camp Vigo were reported to have wrecked the print shop of the Terre Haute *Journal* because of its anti-administration views. Pigg, Civil War Sentiment in the Lower Wabash Valley, pp. 41-42.

liberty Voorhees cried defiantly to the opposition: "I have no doubt you consider me disloyal, for this speech. What do you suppose I care for your opinion whether I am disloyal or not? I return the compliment most heartily and sincerely. I think you are disloyal and there we are even."[50]

Some of the bitterest denunciations by Democrats were against the arrest of civilians by military authorities. As previously noted the order of Lincoln in September, 1862, suspending the writ of habeas corpus and subjecting suspected persons to martial law, and the wave of arrests which followed contributed to the Democratic victory in the elections of that year. A proposal in Congress for legislation which would have the effect of retroactively giving legal sanction to the order of the President called forth one of Voorhees' most bitter harangues against the administration. In the 1863 legislative session several measures were introduced criticizing past arrests and seeking to curb the power to make such arrests when civil courts were open.[51]

The House of Representatives created a special committee to investigate arbitrary arrests. After examining witnesses and gathering testimony in connection with forty-three cases, the Democratic majority of the committee issued a report which condemned the arrests. They asserted that they had been made merely for the purpose of intimidating and suppressing expression of opinions without any expectation that the persons arrested would ever be convicted. In most instances those arrested were never brought to trial but were released after being held for several weeks. The report of the Republican minority denied that the arrests were "arbitrary, unjust, and illegal . . . or dangerous to the liberties of the people," but rather were necessary for crushing the rebellion. In a rather remarkable defense of the suspension of the writ of habeas corpus they argued that "all such as would, in times of war, make the civil authority supreme and above the mili-

---

[50] Indianapolis *Daily Sentinel,* March 23, 1863; Voorhees, *Speeches,* p. 121.

[51] Voorhees, *Speeches,* pp. 62 ff; Indiana *House Journal,* 1863, pp. 26-29, 265, 297, 580-582, 645-647; Indiana *Senate Journal,* 1863, p. 520.

tary power, were begotten and brought forth by either *ignorance* or *treason."* All persons who were "constantly talking of the *habeas corpus,"* and were alarmed over threats to personal liberty were declared to "need more patriotism."[52]

The Indiana Supreme Court, speaking through Judge Samuel E. Perkins, issued two protests against the authority of military officials to arrest and imprison civilians who violated orders issued by the military. One arrest arose out of an order issued by the brigadier general of the District of Indiana and Michigan which called for the arrest of persons who stole or prevented the delivery of property to which the United States had a just claim. A man was arrested by the deputy provost marshal of Ripley County and placed in the county jail for allegedly stealing a horse which belonged to the United States. He was released from jail by the local judge on a writ of habeas corpus because "no verified charge of any offence whatever" had been brought against him.[53] In the second case, an order had been issued by the military authorities prohibiting the sale of liquor to enlisted men. An Indianapolis saloonkeeper was arrested and jailed by a military officer for violating the order. After serving the term imposed upon him, he sued the officer for false imprisonment.[54] In both cases the Supreme Court held that the military officer had acted without authority. Perkins stressed that the men in question had not been charged with violating any law and denied that the military had jurisdiction over civilians when civil courts were open and functioning. The fact that the military acted under authority derived from the Presidential orders did not justify their actions. Said Perkins: "In all parts of the country where the courts are open, and the civil power is not expelled by force, the Constitution and laws

[52] Indiana *House Journal,* 1863, pp. 26-29, 40; *Report and Evidence of the Committee on Arbitrary Arrests, in the State of Indiana, authorized by Resolution of the House of Representatives, January 9, 1863* (Indianapolis, 1863), pp. 6, 8, 123, 127.

[53] Skeen *v.* Monkeimer, 21 Ind. 1-4 (1863).

[54] Griffin *v.* Wilcox, 21 Ind. 370 (1864).

rule, the President is but President, and no citizen, not connected with the army, can be punished by the military power of the *United States,* nor is he amenable to military orders."[55]

In the opinion of the Indianapolis *Journal* the decision of Perkins was "very brilliantly copperplated" and "a skeleton of treason clothed in judicial arguments," but his arguments as to the jurisdiction of the military anticipated the line of reasoning which the United States Supreme Court followed in the celebrated Milligan case in 1866.[56]

§ § § § § §

Early in 1864 Morton wrote to Lincoln: "Considerations of the most vital character demand that the war shall be substantially ended within the present year." Republicans faced the approaching political campaign of that year apprehensively. Increasing weariness with the war might continue the surge of Democratic strength which had been shown in 1862. Republican prospects were also weakened by internal dissensions. There was some dissatisfaction with Lincoln and some sentiment for the nomination of Secretary of the Treasury Chase or General Frémont who was admired by the radical German element. But the supporters of Lincoln seized the initiative at the Union state convention February 23, by introducing resolutions instructing the delegates to the national convention to vote for Lincoln and calling for the nomination of Morton for the governorship by acclamation. The resolutions were carried without dissent. The state platform called for the re-election of Lincoln "as essential to the speedy and triumphant end of the war." The platform also called for the nomination of Andrew Johnson for the vice-presidency. It ignored such issues as the tariff and banking and concentrated on the war issues, praising the conduct of the Union armies and promising no compromise with traitors. Morton was

---

[55] *Ibid.,* p. 386.

[56] Indianapolis *Daily Journal,* February 3, 1864; *Ex parte Milligan,* 4 Wallace 2 (1866); Thornbrough, "Judge Perkins, the Indiana Supreme Court, and the Civil War," *Indiana Magazine of History,* LX, 85-90.

nominated for the governorship by acclamation in spite of the fact that the state constitution stated that the governor "shall hold his office during four years, and shall not be eligible more than four years, in any period of eight years" (Art. V, sec. 1). Challenges to his eligibility were answered simply by asserting that in 1860 he had been elected as lieutenant governor rather than governor. In a long address before the convention Morton set the tone for the ensuing campaign. He attacked the loyalty of the Democratic legislature of 1863, defended his own course of action, denounced talk of peace, and called for a vigorous prosecution of the war. Efforts to win support of War Democrats were apparent in the nomination of other state officers. Gen. Nathan Kimball, a Democrat, was nominated for lieutenant governor but withdrew in April because of rumors of dissatisfaction of the radical Germans with the ticket. Col. Conrad Baker, who was popular with the Germans, was then named for the office.[57]

In spite of the convention's endorsement of Lincoln there continued to be some opposition to him. A group of Germans and other radicals sent delegates to a national convention held in Cleveland which nominated Frémont. During the ensuing campaign Frémont men attacked the alleged "usurpations" of both Lincoln and Morton. Other Indiana radicals, including Julian, might have preferred the nomination of Chase, but they made no active move to oppose Lincoln. War-weary Indianans generally accepted the renomination of Lincoln without any great enthusiasm.[58]

The summer of 1864 was one of despondency. After the terrible slaughter in the Wilderness in May the capture of Richmond seemed as far away as ever, and in the advance

[57] Stampp, *Indiana Politics*, pp. 217, 220-224; Morton, *Speech . . . at Union State Convention;* William F. Zornow, "Indiana and the Election of 1864," *Indiana Magazine of History*, XLV (1949), 19; Henry (comp.), *State Platforms*, pp. 26-27.

[58] Indianapolis *Daily Sentinel*, July 18, August 26, September 16, 17, 18, 1863; Winfred A. Harbison, "Indiana Republicans and the Re-election of President Lincoln," *Indiana Magazine of History*, XXXIV (1938), 54-57; Stampp, *Indiana Politics*, pp. 224-225.

from Chattanooga Sherman had not yet begun to win impressive victories. It was increasingly difficult to fill military quotas, and Indiana was faced with the necessity of a draft as a result of a call by Lincoln in July for five hundred thousand more men.

Democrats approached the political campaign with the hope that dissatisfaction with the war would play into their hands. Instead of holding their convention as usual on January 8, they waited until July 12. The call for the convention invited the support of all those who favored the maintenance of the Union and who were opposed to the "corrupt, destructive, and revolutionary abolition policy of the National and State Administrations."[59] But Democrats were not all of one mind. Some of them, like former Governor Wright, had already deserted the Democracy to support the Union ticket. Of those who remained in the party the vast majority supported the prosecution of the war to a victorious conclusion. All Democrats were critical of both Lincoln and Morton but in varying degrees. Among the more moderate critics were men like Senator Hendricks and Representative William S. Holman, Michael Kerr, and Joseph E. McDonald. Men of this sort were embarrassed by the extremists in the party.[60] More vociferous and irresponsible were men like Voorhees and Judge Perkins who sometimes appeared to support the war, while assailing the administration, but sometimes appeared to favor an armistice. Some local Democratic meetings called for peace—but nearly always on terms which would include the restoration of the Union. There was a small coterie of "peace at any price" Democrats, a few of whom were actually engaged in disloyal activities.

The moderates controlled the Democratic convention. Joseph E. McDonald, an able lawyer and former attorney

[59] Stampp, *Indiana Politics,* p. 230.

[60] After Vallandigham had been defeated in his campaign for the governorship of Ohio in 1863, Holman had privately expressed the opinion that his defeat was "a fortunate event not only for the country but for the Democratic party." Holman to Allen Hamilton, October 9, 1863, Hamilton Papers.

general who had maintained a personal friendship with Morton for many years, was nominated for the governorship over the "peace" candidate, Lambdin P. Milligan, by a vote of 1,097 to 160.[61] The peace men failed to insert an amendment which they desired into the party platform. The platform which was adopted declared: "A faithful adherence to the Constitution of the United States, to which the Democracy are pledged, necessarily implies the restoration of liberty, and the rights of the States under that Constitution unimpaired, and will lead to an early and honorable peace." The valor of Indiana troops was praised, while Morton's conduct was condemned as "revolutionary" and "subversive." Suspension of the writ of habeas corpus, military arrests, and suppression of freedom of speech and the press were also condemned.[62]

The nomination of Gen. George B. McClellan for the presidency was applauded by Indiana Democrats. McClellan was

[61] In a letter dated June 21, 1864, in which he addressed a group of men who were asking him to be a candidate for governor, Milligan pledged that he would take steps to end the war as quickly as possible, declaring: "The restoration of peace without a separation of the agricultural states of the Union is the only means by which the people of Indiana can be saved from absolute and irreparable subjugation from a system of class legislation, exactions and oppression dictated alone by puritanic rapacity." The history of the "anti-Democratic party," for half a century, he said, had revealed the purpose of reducing the people of the West "to a state of pecuniary vassalage to the commercial and manufacturing interests of the East." This could be accomplished only "by dividing the agricultural states and reducing the Democratic vote in Congress. Hence their persistent effort to sever the South from the West. . . . For this purpose was the war inaugurated and is now maintained. . . ." Indianapolis *Daily Sentinel,* July 8, 1864.

Joseph E. McDonald was a native of Ohio who came to Montgomery County, Indiana, as a boy. At the age of twelve he was apprenticed to a saddler, but he later attended Wabash College and graduated from Indiana Asbury in 1840. In 1843 he began the practice of law in Crawfordsville. He was twice elected prosecuting attorney and in 1849 was elected to Congress. In 1856 and 1858 he was elected the state attorney general. In spite of their political differences McDonald and Morton remained lifelong friends. Joseph E. McDonald in *Dictionary of American Biography;* Foulke, *Morton, passim.*

[62] Henry (comp.), *State Platforms,* pp. 25-26; Stampp, *Indiana Politics,* pp. 233-234.

"for peace upon the basis of Union . . .," declared the Indianapolis *Sentinel*. "Can more be conceded than this without consenting to a dissolution of the Union and the establishment of separate Confederacies?"[63]

During the campaign some Democrats engaged in extreme vituperation of Lincoln and blamed him and his abolition policies for prolonging the war. A meeting at Fort Wayne which was addressed by Milligan declared that upon Lincoln rested "the crimes and all the horrible sins that are attendant upon the prosecution of an unjust and unnecessary war." McDonald accused the administration of following a dictatorial and unconstitutional course, but his speeches were on the whole restrained and moderate. As was customary, the two candidates for governor made a series of joint appearances in which Morton usually seemed to be the more effective speaker and to have the advantage.[64]

Throughout the campaign Morton and the Indianapolis *Journal* impugned the loyalty of the Democratic party. "How long," asked the *Journal* on July 7, "will it take the few men in that party, who have any semblance of patriotism left, to learn that they are out of place in its ranks? It is about time that *Democrats* had learned that they are aliens in the Copperhead camp." The same paper thought that it must have been "a great oversight" that the Union flag adorned the hall where the Democratic convention met.[65]

Soon after the convention certain sensational developments appeared to give substance to the oft-repeated charges of disloyal activities. Ever since the beginning of the war there had been rumors of secret societies which were supposed to be engaged in plots leading to secession and the formation of a Northwestern Confederacy. It was claimed that they had infiltrated the Union army with the object of encouraging desertion. Governor Morton was deluged with letters from

63 Indianapolis *Daily Sentinel,* September 10, 1864.
64 *Ibid.,* July 13, 22, August 16, 1864; Foulke, *Morton,* I, Chapters 25 and 26.
65 Indianapolis *Daily Journal,* July 7, 13, 1864.

all over the state warning him of secret subversive organizations.[66]

Some Democrats did join the organization known as the Knights of the Golden Circle, although the number of members fluctuated greatly and the figures cited by Republicans are grossly exaggerated. The KGC had been founded in the 1850's with the objective of bringing about the incorporation of Mexico into the United States. Later it became identified with sympathy for the southern cause. According to tradition the first chapter of the order was introduced into Indiana by Dr. William A. Bowles of Paoli, who was regarded as an advocate of slavery. From the beginning of the war the Indianapolis *Journal* claimed that secret societies affiliated with the KGC operated in several counties of the state to obstruct the war effort. A grand jury investigation in May, 1862, heard evidence that members of the order met regularly and conducted military drills. In the 1863 legislature resolutions were introduced by Republican members for an investigation of secret political and military organizations, but they were defeated by the Democratic majority.[67]

[66] Indianapolis *Daily Journal,* January 17, 1863. The Morton Papers in the Archives Division of the Indiana State Library are full of such letters. See also Harvey Wish (ed.), "Civil War Letters and Dispatches," *Indiana Magazine of History,* XXXIII (1937), 65-69.

[67] Fesler, "Secret Political Societies," *Indiana Magazine of History,* XIV, 189, 200-203, 205-207; Klement, *Copperheads in the Middle West,* pp. 134-137. The report of the grand jury to the Federal District Court is printed in Terrell, *Report of the Adjutant General,* I, Appendix, document 90.

The following account of secret societies is based principally upon the article by Fesler, Stampp, *Indiana Politics,* pp. 231-232, 241-249, and Klement, *Copperheads in the Middle West,* pp. 134-135, 154-156, 163-166, 171-175, 187-198. All three men have come to similar conclusions concerning the nature of the societies and the alleged conspiracies. Stampp and Klement agree as to the political motivation for the arrests and trials and minimize the seriousness of the conspiracies. Klement takes the tradition of disloyalty even less seriously than does Stampp. He has performed a painstaking piece of scholarship and detective work in unraveling the evidence on which the charges of disloyalty and conspiracy were based. He shows that much of the evidence is flimsy and suspect.

Morton meanwhile encouraged the growth of pro-administration societies—Union Clubs and Union Leagues—to counteract the alleged menace of secret orders made up of Democrats. These were armed groups whose purpose was to ferret out the secrets of "disloyal" organizations and to stand ready to suppress armed uprisings. The Democrats saw in them an attempt to overawe and intimidate them and regarded them as further evidence that the administration sought to crush constitutional liberties. The existence of secret societies identified with each political party increased tensions and exacerbated an already explosive situation.[68]

Democrats publicly scoffed at the charges that there were treasonable societies. "The Governor and his partisan friends have the nightmare over secret political organizations," said the Indianapolis *Sentinel.* "They have dreams and visions, and scares which only diseased imaginations suffer."[69] But the Republicans insisted that the members of the Knights of the Golden Circle planned an armed uprising in connection with the Democratic convention in Indianapolis in May, 1863. As already shown, if any such plot existed, it failed to materialize.

The Knights of the Golden Circle was such a loosely knit organization that evidence that the secret societies in Indiana were actually affiliated with it is tenuous. In 1863 a new order, similar to the KGC, the American Knights, appeared which absorbed many of the secret societies. A few months later it merged into the Sons of Liberty. By 1864 there were reported to be lodges in forty counties in Indiana. The principal tenet of the new order was devotion to states'-rights principles as embodied in the Virginia and Kentucky Resolutions. Such military plans as may have existed were known only to the leaders who had attained the highest degree in

68 Fletcher Diary, January 11, 1863; Tredway, Indiana against the Administration, pp. 169-174; Klement, *Copperheads in the Middle West,* pp. 149, 161-162, 210.

69 Indianapolis *Daily Sentinel,* April 21, 1863.

the order. Clement Vallandigham, the Ohio Copperhead, was Supreme Commander of the Sons of Liberty. In Indiana the Grand Commander was Harrison H. Dodd, an Indianapolis printer and minor Democratic politician, who was obsessed with the belief that a secret organization was necessary to fight to preserve constitutional liberty against the "despotism" of the Lincoln and Morton administrations. Among the members of the order was the aged Dr. William A. Bowles, publisher of the Paoli *Eagle,* which blamed the North for causing secession. Another was Lambdin P. Milligan, the Huntington lawyer, who unsuccessfully sought the Democratic nomination for governor in 1864. Milligan was an extreme agrarian and strict constructionist who had been bitterly critical of Lincoln and the war from the start. Another member was Andrew Humphreys, a former member of the state legislature from Greene County.[70]

In reality the activities of the Sons of Liberty were not very secret since Governor Morton's aides succeeded in penetrating into the innermost recesses of the order and were fully informed of their every movement. A corps of detectives reported regularly to Morton and Gen. Henry B. Carrington, commander of the Indiana District, on their activities. Felix Stidger, the ablest of the lot, was initiated into the order, became an intimate of Dodd, and revealed to Morton a mad scheme which he said Dodd and a handful of other members were plotting. Dodd, Dr. Bowles, and John C. Walker, all members of the Sons of Liberty, along with Vallandigham of Ohio, had been in contact with agents of the Confederate government in Canada who were trying to foment insurrec-

[70] Fesler, "Secret Political Societies," *Indiana Magazine of History,* XIV, 228-229, 231-233; Stampp, *Indiana Politics,* pp. 166, 232-233. See Klement, *Copperheads in the Middle West,* pp. 163-165, for an account of the harassment which Dodd had suffered which may well have contributed to his apprehension over the future of personal liberty. Good sketches of Bowles, Milligan and Humphreys are found in Tredway, Indiana against the Administration, pp. 189-203, 219-232. See also Florence Grayston, "Lambdin P. Milligan—A Knight of the Golden Circle," *Indiana Magazine of History,* XLIII (1947), 379-391.

tions in the Old Northwest. From them Dodd, Bowles, and Walker received funds to purchase arms, Stidger reported. Plans were made for an uprising in Indianapolis which would result in the seizure of the government arsenal and release of Confederate prisoners held at Camp Morton.[71]

But the conspiracy never got beyond the stage of mere talk. Dodd revealed the plot to J. J. Bingham, editor of the Indianapolis *Sentinel* and chairman of the Democratic state central committee. Michael C. Kerr, a member of the Sons of Liberty and candidate for Congress from New Albany, also got wind of it. Bingham and Kerr, horrified, not only because the plan was treasonable but also because of the disastrous effect that its revelation would have upon Democratic prospects in the coming election, consulted with McDonald. McDonald and other Democratic leaders extracted from Dodd a promise that the uprising would not be attempted. August 16, the appointed date, passed, and nothing happened.[72]

Morton bided his time. In full possession of the details of the plot as the result of Dodd's revelations to Stidger, he did not act until after the date set for the uprising had passed. A sensation was created a few days later when military authorities seized Dodd's private correspondence, papers relating to the Sons of Liberty, and four hundred revolvers which had been shipped to Dodd's office. The next step was the arrest of Dodd on orders of Gen. Alvin P. Hovey, who had recently been made commander of the Indiana District, and who acted at Morton's instigation. On September 22, on the eve of the state elections, Dodd was brought to trial before a military court. The chief witness against him was Stidger, who revealed at length what Dodd had told him of the conspiracy. But Stidger's testimony did not reveal any overt act, which the Constitution requires to prove treason.

[71] Fesler, "Secret Political Societies," *Indiana Magazine of History,* XIV, 243-248.

[72] *Ibid.,* pp. 248-249; Stampp, *Indiana Politics,* pp. 244-245.

He revealed the secrets of the Sons of Liberty, but his testimony did not actually prove that the order was involved in a military plot. He admitted, on cross examination, that he had no firsthand knowledge of the military branch of the Sons of Liberty and had never seen any of its members engage in military drill. During the course of the trial, Dodd escaped and fled to Canada. His escape was declared by Republicans to be proof positive of his guilt. But Democrats hinted that Morton and the military had connived at his escape. After he fled, Dodd was found guilty *in absentia* and sentenced to hang.[73]

Meanwhile a group of alleged accomplices had been arrested —Bowles, Stephen Horsey, Horace Heffren, Milligan, Humphreys, and Bingham of the *Sentinel*. The last, whose arrest was clearly a political gesture, was released when he agreed to turn state's evidence and appear as a witness for the prosecution. Bowles, Milligan, and Horsey were found guilty and sentenced to hang. Humphreys was sentenced to hard labor for the duration of the war.[74]

Democrats charged that the arrests were politically motivated. "We have no hesitation in declaring that O. P. Morton has been, and is to-day, the most desperate and unscrupulous politician that ever disgraced political station in Indiana," exclaimed the *Sentinel* after the arrests.[75]

[73] Stampp, *Indiana Politics*, pp. 245-257; Fesler, "Secret Political Societies," *Indiana Magazine of History*, XIV, 251, 259-262.

[74] Fesler, *op. cit.*, pp. 263-266. For a good sketch of Heffren see Tredway, *Indiana against the Administration*, pp. 209-219. Heffren, editor of the Salem *Democrat*, had at first denounced the war but had later enlisted and served as lieutenant colonel in the Thirteenth and Fiftieth Indiana regiments. He resigned from the army in September, 1862, after having acquired a reputation for brutality as an officer. He was rabidly opposed to emancipation.

[75] Indianapolis *Daily Sentinel*, October 8, 1864. After the arrest of Bingham the *Sentinel* said: "We charge O. P. Morton, Governor of Indiana, as being the prime mover of all military arrests of citizens made in this State. It is by his advice and sanction, that Mr. Bingham was arrested; and we call on all Indianians who respect the rights and liberties of the citizen, to cast their votes against him at the ensuing election." *Ibid.*, October 7, 1864.

There is no reason to doubt that Dodd and some of the others were involved in a treasonable, if harebrained plot. But efforts at the trials to prove that there was a widespread conspiracy involving all members of the Sons of Liberty were not convincing. If there had been a real danger Morton surely would have acted more promptly and arrested the conspirators before the day on which the uprising was scheduled to occur instead of playing a cat-and-mouse game with them.[76]

§ § § § § §

Charges of treason and military arrests were but one weapon which Morton used to save Indiana for the Union

[76] Morton's principal biographer says regarding Morton's role that those who have examined the reports made to Morton concerning the secret societies and the alleged conspiracy "can understand how completely these organizations were under his control, how he played with them as a cat with a mouse, how he even permitted them to grow and develop that he might fasten conviction more securely upon them and overthrow them utterly when the time should be ripe for their destruction." Foulke, *Morton*, I, 374.

After their conviction the prisoners were confined in a military prison in Columbus, Ohio, awaiting their execution. On May 30, 1865, President Andrew Johnson commuted their sentences to life imprisonment. Meanwhile, counsel for the prisoners had filed petitions for their release under the terms of the act of Congress passed in 1863 which provided that persons arrested by military authorities should be released if they were not indicted by the grand jury. The Federal grand jury had met in Indianapolis but no indictment had been made against them. After the petition for their release was filed an indictment charging them and some other members of the Sons of Liberty with conspiracy was presented in June, 1865. The appeal for the release eventually reached the United States Supreme Court, which decided in a celebrated case in April, 1866, that the trial of the men by the military court had been unconstitutional (*ex parte Milligan,* 4 Wallace 2). The men were immediately released on orders of the Secretary of War. Meanwhile, the indictments which had been made by the grand jury were kept alive while they were in prison, but the cases were not pressed after their release. In 1867 nolle prosequis were entered and the cases were dropped. In March, 1868, Milligan brought suit for false imprisonment against the military authorities. The case, which was tried in May, 1871, in the Federal Circuit Court in Indianapolis (Milligan *v.* Hovey, 17 Fed. Cas. 380), was given political overtones by reason of the fact that Benjamin Harrison served as counsel for the defense, while Thomas Hendricks represented Milligan. The jury found

party in 1864. During the first part of the campaign, while military prospects remained discouraging, he was apparently fearful of a Democratic victory. The absence from the state of large numbers of men of voting age who were in military service added to his apprehensions. Indiana had no law, as did some states, which permitted men in the field to vote. Morton early began a strenuous campaign to secure furloughs for Indiana troops which would enable them to return to Indiana to cast their ballots. In April he wrote to Lincoln requesting that Indiana troops be furloughed to vote. Schuyler Colfax also repeatedly made similar appeals to General Sherman and to Lincoln. When Sherman was cold to the suggestion, Morton made two trips to Washington to entreat with Lincoln.[77]

Morton's zeal for bringing home the soldiers arose from his conviction that the soldier vote would be overwhelmingly for the Republican-Union ticket. In the months preceding the election he attempted through agents in the field to ascertain the political sentiments of various regiments. Dr. Calvin J. Woods, one of the agents of the Sanitary Commission, visited several regiments in Tennessee and Alabama in August for the purpose of taking a political canvass. He reported to the Governor that the vast majority of the soldiers would vote for Lincoln and Morton if given the opportunity. In several companies he found that there was greater enthusiasm for Morton than for Lincoln. On the other hand, he found some support for McClellan and the Democrats. He warned Morton against sending home the Fifty-Ninth Regiment because its men, including its officers, were "coppers." He admitted that the regiment was as good a fighting unit as any of the

for Milligan and awarded him nominal damages of five dollars. The statute of limitations ran against his claim for damages for the period prior to March 13, 1866. Samuel Klaus (ed.), *The Milligan Case (American Trials,* New York, 1929), pp. 40-45.

[77] Stampp, *Indiana Politics,* pp. 250-252; Zornow, "Indiana and the Election of 1864," *Indiana Magazine of History,* XLV, 31-32; Smith, *Schuyler Colfax,* p. 200.

others but opposed a furlough because of its political complexion.[78]

In September Morton and the Union party Congressional candidates addressed a long letter to Secretary of War Stanton to be transmitted to Lincoln in which they pleaded that the pending draft be delayed until after the election and that fifteen thousand troops be returned to Indiana in order to vote in the state elections in October. The letter emphasized that the outcome of the state contests in Indiana would have an important influence upon the presidential election in November. Lincoln refused to delay the draft, but he wrote to Sherman urging him to let as many soldiers go home to vote in October as he could safely spare. The loss of Indiana "to the friends of the Government," wrote the President, "would go far towards losing the whole Union cause. The bad effect upon the November election, and especially the giving the state Government to those who will oppose the war in every possible way, are too much to risk, if it can possibly be avoided."[79]

With Sherman military considerations outweighed the political; consequently, few soldiers in the field were furloughed. But Morton was more successful in securing the return of sick and wounded soldiers to Indiana. As the result of his importunities Stanton issued orders to the surgeon general for the furlough of such men as were able to travel to return to Indiana. Transportation both ways was to be paid by the government. Special agents were sent out by Morton into the South and East to round up as many wounded and sick as possible. After almost frantic efforts about nine thousand

[78] Woods's mission is described in a series of letters in the Morton Papers, Archives Division, Indiana State Library. See Woods to Morton, August 17, 19, 23, 25, 29, 1864.

[79] Zornow, "Indiana and the Election of 1864," *Indiana Magazine of History,* XLV, 26; Foulke, *Morton,* I, 366-369; Lincoln to Major General Sherman, September 19, 1864, in Roy P. Basler (ed.), *The Collected Works of Abraham Lincoln* (8 volumes and index, New Brunswick, New Jersey, 1953-1959), VIII, 11.

returned in time to vote—a number large enough to have a considerable influence on the outcome. The men were originally furloughed only long enough to vote in the October elections, but once they were home Morton persuaded Stanton to arrange for an extension of their furloughs until after the November election.[80]

Democrats were by no means as convinced as was Morton that the soldier vote would be overwhelmingly for the Republican-Union ticket. In July Bingham, chairman of the Democratic state central committee, had joined with Morton in asking for furloughs to enable men in the field to vote. Later Democrats charged that in some regiments only men who promised to vote for Lincoln and Morton were furloughed. Government employees in Washington also returned to Indiana as did railroad employees. Many felt that the fate of the Union hung on the outcome of the election.[81]

Morton's effort to bring home soldiers to vote proved unnecessary. The Republican-Union ticket was victorious by a margin of twenty thousand votes in the October elections. The Republican party regained control of the General Assembly and won eight of the eleven Congressional seats. In November Lincoln carried the state by about the same margin as Morton had in October. During the closing weeks of the

[80] The arrangements for the furloughs and the transportation of the troops are shown in Telegraphic Correspondence, volumes V and XIII, in the Morton Papers in the Archives Division of the Indiana State Library. See especially Morton to Stanton, September 20, 1864; J. K. Barnes to Morton, September 24, 1864; Morton to Lincoln and Stanton, October 12, 1864; Stanton to Morton, October 14, 1864, Telegraphic Correspondence, V, 284-285, 300, 304, 306, 316.

[81] Zornow, "Indiana and the Election of 1864," *Indiana Magazine of History*, XLV, 36; Indianapolis *Daily Sentinel*, October 4, 1864; Fletcher Diary, October 11, 1864. Just before the election Morton wired Gideon Welles, Secretary of the Navy, that there was apprehension that Lieut. Comdr. Le Roy Fitch, who commanded a naval patrol on the Ohio River with headquarters in Evansville, intended to bring his men to Evansville to vote the "Copperhead" ticket. Morton urged Welles to issue orders to Fitch to remain at Cairo, Illinois, until after the election. Morton to Gideon Welles, October 7, 1864, in Telegraphic Correspondence, V, 296; Feigel, Civil War in the Western Ohio Valley, p. 76.

campaign the Indianapolis *Sentinel* had sought to sway voters
by proclaiming on its masthead:[82]

THE ARGUMENTS IN A NUT SHELL

LOOK AT THIS PICTURE	THEN ON THIS
Elect	Elect
LINCOLN	McCLELLAN
and the	and the whole
BLACK REPUBLICAN TICKET	DEMOCRATIC TICKET
You will bring on NEGRO	You will defeat NEGRO
EQUALITY, more DEBT,	EQUALITY,
HARDER TIMES, another	restore PROSPERITY
DRAFT!	re-establish the
Universal anarchy, and ultimate	*UNION!*
RUIN!	in an Honorable, Permanent
	and Happy
	PEACE!

Such an appeal might have been persuasive if the elections
had been held a few months earlier, but by the fall of 1864
forces were in operation which resulted in a Republican-Union
victory of proportions which had seemed impossible at the
beginning of the campaign. Sherman's capture of Atlanta
and Sheridan's victories in the Shenandoah contributed to the
outcome. At the same time the treason trials had the effect
of demoralizing Democrats and discrediting their cause. These
two factors—Union military victory for which Republicans
took credit and the stigmatizing of Democrats as the party
of treason—not only contributed to political victory in 1864

82 Indianapolis *Daily Sentinel,* October 3, 1864; Stampp, *Indiana Politics,*
p. 253. Morton received 152,084 votes to 131,201 for McDonald; Lincoln 150,238
votes to 130,233 for McClellan. Lincoln's percentage of the total vote was
53.59, that of Morton was 53.68. In the central and extreme southeastern part
of the state the Republicans increased their vote over that which they received
in 1860, but in the southwestern part of the state they failed to receive as many
votes as in 1860. Harbison, "Indiana Republicans and the Re-election of
President Lincoln," *Indiana Magazine of History,* XXXIV, 61 and footnote;
Pigg, Civil War Sentiment in the Lower Wabash Valley, p. 137.

but accounted in large measure for Republican ascendancy in the postwar years.[83]

[83] Calvin Fletcher wrote in his diary that he viewed persons who voted for McClellan, "knowing the true issue, as traitors & copperheads." In his opinion they voted for a man whom history would label at least a coward, if not a traitor. "To tell the grandson or child that his father voted for a candidate for president who was running upon the issue that the war was a failure & we should make peace with the enemy will be a disgrace to such a descendant," he predicted. Fletcher Diary, November 9, 1864.

CHAPTER VI

POLITICS AND LEGISLATION OF THE RECONSTRUCTION ERA

FOR SEVERAL YEARS after Appomattox wartime issues and problems growing out of the war dominated Indiana politics. The southern question—the position of the former Confederate states, the treatment of former rebels, the status of the freedmen—overshadowed other issues. The granting of civil and political rights to southern Negroes incidentally had the effect of giving these rights to Indiana Negroes and thereby kept alive the race issue in Indiana politics. The Republican party, ebullient from its victories in 1864, continued as the dominant party in the postwar years. Republicans never ceased to attack the loyalty of Democrats and their alleged treason during the war years and to claim for their own party sole credit for having preserved the Union. Veterans of the war were an important source of strength to the Republican party. The Grand Army of the Republic was virtually an adjunct of the party, and former Union officers were conspicuous among the men chosen for public office. But the Democrats, although demoralized, were by no means defunct. Except in the elections of 1866 the Republican margin of victory was narrow. In 1870 Democrats gained control of the legislature, and in 1872 they elected the governor. The revival of Democratic strength was due to growing weariness with the war issues, a reaction against Radical Reconstruction policies, especially as they related to Negroes, and to economic factors. Monetary policy became an important political issue as the result of economic readjustments following the war. Democrats attempted to capitalize on economic discontent and thereby divert attention from wartime issues.

Until his death in 1877 Oliver P. Morton was the most powerful figure in the Republican party, enjoying a domination comparable to that which Jesse Bright had exercised over the Democracy in the fifties. From the governorship Morton went to the United States Senate in 1867, but he retained a firm grip on Indiana politics. Schuyler Colfax, first as speaker of the United States House of Representatives and later as Vice-President during Grant's first term, held offices of greater prestige than Morton, but he did not exercise comparable influence in party circles. Some Republicans grumbled at Morton's dictatorship, but no one successfully defied him. His critics accused him of ruthlessly killing off potential rivals and using his position for his own advantage and to reward his favorites. "We see a party run for one man and such men as he rewards," declared the Indianapolis *News,* a politically independent newspaper, in 1872. "Whoever will not serve him, or who has a bit of talent or manliness . . . is put down, whether he aspires to a seat in the United States Senate or to the staff of a Constable."[1]

Among Democrats there was no leader comparable to Morton, and consequently the Democracy spoke through several voices. Although times were changing rapidly the Democrats for the most part kept their eyes resolutely on the past and resisted change. They opposed with great bitterness every aspect of Radical Reconstruction, involving as it did centralization of power in the Federal government and increased rights for Negroes. They continued to deplore Republican-sponsored tariffs, national banks, and alleged Republican extravagance and corruption.

Most prominent among Indiana Democrats in the postwar years was Thomas A. Hendricks, who served in the United States Senate until 1869, was nominated and defeated for the governorship in 1868, and finally elected governor in 1872. Hendricks' popularity must be attributed to his amiability and his conciliatory disposition rather than any positive program or profound convictions. His record in the Senate was largely negative as he unsuccessfully opposed every

---

[1] *Indianapolis News,* July 13, 1872.

Radical move and deplored the treatment of southern whites. On issues not immediately connected with Reconstruction Hendricks was known as a "trimmer," following an opportunistic course. His opponents characterized him as the "American Talleyrand," as a "bundle of very convenient negatives, with a private character of negative excellence," but in his public life they said he was "artful" and "impure." His amiability was ascribed to the fact that he had "not enough sincerity to be irritated by opposition."[2]

§ §

The temper of the Republican-dominated legislature which met in January, 1865, as the war was drawing to a victorious close, was very different from that of the stormy session of 1863. Although some Democrats engaged in bitter attacks upon Morton's record and indulged in delaying tactics, the wartime acts of the Governor were vindicated by the majority. W. H. H. Terrell submitted a report of the expenditures of the bureau of finance which a joint legislative committee found in good order. The military auditing committee expressed approval of the operation of the state arsenal. A bill was passed to repay the money advanced by Winslow, Lanier and Company with interest at 7 per cent. The same session also ratified the Thirteenth Amendment to the United States Constitution over the protests of Democrats who saw in it the death knell of white supremacy.[3]

A few weeks later the assassination of Lincoln tempered rejoicing over the end of the war and threw Republican poli-

[2] Indianapolis *Daily Journal,* June 13, 1872. During the war Hendricks opposed conscription, emancipation, the issuance of greenbacks, and the Thirteenth Amendment, but he voted for the supplies necessary to carry on the war. After the war he opposed the Freedmen's Bureau, the Civil Rights Law of 1866, the Fourteenth and Fifteenth amendments. He supported President Andrew Johnson and opposed his impeachment. Thomas A. Hendricks, *Dictionary of American Biography.* He was elected Vice-President in 1884, but died during his first year in office.

[3] Indiana *House Journal,* 1865, pp. 219-224, 375-380; Indiana *Laws,* 1865, pp. 77, 135; Stampp, *Indiana Politics,* pp. 257-258; Thornbrough, *Negro in Indiana,* p. 204.

ticians into a turmoil. Some of the more radical leaders regarded the accession of Andrew Johnson as strengthening their position. Julian at first had high hopes that the new President would be more amenable to the Radicals than was Lincoln. Schuyler Colfax praised Johnson as a man of "sterner mold" than his predecessor. But Morton, who headed a delegation of Indiana politicians who called upon the new President to assure him of their support, attempted to commit him to a moderate course. Republicans of all shades of opinion were at first loud in their protests of allegiance to Johnson, and he in turn expressed an especial attachment to Indiana Republicans since they had first urged his nomination as Vice-President.[4]

At the outset the Indianapolis *Journal,* in an editorial notable for its lack of prophetic insight, declared that Johnson had the good fortune to assume office "under more encouraging auspices than have greeted any of his predecessors for the last forty years." It predicted that the new President would have a Congress sympathetic to him and expressed the opinion that the tragic death of Lincoln had "softened political asperities, and tempered the virulence of partisan antagonism." In June it was still predicting that events since Johnson's accession "presage a successful and brilliant administration." The *Journal* at first approved Johnson's moderate policy toward the South, expressing the view that it would result in the establishment of loyal governments. In September it denied that there was any hostility between Johnson and the Radicals in Congress, averring that such stories were merely the inventions of the Democratic press. In a speech at Richmond, September 29, Morton expressed support for Johnson, insisting that he was faithfully trying to carry forward the Reconstruction policy which had been bequeathed to him by Lincoln. After the speech the New Albany *Commercial*

4 Julian, *Political Recollections,* pp. 259, 260-262; Foulke, *Morton,* I, 440-442; Smith, *Schuyler Colfax,* p. 218; Indianapolis *Daily Journal,* April 17, 24, 26, 1865.

declared that Morton had shown the "mendacity" of the Democratic papers which were reporting attacks by the Radicals on the President. "There are no such attacks," it declared.[5]

On the question of the status of the Negro and Negro suffrage Morton and the Indianapolis *Journal* appeared to be in sympathy with the cautious policy which Johnson was following. Editorially the *Journal* continued to support the idea of a separate country for Negroes and to express the opinion that both races would benefit from a policy of separation. It predicted that Negroes would be unable to achieve equality in the United States for generations.[6]

Morton's Richmond speech was especially noteworthy for what he had to say on the subject of Negro suffrage. He declared flatly that the freedmen were not ready to vote. "Can you conceive that a body of men, white or black, who, as well as their ancestors, have been in this condition, are qualified to be lifted immediately from their present state into the full exercise of political power . . . ?" he asked. "To say that such men—and it is no fault of theirs, it is simply their misfortune, and the crime of the nation—to say that such men, just emerging from this slavery are qualified for the exercise of political powers, is to make the strongest pro-slavery argument I ever heard." He warned that Negro suffrage in the South would mean Negro-dominated governments in those states and would lead to the exodus of whites. "I submit, then," he said, "That however freely we may

[5] Indianapolis *Daily Journal*, April 28, June 22, 29, September 19, 1865; Foulke, *Morton*, I, 447. Johnson considered Morton's speech the ablest defense of his policies which had yet been made. *Ibid.*, p. 451; New Albany *Commercial*, quoted in Indianapolis *Daily Journal*, October 5, 1865. The Lafayette *Courier* praised Morton's speech, saying: "his high indorsement of the Administration, and his glowing tribute to the statesmanship and patriotism of Andrew Johnson is well timed, and it will do much to remove the mists of prejudice with which unreflecting minds and political tricksters have obscured his principles and policy." The *Courier* called for "zealous and unreserved support of the administration of Andy Johnson." Lafayette *Courier*, quoted, *ibid.*

[6] Indianapolis *Daily Journal*, August 19, October 24, November 1, 1865.

admit the natural rights of the Negro, colored state governments are not desirable; that finally they will bring about a
war of races. . . ." Instead of immediate conferral of Negro
suffrage Morton urged a period of education and probation
and the apportionment of representation on the basis of the
number of voters rather than population.[7]

The only prominent Indiana Republican to advocate Negro
suffrage at this time was George W. Julian, whose views
on the subject were well known. In November, 1865, he
made a speech before the state legislature, which was then
in special session, in which he took issue with Morton on the
question of suffrage and Reconstruction. About this time
the Indianapolis *Journal,* which usually reflected Morton's
views, began a vituperative attack upon Julian. Julian and
Charles Sumner, it asserted, by their "ultra dogmas" were
threatening to disrupt the Republican party. Declaring that
Julian's "utter selfishness long ago made him odious to a large
portion of the best Republicans of [his] district," it added that
only his "overweening vanity" caused him to criticize Morton.[8]

In his message to the special session of the legislature,
Morton expressed gratification that the "heresy of State
sovereignty" had "been extirpated" and declared that it must
be established that "treason is a crime," and again expounded
views in opposition to Negro suffrage similar to those which
he had expressed at Richmond. He declared that under the
Constitution the question of suffrage belonged to the States

[7] Foulke, *Morton,* I, 448-451. This last proposal, which would have the
effect of limiting the influence of whites in the South and would serve as an
incentive for ultimately giving Negroes the right to vote, found its way in a
modified form into the Fourteenth Amendment. Morton's proposal grew in
part, no doubt, out of the fact that the ratification of the Thirteenth Amendment, abolishing slavery, would have the effect of nullifying the "three-fifths
clause" of the Constitution, under which three fifths of the slave population
was counted for purposes of apportioning representation. If the entire population of the South was to be counted in apportionment of representation obviously
the number of representatives from the South would be increased—a possibility
which worried the Republicans.

[8] Clarke, *George W. Julian,* pp. 281-291; Indianapolis *Daily Journal,* November 3, 18, 22, 1865.

and that it could not be taken away from them "without a violation of the letter and spirit of that instrument." But he did declare himself in favor of a constitutional amendment giving Federal protection to the civil rights of Negroes and one changing the basis of representation in Congress to the actual number of voters. Morton also pointed out that Indiana was scarcely in a position to urge Negro suffrage and civil rights upon the South when Indiana Negroes were subjected to legal disabilities. He recommended the repeal of the ban on the testimony by Negroes in courts of justice and recommended the enactment of legislation providing for the education of Negro children. The legislature modified the ban on testimony but took no action on the recommendation for education.[9]

After the close of the legislative session Morton, who had suffered a paralysis of the lower part of his body in October, left for Europe at the insistence of his doctors to seek rest and a cure if possible.[10] When he returned home the following March he found that the political atmosphere had changed drastically.

When Congress assembled in December, 1865, it refused to seat the members elected under the governments which Johnson had set up in the former Confederate states. Henceforth the cleavage between Johnson and the Republicans in Congress deepened until a complete breach had developed. Among the Republicans who had become disenchanted with the Presi-

[9] Indiana *House Journal*, special session, 1865, pp. 36, 37-39; Thornbrough, *Negro in Indiana*, pp. 233, 320-321. The Indianapolis *Journal* repeatedly urged a constitutional amendment basing representation on the number of qualified voters and claimed that the editor of the *Journal* had originated the proposal for such an amendment. The Democratic Indianapolis *Herald* was strongly opposed to such an amendment, which it regarded as a device "to deprive the Southern States of a large portion of their Representatives, and reduce them to helplessness." Indianapolis *Daily Herald*, November 11, 1865.

[10] Prior to his departure for Europe Morton stopped in Washington to call upon Johnson. Afterwards it was reported: "The Governor finds President Johnson in full accord with his own lately expressed views on 'reconstruction' and the question of negro suffrage." Indianapolis *Daily Journal*, November 18, 1865.

dent was Colfax. As Speaker of the House he took a leading
part in excluding southern members until there could be no
question that southern state governments were under the
control of men who were loyal to the Union and ready to
guarantee the rights of the freedmen.[11]

Most Indiana Republicans at first tried to minimize and
reconcile the differences between the President and Congress.
The state platform adopted by the Republican convention
which met on February 22, 1866, adopted a resolution expressing its full faith in Johnson, whom it called "a patriot tried
and true." But at the same time it declared that it was "the
province of the legislative branch of the Government to
determine the question of reconstruction" and that the states
should not be restored until they had demonstrated their
loyalty. When Johnson vetoed the Freedmen's Bureau bill, the
Indianapolis *Journal* expressed regret that there was not
better agreement between the President and Congress but
called for "forbearance" and "calm" and said there was nothing in Johnson's veto message to cause a split in the party.
Even after Johnson vetoed the civil rights bill and Congress
overrode his veto, the *Journal* was still hopeful of a reconciliation between the two branches of government.[12]

Meanwhile, Indiana Democrats were showing more and
more admiration for the President and his policy toward the
South. In their state platform adopted on March 15, 1866,
they expressed approval of the principles governing Reconstruction which Johnson had avowed and applauded his veto

[11] Smith, *Schuyler Colfax,* pp. 221-228. The Indianapolis *Journal* asserted
that large numbers of Southerners seeking seats in Congress were men who
could not honestly subscribe to the required oath that they had never given
voluntary aid to the rebellion. "We are in favor of treating the South gener-
ously if it gives satisfactory assurances of future fidelity to the Union, but
the attempt to force representatives into Congress who are disqualified by
law from holding seats there, is to say the least of it, rather an ungracious
return for the leniency which has been extended to the 'wayward sisters.' "
Indianapolis *Daily Journal,* November 7, 1865.

[12] Indianapolis *Daily Herald,* February 23, 1866; Indianapolis *Daily Journal,*
February 21, April 13, 19, 1866.

of the Freedmen's Bureau bill. In Congress Daniel Voorhees introduced resolutions endorsing the President's program. The Republican press looked askance at the *rapprochement* between Johnson and the Democrats. The Indianapolis *Journal* saw in Voorhees' resolutions merely an attempt to create a split between the President and his Republican supporters. It found the endorsement of Johnson in the Democratic platform "as impudent as it was dishonest."[13]

But by midsummer even moderate Republicans had ceased to defend Johnson and were accusing him of protecting southern traitors and infringing upon the powers of Congress. "Hastily assuming powers which belonged alone to the National Congress," declared the *Journal,* "the President had invited the rebels to reorganize their State governments, which they did to the exclusion of loyal men. . . ." Later the *Journal* went so far as to advance the doctrine that the Founding Fathers had made "the Legislature the first and Supreme department of the Government," and that the President had "not a single duty to perform except in the mode and manner presented by Congress." At a Union meeting one speaker declared that by his vetoes "the President had deserted his friends, and joined hands with those whom he had once been swiftest to denounce as the country's enemies." In similar vein Schuyler Colfax declared: "The President don't talk now like he used to. . . ." He insisted that Johnson had "grievously betrayed" the American people "in abandoning his friends and rushing into an unnatural embrace with the enemies of the country." Even Senator Henry S. Lane was proclaiming that he was "proud to be a radical in the most

13 Henry (comp.), *State Platforms,* pp. 27-29; Indianapolis *Daily Journal,* January 13, 16, 1866. In February, 1866, the House of Representatives voted to seat Col. Henry D. Washburn, a Republican, and to oust Voorhees on the grounds that there were frauds in the votes cast for Voorhees. The Indianapolis *Journal* rejoiced at the seating of Washburn, who, it said, "served in the Union army while Voorhees was serving the rebellion as a member of Congress." Voorhees on leaving the House declared himself to be the friend of Andrew Johnson, personally and politically, which, the *Journal* said, was "hard on Johnson." *Ibid.,* February 24, 1866.

Radical Congress that ever assembled. . . . The Radicals constitute one side, rebels and traitors are the other side."[14]

This theme was constantly reiterated during the political campaign of 1866. The strategy of the Republicans was to attack the war record of the Democrats and win the support of the Union veterans. Morton, who had won the name of "soldiers' friend" during the war, assiduously cultivated the support of the returning soldiers. In the months following the war he welcomed the homecoming regiments in elaborate ceremonies. On these occasions he reminded them that while they had been fighting for the Union disloyal men had been active at home. After his return from Europe in 1866 he actively promoted the growth of the G. A. R. in Indiana. The first posts of the Grand Army of the Republic had been organized in Illinois after the end of the war as radical secret societies. From Illinois they spread into Indiana. Morton immediately realized their political possibilities. Behind the scenes he supplied leadership in promoting the growth of the organization. One of the men most prominent in the establishment of the G. A. R. on a nationwide scale, Maj. Oliver M. Wilson, gave Morton full credit for being the first person to envision the possibility of making the organization a "power in the land." Postwar political campaigns in Indiana, said Wilson, "meant the marshaling of every soldier in the party that supported him as governor during the war. . . . His first wish was to preserve unsullied the record of Indiana's soldiers from the taint of affiliation with the political party that had opposed the war." Union uniforms were conspicuous at every Republican rally as former officers sought to revive wartime feelings. In August, 1866, a statewide rally of veterans was held in Indianapolis. In November, following the election, the first national convention of the Grand Army of the Republic was held in the same city.[15]

14 Indianapolis *Daily Journal,* July 30, August 6, 8, 20, 31, 1866.

15 Oliver M. Wilson, *Grand Army of the Republic,* p. 16, quoted in Mary R. Dearing, *Veterans in Politics: The Story of the G. A. R.* (Louisiana State University Press, 1952), pp. 92, 93; *Proceedings of the First Meeting of the*

The central theme of the Republican campaign in 1866 was Democratic treason. One campaign pamphlet entitled *Treason Exposed: Record of the Disloyal Democracy* reprinted accounts of the treason trials of 1864 and excerpts from wartime Democratic speeches and editorials critical of the war effort. Another declared succinctly that the reader would find "that those who are with Johnson are with the Northern Copperheads; that those who are with the Northern Copperheads are with the original rebels; and that those who are with the original rebels are on the direct route, with baggage checked through, to the hottest part of the dominions of Prince Lucifer."[16]

Morton set the tone for the campaign at an opening rally with a speech which was extreme, even for him, in its vilification of the Democratic wartime record. "In short," he concluded, "the Democratic party may be described as a common sewer and loathsome receptacle, into which is emptied every element of treason North and South, and every element of inhumanity and barbarism which has dishonored the age." In another speech directed especially at veterans Morton asked former soldiers if they wanted men "whose garments were yet red with the blood of their comrades to legislate for them, to say how much bounty they should have and what pensions they and the widows and families of their slaughtered brethren should have, if any." At another rally a former colonel dededeclared that men like Voorhees and McDonald should be hunted down and hanged and declared that Democratic "scoundrels" deserved "the punishment that is waiting for them in hell."[17]

National Encampment, Grand Army of the Republic. Held at Indianapolis, Indiana, Nov. 20th and 21st, 1866 (Philadelphia, 1876).

[16] *Treason Exposed! Record of the Disloyal Democracy, Resolutions of their Conventions, Speeches, Letters, Etc., Etc.,* Compiled from Authentic Sources, for the Union State Central Committee (Indianapolis, 1866); James M. Hiatt, *The War for the Democratic Succession* (Indianapolis, 1866), Preface. Hiatt dedicated his booklet to Morton, "The Great Union Worker, and the Soldier's True and Abiding Friend."

[17] Foulke, *Morton* I, 469-476; Indianapolis *Daily Journal,* June 20, August 13, 31, 1866.

The enraged Democrats countered by personal attacks, which included speculations as to the causes for Morton's physical disability. The Indianapolis *Journal* felt compelled to answer Democratic newspapers which had "often insinuated, and sometimes directly charged, that Governor Morton was not suffering from paralysis, but that his disease was the result of licentious habits." Two of Morton's personal physicians addressed letters to the Indianapolis *Herald* saying that Morton's condition was due to mental anxiety and overwork.[18]

Meanwhile, the attacks on Johnson intensified. An advertisement for a Union rally at Centerville called upon people to turn out to express their indignation at "the treacherous acts of an imbecile Executive." The climax came when Johnson visited Indianapolis in his "swing around the circle" in which he sought the election to Congress of members who would support his policies. Before his arrival the *Journal* asserted that he was coming, not as President of the United States, but as "a partisan to harangue the people for the benefit of the Copperheads and to build up a party composed almost exclusively of men who were disloyal to the government during the terrible civil war. . . ." No loyal men, it said, could participate in the ceremonies attending his visit "without being insulted by the man who has basely betrayed them."[19]

Johnson, who was accompanied by secretaries Seward and Welles and General Grant and Admiral Farragut, went from the railroad station to his hotel preceded by a brass band, but a crowd which assembled outside the hotel proved to be hostile. When the President appeared on the balcony and attempted to address them, he was met with hisses and groans and shouts for General Grant. According to the account in the *Journal*, when an attempt was made to introduce Johnson, "never before was such a scene of frantic tumult and con-

---

18 Indianapolis *Daily Journal*, July 4, 1866; Foulke, *Morton*, I, 477.
19 Indianapolis *Daily Journal*, September 10, 11, 1866.

fusion witnessed in our city. Johnson, with all his brazen facedness, had not the hardihood to endeavor to stem this storm of honest indignation. After standing upon the balcony a few minutes, he gave it up in despair. . . ."[20]

After the President retired there was a riot between Democrats, who were attempting to hold a torchlight procession, and Republicans. Shots were fired, several men were wounded, and one man, a Republican, was killed. The following morning Johnson spoke briefly to a crowd outside his hotel before departing for Madison. Democrats charged that the disorders attending Johnson's visit were the result of preconceived Republican plans—that Morton, who was in Philadelphia, had sent instructions and that members of the G. A. R. had planned to break up the meeting. The Republicans indignantly denied such accusations. The *Journal* expressed regret that the crowd had not allowed the President to speak but insisted that the outburst against him was entirely spontaneous and unplanned and that Union men were in no way responsible for the disorders which occurred.[21]

Issues other than Democratic disloyalty and the President's southern policy received little attention during the campaign. Republicans attempted to woo the Irish vote, which was normally Democratic, by assailing Johnson for ordering American citizens to desist from assisting the Fenians, who were attempting to use American soil as a base from which to attack Canada. Schuyler Colfax was especially loud in his declarations of sympathy for the oppressed Irish.[22]

The Republican victory on election day was probably not a surprise to anyone, but Republicans may have been disappointed that their margin of victory was surprisingly narrow

[20] *Ibid.,* September 12, 1866.

[21] *Ibid.,* September 11, 12, 13, 14, 1866. At Madison there were more disorders. *Ibid.,* September 13. The Lafayette *Courier* also insisted that the action of the crowds in Indianapolis was merely a spontaneous expression of disgust with Johnson. Lafayette *Courier,* quoted *ibid.,* September 13.

[22] Indianapolis *Daily Journal,* August 8, 18, 1866; Smith, *Schuyler Colfax,* pp. 240-242.

in some contests. The Republican state ticket was elected by a margin of about 14,000 votes—a decline from the vote in 1864. Eight Republicans were elected to the United States House of Representatives and three Democrats. Republicans retained control of both houses of the state legislature.[23]

Morton's message to the legislature which convened in January, 1867, showed how completely he had gone over to the Radical position. In urging the ratification of the Fourteenth Amendment he predicted dire consequences if the southern states rejected the amendment. "Now the blood of the nation is up," he said, "and the cry for vengeance is abroad in the land. Let the people of the South flee from the wrath to come. Let them put away the prepared traitors who hurried them into rebellion, and now darken their councils, and make haste to abandon their sins, and accept the proffered terms." For the first time Morton urged Negro suffrage for the South—and by simple act of Congress. Ordinarily, he said, the subject of suffrage belonged to the states, but if loyal governments could be created only by extending suffrage to a group to whom it had been denied by state law, then it was within the power of Congress to grant suffrage.[24]

Soon after the beginning of the legislative session Morton was elected to the United States Senate as the successor of Henry S. Lane. Some Republicans, as well as Democrats, thought that Morton was ineligible to be elected to the Senate while he held the office of governor. Two Republican members of the state Senate refused to vote for him on these grounds, but the rest supported him. The Democratic minority voted for Voorhees. Morton's political opponents could find no words of praise for the departing governor. The leading Democratic paper declared that as governor his "pecuniary condition was benefitted. He trafficked in the blood of the country, in its woes, to advance his personal interests." His every act as governor, it said, was motivated by personal and

23 *Appletons' Annual Cyclopædia*, 1866, pp. 405-406.
24 Indiana *Senate Journal*, 1867, pp. 43-44.

selfish considerations and "not a public duty was discharged by any citizen of the state, which His Excellency did not endeavor to appropriate to his own aggrandizement." On the other hand, the same paper declared that Conrad Baker, who succeeded Morton as governor, although as much a partisan as his predecessor, was "a straightforward, honest, honorable and Christian gentleman."[25]

In their state platform in 1868 the Democrats endorsed Johnson and his policies and expressed "abhorrence and condemnation" of Radical Reconstruction as a policy which had as its object the continuation in power of "the most venal and corrupt party that ever dishonored any civilization"—a policy "vindictively enacted and mercilessly prosecuted with the unconstitutional purpose of centralizing and perpetuating all political powers of the Government in the dominant Radical party. . . ." Negro suffrage was expressly opposed and the right of the Federal government to interfere with suffrage in the states was denied. Once more the Democrats nominated Hendricks for the governorship.[26]

In their state platform Republicans defended Radical Reconstruction measures as having been made necessary "by the continued rebellious spirit of the Southern people." Negro suffrage in the South was also declared to be necessary because of the rebellious spirit of southern whites, but the framers of the platform, out of deference to the well-known prejudices of Indiana voters, were careful to add that "the question of suffrage in all the loyal States belongs to the people of those states under the Constitution of the United States."[27]

25 Foulke, *Morton*, I, 487-488; Indianapolis *Daily Herald*, January 23, 26, 1867. Conrad Baker was born in Pennsylvania in 1817. He attended Gettysburg College and studied law in the office of Thaddeus Stevens. In 1841 he settled in Evansville, Indiana, which was his official residence until he became governor. During the war, as already seen, he had served as a colonel of a cavalry regiment and as provost marshal general for Indiana. Nowland, *Prominent Citizens*, pp. 228-230.

26 Henry (comp.), *State Platforms*, pp. 32-34.

27 *Ibid.*, pp. 34-35; Indianapolis *Daily Herald*, February 21, 1868.

Conrad Baker was nominated for the governorship by the Republican convention, which also endorsed General Grant for the presidency and Schuyler Colfax for the vice-presidency. Colfax had the active support of such important Republicans as John D. Defrees and Henry S. Lane and the support of the Indianapolis *Journal*. Morton, while not enthusiastic in his support, at least did not oppose him. At the national convention Colfax was nominated on the fifth ballot, becoming the first Indianan to be named by a major party for the vice-presidency.[28]

In the ensuing campaign the Republicans made the usual charges of treason or sympathy with treason against the Democrats, while the latter, as usual, raised the race issue. They insisted that the recently adopted Fourteenth Amendment, which made Negroes citizens, was intended to make voters of them. This Republicans vigorously denied, pointing out that both their state and national platform declared that in the "loyal" states the question of who should vote belonged to the states.[29]

Veterans of the recent war were conspicuous in the campaign. In an effort to counteract charges that they had not supported the war the Democrats organized the "White Boys in Blue," who invited to membership all veterans who were opposed to "radicalism," the "revolutionary" policies of the Republican Congress, and the continued exclusion of Confederate states from the Union. The Republicans countered by organizing the "Fighting Boys in Blue." During the campaign several clashes were reported between members of the two groups. As election day approached there were the usual

[28] Smith, *Schuyler Colfax*, pp. 275-276. See *ibid.*, pp. 274-275 for a letter from Colfax to Charles Heaton, February 11, 1868, in which Colfax expressed the opinion that Morton himself cherished an ambition for the vice-presidential nomination. On the other hand, correspondence between Morton and Baker shows that Colfax gave the impression that he had support for the gubernatorial nomination which Baker sought. Morton told Baker that Colfax treated him with "marked neglect." Morton to Baker, January 19, 21, 1868, in Governor Conrad Baker Papers, Indiana Historical Society Library.

[29] Thornbrough, *Negro in Indiana*, pp. 242-243.

charges by members of both parties that their rivals were planning to win by fraudulent votes. In spite of a recently enacted voter registration law Democrats insisted that Republicans were planning to "colonize" voters in doubtful counties. On the eve of the state election it was reported that Republican "carpet-baggers" had arrived in Indianapolis and would attempt to register to vote. Republicans in turn charged that Democrats were importing voters from Kentucky. When Conrad Baker was victorious over Hendricks by a margin of less than one thousand votes the Democrats charged that his victory was due to "the most stupendous frauds and the most lavish and corrupt expenditure of money" of any election to date. A few weeks later Grant carried the state by over nine thousand votes. In the Congressional elections Democrats won four seats, a gain of one, while Republicans won seven. One of the victorious Republicans was George W. Julian, who was re-elected in spite of continued efforts of Morton to bring about his defeat. In 1867 the legislature, which was subservient to Morton, had redistricted the state in such a way that three solidly Republican counties were taken from Julian's district and four counties in which Democrats were numerous were added. In spite of this maneuver Julian carried the district by a narrow margin, but in 1870 he failed to secure endorsement from the Republican primary in his district.[30]

Republicans controlled both houses of the 1869 session of the legislature by large margins, but became embroiled in a prolonged intra-party squabble over the election of a successor to Democratic Senator Hendricks. At first it appeared that the choice would be the lieutenant governor, William Cumback, who had received the nomination of the party caucus and apparently had the support of Morton. But Cumback's enemies brought to light correspondence which he had had with Governor Baker the previous year which proved to be

---

30 Indianapolis *Daily Herald,* April 9, 1868; Indianapolis *Daily Sentinel,* August 21, October 2, 6, 7, 9, 10, 12, 17, 1868; *Appletons' Annual Cyclopædia,* 1868, pp. 378-379; Julian, *Political Recollections,* pp. 303, 320-321; Clarke, *George W. Julian,* pp. 306, 328, 334.

his undoing. In January, 1868, Cumback had asked Baker to appoint him to the Senate in the event that Hendricks resigned in order to campaign for the governorship. He had indicated that if he received assurances that he would receive the appointment he would not seek a state office, which apparently meant that he would not oppose Baker for the gubernatorial nomination. Baker interpreted the letter as an attempt to bribe him, and the same interpretation was put upon it when its contents were revealed to the legislature. As a compromise Daniel D. Pratt was finally elected to the United States Senate. He was a lawyer from Logansport who had recently been elected to the United States House of Representatives. In the Senate Pratt, who was reserved and no orator, had a colorless and undistinguished but honorable record. His relations with his colleague Morton were not especially cordial.[31]

A more serious and dramatic legislative crisis arose over the ratification of the Fifteenth Amendment. In spite of the fact that both national and state Republican platforms in 1868 had declared that the question of suffrage in the "loyal"

[31] *Brevier Legislative Reports,* X (1869), 35-39, 45-55, 67-70, 78-79, 108-115; Foulke, *Morton,* II, 62-63; Joseph E. Holliday, "Daniel D. Pratt: Lawyer and Legislator," *Indiana Magazine of History,* LVII (1961), 122-123; Joseph E. Holliday, "Daniel D. Pratt: Senator and Commissioner," *ibid.,* LVIII (1962), 17-51 *passim.* The Indiana Senate passed a resolution censuring Cumback for "an improper attempt to tamper with the integrity and destroy the independence of the appointing power vested in the governor." In the Senate there were 33 Republicans, 17 Democrats; in the House 57 Republicans, 43 Democrats. *Appletons' Annual Cyclopædia,* 1868, p. 379.

The letter which created the furor is as follows: "Dear Friend: If I had not a thousand things to demand my attention this week I would come up and see you. I will therefore venture to make this suggestion. I think Hendricks will be chosen by the democrats and he will certainly (if he intends to inspire hope of success among his friends) resign his position. The person appointed by you will other things being equal stand the best chance to be chosen by our Legislature. If you will assure me of the appointment I will withdraw from the contest for any position on the State ticket and take the position of elector at our State Convention. If this proposition does not meet with your approbation please return this letter to me. Let me have your reply at an early day. I do most earnestly hope for the unity of the Republican party." Will Cumback to Conrad Baker, January 6, 1868, Conrad Baker Papers, Archives Division, Indiana State Library.

states was one entirely reserved to the states, the election was scarcely past when the amendment prohibiting a state to deny the right to vote because of race was under consideration in Congress. Morton, in a remarkable *volte face,* became one of the principal advocates of the measure. Democrats accused Republicans of bad faith in so rapidly abandoning their election year pledges. Although Democrats were in a minority in the Indiana legislature, they were determined to block ratification of the amendment and to compel the issue to be taken to the voters. In order to break a quorum and thereby prevent a vote on the amendment seventeen Democratic senators and thirty-seven representatives resigned. An address prepared by the Democratic members reiterated the old argument that the government had been created by white men for white men and denounced the proposed amendment as a Republican scheme to win votes by placing the ballot "in the hands of those whom they hope to control—an ignorant, irresponsible and depraved race. . . ." Throughout the state Democrats held protest meetings. The resignations not only prevented action on the amendment but on other necessary financial legislation. A special session of the legislature was therefore necessary, and special elections were held to fill the seats made vacant by the mass resignations. All of the members who resigned were triumphantly re-elected—evidence in the eyes of Democrats that public opinion was opposed to ratification of the proposed amendment.

At the special session Democrats again attempted to forestall action by resigning in sufficient numbers to make a quorum impossible. This time their purpose was thwarted by the resourceful and audacious Morton, who arrived from Washington to take charge just as they were preparing to bolt. The state constitution expressly stated that a quorum consisted of two thirds of each house. In spite of long-established precedent to the contrary Morton now insisted that this merely meant two thirds of the members who remained after the resignations. The Republicans went ahead and voted for the amendment, the vote was certified to Washington, and Indiana was counted as one of the states ratifying the amendment, even though Democrats and some Republicans thought the action illegal.[32] The same session of the legislature which conferred suffrage upon Indiana Negroes by these highly irregular proceedings also adopted the first legislation which provided for public schools for Negro children.[33]

Political reverberations over the ratification of the Fifteenth Amendment continued in the 1870 campaign. In their state platform Democrats protested the counting of Indiana among the states which had ratified and declared their "unalterable opposition to its ratification." At the 1871 session of the legislature they introduced resolutions saying the "pretended ratification" was null and void. But the Republican members countered with resolutions that the ratification was valid and that it was "too late for any political party to file a special demurrer to the methods or manner by which this grand result was accomplished."[34]

The Republican state platform of 1870 declared: "We rejoice in the ratification of the Fifteenth Amendment . . . and we extend to the colored man a helping hand to enable him in the race of life to improve and elevate his condition." In the ensuing campaign Republicans wooed the newly enfranchised voters by emphasizing the debt which Negroes owed the party of Lincoln for emancipation and civil rights and by dubbing the Democrats the party of slavery and white supremacy. These tactics were used successfully for many

[32] Thornbrough, *Negro in Indiana*, pp. 243-248. The ratification of the Fifteenth Amendment had the effect of nullifying the parts of the Indiana constitution which limited the right to vote to white persons. Earlier decisions of the Indiana Supreme Court had already nullified Article XIII of the constitution, which barred Negroes from coming into the state. Nevertheless the provisions which made distinction as to race were not finally removed from the constitution by constitutional amendment until 1881. *Ibid.*, pp. 234-235, 249-250.

[33] *Ibid.*, pp. 323-324.

[34] *Ibid.*, p. 249.

years in winning and holding the allegiance of Negroes to the Republican party.[35]

The number of Negro voters in Indiana was not large. Although Republicans won their votes they probably alienated some white voters by championing Negroes. Reaction against the highhanded methods which were used to secure ratification of the Fifteenth Amendment may have played a part in the elections of 1870 when, for the first time since 1862, Democrats won control of the state legislature. Reaction against revelations of corruption among Republican officeholders also probably played a part in the outcome. In Marion County Democrats ran on a "reform" ticket calling for economy and retrenchment and an end to corruption. "There must be something wrong in the conduct of public affairs," cried the Indianapolis *Sentinel*, "when public officers become rich in a term or two . . . when candidates are willing to and do spend large sums of money to secure official position." Germans, who felt they had been slighted at the hands of the regular Republican organization, were active in the "reform" movement, which foreshadowed the coalition of Democrats and Liberal Republicans in 1872.[36]

In 1870, instead of basing the campaign principally upon charges of past disloyalty of Democrats, as in previous years, the Republicans were compelled to take a defensive position. "The Republican party has doubtless had bad men in high places," Morton admitted in a speech at Lafayette, but he added that when scoundrels were discovered they were forced to vacate their positions. Perhaps Morton was active in campaigning for a Republican legislature because he hoped to resign from the Senate and become minister to Great Britain, a post which he could use as a stepping stone to the White House. The Senator's hopes were dashed by the outcome of the elections. Democrats gained control of both

---

35 *Ibid.*, p. 253. For an account of the role of the Negroes in Indiana political life in the late nineteenth century see *ibid.*, pp. 288-316.

36 Indianapolis *Daily Sentinel*, August 20, September 24, 1870.

houses of the legislature, which meant that Morton dared not resign from the Senate because anyone elected to replace him would be a Democrat. The entire Democratic state ticket was elected by a margin of about 2,800 votes, and Democrats elected five of the eleven Congressmen—a gain of one over 1868.[37]

By 1872 more revelations of corruption and incompetence in the Grant administration and increasing weariness with the southern policy of the Radicals gave an impetus to demands for reform and new hope to the Democrats. "The extravagance and corruptions of the partisans in power, the class interests that have grown out of Radical rule, and the grinding public burdens which have been imposed upon the country," the Indianapolis *Sentinel* declared, "have awakened the people to the necessity of reform, of a change in public policy that can only be brought about by a change in the administration of the Government."[38]

The Evansville *Courier,* a Democratic paper, urged that Democrats and Liberal Republicans emulate the example of Missouri and join together to elect a President. In reply the Republican Indianapolis *Journal* warned that the Liberal Republican movement was a Democratic plot. How, it asked, could any Republican contribute "even in the remotest degree, to the success of a party so utterly odious, so universally disloyal, so thoroughly corrupt, as the Democracy of the present day?" But even the *Journal* admitted the need for reform within the Republican party and was critical of the Grant administration on a number of scores.[39]

The Republican state platform denounced corruption in general terms and expressed approval of "exposures" of

[37] Indianapolis *Daily Sentinel,* September 30, October 15, 1870; Foulke, *Morton,* II, 144; *Appletons' Annual Cyclopedia, 1870,* p. 404. According to the Indianapolis *Sentinel,* October 15, 1870, the New York *Herald* reported that Morton had personally raised $15,000 for use in the Indiana campaign while on a trip to New York.

[38] *Ibid.,* January 26, 1872.

[39] Indianapolis *Daily Journal,* January 30, 1872; Evansville *Courier,* quoted *ibid.*

corrupt officials but endorsed the renomination of Grant and Colfax. The Grant administration was commended for bringing all citizens under the protection of national authority, and adherence to the principle of the authority of the national government over "the false theories of states' rights" was proclaimed. For governor the Republicans nominated Thomas M. Browne, who as a member of the 1863 legislature had opposed the "treasonable" activities of the Democrats and then resigned to enlist in the Union army, in which he attained the rank of brigadier general. Browne was nominated over two other aspirants both of whom were better known than he—Godlove S. Orth and Benjamin Harrison. Morton was rumored to have blocked the nomination of Harrison because he feared he might become a rival for the senatorship if elected.[40]

At the national convention the Indiana delegation supported Colfax for the vice-presidency, but Henry Wilson was nominated. Colfax had taken a rather equivocal position on the subject of his renomination. In 1870 he had announced his intention of retiring from public life in 1872 although it seems doubtful if he really meant to retire. As the 1872 convention approached he began to encourage his friends to work for his renomination, but he had lost much support both among politicians and in the press. He did not have the active support of Grant. At the time of the convention Colfax's relations with the Crédit Mobilier had not been publicized, but two months later it was revealed that he held stock in that discredited organization. Although he persistently denied that he had done anything blameworthy in receiving the stock, his reputation suffered irreparable damage and Grant was no doubt relieved that he was not his running mate.[41]

[40] *Ibid.*, February 23, 1872; Harry J. Sievers, S. J., *Benjamin Harrison, Hoosier Statesman, From the Civil War to the White House 1865-1888* (New York, 1959), pp. 57-59, 61.

[41] Smith, *Schuyler Colfax*, pp. 349-355. See *ibid.*, pp. 393-399 for a summary of Colfax's relations with the Crédit Mobilier. Although Colfax received

The Indianapolis *Journal* labeled the Republicans who attended the Liberal convention in Cincinnati which nominated Horace Greeley for the presidency as merely "soreheads," who had failed to receive the favors which they sought from the Grant administration. But among the Indiana delegates were George W. Julian, John Defrees, and David Kilgore, all of whom had helped found the Republican party in Indiana.[42]

The Democrats postponed their state convention until after the Cincinnati convention. The Indianapolis *Sentinel* spoke highly of Greeley's character and intelligence. While admitting that there might be features of the Liberal Republican platform which all Democrats could not endorse, it urged the Democracy to unite with the Liberals "in the patriotic effort to wrest the Government from the spoilers and corruptionists, and to aid in the restoration of honesty, purity, and economy in the conduct of public affairs." Thomas Hendricks immediately announced that he would support Greeley if the Democratic convention endorsed him, but other Democratic leaders held back. Joseph E. McDonald was quoted in the Republican press as saying that he regarded the nomination of Greeley as "disastrous," but at the state convention he promised to abide by the decision of the national convention.[43]

stock in the organization there is some doubt that he was actually paid any dividends and no evidence that he used his position in Congress to further the interests of the Union Pacific Railroad.

[42] Indianapolis *Daily Journal*, May 3, 1872. In a letter to the Indianapolis *News*, July 5, 1872, Defrees defended his support of Greeley instead of Grant. Greeley, he said, was "as well known throughout the world, and as much respected for his great ability, intelligence, and correct personal habits, as any other American.

"It is a melancholy fact that this can not be truthfully said of the present incumbent—but, I forbear. It is a subject too humiliating to an American to contemplate."

In spite of the high moral ground which Defrees appeared to take, the fact that he had lost his position as public printer in 1869 may have contributed to his espousal of the Liberal movement. See Smith, *Schuyler Colfax*, pp. 316, 354, for an account of the break between Defrees and Colfax over patronage

[43] Indianapolis *Daily Sentinel*, May 4, 1872; Indianapolis *Daily Journal*, May 11, June 13, 1872.

In a speech in the House of Representatives in May Voorhees declared that Greeley's record on the tariff and other questions made him wholly unacceptable as a Democratic candidate, but during the campaign he gave Greeley lukewarm support. The Democratic party, "even with Horace Greeley as its candidate," he said, was preferable to the party of "Grant and the profligate managers by whom he is lead [sic] on to his own and his country's ruin."[44]

The Democrats once more nominated Hendricks for the governorship and adopted a platform in which they endorsed the principles stated in the Liberal Republican platform and avoided committing themselves on any economic questions which might alienate Republican support. They attacked the corruption of the Grant administration and called for the immediate restoration of all political rights of former Confederates—for "universal amnesty and universal suffrage."[45]

The Grant Republicans were especially bitter toward the Liberal Republicans. The Indianapolis *Journal* labeled the fusionists as "Hermaphrodites" and insisted that the alliance of Greeley and the Democrats was motivated by sheer opportunism. Julian was described not merely as a "sorehead" but as a "renegade," "apostate," and "trusted ally of Copperheads." When he spoke in Indianapolis the *Journal* advised: "Let all good Republicans who want to have their faith strengthened and learn how to escape political infamy, go and hear Julian's advice tonight and then do the opposite."[46]

During the campaign the Democrats pleaded that the past be forgotten. The Indiana delegation to the Baltimore convention declared their desire to "ignore all past party differences, especially on obsolete issues," and promised to cooperate with former political opponents in a move to overthrow the Grant administration, "with its corruption and

44 Indianapolis *Daily Journal*, May 14, 1872; *Speech of Hon. Daniel W. Voorhees, Delivered at Spencer, Ind., July 18, 1872. Grant's Administration the Most Infamous in History* (n.p., n.d.).

45 Indianapolis *Daily Journal*, June 13, 1872.

46 *Ibid.*, June 12, July 8, 1872; Indianapolis *News*, July 18, 1872.

imbecility."[47] The platform and ticket of the Liberal Republican party were accepted without change by the Democrats in their national convention. A straight-out Democratic ticket was subsequently nominated, composed of Charles O'Connor for President and Charles Francis Adams for Vice-President.

But Morton, who was the master mind of the Republican campaign and who was fighting for his own political survival, would not let the past be forgotten. He leveled his sharpest attacks against Hendricks' war record and compared it invidiously with his own. In failing to elect Hendricks as governor in 1860 he said the state had "avoided a vast calamity" and that Hendricks' election to the United States Senate "by the treasonable legislature of 1863" was due to the fact that "he was a recognized enemy of the war."[48]

It was a bitter campaign, marked by more than the usual amount of personal abuse. The Indianapolis *Journal* spoke of Hendricks as a candidate who was "cloaked with political infamy." The Democrats reiterated the old gossip that Morton's paralysis was due to "dissipation" and that members of Indianapolis society refused to associate with him. Democratic charges that Browne, the Republican candidate for governor, was a drunkard, were so widespread that the *Journal* felt compelled to deny them. Later it attributed his defeat "almost entirely" to "the infamous calumny of intemperance" which had been repeated "with the most shameless and persistent wickedness." When Greeley spoke in Indianapolis the *Journal* headlined the account: "GRANDMOTHER GREELEY GIBBERS" and ridiculed him as the "bran-bread philosopher" with "childish face."[49]

Accusations of corruption at the ballot box were also unusually vehement. Both parties accused the other of importing voters from Kentucky and of plans to stuff the ballot box. But on the day of the state election in October all was quiet

[47] Indianapolis *Daily Journal*, July 10, 1872.
[48] Foulke, *Morton*, II, 257-258, 261.
[49] Indianapolis *Daily Journal*, July 9, September 24, October 15, 16, 1872.

and orderly. This time Hendricks, who had barely missed election in 1868, was elected by a narrow margin. One other Democrat on the state ticket was elected, the Superintendent of Public Instruction, but Republicans were victorious in the other state contests, and Republicans gained control of the state legislature with a majority of twelve on joint ballot.[50]

After the state election Republicans redoubled their efforts to carry the state for Grant. There were reports of enormous expenditures of money, which were indignantly denied. Grant's margin of victory was over 21,000—larger than in 1868. The Indianapolis *Journal* rejoiced in headlines which proclaimed: "HOOSIERDOM TAKES HER PLACE IN THE RANKS OF CIVILIZATION! SHE REDEEMS HERSELF FROM THE INFAMY OF HENDRICKS' ELECTION!"[51]

It was obvious that many persons who had voted for Hendricks had failed to vote for Greeley. A few weeks before the state election a "straight out" Democratic convention had met in Indianapolis and denounced the endorsement of Greeley as "a fraud and swindle." Their efforts to persuade Alfred P. Edgerton of Fort Wayne, who had been the Democratic candidate for lieutenant governor in 1868, to accept the nomination for governor were unsuccessful. Edgerton announced that he would support Hendricks, but declared his uncompromising opposition to Greeley, a position which apparently thousands of Indiana voters shared. On the other hand there were Republicans who supported the Liberal movement in 1872 who never returned to their former allegiance. Of these the most prominent was George W. Julian.[52]

During the campaign there was some speculation that if the Democrats won control of the legislature they would

50 *Ibid.*, October 3, 4, 5, 7, 8, 9, 1872; *Appletons' Annual Cyclopædia*, 1872, p. 397.

51 Indianapolis *Daily Journal*, October 17, November 6, 1872; *Appletons' Annual Cyclopædia*, 1872, p. 397.

52 *Appletons' Annual Cyclopædia*, 1872, p. 397; Indianapolis *Daily Journal*, September 20, 1872. Morton was accused of fomenting the "straight out" movement in order to weaken Greeley but indignantly denied the charge. Foulke, *Morton*, II, 265.

elect Hendricks to the United States Senate, an office which he was reported to prefer to the governorship. But Republican control of the new legislature thwarted any such ambitions which Hendricks may have harbored and insured the re-election of Morton.

There was some talk that Democrats might seek a coalition with disaffected Republicans in order to defeat Morton. No Republicans could be found who would publicly lend themselves to such a scheme, but Morton was sufficiently worried that he had Baker call a special session soon after the election before the opposition could coalesce. It was reported that all members of the Republican caucus were compelled individually to go on record as favoring Morton, and he was re-elected. "Thus the Senator has not only secured his re-election, crushed the probability of a bolt and got his course as completely endorsed as any man's could be," admitted the Indianapolis *News* with grudging admiration, "but he has destroyed all opposition to himself and buried his enemies in his own party so deep that they will not get up again much, if any, before the general resurrection. He has made himself the Republican party of Indiana, and has achieved the greatest triumph of the political fight this year. . . ."[53]

§ § §

Next to the southern question and the status of Negroes the most highly publicized political issue of the postwar years was money. Primarily this involved the policy with regard to the treasury notes or greenbacks which had been issued as a wartime measure. A related question was the extent to

[53] Indianapolis *News*, November 14, 1872. Both Colfax and Richard Thompson had been mentioned as possible contenders for Morton's seat but both refused to oppose him. Foulke, *Morton*, II, 268. Conrad Baker himself made no move to seek election to the Senate after filling his term as governor as so many of his predecessors had done. Apparently he had no further political ambitions. After he left the governorship Baker became a partner in the law firm of Baker, Hord, and [Abram W.] Hendricks, taking the position in the firm which Thomas A. Hendricks resigned when he assumed the governorship. After Hendricks retired from the governorship he once more joined the firm.

which the currency should consist of national bank notes. The system by which the national banks were apportioned gave a disproportionate number to the eastern states and relatively few to the West. This caused some critics to seek to abolish the national banks entirely, while others advocated a free banking law.[54] The money issue had potency because the wartime boom was followed by a period of economic readjustment and falling prices. Democrats were especially eager to exploit economic discontent as a means of distracting attention from their war record, but in Indiana their efforts were frustrated somewhat by reason of the fact that there was no clear-cut distinction between them and Republicans on the money question. Instead there were divisions within both parties and many inconsistencies on the part of individual politicians.

Hugh McCulloch, the Fort Wayne banker who was Secretary of the Treasury at the end of the war, was a staunch advocate of contracting the currency by withdrawing the greenbacks from circulation and returning to specie payment with all possible speed. He declared that God Almighty had created gold and silver as the only true measures of value and considered the greenbacks a "dishonored and disreputable currency" and the fact that they were legal tender he considered "dishonorable to the government and subversive of good morals." In March, 1866, McCulloch received from Congress authority to begin the withdrawal of greenbacks from circulation.[55]

On the other hand, Morton, who was more representative of Middle Western Republican opinion than McCulloch, opposed a policy of rapid contraction. In his message to the

54 George L. Anderson, "Western Attitude toward National Banks, 1873-74," *Mississippi Valley Historical Review*, XXIII (1936-1937), 205-216. See below pp. 433-439, for a further discussion of national banks.

55 Robert P. Sharkey, *Money, Class, and Party. An Economic Study of Civil War and Reconstruction* (Johns Hopkins University *Studies in Historical and Political Science*, Series LXXVII [1959], No. 2), pp. 59-60, 80, 117; Hugh McCulloch, *Our National and Financial Future. Address of Hon. Hugh McCulloch, Secretary of the Treasury at Fort Wayne, Indiana, October 11, 1865* (Fort Wayne, 1865), pp. 12-15.

legislature in 1867 he expressed himself as favorable to a return to specie payment as soon as was "consistent with maintaining business prosperity," but warned that too rapid contraction would "hazard general disaster and bankruptcy." In what was perhaps an oblique thrust at McCulloch he spoke disparagingly of "cast iron theories of finance which do not yield to the circumstances of the times" and declared that it was "the part of wisdom to make the theory . . . submit to the temporary condition of the people."[56]

The difference between McCulloch and Morton reflected the lack of unity among Republicans. On the aforementioned measure authorizing the withdrawal of greenbacks Senator Lane had voted for contraction. In the House of Representatives three Indiana Republicans had voted for contraction, while three had voted against. On a measure to halt further contraction in December, 1867, all seven Republicans from Indiana in the House voted against contraction and against McCulloch. Morton, who was in the Senate by this time, also voted against further contraction.[57]

More significantly, Hendricks, Morton's Democratic colleague, voted with Morton on the measure, and in the House all three Indiana Democrats also voted against withdrawing the greenbacks. This vote reflected a remarkable change in position. The original measure for issuing the greenbacks and making them legal tender had been passed in 1862 by

[56] Indiana *Senate Journal*, 1867, pp. 39-40. Morton and McCulloch were also at odds over Reconstruction policy. McCulloch made speeches in support of Johnson during the political campaign of 1866. William G. Carleton, "The Money Question in Indiana Politics, 1865-1890," *Indiana Magazine of History* XLII (1946), 109. N. G. Olds, a spoke and hub manufacturer in Fort Wayne, wrote to Senator John Sherman, December 11, 1866, sending him several clippings from newspapers opposing contraction and saying: "We the people endorse every word contained in the slips herewith enclosed. We demand that something be done for the improvement of our finances at once. We think it quite as necessary to look after Hugh McCulloch as His Accidency, A. J." Sharkey, *Money, Class and Party*, p. 156.

[57] *Ibid.*, p. 75; Carleton, "The Money Question in Indiana Politics," *Indiana Magazine of History*, XLII, 108.

Republican votes and over the opposition of Democrats. During the war years Democrats as hard money disciples of Andrew Jackson had been unsparing in their denunciation of greenbacks. A typical editorial in the leading Democratic newspaper in Indiana in November, 1865, expressed unalterable opposition to any increase in the amount of paper money in circulation and advocated the retirement of paper money and the increased use of gold and silver.[58]

In voting to accept greenbacks as part of the currency in 1867 Indiana Democrats were following the lead of Ohio Democrats who first advocated a series of proposals which were known variously as the "Ohio idea" or the "Pendleton Plan." The basic idea was that the war debt which had been contracted in depreciated currency should be paid in the same currency. A more conservative proposal was to give bondholders the option of being paid in greenbacks or exchanging bonds for new bonds which would pay lower interest and would be subject to taxation. Closely related to these proposals were proposals for abolishing the national banks and substituting greenbacks for bank notes and thereby saving the costs of interest.[59]

Although political expediency was undoubtedly the most important force in causing Democratic disciples of Jackson to abandon their devotion to hard money, there was a certain ideological consistency in their seeming inconsistency. A fundamental tenet of Jacksonianism had been dislike of banks and bank notes and a belief that all money should be issued

[58] Carleton, op. cit., p. 108. Indianapolis *Daily Herald,* November 27, 1865. The three Democrats in the House who voted against withdrawal of the greenbacks were William E. Niblack, William S. Holman, and Michael Kerr, all three of whom later became hard money men. See above, pp. 194-195, for the position of the Democrats on the greenbacks during the war.

[59] In Ohio George H. Pendleton, who had always been a hard money man, was persuaded to accept these proposals as a platform on which Democrats might hope to win in 1868. Sharkey, *Money, Class, and Party,* pp. 97-100. See Chester McArthur Destler, *American Radicalism 1865-1901: Essays and Documents (Connecticut College Monograph No. 3,* New London, Connecticut, 1946), pp. 32-43, for a detailed account of the genesis of the Pendleton Plan.

exclusively by the government. After the Civil War insistence upon an exclusively metallic currency would have meant drastic deflation, which would have worked such a severe hardship as to be politically impossible to many Democrats. But to avoid deflation by withdrawing greenbacks and increasing the issue of bank notes was equally unacceptable. It was easier for Democrats to accept greenbacks, "the money of the people," issued directly by the government, than to accept bank notes.[60]

By September, 1867, Judge Samuel Perkins, who as chief justice of the Indiana Supreme Court during the war had handed down two opinions denouncing greenbacks, was advocating paying for government bonds in paper money and denouncing as "wicked" legislation which required that "rich" bondholders be paid in gold "while the laborers are compelled to take depreciated currency." Daniel Voorhees was also urging that the national debt be wiped out by redeeming bonds in legal tender. Thomas Hendricks, who in 1851 in the state Constitutional Convention had denounced paper money as "a monstrous imposition and a strange delusion," was also converted to the advocacy of greenbacks to pay the national debt. Joseph McDonald, in later years a hard money man, called for the payment of the debt in greenbacks at a workingmen's rally.[61]

Democratic hopes for victory in 1868 were raised by signs of opposition to contraction in business circles. For example, a citizens' meeting in Indianapolis, which included businessmen and some bankers, called for a cessation of contraction and for the postponement of payment of the principal of the na-

[60] Sharkey, *Money, Class, and Party,* p. 106.

[61] Indianapolis *Daily Herald,* September 27, October 4, 7, 1867; Carleton, "Money Question in Indiana Politics," *Indiana Magazine of History,* XLII, 112-113. McDonald also served on the committee which drafted the money planks in the national Democratic platform in 1868. As early as July 31, 1867, the Indianapolis *Daily Herald,* the leading Democratic newspaper, had given endorsement to a pamphlet which proposed that Congress issue legal tender currency as a means of paying the national debt.

tional debt "until the people are able to pay the same without distress or impoverishment to themselves." In their state platform Democrats embraced the various features of the "Ohio idea"—payment of government bonds in greenbacks except where the law expressly called for gold, taxation of government bonds, and the abolition of national banks and the substitution of treasury notes for bank notes.[62]

Except that they did not condemn national banks, Indiana Republicans took a position almost identical with that of the Democrats on fiscal policy in 1868. Their platform called for the payment of the public debt in "legal tenders, commonly called greenbacks," except where payment in gold was specified. Republicans in Congress were praised for voting against contraction, while Democrats were blamed for having previously sanctioned contraction. Early in 1869 Morton presented to the United States Senate a joint resolution passed by the Republican-controlled Indiana legislature which opposed any law which would "reduce the present volume of the paper money in use among the people of the United States." But while Morton opposed further contraction of the currency he had begun to advocate preparation for a return to specie payments by building up a gold reserve in the treasury to use to redeem treasury notes. In December, 1868, he introduced a bill for the accumulation of gold to resume specie payment which was almost identical with the resumption law which was ultimately adopted in 1875, but the Senate committee on finance rejected his measure.[63]

By 1870 Republicans had become more cautious and equivocal on the money question. In their state platform they suggested that the Democratic proposals for paying the na-

[62] Indianapolis *Daily Herald,* January 3, 1868; Henry (comp.), *State Platforms,* p. 32. A typical editorial in the Indianapolis *Daily Herald,* January 30, 1868, condemned national bankers as "a small and privileged class," who were making immense amounts of money. It demanded that $300,000,000 in currency be issued directly by the government.

[63] Henry (comp.), *State Platforms,* p. 34; *Appletons' Annual Cyclopædia,* 1869, p. 356; Indiana *Laws,* 1869, pp. 33-34; Foulke, *Morton,* II, 74-88, 97.

tional debt constituted repudiation. They called for a "currency founded on the national credit, as abundant as the wants of the trade and commerce of the country demand." On the other hand the Democrats, in a year when the price of corn had fallen to thirty-eight cents a bushel, were more frankly inflationary than before. They opposed contraction "in the interest of the bondholders" and declared that the business interests of the country required "an increased and maintained volume of the currency." Their platform reiterated the demand for the abolition of the national banks. During the compaign the Grant administration was attacked for its policy of payment of interest in gold, and barbs were aimed at "the kid gloved aristocracy," who drew their interest in gold, "while the soldier and laborer must be content with a currency that is depreciated."[64]

In 1872 Democrats ignored all mention of money in their state platform out of a desire to avoid taking a position which might offend Liberal Republicans. Republicans praised the monetary politics of the Grant administration for having given "stability, security and increased confidence" to the business interests of the country.[65] But although the greenback question was quiescent it was by no means dead. In 1872 some Democrats undoubtedly refused to vote for Greeley because of his well-known support of hard money. The onslaught of depression in 1873 caused an intensification of interest in currency expansion which made it a powerful issue during the remainder of the decade.

§ § § §

While issues growing out of the war were dominant in national politics, at the state level there was a revival of interest in some of the reforms which the war had forced into abeyance. Among them was the question of woman's

---

[64] Henry (comp.), *State Platforms*, pp. 36-40; Indianapolis *Daily Sentinel*, January 26, September 27, 1870.

[65] Carleton, "Money Question in Indiana Politics," *Indiana Magazine of History*, XLII, 115; Indianapolis *Daily Journal*, February 23, 1872.

rights. The movement to give the ballot to Negroes gave an added impetus to the movement to enfranchise women, but the first proposal for woman suffrage was made by a Democrat, Charles B. Lasselle, who was a strong opponent of Negro suffrage. In the special session of the legislature in 1865 Lasselle introduced a resolution to amend the state constitution so as to extend suffrage to females, and the committee to which the resolution was referred favored its adoption, but it was tabled.[66]

In Congress George W. Julian, Radical Republican, led the way for an amendment to the United States Constitution by proposing in December, 1868, that suffrage be granted all citizens "without any distinction or discrimination whatever founded on race, color or sex." At the next session of Congress, after the Fifteenth Amendment had been framed, he proposed a Sixteenth Amendment prohibiting the denial of the right to vote because of sex.[67]

Meanwhile, the former Woman's Rights Association had been revived and had taken the name Indiana Woman's Suffrage Convention. Its 1869 convention endorsed Julian's proposal and called on "all true patriots and lovers of temperance and moral purity to unite upon Woman's Suffrage, as presented in the 16th Amendment, as the rallying cry of the next political canvass." They added: "While our laws are being reconstructed so as to give the elective franchise to colored men, they should not forget the women of the country, who are surely as competent to use that power judiciously as those who have so recently been in the degradation of chattel slavery."[68]

---

[66] Indiana *House Journal*, special session 1865, pp. 316, 455.

[67] Clarke, *George W. Julian*, p. 315.

[68] *Appletons' Annual Cyclopædia*, 1869, p. 360; Minutes of Woman's Rights Association, p. 51. In other resolutions adopted in 1869 the women declared: "That woman's possession of the elective franchise would eventually be the means of the entire overthrow of the liquor traffic throughout the land." They also declared that "it would be unworthy of the philanthropic character of woman, to oppose the ratification of the 15th amendment to the Constitution,

In 1871 a committee of the women appeared before the legislature to ask for the removal of political restrictions against their sex. Their memorial was presented to the committee on rights and privileges, which made a report in which the majority expressed the opinion that it was not expedient to submit the question of woman's suffrage to the voters at the present time, but the minority recommended a constitutional amendment.[69]

The report led to the most serious debate on the subject which had yet been heard in the legislative halls of Indiana. One of the supporters of the proposal ridiculed the argument that women should not vote because the atmosphere at the polls was not a suitable place for women. This he said was really an argument for the disfranchisement of men. "Where you find a man opposed to putting any other human being on an equality with himself as far as political rights are concerned—if opposed to giving either man or woman equal chances with him in the race of life," he said, "I will show you a man who is a coward . . . fearful of being left way behind in the race."

To such unconventional views another member replied that there was no evidence that a majority of either sex wanted the amendment—an amendment which he declared would "revolutionize society, array the sexes against each other and against themselves." God, he said, had prepared woman for a different role from that of man—a deduction he found "warranted by Revelation and by the anatomy of the two sexes." Moreover if women were allowed to vote they would want to hold offices, and in order to be elected a woman would have to "throw off the mantle of her modesty, banish all her female qualities." Such results he felt would be "suicidal to society," and he predicted that women would refuse "to expose themselves to the vulgar rowdyism of men on election days."

<hr/>

although the framers of it refused to recognize the equal rights of woman in that amendment." Minutes of Woman's Rights Association, pp. 50-51.

[69] *Brevier Legislative Reports,* XII (1871), 125, 278-279, 292-293; Indiana *Senate Journal,* 1871, p. 603.

By a vote of 27 to 20 the Senate voted to reject the recommendation for an amendment.[70]

Governor Baker transmitted a memorial of the American Woman Suffrage Association to the 1873 session of the legislature. He asked that it be given thoughtful consideration, adding that he himself was willing to support giving women the right to vote "whenever they shall with any considerable degree of unanimity signify a desire to assume the responsibilities which such a change in their relations to the State would impose." This argument, that most women were not interested in voting, was used frequently. One member of the House introduced a resolution that a referendum be conducted among the female population of the state with the proviso that if a majority of adult women voted in favor of suffrage that women should thereafter be allowed to vote on equal terms with men.[71]

In spite of rebuffs the suffragists persisted. No serious consideration was given their pleas during the remainder of the seventies, but in 1881 both houses of the legislature adopted resolutions for a constitutional amendment which would remove the word "male" from the constitutional article on suffrage. This seeming victory proved illusory, however. At the next session the House again passed the resolutions, as required by the state constitution before an amendment could be submitted to the voters. But the Senate failed to take action, thereby killing the amendment.[72]

Meanwhile, even though they did not have the right to vote, women continued to be active in the crusade for legislation outlawing the manufacture and sale of strong drink. But in spite of the efforts of women's groups and church groups politicians showed little inclination to press for stronger

[70] *Brevier Legislative Reports*, XII (1871), 494-497; *Appletons' Annual Cyclopædia*, 1871, p. 407.

[71] Charles Kettleborough, *Constitution Making in Indiana* . . . (3 volumes, *Indiana Historical Collections*, I, II, XVII, Indianapolis, 1916, 1930), II, 124-126. See a typical editorial in Indianapolis *Daily Journal*, June 2, 1874.

[72] Kettleborough, *Constitution Making in Indiana*, II, 194-195, 232-233.

temperance legislation. An important reason for this was the fact that Germans, who constituted a substantial number of voters, made it clear that they would support no party which advocated prohibitory laws. "We want no more oppressive Temperance Laws under any guise or shape whatever," announced an address by Germans to state party leaders in 1866. "What have the mischievous men, agitating such prohibitory laws, accomplished in the past? Nothing. What will they accomplish in the future? Nothing." On the contrary, temperance agitation, said the Germans, "stirs up strife and hatred among the citizens, increases secret vice, hypocrisy and espionage, burthens our courts with thousands of infamous suits," and discouraged Germans from settling in the state.[73]

But the temperance cause remained alive in the churches, and in 1868 a State Temperance Alliance made up of church groups was organized. In 1872 they prepared to fight for "total prohibition" and "utter extirpation" of the manufacture and sale of intoxicants. They went so far as to advocate a constitutional amendment which would require all state officers to take an oath that they would abstain from the use of intoxicants during their term in office.[74]

Prohibition advocates were divided among themselves as to whether to organize a third party. One group insisted that both major parties ignored the temperance cause and that therefore a separate ticket should be organized. Others felt that a separate ticket would hurt the temperance cause by drawing away Republican votes and thereby benefit the Democrats. The Indianapolis *Journal* repeatedly expressed opposition to such a third-party movement. Nevertheless in 1872 a small group insisted upon nominating a state Prohibition ticket, which polled only an infinitesimal vote. So far

[73] Minutes of Woman's Rights Association, p. 50; Indianapolis *Telegraph* quoted in Indianapolis *Daily Herald*, February 22, 1866.

[74] Goodwin, *Seventy-six Years' Tussle with the Traffic*, p. 24; Dunn, *Indiana and Indianans*, II, 1056; Indianapolis *Daily Journal*, February 8, March 1, 1872.

as the two major parties were concerned, except for reference to Thomas Browne's personal habits, the temperance question played no part in the 1872 campaign. But at the 1873 session of the legislature, a new liquor law known as the "Baxter Bill" was adopted. The measure, which resembled the law of 1853, which had been invalidated by the state Supreme Court, did not require a special election as that law had done, but provided that an application for permission to sell liquor could be granted only if a majority of voters in any ward, town, or township signed a petition. The measure was passed primarily by votes of Republicans, who were in a majority in both houses, but it was signed by Hendricks, the Democratic governor, without comment. It was strongly opposed by German groups and by the liquor interests, but its constitutionality was upheld in a test case.[75]

As soon as the law was passed a fight to repeal it was begun, while temperance forces girded themselves for the struggle to keep it on the statute books. Early in 1874 the German State Press Association adopted resolutions which denounced the Baxter law and criticized efforts "to produce general sobriety by the enactment of more or less stringent prohibitory laws." The association declared that they would not support any candidate for office who favored the Baxter law. About the same time women in various parts of the state embarked upon a crusade of "moral suasion," intended to bring about the complete abolition of the liquor business. Their method was to visit all saloons and liquor stores, where they offered prayers for the proprietors, entreated them to give up their business, and sought to force them to sign pledges that they would do so. In one town where they were

75 *Ibid.,* April 3, 4, 1872; February 21, 1873; Indiana *Laws,* 1873, pp. 151-158; Dunn, *Indiana and Indianans,* II, 1056; Groesch *v.* the State, 42 Ind. 547 (1873). The Supreme Court held that the act did not violate Sec. 1, Art. IV of the Indiana constitution by committing the legislative power to the people, nor did it violate the prohibition against the enactment of local or special legislation. The National Prohibition party appeared for the first time in a national election in 1872.

refused admittance to a saloon a band of ladies knelt in the street and prayed during a severe snowstorm. The crusade, which began in Shelbyville in January, 1874, spread like wildfire through the state causing great excitement.[76]

The temperance question played an important part in the city elections in the spring of 1874. At Crawfordsville, Bloomington, Wabash, Anderson, Franklin, and New Albany temperance forces were victorious. But at Goshen, Richmond, Angola, Muncie, Peru, and Jeffersonville anti-temperance tickets were reported to have triumphed. In Indianapolis, where there was an unusually lively campaign and a larger vote than usual, Democrats won control of the city council for the first time in fourteen years. Undoubtedly unrest arising from the economic depression played a part, but the outcome was also a victory for the anti-temperance forces. The Indianapolis *Journal* attributed the Republican defeat to the "ill-conceived and misdirected zeal of the so-called temperance people"—especially the activities of the women crusaders, who were conspicuous at the polling places.[77]

In their state platform in 1874 the Republicans endorsed the Baxter law, but in the ensuing campaign they ignored the temperance question. The Democratic platform called the Baxter law a failure and demanded a license law. At the state convention Hendricks said that he disapproved of the Baxter law but had signed it because it represented the will of the legislature and did not violate the constitution. The Democrats were victorious in the state elections and won control of the legislature. The outcome was probably more a symptom of economic unrest than a mandate for the repeal of the Baxter law, but a new liquor law was adopted in 1875. It

[76] Dunn, *Indiana and Indianans*, II, 1059-1060; Indianapolis *Daily Journal*, January 22, February 26, March 13, 1874. Within a month there were reports of activities by women crusaders in Cambridge City, Columbus, Lafayette, Jeffersonville, Lebanon, Anderson, Richmond, Valparaiso, La Porte, Princeton, Terre Haute, Ellettsville, Union City, and Noblesville. *Ibid.*, February 14, 16, 18, 19, 20, 21, 24, 1874.

[77] *Ibid.*, May 6, 1874.

gave the county commissioners authority to license persons selling liquor.[78]

The temperance forces grew in number in spite of their failure to win political support. During the late seventies the "ribbon movements" swept Indiana. One of these was the "Blue Ribbon" movement, founded in the East in 1876 by an ex-drunkard named Murphy, who persuaded thousands to sign a pledge not to drink and to don a blue ribbon as a sign. There were Blue Ribbon groups in Indiana, but the Red Ribbon movement, which had similar objectives, appears to have won more adherents. It had some of the fervor of a religious revival. Night after night reformed drunkards testified at revival-like meetings, pleading with their audience to take the pledge. In Indianapolis during the spring of 1877 hundreds were reported to be signing the pledge every night. By 1879, in addition to the Blue Ribbon Order, the Red Ribbon Order, and the Ladies White Ribbon Club, there were in the state the Women's Christian Temperance Union, the Independent Order of Good Templars, the Prohibition League, the State Reform Club, and a Prohibition party— all dedicated to the extermination of the liquor traffic. In 1879 all of these groups united into a Grand Council for the purpose of working for an amendment to the state constitution prohibiting the manufacture and sale of intoxicants.[79]

Although the state legislature failed to enact the woman's suffrage amendment or prohibition measures, both of which were being urged on moral grounds, it took a step in the direction of moral reform in 1873 when it amended the law on divorce. A law adopted in 1852 provided that divorces should be granted on specific grounds such as adultery and cruel treatment or for "any other cause for which the court shall deem it proper that a divorce shall be granted." Per-

[78] *Ibid.,* June 11, 1874; Goodwin, *Seventy-six Years' Tussle with the Traffic,* p. 26; Dunn, *Indiana and Indianans,* II, 703; Indiana *Laws,* special session, 1875, pp. 55-59.

[79] Indianapolis *Daily Journal,* May 1, 2, 7, 14, 1877; May 15, 22, August 13, 1879; Dunn, *Indiana and Indianans,* II, 1060.

sons seeking divorce were required to prove "to the satisfaction of the court" that they had resided in the state for
one year. These lax requirements made Indiana a mecca for
persons seeking quick dissolution of matrimonial bonds. Critics
called the law "almost a realization of the hopes of the most
progressive free lover." The *New York Medical Gazette*
reported that immense numbers of divorces were granted in
Indiana each year, and that probably a majority of the applicants were persons who took up temporary residence solely
for the purpose of taking advantage of the law. "Any discontented couple can be released from marital bonds by our
courts whenever they ask for it," said the Indianapolis *Journal.* It admitted that occasionally young attorneys with ob-
scure clients were unsuccessful. "But if any of our married
and discontented friends will secure a high pressure firm of
lawyers to prepare their papers . . . the irreversible decree
of divorce will surely come."[80]

In his message to the legislature in 1871 Governor Baker
advocated the tightening of the divorce law so that "Indiana
divorces would cease to be advertised in any of the Atlantic
cities as marketable commodities. . . ." In 1873 the legislature changed the law so as to require a bona fide residence
of two years and forbade the person obtaining a divorce to
remarry for two years. Divorces were to be granted for only
those causes specifically stated in the law.[81]

Another field where reform was badly needed was the legislation governing voting requirements and the conduct of
elections. For years before the war governors had been pointing out the abuses which resulted from lax laws. In his mes-

[80] *Revised Statutes of Indiana* 1852, II, 234-235; Gavin and Hord (eds.),
Statutes of Indiana (2 volumes, Indianapolis, 1870), II, 350-351; Indianapolis
Daily Journal, June 22, 1871; *New York Medical Gazette,* quoted *ibid.,* Jan-
uary 5, 1871.

Indiana's lax divorce laws led German-born Heinrich Schliemann to come
to Indianapolis in the spring of 1869 to obtain a divorce from his Russian wife.
See Eli Lilly (ed.), *Heinrich Schliemann in Indianapolis* (Indiana Historical Society, 1961).

[81] Indiana *Senate Journal,* 1871, p. 62; Indiana *Laws,* 1873, pp. 107-112.

sage of 1867 Morton pointed out that it was "a notorious
fact" that under the law "men go to the polls and vote, who
at the time have not the right to vote anywhere; that men
vote in precincts and townships where they do not reside, and
often vote several times on the same day, at difference places,
and sometimes at the same place." After considerable wrangling a measure was enacted which provided that voters must
reside in a township, city, or ward for twenty days prior to
an election and must be registered by a bipartisan board. The
law also provided that all ballots must be plain white paper
without any distinguishing marks. In 1869 this measure was
revised, and a provision was added which prohibited persons
who had bet on the outcome of an election from sitting on
election boards! Two years later the requirement of twenty
days residence was declared unconstitutional on the grounds
that the state constitution provided only that a voter reside
in a township or precinct and did not specify the length of
time.[82]

At the 1873 session of the legislature Hendricks recommended a constitutional amendment fixing a residential requirement for voting. A resolution was adopted by both
houses proposing an amendment which required a residence
of one year in the state (instead of six months), three months
in the county, and thirty days in the township or precinct.
Another resolution, which also was recommended by Hendricks, provided that general elections be held in November
instead of October. This would have the effect of making
state and Federal elections occur at the same time and would
bring Indiana into line with the practices of other states. At
the same session other resolutions were passed for amendments to delete the constitutional provisions limiting suffrage
to whites and providing for the exclusion and colonization of
Negroes—provisions which had already been made inopera-
tive by judicial decisions and the Fifteenth Amendment. For

[82] Indiana *Senate Journal,* 1867, pp. 26-27; Indiana *Laws,* 1867, pp. 113-120;
special session, 1869, pp. 58-61; Quinn *v.* the State, 35 Ind. 485-486 (1871).

Article XIII, the Negro exclusion article, it was proposed to substitute an article limiting the bonded indebtedness of municipalities.[83]

All of these proposed constitutional amendments were killed when the 1875 session failed to vote favorably upon them. Consequently the whole process of enacting them had to begin again. In 1877 similar resolutions were passed. The only significant change was in the article dealing with the residence requirement for voting. It retained the existing requirement of six months' residence in the state but added a requirement of sixty days' residence in the township and thirty days in the ward or precinct. In 1879 these proposed amendments were passed a second time, as required by the constitution. The next step was to submit them to the voters. This was done at the regular spring elections in April, 1880. A majority of the persons voting on the amendments voted in favor of them, and Governor James D. Williams accordingly declared them adopted. But a few months later the Indiana Supreme Court held that they were not in force. The opinion of the court rested on the interpretation of the provision in the constitution which required that a "majority of the electors" vote in favor of proposed amendments. Although a majority of the persons who voted on the amendments had voted in favor of them, many persons who voted in the election for local officials held at the same time failed to vote either for or against the amendments. Hence the total number of persons voting for the amendments did not constitute a majority of the electors voting in the election. In consequence of this decision a special election was called in 1881 for the sole purpose of voting on the amendments. At this election a majority voted for them and they were finally declared to be a part of the constitution.[84]

[83] Indiana *House Journal,* 1873, pp. 79-80; Kettleborough, *Constitution Making in Indiana,* II, 117-120, 123-124, 140-141.

[84] *Ibid.,* pp. 130-131, 137, 151-155, 166-169, 204-207; State *v.* Swift, 69 Ind. 505 (1880).

Meanwhile, the legislature had attempted to reform itself by outlawing the practice of bolting, which had been used at various times by both parties to block legislation. A law passed in 1867 provided that whenever there was no quorum by reason of "the wilful, or intentional absence of any member" with the intent "to defeat, delay, or obstruct legislation," the absent member was declared to be guilty of a misdemeanor and subject to a fine of one thousand dollars. The law put an end to the old system of bolting but led to the adoption of new obstructionist tactics. As has already been shown Democrats resorted to mass resignations in 1869 in an attempt to block ratification of the Fifteenth Amendment. In 1871 thirty-four Republicans brought the legislative session to an abrupt close by resigning and thereby making a quorum impossible. Their resignation was in protest against a reapportionment bill which they said was unconstitutional. At the special session of 1872, which was controlled by Republicans, the state was redistricted for both legislative and Congressional representation. This time the Democratic minority cried that the reapportionment was an outrageous gerrymander. Reapportionment continued to be a source of partisan wrangling. In 1876 Republicans won nine of thirteen Congressional seats although in the state as a whole Democrats cast seven thousand more votes for members of Congress than did Republicans. Democrats regarded this as evidence of the inequity of the apportionment. In 1879 a Democratic-controlled legislature passed an apportionment bill which the Democratic governor, Williams, signed, saying it met with his entire approval. The Indianapolis *Sentinel* considered it "a vast improvement" over the "Republican gerrymander" which it superseded, but the Republican *Journal* disagreed.[85]

85 Indiana *Laws*, 1867, p. 131; *Appletons' Annual Cyclopædia*, 1871, p. 408; 1872, p. 398; Indianapolis *Daily Sentinel*, March 12, 21, 1879. According to the Indianapolis *Sentinel*, if the whole voting population of the state could have been divided equally each district would have contained 34,694 voters. The bill

The violence and the tendency for private groups to take the law into their own hands which had characterized the fifties and the war years continued into the postwar period. Examples of lynchings were numerous. Early in 1867 two men who were charged with murdering an old woman in an attempted robbery were taken from the jail in Jackson County by a mob and hanged. The lynchers wore no disguises and according to reports "did their work in a quiet and orderly manner." Later in the same year a similar group broke into the Johnson County jail and carried off and hanged a man who was charged with murder in connection with a robbery.[85]

A daring railroad robbery in 1868 resulted in two separate hanging bees. In May, 1868, a gang of desperadoes robbed a car belonging to the Adams Express Company on the Jeffersonville Railroad. Some of the robbers were arrested soon afterwards and jailed in Cincinnati. While they were en route to Seymour for trial the train on which they were riding was stopped by members of the vigilance committee of Seymour. The prisoners were carried off, compelled to confess, and summarily hanged. The vigilance committee then published a proclamation in which they declared their intention of treating all thieves in a similar manner. If property was stolen or honest men harmed, they warned: ". . . we will *swing by the neck,* until they be dead, every thieving character we can lay our hands on, *without inquiring whether we have the persons who committed that particular crime or not.*" In December the committee completed its work by breaking into the New Albany jail and seizing and hanging four more men who were accused of taking part in the robbery.[87]

passed in 1879 created districts in which the number of voters ranged from 31,000 to 35,000. Indianapolis *Daily Sentinel,* March 11, 1879.

86 Cincinnati *Commercial,* quoted in Indianapolis *Daily Herald,* April 2 and November 2, 1867.

87 Indianapolis *Daily Sentinel,* May 25, December 14, 1868; *Appletons' Annual Cyclopædia,* 1868, p. 379. The robbers seized the train south of Seymour when it had stopped for water. They knocked the engineer senseless, detached the engine and baggage car from the rest of the train, and roared away at high speed. They abandoned the train after rifling the baggage car of as

In his 1869 message to the legislature Governor Baker reported that during the past two years more than a dozen prisoners had been taken from the authorities and hanged. He urged the legislature to make it a felony to join an organization which had as its object "the usurpation of the functions of the judiciary by condemning and punishing others for real or pretended offenses." But the legislature failed to act.[88]

In 1871 a mob stormed the jail at Charlestown in Clark County and carried off three Negroes and hanged them. The victims had been jailed on very flimsy evidence in connection with the murder of a white family. They were probably not guilty and the grand jury had failed to return an indictment against them. This mob action led Governor Baker to issue a proclamation calling upon local authorities to suppress illegal organizations. He threatened to call upon the Federal government (under the Force acts passed in connection with Reconstruction) for assistance in quelling illegal mobs. No such action was taken, however, and the press continued to carry frequent accounts of mob activity.[89]

In 1873 a mob of masked men broke into the office of the clerk of Crawford County and mutilated records and carried off public papers in order to prevent the further prose-

---

much as $42,000. The vigilantes, who came from Seymour to New Albany by rail, were masked and heavily armed. They gained access to the jail by shooting the sheriff in the arm and taking his keys. The hangings were performed within the jail.

[88] Indiana *Senate Journal*, 1869, pp. 46-47. A joint resolution was introduced in the Senate to appropriate $10,000 for the governor to expend in order to detect and bring to punishment persons guilty of high crimes. The sponsor of the resolution said that the appropriation was needed because local authorities did not offer rewards and were not active in apprehending those responsible for lynchings. The resolution failed to pass. *Brevier Legislative Reports*, X (1869), 264-268.

[89] James M. Hiatt, *Murder and Mob Law in Indiana! The Slaughter of the Park Family!! and the Lynching of the Negroes Taylor, Davis, and Johnson* (Indianapolis, 1872); Thornbrough, *Negro in Indiana*, pp. 277-278; Indianapolis *Daily Sentinel*, November 24, 1871; *Appletons' Annual Cyclopædia*, 1871, p. 410.

cution of a case pending in court. About the same time a notorious criminal was lynched at Salem in Washington County. These events caused Governor Hendricks to issue a proclamation calling for the end of secret vigilance bands and calling upon local law enforcement officials to bring criminals to speedy justice so that there would be no excuse for defiance of the law. But in spite of the action of the Governor, lynchings and other activities by vigilance groups continued unabated. During July, 1874, for example, one group of regulators almost beat a man to death in Brown County, while in Orange County another group hanged a feeble-minded man who was suspected of theft. In 1878, in an especially shocking episode, a mob overpowered the guards of the jail in Mount Vernon in Posey County and seized five Negroes who had been arrested for forcing their way into a house of white prostitutes. One of the prisoners was butchered on the spot, while the other four were marched to the town square and hanged. There had been rumors that the Governor was sending militia to prevent the lynching, but there is no evidence that local authorities requested troops and none were sent. In 1879, when the sheriff of Washington County asked for troops, the Governor sent fifty militia men to prevent a prisoner who was accused of murder from being lynched. But local officials seldom requested assistance and usually made no effort to prevent mob law.[90]

Some lynchings were carried out by groups organized as the result of a particular incident. But in some counties, especially in the southern part of the state, vigilance committees apparently operated more or less continuously. For example, in 1879 it was reported that a group of regulators in Harrison County had served notices on several people, warning them to "walk a bee line in the way of good behavior" toward their community and families or face the

[90] Indianapolis *Daily Journal,* July 1, 12, 1873; November 1, 1879; Indianapolis *Daily Sentinel,* July 4, 22, 1874; Thornbrough, *Negro in Indiana,* pp. 278-279.

prospect of a whipping.[91] Activities of vigilance groups were frequently defended on the grounds that local law enforcement officials were lax or corrupt. These same officials acquiesced in the beatings and lynchings perpetrated by the vigilantes. They made little or no effort to prevent them from breaking into jails. The identity of the leaders was usually well known, but no efforts were made to indict them. Governors deplored mob activity but did little to use the authority of the state to suppress it, and the legislature failed to do anything to penalize lynchings or to strengthen local law enforcement.

[91] Indianapolis *Daily Sentinel,* March 28, 1879.

CHAPTER VII

DEPRESSION AND POLITICS 1873-1879

IN SEPTEMBER, 1873, the failure of Jay Cooke and Company signalled the beginning of the Panic of 1873. The failure of the famous New York banking house was quickly followed by the announcement of the closing of other banks and the bankruptcies of many railroads and businesses. What appeared at first to be a financial panic developed into a prolonged depression of unprecedented severity. Although Indiana remained primarily rural and agricultural, the Panic of 1873 had a profound impact upon the state. Depression had consequences which significantly affected politics and government. Old issues like Reconstruction and the corruption of the Grant administration were overshadowed by economic problems. The state was confronted with unemployment and bankruptcies which led to demands for government action. Depression increased the clamor against railroads and other corporations. Hard times stimulated political activity on the part of both workers and farmers. But the most obvious political result of depression was greatly increased interest in the money question. No other issue received as much attention in the seventies. The position of both the old parties was wavering and equivocal. Their failure to give unqualified support to inflation gave an impetus to formation of a third party. Much of the genesis of the Greenback party movement came from Indiana, and the "Indiana Plan" became its platform.

The immediate reaction in the press and in business and financial circles was to minimize the importance of the financial panic and to insist that it was an eastern phenomenon which could have little effect upon Indiana. A typical editorial in the Indianapolis *Journal* was entitled "Keep Cool."

Business in Indianapolis, it said, was better than ever before. "There is no danger if we don't make it ourselves." The next day it was reported that Indianapolis banks were confident and that the "scare" was over, although depositors were advised against panicking and thereby forcing the banks to close. From Fort Wayne came reports that all was "serene" in that city and that "no one shows the least symptom of uneasiness." A few days later an Indianapolis man compared the "late panic" to the "epizootic, which commenced in New York and traveled westward." It had passed over Indianapolis, he said, "leaving business dull, but not materially damaging trade."[1]

Press dispatches were determinedly optimistic, but it was apparent that Indiana as well as New York was in a financial panic which was soon affecting business generally. Banks were refusing to pay out more than small sums of money. Almost immediately a group of representatives of banks and industries in Indianapolis met to discuss their common problems, especially whether to reduce wages or to dismiss employees. Some employers at once announced plans to pay workers on a monthly rather than a weekly basis in view of the currency stringency. Both Indianapolis and Lafayette began paying their city employees in warrants because there was no money in their treasuries due to the banking crisis. In Lafayette the workers had difficulty in disposing of their warrants even at a discount of 10 per cent. At a second meeting a group of Indianapolis manufacturers adopted resolutions in which they said that there was no panic except in banking. They agreed that it would be unwise for manufacturers to enter into any sort of agreement to cut wages or employment. Instead each establishment was left free to pursue whatever course seemed best for it.[2]

Within a few weeks there were reports of hundreds of unemployed vainly seeking work at the pork-packing establishments

1 Indianapolis *Daily Journal*, September 26, 27, October 1, 1873.

2 *Ibid.*, October 1, 2, 6, 1873.

in Indianapolis. Even earlier the Ohio Falls Car and Locomotive Company at Jeffersonville had suspended operations,
throwing seven hundred men out of work. Everywhere there
were reports of reduction of working forces or at least reduction in hours and wages. When workers at the New Albany
Rolling Mills struck in protest over wage cuts, the Indianapolis *Journal* reported that the manager was glad that the
men had struck. "He did not wish to stop the works, but
as the men have taken the matter in hand and stopped for
him, he is satisfied to let them shoulder the responsibility."
The *Journal* correspondent predicted that the strikers would
suffer more than the owners and they would "be glad to work
at even a greater reduction before next spring sets in." In
December of 1873 workers at rolling mills in Indianapolis
protested a wage cut of 20 per cent and being paid partly
in notes rather than cash. But they were reported returning
to work on these terms—because, like other workers in Indianapolis, they had "concluded that winter work at a reduced
scale of prices is preferable to idleness." At the year's end
all engineers on the railroads operated by the Pennsylvania
Company went on strike in protest against wage cuts.[3]

Even before the end of October the Ladies Relief Society
of Indianapolis was making arrangements for a soup kitchen
to feed the "suffering poor" during the coming winter. A
debate developed over where the money to take care of the
needy was to come from. Plans were made to have an evening
of entertainment at the Academy of Music to raise funds, and
the Indianapolis *Journal* urged a series of lectures to provide
money for relief activities.[4]

It was soon obvious that purely voluntary methods were
going to be inadequate. A committee composed of representatives of private charitable societies in Indianapolis asked that
all charitable activities be co-ordinated under a commissioner

[3] Indianapolis *Daily Journal*, September 30, November 3, 6, December 8,
1873. See below, Chapter X, pages 451-460, for a more detailed account of
labor troubles in this period.

[4] Indianapolis *Daily Journal*, October 28, November 4, 10, 1873.

appointed and paid by the city council. They expressed the opinion that fund raising would be "more equitably distributed by appropriations from the public treasury" and urged that the city council at once put under way all public works which had been planned for the following year in order to furnish employment. The Indianapolis *Journal* opposed appropriating city funds for a soup kitchen or to pay a commissioner of charity, but it was favorable to accelerated spending of city money on public works. "The idea of dispensing with private organizations and individual effort and pensioning the city poor, deserving and undeserving, on the city treasury," it declared, "is wrong in principle and would be demoralizing in practice." The city council refused to vote for the commissioner but agreed to appropriate the sum of $2,000 for poor relief! The working men of the city replied by sponsoring a rally at which they called for public works to provide employment "for the numbers of working men now suffering destitution and almost starvation."[5]

The hard times of the winter of 1873 were but the prelude to several years in which economic conditions grew progressively worse. Year after year the number of business failures in Indiana increased, the ranks of the unemployed grew, and farm prices continued to plummet.[6] Workers resorted to strikes in futile protest against wage cuts. The unemployed increasingly demanded that government take steps to ameliorate their condition. In May, 1876, over a thousand jobless workers met in the State House yard to consider ways of

[5] *Ibid.,* November 7, 12, 13, 25, December 2, 22, 1873.

[6] Failures of Businesses in Indiana, 1872-1877

1872	80	$ 991,000
1873	134	2,200,000
1874	167	2,397,000
1875	332	4,804,052
1876	362	4,787,400
First half of 1877	178	2,234,886

These figures were compiled by R. G. Dun and Co. and were published in the Indianapolis *Daily Sentinel,* July 14, 1877.

alleviating their distress. The meeting was an orderly one. The principal speaker declared that "earnest desire for honest work must not be mistaken for threats of communism." He urged a move to persuade the city council to put two thousand men to work on city improvements. "We want work, and will have it," he insisted. The city council responded by increasing the force of the street commissioner somewhat and by creating a Citizens Relief Committee, which raised funds from private sources for immediate relief. Governor Hendricks sent a message to a second mass meeting of unemployed in which he stated that the state could do nothing for their relief which was not provided for by law. He expressed sympathy for their plight, promising as rapid action as possible in carrying out construction projects which had already been authorized by the legislature.[7]

Mayor John Caven, a Republican, who had just been elected, responded more imaginatively to the unemployment problem by recommending the establishment of a Union Stockyards and a Belt Railroad for the use of all railroads coming into Indianapolis. These projects, which were to be privately owned, would be underwritten by public funds, and would serve the dual purpose of creating employment and bringing business to the city. There were expectations that about four hundred men would be employed.[8]

Unfortunately work on the project could not begin until after the 1877 session of the legislature had adopted special legislation authorizing the city to underwrite it. As plans advanced several hundred more unemployed men came to the city in hopes of securing construction work, but it was announced that only bona fide residents of Indianapolis would be hired.[9]

When work on the Belt Railroad failed to materialize, two or three hundred workers met and prepared a petition to the

[7] Indianapolis *Daily Sentinel,* May 31, June 2, 3, 4, 1876.
[8] Indianapolis *Daily Journal,* April 26, 1877.
[9] *Ibid.,* April 3, 11, 1877.

mayor and city aldermen, saying: "We . . . who have exhausted all the means in our power to obtain employment and failed, do now most respectfully ask and pray that you give us work or devise some means by which we can relieve our suffering families." The city council said it had no funds and asked the mayor to appoint a committee of influential citizens to propose ways of dealing with the emergency.[10] The committee simply referred the whole question back to the city government, expressing the hope that work on the Belt Railroad would solve the problem. They came to the not surprising conclusion that the demand for labor in Indianapolis was not sufficient to employ all workers and advised that the "only permanent remedy for existing evils" was "the withdrawal of a reasonable number of laborers from this field." "We believe," they concluded, "that if a few hundred could find employment elsewhere there would be a sufficient demand for labor here to employ the rest." They recommended that the unemployed be encouraged to seek work on farms, where there were "untold millions of uncultivated lands and remunerative prices for farm products."[11]

This exercise in futility was scarcely over when Indianapolis and other railroad centers in the state were confronted by a far more serious threat to law and order—the great railroad strikes of the summer of 1877, which in Indiana, as in the rest of the country, were the most serious labor troubles of the depression years. Earlier strikes, during the administration of Governor Hendricks, had led to the use of troops on a small scale. In the spring of 1873, after a prolonged and bitter strike in the coal mines of Clay County, a riot

10 *Ibid.*, May 30, June 2, 1877.
11 *Ibid.*, June 6, 1877. At a second meeting of the unemployed where there were threats of staging a demonstration if the city did not act, the Indianapolis *Journal* professed to find "considerable communistic feeling." The *Journal* urged the churches in the city to take up a special collection for the needy. It advised the workers: "The sooner you stop holding public meetings and listening to inflammatory harangues from self-constituted leaders, the better it will be for both yourselves and the city. You do your cause great injury by these proceedings." *Ibid.*

occurred between striking white miners and Negro strike breakers. At the request of local authorities Hendricks sent in about eighty guardsmen.[12] The following winter there was a strike by employees of the Pennsylvania Railroad which was the largest strike in the United States up to that time. In Indiana disorders at Logansport led the sheriff to call for aid, and Hendricks sent in a few guardsmen, but the Indianapolis *Journal* was critical of him for not taking more drastic action and not acting in Indianapolis and other places where transportation was paralyzed. During the summer of 1876 employees of the Ohio and Mississippi Railroad in towns in Indiana went on strike after prolonged failure of the company to pay wages was followed by an announcement of an additional wage cut. Sheriffs of the counties involved called upon the governor to send troops. The strike occurred during the political campaign when Hendricks was the candidate for Vice-President. He was out of the state at the time the strike began. On his return he issued a statement in which he said that failure to pay wages was no excuse for the strike and that the workers should seek redress through the courts. He called upon the strikers to go back to work but left the matter of law enforcement up to local authorities and did not send in any troops.[13]

The strikes of 1877 involved larger numbers and had more serious consequences than these earlier labor disputes. They began in the East as the result of the announcement of wage cuts and spread westward. Almost simultaneously there were work stoppages in Fort Wayne, Indianapolis, Terre Haute, Evansville, and in lesser centers, like Elkhart and Vincennes. Movement of freight trains on most lines came to a standstill at once. At first passenger trains were allowed to run, but later they too were stopped, and transportation throughout the state was paralyzed. In Fort Wayne, where

[12] Indianapolis *Daily Journal,* April 16, 17, 1873. See Chapter X, pages 451-452.

[13] Indianapolis *Daily Journal,* December 27, 29, 30, 31, 1873; Indianapolis *Daily Sentinel,* August 12, 15, 16, 1876.

there was some violence, the mayor called upon Governor Williams for troops. The Governor replied that he would send troops only as a last resort—and only to protect life and property and not to interfere between the companies and their employees. The Adjutant General had the militia in a state of readiness but announced that in no case would they be used to assist in running trains. In Indianapolis all transportation was at a standstill, and huge crowds were assembled at the Union depot, but there were no serious disorders. Both Mayor Caven, who was a Republican, and Governor Williams, a Democrat, adopted a conciliatory attitude toward the strikers and refused to be pushed into using force. Both the Indianapolis *News* and the *Journal* were impatient with Williams. The *Journal* probably spoke the truth when it declared: "There is great regret on the part of many citizens that Senator Morton is not Governor of Indiana now."[14]

The railroad operators, unable to persuade Williams to call out the militia, turned to Walter Q. Gresham, Federal District Judge. A peculiar legal situation existed because of the fact that several of the lines which were on strike were in the hands of receivers appointed by the Federal courts. Gresham, who was less sympathetic with the strikers than Williams and more fearful of violence, on his own initiative asked President Hayes for troops, but was informed that none were available. From Judge Thomas Drummond, of the Federal Circuit Court, Gresham received an opinion that in the present circumstances a United States marshal had the authority to call for whatever assistance was needed to protect life and property. Gresham thereupon declared that the community was in the hands of a mob and called for the organization of a committee of public safety and proceeded to enroll troops to use if necessary. The committee named by Gresham included such distinguished persons as

14 Indianapolis *Daily Sentinel,* July 23- 26, 1877; Indianapolis *Daily Journal,* quoted *ibid.,* July 26, 1877.

ex-Governor Baker, Senator McDonald, and Benjamin Harrison.

Governor Williams then issued a proclamation in which he said that the peace of the community was threatened and that court processes were the remedies for the grievances of the strikers. He called upon the strikers to desist lest he be compelled to take more extreme measures. A committee of arbitration was named to hear reports from both employers and strikers. Judge Gresham told the strikers to go back to work, and members of the committee assured them that justice would be done them. After this the strike began to collapse. By August 1, the strikes, which had begun on July 22, were virtually at an end. Most of the men returned to work without any promise of wage restoration. Federal troops arrived in Indianapolis to be present when the freight trains started rolling, but there were no disorders and the troops were not needed.[15]

After the strikes were over, fifteen of the men who had participated in them were arrested and charged with contempt for interfering with the operation of lines which were in receivership. They were found guilty in Federal court by Judge Drummond, Gresham having disqualified himself from hearing the case. They were sentenced to three months in jail for interfering with property over which the court had control.[16]

The arrests had far-reaching and bitter repercussions. The strikers regarded the arrests as a betrayal of pledges made by the committee on arbitration. Mayor Caven was embarrassed by them and personally testified in behalf of the

15 Indianapolis *Daily Journal,* July 27, 28, 1877.

16 *Ibid.,* August 4, 1877; Matilda Gresham, *Life of Walter Quintin Gresham 1832-1895* (2 volumes, Chicago, 1919), I, 402-408; King *v.* Ohio and Mississippi Railway, 14 Fed. Cas. 539. For a discussion of the legal aspects of the cases, especially as a precedent for the use of the Federal injunction in later labor disputes, see Walter Nelles, "A Strike and Its Legal Consequences—an Examination for the Receivership Precedent for the Labor Injunction," *Yale Law Journal,* XL (1931), 507-554.

one striker who was acquitted. The Democratic Indianapolis *Sentinel* heaped abuse upon Judge Drummond and the railroad executives who had instigated the arrests. The trials, it declared, "compel honest men and patriots to hang their heads in shame." Drummond was castigated as a judge who simultaneously played the role of "prosecutor, pettifogger, jury and judge" and who should be impeached. "With such a creature tricked out in the robes of office innocence counts as nothing against prejudice and the demands of a souless corporation."[17] Republicans continued to be critical of Governor Williams for not having called out troops to quell the strikers. They frequently asserted that the strikes had been fomented by "communists." On the other hand, a Workingman's Convention which met in Indianapolis soon after the strikes commended Williams, Mayor Caven, and the *Sentinel* for the course they had followed.[18]

The depression also led to some abortive efforts at political activity on the part of labor. Earlier a Workingmen's party had appeared in the municipal election of 1867 in Indianapolis. The principal demand of the group was eight-hour-day legislation. During the campaign it had co-operated with the Democrats, which caused the Indianapolis *Journal* to speak of the "copperhead control of the workingmen's movement in this city" and to characterize it as "a swindle upon our industrial population." During the seventies several workingmen's conventions were held which passed resolutions calling for the election of representatives of labor to legislative bodies.[19] In 1877 there were efforts to form a branch of the

---

17 Indianapolis *Daily Sentinel*, July 29, August 4, 1877. In another editorial the *Sentinel* declared: "Railroad presidents, manufacturers and operators of various kinds may form protective unions, rings, cliques or what not, without exciting any remark or criticism, but let the railroad employee, the workman or the miner combine with his brother employee for protection, then begin exhaustless, unfavorable and derogatory criticisms from almost every quarter." *Ibid.*, August 13, 1877.

18 *Ibid.*, August 14, 1877.

19 Indianapolis *Daily Herald*, March 22, 25, April 5, 1867; Indianapolis

Workingmen's National party, which resulted in the nomination of a ticket of candidates for the city election in Indianapolis. The platform of these labor groups denounced monopolies and called for such reforms as an income tax and woman suffrage. At the state and local level they favored compulsory education and free textbooks. But the issue which was stressed far more than any other was monetary reform. There was a close alliance between the Greenback party discussed below and these labor groups.[20]

The speeches and the resolutions adopted at the labor conventions were almost invariably moderate in tone. They expressly deplored violence and approved arbitration as a means of settling disputes. But the Indianapolis *Journal* dubbed some of their ideas "communistic sentiment and rant," and some laborers were accused of being communists.[21]

Ideologically more radical, but more philosophical, was a small group of Socialists. Nearly all of them were Germans who met regularly to discuss economic questions.[22] In 1879 a Socialistic Labor group which endorsed the platform of the Socialistic Labor party of the United States nominated a mayoralty candidate in Indianapolis. They demanded that the city create a program of public works and asked that

Daily Journal, May 5, 7, 1867; December 22, 1872; February 23, May 6, 1874; Indianapolis *Daily Sentinel,* February 25, 1876.

[20] Indianapolis *Daily Journal,* April 3, 4, 1877. Typical resolutions adopted by a Workingmen's convention in Indianapolis in 1877 declared that a specie basis for money was "productive of the wildest inflation and the greatest contraction of money" and called for the free coinage of silver and the issuance of treasury notes. Indianapolis *Daily Sentinel,* August 14, 1877.

[21] *Ibid.,* February 25, June 6, 1876; Indianapolis *Daily Journal,* December 22, 1873, February 23, 1874, February 2, 1875, April 3, 1877. The *Journal* sarcastically dubbed the Workingmen's party "The Great North American Union Labor Savings Association for the Suppression of Work," and said that the "genuine workingmen" of the city repudiated it. Indianapolis *Daily Sentinel,* July 2, 1876.

[22] Indianapolis *Daily Sentinel,* May 2, 11, 1876; Indianapolis *Daily Journal,* May 4, 1878. "As an organization the socialists of this city are opposed to violent revolutionary methods," the Indianapolis *Journal* admitted, "but many of its members are extremists and would not hesitate, if the opportunity was offered, to go almost any length to achieve their purposes." *Ibid.*

the water works, gas works, and street railroads be operated by the city.[23]

Farmers as well as laborers were aroused to united action as never before by the depression. In Indiana the spectacular growth of the Patrons of Husbandry or the Grange coincided with the early years of the depression. At the beginning of 1873 there were only 54 Granges in the state. By the end of the year there were 650 and they were reported to be multiplying at the rate of thirty or forty a week. By the middle of 1874 there were almost two thousand; by January 1875 almost three thousand. At the end of 1873 the secretary of the State Board of Agriculture reported "a sudden awakening of the farming community to arouse and assert their rights, and claim the position to which they are entitled." The Indiana Granges showed less inclination toward political activity than did those in Illinois, but Grange influence was significant in several elections—and especially so in the election of the legislature of 1874. In the next session which was known as the "Farmers' legislature," some forty members of the House of Representatives organized themselves as a sort of "Granger Conclave" to discuss legislation which was of especial interest to farmers. Granges in various parts of the state sent petitions to the Assembly in which they asked for a wide variety of measures. These petitions and resolutions passed at the state Grange meetings showed the Granges to be interested in reducing the costs of government and in regulating railroad rates and eliminating special favors to railroads. They also complained against high interest rates. But Grangers, like labor groups, showed greater interest in monetary reform than in any other issue.[24]

§ §

The bank failures which ushered in the panic caused many people—workers, farmers, and businessmen—to embrace the

[23] Indianapolis *Daily Sentinel,* March 17, 1879.

[24] *Ibid.,* July 16, 1874; Indianapolis *Daily Journal,* December 1, 1873, February 3, 1875; Carleton, "Money Question in Indiana Politics," *Indiana Maga-*

idea that the cure for economic ills lay in the issuance of more money and in curtailing the power of private banks. As soon as the panic struck, Indianapolis businessmen, merchants, and bankers began a series of meetings to consider measures which might be adopted to improve the situation. At the first meeting William H. English, a prominent banker and a future Democratic candidate for the vice-presidency, expressed what he regarded as "unpalatable truths"—that no country could have permanent prosperity without a gold-backed currency. His views clearly did not reflect the sentiment of most of the gathering, where currency expansionists were in a majority. One speaker said that nine tenths of the businessmen of the country wanted more currency. At a larger meeting a week later the group, which took the name Citizens and Business Men's Committee, discussed numerous resolutions on monetary policy. One declared that currency equal in value to and redeemable in gold or silver was inadequate and "the sooner theorists and book financiers submit to the logic of facts and experience the better it will be for the practical men who drive the business, produce the wealth and develop the resources of the country."[25]

At the third meeting, James Buchanan, the editor of the Indianapolis *Sun,* and a prime mover behind the meetings, introduced a series of resolutions as a substitute for all other resolutions that were pending. These embodied the essential features of the "Indiana Plan," which later were incorporated into the platform of the Greenback party. They declared that the present crisis was due to insufficient money and that attempts to force specie payment would be ruinous. The circulating medium should be so arranged that it could be increased or diminished as business necessities required, and it was the duty of Congress (not banks) to furnish the people

zine of History, XLII, 117; Indiana State Board of Agriculture, *Annual Report,* 1873, p. 9; Indiana State Grange, *Proceedings,* 1874, pp. 11, 33; 1877, p. 19; *Brevier Legislative Reports,* XV (1875), 56-57. For a more complete treatment of the Grange in Indiana see Chapter IX, pages 397-403.

25 Indianapolis *Daily Journal,* October 27, November 3, 1873.

with a supply of money adequate to carry on the needs of business. The heart of the plan was a proposal that Congress pass legislation which would permit people to deposit United States bonds in the United States Treasury and receive in return legal tender notes to the value of the bonds. In the period during which the bonds were deposited in the treasury the interest which they accrued would go to the government, but the bonds were to be returned to the owner whenever he redeemed them in legal tender notes.[26]

At a fourth meeting resolutions along the lines which Buchanan recommended were adopted, and it was agreed that meetings of businessmen and other interested citizens be called throughout the state to discuss them and to urge Congress to pass legislation "to restore confidence and relieve the present pressing money panic. . . ." Buchanan was named chairman of a committee which was to correspond with members of Congress and businessmen.[27]

A few days later, under the sponsorship of the Citizens and Business Men's Committee, Buchanan addressed a large meeting at Masonic Hall in Indianapolis. Businessmen continued to show interest in currency expansion, although not necessarily all the details of the Indiana Plan. In March, at a meeting at which Thomas D. Kingan, head of the largest pork-packing business in the United States, presided, Indianapolis businessmen called upon Congress to issue in Greenbacks the $44,000,000 which was held in reserve and to increase the number of national banks. A mass meeting in Evansville, which included merchants, manufacturers, and businessmen, also asked for expansion of the currency through the issuance of legal tender notes.[28]

Meanwhile, members of the laboring force, who were especially hard hit by the panic, were being converted to currency expansion. A workingmen's rally in Indianapolis in De-

[26] *Ibid.*, November 6, 1873.

[27] *Ibid.;* Carleton, "Money Question in Indiana Politics," *Indiana Magazine of History,* XLII, 118.

[28] Indianapolis *Daily Journal,* December 6, 1873, March 3, 17, 1874.

cember, 1873, called for the payment of wages in money rather than in scrip and endorsed a "purely national circulating medium, based on the faith and resources of the nation." A mass meeting of coal miners in Brazil, called to protest wage reductions, asked for an expansion of the national currency.[29]

During these early stages there was no evidence that the supporters of the Indiana Plan were thinking of a third-party movement. Members of the old parties continued to be divided over monetary policy, but at first certain Republicans appeared to be especially sympathetic to the Indiana Plan. At one of the meetings of the Citizens and Business Men's Committee, Representative John Coburn had declared that he had consistently voted against all forms of currency contraction and that he favored a moderate amount of currency expansion. More significantly Representative Godlove S. Orth introduced into the United States House of Representatives a measure which embodied the essentials of the Indiana Plan for the issuance of treasury notes which could be received in exchange for bonds.[30]

As soon as the panic had begun, Morton had urged Grant to use the whole reserve of greenbacks to relieve the financial stringency. In the Senate he led the fight for a bill to increase the amount of legal tender notes by $18,000,000. His Republican colleague, Pratt, also voted for the measure. In the House the nine Republican representatives voted for it, while two Democrats voted against it. One Republican member and one Democratic member refrained from voting. When Grant vetoed the measure, the Republican press in Indiana was generally critical. The Indianapolis *Journal* expressed the opinion that Grant had been "largely controlled by Eastern capitalists in this matter, and that the voice of the West and South in favor of a moderate increase of the currency, has been unable to make itself heard over the loud and

29 Indianapolis *Daily Journal,* December 22, 1873, January 10, 1874.
30 *Ibid.,* November 5, 1873, January 28, 1874.

imperious protests of the rich men and money kings of the East." A mass meeting in Indianapolis at which James Buchanan spoke protested Grant's veto and commended the course of Indiana's senators and representatives.[31]

Soon after Grant's veto some of the supporters of currency expansion called for a statewide convention of all groups who were interested in "reform." The group of about five hundred which assembled in Indianapolis on June 9 was made up primarily of farmers, including members of the Grange. E. A. Olleman, editor of the *Indiana Farmer,* who had been prominent in the launching of the Indiana Plan, was a leader in the movement. After some debate it was decided to start a new party under the name of Independent party. The address of the permanent chairman emphasized that questions like the Negro question and the tariff, over which the old parties wrangled were outmoded. On really vital issues he insisted there was no difference between the major parties and neither of them offered any remedy for corruption.

The platform adopted by the new group called for the abandonment of "the gold base fallacy" in favor of a paper currency issued directly by the government rather than bank notes. This currency was to be convertible for government bonds. The platform also condemned monopolies of all kinds —in banking, railroad, manufacturing, and grain. A full slate of state officers was nominated, which was made up about equally of Republicans and Democrats, but no prominent members of either of the major parties were identified with the new movement.[32]

The platform of the Republican state convention which met a few days later reflected an awareness of a potential

31 Foulke, *Morton,* II, 317-318; Carleton, "Money Question in Indiana Politics," *Indiana Magazine of History,* XLII, 119-120; Indianapolis *Daily Journal,* April 23, 27, 1874. The two Democrats voting against the measure were William Niblack and William S. Holman.

32 Indianapolis *Daily Journal,* June 11, 1874; *Appletons' Annual Cyclopædia,* 1874, pp. 412-413. Some of the men named at the convention refused the nomination and others were then named to replace them.

threat from the new party and the growing strength of the Grange. Although the language was equivocal the platform called for the issuance of such additional amounts of currency as might "be necessary to meet the wants of the agricultural, industrial, and commercial interests of the country." This money was to be distributed in such a way as to prevent "capitalists and combinations of capital from controlling the currency of the country." "Cheap transportation and profitable markets for the products of agricultural and manufacturing labor" were endorsed. The planks were obviously worded in such a way as to avoid a party split over money, but some Republicans, including Benjamin Harrison and Walter Q. Gresham, were chagrined that there had not been a flat endorsement of hard money.[33]

The Democrats too were divided. Just prior to their state convention the Indianapolis *Sentinel,* which was temporarily voicing hard money views, declared that inflationists belonged in the Republican camp. "It is clear," it said, "that the real financial policy of the country is to return to specie payments as the only safe course. . . . The policy of resumption should be firmly maintained by all wise men." In a speech at the convention Hendricks, as usual, took a rather ambiguous position, saying that a return to specie payments was desirable but that the present state of the country made it necessary to continue the use of paper currency for the foreseeable future. Probably inflationists were in a majority at the convention, but the platform represented a compromise, calling for a return to specie payment as soon as business interests of the country permitted, but at the same time asking for legislation to adjust the volume of the currency to commercial and industrial needs and the abolition of the national banking act and the substitution of greenbacks for bank notes.[34]

[33] Indianapolis *Daily Journal,* June 18, 1874; Carleton, "Money Question in Indiana Politics," *Indiana Magazine of History,* XLII, 121.

[34] Indianapolis *Daily Sentinel,* July 14, 16, 1874.

Hard money advocates were disappointed. The *Sentinel* regretted that Democrats had missed an opportunity to take a position basically different from that of the Republicans and Independents by announcing themselves "champions of the policy of a return to specie payments." During the campaign two of the most influential men in the party forthrightly denounced inflation. Michael Kerr of New Albany, who became the Speaker of the United States House of Representatives at the next session, campaigned vigorously for hard money. In a typical speech before a gathering of farmers he spoke of the disastrous effects of inflation upon farmers. "What our people need is not more money," he said, "but most emphatically better money. . . ." Joseph E. McDonald, chairman of the Democratic State Central Committee, who spent much time campaigning for Kerr, openly repudiated the inflationary planks of the state platform. In a speech at Greencastle he admitted to having some "old fashioned ideas" on the subject of money and expressed doubt whether in normal times Congress had the power to "coin money out of paper." On the other hand, Voorhees, who had a large popular following and who hoped for election to the United States Senate, was an ardent advocate of greenbacks.[35]

The new Independent party flayed the old parties for their inconsistency. "To act with either the Democratic or Republican parties as they have now placed themselves before

[35] *Ibid.,* July 3, 17, August 16, 1874; Carleton, "Money Question in Indiana Politics," *Indiana Magazine of History,* XLII, 121-122.

Michael Kerr, who was born in Pennsylvania in 1827, migrated to Kentucky as a young man. After receiving a law degree from the University of Louisville he took up permanent residence in New Albany. He represented Floyd County in the General Assembly in 1857. In 1864 he was elected to the United States House of Representatives and was re-elected in 1866, 1868, 1870, and 1874. After his victory in 1874 he was elected Speaker during the 44th Congress when Democrats gained control of the House for the first time since before the Civil War. His term as Speaker was marred by ill health, and he died in August, 1876. Kerr was one politician whose record apparently was unblemished and who was deeply respected by both Democrats and Republicans. Woollen, *Biographical and Historical Sketches,* pp. 335-343.

the people," said the party organ, "is to surrender both integrity and manhood."[36]

There was no doubt that the Independent movement was
winning support and causing concern among seasoned politicians of the old parties. By September it was reported that
there were Independent organizations in at least 67 of the
92 counties. In many counties a separate slate of county
officers was nominated. In four of the thirteen districts Independents nominated their own candidates for Congress. In
the Seventh District, which included Indianapolis, there was
no Independent candidate. Both the Republican incumbent,
John Coburn, and his Democratic opponent, Franklin Landers,
favored currency expansion. But Landers was regarded as
more sympathetic to Independent views and received their
support. In the Second District the regular Democratic organization was compelled by pressure from the Grangers to
nominate James D. Williams instead of the man whom the
managers had at first intended to support.[37]

During the campaign money was the most publicized issue.
Democratic efforts to exploit alleged corruption in the Republican national administration appeared to arouse little
interest. Nor did Republican efforts to play upon southern
outrages stir the Indiana voters. The outcome clearly reflected the political unrest and desire for change which
stemmed from the depression. Democrats swept the state,
electing the entire state ticket by a margin of about seventeen thousand over the Republicans. Eight Democrats were
elected to Congress, among them the Greenback sympathizers,
Williams and Landers, but also the hard money Kerr. Democrats won control of the state House of Representatives and
had a majority of the vote in joint session, which meant that
they could elect the next United States senator. The Independent party polled between sixteen and nineteen thousand

36 Indianapolis *Sun*, August 1, 1874.

37 *Ibid.*, August 15, September 12, 26, 1874.

votes for state offices. Five Independents were elected to the state Senate and eight to the House.[38]

Independents as well as Democrats were jubilant over the outcome. "The Republican party in the State with its festering pollution, is broken and utterly destroyed," exulted the Independent paper. It predicted that the Democratic party would be "next in the order of pulling down of strongholds of political heresy and oppression." Soon after the election an effort to launch the Independent party on a national scale was made. A convention was called to meet in Indianapolis at the same time as the meeting of the State Grange. Only a few people assembled, nearly all of them from Indiana, but plans were laid for a national convention in Cleveland the following March.[39]

The Independents' disgust with the old parties was intensified when the legislature elected Joseph E. McDonald, exponent of hard money views, to the United States Senate. Although many Democratic members had inflationist sympathies the party caucus decided to support McDonald instead of Voorhees. This was apparently the result of an agreement whereby Hendricks threw his support to McDonald in return for a promise that the McDonald forces would support him for the presidency in 1876. Voorhees' followers were unhappy, but Voorhees withdrew from the contest and only two Democrats failed to vote for McDonald. The latter received 76 votes, the incumbent Pratt 41 votes, and James Buchanan all of the 13 Independent votes. The Independents declared bitterly that by the election the Democrats had betrayed every campaign promise and stood revealed as "the betrayer of the hopes and confidences of the laboring masses of our

[38] Carleton, "Money Question in Indiana Politics," *Indiana Magazine of History*, XLII, 123-124.

[39] Indianapolis *Sun*, October 17, November 28, 1874; Indianapolis *Daily Sentinel*, November 26, 1874. The platform adopted at this meeting emphasized financial grievances, called for paper money issued directly by the government, and deplored "extortionate rates for transportation."

people, and convicted of a baseness and a fraud upon the producing interests of the country never before equalled in the breadth and depth of perfidy by any political party in any age."[40]

As the depression dragged on money continued to be a paramount issue at both the national and state levels. Indiana's two leading politicians, Morton and Hendricks, both of whom cherished presidential ambitions, as well as lesser politicians, pursued a tortuous and sometimes inconsistent course. Both sought to placate the inflationist groups at home and at the same time to avoid offending the hard money interests of the East. As a member of the United States Senate, where he actually had to vote on money issues, Morton's role was somewhat more difficult. During the campaign of 1874, while supporting some currency expansion, he had tried to represent the Democrats as being dangerous inflationists.

During 1875 the positions of both Indiana Republicans and Democrats continued to shift. When the Resumption of Specie Payment Act, which provided that after January 1, 1879, all greenbacks should be redeemable in gold, came before the Senate, both Morton and Pratt voted for it. In the House nine Indiana Republicans also voted for the measure. This vote was a complete reversal of the position which the Republican members had taken just nine months before. Among Democrats Holman and Niblack reversed their previous position by voting against resumption.[41]

By the summer of 1875 the Indianapolis *Journal,* which usually reflected Morton's views, was flaying Greenbackers and insisting that return to specie payment and some deflation were necessary to get the country back on a sound economic

---

[40] Carleton, "Money Question in Indiana Politics," *Indiana Magazine of History,* XLII, 124; Indianapolis *Daily Journal,* January 6, 1875; Indianapolis *Daily Union,* January 20, 1875; Indianapolis *Sun,* January 23, 1875. The Indianapolis *Daily Journal,* January 15, 1875, labeled McDonald "a Hard Money Democrat Standing Upon a Repudiation Platform."

[41] Carleton, "Money Question in Indiana Politics," *Indiana Magazine of History,* XLII, 125.

basis. But within Republican ranks there continued to be a substantial element favorable to greenbacks. Within a few months the *Journal* had again shifted and was calling for repeal of the Resumption Act because it was impossible to carry it into effect and it was injurious to business.[42]

In 1876 it was evident that the currency question would once again be important in the political campaign. The Independents, who were now generally known as the Greenback party, had formed a national organization at Cleveland in March, 1875, and adopted a platform which denounced the Resumption Act and endorsed most features of the Indiana Plan. E. A. Olleman of the *Indiana Farmer* was chairman of the new party, while James Buchanan was secretary. Greenback clubs consisting of farmers and disgruntled laborers were being organized throughout Indiana. In February, 1876, more than three hundred Greenbackers converged upon Indianapolis for a state convention. Franklin Landers, who had been elected to Congress in 1874 through the combined support of Democrats and Independents, was nominated for governor while Anson Wolcott, a former Republican, was named for lieutenant governor. In May delegates from eighteen states met in Indianapolis for the first national Greenback convention and nominated Peter Cooper of New York for their presidential candidate.[43]

The Republican state convention, confronted with the dilemma of how to cater to inflationist sentiment in Indiana without jeopardizing Morton's chances nationally, framed a platform which favored "ultimate redemption in gold and silver," but asked for repeal of the law (which Morton had voted for) fixing a definite date for resumption. Democrats were accused of seeking to destroy the currency, and it was declared that the welfare of the country demanded that the

[42] Indianapolis *Daily Journal*, August 24, September 16, 1875; O. B. Carmichael, "The Campaign of 1876 in Indiana," *Indiana Magazine of History*, IX (1913), 277.

[43] Carleton, "Money Question in Indiana Politics," *Indiana Magazine of History*, XLII, 125-126; Indianapolis *Daily Sentinel*, February 16, 17, 1876.

currency be left "in the hands of its friends and not turned over to its enemies."[44]

The Republican state platform declared that Oliver P. Morton "possesses in an eminent degree the ability and qualities which fit him for the office of President of the United States." An enthusiastic group from Indiana went to Cincinnati to support their favorite son, but the Indiana delegation was not unanimously for Morton. A small "reform" element in the Republican party opposed his domination of the state machine and refused to support him for the presidency. Among the Indiana delegates to Cincinnati Walter Q. Gresham and John H. Holliday, editor of the Indianapolis *News*, supported the nomination of Benjamin Bristow, the Secretary of the Treasury who had exposed the Whiskey Ring. Except for some southern delegations Morton had no support outside Indiana, and his presidential hopes collapsed on the first ballot. The Indiana delegation eventually threw its support to Governor Rutherford B. Hayes of Ohio.[45]

The Democrats paid tribute in their platform to "our ancient doctrine that gold and silver are the true and safe basis for the country," but opposed contraction in the volume of the currency. They again urged the gradual retirement of national banks notes and their replacement with greenbacks. They demanded immediate repeal of the Resumption Act. There was a three-way contest for the Democratic nomination for governor among James D. Williams, William S. Holman, and Franklin Landers. Holman was regarded as more of a hard money advocate although he had voted against resumption, while both Williams and Landers had Greenback tendencies. The latter had already been nominated by the Greenback party and for this reason expected the Democrats to endorse him. At the convention, which was unusually tumultuous, even for a Democratic gathering, a bitter dispute

---

[44] *The Indiana Republican Hand Book for the Campaign of 1876* (Issued by the Republican State Central Committee, n.p., n.d.), pp. 47-48.

[45] *Ibid.*, p. 51; Foulke, *Morton*, II, 397-402.

developed between the Holman and Landers forces, which redounded to the benefit of Williams, who was nominated on the second ballot.[46]

The Greenbackers were offended that Landers was not nominated and branded the Democratic platform and the nomination of Williams as another betrayal of the people. But after the nomination of Williams, Landers withdrew as the Greenback candidate and was replaced by Wolcott.[47]

At the Democratic national convention Hendricks, who had been endorsed for the presidency by the Indiana convention, had to be satisfied with the vice-presidential nomination. Hendricks' record on the currency question was equivocal, but Samuel J. Tilden, the presidential candidate, had consistently taken a hard money position. The money plank in the national platform was somewhat ambiguous. It was unsatisfactory to the Indiana delegation, which had tried to secure the incorporation of a resolution calling for repeal of the Resumption Act. The Indianapolis *Sentinel* interpreted the convention as "a hard money victory all around"—a fact which caused Voorhees and the inflationist element in Indiana some chagrin. During the campaign Republicans gibed at the Democracy for the inconsistency between the position taken by state and national conventions and the inconsistency between the positions of the presidential and vice-presidential candidates.[48]

In James D. Williams the Democrats had one of the most colorful candidates in the entire history of Indiana politics. After a boyhood of privation, in which he received only a

[46] Henry (comp.), *State Platforms*, pp. 49-51; Carmichael, "Campaign of 1876," *Indiana Magazine of History*, IX (1913), 285; Carleton, "Money Question in Indiana Politics," *ibid.*, XLII, 128-129.

[47] Headlines in the Indianapolis *Sun*, the Greenback organ, April 22, 1876, proclaimed the nomination of Williams a "betrayal of the people" and accused the Democrats of selling out to the "bankers and money sharks."

[48] Carleton, "Money Question in Indiana Politics," *Indiana Magazine of History*, XLII, 130-131; Indianapolis *Daily Sentinel*, quoted in Carmichael, "Campaign of 1876," *ibid.*, IX, 293. Richard Gregg replaced Wolcott, the original nominee for lieutenant governor.

fifth-grade education in a log building, Williams became a successful farmer in Knox County, where he owned some three thousand acres of land. He was known for his interest in scientific farming, had served on the State Board of Agriculture, and had won several awards at the Indiana State Fair. After serving for almost thirty years in the state legislature, in 1874 he was elected to Congress with the support of the Grange and the Greenbackers. In Washington he presented an unusual figure, dressed in a distinctive suit made of the material from which blue jeans were made—a costume which earned him the sobriquet of "Blue Jeans." He became the butt of numerous jokes because of his appearance and because of his constant harping on the necessity for economy in government. Republicans tried to ridicule him for his rusticity and uncouth appearance, which his friends compared to that of Lincoln.[49]

The very qualities which his opponents ridiculed appealed to many voters, and Williams astutely capitalized on them. During the campaign his followers wore blue jeans. Blue Jeans clubs were formed throughout the state which sang songs like the following about their hero:

> Delighted and hopeful we anchor
> Our trust in all virtuous means,
> For this as a weapon will conquer
> In the hands of our leader, "Blue Jeans".[50]

While Republicans scoffed at Williams, Godlove Orth, their own original gubernatorial candidate, became such a source

[49] Howard R. Burnett, " 'Blue Jeans' Williams, Last Pioneer Governor," *Indiana Magazine of History*, XXII (1926), 101-130 *passim*. The Indianapolis *Daily Journal*, September 7, 1876, thus described Williams: "Abraham Lincoln was an Admiral Crichton in comparison. . . . The English language would never recover from the shock of a detailed and accurate description of his general appearance. . . . He is as handsome as a black India-rubber baby drawn out to its greatest possible length and its face pinched out of shape. . . ."

[50] Burnett, " 'Blue Jeans' Williams," *Indiana Magazine of History*, XXII, 121.

of embarrassment that he withdrew from the ticket. At the state convention Orth, who was serving as minister to Austria at the time but who had the backing of Morton for the governorship, was nominated without opposition. Prior to the convention there had been a movement to nominate Benjamin Harrison, grandson of President William Henry Harrison, who was popular with the reform element in the party and also with veterans. But Harrison, who disliked Morton but who was reluctant to challenge him, refused to allow his name to be presented.[51]

As soon as Orth was nominated, the Democratic press began to assail him for his former Know Nothing affiliation and to cast doubts on his integrity. Reform Republicans also had reservations about him. The Indianapolis *News* was especially persistent in raising questions about his conduct while he was serving as minister to Venezuela during the Johnson administration and later as a member of Congress. There was never evidence that Orth had actually violated any law, but a Congressional investigation indicated that he had been in collusion with a corrupt group which speculated in Venezuelan bonds and claims arising under a treaty between the United States and Venezuela. The investigation also showed that Orth had continued to act as paid legal counsel for speculators seeking favors from Congress after taking his seat in that body. After he returned from Austria to campaign for the governorship, he persistently refused to answer questions about the Venezuelan affair. Finally the Indianapolis *News* accused him of aiding and abetting "one of the most disgraceful swindles ever perpetrated in the name of the National Government" and of prostituting his office to that of "procurer for thieves and swindlers." On July 31 the *News* declared editorially: "Mr. Orth Must Retire," and even Republican leaders had to agree. Two days later Orth withdrew from the race. To replace him the Republican Central Committee

[51] Sievers, *Benjamin Harrison, Hoosier Statesman*, pp. 79-81.

named Benjamin Harrison who was only forty-three years old, but was a successful lawyer and staunch Presbyterian and had been active in the Republican party since its founding. The only elective office which he had held was that of Indiana Supreme Court Reporter, but he had a fine war record and had attained the rank of brigadier general.[52]

The new Republican candidate presented an interesting contrast to the homespun Williams. With Harrison on the ticket the Republicans tried to recapture the spirit of the 1840 campaign, but their efforts appeared somewhat ludicrous in view of the candidate's personality. The Democratic press insisted that Harrison was an aristocrat by birth and feeling with no sympathy for the common people—"as cold as an icicle" and having "more brains than feelings." He was labeled the "kid gloves candidate." "Give Harrison a kid-glove client and a two thousand dollar fee," said the Indianapolis *Sentinel*, "and no matter how guilty the culprit may be, his intellectual grasp will readily separate crime from such respectability."[53]

The money question received more attention than any other national issue during the campaign. Democrats tried to blame hard times on Republican policies—especially contraction. In his opening campaign speech at Salem in August, Williams denounced resumption and called the "greenback currency . . . good enough for practical purposes . . . the best currency we can get." On the other hand Harrison came out firmly for resumption and denounced the Greenback movement as a snare and a delusion in his opening speech at Danville. He warned that the laboring classes especially suffered from a currency which fluctuated in value.[54]

[52] Indianapolis *Daily Sentinel*, May 26, 1876; Indianapolis *News*, July 26, 31, 1876; Carleton, "Money Question in Indiana Politics," *Indiana Magazine of History*, XLII, 133; Sievers, *op. cit.*, pp. 98-99 and *passim*.

[53] Sievers, *op. cit.*, p. 108; Indianapolis *Daily Sentinel*, August 9, 1876; Burnett, " 'Blue Jeans' Williams," *Indiana Magazine of History*, XXII, 122, 124.

[54] Carleton, "Money Question in Indiana Politics," *Indiana Magazine of History*, XLII, 133; Sievers, *op. cit.*, p. 113.

Democrats also harped on the corruption issue and the need for reform. Their state platform asserted that "repeated exposures of corruption" in the Republican administration showed the necessity for "a general and thorough change." Throughout the campaign Democratic speakers stressed this theme. Republicans, anticipating the attack, expressed "fullest confidence and approbation" in the Grant administration and commended the President for "the example he will leave to his successors of removing from office those of his own appointment when he has found them to be unfaithful. . . ." "The Republican party has hunted down and punished its own offenders," claimed the Indianapolis *Journal*. "It inaugurated that war against corruption. . . . As a whole, the Republican party is the only untainted party. The other smells of treason, rebellion, and secession."[55]

In their state platform Republicans expressed themselves as "willing and anxious to restore amicable relations" between the people of the North and South and expressed a willingness "to forgive and grant amnesty to all those who desire to be forgiven and amnestied." But throughout the campaign they tried to distract attention from the record of malfeasance of the Grant administration by reviving charges of Democratic wartime treason. Harrison, in spite of his aristocratic aloofness, waved the bloody shirt almost as vigorously as Morton had ever done. He told a veterans' rally: "I accept the banner of the bloody shirt. I am willing to take as our ensign the tattered, worn-out, old gray shirt, worn by some gallant Union hero, stained with his blood as he gave up his life for his country. . . . When they [the Democrats] purge their party of the leprosy of secession . . . we will bury the 'bloody shirt' in the grave with the honored corpse who wore it and not before." A popular campaign ditty proclaimed:

55 *Indiana Republican Hand Book . . . 1876*, pp. 50, 53; Indianapolis *Daily Journal*, April 14, 1876, quoted in Carmichael, "Campaign of 1876," *Indiana Magazine of History*, IX, 291.

> The Boys in Blue and soldiers true
> Are shouting loud for General Ben.
> While from the river to the lakes
> He draws a host of loyal men.
> But nowhere in the Hoosier State
> A single voice or vote he gains
> From Copperheads or ex-Confeds
> For they all march with Uncle James.[56]

The Boys in Blue were very active in the campaign, and there was a feeling that they alone could save the Indiana Republican party from defeat. A mass encampment of Boys in Blue from all parts of the country was held in Indianapolis prior to the election. One worker who was making arrangements for the encampment wrote to another: "I desire to see that the colored troops, especially, shall all be there— if a few thousands of them should come, from the south and remain to vote—it will do no harm."[57]

The Democratic press tried to epitomize the issues by headlines which proclaimed:

REFORM THE ISSUE OF THE DAY

Grant, Morton, Hayes, Corruption, Crime, Outrage and the
Bloody Shirt; Tilden, Hendricks, Reform Honesty,
Patriotism, and Pure Government.

"We are not fighting the war now against the South," declared Voorhees. "We are fighting the battle of honesty and reform in public office." The Republicans countered by calling Tilden "a notorious sham," a "colossal fraud," and "a friend and companion of Boss Tweed."[58]

Both old parties showed signs of alarm at the prospect of losing votes to the Greenback party. The Democratic Indi-

---

[56] *Indiana Republican Hand Book . . . 1876*, p. 46; Sievers, *Benjamin Harrison, Hoosier Statesman*, pp. 117, 122.

[57] Dearing, *Veterans in Politics*, pp. 225-226; L. S. Hart to James G. Garfield, July 13, 1876, quoted *ibid.*, p. 226.

[58] Indianapolis *Daily Sentinel*, September 4, 1876, quoted in Carmichael, "Campaign of 1876," *Indiana Magazine of History*, IX, 290, 294; Burnett, " 'Blue Jeans' Williams," *ibid.*, XXII, 123.

anapolis *Sentinel* urged the Greenbackers "to throw their strength with that party that most nearly represents their views," which in Indiana was clearly the Democratic party. Although the Greenbackers were offended when the Democrats failed to nominate Landers, Williams embraced the Greenback program. Throughout the campaign he and Voorhees emphasized the money issue. As a result of this, there seemed to be little reason to fear that disgruntled Democrats would vote the Greenback ticket. On the other hand the hard money position of Harrison and other Republicans caused predictions that the Republicans would lose votes to the new party. This possibility appeared to be reduced somewhat when almost on the eve of the state elections Wolcott withdrew as the Greenback candidate for governor and urged the election of Harrison. This last minute development created a sensation. Democrats at once cried that there had been a deal between Wolcott, who had formerly been an active Republican, and the Republican organization. This Wolcott vigorously denied as did E. A. Olleman, but the charges of collusion were widely believed. Many Greenbackers were bitter against Wolcott, but his action seems to have had little effect upon the outcome of the election.[59] Once again the Democrats elected a governor. Williams was victorious over Harrison by a margin of about five thousand votes. In the presidential election Tilden carried the state by almost exactly the same margin. Henry W. Harrington, who was named at the last moment as the Greenback choice for governor, received almost thirteen thousand votes, but Peter Cooper, the presidential candidate, received less than ten thousand. Republicans won nine of the thirteen Congressional seats. This was due in part, at least, to the fact that the system of districting favored the Republicans. In the Congressional vote for the state as a whole the combined Democratic vote was

[59] Indianapolis *Daily Sentinel,* May 18, 1876; Carleton, "Money Question in Indiana Politics," *Indiana Magazine of History,* XLII, 134; Sievers, *Benjamin Harrison, Hoosier Statesman,* pp. 120-122; Indianapolis *Daily Journal,* October 6, 7, 1876.

more than seven thousand greater than the Republican. Republicans won control of the state House of Representatives. In the Senate there would be 25 Democrats and 24 Republicans and one Greenback Independent.[60]

As might have been expected both parties responded in thoroughly partisan fashion to the dispute which developed over the outcome of the presidential election. Immediately after the November election the Indianapolis *Sentinel* proclaimed that the "day of redemption" had come—that Tilden and Hendricks had been elected. "At last! after many years of gloom," it exulted, "there is the dawn of a better day." But Democratic rejoicing was soon turned to gloom as it became apparent that the Tilden victory was in dispute. At a state convention in January Democrats warned of a "formidable conspiracy" to impose upon the people a President and Vice-President whom they had not elected. The Democratic press denounced the decision of the Electoral Commission, which finally decided in favor of Hayes, as a fraud and continued throughout Hayes's term to insist that he was illegally chosen.[61]

When the Electoral Commission made its report in favor of Hayes, the Republican *Journal* rejoiced that the country had had "a narrow escape from a triumph of fraud." The country, it declared, was to be congratulated upon having escaped the election of the "unscrupulous" Tilden and having secured in Hayes, "a President of the purest patriotism, most incorruptible integrity and unquestioned honor."[62]

[60] Williams received 213,219 votes to 208,080 for Harrison; Tilden received 213,526 votes to 208,011 for Hayes. *Appletons' Annual Cyclopædia,* 1876, p. 411; Carleton, "Money Question in Indiana Politics," *Indiana Magazine of History,* XLII, 134.

[61] Indianapolis *Daily Sentinel,* November 8, 1876; Indianapolis *Journal,* January 9, 1877. The Republican *Journal* expressed "profound disappointment" at the "uncompromising partisanship" of the seven Democratic members of the Electoral Commission because they consistently voted in favor of Tilden's claims to the disputed votes. *Ibid.,* February 9, 1877.

[62] *Ibid.,* February 22, 1877.

The *Journal* also gave its approval to Hayes's southern policy, including the withdrawal of Federal troops, which was accompanied by the collapse of the last of the Radical governments. Other Republican papers expressed similar views. "There are no rebels any more," said the Terre Haute *Express*; "it is time for us to be one people."[63] Democrats, who for years had been urging the withdrawal of troops and a policy of reconciliation, could scarcely quarrel with such sentiments. As a result of Hayes's policies the southern question and passions growing out of the war tended to recede into the background. As a part of his policy of conciliating the South Hayes appointed "Colonel" Richard Thompson of Terre Haute to his Cabinet as Secretary of the Navy. Thompson, who maintained cordial relations with Morton, had placed the latter's name in nomination for the presidency at the Cincinnati convention. In return Morton had recommended him as a possible Cabinet member. Hayes was reported to have told Thompson: "I desired to have in the Cabinet a Republican of the Old Whig element which, in the South particularly, I am anxious to enlist in the work of pacification."[64]

The death of Oliver P. Morton early in the Hayes regime also contributed to the passing of old issues and brought an end to an era in Indiana politics. The passing of the long-time leader was an event of national significance. President Hayes visited Morton at Richmond during his last illness. Cabinet members, senators, and other notables flocked to Indianapolis to attend his funeral and pay him tribute. Even Hendricks called him a great man and said that he chose to forget everything that would disturb pleasant memories. The Democratic press paid him decent respect, but an editorial in the Indianapolis *Sentinel* some months before his death was a more honest, if tasteless, expression of Democratic senti-

63 *Ibid.,* March 8, 1877; Terre Haute *Express,* April 11, 1877, quoted in Charles Roll, "Indiana's Part in Reconstruction," in *Studies in American History Inscribed to James Albert Woodburn* (Indiana University Press, 1926), p. 318.

64 Roll, *Colonel Dick Thompson,* p. 212.

ment. "The indications are that Morton will die," the *Sentinel* had announced, and added: "If Morton could be persuaded to be honest with himself and with his countrymen, what hideous stories he could tell, of malice, hate, corruption, perfidy and crime." To his journal George W. Julian once again confided his estimate of Morton as an opportunist and "servile *follower* throughout his career." "There was a great parade at his funeral, but little sign of real solemnity or sorrow was visible," Julian commented. "The funeral sermon (so called) . . . was a solid stump speech, disgusting to all right-thinking people."[65]

As had been generally expected Governor Williams appointed Daniel Voorhees to the Senate seat of the departed Morton—as fine a piece of political irony as ever occurred in Indiana. In the Senate Voorhees joined other members in paying tribute to his predecessor. "The motives which actuated Senator Morton in his public career are not now open to discussion," he said. "I shall ask the same charity for mine when I am gone that I extend to his. That he was sincere in his convictions no one will ever question. That the general tenor of his convictions upon the relations between the North and South was erroneous, I think history will fully establish."[66]

The *Sentinel* exulted over the appointment of Voorhees because it meant the burial of "the bloody shirt still deeper," but even more because it meant "correct views in regard to the financial policy, and another vote in the interest of business and against John Sherman's bondholding policy."[67] In the Senate, where he served from 1877 until 1897, Voorhees, as expected, proved to be one of the most eloquent champions of currency expansion. He arrived in the Senate at a time when the friends of inflation, unable to bring about the repeal of the Resumption Act, were beginning to embrace the free coinage of silver.

[65] Foulke, *Morton*, II, 502; Indianapolis *Daily Sentinel,* August 17, 1877; Julian Journal, December 2, 1877, in George W. Julian Papers, Indiana Division, Indiana State Library.

[66] Voorhees, *Forty Years of Oratory,* II, 748.

[67] Indianapolis *Daily Sentinel,* November 7, 1877.

Indiana Republicans as well as Democrats at first showed sympathy for silver. In the 1877 session of the Indiana legislature members of both parties combined to pass a resolution asking Congress to enact legislation "restoring the legal-tender quality of the silver dollar." Every member of the Indiana delegation, Republican and Democrat, who voted, voted in favor of the Bland bill for the unlimited coinage of silver which passed the United States House of Representatives in 1877. In the Senate Voorhees voted against the Allison amendment, which limited the amount of silver to be purchased, while McDonald voted for it. But both Indiana senators voted for the final version of the Bland-Allison bill. When Hayes vetoed this measure, every Indiana member in both House and Senate voted to override the veto.[68]

Interest in the money question was kept alive by the continued depression and accompanying economic unrest. In 1877 in Indiana the depression seemed to reach its depth. Business failures, which had been mounting steadily since 1873, continued to increase. Unemployment in Indianapolis became acute. Bands of "tramps" wandered about the countryside and infested the cities. Labor disputes, already described, shook the complacency of the more fortunate and convinced many middle-class citizens that a revolution was imminent. These developments had profound effects upon political events in 1878.

Monetary expansion still appeared the most obvious panacea for economic problems. Throughout 1877 the Democratic press continuously blamed unemployment and suffering upon the "heresy" of resumption. The two most important issues before Congress, declared the Indianapolis *Sentinel,* were "the repeal of the resumption law and the remonetization

---

68 Indiana *Laws,* 1877, p. 163; Carleton, "Money Question in Indiana Politics," *Indiana Magazine of History,* XLII, 135-136. After the great increase in the supply of gold following the gold strikes in California in 1849 silver had been almost entirely driven out of circulation and the silver dollar had disappeared. The currency act passed in 1873 omitted the silver dollar from the list of coins.

of silver." In his keynote address at the Democratic state convention, which met in February, 1878, Hendricks made a plea for silver. "It is not as cheap money that the people demand its restoration," he said, "but as a legal tender and coin contemplated by the constitution." The platform, which was apparently largely the work of Voorhees, unequivocally called for greenbacks as full legal tender, the repeal of resumption, and the restoration of the silver dollar and the unlimited coinage thereof.[69]

The platform also deplored the recent labor troubles and included planks designed to appeal to voters among the working classes. For their principal state office, secretary of state, the Democrats nominated John Gilbert Shanklin, editor of the Evansville *Courier,* a paper which until recently had been an advocate of hard money. Shanklin, who had been educated in Germany and had lived abroad for many years, the Indianapolis *Journal* described as the "most ultra of the swallow-tailed element," adding that his nomination on a ticket "which undertakes to champion workingmen will be looked on as a huge joke in his part of the state."[70]

In their platform the Democrats referred to the denial of the presidency to Tilden as the "monster crime of the age," and during the campaign Hayes was attacked continuously for his allegedly fraudulent election. But the major emphasis was to blame Republican monetary policies for prolonging the depression and to appeal to dissatisfied economic groups, especially those with Greenback tendencies.[71]

[69] Indianapolis *Daily Sentinel,* July 18, December 5, 1877; Indianapolis *Daily Journal,* February 21, 1878.

[70] Indianapolis *Daily Journal,* February 21, 1878.

[71] During the campaign it was announced that Elijah B. Martindale, publisher of the Indianapolis *Jounal,* which supported resumption, had gone into bankruptcy. Martindale had invested heavily in Indianapolis real estate which had shrunk drastically in value as the result of the depression. The Indianapolis *Sentinel* expressed sympathy for him but blamed his misfortunes on the "radical contraction policy," which the *Journal* supported. Indianapolis *Daily Sentinel,* August 21, 1878.

1866. **1866.**

TERRE HAUTE

AND

INDIANAPOLIS RAILROAD.

Four Trains daily, (Sundays excepted), between Terre Haute and Indianapolis. These Trains make close connections at Indianapolis with Trains for

NEW YORK, BOSTON, PHILADELPHIA, BALTIMORE,

WASHINGTON CITY, CINCINNATI,

LOUISVILLE, ETC.,

And at Terre Haute for

SAINT LOUIS

AND ALL POINTS WEST. ALSO, FOR

VINCENNES, EVANSVILLE,

AND POINTS ON THE OHIO RIVER.

Passengers will please procure Tickets before entering the Cars. Through Tickets for all Eastern Cities, etc., to be had at the Ticket Offices. Four Freight Trains each way daily, except Sunday.

Quick time is made by Express Freight Trains from St. Louis to the East. Only one change between St. Louis and Pittsburg, Buffalo and Cleveland. Stock Shippers will find this the most superior route to the East. Through arrangements can be made with **JAMES BEEBE,** cor. Second and Poplar Streets, St. Louis, Mo.

CHAS. WOOD, Sec'y.　　　　　　　**E. J. PECK, Pres't.**
　　　　　R. E. RICKER, Superintendent.

Columbus, Edinburg and Franklin Business Guide, 1865, 1866

Evansville City Directory, 1880

The Republicans countered by branding their opponents as simultaneously "the party of reaction, revolution and agitation." The Democrats were held responsible for delaying recovery by their persistent agitation of the money question. They were blamed for encouraging the strikes of 1877 and arraying capital against labor. Throughout 1878 the Republican press and Republican speakers expressed alarm over the threat of communism and accused Democrats and Greenbackers of being tainted with communism. "The steady growth of communism in the United States is an actual fact, and a matter of serious alarm," warned the Indianapolis *Journal* in a typical editorial. It declared that nine tenths of the "Communistic elements" were in the Democratic party and accused Democratic leaders of "truckling and catering" to communism. The Greenback party was accused by the *Journal* of representing a "class movement" and "a large slice of communism."[72]

The money issue once again presented a dilemma to the Republicans. Hayes had shown himself uncompromisingly opposed to silver, but within Indiana there was obviously much sympathy for silver and greenbacks. The result was an equivocal platform which called for a "sound and stable currency of gold, silver, and paper of the same value" and a cessation of "further financial agitation."[73]

In 1878 the Greenbackers adopted the name National party. Their platform once more emphasized money over other questions but it included planks on several other questions which were designed to appeal to farmers and laborers. It explicitly denounced "red flag communism imported from Europe." Nationals nominated a complete slate of state officers and maintained a separate organization, but in some counties a coalition was effected between them and the Democrats.[74]

[72] Indianapolis *Daily Journal*, February 15, 20, April 22, May 22, 1878.
[73] *Ibid.*, June 6, 1878.
[74] *Ibid.*, May 23, 1878.

In the Seventh District the National candidate for Congress received Democratic endorsement. He was Gilbert De La Matyr, a Methodist minister and former army chaplain, who had been charged by the Indianapolis *News* with being a communist. In seeking the nomination De La Matyr said that "next to preaching the Gospel of Christ, there is no more responsible work than to help unfold the sublime purposes of our civilization in its legislative halls." During the campaign he insisted that the overriding issue was "oppression of the masses by concentrated wealth, swayed by mammon." The masses of people were suffering, he asserted, and calling them "shiftless" and "tramps" and "communists" would not solve the problem. The specific measures which he urged most strongly were monetary reform and lower interest rates.[75]

It was a lively campaign. From the beginning to the end the Democrats breathed confidence. Voorhees, who had hopes of being elected to the United States Senate by the next legislature, stumped the state, deploring the economic hardships of farmers which he blamed on Republican monetary policies and eastern "loan sharks." "These sharks," he said, had "sneaked into Congress" in 1873 and "killed silver money to make it more scarce, knowing that the mines were turning out large quantities of bullion and the poor people might get rich."[76]

Benjamin Harrison, who expected to be the Republican senatorial choice, tried to refute Voorhees' monetary arguments and ridiculed him for his efforts to perpetuate the idea of "a gigantic conspiracy formed in the east to oppress and ruin the farmers of the west." Harrison deplored the "communistic" tendencies of the times and accused the Democrats of fomenting class warfare. The Republicans, he insisted, were the true friends of the working man.[77]

[75] Indianapolis *Daily Journal,* May 6, 1878; Indianapolis *Daily Sentinel,* August 11, 31, 1878.

[76] Indianapolis *Daily Sentinel,* August 24, 1878.

[77] *Ibid.,* August 10, 1878.

The Democrats responded by attacking Harrison as cold-blooded and at heart opposed to labor. "The United States Senate is too big a place for his narrow prejudices against labor," said the principal Democratic organ. "The west is not falling in love with aristocratic kid gloved Shylocks." In an effort to discredit Harrison and other hard money Republicans and to win votes from Republicans with inflationist tendencies, Democrats even appealed to the memory of the dead Morton. They quoted some of the deceased Senator's statements opposing immediate return to specie payments and declared: "Here we find Mr. Voorhees and Mr. Morton fighting side by side. . . ."[78]

In the election the Democrats swept the state, electing all of the state ticket and gaining seats in both Congress and the state legislature. At the same time the Nationals made a surprisingly strong showing. Their candidate for secretary of state received over 39,000 votes. Each of the major parties carried six Congressional districts. De La Matyr, the National, was elected in the Seventh District.[79] In the Twelfth District (which included Allen and surrounding counties) the Republicans threw their support to the Democratic candidate, Walpole G. Colerick, in order to defeat the Nationals. In the state legislature party designations were somewhat blurred as between Democrats and Nationals in some cases. But

[78] *Ibid.*, August 13, October 5, 1878. In the same editorial in which it attacked Harrison the *Sentinel* pictured conditions under Republican rule as being deplorable. "Human life is cheap in America. Let people starve, or if they complain denounce them as communists and hurry them out of the way by the discharge of Gatling guns manned by federal troops. With millions of idlers, highways lined with tramps, penitentiaries filled with convicts; . . . business men hurrying to the bankrupt court; the sheriff's hammer forever beating the funeral march of estates, unable to stand further shrinkage, are knocked down to the fortunate possessor of a mortgage." *Ibid.*, August 13, 1878.

[79] While in Congress De La Matyr sometimes acted as chaplain of the House. He devoted most of his efforts as a congressman to the money question. One of his proposals was for the government to issue a billion dollars in greenbacks to loan for fifty years to private corporations which were in financial distress. The suggestion was ridiculed—especially by the newspapers of the East. *Ibid.*, May 14, 1879.

according to one count there were 50 Democrats, 39 Republicans, and 11 Nationals in the House. Most of the Nationals came from counties in the northern or western part of the state, where the party showed its greatest strength. The Democrats were able to organize the Senate by the deciding vote of the lieutenant governor. On joint ballot the Democrats would have a clear majority and would be in a position to elect the United States senator. It was a foregone conclusion that Voorhees would be elected to fill the remainder of Morton's unexpired term and for a full six-year term.[80]

The 1878 elections were followed by the usual charges of fraud. In Montgomery County, the Democrats claimed, Republicans imported voters and also permitted Wabash College students, who were not bona fide residents, to vote. They also claimed that in Jefferson County a township trustee, who later absconded, was paid five dollars a vote to stuff the ballot box with Republican ballots and to remove those cast for Democratic candidates. On the other hand Republicans accused Democrats of engaging in a conspiracy to bring a large number of voters into Jennings County. This resulted in a prolonged trial in the Federal District Court before Judge Walter Q. Gresham. Benjamin Harrison figured prominently in the prosecution of the case, which Democrats insisted was instigated by Republicans solely for political reasons. One of the defendants was found guilty, while ten others were acquitted.[81]

That many members elected as Democrats and some Republicans as well had Greenback proclivities was apparent

---

[80] Indianapolis *Daily Sentinel,* January 10, 22, 1879; *Appletons' Annual Cyclopedia,* 1878, pp. 443-444. Carleton, "Money Question in Indiana Politics," *Indiana Magazine of History,* XLII, 138-139. Voorhees received 83 votes, Harrison 60. Three Greenback members voted for James Buchanan for United States senator; the rest voted for Voorhees.

The following counties elected Nationals to the state legislature: Parke, Vermillion, Benton, Jasper, Newton, White, Montgomery, Morgan, Hamilton, Tipton, Putnam, Hendricks, Ohio, and Switzerland. Carleton, *op. cit.,* p. 141.

[81] Indianapolis *Daily Sentinel,* November 2, 1878, February 25, May 9, June 7, 1879; Indianapolis *Daily Journal,* July 31, 1879; Gresham, *Life of Walter Q. Gresham,* II, 473-483.

throughout the 1879 session. Most striking evidence of this was a series of resolutions dealing with financial policies which were carried in the House of Representatives. A resolution asking for the abolition of all bank issues and for the free and unlimited coinage of silver was passed by the overwhelming margin of 85 to 5. Other resolutions, passed by narrower margins, called for repeal of the Resumption Act and for issuance of legal tender paper money to the extent of at least thirty dollars per capita.[82]

§ § §

The monetary policy of the Federal government was the most hotly debated issue of the political campaigns of the depression years. Monetary reform was hailed as the panacea for all economic ills. Other issues lacked the emotional appeal of money as a cure-all, but at the state level many advocates of currency expansion showed an interest in other economic problems.

The power of railroads, especially their discriminatory practices, was a powerful cause of discontent among the farm population. Railroads were one of the principal targets of the Grange. At every legislative session numerous measures were introduced to regulate railroads and curb their powers. But in spite of the strong popular feeling almost no regulatory legislation actually passed.[83]

The depression and popular unrest caused politicians to give increased attention to other economic problems, but the proposals which were made were for the most part moderate and orthodox. In spite of the charges of radicalism brought against them by their opponents Grangers and Greenbackers were essentially farmers who still clung to Jeffersonian ideas of limited government. Depression led to calls for retrenchment and economy and reduction, rather than expansion, of

[82] *Brevier Legislative Reports,* XVII (1879), 37-38. These resolutions were tabled in the Senate. Indiana *Senate Journal,* 1879, pp. 332-333.

[83] See below, Chapter VIII, pages 358-360 for a more detailed treatment of this subject.

government activities. The message which Governor Williams, himself closely allied with Greenbackers and Grangers, sent to the legislature in 1877 was a typical expression of these views. The depression he blamed on "over trading and deceptive speculation." "We have been lured to the embrace of Debt under the flattering guise of Credit," said Williams, "and we can be extricated only by the joint aid of Industry and Economy. We should again seek the ancient landmarks of frugality and republican simplicity, from which too many have unwittingly strayed."[84]

The farmer influence which was powerful in the 1875 session was reflected in an act regulating public warehouses, which was a typical piece of Granger legislation but much milder than the Illinois law, which fixed rates. The Indiana law merely required warehousemen to receive and store any grain which was tendered without "any discrimination between persons desiring to avail themselves of warehouse facilities." It also made provisions for inspection and grading of grain which was stored. In 1879 another act made warehouse receipts negotiable in the same way that bills of exchange were.[85]

Debt-burdened farmers complained of excessive interest rates. The 1874 state meeting of the Grange asked for state legislation fixing the legal rate at 6 per cent. Legislation along these lines was introduced but failed to pass at the 1875 and 1877 sessions. In 1877 the Grange petitioned Congress to fix rates. They complained that interest rates of 10 or 12 per cent were being charged and were "absolutely eating up the laboring and business men, and paralyzing every branch of industry throughout the land." By 1878 even the Indianapolis *Journal,* which earlier had said that usury laws were either "idle" or "tyrannical," was complaining over high interest rates imposed by eastern creditors to the detriment of western debtors.[86]

[84] Indiana *Senate Journal,* 1877, p. 51.

[85] Indiana *Laws,* 1875, pp. 172-177; special session, 1879, pp. 230-233.

[86] Indiana State Grange, *Proceedings,* 1877, p. 19; Indianapolis *Daily Journal,* January 28, 1875, February 11, 1878.

Promises to lower interest rates were an important part of the appeal of the Democratic and Greenback candidates during the 1878 campaign. At the 1879 session at least fifteen bills fixing interest rates were introduced in the House of Representatives. Some of them provided that persons who were charged in excess of the legal rate could sue to recover twice the amount. These proposals led to prolonged debate. Opponents insisted that they constituted "class legislation" and an unwarranted interference with the right to contract freely. An act was finally adopted which fixed 6 per cent as the legal rate and declared that no agreement for a higher rate was valid unless expressly provided for in writing. Under no circumstances was more than 8 per cent to be charged.[87]

Depression, which led to mortgages, foreclosures, and forced sales of property, also led to demands for legislation to protect those faced with these misfortunes. An 1875 act provided that a person whose personal property was sold for taxes might redeem it within thirty days by paying the purchase price plus certain penalties. At the 1877 session of the legislature at least seven bills were introduced to stay or regulate the collection of mortgages, none of which were adopted. At the next session a dozen or so bills were introduced in each house dealing with the sale of property and foreclosure of mortgages. A homestead law was adopted which provided that property valued up to six hundred dollars was to be exempt from sale on execution for any debt growing out of a contract made after the adoption of the law. Another act provided that persons whose property was sold on execution might redeem it at any time during the following year by paying the purchaser the purchase price plus 10 per cent interest. Other legislation attempted to protect Indiana residents from attachment or garnishment of property by persons or corporations outside of Indiana.[88]

87 Indiana *House Journal,* 1879, pp. 17-18 and *passim; Brevier Legislative Reports,* XVII (1879), pp. 87-88; Indiana *Laws,* 1879, p. 43.

88 Indiana *House Journal,* 1877, pp. 17, 85, 105, 131, 137, 139, 157, 236, 265;

Numerous measures were introduced to protect the rights of wage earners but little was accomplished. In 1875 bills were introduced to enable workers to collect wages due them. One provided that workers should be paid once a month in lawful money of the United States. None of these were adopted. In 1877 a law was passed which gave employees of any corporation doing business in the state a first lien upon the property and earnings of the corporation for work done. A supplementary law adopted in 1879 provided that when any corporation or person engaged in manufacturing or construction suspended business or became bankrupt, laborers should be regarded as "preferred creditors" and their claims to wages should be regarded as "preferred debts" against the assets of the corporation or person.[89]

Although the legislature tried to protect the property rights of farmers against foreclosure and the right of workers to their wages, it did nothing for the relief of unemployed workers, whose ranks grew as the depression continued. One of the most alarming aspects of the depression was the hoards of indigent men who roamed the countryside and congregated in the cities. The press was full of references to these "tramps" and "beggars." Early in 1876 the Indianapolis city council passed an ordinance which provided that unemployed persons who loitered around the city should be arrested. The Indianapolis *Journal* observed that most states were passing laws dealing with tramps and urged Indiana to act—"otherwise this state will become the paradise of tramps, and be overrun by a swarm of lazy drones." The *Journal* insisted that most of the tramps did not want work—that they "would rather beg or steal than work" and that compulsory labor was the answer to the problem.[90]

Indiana *Laws,* special session, 1875, p. 76; special session, 1879, pp. 44-45, 115, 127, 176-179.

[89] Indiana *House Journal,* 1875, p. 136; *Brevier Legislative Reports,* XV (1875), 64; Indiana *Laws,* special session, 1877, p. 27; special session, 1879, p. 153.

[90] Indianapolis *Daily Sentinel,* February 25, 1876; Indianapolis *Daily Journal,* January 25, 1877.

To deal with the problem the 1877 Assembly passed a vagrancy law which Governor Williams signed after some hesitation. It defined as vagrants any persons "who shall have arrived at years of discretion, who shall be found without any fixed residence, and without any visible means of support, and idling away their time, and making no effort to procure employment," or who refused labor when it was offered, or who were found wandering about "with no certain place of abode, and no sufficient means of support, and shall be living without labor or employment." Persons charged with being vagrants were to be fined ten dollars. If unable to pay their fines they were to be required to work on the streets or in the workhouse at the rate of fifty cents a day. If a person refused to work he was to be fed on bread and water until he consented to work. The Indianapolis *Journal* praised the adoption of the law but later reported it was not proving effective.[91]

The 1878 elections and 1879 session of the legislature marked the high point of political unrest. In 1879 economic conditions began to improve. A severe crop shortage in Europe increased the demand for farm products and created a favorable trade balance for the United States. The resumption of specie payments, which was carried out according to plan in 1879, took place without a flurry. For the time, at least, interest in monetary expansion subsided. The flirtation of Indiana Democrats with inflation appeared to be over. Indiana Democrats did not protest when the national convention adopted a hard money platform in 1880 and nominated William H. English, a conservative hard money Indiana banker, for the vice-presidency. A political era had ended.

[91] Indiana *Laws,* special session, 1877, pp. 80-83; Indianapolis *Daily Journal,* April 12, 1877.

CHAPTER VIII

THE TRANSPORTATION REVOLUTION

At midcentury Indiana was at the threshold of a revolution in transportation. No other development during the next thirty years had more far-reaching effects upon the state than did railroads. In 1850 there were only about two hundred miles of completed track in the state. By 1880 there was a network of over four thousand miles, reaching into almost every county and connecting Indiana with both the east and west coast. Railroads brought new settlers, broke down rural isolation, transformed villages into cities, brought far-reaching changes in agriculture and everyday life, and hastened the beginnings of mining and industry. Railroad corporations wielded great political power and successfully sought favors from government. After a few years a clamor for government regulation developed.

By the fifties the canal era, which had been hailed with such optimism a generation earlier, was drawing to a close. Competition of the railroads was in large part responsible for this development. By 1855 boats had ceased to make regular runs on the upper part of the Whitewater although the lower end of the canal was used until 1864. The Central Canal was sold by the state in 1859 for the sum of $2,425.[1]

The Wabash and Erie, the most ambitious canal project in the state, reached Terre Haute in 1850, and was finally completed to Evansville in 1853. The upper part of the canal enjoyed a considerable amount of prosperity from 1847 to 1856. Receipts reached the peak in 1852. But the extension below Terre Haute was never profitable, and the later

[1] Carter, Decade of Hoosier History, p. 257; Logan Esarey, *Internal Improvements in Early Indiana* (Indiana Historical Society *Publications,* V, No. 2, Indianapolis, 1912), p. 123.

history of the whole canal was beset with disasters. In 1850 cholera struck and killed one hundred and fifty of the canal workers. The following year the entire canal was closed for a month because of floods. Thereafter floods frequently tied up traffic for months. Frequent and costly repairs to locks, gates, and bridges were necessary. By 1852 railroads parallel to the canal were under construction, and the business of the northern part, which had been relatively prosperous, began to decline as railroads reached Fort Wayne, Lafayette, and Logansport. Rate wars followed, but even drastic reductions in canal tolls failed to hold trade. By 1856 tolls had dropped to $113,000 while expenses for repairs mounted to $60,000, and the stockholders ordered the trustees to close any part of the canal which did not operate at a profit. By 1860 the lower portion of the canal had fallen into complete disrepair and was virtually abandoned.[2] In 1866 the Wabash and Erie Canal Company was organized to operate the canal. Between 1866 and 1874 it spent $436,345 on maintenance and repairs and collected only $274,019 in tolls. In the meanwhile some persons who had invested money in canal securities had begun a movement to have the state assume responsibility for the obligations of the canal. Governor Baker devoted a substantial part of his message to the legislature in 1871 to the canal question, recommending that a constitutional amendment be adopted to preclude the possibility of such action. Accordingly a resolution was passed prohibiting the General Assembly from assuming any liability incurred by the Wabash and Erie Canal. The resolution was passed a second time in 1873, submitted to the voters for ratification, and declared in force. Early in 1874 the company which was operating the canal abandoned it completely, and thereafter it fell into complete disuse.[3]

[2] Esarey, *op. cit.,* pp. 147-153; Carter, *op. cit.,* p. 258.

[3] Annual Report of the Board of Trustees of the Wabash and Erie Canal for the Year 1874, Indiana *Documentary Journal,* 1875, II, Doc. 14, pp. 3-4; Kettleborough, *Constitution Making in Indiana,* II, 80-84, 86, 87, 89-92, 98-112.

During the late forties and early fifties, when the railroad mania hit the state, there was simultaneously a plank-road craze. In fact some champions argued that the solution of Indiana's transportation problems lay in the plank roads rather than steam railways. Planking consisted of laying a timber floor—usually of oak planks—on a dirt roadbed. The completion of the first wooden toll road in New York in 1846 was followed by a wave of enthusiasm in the West, where abundant timber made for cheap construction of the roads. Farmers especially were expected to benefit by quicker means of getting grain to market. Numerous plank-road companies petitioned the Indiana legislature for charters and embarked upon campaigns to sell stock. Newspapers were full of accounts of plans for the new roads, which they heartily endorsed.

"This has become the Plank Road age as well as the Railroad and Telegraph age . . .," declared one. "Build up your towns by Plank Roads to that size which will permit you to erect railroads." Another paper predicted that plank roads would become the most profitable form of investment. Robert Dale Owen, who was the most enthusiastic advocate of plank roads in the state, also expressed the view that at the present stage of development they were more suitable and profitable than railroads. Some four hundred miles of road were built in 1850 and an additional twelve hundred miles were surveyed. At the 1850-51 session of the legislature more than thirty plank-road companies were chartered. Portions of both the National Road and the Michigan Road were planked. An English traveler, who set out from Indianapolis to Terre Haute in 1851, found the experience of traveling on the wooden road a novel but pleasant one. He liked the absence of dust and reported that the planks "rose and sank under us with the elasticity of the floor of a ball room."[4]

4 Evansville *Journal,* December 14, 1849, quoted in Leopold, *Robert Dale Owen,* p. 264; Indianapolis *Indiana State Journal* (weekly), March 30, 1850; letter of Owen in New Albany *Bulletin,* quoted in Indianapolis *Indiana State*

The enthusiasm for the wooden roads declined almost as rapidly as it had developed—partly because sparseness of population meant that traffic was too light to be profitable in many places. More important was the fact that the roads deteriorated rapidly as the planks decayed because of poor drainage. By 1860 many plank roads had been abandoned, but gravel or macadamized toll roads continued to be built and operated until almost the end of the century. With few exceptions these roads, which were operated by private corporations, were the only improved roads in the state. Between New Albany and Paoli was a macadamized road which had been built by the state as part of the internal improvements program of the thirties. From 1840 to 1850 it was operated by the state as a toll road, and in 1851 it was turned over to a private corporation which kept it in repair and collected tolls from it until 1899. In 1850 the Wayne County Turnpike Company took over the operation of the portion of the National Road in Wayne County. The road was graveled and operated as a toll road until 1890. In 1853 another company took over the portion of the road in Henry County.[5]

A general law passed in 1852 provided for the formation of companies to construct macadamized or gravel roads. It authorized groups to file articles of association after stock for the proposed road had been subscribed to the amount of five hundred dollars per mile. Directors of the company were given power to determine the location of the road and to acquire land for it. They could sell bonds and borrow money in other ways to finance the enterprise. As soon as three miles were completed tolls might be collected. Numer-

Sentinel (triweekly), January 1, 1850. Owen published an essay, A Brief Practical Treatise on the Construction and Management of Plank Roads, in June, 1850. Leopold, Robert Dale Owen, p. 266; Indiana Senate Journal, 1850-1851, p. 14; Carter, Decade of Hoosier History, pp. 249-250; J. Richard Beste, The Wabash: or Adventures of an English Gentleman's Family in the Interior of America (2 volumes, London, 1855), I, 298.

5 "The Roads and Road Materials of Indiana," Indiana Department of Geology and Natural Resources, Annual Report, 1905, pp. 33-34, 36.

ous toll roads were constructed, especially in the central and northern parts of the state. Some of them were very profitable projects, paying dividends of 7 to 15 per cent. Later legislation laid the groundwork for a system of free roads. A law passed in 1865 provided that special taxes might be levied to build gravel or macadamized roads. Persons owning property along the route of a proposed road were authorized to form a company to build the road. They were assessed taxes over a three-year period to pay the costs of construction, but they were allowed to collect tolls for the use of the road for a period of twenty years, after which the road was to become toll free. In 1877 the law was changed to authorize county commissioners to lay out and construct new roads and to improve existing roads. A special tax was to be levied on land adjacent to the roads, but the roads could be built only after a majority of the landowners affected had signified their approval. Roads built under this authority were to be toll free. A supplementary law of 1879 authorized county commissioners to keep free gravel roads in repair.[6]

§ §

The plank-road mania was minor compared to the excitement and enthusiasm engendered by railroads. During the forties every session of the legislature was deluged with applications for railroad charters. By 1850, lines, which if completed, would have totaled more than four thousand miles, had been chartered. The purpose of these lines was primarily to supplement the system of waterways. Most of the early charters called for terminals in towns along the Ohio River, where most of the population and business of the state were concentrated. Others were to touch the Wabash and Erie Canal and others the Great Lakes. The location of the state capital in the center of the state was also a factor in determining proposed routes, some of which were to radiate from

6 "The Roads and Road Materials of Indiana," *loc. cit.,* p. 37; Indiana *Revised Statutes,* 1852, II, 394-397, 399; Indiana *Laws,* 1865, pp. 90-93; 1877, pp. 82, 84, 86, 89; 1879, pp. 226-228.

Indianapolis. But out of all the lines which were chartered only one of any consequence had been completed by 1850—the Madison and Indianapolis. This line, eighty-six miles in length, had reached the state capital in 1847. Its construction was considered an engineering achievement of the first magnitude. The ascent of the steep hill to the north of Madison by a train of cars pulled by "a magnificent engine" constructed in England was regarded as something of a marvel by European visitors as well as Americans.[7]

The original part of the line had been built and operated by the state and subsequently leased to a private company which completed it. Because of a prohibition in the new state constitution against the state engaging in this sort of activity the state prepared to sell its share in 1853. This was accomplished by mortgaging the railroad and giving the state the mortgage as security. For a few years the line, with the spurs which were built to connect it with other towns, operated at a profit and was considered one of the most successful roads in the country. Its construction was a major factor in the emergence of Indianapolis as the largest city in the state.[8]

[7] Victor M. Bogle, "Railroad Building in Indiana, 1850-1855," *Indiana Magazine of History*, LVIII (1962), 215; Beste, *The Wabash*, I, 252; Pulszky, *White, Red, Black*, II, 9-10; William Ferguson, *America by River and Rail; or, Notes by the Way on the New World and Its People* (London, 1856), p. 343.

[8] Indiana *Senate Journal*, 1851-1852, p. 21; *American Railroad Journal*, quoted in Indianapolis *Indiana State Sentinel* (triweekly), January 3, 1850; Daniels, *Village at the End of the Road*, p. 89. The state had spent nearly $2,000,000 on the Madison and Indianapolis road but agreed to accept $200,000 payable in four years as payment. But by 1855 none of the payment had been made. This led to an investigation and report of a commission which recommended that the state settle its claim by accepting $75,000 in state bonds. Esarey, *Internal Improvements in Early Indiana*, p. 123. See below, pp. 334-335n. The first president of the Madison and Indianapolis was John Brough, formerly of Cincinnati. After serving as president of the Madison line he served as the second president of the Indianapolis and Bellefontaine and later as president of the Indianapolis, Pittsburgh, and Cleveland. During the Civil War Brough, a former Democrat, was nominated by the Ohio Republicans to oppose Clement Vallandigham in the gubernatorial contest of 1863. He defeated Vallandigham in a record vote but died in 1865. John Brough in *Dictionary of American Biography*.

The success of this pioneer line kindled enthusiasm for other lines. A few men of vision, among whom members of the Whig party were conspicuous, took the lead in projecting railroads which became the basic network connecting Indianapolis with other states. Most prominent among them was Oliver H. Smith, former member of the United States House of Representatives and of the Senate, who was the moving spirit in the building of the Indianapolis and Bellefontaine line, which ran northeastward from Indianapolis to the Ohio state line. Because of his experience in Congress Smith knew persons in the East from whom he was able to secure financial assistance. He served as president of the Bellefontaine line until his death in 1859 and was also the first president of the Evansville and Indianapolis Straight Line.[9] The idea of connecting the new state capital, Indianapolis, by rail with Cincinnati, the metropolis of the West, was conceived as early as 1832 by George H. Dunn of Lawrenceburg. He and a group of prominent Whigs secured a charter for a Lawrenceburg to Indianapolis line that year, and a small amount of track was laid, then the project fell into abeyance. The success of the Madison and Indianapolis Railroad caused a revival of interest, but the Madison line fought the chartering of a rival. Consequently Dunn and his associates sought to achieve their objective indirectly. In 1848 they received from the legislature a charter for a line from Rushville to Lawrenceburg by way of Greensburg. Subsequently the charter was amended to permit extensions. A line from Shelbyville to Rushville was incorporated in 1850 into the Lawrenceburg and Upper Mississippi (formerly the Rushville and Lawrenceburg). Then a line from Shelbyville to Indianapolis

<hr />

[9] Oliver Hampton Smith in *Dictionary of American Biography;* Ared M. Murphy, "The Big Four Railroad in Indiana," *Indiana Magazine of History,* XXI (1925), 117; Oran Perry (comp.), *History of the Evansville and Indianapolis Railroad and Constituent Companies* (n.p., 1917), p. 12. Smith was a native of Pennsylvania who settled in Connersville and established a lucrative law practice. He was first elected to the United States House of Representatives as a Democrat, but he was elected to the Senate in 1836 as a Whig.

was incorporated. George H. Dunn served as president of the companies organized to build these lines which were consolidated into the Indianapolis and Cincinnati line.[10] The moving spirit behind the Lafayette and Indianapolis railroad, and its first president, was Albert S. White of Tippecanoe County, another Whig who had been a member of both the United States House and Senate.[11] Unlike the aforementioned group, Chauncey Rose, who was largely responsible for the building of the highly successful Indianapolis and Terre Haute Railroad, was not politically prominent. Rose, a Terre Haute businessman, was influential in diverting a projected line from Richmond, Indiana, to Springfield, Illinois, to run by way of Terre Haute and was responsible for bringing other lines into that city.[12] The first president of the New Albany and Salem, which eventually connected the Ohio River with Lake Michigan, was a less well-known figure, James Brooks, a New Albany businessman.[13]

The man who played the most important role in the actual surveying and construction of the early lines was Thomas Armstrong Morris of Indianapolis, who embarked upon a career as a civil engineer after graduating from the United States Military Academy. He served as chief engineer of the Madison and Indianapolis Railroad from 1841 to 1847.

[10] Murphy, "Big Four Railroad in Indiana," *Indiana Magazine of History,* XXI, 160-162, 165-169.

[11] *Ibid.,* p. 159; Albert Smith White in *Dictionary of American Biography.* White was a native of New York and a graduate of Union College, where he had been a roommate of William H. Seward. He retired from politics in 1845 to devote himself exclusively to the practice of law and railroad affairs, but in 1860 he was elected to Congress again as a Republican.

[12] Chauncey Rose in *Dictionary of American Biography;* C. C. Oakey, *Greater Terre Haute and Vigo County* . . . (2 volumes, Chicago, 1908), I, 140-143. Rose, who was born in Connecticut, had little formal education. He settled in Indiana in 1818, and at first operated a grist- and sawmill at Rosedale. In 1825 he moved to Terre Haute, where he amassed a fortune in a variety of business enterprises. Rose was noted for his philanthropies. For his contributions to educational institutions see Chapter XI.

[13] Frank F. Hargrave, *A Pioneer Indiana Railroad. The Origin and Development of the Monon* (Indianapolis, 1932), pp. 22-23.

Thereafter he served both the Terre Haute and Richmond line and the Indianapolis and Bellefontaine in the same capacity. In 1852, after these two railroads were largely completed, he became chief engineer of the Indianapolis and Cincinnati. Meanwhile he had also prepared estimates for the projected Peru and Indianapolis line. From 1854 to 1857 he also served as president of the Indianapolis and Cincinnati and from 1857 to 1859 as president of the Indianapolis and Bellefontaine.[14]

The fact that the 1850-51 session of the legislature, the last one under the old constitution, authorized at least twenty-four new railroad corporations is evidence of the general enthusiasm. These early charters authorized the sale of stock, and in many cases permitted county commissioners to buy stock on behalf of the county. They required that construction be begun within a specified time and be completed within a specified time, but the terms were generous. Some companies were allowed as much as twenty or twenty-five years for completion. Under the new state constitution special legislation was prohibited. In 1852 a general act for railroads was adopted which permitted any group of fifteen or more persons with a total capital of at least fifty thousand dollars, or one thousand dollars for each mile of the proposed line, to incorporate. In addition to selling stock such companies were allowed to receive donations and to borrow money by selling bonds and mortgaging their property as security.[15]

In his message to the legislature in 1850 Governor Wright reported that 212 miles of track were in actual use and that more than a thousand more had been surveyed and were

[14] Thomas Armstrong Morris in *Dictionary of American Biography.* From 1862 to 1866 Morris was chief engineer of the Indianapolis and Cincinnati, during which time the section between Lawrenceburg and Cincinnati was completed. From 1866 to 1869 he was president and chief engineer of the Indianapolis and St. Louis line. In 1870 he became receiver for the Indianapolis, Cincinnati and Lafayette. For his role in the Civil War see Chapter IV, pages 127, 143.

[15] Indiana *Local Laws,* 1851-1852, pp. 580-584; Indiana *Revised Statutes,* 1852, I, 409, 417.

under construction. Newspapers were ecstatic over the future of the railroads and the benefits they would bring to the state. Probably more newspaper space was devoted to railroad news and prospects than any other single subject during the early fifties. As a result of railroads, ran a typical bit of journalistic comment, "Prices are to be equalized, districts heretofore remote, will be brought nigh to market. New avenues of trade will be opened. New places of business established. The value of land and its production everywhere advanced."[16]

Railroad conventions were called to stimulate interest in the new form of transportation and to seek money for construction. The newly organized corporations appealed to investors by publishing glowing promotional literature. They sought capital wherever they could find it, from local farmers and businessmen, from eastern and European capitalists, and from government subsidies. At first it was thought that lines could be built principally out of local resources—private and public. The Indianapolis *Journal* reported approvingly that the people of Jefferson, Bartholomew, Brown, and Monroe counties were subscribing stock in the Columbus, Nashville, and Bloomington line. The *Journal* urged people in other counties to "rely upon their own labor and energies, to carry improvements into their midst," assuring them that in a few years they would "own their own roads and their profits among themselves, in addition to receiving an immense increase of price upon all they have to sell. Railroads, as to their construction, are now no mystery. They *can* be made, like all other roads, by the labor of the country." "You who are farmers and land owners along the line ought to *take stock,* and aid in the construction of the road; hold it for yourselves and your children as you do real estate. It will be a good investment," said a brochure of the Jeffersonville Railroad Company.[17]

16 Indiana *Senate Journal,* 1850-1851, p. 14; Indianapolis *Indiana State Sentinel* (triweekly), January 11, 1851.

17 Jeffersonville Railroad Company, *Annual Report,* 1849, p. 6; Indianapolis *Indiana State Journal* (weekly), February 4, 1850.

Crop failure in 1849 made the sale of railroad stock to farmers difficult, but in 1850 a good wheat crop brightened the prospects for sale of stock and for the collection of money pledged earlier. Some of the stock was purchased with money, but a large amount of the subscriptions was exchanged for land. In some instances the right of way was donated. Frequently contractors and construction workers agreed to take stock in payment. For example, in 1851 the Indianapolis and Bellefontaine road reported $232,454 in subscriptions in land; $206,149 in cash; and $41,550 in labor and materials. Lands with an estimated cash value of $450,000 were subscribed to the Evansville to Indianapolis (the Straight-Line) road. Chauncey Rose, president of the Terre Haute and Richmond line (later the Indianapolis to Terre Haute), reported in 1851 that most of the right of way and the lands for depots and machine shops were donated to the company. Most of the stock of the Indianapolis and Cincinnati Junction Railroad Company was taken in real estate. Most of the contracts for construction of the line were partly payable in stock of the company. The promoters originally hoped "to accomplish the enterprise to a great extent, if not entirely, directly on the means the stockholders had furnished, in kind. . . ."[18]

Frequently the slowness of payments of cash subscriptions delayed construction. In 1852 the Jeffersonville Railroad, as the result of shortage of cash, made contracts payable entirely in stock. Contractors in turn were compelled to sell their stock at a discount to pay their laborers.[19]

Appeals were also made to local governments to buy stock. A plea from the Indianapolis and Bellefontaine line urging

[18] Indianapolis *Indiana State Sentinel* (semiweekly), July 10, 1850; Terre Haute *Journal,* quoted *ibid.,* July 20, 1850; Indianapolis and Bellefontaine Railroad Company, *Annual Report,* 1851, p. 9; *Exhibit of the Evansville, Indianapolis and Cleveland Straight Line Railroad Company* (New York, 1854), pp. 8, 9, 13; Lafayette and Indianapolis Railroad Company, *Annual Report,* 1851, p. 5; *Exhibit of the Terre Haute and Richmond Rail-Road Company* (New York, 1851), p. 6; Cincinnati and Indianapolis Junction Railroad Company, *Annual Report,* 1856, p. 6.

[19] Jeffersonville Railroad Company, *Annual Report,* 1852, p. 4.

county governments to contribute assured them that they would in reality only be "lending" the amount which they subscribed since in later years the stock would pay dividends, and the people would have "the great benefits secured, resulting from the road running forever through their counties, adding to the value of their real estate and the products of their farms, as well as greatly increasing the capital and population of those counties, to share in the burdens of taxation in after years."[20]

Governor Wright was opposed to the appropriation of public money for railroads, declaring that it was "wholly foreign to the objects for which municipal corporations are organized and for which the power of taxation is granted." He warned that such appropriations were likely to place local governments in the same difficulties which the state had been involved in as the result of the internal improvements program of the thirties. Apparently most people did not share the Governor's views. As early as 1850 he estimated that cities and counties had subscribed more than a million dollars in railroad stock, and that amount was increased many times over during the next twenty years. Local governments vied with each other to attract railroads, and roads were built along the route which offered the largest assistance. For example, the Lake Erie and Mississippi line, which was to run between Fort Wayne and Logansport, was built through Huntington rather than Liberty Mills, even though this was a longer route, because Huntington's citizens subscribed $22,000 in stock. The city of Evansville subscribed $200,000, consisting of 4,000 shares of stock in the Evansville to Indianapolis line. The stock was to be paid for by issuing city bonds bearing 7 per cent interest to the railroad corporation. The city of Lafayette subscribed $120,000 in 7 per cent bonds to the Lafayette and Indianapolis road. Some interest was also expressed in Federal aid. For example, joint resolutions

[20] Indianapolis and Bellefontaine Railroad Company, *Annual Report*, 1849, p. 7.

asking Congress for assistance in building certain lines which had been projected were introduced into the state legislature in the session of 1851-1852 and defeated by a narrow margin.[21]

Vigorous efforts were made to sell both stocks and bonds to eastern investors. Attempts were made to persuade them that western lines would be more lucrative than eastern— that they could be constructed at lower costs and would have a larger amount of business in proportion to the cost of construction. Oliver H. Smith, president of the Indianapolis and Bellefontaine line, confidently predicted that dividends could not be less than 15 per cent per year, "with a rapid increase from year to year."[22]

Hopes that some railroads could be built with local capital were doomed to disappointment. Some corporations from the beginning, others after a few years, sought additional resources from eastern capitalists. The usual method was to mortgage the line, using the land which had been subscribed as security for the sale of bonds. In its first annual report the Indianapolis and Cincinnati Junction Company reported it would probably be necessary "to anticipate the sale of real estate by mortgaging the road to obtain money for the purchase of iron." In 1851 the Jeffersonville Company issued $300,000 in bonds, secured by a mortgage on the road, to New York investors. At the outset Chauncey Rose proposed to use the lands acquired by the Terre Haute and Richmond Company as security for a bond issue in order to raise money to pay for iron. The Evansville to Indianapolis Straight Line used the lands which it received as security and sent Willard

[21] Indiana *Senate Journal,* 1850-1851, p. 15; 1851-1852, pp. 631, 655, 673-674; Carter, Decade of Hoosier History, p. 264; *Exhibit of the Evansville, Indianapolis, and Cleveland Straight Line Railroad Company,* 1854, pp. 8-9, 13; Lafayette and Indianapolis Railroad Company, *Annual Report,* 1851, p. 5.

[22] *Statement of the Condition and Prospects of the Jeffersonville Rail-Road Company* (New York, 1851), p. 10; *Communication of the President, and Report of the Engineer of the Indianapolis and Bellefontaine Railroad Company, December 4, 1849* (Indianapolis, 1849), p. 6.

Carpenter, the moving spirit of the company, to Europe to sell bonds and purchase rails and equipment. But Carpenter's mission was unsuccessful and construction on the railroad was suspended. The Cincinnati, Peru, and Chicago line which was organized in 1853 was mortgaged to New York capitalists in 1855.[23]

Abundant timber was available locally for superstructures such as bridges and for fuel, but iron for the tracks as well as the locomotives themselves had to be brought from outside —sometimes from England. Rails for the Indianapolis and Terre Haute line were brought from Liverpool to New Orleans and then to Madison. Part of the iron for the Jeffersonville road was shipped from New York via the Great Lakes and canals to Cincinnati; part of it was shipped from Europe to New Orleans. The track used on the Lafayette and Indianapolis road came from Wales. Most of the locomotives were made in the East, principally in Boston or Philadelphia.[24]

Most of the track which was first laid was covered with flimsy strip rail, but after a few years there was a change to the heavier T rails. By 1851 the Madison and Indianapolis Railroad had relaid its track with the heavier type of rail. T rail was much more expensive than the older type, and its use added greatly to the cost of construction.[25] At first the width of track on various lines was not uniform, and there was little interest in making it possible for cars of one line

23 Indianapolis and Cincinnati Junction Railroad Company, *Annual Report,* 1853, p. 7; Jeffersonville Railroad Company, *Annual Report,* 1852, p. 4; *Exhibit of the Terre Haute and Richmond Rail-Road Company,* 1849, p. 6; Oran Perry (comp.), *History of the Evansville and Indianapolis Railroad,* p. 12; Carter, Decade of Hoosier History, pp. 266-267.

24 Oakey, *Greater Terre Haute and Vigo County,* I, 189; Jeffersonville Railroad Company, *Annual Report,* 1852, p. 5; Lafayette and Indianapolis Railroad Company, *Annual Report,* 1851, p. 4; Bogle, "Railroad Building in Indiana, 1850-1855," *Indiana Magazine of History,* LVIII, 229.

25 Bogle, *op. cit.,* p. 228; *American Railroad Journal,* quoted in Indianapolis *Indiana State Sentinel* (triweekly), January 3, 1850; Daniels, *Village at the End of the Road,* p. 105.

to be switched to the track of another. In fact, in a letter to the press in 1850, Oliver H. Smith expressed the opinion that the problems involved in sending cars out of the state—beyond the jurisdiction of the state, where they were liable to accident and might require repairs—"would more than counter balance any inconvenience growing out of transfers at the State line, from one line to another." Later, of course, it was necessary to make adjustments, and Smith's Bellefontaine line was forced to widen the gauge of its tracks. In 1856 an English traveler coming into the state from Ohio reported that in order for the cars connecting with Indianapolis to use the track of the Ohio and Mississippi line a third rail had been laid—"a piece of awkwardness and expense," he observed, which might have been avoided here and elsewhere, had a uniform gauge been adopted for all the states. Most of the track laid in Indiana during the 1850's was 4 feet 8½ inches in width, a gauge which had come to be regarded as standard.[26]

The fifties saw the greatest increase in railroad mileage of any decade in the history of the state, from a mere 212 miles in 1850 to 2,163 miles in 1860. The Madison and Indianapolis completed spurs to Edinburg and Shelbyville in 1850. The Lafayette to Indianapolis line was completed in 1852. The Bellefontaine line, which had reached Pendleton in 1850, expanded rapidly thereafter through Anderson, Muncie, and Winchester to the Ohio border by the end of 1852. The same year the Indianapolis to Terre Haute was completed, and the Indiana Central from Indianapolis to Richmond was completed the following year. In 1853 the Indianapolis and Cincinnati road was completed from Lawrenceburg to Indianapolis via Greensburg and Shelbyville. Meanwhile the Jeffersonville road had been built northward from New Albany to Columbus and Edinburg, and the New Albany and Salem had been extended, reaching Lake Michigan, where it

[26] Indianapolis *Indiana State Sentinel* (semiweekly), March 30, 1850; Ferguson, *America by River and Rail*, p. 323; Bogle, "Railroad Building in Indiana, 1850-1855," *Indiana Magazine of History*, LVIII, 228.

connected with Chicago, in 1854. During the same year the Peru and Indianapolis line was completed, and the Evansville and Illinois completed its road from Evansville to Terre Haute.[27] Most of these early lines ran in a generally north-south direction or radiated from Indianapolis, which more than any other city in the state became the railroad hub. In 1853 a Union Depot was completed in the capital city. By 1855 eight lines were using it.[28]

Meanwhile, some east-west lines were being constructed across both the southern and northern parts of the state. The Ohio and Mississippi, which connected Cincinnati and St. Louis, entered Indiana at Lawrenceburg and ran across the state to Vincennes. In the north the Northern Indiana Company joined with the Michigan Southern Railroad to open a route which extended through Indiana to Chicago, passing through Elkhart, Mishawaka, South Bend, and La Porte. A segment of the Michigan Central, which extended westward from Detroit, entered Indiana at New Buffalo and ran to Michigan City. The Lake Erie, Wabash, and St. Louis (later the Wabash line) was completed from Toledo to Fort Wayne and then followed the valley of the Wabash through Peru and Logansport to the Illinois line. The Pittsburgh, Logansport, and Chicago, a part of which had originally been the New Castle and Richmond, ran diagonally across the state from southeast to northwest, reaching Chicago in 1858.[29]

27 Bogle, op. cit., p. 219; O. H. Smith, "The Railroads of Indiana," in Indiana State Board of Agriculture, Annual Report, 1856, p. 486. By 1856 there were 650 miles of railroads running through 30 counties connecting with the Union Depot in Indianapolis. In addition there were 1,209 miles running through 36 counties, connecting with these lines. Only 25 counties were not reached by railroad at that date. Ibid. See Table, p. 361, showing annual increase of railroad mileage.

28 Daniels, Village at the End of the Road, pp. 101-103; Oliver H. Smith, Early Indiana Trials and Sketches. Reminiscences. by Hon. O. H. Smith (Cincinnati, 1858), p. 424. Engineer Thomas A. Morris was largely responsible for the planning and building of the Union Depot.

29 Bogle, "Railroad Building in Indiana, 1850-1855," Indiana Magazine of History, LVIII, 218-219; Frederic L. Paxson, "The Railroads of the 'Old Northwest' before the Civil War," Transactions of the Wisconsin Academy

The completion of a portion of a line was always the occasion for a celebration with parades and bonfires. Crowds came from far and wide to look with awe at the hissing locomotive and to hear speeches by the governor or other notables. The increased ease and especially the speed which the new form of transportation afforded was a constant source of amazement. "We breakfasted in Terre Haute, dined in Indianapolis, and supped the usual tea-time again in Terre Haute," exclaimed one passenger. "All this may be done any day now —what may come next we are not at present prepared to advise."[30]

In spite of the optimism with which they were begun most lines fell into financial difficulties and failed to make profits for the men who started them. The Indianapolis to Terre Haute, which constantly showed a profit and which was prevented from falling into the hands of eastern capitalists, was one of the few exceptions. Almost from the beginning most lines suffered from ruinous competition. The original line, the Madison and Indianapolis, unsuccessfully sought to forestall the building of the rival lines which ultimately drove it into bankruptcy. It succeeded for a time in preventing the chartering of a company to build a direct line from Indianapolis to Cincinnati, but, as already seen, these efforts were thwarted by the chartering and consolidation of several short lines. However, the building of the Jeffersonville to Indianapolis line proved most disastrous to the Madison line. By 1855 the president of the company reported that "the Madison Road, from occupying the first position among Western Roads . . . has been reduced to the position of a road of inferior class, has been stripped of its business by rivalship and competition, and hangs upon the hands of its owners as a prop-

of Sciences, Arts and Letters, XVII (2 parts, Madison, Wis., 1914), Pt. 1, p. 260.

30 Terre Haute *Wabash Courier*, quoted in Roll, *Colonel Dick Thompson*, p. 135. For examples of celebrations see Indianapolis *Indiana State Sentinel* (semiweekly), September 7, 1850; *ibid.* (triweekly), October 10, 1850; *History of St. Joseph County, Indiana . . .* (Chicago, 1880), pp. 456-457.

erty nearly worthless." By that date the company was in debt to the extent of more than three million dollars, and a state-appointed commission which investigated its affairs declared it was in a state of "hopeless insolvency."[31]

The Jeffersonville road, the principal rival of the Madison line, also complained of the effects of competition which led many western lines to cut rates to ruinous levels in an effort to increase their business, and harm their rivals. In its annual report in 1858 the Bellefontaine road reported that in 1857, a year of depression, for sixty days rates had been reduced to "ruinous figures" as the result of competition. The rate slashing had been followed by a convention of rival companies seeking a remedy for the evil, but it had been impossible to get enough companies to agree, so there was no guarantee that the same situation would not recur. From this it is apparent that the problems of ruinous competition accompanied by rate slashing and efforts at joint action to maintain rates which characterized later railroad history were already present in the fifties.[32]

Although most railroads were not themselves financially successful they contributed greatly to the economic growth and prosperity of the state as a whole. At the time of the death of Oliver H. Smith in 1859 the Bellefontaine line was

31 Murphy, "The Big Four Railroad in Indiana," *Indiana Magazine of History*, XXI, 165, 169; Indianapolis *Locomotive*, January 26, 1850; Report of the President of Madison and Indianapolis Railroad, in Indiana *Documentary Journal*, 1857, I, Doc. 5, pp. 351, 352-353, 370-372. In 1852 the gross earnings of the line were $476,892; by 1855 they had fallen to $225,000. The commission recommended that in view of the bankruptcy of the railroad and the fact that this condition had been brought about in part through the chartering of rival lines by the legislature, that the state should accept $75,000 in 5 per cent bonds as full satisfaction on the mortgage which the state held on the railroad. This settlement was obviously disadvantageous to the state. In 1861 the company was sold for $325,000 and reorganized. In 1864 a controlling interest in the line was acquired by the rival Jeffersonville Company. *Ibid.;* Freda L. Bridenstine, The Madison and Indianapolis Railroad (Master's thesis in History, Butler University, 1931), pp. 72-74.

32 Jeffersonville Railroad Company, *Annual Report*, 1855, p. 11; 1856, p. 3; Bellefontaine Rail Road Line, *Annual Report*, 1858, p. 16.

in financial difficulties. At a memorial service in honor of Smith one speaker said that the railroad would nonetheless be recognized as a "monument" to his memory and a "public benefit." "Although there have been very serious losses to many worthy stockholders," he said, "it is clear that these losses have been vastly overbalanced by the benefits conferred upon the traveling public, and especially upon the farmers and citizens on and near its route."[33] The immediate effect of building short lines was to give farmers easier access to nearby markets. For example, as rail connections were made between Pendleton and Indianapolis and Noblesville and Indianapolis much more produce was shipped from those towns to the state capital, and prices increased.[34] As lines lengthened and junctions were made with other lines or with the Ohio River or Lake Michigan new trade patterns developed or old ones were modified. Markets in the East became more accessible for agricultural products. Railroad transportation was especially important to central and northern Indiana, the parts of the state where population increased most rapidly in the fifties. Livestock production first began to assume importance in the northern counties after railroad transportation to the East became possible. On the other hand most of the products of the southern part of the state, which had formerly gone to New Orleans and other southern cities, continued to go southward although in some cases goods which had formerly gone by water were now transported by rail.[35]

[33] *Proceedings of the Indianapolis Bar on the Death of Hon. Oliver H. Smith, March, 1859* (Indianapolis, 1859), p. 17.

[34] Bogle, "Railroad Building in Indiana, 1850-1855," *Indiana Magazine of History*, LVIII, 226; Indianapolis and Bellefontaine Railroad Company, *Annual Report*, 1851, p. 8. After the first section of the Bellefontaine line was in operation it was reported that flour in Pendleton had increased in price by 37½ cents a barrel and that wheat had increased 10 cents a bushel, while real estate values in the vicinity had increased by one third. *Ibid.*

[35] Kohlmeier, *The Old Northwest*, pp. 212-213. See also, *ibid.*, pp. 89, 112-114, 122-123, 154-155, 161, 204.

§ § §

Although the Civil War disrupted normal trade with the South the war proved a blessing to the railroads and gave most lines a chance to recoup their fortunes, at least temporarily. Business furnished by the state and national governments enabled many lines to pay their debts, buy and repair equipment, and pay dividends, even though wartime conditions increased operating costs. Even the Madison line, which performed valuable services during the war, showed a recovery. The Bellefontaine line, which had been in a state of financial embarrassment from 1855 to 1862, reported that during 1863 and 1864 it was able to make needed repairs and also to declare a 6 per cent dividend. In 1864 the Toledo and Wabash line enjoyed a great increase in both passenger and freight traffic. Its revenues were reported to "have surpassed the conjectures of the most sanguine and hopeful." The company was able to pay interest on all its funded debt, to pay dividends on both preferred and common stock, and to appropriate money for new buildings and equipment as well. In April, 1864, the Indianapolis to Terre Haute paid a stock dividend of 25 per cent, a regular cash dividend of 5 per cent, and an extra dividend of 5 per cent.[36]

The years after the Civil War saw the completion of lines already begun and the construction of new ones. A more striking development was the consolidation of short lines into a few major systems and the transfer of control of most lines to eastern capitalists. By 1880 there were more than four thousand miles of railroads in the state, reaching eighty-five of the ninety-two counties. In the postwar years several new lines were begun and numerous lateral lines were built to connect with major lines. A number of short lines were built to the coal fields in the southwestern part of the state.

36 Bellefontaine Railroad Line, *Annual Report,* 1864, pp. 12-13; Toledo and Wabash Railway Company, *Annual Report,* 1864, pp. 4, 9; Terre Haute and Richmond Railroad Company, *Annual Report,* 1864, pp. 6-7; Terrell, *Indiana in the War of the Rebellion,* p. 489.

Indianapolis was linked to the southwest by the Indianapolis and Vincennes line, completed in 1869. Soon afterwards the Evansville and Indianapolis was begun from Evansville to Worthington, where it connected with the Vincennes line. In 1869 the Indianapolis, Crawfordsville, and Danville line was begun to link Indianapolis with Danville, Illinois. In 1870 it was consolidated with an Illinois line to become the Indianapolis, Bloomington and Western. The Indianapolis and St. Louis was chartered in 1867 and completed in 1870. It ran from Indianapolis to Terre Haute through Greencastle and Clay County, following a more northerly route than the older Indianapolis to Terre Haute line. It was financed chiefly by older companies which expected it to be a good feeder line to lines running eastward from Indianapolis. In 1871 the Indiana and Illinois Central (later the Indianapolis, Decatur and Springfield) from Indianapolis to Decatur, Illinois, was begun.[37]

In the northern part of the state several lines were begun, usually to connect Indiana cities with Michigan or Chicago. Among them was the Fort Wayne, Jackson and Saginaw, begun in 1869, which was soon completed between Fort Wayne, and Jackson, Michigan. The same year the Grand Rapids and Indiana, from Fort Wayne to Mackinac, which had first been chartered in 1854, began building. By 1871 two hundred miles between Fort Wayne and Paris, Michigan, were in operation, and the line was completed in 1873. In 1870 the Fort Wayne, Muncie and Cincinnati line was completed between Fort Wayne and Connersville, and in 1872 the Cincinnati, Richmond and Fort Wayne went into operation. The Peninsular Railroad, connecting South Bend with Lansing, Michigan, was operating by 1871.[38]

[37] Henry V. Poor (comp.), *Manual of the Railroads of the United States* (New York, 1868-   ), 1869-1870, pp. 432, 701; 1871-1872, pp. 67, 467, 487; United States Bureau of the Census, *Tenth Census* (1880), IV: *Transportation* [Pt. 1], p. 328; Murphy, "The Big Four Railroad in Indiana," *Indiana Magazine of History*, XXI, 219-227.

[38] Poor's *Railroad Manual*, 1869-1870, pp. 329, 416; 1871-1872, pp. 287,

Farther west the Chicago, Cincinnati and Louisville line was begun. By 1869 it connected LaPorte with Peru, where it joined the Peru and Indianapolis. By 1874 a portion of the projected Lafayette, Muncie, and Bloomington line had been completed from Lafayette to the Illinois state line. The same year the Eel River line from Logansport to Butler, Indiana, was completed.[39]

Eagerness to tap the coal fields of the southwestern part of the state was an important factor in the projection of several lines during the seventies. Among them were the Evansville, Terre Haute, and Chicago, which was completed from Evansville to Terre Haute and westward to the Illinois border in 1872, and the Bedford, Springville, Owensburg, and Bloomfield, completed in 1876. The Indiana North and South line, which was projected to run from Oxford to Newburgh, and the Cincinnati and Terre Haute, were never completed.[40]

The financial panic which began in 1873 did not bring a halt to the opening of new lines. By 1874 there were twenty-seven lines operating in the state; by 1876 thirty-five lines; and by 1880 a total of sixty-four. This figure embraced many short lines including spurs to the coal fields.[41] While new lines were being built older lines made improvements in track and equipment. During the seventies most of the major lines began to replace the old iron track with new steel rails. Travel was being made more pleasant by improved coaches and the introduction of sleeping cars.[42]

368; 1880, p. 692; United States Bureau of the Census, *Tenth Census* (1880), IV: *Transportation* [Pt. 1], p. 328; Marie Johnston, "The Building of the Grand Rapids and Indiana Railroad," *Indiana Magazine of History*, XLI (1945), 153-154, 160-161, 165-166.

[39] Poor's *Railroad Manual,* 1869-1870, pp. 376-377; 1874-1875, p. 595; 1880, p. 696; United States Bureau of the Census, *Tenth Census* (1880), IV: *Transportation* [Pt. 1], p. 324.

[40] *Tenth Census* (1880), IV [Pt. 1], p. 328; Poor's *Railroad Manual,* 1874-1875, pp. 534, 616, 703-704; 1880, p. 691.

[41] Poor's *Railroad Manual,* 1875-1876, p. xl; 1876, p. xxiv; 1880, p. 690.

[42] United States Bureau of the Census, *Tenth Census,* IV: *Transportation*

Subsidies by local governments played an important part in financing the lines built after the war. In some instances lines appear to have been projected primarily as speculative ventures to enable the promoters to collect the subsidies. The early railroad charters which had been granted by special act of the legislature frequently contained provisions which enabled the local governments to take stock in them. The general act of 1852 for railroad corporations contained no such provisions, but even though there was no authorization in the law for subsidies by counties some railroads received public assistance. In 1866, for example, it was reported that some of the counties through which the Indianapolis and Vincennes line ran were making financial contributions. The commissioners of Montgomery County voted to donate $125,000 to the Indianapolis, Crawfordsville, and Danville Railroad. Although there was apparently a great deal of popular support for the subsidy, one taxpayer tried to block it by seeking an injunction. The railroad had the able legal assistance of Joseph E. McDonald and Lew Wallace. The circuit court refused to issue the injunction, but the Indiana Supreme Court reversed this decision. It held that in the absence of a statute authorizing it a county could not make an appropriation to aid a railroad, therefore the entire transaction in Montgomery County was unwarranted by law.[43]

Meanwhile, the legislature acted to legalize subsidies. Acts passed in 1867 and 1869 authorized cities and counties and townships to subscribe money—by buying either stocks or bonds—and to levy taxes for this purpose. Special elections at which voters were given an opportunity to ratify or reject proposals for such subsidies were required before money could

[Pt. 1], pp. 474, 476, 478, 482, 484; Terre Haute and Indianapolis Railroad Company, *Annual Report*, 1871, p. 7; Indianapolis, Cincinnati and Lafayette Railroad Company, *Report of the President*, 1874, p. 7; Indianapolis *Daily Sentinel*, April 28, 1863, April 24, 1879; Indianapolis *Daily Herald*, March 4, 1867.

43 Indianapolis *Daily Herald*, March 23, 1866, August 6, 1867; Harney *v.* The Indianapolis, Crawfordsville and Danville Railroad Company and others, 32 Ind 244 (1869).

Express Passenger Locomotive built by
Richard Morris & Son, Philadelphia

Freight Locomotive, built by Richard Morris & Son, Philadelphia

RAIL·ROAD
ELECTION NOTICE

The qualified voters of Russell Township, Putnam County, Indiana, are hereby notified that pursuant to the petition of Asa O. Fordyce and 24 other Freeholders of said Township, and the order of the Board of Commissioners of said County upon said petition, the polls of said Township will be opened

On Saturday, December 11, 1875,

At the usual voting place in said Township, to take the vote of the legal voters thereof, upon the subject of said township taking or subscribing stock to the amount of $9,649, not exceeding one per cent. of the taxable property of said township, according to the assessment of 1874, to aid the Indianapolis and Springfield Railroad Company to build their Railroad through said Township.   The voters of said Township are therefore notified that at the time and   place above stated, those in favor of the appropriation will cast their ballots with the words thereon, "in favor of the Railroad Appropriation," and those opposed to said appropriation will cast their ballots with the words, "against the Railroad Appropriation."

By order of the Board of Commissioners of Putnam County, Indiana, made at called session, held November 10th, 1875.

Witness my hand, and the seal of said Board, this 10th day of November, A. D. 1875.
    [L. S.]   H. M. RANDEL, Auditor Putnam County, Ind.

Indiana Historical Society Library

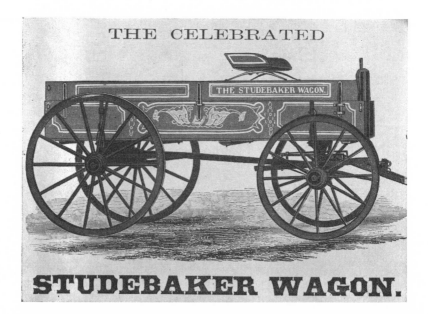

THE CELEBRATED

THE STUDEBAKER WAGON.

STUDEBAKER WAGON.

be appropriated or taxes levied. But there continued to be sharp differences over public subsidies after the legislature authorized them. In 1869 voters in Indianapolis refused by a wide margin to appropriate $75,000 to aid the proposed Indianapolis, Delphi, and Chicago Railroad, even though the press had strongly urged all who wanted "to make a city of Indianapolis" to vote for the subsidy. A few months later, on the other hand, the voters of Center Township in the same city voted to donate $65,000 to the proposed Indiana and Illinois Central Railroad, which was to run from Indianapolis to Decatur, Illinois. Prior to this all the counties west of Indianapolis through which the road would pass had authorized donations.[44]

In 1870 and 1871 two cases challenging the constitutionality of the legislation authorizing appropriations for aid by counties and townships were brought before the Indiana Supreme Court. In both cases the legislation was upheld. The court held that the state itself had the power to make internal improvements directly or to authorize townships or counties to do so, and that the latter could either do the work themselves or authorize corporations to do so. In 1874 the constitutionality of the legislation was again upheld, but in this case there was a dissent by one justice, who insisted that the law was local and special in its operation and had the effect of taking private property from citizens without their consent. In another case the court decided that a corporation had forfeited an appropriation of $100,000 which Decatur County had voted by failure to begin construction within the one-year period which the law required. But in another case it decided that a special tax levied to pay a donation to a railroad in Hamilton County should be collected even though the company had become insolvent and had failed to complete the road.[45]

[44] Indiana *Laws,* 1867, pp. 166-167; 1869, p. 92; Indianapolis *Daily Sentinel,* October 18, 19, November 17, 1869, March 12, 15, 16, 1870.

[45] Lafayette, Muncie and Bloomington Rail Road Company *v.* Geiger, 34 Ind. 185 (1870); John *v.* Cincinnati, Richmond and Fort Wayne Railroad

Charges were made that some railroad corporations collected subsidies and then failed to build roads or failed to build them through communities which had made donations. A notorious case was that of the Cincinnati, Richmond, and Fort Wayne, which was accused of abandoning the route described in its charter after collecting some $220,000 from communities along that route. Instead, the line was relocated at a distance of ten to fifteen miles from the original route. This was said to have been done in order to avoid paying taxes to the city of Fort Wayne which had helped subsidize it.[46]

A major scandal involving charges of attempted bribery of a judge of the Indiana Supreme Court grew out of a donation by Tippecanoe County to the Lafayette, Muncie, and Bloomington Railroad. An attempt was made to prevent the collection of a special tax for the donation by means of an injunction. Complaints were made that there had been irregularities in the special election which authorized the tax. The Tippecanoe County court granted the injunction but the Indiana Supreme Court, in one of the test cases mentioned above, set aside the injunction and upheld the constitutionality of the law providing for county donations. After the case was decided there were reports that Adams Earl, the president of the railroad company involved, had admitted to spending $15,000 to procure an early and favorable decision by the Supreme Court. It was said that the payment of the money was to be contingent upon a favorable decision being rendered within thirty days. Judge Samuel Buskirk, who had written the opinion, indignantly denied that anyone had attempted to influence him and demanded an investigation. In a sworn statement Earl said that no money had been used to influence

Company and another, 35 Ind. 539 (1871); Petty et al. *v.* Myers, Treasurer, et al., 49 Ind. 1 (1874); State ex rel. Scobey *v.* Wheadon, Auditor, 39 Ind. 520-521 (1872); Wilson et al. *v.* the Board of Commissioners of Hamilton County et al., 68 Ind. 507 (1879). In the last case two judges dissented.

46 *The State v. C. R. and Ft. W. R. R Co.* (Pamphlet, n.p., n.d., Indiana Division, Indiana State Library).

the court. In spite of his statement it was not entirely clear what had happened to all of the money which admittedly he had spent on the case. The Indianapolis *Journal* labeled the "so-called investigation" of Earl "rather farcical."[47]

The building of new lines after the war brought services to parts of the state hitherto not reached by railroads, but in some cases railroads were built in excess of needs, and ruinous competition resulted. Competition helped to force into bankruptcy many short lines and many weaker lines, which were then consolidated into longer lines. The consolidated giants in turn engaged in cutthroat practices against each other. Longer lines meant intensified competition for "through" traffic. In order to secure freight, rates were slashed below cost on long hauls. The result was a discrepancy between rates for local traffic and through traffic about which farmers complained bitterly.[48] But railroad operators were also unhappy about the state of affairs. The Indianapolis to Terre Haute line complained of "ruinously low" rates on through traffic after the completion of the rival Indianapolis to St. Louis line. It also protested against the "pernicious practice" by which competitors gave free passes in order to obtain shipments. In 1874 the Indianapolis, Cincinnati, and Lafayette complained: "The tendency with railroads for the past few years has been steadily to low rates, until they have been forced below a paying standard in many cases. . . ." It admitted that "great dissatisfaction" was caused "by the disproportion between through and local rates." Farmers who were dependent upon one railroad did not "readily see the justice in paying ten

[47] Lafayette, Muncie and Bloomington Rail Road Company *v.* Geiger, above, Note 45; Indianapolis *Daily Journal,* March 13, 18, 19, 27, 1873; Lafayette *Journal,* quoted *ibid.,* March 17, 1873. Four thousand dollars of the $15,000 was said to have been paid to the librarian of the Supreme Court, who said he accepted it as a legal fee and denied using it to try to influence the court. Charles A. Ray, one of Earl's lawyers, swore that Earl had agreed to pay him $7,000 for the case—$1,000 as an initial payment, $4,000 more if the decision of the lower court was reversed, and another $2,000 if the decision were reversed in a given time.

[48] See below, pp. 358-360.

cents a bushel for hauling their corn fifty miles to market, when their more fortunate neighbors, a few miles further on, at the junction of two roads, pay but twenty cents for sending theirs a thousand miles." But railroads tried to justify the discrepancy between local and through rates by emphasizing the high cost of handling grain on short hauls.[49]

A report of the Indianapolis Board of Trade for 1877 declared that competition and discrimination had injured small shippers and diverted traffic from Indianapolis. "Rates, throughout the West, were in many instances established by the shipper according to his influence or the magnitude of his business, to the great detriment of smaller shippers and less favored localities," it complained. Agents at points west of Indianapolis frequently gave lower rates on through traffic than those which the Indianapolis lines charged. For example, a miller reported that he could ship his product eastward from Indianapolis via Lafayette sixty miles northwest of Indianapolis for less than he could ship it directly eastward.[50]

In an effort to put a stop to rate slashing and other cut-throat practices competing lines tried to enter into agreements and "pools" to stabilize rates, but these voluntary arrangements usually proved impossible to maintain. In the late seventies a statistical bureau was maintained jointly by the various lines operating in Indianapolis, and efforts were openly made to form a pool to divide up the traffic and fix rates. But efforts of this sort failed in part because other railroad centers undercut the rates fixed in Indianapolis. There were also complaints that favored shippers were secretly charged rates lower than those fixed by the pool.[51]

[49] Terre Haute and Indianapolis Railroad Company, *Annual Report,* 1870, pp. 17-18; 1871, p. 21; Indianapolis, Cincinnati, and Lafayette Railroad, *Report of the President,* 1874, pp. 10-11.

[50] Indianapolis *Daily Journal,* January 25, 1878; Indianapolis *Daily Sentinel,* November 30, 1878.

[51] Indianapolis *Daily Sentinel,* November 30, December 4, 6, 11, 1878; Indianapolis *Daily Journal,* January 25, 1878, September 5, 10, 1879. The report of the Indianapolis Board of Trade mentioned above said that no dependence could be placed on the agreements to stabilize rates—that "guerilla

During the depression years of the 1870's a large percentage of railroads became bankrupt, but even earlier several had experienced financial difficulties. The end of the war meant a termination of military transportation and wartime profits. This was followed by two years of poor crops of wheat, which meant a further decline in revenue. By 1869 it was reported that practically every railroad was operating at a loss. Some of the new lines were in financial trouble almost before they were begun. Most lines never paid a cash dividend, and many were unable to meet the interest on their bonds.[52]

The most consistently profitable line in the state was the Indianapolis to Terre Haute. It continued to make money when other lines reported deficits, partly because it tapped the coal fields. It reached its peak during the war in 1864 when it declared a cash dividend of 18 per cent, and issued a stock dividend of 25 per cent. In 1868 it paid cash dividends of 12 per cent, and even during the depression years of the seventies paid 10 per cent. The Bellefontaine line, which had become a part of the Cleveland, Columbus, Cincinnati and Indianapolis line in 1868, paid dividends of 7 per cent from 1868 to 1870 but not thereafter for several years. By 1880 it was paying 2.5 per cent. During the seventies the reorganized Jeffersonville, Madison, and Indianapolis line consistently paid 7 per cent. By 1880, after the disastrous years of panic, some other lines paid modest dividends. But stockholders on most lines were paid nothing. Although railroads throughout the country had financial problems and few were really profitable, Indiana railroads in the seventies seem to have been relatively less profitable than those of the neighboring states.[53]

warfare" between connecting lines was likely to be renewed at any time. Indianapolis *Daily Journal,* January 25, 1878.

52 Terre Haute and Indianapolis Railroad, *Annual Report,* 1866, p. 5; Indianapolis *Daily Sentinel,* February 1, 1869.

53 Poor's *Railroad Manual,* 1869-1870, p. 145; 1871-1872, p. 261; 1875-1876, pp. xl, xli; 1877-1878, pp. xxiv-xxv. In Indiana in 1878 only $421,000 in divi-

While new lines were being begun, older lines were failing. As early as 1858 the Wabash line was sold under foreclosure. In 1862 the Madison and Indianapolis line was sold under similar circumstances. In 1864 the Evansville and Indianapolis Straight Line was sold by court order to a group of eastern investors. In 1868 it was ordered to be sold again for delinquent taxes, but an agent of the owners was able to buy it back. In 1867 the Ohio and Mississippi line was sold under foreclosure, and in 1876 it was placed in the hands of a receiver a second time. By 1869 the Louisville, New Albany, and Chicago line was in the hands of a receiver. The Peru to Indianapolis road, unable to pay its bonded indebtedness, had been sold, and the stockholders had lost everything they invested.[54] During the seventies financial problems became even more acute, and the number of bankruptcies and foreclosures increased. By 1877 the following were among the lines which were in the hands of receivers: the Ohio and Mississippi; the Indianapolis, Cincinnati and Lafayette; the White Water Valley; the Cincinnati, Muncie and Fort Wayne; the Lafayette, Muncie and Bloomington; the Logansport, Crawfordsville Southwestern; the Logansport and Terre Haute; and the Louisville, New Albany and Chicago.[55]

The bankruptcies and foreclosures of the depression years accelerated a trend which had begun earlier—the consolidation of short lines into a few major systems. An act of the

dends was paid on the 4,000 miles of railroad in the state; in 1879 only $404,162. The following dividends were paid in the neighboring states:

| State | 1878 | | 1879 | |
	Total Miles	Dividends	Total Miles	Dividends
Michigan	3,308	over $1 million	3,308	$1,383,000
Ohio	6,233	over $6 million	6,706	$7,647,000
Illinois	8,624	over $8 million	8,844	$10,032,000

Poor's *Railroad Manual,* 1879, p. vii; 1880, p. vii.

54 Indianapolis *Daily Sentinel,* May 26, 1868, February 1, 1869; Poor's *Railroad Manual,* 1869-1870, pp. 249-251, 407; 1880, pp. 598, 710.

55 Gresham, *Walter Q. Gresham,* I, 379. For an account of the receivership of the Louisville, New Albany, and Chicago and of some of the other lines see *ibid.,* pp. 366-378.

legislature, in 1853, authorized railroad companies to consolidate their stock with the stock of railroad companies in Indiana or adjoining states and to connect their roads with the roads of other companies,[56] but it was not until after the war that the trend toward consolidation became pronounced. As a result of reorganizations by 1880 most of the major lines in Indiana had become part of larger systems controlled from outside the state.

In 1869 the Indianapolis *Sentinel,* commenting on the trend toward consolidation, predicted that within a few years all the railroads in the United States would be controlled by two or three large corporations. Three years later a letter in the Indianapolis *Journal* complained that nearly all the early lines in Indiana had "passed under the control of combinations foreign to our State, whose local interests and business sympathies are elsewhere than in Indiana," even though private citizens and towns had invested heavily in their construction. "By a system of manipulation known only in railroad circles," the writer complained, "many of these lines have been secured to the present managers for less than the cost of the rails— all the remainder being lost to those paying it." He asked: "Are the untold millions of treasure contributed by our people, the priceless franchises granted, the many inconveniences endured to go for naught but to enrich a comparatively few men of the seaboard?"[57]

The answer seemed to be that there was little that the original investors could do except complain. One or two examples of the type of "manipulations" about which the writer complained will suffice to show why there was sometimes great bitterness against the outside corporations. One case was that of the Cincinnati and Chicago Railroad (formerly the Pittsburgh, Logansport, and Chicago). It was alleged

[56] Gavin and Hord (eds.), *Statutes of Indiana* (2 volumes, 2d edition, 1862), I, 526-527.

[57] Indianapolis *Daily Sentinel,* April 12, 1869; Indianapolis *Daily Journal,* December 6, 1872.

that an eastern firm to which the line had been leased had deliberately driven it into bankruptcy, thereby defrauding the original stockholders. It had failed to pay interest on the bonds of the railroad, thus ruining its credit and forcing an order that it be sold. As a result the road was sold for a fraction of its actual value.[58] After the board of directors of the Cincinnati, Richmond, and Fort Wayne road leased it to the Pennsylvania system the original stockholders were powerless to prevent actions which they regarded as prejudicial to their interests. The stockholders protested against the lease and against a new issue of "watered" stock, but they were unable to stop them. After the Ohio and Mississippi line had been placed in the hands of receivers in 1876 some of the stockholders brought charges of fraud against the officers and some members of the board of directors. They complained that they had misrepresented the facts about the company and had placed it in receivership without informing the stockholders.[59]

By 1880 the Pennsylvania Railroad Company controlled a network of lines in Indiana including the Cincinnati, Richmond and Fort Wayne. In 1869 the Columbus, Chicago and Indiana Central Railroad, after having been placed in a receivership, was leased to the Pittsburgh, Cincinnati and St. Louis. The terms of the lease were guaranteed by the Pennsylvania Railroad Company. The Indianapolis and Vincennes road was owned and controlled outright by the Pennsylvania. The old Madison and Indianapolis line and the Jeffersonville line, which had been consolidated in 1864, were leased to the Pennsylvania in 1873. The Indianapolis and St. Louis line was operated under a ninety-nine year lease by the same company. The Grand Rapids and Indiana line was also operated by the Pennsylvania.[60]

58 Cincinnati *Gazette,* quoted Indianapolis *Daily Journal,* January 19, 1872.
59 *Ibid.,* April 27, 1872, January 20, 1877.
60 Poor's *Railroad Manual,* 1880, pp. 694-696, 706, 709-710.

In 1864 the Bellefontaine line was formed by the consolidation of the Bellefontaine and Indianapolis and the Indianapolis, Pittsburgh, and Cleveland lines. In 1868 it was consolidated into the Cleveland, Columbus, Cincinnati, and Indianapolis, which was popularly known as the "Bee Line." In 1866 the Lafayette and Indianapolis road sold out to the Indianapolis and Cincinnati line to form the Indianapolis, Cincinnati and Lafayette company with headquarters in Cincinnati. Thereafter, the new company fell into financial difficulties and was in and out of receivership three times before 1880. In 1880 it was sold under foreclosure and reorganized as the Cincinnati, Indianapolis, St. Louis and Chicago.[61]

Running across the northern part of the state was the Wabash, St. Louis, and Pacific line, which was formed in 1879 by the consolidation of several smaller lines. The Indiana portion was part of a system extending from Toledo to Kansas City. The Eel River line, which was sold under foreclosure in 1877 and reorganized, was leased in 1879 to the Wabash line.[62]

Farther north was the Lake Shore and Michigan Southern, also formed out of the consolidation of several small lines. It was part of a line running from Buffalo to Chicago and was controlled by the Vanderbilt interests. Across the southern part of the state was the Ohio and Mississippi, which was part of a system extending from Baltimore to St. Louis. Running north and south one of the longest lines in the state was the Louisville, New Albany and Chicago (later known as the Monon). Another one of the longer lines in the state in 1880 was the Indianapolis, Peru, and Chicago, running from Indianapolis to Michigan City. It was formed by the consolidation of the old Peru and Indianapolis line with the Cincinnati, Peru, and Chicago and the LaPorte and Lake Michigan lines. The Cincinnati, Wabash and Michigan

[61] *Ibid.,* 1869-1870, p. 360; 1880, pp. 703-705; Murphy, "Big Four Railroad in Indiana," *Indiana Magazine of History,* XXI, 139, 197, 199, 207, 212.
[62] Poor's *Railroad Manual,* 1880, pp. 696-697, 720.

INDIANA RAILROADS IN 1880

1. Anderson, Lebanon, St. Louis (Anderson to Noblesville), 19 m.
2. Baltimore, Ohio, and Chicago (formerly Baltimore, Pittsburgh, and Chicago), 146 m.
3. Bedford, Springville, Owensburg, and Bloomfield, 41 m.
4. Chicago and Block Coal (Attica to Veedersburg), 15 m.
5. Chicago, Cincinnati, and Louisville (Peru to LaPorte), 71 m.
6. Chicago and Eastern Illinois (Bismark, Ill., to Coal Creek), 19 m.
7. Chicago and Grand Trunk, 56 m.
8. Cincinnati, Hamilton, and Indianapolis, 78 m.
9. Cincinnati, Lafayette, and Chicago (Lafayette to state line), 23 m.
10. Cincinnati, Richmond, and Fort Wayne (Fort Wayne to Richmond), 83 m.
11. Cincinnati, Rockport, and Southwestern (Rockport to Jasper), 38 m.
12. Cincinnati, Wabash, and Michigan (Anderson to Goshen), 111 m.
13. Cleveland, Columbus, Cincinnati, and Indianapolis (formerly Bellefontaine), 84 m.
14. Columbus, Chicago, and Indiana Central (Indianapolis to Richmond to Chicago), 416 m.
15. Eel River (Logansport to Butler), 93 m.
16. Evansville and Terre Haute, 108 m.
17. Evansville, Terre Haute, and Chicago (Terre Haute to Danville, Ill.), 43 m.
18. Fairland, Franklin, and Martinsville, 38 m.
19. Fort Wayne, Jackson, and Saginaw (Fort Wayne to Jackson, Mich.), 54 m.
20. Fort Wayne, Muncie, and Cincinnati (Fort Wayne to Connersville), 104 m.
21. Frankfort and Kokomo, 26 m.
22. Grand Rapids and Indiana (formerly Grand Rapids and Fort Wayne), 104 m.
23. Indiana Block Coal (Otter Creek to Brazil), 17 m.
24. Indiana, Bloomington, and Western, 78 m.
25. Indianapolis, Cincinnati, and Lafayette, 163 m.
26. Indianapolis, Decatur, and Springfield, Ill., 65 m.
27. Indianapolis, Delphi, and Chicago (Rensselaer to Delphi), 38 m.
28. Indianapolis, Peru, and Chicago (Indianapolis to Peru), 72 m.
29. Indianapolis and St. Louis (Indianapolis to Terre Haute), 71 m.
30. Indianapolis and Vincennes, 116 m.
31, 31a. Jeffersonville, Madison, and Indianapolis, 185 m.
    31b. Rushville extension, 18 m; Cambridge City extension, 20 m.
32. Lake Erie, Evansville, and Southwestern (Boonville to Ill. line), 17 m.
33. Lake Shore and Michigan Southern (including old Indiana Railroad), 167 m.
34. Lake Erie and Western (Muncie to Ill. state line), 158 m.
35. Louisville, New Albany, and Chicago (Monon), 288 m.
36. Louisville, New Albany, and St. Louis (New Albany to Milltown), 18 m.
37. Logansport, Crawfordsville, and Southwestern (Logansport to Terre Haute), 114 m.
38. Michigan Central, 43 m.
39. Michigan City and Indianapolis (Michigan City to LaPorte), 12 m.
40. Ohio and Mississippi (including spur from North Vernon to Jeffersonville), 266 m.
41. Pittsburgh, Fort Wayne, and Chicago, 153 m.
42. Terre Haute and Indianapolis, 79 m.
43. Terre Haute and Southeastern (Terre Haute to Clay City), 40 m.
44. Toledo, Delphos, and Burlington (Kokomo to Ohio state line), 37 m. completed.
45. Wabash, St. Louis, and Pacific (Lake Erie and Mississippi), 166 m.
46. Whitewater (Harrison, Ohio, to Hagerstown), 62 m.

RAILROADS
in INDIANA
in 1880

extended from Anderson to Goshen, a distance of 111 miles. The Fort Wayne, Muncie, and Cincinnati ran from Fort Wayne to Connersville, 104 miles.[63] In addition to these lines there were still numerous small independent lines which had not yet been merged with larger systems.[64]

The frequent changes in names which resulted from the many consolidations of shorter lines into longer lines and the many reorganizations resulting from foreclosures make it confusing to attempt to trace the history of various lines. The two most reliable sources of information are the volume on transportation in the Tenth Census and Poor's *Railroad Manual*, which was published annually. There are a few minor discrepancies between the two, but on the whole they are in agreement.[65]

§ § § §

The impact of the railroads upon economic life in turn produced repercussions in the political realm. As has been seen, the advent of railroads had been hailed with great public enthusiasm. The state legislature had been generous in the terms of the charters which were granted, and local governments vied with each other to extend financial aid. During the fifties there was almost no criticism, but as railroads became more and more powerful and as the lives of many people, especially farmers, became more dependent upon them, complaints began to be heard. Following the Civil War in every session of the legislature there were debates on railroads and

[63] Poor's *Railroad Manual,* 1871-1872, p. 538; 1880, pp. 693, 701, 706, 714.

[64] The most important example of an independent line still operating in 1880 was the Indianapolis to Terre Haute. The president of the line was William R. McKeen, a Terre Haute banker, who had become president in 1867. All of the members of the board of directors were residents of Terre Haute. *Ibid.,* p. 719; *Encyclopedia of Biography of Indiana,* I, 80.

[65] See pages 350-351 for a list of railroads in 1880 and a map showing their routes, compiled from Poor's *Railroad Manual,* 1880, pp. 689-690 and United States Bureau of the Census, *Tenth Census* (1880), IV [Pt. 1], 509-515. The list does not include some very short segments of lines which were principally out-of-state lines, nor does it include some short coal lines nor the Indianapolis Belt Line.

proposals to curb abuses attributed to them. Opposition was intensified during the seventies by prolonged depression. But although party platforms condemned the power of railroads and lawmakers introduced many regulatory measures, little legislation was adopted, and railroads remained almost entirely free from governmental restraints.

The first proposals for legislation arose out of the fact that the new form of transportation frequently involved hazard to life and limb of passengers and nonpassengers, and even more frequently to farm animals. Newspapers were full of sensational stories of railroad accidents. In 1852 the legislature enacted a measure "to prevent the destruction of, or injury of animals, and the destruction of human life by railroads, and to provide compensation for the same." It made railroads liable to pay damages to the heirs of persons killed through negligence of railroad employees or as the result of defects in the railroad or equipment. Owners of animals killed by trains could collect damages without proof of negligence or wilful misconduct on the part of railroad employees. Similar provisions continued to be found in later revisions of the laws.[66] Suits against railroads for damages arising from accidents, and especially from the killing of farm animals, were common. An examination of the Indiana Supreme court reports shows that of the cases involving railroads which came before it by far the largest number were damage suits.

It was during the wartime session of the legislature in 1863 that railroads first became the object of serious criticism. It has already been seen that dissatisfaction with the railroads was one ingredient in so-called "Copperheadism." During the course of the 1863 session one speaker complained that

[66] Indiana *Revised Statutes,* 1852, I, 426. In 1855 Governor Wright called attention to the number of accidents caused by flimsy construction, defective locomotives, and careless employees. He recommended the creation of a state commission to enforce the law, but the legislature failed to act. Indiana *House Journal,* 1855, pp. 31-32. This appears to have been the only regulatory measure of this sort introduced before 1863.

the people were being "ground down" by the railroads. Another complained that although the railroads had been originally financed mainly by people who lived near the lines,
"the stocks were now being held by capitalists who bought
them up for a mere song." Much dissatisfaction with discriminatory practices was shown. One member pointed out that
transportation for through freight was always available to
shippers in Indianapolis because of the competing lines in
the city. But at local stations "the roads knew that they had
the freight anyhow, and no competition could take it from
them," with the result that they delayed shipment, and shippers of livestock, especially, were put to much inconvenience.
Another member urged measures which would "correct the
discrimination against the local business"—whereby passengers
and freight were carried more cheaply for the whole length
of the line than those going shorter distances. Proposals were
made that the legislature fix rates and require that they be
uniform.[67]

The dissatisfaction expressed in 1863 arose in part out of
wartime conditions, but the criticism contained the principal
elements of the evils which were to be complained of for a
generation or more—control by outside capitalists, discriminatory practices, and especially disparity between local and
through rates. In the 1865 session resolutions were introduced proposing legislative regulation of rates, and complaints were made against the practice of "charging more for
freight from intermediate stations along the line of the roads,
than more remote" points.[68]

In 1867 numerous regulatory measures were introduced fixing railroad rates and requiring that they be uniform. There
was strong opposition to all the proposals. During the debate it was shown that part of the opposition was led by a
member who was an attorney for the Peru line, and by the
speaker of the House, who had "been all his life in the rail-

[67] *Brevier Legislative Reports*, VI (1863), 78-79, 153-154.
[68] *Ibid.*, VII (1865), 31, 46, 49.

road interest."[69] In 1869 there were more proposals for rate regulations, but none of them were adopted.[70] At the 1867 session, there were charges that failure to pass regulatory measures was due to the corruption of legislators by railroad lobbyists. In consequence a committee was appointed to investigate evidences of corruption, but, not surprisingly, it failed to report any proof of wrong doing. "God save Indiana from another such Legislature," cried one newspaper at the session's end, "made up of aspiring and venal politicians, old party hacks, bargainers in corruption, tools of wealthy corporations, vassals—labelled and yoked—of rich companies." It declared that members of both parties sold their votes, that "important acts were passed, and important measures and reports suppressed, solely by the power of money."[71] But whether or not members of the legislature accepted money bribes from railroads, there was no doubt that the practice of accepting free passes was widespread. In 1869 a bill to prohibit members from accepting free passes was introduced and referred to a committee but never heard of again.[72]

Editorially the Indianapolis *Sentinel* declared that the greatest threat to the general welfare of the mass of people arose from the growing power of monoplies, and that the most powerful monopolies were the "railroad interest," which represented "a capital equal to, if not greater than the national debt," which sought to control the public policy of the country. "It is well known," it declared, "that these monopolies have a controlling influence over both National and State Legislatures."[73]

Considerable concern was shown by legislators over the trend toward consolidation and control by outside interests.

69 *Ibid.,* IX (1867), 36, 310, 321, 336, 360, 373, 438-439.
70 *Ibid.,* X (1869), 514-515; Indiana *House Journal,* 1869, pp. 759-760.
71 Indianapolis *Daily Herald,* March 12, 1867; New Albany *Commercial* (a Democratic paper), March 16, 1867; *Brevier Legislative Reports,* IX (1867), 336; Indiana *House Journal,* 1867, p. 774.
72 Indiana *Senate Journal,* 1869, p. 262.
73 Indianapolis *Daily Sentinel,* October 15, 1869.

In 1869 numerous petitions were received asking for legislation to remove "the evil growing out of Railroad Combinations" as well as to fix rates. A bill which provided that lines which consolidated lost the special privileges conferred upon them in their original charters passed the Senate in spite of stiff opposition, but it failed of adoption because the House and Senate could not agree on amendments.[74]

At the legislative sessions of 1871, 1872, and 1873 various measures were introduced and debated to curb exorbitant charges. To meet objections that rate fixing was not within the scope of legislative power, constitutional amendments expressly granting the power were introduced in 1871 and 1873. None of these proposals were adopted.[75]

The panic of 1873 and the rise of the Grange in the early seventies intensified the demand for railroad regulation. The newspapers of both political parties were increasingly critical. Even before the depression began the Indianapolis *Journal* editorially attacked the railroad "monopoly." It pointed out that legislatures had been generous in granting favors, but in return railroads had disregarded the public interest—had "managed all their affairs with . . . little reference to the needs of the country" and had "worked wholly for themselves and never for the people." As a result of consolidation and outside control, the *Journal* complained, "the transportation of our people is at the mercy of men who never see us, who know nothing of us, and care nothing for us." Railroads should

[74] Indiana *Senate Journal,* 1869, pp. 189, 276, 283, 344-345, 510, 535, 536, 650, 651; *Brevier Legislative Reports,* IX (1867), 310, 321, 401-402; X (1869), 124, 128, 145, 152, 170. The only regulatory measure with regard to railroads which was actually adopted was a mild one enacted in 1867. It required that corporations which abandoned or failed to complete lines would lose their charters, and it required railroads to file statements with the auditor of state showing their gross receipts, their expenditures, and the dividends paid. Indiana *Laws,* 1867, pp. 160-161.

[75] *Brevier Legislative Reports,* XII (1871), 98; XIII (1872), 258; XIV (1873), 519-533; Kettleborough, *Constitution Making in Indiana,* II, 92-93, 126-127.

not be surprised "if the public seek some remedy through State or Federal interference."[76]

The Grange, which showed a spectacular growth in Indiana in the early seventies, was made up of farmers who were at the mercy of the railroads.[77] Grange meetings showed concern over railroads, but the resolutions adopted by Indiana Grangers were restrained in tone and emphasized that the interests of farmers and railroads were inseparable. Resolutions adopted at a Grange meeting in 1873 complained of financial mismanagement and the methods by which railroads made "large dividends on watered stock," and urged the construction of more competing lines. The 1874 meeting of the state Grange asked for legislation which would be "just to the railroad interests of the country" but which would make the railroads "serve the people instead of ruling them," and which would compel rates to be fixed according to actual costs.[78]

Grange influence in the 1875 legislature was powerful, and it was expected that some regulatory measures would pass. In his message Governor Hendricks referred to popular complaints and said that railroads should not "take advantage of the absence of competition" in order to make unreasonable charges. He recommended that the lawmakers consider regulation. Several regulatory measures were introduced in both houses.[79] While the measures were under consideration operators of the railroads met with members of the legislature to plead with them not to adopt them. The principal spokesman for the railroads was M. E. Ingalls, of the Indianapolis, Cincinnati, and Lafayette. In his defense of the railroads he pointed out that they were suffering from a decline in

[76] Indianapolis *Daily Journal,* November 14, 1872, February 27, 1873.

[77] See Chapter IX, pages 397-403, for a further discussion of the Grange.

[78] Indianapolis *Daily Journal,* December 1, 1873; Indiana State Grange, *Proceedings,* 1874, p. 30.

[79] Indiana *House Journal,* 1875, p. 48. For examples of regulatory measures introduced see Indiana *Senate Journal,* 1875, pp. 102, 273, 562, 687. Several similar measures were introduced in the House.

business. He insisted that they were "honestly and faithfully managed," and that they had "made every body rich but themselves." He admitted that there was strong public hostility to railroads. This he attributed in part to ignorance, in part to "unwise action" on the part of the railroads, and in part to "political demagogues who hope to ride into power on this feeling and care not who is injured by it." He insisted that the Grangers did not understand the magnitude of the railroad interests nor their contribution to the growth of the state. He warned that to cripple the railroads would injure the prosperity of the whole state. He urged the lawmakers "to prevent such hasty and ill advised legislation in this state" as had been adopted in other states. Instead of fixing rates—which was an arbitrary procedure—he recommended that they consider a railroad commission to hear complaints, similar to the one already operating in Massachusetts. Ingalls' plea was apparently effective for none of the proposed regulations were adopted.[80]

In 1877 Governor Williams revived the question of regulation. He emphasized especially the inequities between charges for long hauls and short hauls and urged "earnest consideration" of the problem. But no legislation was adopted.[81] Even the 1879 legislature, the most "radical" of any elected in the seventies, like its predecessors failed to adopt regulatory measures. About a dozen bills relating to railroads were introduced in each house. None of them passed, but the 1879 session was remarkable for the frankness with which some members attacked the lobbyists who were accused of being responsible for blocking legislation.[82]

One method which railroads used to win legislative support was to issue free passes. As early as 1869 a resolution had been introduced into the Senate to provide free transportation to and from the capital for members of the legisla-

---

80 Indianapolis *Daily Journal,* February 16, 1875.

81 Indiana *Senate Journal,* 1877, p. 51.

82 See Chapter VII, pages 315-317, for a further account of this legislature.

ture and at the same time to prohibit members from accepting railroad passes, but it had died in committee.[83] At the next session a resolution was introduced to the effect that free passes were contrary to public policy but it was not adopted.[84]

In 1879, when the resolution appropriating money for the expenses of the members was under discussion, one member proposed an amendment, which of course did not pass, that no money be appropriated for mileage for members who had accepted railroad passes. In the debate on the proposal one member exclaimed: "Look back in the history of State Legislation and show where railroads have ever asked for anything they have not obtained; and it is equally true that nearly every measure the people have asked for to protect themselves from oppression by the railroads has been denied."[85]

Inability to secure action at the state level was undoubtedly one reason why the 1879 legislature turned to Congress. The idea of Federal regulation was not entirely new. As early as 1869 Indiana's Representative William Williams, a Republican from Warsaw, had introduced into Congress a resolution asking for a commission to inquire into the power of Congress to regulate interstate railroad rates under its power to regulate interstate commerce.[86] At the National Agricultural Congress which met in Indianapolis in 1873 there was a prolonged discussion of railroad problems. A resolution was adopted which declared that whenever a railroad corporation owned or controlled lines in two or more states, it was the right and duty of the Congress to regulate freight rates under the constitutional power to regulate interstate com-

83 Indiana *Senate Journal*, 1869, p. 262. It was also customary for railroads to furnish free passes to delegates to political conventions. See, for example, Indianapolis *Daily Sentinel*, July 2, 1868, for a notice that railroads would furnish free passes to delegates attending the National Democratic Convention in New York.

84 *Brevier Legislative Reports*, XII (1871), 79-80.

85 *Ibid.*, XVII (1879), 36.

86 *Danger of Railroad Monopolies and the Duty of Congress to Protect Agriculture. Speech of Hon. William Williams of Indiana, in the House of Representatives, January 29, 1870* (n.p. n.d.).

merce.[87] In the Senate in 1874 Morton urged the adoption of legislation to regulate railroads which were interstate in character. In the same session Democrat William Steele Holman, ordinarily a strong defender of states' rights, also called for Federal regulation and introduced a bill requiring that interstate railroads charge rates which were "fair and reasonable."[88]

These early proposals having come to nothing, the 1879 session of the Indiana legislature adopted a concurrent resolution urging Congress to act. Support for the measure arose in part because of popular opposition to pooling arrangements by which competing railroads kept rates high. One proponent said that the only way the "plain people" could make themselves heard in the face of the powerful lobby of "organized capital" was by an appeal to Congress. "Unless the people can successfully strike against this great monopoly," he said, "no man can ship his surplus produce without bowing in submission to its iron rule."[89]

The resolution as finally adopted declared that "the great transportation corporations," which owned the thoroughfares over which the products of Indiana must pass, had "succeeded in pooling their business, thereby preventing fair competition, and creating a monopoly of the carrying trade." Indiana's delegation in Congress was therefore requested to support the bill then pending in the Senate to regulate interstate commerce.[90]

Congress did not pass the Interstate Commerce Act until 1887, but the debate in the Indiana legislature in 1879 anticipated some of the arguments used in the debate in Congress. Some speakers argued that Federal regulation was uncon-

[87] Indiana State Board of Agriculture, *Annual Report*, 1873, p. 320.

[88] *Railroad Legislation. Speech of O. P. Morton of Indiana in the Senate of the United States, January 27, 1874.* (Washington, D.C., 1874); *Railroad Monopoly. Speech of Hon. William S. Holman of Indiana in the House of Representatives, March 17, 1874* (Washington, D. C., 1874).

[89] *Brevier Legislative Reports,* XVII (1879), 109.

[90] Indiana *Laws,* 1879, p. 56.

stitutional. Others expressed apprehension over centralization of power. But many Democrats who were theoretically dedicated to the preservation of states' rights showed themselves ready to accept Federal regulation when vital economic interests were involved. It was also apparent that the railroad question was a sectional one which cut across party lines. In order to protect themselves from eastern corporations both Democrats and Republicans turned to Congress.

RAILROAD MILEAGE IN INDIANA 1850-1880[91]

Year	Miles	Year	Miles	Year	Miles
1850	228	1860	2,163	1870	3,177
1851	558	1861	2,175	1871	3,529
1852	756	1862	2,175	1872	3,649
1853	1,209	1863	2,175	1873	3,714
1854	1,317	1864	2,195	1874	3,890
1855	1,406	1865	2,217	1875	3,963
1856	1,807	1866	2,217	1876	4,003
1857	1,895	1867	2,506	1877	4,057
1858	1,995	1868	2,600	1878	4,198
1859	2,014	1869	2,863	1879	4,336
				1880	4,454

91 Poor's *Railroad Manual,* 1871-1872, pp. xxxii-xxxiii; 1878, pp. iv-v; 1881, p. lxxviii.

CHAPTER IX

AGRICULTURE

INDIANA REMAINED a predominantly rural state with farming as the principal occupation and way of life throughout the thirty years from 1850 to 1880. In some places life went on very much as it had in the pioneer period, but for the state as a whole several significant changes occurred. One of the most striking was the northward movement of population and the bringing of new lands under cultivation. Improved transportation, especially the building of railroads, helped to begin the breakdown of rural isolation. The greater accessibility of markets which resulted from better transportation stimulated the production of crops for sale rather than consumption. At the same time there was a marked increase in the use of farm machinery and interest in improved methods. The Civil War accentuated the trend toward mechanization by bringing about both an increased demand for farm products and a shortage of man power.

At midcentury Indiana stood at the threshold of a tremendous agricultural expansion. "Rural Indiana, of the 1850's," as one historian has remarked, "was no longer part of the American frontier but a product of it."[1]

The decade from 1850 to 1860 showed the greatest increase in population of any in the history of the state. Most of the growth occurred in the central and northern parts. In 1850 most of the population was concentrated in the southern half of the state, but the rate of immigration to the southern counties was already declining. For the most part the lands in the southern third of the state were inferior to those farther north, and most of the good lands in that

---

[1] Harvey Carter, "Rural Indiana in Transition 1850-1860," *Agricultural History* (Washington, D. C.), XX (1946), 107.

portion were already under cultivation. The center of population was shifting to the central counties. During the next
three decades all three major sections of the state continued
to show an increase in population but the rate of growth was
greater in the central and northern sections. Some of the
older counties in the south continued to show substantial
increases but in some, including Ohio, Switzerland, Washington, Dearborn, Owen, Franklin, and Jefferson, the population
either remained stable or declined slightly. The Whitewater
Valley, the first part of the state to be thickly settled, was
the first part to begin to show a decline. By 1870 the total
population of the central counties exceeded the total in the
south. As might be expected the most spectacular gains were
made in the northern counties, which had been the most
sparsely settled before 1850.[2]

By 1880 almost the entire territory of Indiana had a rural
population which averaged about one family for each eighty
or one hundred acres. The chief exception was the northwestern one eighth of the state and some areas in the south,
especially the hilly country, which extends southward from
Owen County to Spencer and Crawford counties. As late
as 1880 over half of all persons who were classified as engaging in an occupation were engaged in agriculture, and 80
per cent of the population might be classified as rural.[3]

2 Visher, "Population Changes," Indiana Academy of Science, *Proceedings,*
LI (1942), 179, 182-183; Roger H. Van Bolt, "The Indiana Scene in the
1840's," *Indiana Magazine of History,* XLVII (1951), 335-340. See Chapter
XII, pages 536 ff., for a more detailed discussion of population changes from
1850 to 1880.

3 Visher, *op. cit.,* pp. 182-185. In 1880 out of a total of 635,080 persons listed
as being engaged in all types of occupations, 331,240 were engaged in agriculture. The United States census reports classified as "urban" persons living
in cities of more than 2,500. In Indiana the percentages of such persons by
decades were as follows:

1850	4.5 per cent	1870	14.7 per cent
1860	8.6 per cent	1880	19.5 per cent

Ibid., p. 188; United States Bureau of the Census, *Compendium of Tenth
Census* (1880), p. 1356.

At midcentury there was still much uncleared land—even in relatively settled areas. Travelers frequently commented on the vast expanses of forests. One English visitor in the vicinity of Muncie in 1850 reported that bears and wolves still roamed the woods a few miles away. By that date bears, panthers, wild cats, and beavers were seldom seen except in areas where lands had not yet been brought under cultivation, but wolves were still numerous in many places. Deer, raccoons, and opossums were even more common. Another traveler, on a trip by railroad from Cincinnati to Seymour in 1856, traveled much of the distance through dense forest. Around Seymour he found a considerable amount of cleared land, but there had not been a house in the vicinity before the building of the railroad.[4]

As late as 1875 it was estimated that over seven million acres, 39 per cent of the state, were still forest. In eleven counties 50 per cent or more of the land was timberland. Large stands of oak, poplar, black walnut, hickory, ash, basswood, and beech still flourished, but in some places were rapidly being depleted. This was especially true of walnut trees because of the vogue for walnut furniture. Some of the counties in the southern part of the state were already suffering the consequences of deforestation. In Dearborn County, which was said to be typical, farmers were compelled to buy timber for building and fencing and to haul coal for fuel, "where, twenty-five years ago, there was burned in log piles, one hundred cords of wood per acre to clear the ground." As the result of the destruction of timber the velocity and destructiveness of wind storms were reported to have increased greatly and soil erosion to have begun.[5]

[4] John Candler, Extracts from a Narrative of a Journey in Indiana in 1850 (Typed copy, Indiana Division, Indiana State Library); Richard S. Fisher, *Indiana: In Relation to its Geography, Statistics, Institutions* . . . (New York, 1852), p. 20; Ferguson, *America by River and Rail*, p. 324.

[5] United States Department of Agriculture, *Report of the Commissioner*, 1875, pp. 306-309; M. B. Kerr, "Forests of Southern Indiana," Indiana State Board of Agriculture, *Annual Report*, 1874, II, 280-282. In Switzerland County,

By 1849 nearly all of the land in the state had been surveyed—21,487,760 acres out of a total of 21,637,760. Of this more than three million acres remained open for sale and entry. There were six land districts with an office in each for the sale of government lands—the Jeffersonville district, Vincennes district, Indianapolis district, Crawfordsville district, Fort Wayne district, and the Winamac district. In 1850 slightly less than one fourth of the land in the state was under cultivation according to United States census reports. By 1860 it was estimated that more than one third of the land was improved or under some sort of cultivation. By 1880 between one third and one half of the land remained unimproved.[6]

for example, it was reported: "Timber of all kinds is growing scarce, and even wood is so scarce and high that farmers haul coal from the Ohio river to their homes, ten miles in the interior." The eleven counties with the highest percentage of timberland were as follows:

Adams	52.6 per cent	Martin	59.1 per cent
Brown	57.3 "	Perry	65.1 "
Dubois	56.7 "	Pike	50.8 "
Jay	50.3 "	Tipton	52.3 "
Marshall	50.7 "	Wells	53.3 "
		Whitley	51.7 "

United States Department of Agriculture, *Report of the Commissioner,* 1875, pp. 308-310.

6 Fisher, *Indiana,* pp. 23-24; United States Bureau of the Census, *Seventh Census* (1850), p. 791; *Tenth Census* (1880), III: *Agriculture,* [Pt. 1], p. xii, Table VII, pp. 113-114; *Emigration to the United States of North America. Indiana As A Home for Emigrants* (Prepared and published under the direction and by authority of Oliver P. Morton, Governor of Indiana, Indianapolis, 1864), p. 11; John Collett, *The State of Indiana* (Extracted from the *First Annual Report of the Department of Statistics and Geology,* Indianapolis, 1880), pp. 6, 10, 11. According to the United States Census the amounts of improved and unimproved farm lands were as follows:

	Improved Land in Farms	Unimproved Land in Farms
1850	5,046,543 acres	7,746, 879 acres
1860	8,242, 183 "	8,146,109 "
1870	10,104,279 "	8,015,369 "
1880	13,933,738 "	6,487,245 "

Improved land was defined as land which was tilled, including land lying

In 1850 the largest single unimproved and unsettled area was the lands in the north, near Lake Michigan. The Black Swamp in northwestern Ohio deflected immigrants from the most direct land route from the East, and settlers who came by way of the Erie Canal and the Great Lakes tended to by-pass Indiana and go to northern Illinois or southern Michigan or Wisconsin. Sand dunes and lack of harbors on Lake Michigan discouraged settlement in Indiana, but the fact that much of the land south of the lake was swampy was a stronger deterrent. In 1850 Congress passed legislation ceding to the states all public lands which were classified as swamps, with the stipulation that the proceeds from the sale of the lands be applied "exclusively, so far as necessary," to reclamation by means of levees and drains. Indiana received 1,226,706 acres of swamplands in 1851. The following year the General Assembly passed legislation to provide for the sale of the lands and to carry out the reclamation provisions of the act of Congress. The law provided for the appointment by the governor of a commissioner of swamplands in each county, and the latter in turn was to appoint an engineer who was to make arrangements with contractors for drainage of the land. The greatest concentration of swamplands was in the Calumet and neighboring areas—in Lake, La Porte, Porter, Starke, Jasper, Newton, St. Joseph, Marshall, and Fulton counties.[7]

Once the lands were offered for sale by the state they were quickly disposed of—in many instances to speculators who acquired large tracts under dubious circumstances. By 1853 there were only 246,339 acres in the entire state which were unsold and unappropriated.[8]

fallow, grassland in rotation, permanent pastures, orchards, and vineyards. Unimproved land included woodlands, forests, and "old fields" which were not growing wood. Collett, whose statistics are based on assessors' reports, gives a smaller percentage of improved land than do the United States census reports.

[7] Powell A. Moore, *The Calumet Region. Indiana's Last Frontier* (*Indiana Historical Collections,* XXXIX, Indianapolis, 1959), p. 93; Carter, "Rural Indiana in Transition," *Agricultural History,* XX, 109.

[8] Carter, *op. cit.*

The legislation dealing with the drainage and disposal of the swamplands was loosely drawn and more loosely administered. Most counties kept no records or inadequate records, so that a complete account is impossible, but the evidence of laxity and fraud is overwhelming. Some men purchased large tracts of land for $1.25 or less per acre but failed to carry out drainage projects. Contractors took land as pay for building drainage ditches but failed to build the ditches. It was charged that the land law had been deliberately framed so as to benefit speculators and that persons with powerful political connections profited most from it. Among them was Michael G. Bright, brother of Senator Jesse D. Bright, who acquired a large amount of land in the Beaver Lake area in Newton County.[9]

Two legislative committees were appointed to investigate alleged frauds. In most places they found that records had not been kept or were so incomplete as to make legal action against the guilty parties impossible. But evidence of the activities in La Porte County, where records were more complete, throws light on the way in which the law probably operated in most places. There the commissioner agreed to pay the engineer who was in charge of ditching in land since funds for the purpose were soon exhausted. The engineer in turn agreed to advance the cash necessary for paying for the ditching. The commissioner agreed to give the engineer three dollars in ditching certificates for every dollar he advanced.

"The practical effect of their operations is this," said the committee report:

Birch [the engineer] advanced to Fry [the commissioner] one thousand dollars in money; Fry gives Birch a ditching certificate for three thousand dollars, payable in swamp land; Birch, with another ditching certificate, payable also in swamp land, gets from the State Treasury three thousand dollars in money, with which he gets from Fry nine

9 *Ibid.*, p. 110; *Report of the Swamp Land Committee to the General Assembly of the State of Indiana* (Indianapolis, 1859), pp. 4, 10, and *passim;* Report and Testimony of the Swamp Land Committee, Indiana *Documentary Journal,* 1863, II, Pt. 2, Doc. 25, pp. 1270-1271.

thousand dollars in ditching certificates and pays for swamp land with it. In other words, the State sells, through this operation nine thousand dollars worth of land, or seven thousand two hundred acres, for one thousand dollars in money.

The law set a minimum price of $1.25 an acre, but the effect of these operations was to sell it for less than fourteen cents an acre. In Starke County, the committee found, "the opportunity of perpetrating fraud was only limited by the quantity of swampland in the county."[10]

In spite of the fact that by the mid fifties virtually all public lands had been disposed of, vast stretches of the swampland remained totally unimproved for many years. During the fifties and sixties there were also large holdings of unimproved land in Benton, White, Warren, and Tippecanoe counties. Large holdings belonged to absentee owners who were unwilling to spend money to carry out drainage projects and unwilling to pay taxes to build roads and schools.[11]

Speculators who acquired large holdings hoped that the land would be worked and improved by tenants. For example, in 1854 Henry W. Ellsworth advertised 50,000 acres of "farm" land near the Wabash with the provision that if immigrants were unable to buy they could lease the land for two or three years, giving one half of their crops in payment and then receive title to the land. But offers of this sort attracted few settlers. Consequently the great landowners turned to cattle raising, which for several years proved very lucrative. By the seventies increasing land values and taxes caused some cattlemen to turn to a more intensive use of their land. They began to divide pasture lands into quarter, half, or full sections, and drain them and plant them with corn. In most cases such land was worked by tenants who did not have the money to buy land. For example, in 1877 arrangements were made to divide some of the land owned by Moses

10 Report and Testimony of the Swamp Land Committee, *loc. cit.*, pp. 1277, 1286.

11 Paul W. Gates, "Land Policy and Tenancy in the Prairie Counties of Indiana," *Indiana Magazine of History*, XXXV (1939), 18-19.

Fowler and to plant it with corn—with the owner receiving compensation at the rate of twenty-five cents per bushel.[12]

Large holdings and absentee ownership were not typical of the state as a whole and were confined almost entirely to the counties of the northwest. In 1880 there were only two hundred and seventy-five farms of more than one thousand acres in the state. The counties containing the largest number of these farms were as follows: Newton with twenty-three; Jasper with twenty; Benton with seventeen; Lawrence and Warren with fourteen each; Putnam with eleven; and Porter with ten. The typical farm was a relatively small one worked by the owner. In 1850 the average size of farms was 136 acres. By 1880 this had decreased to 105 acres. Farm tenancy was not common. Of approximately 194,000 farms 147,000 were cultivated by the owners. On farms worked by tenants rent was seldom paid entirely in cash. Usually some sort of system of payment by dividing the crop prevailed. In some cases tenants who cleared land which was not ready for cultivation were not expected to pay any rent the first year. Hired agricultural workers were not numerous. Such as there were, were usually seasonal workers.[13]

§ §

During the pioneer period the economy of Indiana had been based on corn and hogs, and these two products continued to be agricultural mainstays, but wheat and cattle became increasingly important. Indian corn was the universal crop. "Corn is the great staple of the State," declared the *Indiana Gazetteer* of 1850. "It is easily cultivated and almost

[12] *Ibid.*, pp. 20-22; Paul W. Gates, "Hoosier Cattle Kings," *Indiana Magazine of History*, XLIV (1948), 9.

[13] United States Bureau of the Census, *Tenth Census* (1880), III: *Agriculture* [Pt. 1], Table V, pp. 46-49; Carter, "Rural Indiana in Transition," *Agricultural History*, XX, 114. Of the 194,013 farms in the state in 1880, a total of 43,403 were between 20 and 50 acres; 64,030 between 50 and 100 acres; 72,103 between 100 and 500 acres; 1,320 between 500 and 1,000 acres; 275 over 1,000 acres.

every farmer has from 20 to 100 acres. A single hand can
prepare the ground, plant and attend to and gather from 20
to 25 acres, according to the state of the ground and character of the season." Corn was described as "the main article
of food for man and stock," capable of being "cooked in a
great variety of ways, so as to be equally acceptable at the
tables of the poor and rich."[14] It was raised principally as
a feed grain for hogs and, increasingly, for stock rather than
for sale. United States census reports show that corn production more than doubled in the period from 1850 to 1880—
from approximately 52 million bushels in the former year to
115 million in 1880. In 1850 and 1860, according to the
census, Indiana ranked fourth among all the states in the
Union in corn production. In 1870, as the result of a temporary decline, she fell to fifth place, but in 1880 she was
again in fourth place. Thereafter her relative position declined. It should be pointed out that census statistics are
useful for showing trends of this sort, but that for a number
of reasons census data are not to be regarded as entirely
reliable. Corn production fluctuated from year to year and
in some instances, as in 1870, the census year was not typical.
There are sometimes marked discrepancies between the census
figures and those compiled by the United States Department
of Agriculture.[15]

[14] *The Indiana Gazetteer, or Topographical Dictionary of the State of
Indiana* (3d edition, Indianapolis, 1850), pp. 35-36.

[15] Census reports usually were based on data collected the previous year.
Taking this into account, the following table shows the comparative figures for
corn production by bushels compiled by the Census Bureau and the Department of Agriculture.

U. S. Census		U. S. Department of Agriculture	
1850	52,964,363	1849	no report
1860	71,588,919	1859	no report
1870	51,094,538	1869	73,000,000
1880	115,482,300	1879	134,920,500

United States Bureau of the Census, *Compendium of the Tenth Census* (1880),
p. 662; United States Department of Agriculture, *Report of the Commissioner,*
1869, p. 29; *ibid.,* 1879, p. 133. Indiana's rank among the leading corn-producing
states at each census from 1850 to 1880 is shown by the following:

As population moved northward counties in the central part of the state became the principal producers of corn. By 1850 Tippecanoe County, in the rich lands of the upper Wabash, was in first place. Of the ten counties with the largest corn production in that year the most southerly one was Bartholomew. Ten years later Tippecanoe was still in first place, but by 1880 it was in second place, and neighboring Benton County was in first place. By 1880 no county in the southern third of the state was among the top ten in corn production.[16]

While corn continued to be the most important crop, wheat production showed a more spectacular increase—from a mere 6 million bushels in 1850 to 47 million bushels in 1880, according to the United States census figures.[17] Nearly all of the

1850: Ohio, Kentucky, Illinois, Indiana
1860: Illinois, Ohio, Missouri, Indiana
1870: Illinois, Iowa, Ohio, Missouri, Indiana
1880: Illinois, Iowa, Missouri, Indiana

United States Bureau of the Census, *Compendium of the Tenth Census* (1880), p. 662.

[16] In 1850 the ten most important corn-producing counties listed in the order of their importance were: Tippecanoe, Rush, Wayne, Montgomery, Putnam, Shelby, Morgan, Parke, Bartholomew, and Marion. In 1860 the ten counties with the largest corn production were as follows: Tippecanoe, Clinton, Rush, Putnam, Shelby, Morgan, Montgomery, Marion, Gibson, Bartholomew. The last two are in the south; the remainder are in the central portion of the state.

In 1880 the ten counties with the largest corn production were as follows: Benton, Tippecanoe, Shelby, Montgomery, Hamilton, Boone, Rush, Marion, Warren, Madison. Figures for 1870 are not included because they are not representative. The 1869 crop on which the 1870 figures are based was abnormally small. United States Bureau of the Census, *Seventh Census* (1850), pp. 791-792; *Eighth Census* (1860): *Agriculture*, pp. 39, 43; *Tenth Census* (1880), III: *Agriculture* [Pt. 1], Table XI, pp. 186-187.

[17] Census figures show wheat production by decades as follows:

1850	6,214,458	bushels
1860	16,848,267	"
1870	27,747,222	"
1880	47,284,853	"

There are marked discrepancies between the census figures for wheat production and those compiled by the U. S. Department of Agriculture, with the figures

wheat was the winter variety. The amount of spring wheat planted was negligible. In 1850 Indiana ranked sixth among all of the states in wheat production. The rapid expansion of the next decade brought her to second place by 1860. By 1870 she had fallen to fourth place, but in 1880 was temporarily again in second place though her relative position declined thereafter.[18]

Wheat growing centered in the northern section of the state, and as the lands in the north were brought under cultivation production sharply increased. As early as 1850 La Porte County, on Lake Michigan, was the largest producer of wheat, followed by Allen, Elkhart, and St. Joseph counties, all of which were in the north. But in the following years the pattern changed somewhat. Most of the wheat continued to be grown in the north, but certain counties in the south on the lower Wabash turned to wheat growing. As a result, in 1880 Gibson County led all counties in the state in the amount of wheat grown, while the neighboring counties of Knox and Posey were in third and fourth place, with Elkhart in second place.[19]

Production of other cereal crops was relatively unimportant. In 1850 the amount of oats grown was almost as great as that of wheat, but by 1880 it amounted to only about a third

of the latter being smaller. Department of Agriculture figures for bushels of wheat are as follows:

| 1869 | 20,600,000 | 1879 | 43,709,960 |
| 1870 | 20,200,000 | 1880 | 49,766,758 |

United States Bureau of the Census, *Compendium of the Tenth Census* (1880), p. 665; United States Department of Agriculture, *Report of the Commissioner,* 1869, p. 29; 1870, p. 31; 1879, p. 133; 1880, p. 191.

[18] In 1870, for example, more than 27 million bushels of winter wheat were grown, and only about 161,000 bushels of spring wheat. United States Bureau of the Census, *Ninth Census* (1870), III: *Statistics of Wealth and Industry of the United States,* p. 139. In 1880 only Illinois, with 51,110,502 bushels, exceeded Indiana in wheat production. *Tenth Census* (1880), III; *Agriculture* [Pt. 1], p. xvii; *Compendium of the Tenth Census* (1880), p. 665.

[19] United States Bureau of the Census, *Seventh Census* (1850), pp. 791-792; *Tenth Census* (1880), III: *Agriculture* [Pt. 1], Table XI, pp. 186-187.

as much. In 1850 Indiana ranked eighth among the states in the production of oats; by 1880 she was in tenth place. Oats were raised principally for consumption on the farm as food for horses and sheep. They were seldom raised for market and never were used for human food. They were regarded by farmers as a "side" crop and were planted to prevent the ground intended for wheat sowing in September from lying fallow. One reason for the failure to increase oats production was the uncertainty of the crop. A drought which would not harm corn or wheat could ruin oats. Very little barley was raised. Such as was produced was used chiefly for manufacture of malt liquors. Rye was cultivated even less extensively than barley.[20]

Tobacco was a relatively unimportant crop confined to a few counties, but production increased sharply after 1850. In 1850 only a little more than a million pounds were being grown annually. By 1870 more than nine million pounds were produced, and in 1880 slightly less. At the last date Indiana ranked eleventh among the states in tobacco production. Nearly all of the tobacco was grown in the southwestern part of the state in the area between the Ohio and White rivers. Spencer County led all the counties in production in 1880, followed by Warrick and Dubois counties.[21]

Hay was a crop of some importance. In the north native prairie and swamp grasses were cut for feed for cattle during the winter. Elsewhere after 1850 there was a rapid increase in production of timothy grass and red clover. With the development of machinery for mowing and raking hay could be raised for market with relatively little labor. By 1880

---

[20] Indiana State Board of Agriculture, *Annual Report,* 1876, pp. 284-285. In 1879 a total of 15,599,518 bushels of oats were grown on 623,531 acres; 303,105 bushels of rye on 25,400 acres; 382,835 bushels of barley on 16,399 acres. United States Bureau of the Census, *Tenth Census* (1880), III: *Agriculture* [Pt. 1], Table I, p. 6; *Compendium of the Tenth Census* (1880), p. 663.

[21] *Tenth Census* (1880), III: *Agriculture* [Pt. 1], pp. xix, 304-306; *Compendium of the Tenth Census* (1880), p. 671.

Indiana was in tenth place among the states in hay production.[22]

A variety of fruits were grown on almost every farm for
home consumption. The northern part of the state was considered as being well suited for apple culture. By the 1870's
this fruit was becoming of some importance as a commercial
crop. The climate of the southern half of the state was better
adapted to the growing of peaches. In a few places peaches
were canned for market before 1880. In addition to apples
and peaches, pears, plums, quinces, cherries, and grapes were
grown quite generally throughout the state.[23]

At midcentury pioneer methods of planting and cultivation
and harvesting were still generally prevalent, but during the
next few decades there was a great increase in mechanization,
although in newly cleared land stumps continued to make the
use of machinery difficult or impossible.[24]

The exhibits of farm machinery were one of the principal
attractions of the state fairs, which began in the fifties. In
addition to displays of the machines there were trial exhibitions
to test them. One of the most elaborate was held by the State
Agricultural Board in 1856 near Richmond. Large numbers of
farmers from both Indiana and western Ohio attended. The
first event was the trial of twelve types of mowers, which were
reported to be the largest number of such machines made by
different manufacturers ever brought together in one place for

[22] Esarey, *History of Indiana,* II, 836-837; Indiana State Board of Agriculture, *Annual Report,* 1876, p. 285; United States Bureau of Census, *Tenth
Census* (1880), III: *Agriculture* [Pt. 1], p. xxi.

[23] Indiana State Board of Agriculture, *Annual Report,* 1876, p. 292; 1852,
pp. 55-58. Detailed information about the many varieties of fruits grown is
given in the *Annual Reports, passim.*

[24] Between 1850 and 1880 the estimated value of farm implements and
machinery in use in the state increased more than threefold. The value of
farm implements as reported in the census was as follows:

1850	$ 6,704,444	1870	$17,676,591
1860	$10,457,897	1880	$20,476,988

Compendium of the Tenth Census (1880), p. 659. These figures do not take
into account the fluctuations in the value of money between 1850 and 1880.

such a purpose. The machines, which were tested in three large meadows which presented a varied terrain, were graded on a scale fixed by the Massachusetts Board of Agriculture. The second day there was a trial of reapers and combined mowers and reapers. At the time of the fair sixty-nine varieties of plows were put on trial in a tract near Indianapolis. Sometimes machines which won awards at trials of this sort did not prove to be durable when put to actual use. Another source of criticism was that the machines which were exhibited were superior to those which were actually offered for sale by the various manufacturers.[25]

By the fifties, although wooden plows were still in use in some places, they were for the most part replaced by cast-iron ones, and these in turn were replaced by steel plows, which were necessary for breaking the sod of the prairies. But the high cost of steel caused continued interest in methods of improving iron. In the fifties James Oliver began experiments which resulted in the development of the first successful chilled-iron plow. He continued to improve his product by additional patents and by the late seventies had established what became the world's largest plow manufacturing establishment at South Bend.[26] A wide variety of plows adapted to different kinds of soil were developed. At a field trial at the State Agricultural College (Purdue) near Lafayette in 1876 thirty-five different kinds of breaking plows were exhibited. In addition there were several types of cultivators. Some of the plows were three-horse sulkies, on which the farmer could sit as he plowed, but these were not widely used before 1880.[27] Various kinds of homemade types of corn

[25] Indiana State Board of Agriculture, *Annual Report,* 1856, pp. 85-87, 89-91, 93-95; 1854-1855, p. 465.

[26] See below, Chapter X, page 420.

[27] Indiana State Board of Agriculture, *Annual Report,* 1876, pp. 30-31; Fred A. Shannon, *The Farmer's Last Frontier: Agriculture, 1860-1897 (The Economic History of the United States,* V, New York, 1945), pp. 128-129; William C. Latta, *Outline History of Indiana Agriculture* (Lafayette, Ind., 1938), pp. 78, 100.

planters were developed at uncertain dates, and by 1860 successful devices had been patented. Only a few major alterations were made thereafter. Wheat drills had been developed by the fifties but came into use rather slowly.[28] By the 1850's mowers and reapers were in use rather widely but they were crude and were greatly improved in later years. Some of the mowers were equipped with changeable parts so that they could be used for both mowing and reaping. Early reapers merely cut the grain and dumped it on the ground. In 1858 the Marsh reaper was invented, with a platform behind on which men could ride and tie the grain as it came from the reel. An aggregate of thirty harvesters were displayed at the State Fair in 1870. These included reapers, mowers, and combined reapers and mowers. In spite of the large number the machines were similar. All of them used essentially the same system of cutting—the McCormick vibrating sickle. Various efforts were made at developing automatic binding devices. A twine binder was in use about 1850, followed by various types of wire binders in the 1870's, none of which were entirely satisfactory. At the field trial at the State Agricultural College in 1876 the Wood's Harvester and Binder was the center of attraction. At the State Fair that year two other binders were displayed both of which appeared to work well, but neither had really been thoroughly tested. "A successful binder appears to be about all that is required to perfect our harvesting machinery," said the State Agricultural Report of that year.[29]

Threshing machines had been introduced before 1850, but the method of trampling out grain on the barn floor was still more common than the use of machinery. The first threshing machines were crude affairs and their operation somewhat uncertain. In one of the early trial exhibitions sponsored by the State Board of Agriculture several of the entries broke

---

[28] Indiana State Board of Agriculture, *Annual Report,* 1857, p. 522; 1869, pp. 136-137.

[29] *Ibid.,* 1870, p. 147; 1876, pp. 31, 75-76; Latta, *Outline History of Indiana Agriculture,* p. 115; Shannon, *The Farmer's Last Frontier,* p. 134.

down. These early machines operated on tread mills or by teams of horses pulling a large rotating wheel. Machines operated by eight horses were the usual type. But there were some smaller machines operated by two or four horses which were expected to be more suitable for the hillier regions in the southern half of the state. By 1870 the small machines apparently were no longer being made. All threshers displayed at the State Fair that year were operated by at least eight horses and sometimes by larger numbers. Steam-operated machines were also exhibited, but their use did not become common until after 1880.[30]

By the 1870's few radical innovations were being made in the farm machinery displayed at the fairs, but the machinery was constantly being improved by being made lighter and less unwieldly and by greater durability. Iron and steel were increasingly used for parts formerly made of wood. A pamphlet published by the State Board of Agriculture in 1876 claimed that the introduction of machinery had reduced the manual labor required in farming by 50 per cent from what it had been forty years before. "Perhaps in no part of the world has [sic] improved implements and labor-saving machinery been more generally introduced among farmers than in Indiana," it asserted. "The polished steel plow, the seed drill, the corn planter, the cultivator, and the harvester are found on almost every farm, and each autumn the threshing machine with its portable steam, or horse power makes its rounds of the neighborhood, and prepares the harvest for market."[31] Perhaps machinery was not as widely used as this suggests, but mechanization had undoubtedly reached a high percentage of Indiana farms and largely revolutionized age-old methods.

In the 1850's mechanical devices for planting corn were just beginning to be used, but most corn was planted by hand

---

[30] Indiana State Board of Agriculture, *Annual Report*, 1854-1855, p. 466; 1856, p. 92; 1870, p. 148; 1878, p. 130; Carter, "Rural Indiana in Transition," *Agricultural History*, XX, 113, 117; Shannon, *Farmer's Last Frontier*, p. 136.

[31] Indiana State Board of Agriculture, *Annual Report*, 1876, pp. 76, 279.

and covered with a hoe. Of persons winning prizes for corn at the State Fair in 1857 eleven had planted by hand and only six had used a drill. By 1880 horse-drawn planters were nearly always used, although on rough land some corn was still planted by hand. It was estimated that a man could plant two or three acres of land a day by hand and more than twice as much with a horse-drawn machine. The seed was checker planted in such a way that the field could be cultivated both lengthwise and crosswise. By 1880 horse-drawn cultivators were in general use.[32] Corn was not used extensively for forage. The stalks were usually allowed to remain in the field until November, when the ears were gathered and put into bins or cribs. There were wide variations in the yield per acre due principally to differences in the quality of soil. In 1856 separate premiums were awarded at the State Fair for corn grown in different kinds of soil. One went to a Montgomery County farmer who had raised 146 bushels on an acre of clay soil; another to a Warren County farmer who raised 153 bushels on alluvial soil; and one to a Sullivan County farmer who raised 171 bushels on prairie soil. In 1870 the premium was awarded for corn grown in bottom land in Fountain County with an average yield of 140 acres. In 1871, a year when crops generally were unusually large, the premium went to a Grant County farmer who raised 197 bushels on an acre. On poor soil there might be a yield of only ten bushels per acre. Anything from thirty to fifty bushels was considered a normal yield on ordinary soil.[33]

For wheat the soil was broken in August or September, and the sowing was usually done in September but sometimes in October. At midcentury sowing broadcast by hand was almost universal. For example, all of the prizes for wheat at the

[32] Indiana State Board of Agriculture, *Annual Report,* 1876, pp. 282-283; Esarey, *History of Indiana,* II, 833-834; United States Bureau of the Census, *Tenth Census* (1880), III: *Agriculture* [Pt. 2], pp. 478, 481.

[33] *Ibid.,* p. 481; Esarey, *History of Indiana,* II, 833; Indiana State Board of Agriculture, *Annual Report,* 1870, pp. 201-202; 1871, pp. 207-208; 1876, p. 283.

State Fair in 1857 went to persons who had sowed in this way. But mechanical drills had come into general use by the 1870's, although some wheat continued to be sowed in the old way. Wheat was harvested in late June or July. By 1880 nearly all of it was cut by machine. A reaper drawn by a team of three or four horses could cut from eight to twelve acres per day. After it was cut wheat was usually bound into sheaves and later threshed. Few individual farmers owned threshing machines. It was a common practice for a machine to travel from farm to farm.[34] As in the case of corn the yield of wheat per acre varied widely. In 1857 a premium was awarded for 48 bushels grown on one acre in Howard County. In 1870 the premium was for 36 bushels grown in Putnam County; in 1871 for 39 bushels grown in Hamilton County. On poor soil or in a bad year the yield was much lower—as little as five bushels an acre. About seventeen bushels was considered a good yield.[35]

The opening up of new lands to cultivation and the use of farm machinery contributed to extensive rather than intensive agriculture. Farmers were slow to adopt measures to conserve or increase the fertility of the soil. As early as 1853 Governor Wright was deploring the emphasis upon corn and hogs and urging diversification. "If we keep on for half a century in the same mode of cultivation that some of us have pursued for the last few years," he warned, "in some portions of the State, we shall not be able to raise a mullen stalk." He urged Indiana farmers: "It is your duty to leave this earth in as good condition, at least, as it was when you found it." But few heeded his advice. In 1869 an observer remarked that farmers tended to "disdain the new-fangled notions of rotation," especially in the older portions of the state, where bottom land was almost always devoted year after year to

34 Esarey, *History of Indiana*, II, 835; Indiana State Board of Agriculture, *Annual Report*, 1876, p. 284; United States Bureau of the Census, *Tenth Census* (1880), III: *Agriculture* [Pt. 2], p. 73.

35 *Ibid.;* Esarey, *History of Indiana*, II, 834-835; Indiana State Board of Agriculture, *Annual Report*, 1870, pp. 199-200; 1871, p. 213.

corn and uplands to hay. A few years later another critic declared: "It can hardly be said that the farmers of Indiana have any well defined system of rotating crops. . . . It is hard to convince the average Indiana farmer that his virgin soils need manures or any artificial helps."[36]

Certainly many farms continued to yield rich results without crop rotation or the use of fertilizers. Premiums at the State Fair were regularly won by farmers who raised corn and wheat on land which had received no enrichment.[37] But productivity of older lands was apparently already declining. In 1879 a professor at the recently established State Agricultural College, Purdue, asserted that although vast amounts of virgin land had been brought under cultivation in Indiana in recent years there had been little increase in the average productivity per acre in either wheat or corn. Statistics prepared by the United States Department of Agriculture appear to support his statement, especially with regard to corn. Although averages for corn fluctuated widely from year to year, the average yield per acre, according to these statistics, was the same in 1864 and 1880. On the other hand wheat production per acre, while fluctuating even more than that of corn, increased somewhat.[38] The increase was undoubtedly due to the opening of new lands rather than to efforts at artificial enrichment. But in spite of widespread indifference or lack of knowledge some farmers were paying increased attention to crop rotation by the 1870's. The amount of clover sowed in Indiana increased fourfold between 1870 and 1880. Some of this was due to the practice of raising clover in fields where

[36] Joseph A. Wright, *Address . . . at Livonia, Washington County*, p. 4; "Letter from Indiana," *The Country Gentleman. A Journal for the Farm, the Garden and the Fireside*, XXXIII (Albany, New York, 1869), 234; Indiana State Board of Agriculture, *Annual Report*, 1876, p. 287.

[37] Of the premium corn mentioned above none appears to have been raised on land which was fertilized in any way. One or two of the prize-winning wheat growers had used stable manure, but the rest had used no form of fertilizer.

[38] C. L. Ingersoll, "Progressive Agriculture," Indiana State Board of Agriculture, *Annual Report*, 1879, p. 176. See below, pp. 390, 391, for tables showing average corn and wheat production.

wheat was sowed in the fall. Some farmers were also beginning to apply stable manure to their fields, but little commercial fertilizer was in use.[39]

§ § §

As far back as records are available hogs were the most important source of cash income for Indiana farmers.[40] Most of the corn grown in the state was fed to hogs. In 1860 Indiana ranked first among all states in the Union in the number of hogs raised. There was always a correlation between the amount of corn grown and the number of hogs. In general the period from 1850 to 1880 showed an increase in both products. But in 1870, when census figures showed a marked, though temporary, decline in corn production, they showed a corresponding decline in the number of hogs. Hog production increased steadily but not as rapidly as that of corn. The amount of corn grown in 1880 was more than twice the amount grown in 1850, but hog production had increased less than 50 per cent.[41] Hogs were grown in all parts of the state, but the largest number were found in the central part. Throughout the period from 1850 to 1880 every census showed Rush County as the largest producer of hogs.[42]

[39] Indiana State Board of Agriculture, *Annual Report,* 1876, pp. 287-288; Barnhart and Carmony, *Indiana,* II, 221; Latta, *Outline History of Indiana Agriculture,* p. 127. In 1880 Indiana was not one of the top thirteen states in the use of commercial fertilizer. Most of the states using the largest amounts of commercial fertilizer were in the East, where soil exhaustion had already caused declining productivity. United States Bureau of the Census, *Tenth Census* (1880), III: *Agriculture* [Pt. 1], p. xxv.

[40] [Paul Farris and R. S. Euler], *Prices of Indiana Farm Products 1841-1955* (Agricultural Experiment Station, *Bulletin 644,* Purdue University, 1957), p. 11.

[41] United States Bureau of the Census, *Compendium of the Tenth Census* (1880), pp. 662, 681. Total hog production was as follows:

| 1850 | 2,263,776 | 1870 | 1,872,230 |
| 1860 | 3,099,110 | 1880 | 3,186,413 |

[42] Hog production by counties is shown in United States Bureau of the Census, *Seventh Census* (1850), pp. 791-792; *Eighth Census* (1860): *Agriculture,* pp. 39, 43; *Ninth Census* (1870), III: *Statistics of Wealth,* pp. 139, 143; *Tenth Census* (1880), III: *Agriculture* [Pt.], Table IX, pp. 150-151.

As in the pioneer period some hogs simply ran wild in the woods and fed upon mast, receiving little or no attention. There was little market for hogs of this type because the meat was oily. But after being fed corn for six or eight weeks they could be marketed. As markets became increasingly important more progressive farmers fed their pigs by turning them into early rye or clover fields and later into corn fields. Hogs were usually sold at about eighteen months of age after they had attained a weight of two hundred to two hundred fifty pounds.[43]

By the fifties most farmers were giving attention to breeding in an effort to improve the quality of meat. In the pioneer period the common hog had been "an ungainly type, with long legs and snout, a sharp back, of a roaming disposition, slow and expensive to fatten." But by 1856 it was reported that there had been such marked improvement in the quality of swine that there was hope that the native or "alligator breed" would soon be completely extinct. "Probably in no other class of livestock," says the leading agricultural history of the period, "was improvement so rapid during this period as in swine."[44] At the early Indiana State Fairs the exhibits of hogs were the largest both as to numbers and breeds. Among the breeds were Polands, Berkshires, Suffolks, Leicesters, Byfields, Graziers, Russians, Bedfords, and Chester Whites. The Poland breed was recommended especially for cross breeding as being best adapted to the needs of Indiana farmers. By the 1870's Poland China hogs had become by far the most popular among breeders. At the State Fair in 1879 one hundred and seventy-five Poland Chinas were exhibited, sixty-five Berkshires, and smaller numbers of other breeds.[45]

[43] *Indiana Gazetteer,* 1850, pp. 37-38; Latta, *Outline History of Indiana Agriculture,* p. 74.

[44] Indiana State Board of Agriculture, *Annual Report,* 1856, p. 99; Percy W. Bidwell and John I. Falconer, *History of Agriculture in the Northern United States, 1620-1860* (New York, 1941), p. 441.

[45] Indiana State Board of Agriculture, *Annual Report,* 1854-1855, p. 453; 1857, pp. 595, 597, 598; 1879, p. 66.

The raising of beef cattle increased at a more rapid rate than hog raising. Part of the increase in corn production was to feed the growing number of cattle. United States census figures show that between 1850 and 1880 the number of beef cattle more than doubled—from a total of 389,891 to 864,-846. According to the census figures, Tippecanoe, Montgomery and Warren were the leading cattle producers in 1850; Montgomery, Tippecanoe, Putnam, in 1860; Putnam, Montgomery and Hendricks in 1870; and Hendricks, Allen, and Montgomery counties in 1880.[46] It seems probable that the census figures do not accurately reflect the burgeoning cattle industry in the prairie counties of the northwest along the Illinois border. These lands, sparsely settled and covered with luxuriant grass, were ideally suited to grazing. At first it was possible to raise cattle on government land and then drive them overland to markets in the East. In 1850 an English traveler, who was visiting near Jonesboro in Grant County, Indiana, recorded meeting "large droves of fine fat cattle on their way to the Eastern cities from the prairies of Illinois: the distant [sic] between the extreme points of travel to these poor beasts is at least 1,000 miles; but they have plenty of grass to feed on by the way."[47]

The combination of grassland, cheap corn, and a growing demand for beef in the eastern cities caused the grazing business to grow rapidly in the fifties. A writer in Clinton County, Indiana, in 1853 described the method as follows:

We have in this county a number of individuals who are engaged in buying cattle in small lots, and taking them to the prairies, where they collect large numbers to sell to the drovers from Ohio and Pennsylvania. These cattle are kept on the prairies in Indiana and Illinois in the following manner: The owner selects his location for grazing early in the spring, hires a man to herd them, and furnishes him with

[46] United States Bureau of the Census, *Seventh Census* (1850), pp. 790-791; *Eighth Census* (1860): *Agriculture,* pp. 38, 42; *Ninth Census* (1870), III: *Statistics of Wealth,* 139, 143; *Tenth Census* (1880), III: *Agriculture* [Pt. 1], Table IX, pp. 150-151.

[47] Candler, Extracts from a Narrative of a Journey in Indiana in 1850.

a pony, and prepares a lot called a "pound" to put them in at night. As soon as the grass starts in the spring, he takes his cattle to the grazing ground, adjacent to some farmer on the edge of the prairie. He starts his cattle out in the prairie early in the morning by themselves. . . . He remains with them until night, when he brings them in and puts them in the pound for the night. The cost of keeping a lot of cattle in this manner, during the summer, is the herdsman's wages and board, and their salt, one hundred dollars will keep four to five hundred head of cattle during the summer.

Native stock was purchased at little cost and turned loose on the prairie from April to December. After the prairie grass was killed by the winter the calves were put into enclosures and fed. Two summers of grazing plus some fattening with corn prepared them for slaughter and they were driven off to market.[48]

This particular phase of the cattle industry was short-lived. The purchase of land by speculators and the appearance of settlers forced the cattlemen to purchase their grazing lands, and public lands quickly disappeared. Building of the railroads brought an end to the necessity for the long drives to market. The Civil War and the increasing importance of Chicago as a meat-packing center caused cattle growing to expand. The heyday of the cattle kings in Indiana was from the outbreak of the Civil War until the eighties.[49]

Most of the great cattlemen were men who had already made fortunes in other enterprises and who invested their surplus in land. Typical were Moses Fowler of Lafayette and his brother-in-law, Adams Earl. After making money in banking, meat packing, and other businesses they bought 20,000 acres in Benton County and 25,000 acres in White and Warren counties on which they raised corn and cattle. Edward C. Sumner, another cattleman, acquired about 30,000 acres

---

48 United States Patent Office, *Annual Report*, 1853: *Agriculture*, p. 6, quoted in Bidwell and Falconer, *History of Agriculture in the Northern United States*, p. 392. Gates, "Hoosier Cattle Kings," *Indiana Magazine of History*, XLIV, 7.

49 Gates, *op. cit.*, p. 21.

on the Indiana-Illinois border, mostly in Benton County, which he used for raising corn and fattening cattle. Still another was Lemuel Milk, who owned some 40,000 acres in Newton County on which he pastured 2,500 cattle and 10,000 sheep. The prairie counties today are dotted with towns named after some of these and other cattle kings. Examples are Fowler, Earl Park, Kentland (named after Alexander Kent), Raub, and Rensselaer.[50]

These were men with feudalistic views, who "refused to accept anything less than despotic control of widespread domains. . . . They owned land by townships instead of sections." They played a major part in the development of the state, but they resisted the payment of taxes for such services as roads and schools. Sumner, for example, was accused of driving his herds of cattle on to lands in Illinois in order to avoid assessment for taxes in Indiana and then driving them back to Indiana to avoid assessment in Illinois.[51] Some of the resentment shown by Grangers and other farmers against land "monopolists" in the seventies was directed against men of this sort.

Raising of dairy cattle also increased steadily although their numbers were smaller than those of beef cattle. In 1850 Wayne County had the largest number of milk cows in the state, followed by Montgomery and Tippecanoe counties. By 1860 Allen County in the far north had become the principal center for dairy cattle, a position which it maintained in 1870 and 1880. In 1860 Montgomery and Tippecanoe counties were in second and third place. By 1870 Lake County had moved into second place, with Montgomery third. By 1880 Lake County remained in second place but Elkhart, another county in the far north, was third.[52]

50 *Ibid.*, pp. 8-21 *passim.*

51 *Ibid.*, p. 16; George Ade, "Prairie Kings of Yesterday," *Saturday Evening Post,* CCIV (July 4, 1931), quoted in *ibid.*, p. 6.

52 United States Bureau of the Census, *Seventh Census* (1850), pp. 790-791; *Eighth Census* (1860): *Agriculture,* pp. 38, 42; *Ninth Census* (1870), III: *Statistics of Wealth,* pp. 139, 143; *Tenth Census* (1880), III: *Agriculture* [Pt. 1], Table IX, pp. 150-151.

As cattle growing expanded there was increased emphasis upon improving breeds. Prior to 1850 few cattle except native "scrubs" were to be found, but during the next few years throughout the state there were reports of marked improvements as the result of introduction of new breeds. Durhams became by far the most popular of beef cattle. Devons were regarded as superior dairy cattle. By the 1870's Jerseys were also becoming popular.[53]

Several Indiana men were pioneers in the breeding of prize shorthorn cattle. In 1853 Dr. A. C. Stevenson of Putnam County imported shorthorns into Indiana directly from England. Somewhat earlier Sol Meredith, who later gained fame as a military figure in the Civil War, had begun the breeding of shorthorns in Wayne County, as had Thomas Wilhoit in Henry County. In the late seventies the aforementioned Adams Earl and Moses Fowler and other cattlemen of the prairie counties began to show an interest in the breeding of Herefords. In 1872 the Indiana Shorthorn Breeders Association was formed with Dr. Stevenson as president. Stevenson was also the first president of the National Shorthorn Breeders Association, which was organized in Indianapolis the same year.[54]

Some of the cattle purchased and bred were of the finest stock in the world and commanded prices which were extremely high for the time. In the 1870's S. F. Lockridge of Greencastle was the owner of a prize bull, Lord Strathallan, bred in Scotland and imported by a breeder in Ontario, Canada. Lockridge purchased him from the latter for $2,500. At a sale at the farms of Meredith and Son in Cambridge City in 1874, at which fifty-three head of shorthorns were sold, breeders were present from Kentucky, Ohio, New York, Michigan, Illinois, Iowa, and Canada as well as Indiana.

[53] Indiana State Board of Agriculture, *Annual Report,* 1854-1855, p. 452; 1856, pp. 109-110; 1857, pp. 562-567; 1878, p. 143; 1879, p. 65.

[54] Latta, *Outline History of Indiana Agriculture,* pp. 190-193, 286; Indiana State Board of Agriculture, *Annual Report,* 1873, p. 239.

Two cows were sold for $2,000 each. The following year another cow was sold by the same breeders for $2,400 and a second brought the extraordinary price of $4,005. The average price of the forty-two cows and heifers at this sale was $979.[55]

At midcentury oxen were still common in Indiana and were considered superior to horses for use in breaking tough prairie sod, but they were outnumbered by horses. By the seventies oxen had almost disappeared,[56] but the number of horses and mules increased steadily. Some of the mules were sold in the South where they were in demand for work on the cotton plantations. There were also profits to be made from raising horses for sale in the newer states and territories west of Indiana.[57] Between 1850 and 1880 the number of horses almost doubled.[58] Many of the animals were the "scrub" variety— a mixture descended from ancestors brought in by settlers from all over the United States. One critical observer of the exhibits at the State Fair in 1855 said that it was hopeless to try to trace the stock of the horses in the various divisions. "Nearly every horse had a stock after his own name, indicating a mixture of breeds not calculated to perfect the horse," he said. The farm horses were so coarse and awkward that

[55] *Indiana Farmer. Weekly Journal of the Farm, Home and Garden* (Indianapolis), May 30, June 6, 1874, June 5, 1875.

[56] According to the United States Census the number of working oxen was as follows:

1850	40,221	1870	14,088
1860	117,687	1880	3,970

United States Bureau of the Census, *Eighth Census* (1860): *Agriculture*, p. cviii; *Compendium of Tenth Census* (1880), p. 677. The figure given for 1860 is so inconsistent with the trends for the rest of the period that it is probably incorrect.

[57] Indiana State Board of Agriculture, *Annual Report*, 1854-1855, p. 458; 1857, p. 544.

[58] According to the United States census the number of horses was as follows:

1850	314,299	1870	497,883
1860	520,677	1880	581,444

United States Bureau of the Census, *Compendium of Tenth Census* (1880), p. 675.

they should not have been exhibited. "The progeny of these coarse brutes fill our State," he remarked, "and at every cross roads one of these two dollar and fifty cent animals may be found."[59]

Although horses were generally of nondescript breed, by the 1850's there was much interest in improving them by the infusion of new blood. Some thoroughbred horses were being imported. The riding horses exhibited at the state fairs were usually descended from Kentucky racers, but with a mixture of other blood. Some of the cattle breeders in the state like Sol Meredith also turned their attention to horse breeding. Some work horses were imported from England for breeding.[60]

While sheep did not play a part comparable to hogs or cattle in the economy of the state, the demand for wool created by the Civil War caused a sharp increase in the number of sheep during the sixties. In 1850 the United States census figures showed a little more than a million sheep in the state, and this number had declined somewhat by 1860. But by the beginning of 1867 there was an estimated total of about three million, according to figures of the Department of Agriculture. In the fifties the average price for wool had been only about 28 cents per pound, but by 1864 it had reached 96 cents. After the end of the war prices fell sharply and the number of sheep declined. During the sixties Indiana ranked fifth among the states in the number of sheep raised.[61] Although the number

[59] Indiana State Board of Agriculture, *Annual Report,* 1854-1855, p. 447.

[60] *Ibid.,* p. 447; 1856, pp. 106-107; 1857, pp. 544-546; advertisements in *Indiana Farmer,* 1874-1875 *passim.*

[61] United States Bureau of the Census, *Compendium of the Tenth Census* (1880), p. 680; United States Department of Agriculture, *Report of the Commissioner,* 1864, p. 588; 1866, p. 67; 1868, p. 46; 1869, p. 48; 1870, p. 48; [Farris and Euler], *Prices of Indiana Farm Products, 1841-1955,* pp. 14-15. In 1866, according to statistics of the United States Department of Agriculture, Ohio ranked first among the states in the number of sheep grown; New York second; Michigan third; Pennsylvania fourth; Indiana fifth. By 1870 although the number of sheep in Indiana had declined sharply the number in other states had declined even more, with the result that Indiana was in fourth place. By 1880 the older states in the East had been far outdistanced

of sheep declined, the amount of wool produced continued to increase.[62]

At the state fairs sheep of both native and foreign stock were exhibited, but the introduction of high-priced thoroughbreds was slow at first because depredations by roving bands of dogs made farmers hesitate to invest money. In 1861 the legislature passed a law for the licensing and taxing of dogs which provided that the funds obtained from it should be used by township trustees to pay for sheep killed or crippled by dogs. By the 1870's various fine imported breeds, including Cotswold and Southdown sheep, were being raised. In 1876 the Indiana Wool Growers Association was formed to encourage interest in improvement of breeding and management of sheep.[63]

§ § § §

For Indiana farmers, as for farmers generally, the years from about 1850 until after the Civil War were years of rising farm prices. Thereafter a long period of deflation began which continued until almost the end of the century. Prices for agricultural products as a whole rose rapidly during

by California and Texas, and Indiana had dropped to ninth place. United States Department of Agriculture, *Report of the Commissioner*, 1866, p. 67; 1870, p. 48; 1880, p. 201. The discrepancies between the figures in the United States census and the Department of Agriculture figures are so great as to raise serious questions as to the validity of data of this sort. For example, the United States census in 1870 shows 1,612,680 sheep in Indiana, while the figures of the Commissioner of Agriculture show 2,100,000. These wide variations may be due to the fact that the data were collected at different seasons of the year.

[62] Wool production in Indiana as shown by the United States census figures was as follows:

| 1850 | 2,610,287 pounds | 1870 | 5,029,023 pounds |
| 1860 | 2,552,318   " | 1880 | 6,167,498   " |

United States Bureau of the Census, *Compendium of the Tenth Census* (1880), p. 667.

[63] Indiana State Board of Agriculture, *Annual Report*, 1856, p. 101; 1876, p. 248; Indiana *Laws*, 1861, pp. 110-112. See Indiana State Board of Agriculture, *Annual Reports, passim* and *Indiana Farmer, passim,* for mention of imported breeds of sheep.

the inflationary period which followed the discovery of gold in California in 1849 and continued to rise until the panic of 1857. In 1858 there was a temporary decline, followed by another rise, which continued until the outbreak of the Civil War. At the beginning of the war prices fell briefly, but this was quickly followed by an upsurge which lasted into the post-war years.[64] In Indiana corn, according to the United States Department of Agriculture figures, reached a high of 95 cents a bushel in 1864, declined to 38 cents in 1865, but in 1869 rose to 70 cents again as the result of an abnormally small crop.[65]

CORN 1864-1880[66]

Year	Average Yield per acre in bushels	Value (average price per bushel)	Total Crop in bushels	Total Acres in corn
1864	29.0	.95	74,284,363	2,561,529
1865	40.4	.38	116,069,316	2,873,003
1866	36.5	.44	127,676,247	3,497,980
1867	29.2	.65	80,757,000	2,765,650
1868	34.0	.52	90,832,000	2,671,529
1869	23.2	.70	73,000,000	3,146,551
1870	39.5	.38	113,150,000	2,864,556
1871	35.7	.37	79,205,000	2,218,627
1872	38.7	.29	85,541,000	2,210,361
1873	25.6	.40	67,840,000	2,650,000
1874	27.0	.51	74,624,000	2,763,852
1875	34.0	.39	95,000,000	2,794,117
1876	30.0	.34	99,000,000	3,300,000
1877	30.0	.34	96,000,000	3,200,000
1878	32.8	.27	138,252,000	4,215,000
1879	33.0	.34	134,920,500	4,088,500
1880	29.0	.40	99,229,300	3,421,700

[64] [Farris and Euler], *Prices of Indiana Farm Products, 1841-1955*, p. 7. According to this study the price of corn per bushel rose from 26 cents in 1861 to 79 cents in 1864. *Ibid.*, p. 17. There are likely to be wide variations in farm prices among statistical studies. This is due in part to seasonal fluctuations in prices and variations from place to place. Because of the wide variations it is possible to draw only the most general conclusions about prices.

[65] See the following table.

[66] The table is compiled from United States Department of Agriculture,

Wheat reached $1.75 per bushel in 1864, declined in 1865, but rose to $2.41 in 1866 as the result of an abnormally small crop. Thereafter prices fluctuated but prior to 1881 did not equal those in 1864 and 1866.[67]

WHEAT 1864-1880[68]

Year	Average Yield per acre in bushels	Average price per bushel	Total Crop in bushels	Total Acres in wheat
1864	14.0	1.75	22,321,376	1,594,384
1865	8.5	1.35	13,020,803	1,531,859
1866	5.9	2.41	9,114,562	1,544,841
1867	10.5	2.21	16,861,000	1,605,809
1868	11.2	1.50	17,366,000	1,550,535
1869	14.4	.93	20,600,000	1,430,555
1870	11.0	1.00	20,200,000	1,836,363
1871	12.0	1.26	19,190,000	1,599,166
1872	12.4	1.32	19,381,000	1,562,983
1873	11.2	1.22	20,832,000	1,860,000
1874	12.2	.94	23,331,000	1,912,377
1875	9.0	.97	17,280,000	1,920,000
1876	11.0	1.02	20,000,000	1,818,181
1877	14.5	1.13	24,600,000	1,696,552
1878	16.0	.81	33,136,000	2,071,000
1879	20.3	1.17	43,709,960	2,153,200
1880	16.8	.99	49,766,758	2,962 307

In 1874 the price of wheat declined sharply to 94 cents. Meanwhile corn prices had begun to drop in 1870 and by 1872 had fallen to 29 cents. Although there were fluctuations thereafter the general trend of prices for both crops was downward during the rest of the seventies. Corn fell to 27 cents in 1878, and wheat to 81 cents the same year.

Reports of the Commissioner, 1864-1880. The figures show the price at which corn sold in the markets on December 1 of each year.

[67] See the following table.

[68] The table is compiled from United States Department of Agriculture, *Reports of the Commissioner,* 1864-1880. The figures show the price at which wheat sold in the market on December 1 of each year. Since most farmers sold their wheat in June, July, or August these figures do not necessarily show the prices which farmers received.

As a rule the price of hogs followed the fluctuations of corn. For example after a general decline for several years hogs rose in 1869-1870 as the price of corn advanced in 1869. Thereafter hog prices fluctuated during the seventies until they reached a low of $2.97 per head at the beginning of 1879; at the same time corn reached a record low.[69]

PRICE OF HOGS 1865-1880[70]

1865	7.08	1873	3.61
1866	6.83	1874	4.40
1867	4.72	1875	5.58
1868	6.84	1876	7.70
1869	6.57	1877	6.55
1870	7.91	1878	5.18
1871	6.04	1879	2.97
1872	4.93	1880	4.70

Cattle prices showed no marked changes from the end of the war until 1873, although as in the case of hogs the high price of corn was reflected in a rise in the price of cattle in 1869-1870. In 1873 prices began to decline, reaching an average low of $17.42 per head at the beginning of 1879 as compared with a high of $28.07 at the beginning of 1870.[71]

PRICE OF CATTLE 1865-1880[72]

1865	22.29	1873	23.98
1866	25.00	1874	20.67
1867	24.55	1875	19.95
1868	24.24	1876	19.65
1869	26.66	1877	17.72
1870	28.07	1878	18.15
1871	26.16	1879	17.42
1872	22.26	1880	18.65

69 See the following table.

70 The table is compiled from United States Department of Agriculture, *Reports of the Commissioner,* 1865-1880. The prices are the estimated price per head of hogs on February 1 of each year. The price for 1865 represents the average price per head for hogs over one year old. The prices for other years are the averages for all hogs without regard to age.

71 See the following table.

72 The table is compiled from United States Department of Agriculture,

Throughout the depression years of the seventies the economic position of the farmer appeared to be steadily deteriorating. More land was constantly being brought into production, the total production of all basic crops increased substantially, but increased production was not reflected in increased farm income. This is vividly illustrated by the following table on corn production.

Year	Total Value of corn crop	Total Bushels of corn	Total Acres of corn
1864	$70,941,567	74,284,363	2,561,529
1870	42,997,000	113,150,000	2,864,556
1878	37,328,040	138,252,000	4,215,000[73]

These figures show that although there was almost a 75 per cent increase in the amount of land devoted to corn and in the total corn crop between 1864 and 1878 the cash value of the crop had actually declined to little more than half what it had been in 1864. Figures on wheat tell the same story. In 1864 the total value of the wheat crop was estimated at $39,062,308 for 22,321,276 bushels grown on 1,594,384 acres. In 1878 the cash value of the crop had shrunk to $26,840,160, although the total crop had increased to 33,136,-000 bushels, and the total acreage to 2,071,000.[74] Between 1870 and 1880 the number of acres of improved land in the state increased from a little more than ten million to almost fourteen million, but the total cash value remained almost stationary.[75]

Reports of the Commissioner, 1865-1880. The prices are the estimated average price per head on February 1 of each year. The price for 1865 represents the average price per head for cattle over three years old. The prices for other years are the averages for all cattle without regard to age.

[73] The figures in the table are compiled from the United States Department of Agriculture, *Report of the Commissioner,* 1864, p. 571; 1870, p. 31; 1878, p. 263.

[74] These figures are taken from United States Department of Agriculture, *Report of the Commissioner,* 1864, p. 571; 1878, p. 263.

[75] In 1870 there were 10,104,279 acres of improved land. In 1880 there were 13,933,738 acres. In 1870 the total value of the land was estimated to be

Figures on declining prices and land values in part merely reflect the deflationary tendencies apparent in the whole economy in the seventies, but other statistics indicate that even in a period of general depression the position of farmers deteriorated more than other elements of the population. For example, United States census statistics show that in 1870 about $650 million was invested in agriculture in Indiana, while agricultural products were valued at about $122 million. Ten years later the total investment in agriculture was $655 million, but the value of farm produce on this investment had shrunk to $114 million. Meanwhile, in 1870 investment in manufacturing in the state amounted to only about $52 million, but the value of manufactured goods was estimated at about $108 million. By 1880 about $65 million was invested in manufacturing, while the value of manufactured goods was placed at about $148 million.[76] In other words, by 1880 the value of manufactured products exceeded the value of farm products, while the investment in manufacturing represented only about one tenth the investment in agriculture. Under the circumstances it is not surprising that farmers turned to political activity and to economic panaceas such as currency inflation as means of alleviating their situation.

§ § § § §

During the fifties an impetus was given to improved farming methods by the creation of the Indiana State Board of Agriculture, the beginning of annual state fairs, county agricultural societies and fairs, and a number of publications devoted to agriculture. The State Board of Agriculture was chartered in 1851 with Governor Joseph A. Wright as the first president and John B. Dillon as secretary. More than any other figure in public life in that period Wright tried to glorify agriculture and to arouse interest in scientific methods. In 1852 during

$634,804,189; in 1880 it was estimated at $635,236,111. United States Bureau of the Census, *Ninth Census* (1870), III: *Statistics of Wealth,* Table III, p. 81; *Tenth Census* (1880), III: *Agriculture* [Pt. 1], xii, Table I, pp. 3-4.

[76] *Ibid.,* II: *Manufacturing* [Pt. 1], Table IV A, p. 111; *Compendium of the Tenth Census* (1880), pp. 684-685.

his governorship the first State Fair was held in Indianapolis. It was regarded as a great success, with an attendance of some thirty thousand persons from all over the state. It featured exhibits of cattle, hogs, horses, poultry, and other products of the farm. In a "Mechanics Hall" were displayed the newest examples of farm machinery, including threshing machines, reapers, plows, corn planters, and wheat drills, and other innovations. The second annual fair, which was held in Lafayette, featured an address by Horace Greeley on "What the Sister Arts Teach as to Farming." In 1854, the fair was held at Madison, in 1855 at Indianapolis again, and in 1856 at New Albany. Because they were not centrally located the fairs held elsewhere than in Indianapolis were financial failures. In 1860 it was decided that a permanent site should be acquired in the capital city. Arrangements were made with railroad companies (which profited from carrying fair-goers) whereby the State Board of Agriculture acquired thirty acres of land which was contributed by the railroads. The board later bought additional land and built horse and cattle stalls. With the coming of the Civil War the fairgrounds were converted into Camp Morton and used successively as a rendezvous for Indiana troops, a camp for Confederate prisoners, and a United States hospital. During the war years fairs were held in Indianapolis, but not at the regular fairgrounds. In 1865 the State Fair was held in Fort Wayne and in 1867 at Terre Haute. In 1868 the fair returned to permanent quarters in Indianapolis, where the buildings had been repaired and rebuilt following their wartime use.[77]

The same legislation which authorized the State Board of Agriculture to hold state fairs also provided for the organization of county agricultural societies in accordance with regulations furnished by the state board. By the end of 1852

[77] Indiana State Board of Agriculture, *Annual Report*, 1852, pp. 1, 23; 1853, pp. 17ff.; 1862-1867 inclusive, pp. 171, 217-220, 339-341; 1869, pp. xxii-xxix, 4.

there were societies in forty-five counties, and twenty of the societies had held fairs. By the 1870's there were seventy-one county agricultural societies plus twenty-one district societies and numerous township societies. County fairs were like the State Fair but on a smaller scale—with exhibits and premiums for farm animals and other farm produce and programs which featured speakers on agricultural subjects.[78]

In addition to the societies which fostered agriculture in general, there were a number of organizations which sought to promote some particular product. For example, the Indiana Society for the Improvement of Domestic Poultry was organized in 1853. It apparently lapsed and was revived in 1875 as the State Poultry Association. In 1860 the Indiana Pomological Society was organized. During the seventies a number of societies were formed to promote raising of improved breeds of farm animals, including the Indiana Shorthorn Breeders' Association in 1872, the Wool Growers' Association in 1876, the Swine Breeders' Association in 1877, and the Dairymen's Association the same year.[79]

Scientific farming was also encouraged by offering premiums for essays on agricultural subjects which were awarded at both state and county fairs and which were sometimes published in the *Annual Reports* of the State Board of Agriculture. Typical were three essays awarded prizes at the first State Fair on "Rendering Useful the Hilly Lands of the State," "Swamp Lands," and "Ditching."[80]

By the fifties a few farmers' periodicals were beginning to appear in Indiana homes. Among them were *The Cultivator,* started in 1834, and *The Country Gentleman,* both published in Albany, New York; they were consolidated in 1866. The *Prairie Farmer,* which was published in Chicago, began

[78] Indiana State Board of Agriculture, *Annual Report,* 1852, p. 1; 1874, II, 10.

[79] *The Farm and Shop* (Indianapolis), I, no. 8 (July 1, 1853), p. 120; *Country Gentleman* XXI (1863), 65; Latta, *Outline History of Indiana Agriculture,* pp. 251, 286-287.

[80] Indiana State Board of Agriculture, *Annual Report,* 1852, pp. 309-328.

in 1844.[81] In addition to these journals, which enjoyed national circulation, there were several published in Indiana. The *Indiana Farmer,* edited by D. P. Holloway and W. T. Dennis, began publication in Richmond in 1851. It was later moved to Indianapolis in 1858. The *Farm and Shop* also appeared in Indianapolis in the fifties, as did the *Indiana Farmer and Mechanic.* In 1854 the *Tippecanoe Farmer* began publication at Lafayette. At Fort Wayne there was the *Western Plow Boy,* and at New Albany, the *Review of the Markets* and *Farmer's Journal.* In 1866 the *Northwestern Farmer, A Monthly Magazine of Agriculture, Horticulture, Home Improvement and Farm Literature,* began publication at Indianapolis. In 1874 this became a weekly and was renamed the *Indiana Farmer.* It served as an organ of the Indiana State Board of Agriculture and included a department of special interest to members of the Patrons of Husbandry. All of these publications contained articles on scientific agriculture, news about agricultural fairs and societies, and advertisements for farm machinery. In addition some of them had a Ladies' Department, with articles on cooking and sewing. Some of them included short stories and poetry.[82] Most farmers' periodicals were short-lived and enjoyed only limited circulation and probably had little influence in bringing about improved methods. One disgruntled reader of the *Country Gentleman* complained of the reluctance of Indiana farmers to learn about agriculture from books. A typical reaction to farm journals, he said, was: *"I am no book farmer;* I have farmed for *forty* years, and I think I know about as much about it as any man who lives in the city and edits a paper."[83]

Agricultural societies and publications of the sort already described had only a limited appeal. The Patrons of Hus-

[81] Bidwell and Falconer, *History of Agriculture in the Northern United States,* pp. 470-471.

[82] Files of these papers, which are in the Indiana Division of the Indiana State Library, were consulted. See also Barnhart and Carmony, *Indiana,* II, 65.

[83] "Hoosier Letter," *Country Gentleman,* VI (1855), 369.

bandry, popularly known as the Grange, was a different kind of organization, which for the first time united Indiana farmers into a mass movement. The Grange, which was founded in 1867, originated as a fraternal organization for farmers. Like other fraternal groups it had a ritual, elaborate titles, and various degrees of membership. It was intended as a means of filling a social need and of associating farmers for cultural and educational purposes and for co-operative action in solving their economic problems. The unrest resulting from the economic depression of the early seventies caused its membership to soar and had the effect of converting it into a political force.[84]

The first Grange in the state was organized in December, 1869, at Honey Creek in Vigo County. A second lodge was chartered at Terre Haute soon after and a third at Indianapolis. The state Grange of Indiana was organized in 1872 with John Weir of Terre Haute as its first master. By the end of the year there were fifty-four Granges in the state, most of them in counties in the northwest. The next year saw a phenomenal increase in numbers and membership. At the end of 1873 it was reported that there were six hundred and fifty Granges in the state, and that they were multiplying at the rate of twenty or forty a week. By the summer of 1874 Indiana had almost two thousand Granges—a number larger than in any other state except Iowa.[85] By January, 1875, the number had grown to almost three thousand. Thereafter the number declined rapidly, in part as the result of consolidation, in part because many Granges soon disbanded after an initial flurry of enthusiasm, and in part because some charters were

[84] The standard work on the subject is Solon J. Buck, *The Granger Movement* (Cambridge, Mass., 1913).

[85] In the Indiana Division of the Indiana State Library are six books of manuscript copies of the applications of local Granges for charters from 1869 to 1874. They show that by April, 1874, when Loogootee Lodge applied for a charter, there were 1,800 lodges in the state. Buck, *Granger Movement*, p. 47; Carleton, "Money Question in Indiana Politics," *Indiana Magazine of History*, XLII, 117; Indianapolis *Daily Journal*, December 1, 1873. There are some discrepancies in the figures given by Buck, Carleton, and the *Journal*.

revoked by the state organization for failure to pay dues. When the movement was at its height Indiana had the largest number of Granges of any state in proportion to its size— one for every eighteen square miles, or an average of two for every township. The number of dues-paying members was relatively small. In 1875 the State Grange paid national dues on 59,981 members.[86]

But the number of dues-paying members was not an accurate measure of the impact of the Grange movement on Indiana farmers. Grange meetings, which usually took the form of huge picnics, were attended by thousands. Farmers came in wagons from miles around. A typical meeting at Tipton in the summer of 1873 was reported to have had an attendance of four or five thousand, while at another at Remington there were said to have been nearly ten thousand, no doubt an exaggeration. Discontent over worsening economic conditions was undoubtedly the chief reason for the rapid growth of the Grange movement. Through organization farmers hoped somehow to improve their situation. At the Tipton rally banners were carried which bore such slogans as "Farmers' Rights!" "The hand that holds the bread—the Farmer." "Who would be free himself must strike the blow." "Corn must go up—monopolies must come down." Speakers regaled the gatherings on the inequities which farmers suffered— especially their exploitation by railroads and political parties. One speaker "showed the rights of the people to control the railroads." In his report for 1873, the secretary of the Indiana State Board of Agriculture observed: "There has been a sudden awakening of the farming community to arouse and assert their rights, and claim the position to which they are entitled."[87]

[86] Carleton, "Money Question in Indiana Politics," *Indiana Magazine of History,* XLII, 117; Buck, *Granger Movement,* pp. 59, 67; Indiana State Grange, *Proceedings,* 1874, p. 11. The Indianapolis *Daily Sentinel,* July 16, 1874, gives the following number of Granges: Iowa, 1,994; Indiana, 1,968; Illinois, 1,481; Kentucky, 1,101; Ohio, 947; Michigan, 400.

[87] Indianapolis *Daily Journal,* August 15, September 1, 1873; Indiana State Board of Agriculture, *Annual Report,* 1873, p. 9.

The address of the Worthy Master to the meeting of the State Grange in 1874 was somewhat anti-capitalistic and anti-monopolistic in tone. The Grange, he said, was opposed by "well organized monopolies of wealth and power to which even the Government, in all of its departments, were [sic] bowing and doing homage." The power of capital had become "insolent" and "oppressive." Taxes had become so heavy and discriminatory that the taxgatherer now claimed the lion's share of the farmer's income. Agriculture, he told his audience, was the chief source of wealth of the country, and "all the illegitimate speculation and stock gambling of the day," came from the farmers' toil, and all the failures resulting from reckless speculation "have to be accounted for in the depreciated price of your products."[88]

As noted elsewhere members of the Grange were active in the Greenback movement in the state.[89] The 1873 state meeting of the Grange adopted a resolution which blamed the "financial derangement" of the period on the "mistaken" policy of contraction and called for expansion of the currency. In Indiana, as in other states of the Middle West, Grange members also attributed their economic plight to practices of the railroads, but the tone of resolutions adopted at the state meetings was mild. In 1873 the resolutions declared that the interests of the farmers and the railroads were inseparable but complained against mismanagement by which railroads made "large dividends on watered stock" and expressed the view that more competing railroad lines were needed. In 1874 the state meeting asked for state and Federal legislation which was "just to the railroad interests of the country," but which would make the railroads "serve the people instead of ruling them."[90]

There was a division of opinion in Grange ranks over the wisdom of resorting to political activity. One speaker at an

[88] Indiana State Grange, *Proceedings,* 1874, p. 11.

[89] See Chapter VII, pages 313-315.

[90] Indianapolis *Daily Journal,* December 1, 1873; Indiana State Grange, *Proceedings,* 1874, p. 30.

early Grange picnic warned against "the folly of the direct antagonism to other classes, and of assuming the role of a political party." There was a feeling that later efforts at political activity detracted from the true purpose of the Grange. Nevertheless, as noted in another chapter, Grange influence was apparent in the 1874 elections, which resulted in sending an unprecedented number of farmers to the state legislature. In the 1875 legislative session petitions were received from local Granges dealing with such diverse matters as railroads, currency, and reduction of the cost of government. But, although there was a "Grange bloc" among the lawmakers, no significant Grange laws of the kind enacted in other Middle Western states resulted.[91]

The most concrete and noteworthy effort at improving the economic condition of farmers was the attempt to eliminate middlemen by operating a Grange store. The State Grange appointed a purchasing agent who dealt directly with manufacturers and wholesale men. A Grangers' Dry Goods Store, which advertised "anti-monopoly" goods, was maintained in Indianapolis. It sold yard goods, linens, and men's and women's clothing. An agent was at first employed on a commission basis, but as he lost money under this arrangement he resigned. Later an agent was employed at a salary and given $15,000 of Grange funds as capital for the purchasing operations. In 1875 the agency was reported to have done business amounting to $300,000, but during 1876 its purchases exceeded its sales, and in December of that year the agent was discharged and the agency closed. The State Grange lost several thousands of dollars in the venture. Bad business conditions in general and especially crop failures were blamed for the failure, but poor management undoubt-

---

[91] Indianapolis *Daily Journal,* August 15, 1874. See Chapter VII for a further account of the political activity of the Grange and its relation to the Greenback movement. In his address to the state convention in 1874 the Worthy Master expressed gratification that the Grange had placed "representatives of our class in high position in both the State and National Governments." Indiana State Grange, *Proceedings,* 1874, p. 11.

edly also played a part.[92] There were also efforts by the
Grange to buy farm machinery directly from manufacturers
and thereby eliminate the middleman's profits. But manufacturers were reluctant to sell directly. In Lake County a Home
Manufacturing Company was chartered for the purpose of
manufacturing for sale to the Grange, but it apparently was
not a success.[93] In 1876 the Worthy Master expressed the
opinion that it was "both unwise and hazardous for the State
Grange to assume financial responsibility on account of any
business enterprise of any character whatever." His successor
urged Grange members to stick to agriculture and not to try
to go into other fields about which they knew nothing. Nevertheless, he recommended that local Granges form co-operatives
for storing grain and preserving meat. The 1877 state meeting adopted a report in favor of the organization of co-operatives modeled after the Rochdale plan.[94]

Failure of political and business ventures caused disillusionment and was blamed for declining membership. In 1879,
after the Grange movement had lost its momentum, it was
reported that lodges were reorganizing in one county "on the
common sense basis of non-interference as Grangers, in politics." It was felt that "diverting the purpose of this organization into politics" had "demoralized and destroyed its influence." Reaction against political activity caused more
emphasis to be placed on the "social, fraternal, and educational" features which had always been the avowed purposes
of the Grange. One Worthy Master asserted that the Grange
had "introduced among the agricultural classes a system of
social communication hitherto unknown," which was probably
true. In his address to the state convention in 1882 another
Worthy Master stressed that "the excitement and furor" of

[92] Indiana State Grange, *Proceedings,* 1874, pp. 12, 16; 1876, pp. 17-18;
1877, p. 22; Buck, *Granger Movement,* p. 248; advertisement in *Indianapolis
Sun,* August 15, 1874; advertisement in *Indiana Farmer,* January 24, 1874.

[93] *Indiana Farmer,* January 10, 1874. See letter, *ibid.,* concerning the refusal
of a plow works in Dayton, Ohio, to sell except through its agents.

[94] Indiana State Grange, *Proceedings,* 1876, p. 6; 1877, pp. 9, 30.

the first few years of the Grange "when all kinds of imprac-
ticable theories, business and political, were indulged by those
ambitious to lead" had given place to "calm thought and
carefully and well digested plans for the advancement of our
agricultural interests." The majority of the members, he
said, were convinced that "ours is a social, fraternal, and
educational organization."[95]

[95] Indianapolis *Daily Sentinel,* April 4, 1879; Indiana State Grange, *Proceedings,* 1876, p. 7; *ibid.,* 1882, p. 12.

CHAPTER X

FOUNDATIONS OF INDUSTRIALIZATION
MINING–MANUFACTURING–
BANKING–LABOR

WHILE INDIANA REMAINED primarily an agricultural state until after 1880, and industrialization proceeded more slowly within her borders than in neighboring states,[1] the foundations of industrialism had been laid by this time. Manufacturing developed principally to utilize native coal and timber and agricultural products and to serve the needs of an agricultural population. At midcentury there was much optimism over the future of Indiana as a center of industry. Governor Joseph A. Wright, known principally as the friend of agriculture, also showed an interest in manufacturing. In a speech in 1853 he outlined what he called a "Home Policy" in which he urged the development of the mineral resources of the state and of manufacturing. "The old world manufactured for the new for a hundred years," he said. "New England has manufactured for us for nearly half a century. A change must take place. We must, if we pursue our true interests, engage in manufacturing articles, not only for home use, but for exportation."[2] An article in the annual report of the Indiana State Board of Agriculture emphasized the advantages which Indiana possessed as a potential manufacturing center. Among them were cheap power from Indiana coal, abundant building

[1] Indiana lagged behind all of the other states in the Old Northwest in the rate of industrialization. In 1860 the total amount of capital invested in manufacturing was smaller in Michigan and Wisconsin than in Indiana, but the per capita value of manufactures was smallest in Indiana. Carter, Decade of Hoosier History, p. 218. But the rate of growth in Indiana, while smaller than in the neighboring states, was more rapid than for the country as a whole. George W. Starr, *Industrial Development of Indiana* (Indiana University *Studies in Business,* No. 14, Bloomington, 1937), p. 12.

[2] Wright, *Address . . . at Livonia, Washington County.*

materials, including clay, timber, and limestone, and cheap labor, since wages were lower than in the East. Proximity of raw materials was stressed. Wool was produced in Indiana, and cotton could be brought more cheaply to Indiana from Arkansas and Tennessee than to Massachusetts.[3]

Forests, which covered a large part of the state, provided the most easily exploitable natural resource. A larger amount of capital was invested in the lumber industry and in the manufacture of wooden products, such as furniture and wagons, and more workers were employed in the cutting of timber and the fabricating of wooden products than in any other field of manufacturing. Because the amount of capital required to start a sawmill was small, many mills employing only a few persons sprang up. In 1880 the state was dotted with more than two thousand sawmills, which cut timber and prepared it for shipment. Building of the railroads caused a steady expansion of the lumber industry by continuing to bring new forests within reach of transportation.

The most valuable wood was walnut, which was found throughout the state. It was in great demand for furniture. The finest trees brought one hundred dollars each—a price far greater than the cost of the land on which they grew. Part of the wood was used in local industry, part of it was shipped to distant markets. For example, in 1875, over $50,000 worth of walnut logs were shipped from Whitley County to Europe by way of New York. So great was the demand that by the seventies the best forests had been depleted in many parts of the state. Other types of trees were cut for lumber for building and for the manufacture of smaller wooden products. Wood from the hickory forests of Crawford and Floyd counties, for example, was shipped out of state for the manufacture of shafts and spokes and for hoops for cooperage.[4]

3 R. T. Brown, "The Manufacturing Capabilities of the Indiana Coal Field," Indiana State Board of Agriculture, *Annual Report*, 1856, pp. 492-511.

4 United States Department of Agriculture, *Report of the Commissioner*, 1875, pp. 306-308.

Hopes that Indiana would become an industrial center rested primarily upon the abundant coal deposits, principally of the bituminous variety, in the southern and western parts of the state. As early as the 1830's some coal was mined in Perry County. The anticipation of finding cannel coal led to the naming of Cannelton in that county and caused a group of eastern capitalists to organize the American Cannel Coal Company. By the late forties about half a million bushels of coal were being mined annually in the vicinity, and the production of coal led to interest in Cannelton as a field for investment in manufacturing.[5]

By the fifties the demand for coal was increasing for use by railroads and river steamers and as domestic fuel as well as for use in industry. Heretofore lack of transportation facilities had prevented the development of mining, but in 1852 the opening of the railroad from Terre Haute to Indianapolis led to a sharp increase in coal production. In 1853 coal shipments began from Brazil Township in Clay County, where the richest deposits were located. The coal was stripped at Otter Creek and hauled by oxen and horses to the railroad and then shipped to Indianapolis. In 1854 the New Albany and Salem Railroad was completed to Gosport. This was east of the important coal fields but was connected with them by the construction of spurs. More important in the development of the coal region was the Evansville, Vincennes, and Terre Haute line, which was completed in 1853 and which for twenty years was the most important coal artery in the state. The completion of the Ohio and Mississippi line in 1857, connecting Cincinnati, Vincennes, and East St. Louis, provided an additional outlet. In 1869 the Indianapolis and Vincennes line, which ran across part of the coal fields, was completed.[6]

[5] Thomas James De La Hunt, *Perry County: A History* (Indianapolis, 1916), pp. 85-87, 130. Coal had been mined as early as 1825 in Warrick County.

[6] Mine Inspector of the State of Indiana, *Annual Report,* 1880-1881, p. 71. Charles A. Blanchard (ed.), *Counties of Clay and Owen, Indiana* (Chicago, 1884), p. 144; Osmond La Var Harline, Economics of the Indiana Coal

Building of the railroads, together with the demand engendered by war and increasing industry and population, was reflected in increased coal production. Between 1850 and 1860 output nearly doubled, but it rose still more sharply in the sixties. In 1870 twenty times as many tons of coal were mined in Indiana as in 1850. At first nearly all mining was strip mining. In some places, such as the bed of Otter Creek in Clay County, it was possible to quarry many tons without going under the surface to any extent. The first shaft was not sunk in Clay County until 1852. Early operations were wasteful because the men in charge were not trained engineers. Conditions in the mines were unhealthful and hazardous. The state mine inspector reported in 1880 that a great many mines in the state had been opened "without any regard to ventilation or system," and that "gouging and robbing the easiest coal that could be got" was the prevalent method in the early days.[7]

After the Civil War geological surveys were conducted to determine the location and extent of coal deposits. Discoveries of large amounts of block coal raised hopes in the early seventies that western Indiana would become a great iron and steel center. It was asserted that steel rails could be produced in Indiana for thirty dollars less per ton than the cost of European rails which were shipped to New York. Publications of the findings of the state geologists and promotional literature circulated in the East stressed the advantages of this area.[8] An address by Oliver P. Morton at the Indianapolis

Mining Industry (Unpublished Ph. D. thesis in Economics, Indiana University, 1958), pp. 64-65.

[7] William Edward Bean, The Soft Coal Industry of Southern Indiana (Unpublished A.B. thesis in Economics, Indiana University, 1922), pp. 19-20; Mine Inspector of the State of Indiana, *Annual Report,* 1880-1881, p. 67. See note 10 below.

[8] Indianapolis *Daily Journal,* March 1, 1872. See for example, J. W. Foster, *Mineral Wealth and Railroad Development: A Series of Letters* (New York, 1872). These letters were originally published in the New York *Tribune.*

Exposition in September, 1873, dwelt on the prospects of Indiana as a steel-producing state. In its coal fields, he said, Indiana had "vast mineral wealth, more valuable than the gold and silver mines of California, Colorado, or Nevada." He predicted a great development of steel production in Indiana as the result of the utilization of the block coal in the Bessemer process.[9]

Optimism of this sort was partly responsible for the building of new railroad extensions into the hilly portions of the western part of the state to tap the coal fields. In 1872 Indiana mines for the first time produced more than a million tons of coal. The depression which began the next year caused a decline. During the next few years production fluctuated, but by 1879 it had risen to over a million and a half tons.[10] The 1880 census showed 216 mines in the state, employing 4,496 persons. Clay County was by far the most important center of coal production, followed by Fountain, Daviess, and Sullivan counties. Several small mines were located in Greene, Owen, Pike, and Vigo counties.[11] In spite of the great increase Indiana continued to rank far behind Ohio and Illinois

[9] Indiana State Board of Agriculture, *Annual Report,* 1873, pp. 80-82.

[10] Production of Coal—Short Tons

Year	Quantity	Year	Quantity
1850	59,784	1872	1,000,438
1854	80,106	1873	812,000
1860	100,280	1875	949,683
1865	320,142	1876	1,000,184
1870	600,483	1879	1,545,327

Bean, The Soft Coal Industry of Southern Indiana, pp. 32-33.

[11] United States Bureau of the Census, *Tenth Census* (1880), XV: *Report on Mining Industries,* pp. 646-647. For a directory of mines in Indiana in 1880, showing the location of the mines, their names, and the names of the operators, see *ibid.,* pp. 880-881. There are wide discrepancies between the census figures and the figures in Mine Inspector of the State of Indiana, *Annual Report,* 1879-1880, p. 39, which gives the total number of mines as only 177 and the total number of men working in the mines as 3,459. According to the latter

in coal production, and hopes that the iron and steel industry would center near Indiana coal fields did not materialize.[12]

Geological surveys also led to interest in the exploitation of Indiana's native stone for building purposes. In the southern part of the state, especially in Owen, Monroe, and Lawrence counties, were located deposits of some of the finest oölitic limestone in the world. The stone was at first used in a small way in the immediate vicinity for such things as bridge foundations and tombstones. In 1838 a geographical reconnaissance by David Dale Owen brought some attention to the quality of Indiana limestone, but it was not until the building of railroads that exploitation of the stone resources really began. The first trains of the New Albany and Salem

the distribution of mines by counties and the number of men employed was as follows:

County	Number of Mines	Number of Men
Clay	39	1,651
Daviess	14	402
Dubois	5	9
Fountain	5	444
Greene	12	33
Gibson	1	7
Knox	3	101
Martin	2	10
Parke	15	250
Pike	10	46
Perry	11	54
Sullivan	15	88
Spencer	19	48
Vermillion	9	45
Vigo	6	66
Vanderburgh	2	93
Warrick	9	112
	177	3,459

12 United States Bureau of the Census, *Compendium of the Tenth Census* (1880), p. 1242. Manufacturing in Indiana did not expand rapidly enough to keep pace with the expansion of mining. By 1880 it was estimated that facilities for coal production exceeded demand by about one third and that there were about one-third more miners than were needed. Mine Inspector of Indiana, *Annual Report*, 1880-1881, p. 72.

Railroad reached Bedford and Bloomington in 1853 and Ellettsville in 1854. At about the same time construction of the Ohio and Mississippi, which crossed the southern end of Lawrence County, was begun. After the Civil War the Indianapolis and Vincennes line, which ran through Owen County, was completed. As these railroads reached the limestone country, several small quarries were opened near them. There are records of fourteen which were opened between 1853 and 1869. The first major building constructed of Indiana limestone appears to have been the United States Customs and Courthouse at Louisville, which was begun in 1853. At first quarrying was done in the most primitive manner. The stone was blasted loose, but most of the work was done by manual labor and horses. The work was seasonal and irregular, and most of the laborers were farmers from the vicinity. At first great difficulties were encountered in moving the stone from the quarries to the railroads since there were no switches to the quarries, but as demand increased switches began to be built.[13]

Surveys by the State Geology Department, which was organized in 1868, led to increased interest. In spite of the panic of 1873 the demand for Indiana stone gradually increased. At the Philadelphia and New Orleans Centennial Expositions in 1876 a number of Indiana quarrymen won awards for the specimens of stone which they exhibited. Some stone was used in Chicago buildings, and the decision made in 1878 to use Indiana limestone for the new Indiana State Capitol gave an impetus to the industry. In 1879 the first Indiana stone was shipped to New York—for use in the residence of William K. Vanderbilt. By 1880 there were twenty-one quarries in operation in the state.[14]

The stone quarries had a relatively small impact on the economy of the state as a whole, but coal and timber were

[13] Joseph A. Batchelor, *An Economic History of the Indiana Oolitic Limestone Industry* (Indiana University *Studies in Business,* No. 27, Bloomington, 1944), pp. 8-13.

[14] *Ibid.,* pp. 14-15, 23-34.

important in the manufacturing establishments which began to develop after 1850. Prior to that time a few special charters had been granted by the legislature to manufacturing corporations (some of which failed to materialize), but the number of such charters was smaller than the number granted to railroads and turnpike and plank-road corporations. In 1850 the state legislature passed "An Act to encourage the investment of capital for manufacturing purposes," which permitted seven or more persons to incorporate.[15] From time to time proposals were made in the legislature to authorize local governments to raise money to subsidize the establishment of industries as they did the construction of railroads, but no such legislation was adopted. There was no such popular enthusiasm over the development of industry as that which the prospect of railroads aroused. There was little public aid for manufacturing establishments. Neither were there so many elaborate promotional schemes to attract outside capital for manufacturing as there were for the railroads. Most industries were owned by local interests.[16]

Such manufacturing establishments as there were in the state at midcentury were with a very few exceptions small, individually owned shops. The United States census for 1850 listed over 4,000 manufacturing establishments, with a total number of employees of only a little more than 14,000, or an average of less than four employees per establishment.[17]

At midcentury the greatest concentration of population was in the Ohio River towns of Madison and New Albany and Jeffersonville, and in these communities and in other older towns like Richmond were found most of the infant industries. Madison was an important pork-packing center. She also

15 Indiana *General Laws*, 1849-1850, pp. 133-135.

16 In 1867 a bill to authorize boards of county commissioners to make appropriations in the aid of construction of manufacturing establishments or machine shops passed both houses of the legislature but failed to receive the approval of the governor. Indiana *Senate Journal*, 1867, pp. 88, 645, 937; Indiana *House Journal*, 1867, pp. 1124-1125.

17 United States Bureau of the Census, *Compendium of the Tenth Census* (1880), pp. 928-931.

boasted several of the largest flour mills in the West. New Albany was second only to Madison as a center of trade and industry in 1850, and the completion of the New Albany and Salem Railroad caused her importance to increase as an entrepôt for the farming region along the line. Optimism was high that New Albany would become a greater center of commerce and industry than Pittsburgh. Flour mills and pork-packing establishments grew rapidly in the fifties and some new industries appeared. The machine shops of the New Albany and Salem Railroad employed as many as two hundred persons.[18]

Of special importance in the river towns in the period before the Civil War was the building of steamboats for the flourishing river trade. During the 1850's a total of about 375 vessels were constructed at Madison, New Albany, and Jeffersonville. Jeffersonville was the most important of the three cities and exceeded even Louisville in the number of boats built, but at one time there were five ship yards in operation in New Albany.[19] The Howard brothers of Jeffersonville built the largest number of boats and their vessels had an especially fine reputation for speed, comfort, and carrying capacity. They built a variety of types and sizes of vessels, ranging from boats like the "Ben Franklin," built in 1854 for the Louisville and Cincinnati United States Mail Line, which measured three hundred feet and was a giant for its day, to much smaller types. Some of the boats were side-wheelers, some were stern propelled, some screw propelled.[20]

The Civil War brought a halt to the building of boats for the southern market, but this was partially offset by orders

---

[18] Woollen, *Biographical and Historical Sketches,* p. 536; Victor M. Bogle, "New Albany: Mid-Nineteenth Century Economic Expansion," *Indiana Magazine of History,* LIII (1957), 131, 140-141, 143-144.

[19] Stephen C. Savage, James Howard of Jeffersonville, Master Builder of Steamboats (Unpublished Master's thesis in History, Indiana University, 1952), pp. 53, 56; *History of the Ohio Falls Cities and Their Counties* (2 volumes, Cleveland, 1882), II, 169-172.

[20] Savage, James Howard . . . Master Builder of Steamboats, pp. 36-37, 96.

from the government. Boats built in the Indiana yards served as transports and hospital boats, and some were converted into naval vessels. After the war the revival of the New Orleans trade created a demand for more boats. Boat building at New Albany declined in the postwar years, but the Howards enjoyed their greatest prosperity from 1866 until the depression of 1873.[21]

In 1850 there were hopes that the textile industry would develop in the river towns because of their easy access to the cotton fields of the South. At that date the largest single manufacturing establishment in the state was the Indiana Cotton Mills at Cannelton, which employed between three and four hundred persons. During the later 1840's the little town in Perry County, on the Ohio River, attracted attention as a potential industrial site. The coal mining in the vicinity first created interest in the development of textile mills. During its 1847 session the Indiana legislature granted twelve charters for manufacturing corporations to be located in Cannelton. Several investors from outside the state showed an interest in promoting these corporations, which included cotton mills, a glass factory, and a foundry. The only one which got beyond the paper stage was the Indiana Mills, which was financed principally by a group of Louisville investors. The factory which housed the mill was built of native stone and was considered one of the handsomest structures of its kind in the United States. The first operatives as well as the machinery were brought from Massachusetts. In 1850 a steamer unloaded the first shipment of cotton. By 1851 there were 372 looms in operation. The company was not at first a financial success, and the dividends of 10 per cent which had been promised investors did not materialize. In 1852 a controlling interest in the corporation was acquired

[21] *Ibid.,* pp. 60, 70, 84. A total of 102 vessels were built at Madison, New Albany, and Jeffersonville during the war years. *Ibid.,* p. 64. From 1866 to 1876 a total of 204 boats were built in the same three cities, most of them at Jeffersonville. *Ibid.,* table 10, p. 85.

by Horatio Dalton Newcomb of Louisville. For the next thirty years the mills were operated successfully by members of the Newcomb family.[22]

After 1860 the river towns showed a relative decline in importance as manufacturing began to develop in Indianapolis and other points farther north, but one of the largest industrial plants to develop in the postwar years was the DePauw Plate Glass Works at New Albany. Several small glass-making establishments were started in the vicinity because of sand which was particularly well suited for this product. But the development of one of the largest works of its kind in the United States was due to the entrepreneurial efforts of W. C. DePauw, a man of remarkable ability and many interests. DePauw, who was self-made and with little education, had been thrown on his own resources at the age of sixteen. He made his first money in a saw- and gristmill and later invested in farming, banking, merchandising, and especially in the grain trade, from which he made large profits during the Civil War. After the war he invested in rolling mills and iron foundries in New Albany and then in the development of the Star Glass Company. In 1872 he acquired the New Albany Glass Works, which had been founded in 1865 and which made window glass and plate glass. The consolidation created one of the largest firms of its kind in the country, and it flourished even during the depression of the seventies. It employed several hundred persons and by 1877 was reported to be worth a million dollars.[23]

The 1860 census showed a larger amount of capital invested in manufacturing in Jefferson County, the site of Madison, than in any other county in the state. Wayne County, site of

22 De La Hunt, *Perry County,* pp. 131-139.

23 *History of the Ohio Falls Cities and Their Counties,* II, 222-224, 230-231; Collett, *State of Indiana,* p. 3. DePauw, a Democrat, was a powerful political figure as well as industrialist and entrepreneur. In 1875 the Indiana legislature passed a joint resolution on his behalf asking Congress for tariff protection against foreign-made glass. Indiana *Laws,* 1875, pp. 185-186. For DePauw's association with DePauw University see Chapter XI, page 513.

Richmond, was a close second, and the number of persons employed in manufacturing was greater in Wayne than in any other county.[24] But the completion of the Madison and Indianapolis Railroad in 1847 set Indianapolis on the way to becoming the commercial and industrial center of the state. During the fifties the number of manufacturing establishments began to increase but in 1860 while Indianapolis was the forty-eighth city in the United States in population, she ranked only ninetieth in the volume of manufactures.[25] The boom period of the sixties saw a marked expansion in manufacturing and an increased interest in attracting outside capital. The panic which began in 1873 was more severe and prolonged in Indianapolis than in most cities and had the effect of retarding her growth. In 1880 she still lagged behind Louisville and Detroit as well as Cincinnati, both in number of manufacturing establishments and in the amount of capital invested.[26] But by that date she had far outdistanced all other Indiana cities as a manufacturing center. The number of manufacturing establishments, the number of employees, and the amount of capital invested in manufacturing in Indianapolis were twice as great as in any other city in the state, while the value of manufactured products was more than three times as great. Evansville, in the extreme south, ranked second in the amount of capital invested in manufacturing; while South Bend, in the extreme north, ranked third. Terre Haute ranked second in the value of manufactured products and Evansville third; while South Bend ranked second in the number of persons employed in manufacturing and Evansville third.[27]

[24] United States Bureau of the Census, *Eighth Census* (1860): *Manufacturing*, pp. 142-143; Bogle, "New Albany: Mid-Nineteenth Century Economic Expansion," *Indiana Magazine of History*, LIII, 139n.

[25] Frederick Doyle Kershner, Jr., A Social and Cultural History of Indianapolis 1860-1914 (Unpublished Ph.D. thesis in History, University of Wisconsin, 1950), p. 9.

[26] United States Bureau of the Census, *Compendium of Tenth Census* (1880), pp. 1050, 1058, 1060.

[27] See table p. 417.

In Indianapolis slaughtering represented the largest business, on the basis of capital investment and value of product. Foundries and machine-shop products were in second place. Flour mills were third, but the value of lumber and wood products combined was greater. In Terre Haute flour mills and gristmills represented the largest industry, both as to investment and value of products, with iron and steel in second place. In Evansville lumber and wooden products were in first place, both as to investment and value of products. Foundries and machine-shop products represented the second largest investment, but on the basis of the value of products flour mills and gristmills were in second place.[28]

For the state as a whole, in 1880 flour mills and gristmills represented a larger capital investment than any other kind of manufacturing, with lumber second. Foundries and machine shops, slaughtering and meat packing, agricultural implements, carriages and wagons, distilled liquors, iron and steel, woolen goods, furniture, and malt liquors followed in that order.[29]

---

[28] United States Bureau of the Census, *Tenth Census* (1880), XIX: *Social Statistics of Cities*, pp. 443, 455, 474-475.

[29] Leading Industries 1880

Type of Industry	Number of Establishments	Capital Invested	Number of Employees
Flour-Grist Mills	996	$9,484,023	3,159
Lumber (Sawed)	2,022	7,048,088	10,339
Foundries-Machine Shops	120	3,993,578	3,930
Slaughtering-Meatpacking	25	3,974,000	1,815
Agricultural Implements	96	3,231,818	2,471
Carriages and Wagons	195	2,732,417	2,906
Distilled Liquors	22	2,300,250	415
Iron and Steel	12	2,283,100	2,048
Woolen Goods	81	2,273,705	1,741
Furniture	251	2,243,250	2,860
Malt Liquors	63	1,609,179	577

United States Bureau of the Census, *Compendium of the Tenth Census* (1880), pp. 965-966.

MANUFACTURING 1880

Counties and Principal Cities in each County	Number of Establishments	Capital Invested	Number of Employees	Total Wages	Value of Production
Allen (Fort Wayne)	(6) 247	(7) $2,926,146	(5) 3,485	(5) $1,182,448	(4) $ 7,178,778
Cass (Logansport)	(4) 276	(9) $1,309,621	(10) 1,342	(10) $ 422,642	(10) $ 2,573,513
Dearborn (Lawrenceburg)	(10) 168	(5) $3,370,859	(8) 1,681	(8) $ 657,525	(8) $ 4,442,878
Floyd (New Albany)	(9) 200	(4) $3,721,562	(6) 3,059	(6) $1,151,690	(7) $ 5,917,951
Marion (Indianapolis)	(1) 809	(1) $10,366,985	(1) 10,470	(1) $4,027,473	(1) $28,425,874
St. Joseph (South Bend)	(8) 213	(3) $3,760,477	(2) 3,953	(3) $1,471,983	(6) $ 6,749,756
Tippecanoe (Lafayette)	(7) 238	(10) $1,213,298	(9) 1,622	(9) $ 584,504	(9) $ 2,866,261
Vanderburgh (Evansville)	(2) 357	(2) $4,823,745	(3) 3,778	(4) $1,391,171	(3) $ 8,439,173
Vigo (Terre Haute)	(5) 269	(8) $2,757,775	(4) 3,638	(2) $1,492,932	(2) $ 9,709,800
Wayne (Richmond)	(3) 332	(6) $2,963,535	(7) 2,938	(7) $1,087,391	(5) $ 6,805,259

Compendium of Tenth Census (1880), pp. 963-965

The above table shows the ten most highly industrialized counties.
The figures in parentheses indicate the rank in the various categories.

A large part of manufacturing consisted of preparing agricultural products for consumption. The most obvious examples were the flour mills and gristmills. Although taken as a whole they represented a large investment, they were almost without exception small-scale businesses. There were almost one thousand of them scattered all over the state. No single community was an especially important center of flour milling. On the other hand, in pork packing, in which Indiana ranked as one of the most important states, a larger degree of concentration developed. In the middle of the nineteenth century Ohio, Indiana, and Illinois were the largest hog-producing states. Before the Civil War Cincinnati was the largest pork-packing city in the United States. Some hogs from Indiana were driven to that city for slaughtering. Within the state the early centers of pork packing were river towns. Terre Haute and Lafayette on the Wabash and Madison on the Ohio were the most important centers, but other river towns like Lawrenceburg did business on a smaller scale. Pork packing was at first a strictly seasonal business which began in November and lasted through the winter. Packing houses were small affairs, usually located on streams into which waste material was thrown. After the hogs were slaughtered, the meat was salted and packed in barrels to be transported to market. Until the Civil War much pork was floated down river to New Orleans.[30]

The development of refrigeration and the building of the railroads brought important changes. In 1857 the use of ice made it possible to begin summer packing in Chicago, which soon outdistanced Cincinnati as the nation's greatest pork-packing center. The same developments brought a decline in the small establishments in the river towns in Indiana and caused Indianapolis to become the center of pork packing in

<hr />

[30] Bernard A. Hewes, The Rise of the Pork Industry in Indiana (Unpublished Master's thesis, Indiana University, 1939), pp. 4, 11, 57-62; John J. Schlicher, "Terre Haute in 1850," *Indiana Magazine of History*, XII (1916), 250.

the state. Several meat-packing companies developed in the capital city, the most important being Kingan and Company. This firm, which already had interests in Ireland, England, and Australia, began operation in Indianapolis in 1864. Kingan's was the first establishment in Indiana to start the practice of killing and packing through the whole year by the use of refrigeration. By the middle of the 1870's the firm employed from three hundred to six hundred persons and was one of the largest packing houses in the world. Much of the pork packed in Indianapolis was shipped to Liverpool. Although the number of hogs slaughtered fluctuated widely from year to year, Indianapolis ranked fourth among the cities in the nation as a pork-packing center by 1875. There were also stockyards in Indianapolis and some establishments for the slaughtering of beef cattle. Most of the beef was sold locally, and the beef industry was considerably less important than pork packing.[31]

By 1880 the amount of capital invested in breweries and distilleries, which used some of the grain products of the state, was nearly as large as the investment in meat packing. Numerous small establishments were scattered over the state with the largest numbers in Indianapolis, Evansville, and Terre Haute. Terre Haute claimed to have the largest distillery in the world, but it is doubtful if she really merited this distinction.[32]

[31] Hewes, Pork Industry in Indiana, p. 63; Indianapolis Daily Sentinel (Centennial Issue), February 22, 1876; W. R. Holloway, Indianapolis. A Historical and Statistical Sketch of the Railroad City (Indianapolis, 1870), pp. 379-381; Berry R. Sulgrove, History of Indianapolis and Marion County, Indiana (Philadelphia, 1884), pp. 444-445; Collett, State of Indiana, p. 3; United States Department of Agriculture, Report of the Commissioner, 1875, p. 96; 1878, p. 314. The six largest centers of pork packing in the 1870's, ranked according to the number of hogs slaughtered annually, were as follows: Chicago, Cincinnati, St. Louis, Indianapolis, Milwaukee, Louisville. Hammond, in Lake County, became a center for the packing and shipping of beef in the 1870's. Moore, The Calumet Region, pp. 147-151.

[32] Footnote 29 above; Collett, State of Indiana, p. 3; H. W. Beckwith, History of Vigo and Parke Counties, together with Historic Notes on the Wabash Valley (Chicago, 1880), pp. 144-145.

Manufacture of farm implements was an important industry. There were many small shops scattered over the state in which threshers, drills, and other equipment were made. Every city had several small establishments. One of the most important centers was Richmond, where, in 1841, the first thresher in Indiana was built. In 1849 the shop which made it became A. Gaar and Company, a leading manufacturer of farm machinery. By 1870 it was worth $400,000 and employed two hundred persons. Smaller concerns in Richmond made other types of farm machinery. In South Bend there was the Oliver Plow Works, which became international in scope. The founder was James Oliver, a Scotsman who came to South Bend in 1855 and bought a part ownership in a foundry where he began the manufacture of plowshares. In 1857 the foundry made fewer than fifty plows, but by 1864 the output had increased to about a thousand a year. In 1857 Oliver received a patent for a new process of casting plowshares known as chill hardening; this and later improvements in the chilling and casting process completely revolutionized the industry. By 1879 Oliver had opened a branch in Texas and had made a contract for the sale of his plows in Great Britain.[33]

Also in South Bend was the Studebaker Wagon Works, by far the largest establishment of its kind in the state. In 1852 Henry and Clem Studebaker, descendants of a Dutch ancestor who had come to Philadelphia in 1736, opened a blacksmith and wagon shop with two forges. A few years later their capital was increased by $8,000, contributed by a brother who had gone to California during the gold rush. In 1868 the Studebaker Corporation was formed. During the seventies business expanded until by 1880 it had grown to about one and a half million dollars a year. By that date branches and

[33] Andrew W. Young, *History of Wayne County, Indiana, from its First Settlement to the Present Time* (Cincinnati, 1872), pp. 379-386; Douglas Laing Meikle, James Oliver and the Oliver Chilled Plow Works (Unpublished Ph.D. thesis in History, Indiana University, 1958), especially pp. 33-35, 46, 49, 81, 113-114, 193, 209.

agencies had been established at several places in the United States, including one in San Francisco. In 1878 Studebaker wagons were displayed at the Paris Exposition. Some fashionable carriages and landaus were manufactured by Studebaker, but wagons were by far the most important product.[34]

The Studebaker Corporation was the largest of many Indiana establishments making wagons and carriages. In 1880 there were almost two hundred such shops scattered over the state. The building of railroads also led to shops for building passenger and freight cars for railroads. The abundant timber in Indiana was an important factor in the development of these enterprises which were found in a number of cities.

Many other industries and crafts used wood. One of the most important of these was furniture making. In every town there were several shops employing only two or three persons. In Indianapolis and Evansville there were some larger shops. One of the most rapidly growing industries of the period, the manufacture of sewing machines, was attracted to Indiana because of the availability of timber for cabinets. In 1868 the Singer Sewing Machine Company established a branch in South Bend for making cases and cabinets. Several cities vied with each other in offering inducements when it was learned that the Howe Sewing Machine Company planned a similar factory. In 1870 the company decided to locate a branch in Peru. In Indianapolis was a factory for the manufacture of cabinets for the Wheeler and Wilson Company which had its headquarters in Connecticut. Throughout the state there were many small establishments which made staves and barrels and such wooden products as spokes, shafts, and axles. Some of the larger companies owned their own sawmills.[35]

[34] Albert Russell Erskine, *History of the Studebaker Corporation* (The Studebaker Corporation, 1924), pp. 3, 7, 10, 17, 19, 21, 27; Stephen Longstreet, *A Century on Wheels. The Story of Studebaker . . . 1852-1952* (New York, 1952), pp. 37, 39, 43, 44, 45-46; John B. Stoll (ed.), *An Account of St. Joseph County from Its Organization* (Dayton, Ohio, 1923), pp. 157-159.

[35] Meikle, James Oliver and the Oliver Chilled Plow Works, p. 101;

As noted earlier, after the Civil War the discovery of block coal in Clay County raised hopes that Indiana might become a center of iron and steel production. Between 1867 and 1872 eight blast furnaces were built in Vigo and Clay counties. All of these were owned by the coal mines. Iron ore from Missouri and the Lake Superior region was used in them. The largest of these was the Wabash Iron Company in Terre Haute, which employed about two hundred men. None of these iron works proved a lasting success. Cheap water transportation caused the iron ore from the Lake Superior region to go to ports on the Great Lakes instead of being carried by rail to Indiana. Other sources of iron ore proved inferior in quality or were exhausted.[36]

Although the manufacturing of iron and steel failed to develop, many establishments which fabricated iron products flourished. In Indianapolis by 1870 there were two successful rolling mills, one of which employed 365 persons and manufactured rails which were said to be as good as those produced in England. In Indianapolis, Terre Haute, and other cities there were many small foundries and machine shops which made a variety of iron products. The manufacture of farm machinery and implements has already been mentioned. In addition there were shops which manufactured boilers, steam engines, stoves, and all sorts of iron castings ranging from mill castings to small objects like hinges and latches. One of the largest establishments in the state comprised the shops of the Chicago and Great Eastern Railroad which were established in Logansport in 1863 and which built and repaired cars and locomotives. In 1869 the city subscribed $50,000 to induce the company to locate additional shops

Holloway, *Indianapolis*, pp. 360-361; Indianapolis *Daily Sentinel*, March 22, 1869, March 18, May 22, 1870; Indianapolis *Daily Journal*, January 17, 1871; United States Department of Agriculture, *Report of the Commissioner*, 1875, pp. 306-309; Thomas B. Helm (ed.), *History of Cass County, Indiana. From the Earliest Time to the Present* (Chicago, 1886), pp. 465-466.

36 Alden Cutshall, "Terre Haute Iron and Steel: A Declining Industry," *Indiana Magazine of History*, XXXVII (1941), 238-240.

there. There were similar smaller railroad shops in several cities.[37]

Hopes that Indiana would become an important textile-manufacturing center failed to materialize. The cotton mills at Cannelton already mentioned continued to operate, and there were a few small cotton mills in other towns, but they were relatively unimportant. There were many small woolen mills, and the increase in sheep raising during the Civil War period, noted in another chapter, led to hopes that the woolen industry would become important. In 1870 a Woolen Exposition was held in Indianapolis at which machinery and textiles were exhibited. Cloth woven at mills in Richmond, Peru, Lawrenceburg, Terre Haute, Columbus, and Indianapolis, was displayed. Most of the woolen cloth made in Indiana was of coarse quality—for jeans and blankets principally—although there were claims that some cloth as fine as that of eastern mills was produced.[38]

By 1880, according to United States census figures, a total of more than sixty-five million dollars was invested in manufacturing in Indiana. This was only about one tenth the amount invested in agriculture, but it represented more than an eightfold increase over the less than eight million dollars invested in manufacturing at midcentury. In 1850 there were fewer than fifteen thousand persons employed in manufacturing; in 1880 there were almost seventy thousand. But the total employed in agriculture at the latter date was still more than four times as great—331,000. Although there were a few companies in the state in 1880 which employed hundreds of workers, most manufacturing establishments continued to be small-scale affairs. The average number of employees in 1880 was only slightly more than six persons. In 1880 Indiana ranked sixth among all the states in the number of manu-

37 Holloway, *Indianapolis,* pp. 352-356; Beckwith, *Vigo and Parke Counties,* pp. 143-144; Helm (ed.), *Cass County,* p. 465.

38 Indianapolis *Daily Sentinel,* April 18, 1869, August 6, 1870; Indianapolis *Daily Journal,* January 17, 1871; Holloway, *Indianapolis,* pp. 364-365; Young, *Wayne County,* pp. 387-388.

factured products, but she was twelfth in the amount of capital invested and tenth in the total value of manufactured products. Not only Ohio and Illinois but Michigan and Wisconsin outranked her in the amount of capital invested.[39]

§ §

The beginnings of industrialization and the expansion of markets for farm products which accompanied the development of railroads created a demand for more banking facilities. Since 1834 the banking needs of the state had been served by the Second State Bank and its branches. This bank had a long and honorable history in sharp contrast to the record of most state banks of the era.[40] It weathered the storms of the Panic of 1837 and the debacle over the internal improvements program. But by 1850 it was criticized as failing to meet the needs of the expanding economy, for not providing needed capital, and for not having a sufficient number of branches throughout the state. Its charter would not expire until 1858, but by 1850 the question of whether it should be continued or replaced by another system was already being discussed. The bank question was one of the important

[39] The twelve states with the largest amount of capital invested in manufacturing were as follows: New York, Pennsylvania, Massachusetts, Ohio, Illinois, Connecticut, New Jersey, Michigan, Rhode Island, Wisconsin, Missouri, Indiana. United States Bureau of the Census, *Tenth Census* (1880), II: *Manufactures* [Pt. 1], p. xii.

Growth of Manufacturing 1850-1880

	1850	1860	1870	1880
Number of Establishments	4,392	5,323	11,847	11,198
Capital Invested in Manufacturing	$ 7,750,402	$18,451,121	$52,052,425	$65,742,962
Value of Manufactured Products	$18,725,423	$42,803,469	$108,617,278	$148,006,411
Number of Employees	14,440	21,295	58,852	69,508

United States Bureau of the Census, *Compendium of the Tenth Census* (1880), pp. 928-931.

[40] Logan Esarey, *State Banking in Indiana 1814-1873* (Indiana University *Studies*, No. 15, Bloomington, 1912), Chapter IV.

reasons for the calling of the Constitutional Convention of 1850-1851, and the issue was debated at length by the delegates. Within the convention there were three rather clearly defined groups. One favored the continuation of a state bank. Another favored a system of "free banking" or general banking under which there would be numerous banks competing with each other instead of a single institution enjoying a monopoly. There was a third group of hard money men who were theoretically opposed to any form of banking which involved the issuance of bank notes. No one of these groups was able to control the convention, and the finished constitution represented a compromise which embodied some of the views of each group.[41] The General Assembly was permitted to charter a bank with branches, but the state was prohibited from owning stock in or extending the credit of the state to any banking institution. Free banking under a general banking law was permitted in accordance with an article in the bill of rights prohibiting the legislature from granting privileges and immunities to any group of citizens which did not apply equally to all groups of citizens. Except for a state bank no bank was to be authorized except by a general code. All bills issued by all banks must at all times be redeemable in gold and silver, and no law was ever to be passed "sanctioning, directly or indirectly, the suspension, by any bank or banking company of specie payments."[42]

As the date for the expiration of its charter grew near, the directors of the State Bank considered whether to apply for a new charter which would permit it to continue even though the state would not own stock in it. There were intimations that a renewal could be obtained from the legislature by the expenditure of ten thousand dollars, but this suggestion of use of outright bribery was rejected. Instead it was decided

[41] See Barnhart and Carmony, *Indiana*, II, 71-73 for a good brief discussion and Esarey, *State Banking in Indiana*, Chapter V.

[42] Constitution of Indiana, Article I, section 23, and Article XI, especially sections 1, 2, 3, 4, 7, 12.

not to apply for a renewal but to wind up the affairs of the bank and close it. At the same time some of the principal investors decided to seek a charter for a new institution. As shown earlier, the bank issue was not publicized in the political campaign of 1854, but behind the scenes work was done quietly and efficiently to elect men who would favor the bank regardless of their political affiliation.[43] A bill to charter a new state bank passed the legislature in the closing days of the 1855 session. It was vetoed by Governor Joseph A. Wright and promptly passed over his veto. Wright's veto message emphasized that the bank issue had not been discussed in the political campaign and that the voters had not been given an opportunity to express their views. The Governor also opposed the bill because he thought that it could lead to a money monopoly.[44]

In his message to the legislature in 1857 Wright said that the circumstances under which the passage of the bank act was achieved constituted a "dark page of fraud" and that the location of the branches and the privilege of subscribing stock had been actually sold. "Books for the subscription of stock," he said, "were kept open but a few minutes, and were then only accessible to parties to the fraud; in other instances they were opened in out-of-the-way places, known only to a few; and, in scarcely any instance, was full and free opportunity given, for citizens generally, to subscribe." Wright asserted that a majority of the stock in the seventeen branches of the bank which were first organized was subscribed by twenty-eight persons, most of whom were not bankers. These subscribers in turn immediately transferred much of the stock to bankers at a premium.[45] As the result

43 See above, pp. 67-68; Esarey, *State Banking in Indiana*, pp. 288-289; Hugh McCulloch, *Men and Measures of Half a Century: Sketches and Comments* (New York, 1888), p. 127; *Journal of the Bank Investigating Committee: A Select Committee of the Indiana Senate, 1857* (Indianapolis, 1857), *passim.*

44 Indiana *Laws,* 1855, pp. 229-251; Indiana *Senate Journal,* 1855, pp. 713-716.

45 Indiana *Documentary Journal,* 1857, I, 307-309.

of Wright's prodding a legislative investigation was undertaken which seemed to confirm most of his accusations. The commissioners named in the bank charter were politicians from both parties. Sale of stock was arranged in such a way that the favored group were able to buy up the stock in a few hours—or even minutes. In Indianapolis the books for subscription of stock were kept open for only fifteen minutes, at Bedford only half an hour. In several places there were complaints that the sale of stock had been arranged in advance so that local investors had no opportunity to subscribe. At Indianapolis, Bedford, Evansville, and South Bend a large percentage of the stock was acquired on behalf of W. C. DePauw. At Madison, Lawrenceburg, and Logansport, Michael Bright, brother of Jesse Bright, acquired a large share of stock. From Bright the controlling interest in the Madison bank passed to the New York firm of Winslow, Lanier and Company. Bright was said to have made a profit of $14,000 on the transaction. A large proportion of the stock of the Vincennes branch passed into the control of the same New York bankers.[46]

Most of the stock of the new bank, the Bank of the State of Indiana, came into the possession of the principal stockholders of the old State Bank. Hugh McCulloch, who had been manager of the Fort Wayne branch of the old bank, was elected president of the new one. Branches of the new bank were located in the same places as branches of the earlier bank, but there were other branches in addition. Between fifteen and twenty branches were opened for business in 1857 and continued in operation until 1865. Under McCulloch's direction the organization and policy were essentially the

---

[46] *Journal of the Bank Investigating Committee . . . 1857,* pp. 379, 410-411, 412, 416, 417-418, 421, 425-426, and *passim.* In his diary Indianapolis banker Calvin Fletcher recorded that he had parted with old friends over the circumstances of the acquiring of the charter of the new bank because they bought the privileges of a bank whose charter was obtained by fraud. "I looked upon it as being no better than the holding of stolen goods," he wrote. Fletcher Diary, March 9, 1857.

same as under the earlier bank.[47] The unsavory circumstances under which it was launched at first caused a lack of public confidence, but the bank proved to be a sound and successful institution. "If it was conceived in sin, as was charged by Governor Wright . . .," said McCulloch, "it brought forth in a large measure the fruits of a well-conducted business." It was one of the very few banks in the entire country which did not suspend specie payment during the panic of 1857, and it successfully met the crises created by the Civil War. A recent historian considers it "one of the most distinguished and honored financial institutions" of the period.[48]

Meanwhile, in 1852 the legislature had passed a free banking bill. Under it banks were required to have a capitalization of at least $50,000. They were to deposit with the state auditor securities consisting of United States and Indiana bonds and those of some other states. Specie equal to at least 12 per cent of the amount of the notes in circulation was required to be kept on reserve. Failure to redeem in specie at any time was to lead to immediate closing of a bank. The adoption of the law, which was passed during a period of prosperity and economic optimism, was followed by a proliferation of banks. Six months after the law went into force there were fifteen free banks in the state. By the end of January, 1855, ninety-one had been opened.[49] Governor Wright, a hard money disciple of Andrew Jackson, had signed the bank bill with some reluctance. In his message to the legislature in 1853 he pointed out some of the abuses which had already arisen from the operation of the law. At that date sixteen banks had been organized. Of these six were regarded as doing a legitimate business, five had not yet actually started

[47] McCulloch, *Men and Measures*, pp. 127-130; Bray Hammond, *Banks and Politics in America from the Revolution to the Civil War* (Princeton, N. J., 1957), p. 621.

[48] McCulloch, *Men and Measures*, pp. 133-138; Hammond, *Banks and Politics*, p. 621.

[49] Indiana *Revised Statutes*, 1852, I, 152-161; Esarey, *State Banking in Indiana*, pp. 281-287.

business, but the remaining ones had been organized for purely speculative purposes. These banks had merely a nominal location in Indiana. Their backers deposited securities of dubious value with the auditor of state, received packages of bank notes in return, and hastened to take them out of the state to put them in circulation in some spot where it would be impossible for persons receiving them to attempt to redeem them. The operation was described by Wright:

The speculator comes to Indianapolis with a bundle of bank notes in one hand and his stock in the other. In twenty-four hours he is on the way to some distant part of the Union, to circulate what he denominates as legal currency authorized by the legislature of the State of Indiana. He has nominally located his bank in some remote part of the State, difficult of access, where he knows that no banking facilities are required, and intends that his notes shall go into the hands of persons who will have no means of demanding their redemption.[50]

Wright urged that the law be amended to require that only bonds of the United States or the State of Indiana be used as securities and to require that a majority of the directors of a bank live in the county where the bank was located. In 1854 a man in Washington, Pennsylvania, sent Wright forty-five dollars in notes on Indiana banks with the request that he exchange them for him. "The paper of your Free banks," he wrote, "can't now be passed here except at heavy discount at the Brokers—I think the System must be rotten or it would not have went down so soon."[51]

The proliferation of banks and unrestricted expansion of currency continued. "Men without capital or with barely credit sufficient to borrow a few thousand dollars of stocks, have been furnished facilities under the law, to become bankers to the extent of millions," Wright declared in 1855, in renewing his plea for a more stringent law. "With the currency procured upon the first deposit of stocks, other securi-

[50] Indiana *Senate Journal,* 1853, pp. 14-16.

[51] *Ibid.,* pp. 16-18; Joseph Henderson to Wright, October 17, 1854, quoted in Crane, Joseph A. Wright, p. 188.

ties have been purchased and other notes procured, and thus a large circulation has been created without a dollar of actual capital." As the result of rapid depreciation of the value of these notes and frequent bank suspensions, farmers and workers suffered.[52]

The Bank of Indiana had provided for a circulation of about $3,500,000 or $4,000,000. In addition, notes from banks outside of the state in about the same amount were in circulation. The new free banks quickly ran their circulation up to $9,500,000. In one six-month period more than $6,000,000 in notes were issued. In 1854 this period of wild expansion was followed by a sharp contraction which caused many of the new banks to close their doors. In less than a year about one half of the notes were withdrawn from circulation. A large part of those which remained circulated at only a fraction of their face value. In view of these wild fluctuations, "how can any people have stability under this state of monetary affairs," Wright asked. He blamed part of the evils of the system on the discretion which the law gave to the auditor of state and urged that a state board be created to supervise the banks. The 1855 legislature revised the law somewhat but not sufficiently, in Wright's opinion, to correct the deficiencies. The powers of the auditor were not restricted, and the provisions which permitted worthless securities from other states to be deposited as collateral for the issuance of notes were not changed. Wright vetoed the bill but it was passed over his veto.[53]

52 Indiana *Senate Journal,* 1855, p. 22.

53 *Ibid.,* pp. 22, 24, 721-725; Esarey, *State Banking in Indiana,* pp. 282-287; Hammond, *Banks and Politics,* p. 619; Indiana *Laws,* 1855, pp. 23-48. A contemporary banking journal described the process by which some of these banks operated. "One bank was made the basis of another, and that of a third, and that of a fourth," it observed. "By these cunning operations, three or four banks could be organized in four widely separated corners of the state, inaccessible during the winter season; and by the use of each other's bills, at the remotest point, they easily managed to keep in circulation a large amount of currency." *Bankers Magazine,* quoted in Hammond, *Banks and Politics,* p. 620.

As might have been expected, few of the banks founded on such shaky foundations survived long. Fifty-one banks were reported as having failed by the time the free banking law was three years old. Some of the free banks had adequate securities and not all of them were laxly or dishonestly managed. But the weaknesses of many of them put a strain on all of them. Lack of public confidence led to frequent runs. Even the soundest banks did not have sufficient specie to meet all demands for payment. Brokers and members of rival banks and even persons associated with the state sometimes made a practice of presenting notes for redemption and thereby forced the closing of some banks. Few of the free banks weathered the panic of 1857. In 1861 there were seventeen free banks in operation in the state.[54]

The banks chartered under the free banking law and the Bank of the State of Indiana were banks of issue. The word "bank" in the state constitution apparently was intended to apply only to banks of issue, but in addition to these institutions there were many private banks of discount and deposit which were not chartered under the banking laws. They were usually small institutions without sufficient capital to qualify under the free banking law, and information about them is meager. Although they did not have the privilege of issuing notes, the Indiana Supreme Court in a decision in 1858 said that they were "numerous" and were "discharging a large portion of the banking business" of the state.[55]

The secession crisis and the Civil War which followed put new strains upon existing banks and led to the establishment of the system of national banks. Secession caused a sharp decline in the value of securities of southern states and thereby

54 *Ibid.;* McCulloch, *Men and Measures,* p. 126; Barnhart and Carmony, *Indiana,* II, 75; Esarey, *State Banking in Indiana,* p. 284; Indiana *Auditor's Report,* 1861, p. 139. Esarey says that a banking house was opened in Indianapolis in 1856 for the sole purpose of presenting bills to Indiana bankers and thus getting coin. During the three months it operated it was said to have sent $2,000,000 in coin to the "gougers" in Cincinnati.

55 Davis *v.* McAlpine, 10 Ind. 137-139 (1858).

reduced the value of reserves of some Indiana banks. Banks holding these securities were required to reduce the amount of notes which they had in circulation or to increase their reserves. But such free banks as had survived the panic of 1857 were relatively strong and able to survive this crisis. Between 1860 and 1862 no banks in Indiana failed.[56] The issuance of United States treasury notes (called greenbacks) as legal tender during the war created a serious problem for the Bank of the State of Indiana and its branches as well as the free banks, all of which were required to be ready at all times to redeem their notes in coin. The greenbacks were declared by Congress to be lawful money for the payment of all debts, and throughout the country banks began using them to discharge obligations which called for payment in coin. Under the circumstances the prospect of being compelled to redeem their notes in coin placed an unbearable burden on Indiana banks. In order to receive an early decision on the question the officers of the Bank of the State of Indiana hastened to institute a case before the Indiana Supreme Court. The court unanimously upheld the right of the bank to redeem its notes in treasury notes rather than coin in spite of the charter provisions which prohibited it from refusing payment in gold or silver. The opinion declared that if Congress could make treasury notes legal tender in payment of debts between individuals, it could make them legal tender in transactions between banking corporations and individuals. The true interpretation of the bank charter, said the court, must be that "the bank shall not refuse to redeem her bills in what the Congress shall constitutionally make legal tender money." The bank could not be compelled to receive the treasury notes on the one hand and to pay out gold on the other. The opinion was written by Judge Samuel E. Perkins, a Democrat of the Jacksonian hard money school. He obviously viewed the issuance of the greenbacks with distaste and thought that Congress had

56 Indiana *Auditor's Report,* 1861, pp. 139-140; 1862, p. 286.

exceeded its power in making them legal tender. Nevertheless, he hesitated to render an opinion to that effect because of "the disastrous consequences to the country that must follow a denial of the validity of that exercise of power." He held that the legal tender legislation was valid until the United States Supreme Court should declare otherwise.[57]

In 1863 Congress took an important step toward the creation of a uniform national paper currency by the adoption of the National Banking Act. Banks established under the act could issue notes backed by United States bonds and guaranteed by the Federal government. By an act adopted in March, 1865, to become effective in July, 1866, a tax was placed upon the state bank notes in order to drive them out of circulation. In general Indiana Republicans in Congress supported the enactment of the banking measures while Democrats opposed. Democrats objected especially to the provision for the tax on state bank notes. Hugh McCulloch, who served as Comptroller of the Currency from April, 1863, to March, 1865, had more to do with the establishment of the national banking system than any other single individual.[58]

Indiana bankers were quick to avail themselves of the provisions of the national banking law. Existing state banks with a capital of more than $75,000 had an advantage in securing charters. As a result many of the branches of the Bank of the State of Indiana became a part of the new system even before the tax on state bank notes was imposed. By 1864 there were already thirty-four national banks in

[57] Reynolds *v.* the Bank of the State of Indiana, 18 Ind. 467-474 (1862). The case arose from the refusal of the South Bend branch of the bank to redeem in gold or silver on demand. The St. Joseph Circuit Court upheld the right of the branch to redeem in treasury notes, and this decision was appealed. Perkins, like many other Democrats, later became an advocate of greenbacks, reversing his earlier opposition to them.

[58] George La Verne Anderson, The National Banking System, 1865-1875: A Sectional Institution (Unpublished Ph.D. thesis in History, University of Illinois, 1933), pp. 26, 29, 36. The constitutionality of the tax on state bank notes was upheld by the United States Supreme Court in 1869. Veazie Bank *v.* Fenno, 8 Wall. 533.

Indiana, and by 1866 there were seventy-two. The amount of capital ranged from the minimum requirement of $50,000 in the smaller banks to $300,000 in the Madison bank and $250,000 at Evansville, Indianapolis, and Lafayette.[59]

Between 1862 and 1864 the circulation of the Bank of the State of Indiana dropped from about $5,000,000 to $1,500,-000. In April, 1865, the bankers of Indianapolis gave notice that they would no longer purchase or receive state bank notes except at a discount. As a result, the notes of the state banks were quickly withdrawn from circulation and turned into the department of the state auditor, where they were burned. During a six-month period over a million dollars worth of state bank notes were destroyed. By 1867 nearly all outstanding state bank notes had been redeemed. No financial panic occurred as the result of the withdrawal of the old notes, and the transition to the new currency took place smoothly. Since the National Banking Act had the effect of forcing state banks to stop issuing notes, most of them ceased operation. By 1866 all but three of them had given notice of their intention of closing operations. Most of the branches of the Bank of the State of Indiana received charters as national banks and continued their existence under the new system.[60]

After the Civil War the number of national banks showed a steady increase. In sharp contrast with the record of the state banks, very few of the national banks closed. By 1873 there were ninety-two national banks in operation in the state out of the ninety-seven that had been organized. Even during the depression years which followed 1873 new banks continued to be organized. The number of failures of national

[59] United States Treasury Department, *Report of the Secretary*, 1864, p. 46; *ibid.*, 1866, p. 65; *Emigration to the United States of North America. Indiana As A Home for Emigrants* (1864), pp. 32-33; Anderson, The National Banking System, p. 19.

[60] Harold Knight Forsythe, "Growth of State and National Banks in Indiana," *The Hoosier Banker*, November, 1920, p. 44; Indiana *Auditor's Report*, 1865, pp. 31-32; 1866, p. 29.

banks was surprisingly small in view of the severity of the depression. Up to 1875 only two national banks in the state had failed, and as late as 1879 there had been a total of only five failures. Up to 1880 a total of 117 banks had been organized since the establishment of the system of which 92 were still in operation. In addition to the five which had failed there were twenty which had closed or were in the process of liquidation.[61]

The legislation setting up the national banks fixed the total amount of notes at $300,000,000. The system of apportioning this among the states resulted in the concentration of national banks in the East. Western states received relatively few national banks, while in the South they were almost non-existent. Indiana received a larger number of national banks relative to her population than did Illinois or any of the states farther west.[62] The inequity of apportionment created much dissatisfaction and was one of the reasons that many Westerners embraced the Greenback movement. Other Westerners sought to amend the national banking act to permit free banking—i.e. an unlimited number of banks. The Panic of 1873 gave an impetus to demands for this reform. Although Indiana fared relatively well in the apportionment of bank charters, Indiana Republicans favored a free banking law. In the Senate, Morton was one of the principal advocates of legislation to expand national banking circulation. As the result of pressure from the western states, Congress changed the law in 1875 to provide for free banking.[63]

After the Federal tax was imposed on state bank notes, state banks ceased to operate as banks of issue, but many

---

[61] United States Comptroller of the Currency, *Annual Report*, 1873, p. viii; 1875, p. xxiii; 1879, p. xxxiv; 1880, p. lxxxv.

[62] Anderson, The National Banking System, pp. 18, 19, chart p. 93. By 1867 the New England states, New York, and Pennsylvania had 999 of the 1,647 national banks in the entire country and $217,607,683 of the entire circulation, leaving only $75,064,070 for the remainder of the country. *Ibid.*, p. 107.

[63] *Ibid.*, pp. 316-320, 351, 357, 367, 368; Foulke, *Morton*, II, 100, 323-334.

private banks of discount and deposit continued to operate. These were partnerships which usually called themselves "firms." They did not operate under any banking law and were liable to their depositors only as other partnerships organized for other purposes were liable for indebtedness. Private banks of this kind were usually small institutions in agricultural communities where they furnished credit to farmers. But some were found in larger cities.[64] In 1873 the state legislature passed a law which permitted the organization of state banks with a minimum capital of $25,000. The measure was modeled in some respects after the National Banking Act and gave the state auditor powers of supervision similar to those exercised by the Comptroller of the Currency. Periodic examinations and reports were required. Private banks were not required to be organized under the act, but it was expected that some of them would choose to do so because the act enabled businesses to continue to be carried on after the death of a partner, whereas those private banks which were partnerships were dissolved by the death of a partner.[65]

Surprisingly few state banks were organized under the new law. By 1875 there were only thirteen, and only twenty in 1880. These represented only a small fraction of the banking business in the state. In 1876 there were reported to be a total of 143 banks in the state exclusive of the national banks. They had a total capital of almost six million dollars. Of these only thirteen, with a total capital of less than nine hundred thousand dollars, filed reports with the state auditor under the requirements of the law of 1873. The others filed

[64] George E. Barnett, *State Banks and Trust Companies Since the Passage of the National-Bank Act* (National Monetary Commission Report, *U. S. Senate Documents,* 61 Congress, 3 Session, II, No. 659, Washington, D. C., 1911), p. 206.

[65] Indiana *Laws,* 1873, pp. 21-27; *Brevier Legislative Reports,* XIII (Special session 1872), 322; Forsythe, "Growth of State and National Banks in Indiana," *Hoosier Banker,* November, 1920, p. 45, December, 1920, p. 12.

Horse-drawn Car Used in Fort Wayne between 1872 and 1892

The "Robert E. Lee" Built at New Albany in 1866 for
Capt. John W. Cannon
Painted from a contemporary lithograph

Scenes at the Fairgrounds at Lafayette, 1876

Elkhart County Farm, 1874

no reports and were not subject to examination by authorities appointed by the auditor.[66]

A few savings banks were organized under a law passed in 1869. The purpose was to give persons of low income a place in which they could invest their small savings, but the law was a curious one. No capital stock was required to organize a bank, and no individual or corporate responsibility was attached to the trustees. Trustees had complete control over the use of funds but were not even required to be depositors. The only liability was for damage due to *wilful* misconduct or neglect. The obvious defects of the law drew sharp criticism from the state auditor, who described it as an "anomaly" because the depositors were the stockholders but had no voice in the management of funds. He urged that trustees and officers be made legally responsible. Several savings banks were organized which failed during the depression. By 1880 only seven were included in the report of the state auditor.[67]

Although the number of national banks was smaller than the number of private and state banks, their financial power was much greater. In 1876, when the aggregate capital of all state and private banks amounted to a little less than six million dollars, the aggregate capital of the national banks in the state was more than seventeen million dollars.[68]

The most powerful of the national banks, as was to be expected, were found in the larger cities. The First National Bank of Indianapolis, organized by William H. English and ten associates in 1863, was apparently the first bank organized under the new law in Indiana and the fifty-fifth in the country. It became the largest bank in Indianapolis, and one of the largest in the Middle West. The Indiana National Bank in

[66] Indiana *Auditor's Report,* 1875, p. 101; 1878, pp. 116-117; 1879, p. 171; 1880, p. 82; Barnett, *State Banks and Trust Companies,* Appendix, Table I.

[67] Indiana *Laws,* special session, 1869, pp. 104-116; Indiana *Auditor's Report,* 1878, pp. 139-141.

[68] Indiana *Auditor's Report,* 1878, p. 117.

the same city had its inception as the Indianapolis branch of the Bank of the State of Indiana in 1857. In 1865 it was reorganized as a national bank. There was also the Indianapolis National Bank, which was under the control of the same interests as those which controlled Fletcher and Sharpe's Bank. The latter was found by Calvin Fletcher and Thomas Sharpe. Fletcher had previously been president of the Bank of Indiana. After the demise of that institution the Indianapolis Branch Banking Company, a private bank, had been started as a successor to it, and in 1868 the name was changed to Fletcher and Sharpe's. After the death of Calvin Fletcher in 1866, his interest was passed to his sons. In 1880 this bank had the largest number of depositors in the state. Another large private bank, S. A. Fletcher and Co., was controlled by the same interests.[69]

In Evansville in 1857 the branch of the State Bank of Indiana became the branch of the Bank of the State of Indiana. In 1865, in turn, it became the Evansville National Bank. The Evansville "Canal Bank," which was operated for several years under the free banking law, became in 1863 the First National Bank of Evansville.[70]

In Fort Wayne the principal stockholders of the Fort Wayne branch of the old State Bank became the principal stockholders of the branch of the Bank of the State of Indiana, which in 1865 was reorganized as the Fort Wayne National Bank. Earlier the Citizens Bank, formed in 1861, became the First National Bank of Fort Wayne in 1863. One of the most powerful financial institutions in the state for many years was Allen Hamilton and Company, organized in 1853 as a private bank, not operating under any banking law.

[69] Holloway, *Indianapolis*, pp. 302-304; Jacob P. Dunn, *Greater Indianapolis. The History, the Industries, the Institutions, and the People of a City of Homes* (2 volumes, Chicago, 1910), I, 351; *Manufacturing and Mercantile Resources of Indianapolis, Indiana* . . . (Part IV, *Resources and Industries of Indiana*, n. p., 1883), pp. 411, 416, 438, 514.

[70] Frank M. Gilbert, *History of the City of Evansville and Vanderburg County Indiana* (2 volumes, Chicago, 1910), I, 234-235.

It was founded by Allen Hamilton, president of the Fort Wayne branch of the Bank of the State, Hugh McCulloch, and Jesse L. Williams. In 1874 it was reorganized as the Hamilton Bank under the banking law of 1873. In 1879 it became the Hamilton National Bank.[71] In South Bend the First National Bank was formed in 1863. In 1871 the South Bend National Bank was organized as the successor to the branch of the Bank of the State of Indiana.[72]

§ § §

As late as 1880 the United States census showed that less than one fifth of the working force in Indiana was made up of persons employed in manufacturing and mining, while persons in agriculture made up more than one half of the total.[73] Among those employed in manufacturing and mining the overwhelming majority—more than 80 per cent—were native born. Of the foreign born, Germans made up 57.79 per cent, British 16.37 per cent, Irish 12 per cent, and other

[71] Robert S. Robertson, *Allen County Indiana* (Volume II of *History of the Maumee River Basin*, 3 volumes, Indianapolis and Toledo, 1905), pp. 120-121, 125-127. Allen Hamilton was a native of North Ireland, who came to Indiana after brief sojourns in Quebec and Philadelphia. In 1820 he settled in Lawrenceburg, where he studied law under his uncle, General James Dill, clerk of Dearborn County. In 1823 he moved to Fort Wayne, then a frontier outpost, where he became a wealthy merchant. Much of his wealth was first made in trade with the Indians. He was active in politics as a Whig although he later became a Democrat after the demise of the Whigs. As a member of the Constitutional Convention of 1850-1851 he was an advocate of free banking. *Representative Men of Indiana*, II, District 12, pp. 30-32.

[72] Stoll, *St. Joseph County*, pp. 64, 66. The *Hoosier Banker*, February, 1963, a special number commemorating the centennial of the establishment of the National Banking system, contains brief histories of a number of national banks in Indiana.

[73] Of a total of 635,080 persons engaged in all types of occupations the distribution was as follows:

Agriculture	331,240
Professional and personal services	137,281
Trade and transportation	56,432
Manufacturing and mining	110,127

United States Bureau of the Census, *Compendium of Tenth Census* (1880), pp. 1356-1357.

nationalities 13.84 per cent. Almost none of the workers from southern and eastern Europe who came in large numbers in later decades had arrived in 1880. Few Negro workers (who were included among the native born in the census) were found among industrial workers. Almost 90 per cent of the labor forces in manufacturing and mining were men. About 5 per cent were women and about the same per cent were children under fifteen years of age. The largest group of women were employed in the manufacture of men's clothing, an industry of little importance in Indiana at that time and one which was carried on mostly in small tailoring shops. The second largest group of women were found as operatives in the woolen mills.[74]

Accurate information is meager but, measured by the standards of a later day, wages were low and hours of work long. In many occupations a twelve-hour day was the rule and there were few in which it was less than ten hours. In some occupations a seven-day work week was customary. Among the groups who worked the longest hours were teamsters and employees of flour mills and breweries. All of these might work as much as fifteen hours per day. A normal day for teamsters and brewers began at half past three in the morning and ended at seven in the evening.[75]

Wages in general appear to have risen sharply during the years of the Civil War and to have continued high, although declining somewhat, until 1873. During the period from 1873 until 1879 they fell sharply. For example, machinists and blacksmiths in Lafayette were paid about $1.50 a day in 1850, $2.00 in 1860, and $3.00 by 1865. By 1870 their pay had fallen to $2.50 and by 1879 to $2.25 and $2.00. A miller in Fort Wayne was paid $2.50 a day in 1856. By 1863, he received $3.50, $3.20 in 1870, and only $2.30 in 1878. A

[74] United States Bureau of the Census, *Compendium of the Tenth Census* (1880), pp. 965-966; *Tenth Census* (1880), II: *Manufactures* [Pt. 1], pp. xxxv, xxxvii; Thornbrough, *Negro in Indiana*, pp. 349-351.

[75] United States Bureau of the Census, *Tenth Census* (1880), XX: *Report on Statistics of Wages* [Pt. 1], pp. 24, 61.

common laborer in the milling industry in the same city was paid $1.25 in 1861, $1.50 in 1863, $1.35 in 1873, and in 1877 only $1.15. In the building trades in Indianapolis beginning wages averaged from $1.50 to $1.75 per day at the beginning of the war and had risen to $2.50 to $2.75 by 1864. Some members of the trade received as much as $3.50. Between 1873 and 1879 the average daily wages of members of the Indianapolis Carpenters' Union declined from $2.40 to $1.43. The average wages of workers in a carriage company declined from $2.50 to $1.42 in the same period. An overseer in a boot and shoe factory in Lafayette received $66 a month in 1860, $100 in 1865, $150 in 1866, $100 in 1873, $125 in 1880. Figures on daily or monthly wages do not reveal the full shrinkage in income during the depression because they do not show the decline in the number of days of work. A large percentage of industry operated only part of the time during the seventies. It is probable that workers were fortunate to be employed eight or nine months a year. During the depression it was not uncommon for workers to be paid wholly or partly in scrip or store orders rather than in cash. Work in the mines was especially subject to seasonal fluctuations. On an average employees at the Brazil and Chicago Coal Company in Clay County worked nine months a year during the 1870's. The average pay per ton of coal mined in 1870 was $1.00, but between 1875 and 1878 it had fallen to 65 or 75 cents. Miners were required to furnish their own tools and also the powder which they used for blasting, which cost about 10 per cent of their earnings. Part of their pay was in cash, part in store orders.[76]

In 1880, census figures show, the average yearly wages for industrial workers in Indianapolis were $391. In Evansville and Fort Wayne they were slightly less—$372 and $373 re-

76 *Ibid.* [Pt. 1], pp. 6, 16-17, 60-61, 142, 171, 243, 414, 465; Kershner, Social and Cultural History of Indianapolis, p. 182; Indianapolis *Daily Sentinel,* March 21, 1864; *Emigration to the United States of North America: Indiana as a Home for Emigrants* (1864), pp. 20-22.

spectively—and in Terre Haute slightly higher—$416.[77] Fig-
ures taken from the same census indicate that the cost of
shelter and food was relatively high. Rent for a four- or
six-room house in one of the smaller cities ranged from $120
to $180 a year and would, no doubt, have been higher in
Indianapolis, Evansville, or Fort Wayne.[78]

The depression of the seventies gave an impetus to efforts
of workers to join together to protect their interests, but
even before the Civil War there were some examples of
organizations of workers. These were usually, but not always,
made up of men in a particular trade. Some of them had as
their sole object the improvement of their economic position
but others stressed fraternal and benevolent activities. In
1850 several groups of artisans banded together to form the
"Mechanics Mutual Protections." At a state convention in
Indianapolis in June, 1850, the groups adopted a constitution
and drew up a statement of their objectives. These included
securing "remunerative wages" and educational programs for
apprentices to enable mechanics "to assume a better station in
society than has yet been awarded to them." In addition each
"protection" was to provide against "pecuniary distress during
the sickness of its members, and to extend care and relief to
their destitute families." A final objective was "to cultivate a
proper understanding between the employer and the employed." The other labor groups had more limited objectives.
In Terre Haute the coopers formed a union to maintain uniform prices for barrels, and the carpenters banded together
and agreed not to work for less than $1.25 per day.[79]

77 United States Bureau of the Census, *Tenth Census* (1880), XIX: *Social
Statistics of Cities,* pp. 443, 448, 456, 475. Wages in other cities in the Middle
West were comparable. In Cleveland they were $391, the same as in Indian-
apolis. In Cincinnati they were $358, slightly lower than in the leading cities
of Indiana. In Chicago they were somewhat higher—$436. *Ibid.,* pp. 376,
389, 513.

78 *Ibid.,* XX: *Statistics of Wages* [Pt. 1], p. 104. See *ibid.,* pp. 54-57 for
some statistics on the cost of food.

79 *Locomotive,* June 1, 1850; Schlicher, "Terre Haute in 1850," *Indiana
Magazine of History,* XII, 250.

By the time of the Civil War there were several craft unions. Conditions created by the war caused them to press demands for higher wages. Several strikes occurred as a result. In Indianapolis the journeymen shoemakers formed a union and attempted to force employers to agree to a uniform scale of wages. They published the names of employers who agreed to their demands. The businesses of those employers who agreed were listed as "society shops," while those who failed to agree were listed as "non-society," and persons who worked for them were branded as "scabs"— "not worthy the consideration or respect of any mechanic or well meaning public."[80]

In Indianapolis, the Typographical Union, which was one of the earliest to be established in the state, attempted to force the publishers of the *Sentinel* to give a wage increase of 20 per cent in 1863 and went on strike when their demands were not met. The *Sentinel* promptly dismissed the members of the union and advertised for new employees, announcing, "no member of a typographical union need apply." At the time of the strike union members appealed to fellow members in Madison for support. This caused the Madison *Courier* to comment that the members of the executive committee of the union were "making great asses of themselves" and admonished them to "go to the devil." "Labor and prices should be left to the laws of demand and supply, which will establish them on a permanent and fair basis," it declared. "We advise the members of the Typographical Union to study political economy. Its principles will show them clearly the unjustifiableness and foolishness of 'strikes.' "[81] In 1864 blacksmiths and machinists in Indianapolis went on strike. It was reported that the Blacksmiths and Machinists Union had $25,000 in their treasury to pay members who were thrown out of work by the strike—obviously a grossly exaggerated figure.[82]

[80] Indianapolis *Daily Sentinel,* September 21, 1864.
[81] *Ibid.,* April 13, 14, 1863; Madison *Courier,* quoted *ibid.,* April 16, 1863.
[82] *Ibid.,* November 10, 1864.

By the sixties railroad employees had also begun to organize. Most early railroad unions were formed primarily for the purpose of mutual benefits in case of accident or death arising from a highly hazardous occupation. By 1864 there were locals of the Brotherhood of Locomotive Engineers in Indiana. In 1876 the grand lodge of the Brotherhood of Locomotive Firemen was organized in Indianapolis. Indianapolis served as general headquarters for the national union from 1876 until 1880, when the headquarters were moved to Terre Haute.[83] By the end of the war, in addition to unions already mentioned, there are records of unions of iron molders, stone cutters, bricklayers, plasterers, coach makers, gas fitters, sheet iron workers, and tin- and coppersmiths.[84] There were probably others of which no mention has been found.

From time to time there were efforts at federation of the various trade unions. In 1873 delegates from all over the state assembled to form a permanent trades assembly. Among the unions represented were the Carpenters, Coopers, Typographical, Machinists and Blacksmiths, Cigar Makers, Bricklayers, Iron Moulders, and Puddlers. The constitution adopted at the meeting said that the purpose was to unite the trade unions of the state into "one brotherhood for the defense of the rights and the protection of the interests of the laboring masses" and "to so concentrate labor as to enable it to successfully compete with concentrated capital, in controlling the law making power of the country."[85]

In addition to unions made up of members of a particular trade there continued to be efforts at organizations of a broader type which embraced all kinds of workers. Among

[83] Griswold, *Pictorial History of Fort Wayne*, I, 471; H. C. Bradsby, *History of Vigo County, Indiana, with Biographical Selections* (Chicago, 1891), pp. 612-613; Indianapolis *Daily Journal*, December 27, 1873.

[84] Indianapolis *Daily Sentinel*, September 17, 1854; Indianapolis *Daily Herald*, February 7, 1867; Kershner, Social and Cultural History of Indianapolis, p. 180.

[85] Indianapolis *Daily Journal*, April 15, 1873.

these was the Ancient Order of United Workmen, which was founded in Pennsylvania in 1868 and established a branch in Terre Haute in 1873. Its object was to unite all classes of mechanics or persons employed in the "mechanical arts" for the purpose of adjusting differences between employers and employees, aiding members in distress, and working for the moral and social elevation of all laborers. By 1878 it was reported to have thirty-seven lodges in Indiana with a membership of 1,900. A similar organization was the Independent Order of Mechanics, which held a national convention in Indianapolis in 1877.[86]

During the seventies there were some unions of the Knights of Labor in Indiana, but because before 1881 they were a secret organization almost nothing is known of them. The United States census of 1880 reported twenty-three locals of the Knights in the state. Most of these were apparently in the mining districts. The state headquarters was at Knightsville.[87] There was an abortive effort to form an organization of women workers in Indianapolis in 1874, but internal differences as to objectives and methods caused it to founder. One group wanted to work to raise wages and to go on strike when necessary to achieve its objectives. Another group thought it should confine itself to caring for members during sickness and to pay death benefits.[88]

The United States census of 1880 reported a total of seventy-seven labor unions in Indiana, including both those affiliated with national organizations and locals without any such affiliation. The Knights of Labor mentioned above constituted the most numerous group. There were fourteen unions of railroad employees—seven of locomotive engineers and seven of firemen. In the building trades were one union of car-

[86] *History of Vanderburgh County* (1889), p. 390; Indianapolis *Daily Journal,* May 3, 1877; February 20, 1878.

[87] *Ibid.,* May 4, 1878; United States Bureau of the Census, *Tenth Census* (1880), XX: *Statistics of Wages* [Pt. 3], p. 16.

[88] Indianapolis *Daily Journal,* May 1, 1874.

penters and two of bricklayers; there were seven unions of coopers, five locals of the Typographical Union, five of cigar makers, and one of boot makers and shoemakers affiliated with the Knights of St. Crispin. A few unions made up of industrial workers were reported—five affiliated with the Amalgamated Association of Iron and Steel Workers, four of iron molders, and one of the Amalgamated Society of Engineers, Machinists, Millwrights, Smiths and Pattern Makers. The number of unions in Indiana, according to the census, was much smaller than the number in either Ohio or Illinois at the same date.[89]

Early unions were concerned principally with wages and "protective" functions such as care for sick members and their dependents and death benefits, but some members also sought to improve the condition of the working class through political activity. Immediately after the Civil War a state convention was held in Indianapolis to launch a movement for the eight-hour day. The leading figure in this effort appears to have been John Fehrenbatch of Indianapolis, who was a member of the Machinists and Blacksmiths Union and who was elected president of the international union in 1870. Fehrenbatch continued for years to be the leader in the political activity of labor groups in Indiana. The Workingmen's convention which met in Indianapolis in November, 1865, called for the organization of eight-hour leagues in all states and for the use of "all lawful and suitable means for success," including refusal to support candidates for office who did not favor the eight-hour day. "In consequence of the large amount of labor-saving machinery now in use, and the excess of laborers for the labor required to be performed," they declared, "henceforth, *eight hours shall constitute a day's work!*" Politicians were sufficiently impressed with the strength of the Eight Hour League that both the Democratic and Republican state platforms of 1866 included planks

89 United States Bureau of the Census, *Tenth Census* (1880), XX: *Statistics of Wages* [Pt. 3], 14-16. The number of unions in Ohio was reported to be 252; in Illinois, 226. *Ibid.,* p. 2.

calling for eight-hour-day laws to be enacted by the next legislature.[90]

The Eight Hour League in Indiana was one of several such movements which, along with trade union assemblies, led to the calling of the National Labor Congress which met in Baltimore in 1866. The congress in turn gave an added impetus to political activity by local labor groups. In 1867 a workingmen's party was organized in Indianapolis. Its platform, which was reminiscent of resolutions adopted at Baltimore, declared that the time had come for independent political action by labor since history showed that no dependence could be placed on the old political parties, "so far as the individual classes are concerned, while capitalists engaged in every class of monopolies press their claim for protection successfully." The first and most important demand of the new party was the eight-hour day. In succeeding years there continued to be interest in political activity and in co-operation with the National Labor Union, which stressed political activity. Two delegates from Indianapolis were sent to the National Congress of Laboring Men which met in Chicago in 1870.[91]

After 1870 the National Labor Union quickly disintegrated, in part because of the withdrawal of support by trade unions which were opposed to emphasis upon political action. In 1873 there was an attempt to form another national organization, the Industrial Congress of the United States. The impetus came from the trade unions, and the organization anticipated in structure and program the American Federation of Labor. John Fehrenbatch of Indianapolis was one of the leaders of the congress, serving as permanent chairman of the first convention, which met in Cleveland in July, 1873.[92]

90 Indianapolis *Daily Herald,* November 24, 1865, February 22, March 16, 1866; Indianapolis *Daily Sentinel,* October 8, 1870.

91 Indianapolis *Daily Sentinel,* August 6, 8, 1870. See also Chapter VII, above, pages 283-285, for an account of the political activity of labor.

92 John R. Commons *et al., History of Labour in the United States* (2 volumes, New York, 1918), II, 159-165.

The depression which began a few months later weakened the movement and caused a revival of interest in political activities as workers sought relief from economic distress. Some of the leaders of the congress embraced the idea of currency reform as the solution to economic problems. As shown in an earlier chapter, the money question was especially conspicuous in Indiana politics in the seventies, and labor groups were attracted to the Greenback movement. In December, 1873, a workingmen's rally called by the Trades Assembly of Indianapolis heard a speaker attribute the panic to the monetary system. Resolutions were adopted calling for "a purely national circulating medium, based on the faith and resources of the nation" and for wages paid in money rather than in scrip. A meeting called by the same groups the following February called for political organization by all workers and denounced the system of the national banks as a "curse to the country." The same meeting urged a compulsory education law and expressed opposition to contract labor in penal institutions. In May, 1874, a member of the Indianapolis City Council was elected who had been nominated by a workingmen's convention.[93]

In 1876 there was another effort at organizing a workingmen's party. A meeting in Indianapolis adopted a platform which declared that members of the working classes should be elected to legislative bodies. They also declared in favor of a graduated income tax and woman's suffrage as well as calling for the replacement of bank notes with greenbacks. One workingman's candidate for the legislature was nominated. During the campaign there were efforts at co-operation between the labor group and the Greenback party.[94]

In 1877 there were renewed efforts to form a branch of the Workingmen's National party, which resulted in the nomination of a ticket of candidates for the city election. In city politics the group favored free textbooks for children

---

93 Indianapolis *Daily Journal*, December 22, 1873, February 23, May 6, 1874.
94 Indianapolis *Daily Sentinel*, February 25, June 6, 1876

in the public schools. But in national politics they stressed the money question to the exclusion of almost all other issues.[95]

On the whole the efforts at political activity by workingmen were ineffectual. The state platforms of the major parties usually contained general statements affirming interest in the welfare of workers, but seldom contained any specific pledges to labor. Few measures of particular interest to labor were introduced in the legislature, and almost no labor legislation was adopted. One reform which was expressly endorsed was the eight-hour day, to which platforms of both parties promised support in 1866. In 1867 a bill to carry out the pledge was introduced, but the committee to which it was referred recommended that it be tabled. This caused the sponsor of the bill to ask whether or not party platforms were mere "political claptrap." "You have no right," he told his fellow legislators, "to treat laboring men in that way:—You have no right to say to them before election that you are in favor of this measure, and after election indefinitely postpone it or lay it upon the table." But in spite of his remarks nothing more was heard of the bill. The same legislature adopted a law which prohibited a cotton or woolen mill from employing any person under the age of sixteen for more than ten hours a day. There was opposition even to this on the grounds that it would "interfere with the duties and responsibilities of parents and guardians" and that "manufacturing companies" could "best arrange the working hours of their several establishments."[96]

During the depression several measures were brought forward to protect the rights of wage earners. In 1875 bills were introduced to enable workers to collect wages due them. One provided that workers should be paid once a month in

[95] Indianapolis *Daily Journal,* April 3, 4, 1877; Indianapolis *Daily Sentinel,* May 26, 1876, August 14, 1877.

[96] *Brevier Legislative Reports,* IX (1867), 71, 134; Indiana *House Journal,* 1867, pp. 324, 799, 802-803; Indiana *Laws,* 1867, p. 232.

lawful money of the United States. None of these were adopted. In 1877 a law was passed which gave employees of any corporation doing business in the state a first lien upon the property and earnings of the corporation for work done. A supplementary law adopted in 1879 provided that when any corporation or person engaged in manufacturing or construction suspended business or became bankrupt, laborers should be regarded as "preferred creditors" and their claims to wages should be regarded as "preferred debts" against the assets of the corporation or person.[97]

The 1879 legislature also finally passed a law for the protection of workers in coal mines—a measure which had been considered in four previous sessions[98] and which had been endorsed by the platforms of both the Democrats and Republicans but which had been fought vigorously by the mine operators. One senator opposed the law because, he said, he was "in favor of cheap fuel for every inhabitant of the state." Another predicted that the law would destroy the mining interests of the state. Others opposed it because it was sought by the miners, and miners had participated in bloody strikes. One member declared the proposal "the worst and most dangerous bill" ever proposed in the General Assembly. "If the friends of the miners want legislation for their protection inside the mines," said he, "there should also be laws made to protect the miner outside the mine, and the operator's property should be protected." Another argued that it placed "coal-miners—probably a member of a communistic order—in charge of the entire mining interests of the state."[99]

---

[97] Indiana *House Journal*, 1875, p. 136; *Brevier Legislative Reports*, XV (1875), 64; Indiana *Laws*, special session, 1877, p. 27; special session, 1879, p. 153. For examples of additional bills proposing protection for wage earners see Indiana *House Journal*, 1879, pp. 105, 705, 1141-1142; Indiana *Senate Journal*, 1879, pp. 216, 261.

[98] See Indiana *House Journal*, special session, 1872, pp. 118, 242-243, 461-462, 636-637 for first discussion of mine inspection law.

[99] *Brevier Legislative Reports*, XVII (1879), 190, 200-201.

Others defended the measure as humanitarian and a necessary safety measure. The Indianapolis *Sentinel* pointed out that the bill said nothing about wages or prices and conferred no rights upon miners—it was simply a safety measure. Yet operators were lobbying against it with every means at their command. The *Sentinel* described it as "prudent and practical, humanitarian and utilitarian" and urged its adoption. The law in its final form created the office of a mine inspector who was to be appointed by the governor and required mines which employed more than ten persons to provide certain outlets for entrances and exits and to make provisions for ventilation. It also gave employees a lien on the property and earnings of the mine for the payment of their wages.[100]

More indicative than political activity of the unrest among workers which the depression of the 1870's created were the strikes. During the early months of the depression there were numerous strikes against wage cuts. As the depression worsened there continued to be scattered strikes in factories and in the building trades. These involved small numbers of workers and were of short duration, but in the coal mines in the western part of the state and on the railroads there were prolonged strikes involving large numbers of workers and unprecedented violence.

Labor troubles in the coal mines, where employment was likely to be seasonal and wages unstable, antedated the general depression. During the summer of 1871 miners in Clay County went on strike and succeeded in getting an increase in pay of ten cents per ton. In October, 1872, at the beginning of the busy season they again demanded an increase of twenty cents a ton and to be paid every two weeks instead of once a month. The operators, eager to fulfill their contracts, yielded without much resistance and increased the price of coal to pay for increased labor costs. Then after most of the winter contracts had been filled, the Clay County

---

[100] *Ibid.*, p. 190; Indianapolis *Daily Sentinel*, February 27, 1879; Indiana *Laws*, 1879, pp. 19-25.

Coal Association, an organization of operators, announced a wage cut of twenty-five cents a ton and a return to monthly wage payments. The result was a strike which idled nearly all the mines in the county. After waiting a month the operators retaliated by attempting to replace the idle men with Negro strikebreakers who were brought into the state from Virginia. The presence of the Negroes created tensions. Daniel Voorhees publicly denounced the use of the strikebreakers, but others defended the action of the operators. "That the operators had a right to employ any kind of men they please to work in their mines could not be denied," declared a letter to the Indianapolis *Journal.* "That a few foreigners should attempt to control the mines of Indiana . . . and drive from the mines all who do not join their union, is passing strange, and yet such are the facts in the case." As the strike dragged on, some miners left the county, and others who had been members of the union resigned from it. After about two months, during which the mines had been kept open by Negroes and "black legs" (nonunion white miners), the strike was broken and the workers were ready to return on the operators' terms.[101]

Meanwhile, there were prolonged labor troubles at the Western Iron Company which was under the same ownership as some of the coal mines. In the summer of 1871 about nineteen puddlers had been fired, allegedly for union activity, and a strike had followed. The mill was idle until 1873, when Negro strikebreakers were brought in at the same time the Negro miners were brought in. On the day that the strike in the mines was ended and the miners agreed to return to work, there was a celebration at which the operators dispensed free beer. This was followed by a clash between white miners and Negroes which developed into a wild riot, involving not only the miners but the idled puddlers and the Negroes

[101] Indianapolis *Daily Sentinel,* October 23, 1871; Indianapolis *Daily Journal,* February 21, 22, March 26, 28, April 17, 1873; Terre Haute *Journal,* quoted *ibid.,* March 29, 1873.

employed in the iron works. Shots were exchanged and several persons were badly beaten but no one was killed.[102]

The following year there was another strike in the Clay County mines over wages. The miners agreed to accept a reduction in pay if they were guaranteed steady work—a condition which the operators were unable to fulfill. Nearly all the miners went on strike, but a few weeks later were persuaded to return to work by the president of the Miners National Union who convinced them that their course was futile.[103] In 1875 there was another strike over pay cuts and again strikebreakers—both white and Negro—were employed. After a time the strikers began to return to work without having gained anything.[104]

In 1877 and 1878 there were strikes and disorders arising from the use of Negro strikebreakers in the coal mines of Fountain County. Before March, 1877, the Coal Creek mines in that county had been worked by union miners, who were paid more than those employed in Clay County. The trouble began when a nonunion weight master was hired. Four or five hundred men went on strike in protest. The operators then announced a reduction in wages, and when the men refused to return to work they brought in nonunion workers, including Negroes, who worked at wages less than those paid the white miners. The strikers finally returned to work at reduced wages. The following year there was another strike when wages were reduced once more. Again Negro miners were imported and were given firearms for their own protection. In April, 1878, there were clashes between them and armed members of a white militia company which was made up partly of men who had formerly worked in the mines, some of whom had been replaced by the Negro strikebreakers. Four Negroes were reported to have been driven out of town and shot to death. At the request of

102 Indianapolis *Daily Journal,* April 16, 17, 1873.
103 *Ibid.,* March 23, April 20, 1874.
104 *Ibid.,* February 8, 15, 1875.

the circuit court judge of Fountain County, Governor Williams sent troops from Indianapolis to preserve order, and the Negro miners returned to work under their protection. The local militia company whose members had been involved in the disorders were disarmed. Some of the men were charged with murder, but they were acquitted. A group of nonunion miners, including both whites and Negroes, adopted resolutions in which they thanked the Governor for his intervention, declared their opposition to union membership, stated that their pay was "fair and reasonable," and promised that they would be "faithful" to their employers. The strike and its unfortunate aftermath appeared to have eliminated the union from the mines of Fountain County. But peace had not come to the mines. In spite of repeated failures miners continued to go on strike. At the end of 1879 all the miners in Clay County—nearly three thousand in number—were reported on strike.[105]

Strikes on railroads involved more workers and were accompanied by violence on a larger scale than those in the coal mines. In December, 1873, cuts in wages set off a strike on all the lines operated by the Pennsylvania Railroad Company, which included several lines in Indiana. Begun by members of the Brotherhood of Locomotive Engineers, who were soon joined by firemen, it became the largest strike in the United States up to that time. The strikers resorted to a variety of methods to prevent trains from running. At several points in Indiana violence developed. The most serious rioting was at Logansport, where Governor Hendricks sent some guardsmen at the request of the sheriff. The engineers denied any responsibility for the disorders and destruction of property which accompanied the strike, and press accounts admitted that most of the lawlessness was due to acts of outsiders. The strikers had the sympathy and support of other unions, but the general public was alienated by the

---

[105] Indianapolis *Daily Journal,* April 23, 25, 26, 30, May 25, June 20, 1878, December 2, 1879; Indiana Adjutant General, *Report,* 1878, pp. 72-73.

paralysis of transportation and the violence. After a few days engineers were imported from the West in an attempt to break the strike. Gradually operations were resumed as employees were supplied by other lines. Some of the strikers returned to work, and the strike ended in failure.[106]

In August, 1876, the Ohio and Mississippi Railroad, which had not paid its employees for three months, announced a reduction in wages. This set off a strike by employees along the portion of the line which ran across Indiana. The strategy of the strikers was to stop the movement of freight by removing all links and pins from the cars which pulled into Seymour. Troops were sent from Cincinnati to Seymour, but there was no violence, and they refused to interfere. The men at Seymour agreed after a day or two to call off the strike. Trains started moving again, but when they reached North Vernon, they were stopped once more. When executives of the company tried to bring in police and machinists from St. Louis to break the strike, striking employees at Vincennes ran the car in which they were riding onto a side track. Governor Hendricks, who was out of the state when the strike began, returned and announced that the strike must stop. The remedy for the strikers' grievances lay with the courts, he said, and he called upon the men to go back to work. He also called upon the civil officers to use their authority to break up the "combination" of strikers and "to bring guilty members who may remain contumacious to punishment." But Hendricks refused to send Indiana militia to the strike-torn areas even though the sheriffs of the counties involved requested it. The strike abated when some of the strikers were paid wages due them and discharged, but among the workers who remained in the employ of the Ohio and Mississippi dissatisfaction and unrest continued.[107]

106 Indianapolis *Daily Journal,* December 27, 29, 30, 31, 1873; January 1, 2, 3, 6, 24, 1874.

107 Indianapolis *Daily Sentinel,* August 11, 12, 14, 16, 1876.

The railroad strike of 1876 was the prelude to the great strikes of the summer of 1877. These strikes, which came about principally as the result of the announcement of successive wage cuts, began in the East and spread westward to Indiana. Within a few days almost every railroad line in the state was involved. Work stoppage in Indiana began in Fort Wayne, on July 21 on the Pittsburgh, Fort Wayne, and Chicago line. Employees of the Wabash line in that city soon joined the strike. Officers of the former line were determined that the trains should run but were driven back by strikers when they attempted to operate them.

When the mayor ordered the strikers to disperse, he was hissed down, and a call from the city council also was ignored. The strikers took possession of depots, yards, and railroad shops. They adopted resolutions to prevent violence or destruction of property and urging the men to "do as you would be done by." All saloons were closed by the city government and some two hundred extra police were enrolled. There was some violence, but Governor Williams told the mayor that he would send troops only as a last resort. The striking employees themselves took possession and began operating the passenger trains, but freight traffic was at a complete standstill and public indignation mounted at the stoppage. A citizens' committee pledged support in putting down the strike. Resistance by the strikers was weakened when news came that employees of the Pittsburgh line had surrendered in Pennsylvania as the result of the appearance of Pennsylvania troops. The men voted to return to work when they were promised that no one would be fired for taking part in the strike. Employees of the Wabash line agreed to return to work when company officials promised them that they would raise wages as soon as the business of the company would permit.[108]

[108] Edward Winslow Martin [pseud.], *History of the Great Riots: Being a Full and Authentic Account of the Strikes and Riots of the Various Railroads of the United States and in the Mining Regions* (Philadelphia, 1877), pp. 355-359, 362-364; Indianapolis *Daily Sentinel,* July 24, 1877.

Meanwhile, the employees of one after another of the lines running through Indianapolis went on strike. The Vandalia line employees were the first to stop working and refused to allow freight trains to leave the city. They were followed by employees of the Bee line, the Indianapolis and Peru, the Indianapolis and Vincennes, and other lines in the city. The superintendent of the Jeffersonville, Madison and Indianapolis line attempted to counter the strike by issuing an order suspending all business, which had the effect of throwing the men in the shops as well as the operating employees out of work. At first only freight trains were stopped by the strike, but later passenger service also ceased, and only postal trains continued to operate. Business generally felt the effects. Resentment was especially strong because the strike came at the season when large amounts of grain were in transit and much damage resulted from the stoppage of transportation. Huge crowds assembled around the Union Depot, but considering the number affected by the strike, there was little violence. The press attributed such disorders as did occur to outsiders rather than to railroad employees. The strikers passed resolutions prohibiting the men from drinking, and Mayor Caven ordered all saloons closed.[109]

The Mayor and Governor Williams insisted that there was no need for the use of state militia, but as has been related earlier, Federal Judge Walter Q. Gresham intervened to preserve law and order on the grounds that most of the railroad companies involved were in receiverships under court order. After Gresham called for the creation of a committee of public safety and asked President Hayes to send troops, the Governor issued a proclamation ordering the men to return to work and asserting that remedy for their grievances lay with the courts.[110]

A committee of arbitration made up of prominent citizens, which heard reports from both strikers and operators, de-

109 *Ibid.,* July 24, 25, 1877.
110 *Ibid.,* July 27, 1877. See above, Chapter VII.

clared that there should be redress for the wage cuts which
had caused the strikes, but declared that redress was impossible until transportation was resumed. The committee
gave "unqualified condemnation" to the strike as a weapon.
Strikes were declared to be "in violation of law" and "deeply
injurious to innumerable persons against whom they [the
strikers] profess no grievance." Judge Gresham told the
men to go back to work. Congressman Franklin Landers,
a member of the committee, assured the strikers: "If you will
permit business to resume its usual channel, you will have the
good will of the people of Indianapolis, who will honor you
and see that justice is done you." After this the strike began
to collapse, and men began to return to work, in most cases
without any promise of wage restoration. One exception to
this was the Bee line—the Cleveland, Columbus, Cincinnati,
and Indianapolis—which promised that the 10 per cent wage
cut would be restored.[111]

At Terre Haute all lines except the Terre Haute and
Evansville, which had not reduced wages, were struck. The
strikers passed resolutions calling upon fellow citizens for
"sympathy and aid" in resisting "the encroachments of capital
upon unprotected labor," but at the same time they deprecated
vandalism and violence and assisted in organizing a police
force to maintain order and protect property.[112] Farther
south transportation on the Ohio and Mississippi line was
at a standstill. In the extreme north at Elkhart, transportation on the Lake Shore and the Grand Rapids and Indiana
lines was halted, but there appeared to be a question as
to whether it was the result of a strike or lockout. There
were reports of violence and a large number of arrests were
made for rioting among discharged railroad hands and
"tramps" who gathered in the city.[113]

111 Indianapolis *Daily Sentinel,* July 28, 1877.
112 *Ibid.,* July 25, 26, 1877. In Terre Haute Daniel Voorhees addressed
the strikers, expressing sympathy for them but urging moderation and order.
113 *Ibid.,* July 26, 27, 1877.

By the first of August the strikes were virtually at an end. As shown elsewhere fifteen of the strikers were later held to be guilty of contempt and were sentenced to prison by a Federal judge.[114] The arrests were the unhappy finale of an unhappy chapter in the history of labor relations. The railroad strikes of 1877, like the other strikes of the depression years, were largely a manifestation of frustration and desperation in the face of steadily worsening economic conditions over which workers had no control. Their failure, like the failure of the other strikes in this period, demonstrated the futility of strikes in a period of depression. There were no other strikes of comparable size in Indiana during the remainder of the seventies. By 1879 economic conditions appeared to be improving, and a few workers went on strike to regain losses suffered previously. For example, stove molders at New Albany and Jeffersonville, who had consented to a 20 per cent wage cut in 1878, struck to force a restoration in 1879.[115]

Nearly all of the strikes of the seventies were over wages. In most instances, although not always, all or part of the strikers were union members. As has been shown, in a number of cases union members were replaced by nonunion members, and there was no legal protection against this practice. In 1879 employees of the Indianapolis newspapers sought union recognition. After negotiations the management of the *Sentinel* agreed. But the *News* and the *Journal* refused and demanded that printers employed by them must give up union membership. When *Journal* printers were required to sign a statement that they were dissolving connections with the union, they refused to do so and went on strike. The management responded by announcing that henceforth it would employ only nonunion printers. "There are more nonunion printers than union printers, and they are entitled to equal consideration," declared a *Journal* editorial. "The

114 See Chapter VII, pages 281-282.
115 Indianapolis *Daily Sentinel,* June 10, 11, 1879.

unions exclude all nonunion men from the composing rooms they control, and the managers of the Journal propose to exclude all union men from the composing room they control." The *Journal* no doubt reflected prevailing opinion when it declared that it was "preposterous" for the Typographical Union to attempt to tell the *Journal* what wages it should pay its employees. Only a "knave" or a "coward" would submit to such dictation, the *Journal* loftily declared, "and it is the privilege of publishers to employ men who do not belong to such an institution."[116]

[116] Indianapolis *Daily Journal,* July 16, 17, 1879.

CHAPTER XI

EDUCATION

THE YEARS FROM 1850 TO 1880 constitute one of the most important chapters in the history of education in Indiana. It was in these years that free elementary schools for all pupils became a reality, and the opening of public high schools commenced. The idea of teaching as a profession requiring special training began to be accepted. Indiana University, while not yet meriting the title "university," was at least firmly established as a state institution, and a second state institution, Purdue University, embodying a different concept of state-supported higher education, was founded. Within this period many private academies flourished, but by 1880 most of them had disappeared. On the other hand, private denominational colleges continued to play an important part in higher education.

Although the first state constitution declared that it was the duty of the General Assembly, as soon as circumstances permitted, "to provide by law for a general system of education, ascending in a regular gradation from township schools to a State University, wherein tuition shall be gratis and equally open to all,"[1] public education had made little progress before 1850. Numerous laws on the subject of schools were passed—the school law in the Revised Statutes of 1843 covered twenty pages—but the school system envisaged existed only on paper. Census figures revealed the embarrassing fact that Indiana had the highest rate of illiteracy of any northern state—a point about which political leaders showed considerable sensitivity, and one of the reasons why

[1] Article IX, section 2.

the terms "Hoosier" and Indiana connoted ignorance and backwardness.[2]

In the Constitutional Convention of 1850-1851 one delegate said that there was a general impression that Indiana had done a great deal for education. This arose, he said, "in part from the fact that it always makes a prominent item in the stump speeches that are annually made. Many prophesy in its name, and teach upon the streets and cross-roads, and are great and devoted friends of common schools just before an election. . . ." But actually the state itself had never levied a tax or paid out money for an educational purpose.[3]

The crux of the school question was whether or not the public was willing to pay the taxes necessary to make free schools a reality. In the late 1840's a debate on the subject of public education began which continued for several years, in the legislature, in the Constitutional Convention, and in the press. Probably the man who was most responsible for sparking the debate and shaping the public school system which grew out of it was Caleb Mills, professor of Latin and Greek at Wabash College. Under the nom de plume "One of the People," Mills wrote six "educational messages" over a period of several years in which he persuasively presented to the legislature and Constitutional Convention pleas for public schools with specific recommendations for a system embodying the principles which he advocated. In his first message, in 1846, Mills pointed out that Indiana had borrowed millions for internal improvements but had not as yet raised a dollar by ad valorem taxation to cultivate the minds of her children. "We can better meet the expense of the

[2] In his message to the legislature in 1851 Governor Wright said that the United States census of 1850 showed that there were 75,000 persons over the age of twenty in Indiana who could not read or write. "This number, believed by many to be more than we really have," he said, "has been greatly enlarged, at a distance, in the public journals." Indiana *Senate Journal,* 1851-1852, p. 16.

[3] Quoted in Richard G. Boone, *A History of Education in Indiana* (New York, 1892. Reprinted by Indiana Historical Bureau, Indianapolis, 1941), pp. 143-144.

proper education of the rising generation, than endure the consequences resulting from the neglect of it," he insisted.[4] The basic argument in behalf of tax-supported schools was that universal education was necessary for the preservation of republican institutions. In 1849 Governor Paris C. Dunning urged the legislature to turn its attention to the subject of free common schools upon which "our country mainly relies for her permanent peace and prosperity." At least a good elementary education should be available to every child, he said. "If he has this, he is capable of understanding the tendency and bearing of all political questions which are brought forward for public discussion—he is capable of appreciating his rights and maintaining them—he can analyze public measures, examine into the conduct of public men, and hold them to strict accountability."[5]

One of the obstacles to the establishment of a comprehensive system of free schools was the widely held view that free schools were "pauper schools." Closely related to the argument in favor of public schools as a necessity for an intelligent citizenry was the argument that public schools should be for children of all classes without distinction as to wealth. Friends of public education tried to combat the idea that free schools were for the children of the poor only. In some parts of the state, according to one newspaper, "it has been deemed almost disreputable to attend them. It seems to have been taken for granted that none but the lower classes would send children to them and that consequently they could not be good schools." Another newspaper urged that public schools should be made good enough to attract the children of the well-to-do as well as the poor. They "should be conducted so as not to wound the feelings or mortify their pride by continually keeping the fact before them that their

4 Charles W. Moores, *Caleb Mills and the Indiana School System* (Indiana Historical Society *Publications,* III, No. 6, Indianapolis, 1905), pp. 363-368, 409, 414.

5 Indiana *Senate Journal,* 1849-1850, p. 27.

children are educated at the expense of their more affluent neighbor." Unless this was done, it warned, free schools would have the effect of "arraying one class of citizens against another, and creating ill feeling between the classes."[6]

Another obstacle to an adequate school system was the feeling that schools were a purely local responsibility and that people of one locality should not pay taxes in support of schools for children in another locality. In a debate over a proposal for state support for schools one member of the legislature spoke of "robbing one county for the benefit of another" as "piracy." "If the doctrines of rewards and punishments are true *here* or in the 'kingdom come,' " he declaimed, "no good, I think, could accrue to a child educated with a fund under such a procurement. . . ." On a proposal for a general system of public schools one senator, while professing to favor common schools, declared he was opposed to a system "by which his constituents were annually bled, to the tune of thousands of dollars, to feed the hungry office-holders, that swarm around the school fund." He was opposed to taxing his people to educate the children of other counties.[7]

In the Constitutional Convention of 1850-1851 debates over education occupied much of the time of the delegates. All of the arguments over the question of the responsibility which the state should assume were heard at length. Friends of public schools actively sought to win support by deluging members of the convention with propaganda. But among

[6] Indianapolis *Indiana Free Democrat*, February 16, 1854; Indianapolis *Locomotive*, August 31, 1850. The report of a legislative committee which presented a school bill to the legislature in 1848 stressed that: "Common schools must be made respectable. . . . They should be so elevated that all classes will feel that they are in every way suitable for the education of their children. . . . It is therefore, *indispensably necessary* that the rich, the learned and more polished part of the community, should feel that the public schools are *the* schools—the *only* schools in which their children are to be qualified for the common business of life." Indiana *Documentary Journal*, 1847-1848, II, Doc. 15, p. 359.

[7] *Brevier Legislative Reports*, II (1859), 262, 269.

the delegates there were some who wanted to limit the role of the state. There were proposals that free schooling be made available only to those who lacked the funds to attend private schools or that the public school system be limited to elementary schools only and the state university be abolished and its property sold with the proceeds going to the common schools.[8]

The finished constitution made it mandatory for the General Assembly "to provide by law for a general and uniform system of common schools, wherein tuition shall be without charge, and equally open to all." It also made it the duty of the Assembly "to encourage by all suitable means, moral, intellectual, scientific, and agricultural improvement," but did not mention expressly the state university or any type of educational institution except the common school.[9]

The new constitution provided for a state superintendent of public instruction who was to be elected by the voters and whose duties were to be prescribed by the legislature.[10] The school law of 1852 gave the state superinendent general charge of examining and licensing teachers and created a state board of education with the superintendent as its chairman. The duties of the board were largely advisory, but it was authorized to introduce uniform school textbooks.[11] Because the office of state superintendent was elective it was associated with party politics. But in spite of its partisan character, the office attracted some able men. The first superintendent was a Democrat, William C. Larrabee, who held the office from 1852 to 1855 and again from 1857 to 1859. He was a native of Maine, a graduate of Bowdoin College, and a professor of mathematics at Asbury University. Caleb Mills, who had been conspicuous in the fight for public schools, was elected superintendent in the fusion victory of 1854. Like his

8 Boone, *Education in Indiana*, pp. 134-138.
9 Article VIII, section 1.
10 Article VIII, section 8.
11 Indiana *Revised Statutes,* 1852, I, 448-450, 457.

predecessor he was a New Englander, a graduate of an eastern school, Dartmouth, and an academic figure—a professor of Greek at Wabash College. Among other men who held the office were George W. Hoss, who was elected in 1864 and 1866. At various times he was associated with Indiana Female College in Indianapolis, North Western Christian University, and Indiana University, and also served as one of the first superintendents of the Indianapolis schools. Barnabas C. Hobbs, who was elected in 1868, was the first president of Earlham College. James H. Smart was superintendent of the Fort Wayne schools for ten years before being elected state superintendent in 1874.[12] Though the powers of the office of superintendent were limited, the men who held it contributed to raising educational standards and to creating a uniform school system. The reports of the state superintendent to the legislature constitute the most complete record available of the state educational system and contain recommendations for improving the system which had some influence with the lawmakers.

The 1852 school law, passed by the first legislature under the new constitution, laid the foundations for a system of public schools supported by state taxation. Some of the features of the law had been included in earlier laws, especially that of 1849, but they had been merely permissive and had not actually been carried out. The 1852 law made the civil township the unit for the administration of schools and placed the township trustees in general charge, with authority over buildings and the employment of teachers. The trustees were

[12] For brief sketches of the early state superintendents see James H. Smart (ed.), *The Indiana Schools and the Men Who Have Worked in Them* (Cincinnati, 1876), pp. 90-97; Indiana State Superintendent of Public Instruction, *Twenty-Second Biennial Report* (1903-1904), 32-42. The list of state superintendents and the years in which they were elected are as follows: William C. Larrabee, 1852, 1856; Caleb Mills, 1854; Samuel Rugg, 1858, 1862; Miles J. Fletcher, 1860; Samuel K. Hoshour, appointed in 1862 to fill the unexpired term of Fletcher, who was killed in a railroad accident; George W. Hoss, 1864, 1866; Barnabas C. Hobbs, 1868; Milton B. Hopkins, 1870, 1872; James H. Smart, 1874, 1876, 1878.

empowered to establish in each township "a sufficient number of schools for the education of the children therein." The law permitted the establishment of "graded schools or a modification thereof, where such establishment is practicable and convenient." For the first time a state property tax for the support of common schools was provided. In addition the law authorized townships to levy property and poll taxes for buildings and equipment and for continuing schools after state funds were exhausted. Another innovation was the provision that incorporated cities and towns should constitute school corporations independent of the townships with the power to levy taxes for the support of the schools after state funds had been exhausted.[13]

The enactment of the 1852 law gave an impetus to the opening of new schools and to the lengthening of school terms where schools were already in operation. But these results were short-lived. There was considerable confusion as to just what the respective responsibilities of the state and the local governments were under the law. There was by no means universal support for the taxes authorized, and various efforts were made to block the operation of the law. The result was a decision of the Indiana Supreme Court in December, 1854, invalidating the portion of the law which permitted townships to levy a special tax for school purposes.[14]

Judge Alvin P. Hovey who wrote the decision found that the tax provision violated the article of the new constitution which prohibited local or special laws regarding "common schools and the preservation of school funds." His argument was that if the townships could tax for school purposes, the

[13] Indiana *Revised Statutes,* 1852, I, 439-442, 444, 454. The real author of the law was James R. M. Bryant, a Whig from Warren County. Leopold, *Robert Dale Owen,* p. 287.

[14] Greencastle Township in Putnam County and Earl R. Kercheval, County Treasurer, &c., *v.* Alexander Black and others, 5 Ind. 556-566 (1854). In the April election, 1853, the voters of Greencastle Township voted to levy a property tax and poll tax for school purposes. Alexander Black sought to enjoin the collection of the tax.

power of controlling the schools would pass to a large extent
from the hands of the state into the hands of the townships
and that "the uniformity" of the common school system which
the constitution required "would be at once destroyed." This
argument was reiterated and expanded by Judge William Z.
Stuart in a petition for a rehearing. The constitution, said
Stuart, contemplated common schools "as a State institution,
under the superintendent of Public Instruction." They were
"to be supported, as to tuition, by State funds." A state school
system which was general and uniform could not admit the
levying of local taxes. "Uniformity" meant that the state
raised a common school fund by uniform assessment and taxation and by distributing the fund equally to all entitled to it.
"When a tax is levied in one township for common school
purposes, which is not a state tax . . . the law itself creates
the want of uniformity. Such diversity, where uniformity is
attainable, is in violation of the Constitution."[15]

The decision of the court brought consternation to the
friends of public schools. In an editorial entitled, "The School
Law Ruined," the leading Democratic newspaper sharply
criticized the Hovey opinion, even though it had been handed
down by a Democratic judge. "Our public schools were just
beginning to be appreciated," it lamented, "and the efforts of
teachers and officers had cleared the way for a profitable
administration of the law. The court destroys the law and
leaves our whole public school system to be rebuilt, and the
rubbish is to be cleared out again." In some quarters it was
thought that the entire school law had been declared unconstitutional; as a consequence, some schools were closed, others
shortened their terms.[16]

[15] Greencastle Township in Putnam County and Kercheval, County Treasurer, &c. *v.* Black, 5 Ind. 563-564, 566-577 (1854).

[16] Indianapolis *Daily Sentinel,* December 30, 1854, quoted in Everett E.
Jarboe, The Development of the Public School System in Indiana from 1840
through 1870 (Unpublished Doctor of Education thesis, Indiana University,
1949), p. 129; Boone, *Education in Indiana,* p. 156.

Tell City Brewery, 1875

Employees of Tell City Woolen Mills, 1875

Distillery and Warehouses of T. and J. W. Gaff & Company,
Aurora, 1876

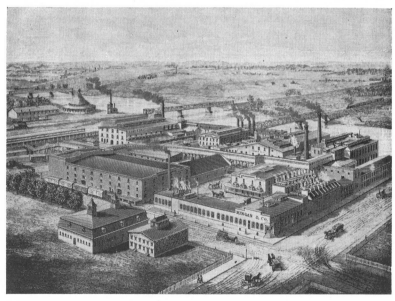

Kingan & Company Packing House, Indianapolis

The court was actually speaking only of taxes for tuition. The law was declared unconstitutional "as to the mode of levying the tax and paying tuition." This meant that taxes for tuition could originate only in the legislature, but it left unanswered the question of the right to levy taxes for building purposes. In a suit brought from Warren County the Supreme Court in 1857, speaking through Judge Samuel Perkins, held that although townships could not levy taxes to pay teachers because that power was vested in the legislature alone, townships could levy taxes for buildings. In the case of buildings "no more uniformity can be required as to them than there can be as to those for building court houses and jails in the different counties."[17]

Following the Hovey decision the school law was revised in 1855 to require that tuition in all public schools be furnished by the state, but that school buildings and equipment be furnished by the local government. The effect of this compromise was not altogether satisfactory. The state legislature was reluctant to levy school funds, and local governments, unable to supplement state funds in paying teachers, hesitated to build schoolhouses which would probably stand unused most of the year. In spite of uncertainties some progress was made in the 1850's in building. The report of the State Superintendent of Public Instruction for 1853 stressed the total inadequacy of existing schoolhouses. In some townships there was not a single schoolhouse. In others there were "a few old, leaky, dilapidated log cabins, wholly unfit for use even in summer, and in winter worse than nothing." At least 3,500 buildings were said to be needed. In 1859 it was reported that 666 new schoolhouses had been constructed, but the extreme limitations of the structures is shown by the fact that the average cost per building was $439.67![18]

17 Adamson *v.* the Auditor and Treasurer of Warren County, 9 Ind. 174-175 (1857).

18 Indiana *Laws,* 1855, p. 162; Indiana State Superintendent of Public Instruction, *Second Annual Report* (1853), 4; *Eighth Annual Report* (1859), 6.

Even more glaring than the lack of adequate buildings was the lack of money to pay teachers. Funds were so limited that in 1854 the average length of the school term in all the schools in the state was estimated to be only a little more than two and one-half months. But there were wide variations from the average, sometimes even in the same township. The trustees divided available funds among the schools in the township, either equally or according to enrollment. But there was no uniformity as to the length of term or even when the term was taught. In the same township, reported the state superintendent, "some schools are taught in summer, some in autumn, and some in winter. Some are kept up one month, some two months, some three months." In 1859 in the state as a whole terms ranging from 22 days to 246 days were reported.[19]

In most places the pay of teachers was so woefully small that teaching could not be regarded as a full-time occupation. In 1853 the average monthly wage of men teachers was less than $18.00, in 1854 about $24.00. Women teachers earned less than $10.00 a month in 1853 and less than $16.00 in 1854. This meant annual pay for men of $50.00 or $60.00. And after the power of townships to tax to pay teachers was denied by the Supreme Court, even these pittances declined. During 1859 the entire school revenue of every kind—state and local—distributed to the schools averaged 94 cents per child—or $68 to each of the 6,500 schools.[20]

The average figures on school terms are for all schools in the state, those in towns and cities as well as rural districts. The overwhelming majority of schools were rural one-room schools, but in the fifties, under the authority of the 1852 law, some incorporated towns and cities began to set up their own

[19] Indiana State Superintendent of Public Instruction, *Third Annual Report* (1854), 29; *Seventh Annual Report* (1858), 8-9; *Eighth Annual Report* (1859), 5.

[20] Indiana State Superintendent of Public Instruction, *Second Annual Report* (1853), 12-13; *Third Annual Report* (1854), 29; Boone, *Education in Indiana*, p. 219.

systems. Prior to that law children in towns either attended township schools or private schools. The 1852 law, it will be recalled, gave the corporation the power to levy taxes for school purposes. In 1855 a separate law dealing with free public schools in cities and towns was passed, giving cities and towns the power to levy taxes for both tuition and buildings even though the Supreme Court had ruled that township taxes for tuition were unconstitutional. It also gave authority to recognize private schools as part of the public system and to appropriate money for them.[21]

In the towns as well as in rural districts there was reluctance to support public schools although not necessarily for the same reasons. In some towns there were already private academies which were regarded as adequate to the needs of the community. Well-to-do parents preferred to send their children to private schools and did not want to pay taxes for public schools. The law of 1855 made it possible to incorporate private schools which were already established into the public system.

By 1856, of about one hundred corporate towns and cities in the state perhaps one half had instituted their own system. In a number of cases private academies were purchased or rented and became public schools. In 1852 Richmond and Madison opened free schools which were among the first examples of graded schools. The following year in Indianapolis a system of ward schools was opened. They were at first supported in part by fees paid by pupils. By 1856 there were twenty public schools in the city with an enrollment of over fifteen hundred. That year one building was opened which would accommodate three hundred children and six teachers. In 1857 a system of graded schools was introduced, and the school term was extended to thirty-nine weeks. The first public schools were opened in Fort Wayne in 1853. The most expensive schoolhouse built in the decade was built in that city at a cost of more than $18,000. In Evansville a

21 Indiana *Laws*, 1855, p. 184.

beginning of public graded schools was made. At first classes were held in churches and private homes, but in 1856 a building with six rooms which would accommodate eight or nine hundred pupils had been completed at a cost of $10,000. In Lafayette free schools were first opened in 1854. By 1856 there were three school buildings accommodating eight hundred pupils.[22]

Some other cities lagged in their efforts. Among the larger communities Terre Haute was described by the state superintendent in 1857 as presenting "the least hopeful prospects in regard to public education." In 1853 a public school was opened, but in 1854 the school trustees voted to suspend public education, and no more schools were held until 1860. In Crawfordsville there were two schools, one in a room fourteen by six feet in dimension, and the other in an old paint shop. Both rooms were dirty and were furnished with broken furniture. The classes were said to be disorderly and recited and read badly. In some other towns schools were maintained sporadically, being opened for a few months some years, and not at all in other years.[23]

These early efforts, feeble though they were in some cases, were weakened by another adverse decision of the State Supreme Court early in 1858. The earlier decisions of the court which denied the power of local governments to tax for tuition purposes had applied only to the townships, but the same issue was raised by the legislation which gave incorporated towns and cities the power to tax to supplement state school funds. In a case appealed from the Tippecanoe Circuit Court, Judge Samuel E. Perkins held that the provision of the 1855 law conferring the power to tax for school purposes upon

---

[22] Boone, *Education in Indiana*, p. 161; Harold Littell, "Development of the City School System of Indiana—1851-1880," *Indiana Magazine of History*, XII (1916), 196-198; Indiana State Superintendent of Public Instruction, *Eighth Annual Report* (1859), 6; *Twenty-Sixth Report* (1877-1878), 313-315, 319-321, 325.

[23] *Ibid., Twenty-Sixth Report*, p. 330; Littell, "Development of the City School System," *Indiana Magazine of History*, XII, 195-196.

towns and cities violated the constitutional requirement that
the legislature provide a "general and uniform system of
common schools." The system must operate equally in the city
and the country, said Perkins; otherwise it was not uniform.[24]
On a motion for a rehearing, which he denied, Perkins reiterated and expanded the arguments he used in his first
opinion. He held that the 1855 law not only violated the
requirement of uniformity but that it also violated the prohibition against local laws. The 1855 law was said to be a
local law because it operated only on a portion of the people
and property of the state and because it was operative in only
a portion of the school districts and created one scale of taxation for one part of the school district and another for the
other part.[25]

The decision meant, as one newspaper put it, that "no
matter how willing and ready the people may be to tax themselves for the laudable purpose of supporting their common
schools, the Supreme Court says they cannot do it." Republican newspapers throughout the state attacked Perkins for the
decision, which they declared showed him to be an enemy of
the public schools. (The decision, of course, followed the
same line of reasoning as to what constituted "uniformity"
as had earlier decisions.) Perkins felt compelled to defend
himself by saying that he himself was "part and parcel of the
free school system," and had cheerfully paid his own taxes
and sent his children to public schools. But he repeated that
the law violated the constitutional requirement of uniformity.[26]

As a result cities and towns drastically curtailed their educational efforts or abandoned them entirely. In some places

---

[24] City of Lafayette and Martin, County Treasurer, *v.* Jenners, 10 Ind. 70-73
(1858). The case arose when a taxpayer sought an injunction against the
collection of the school tax. The circuit court granted the injunction and the
Supreme Court upheld its action.

[25] City of Lafayette *v.* Jenners, 10 Ind. 74-82 (1858).

[26] Vincennes *Daily Gazette*, February 2 and 3, 1858; Jarboe, Development
of the Public School System, p. 151.

public school buildings were rented to groups who operated them as private schools. In others there were efforts to keep the schools open by soliciting voluntary contributions to supplement the funds contributed by the state, but these were largely unsuccessful. Many teachers were dismissed, and there was a general exodus of trained superintendents and principals to other states. In Indianapolis all the schools except one were closed, and more than two thirds of the children of school age were without schooling. There is no record of the payment of any public money to teachers from the time of the court decision until 1860. For five years the city employed no superintendent of schools.[27]

§ §

It was not until the years following the Civil War that the public school system was firmly established throughout the state. About 1860 the city schools which had been paralyzed by the adverse court decision began to revive. Several corporations began to levy school taxes in spite of the court rulings, and schools which had been closed were reopened. In some places, especially in the southern part of the state, the impact of the Civil War retarded progress. For example, in New Albany, where schools had been closed in 1858, they were reopened in 1860, but most of them were closed again from June, 1861, to September, 1864, because the buildings were rented to the United States government.[28]

The fundamental problem for all schools, as has been shown, was that of raising money. In 1861 two resolutions to amend the state constitution to give cities, towns, and townships the power to levy taxes to raise revenues in addition to revenues derived from the state passed the General Assembly. But failure of the 1863 session to pass them again,

27 Littell, "Development of the City School System," *Indiana Magazine of History,* XII, 200-202; Boone, *Education in Indiana,* p. 220; Indiana State Superintendent of Public Instruction, *Twenty-Sixth Report* (1877-1878), 315.

28 *Ibid., Twenty-Sixth Report,* pp. 343-346; Littell, "Development of the City School System," *Indiana Magazine of History,* XII, 203-205.

as required by the constitution, killed them. In 1865 similar
resolutions authorizing supplemental school levies by local
governments were introduced but were not passed. Instead of
trying to overcome the obstacles created by the Supreme
Court decisions by means of constitutional amendment the
1867 legislature simply adopted a law which re-enacted features of the laws previously invalidated. It gave townships,
cities, and towns the power to levy taxes of as much as twenty-
five cents on each one hundred dollars of taxable property and
poll taxes of twenty-five cents. Funds raised by local taxes
could be spent in the same way and for the same purposes
as state taxes for the common school fund.[29]

Evidently the lawmakers hoped that a test case could be
avoided or that if one were brought, the Supreme Court
would reverse its earlier decisions. Their optimism was justified. Apparently public opinion on the subject of public schools
had undergone such a change since the 1850's that the new
law was not challenged for many years. Finally in 1885 a
test case was brought and the law was upheld, the court holding that the state constitution did not require that all school
taxes be levied by the legislature nor did it prohibit the legislature from providing by general law for the levying of school
taxes by local authorities. A law which secured equal and
uniform rights to all the subdivisions within the state was
held to meet the requirement of uniformity.[30]

Meanwhile, progress was being made in providing better
school buildings. As has been shown, the court decisions on
local taxation had applied only to the payment of teachers
and had no effect on the power to raise money for buildings.
Some communities had built schoolhouses which were rented
to private schools. At the end of the Civil War there were
7,403 schoolhouses in the state. By 1876 the number had increased to 9,434. Most of these were one-room frame build-

[29] Indiana *Laws,* 1861, p. 186; 1867, pp. 30-31; Kettleborough, *Constitution
Making in Indiana,* II, 50, 57.
[30] Robinson, Treasurer, *v.* Schenck, 102 Ind. 307 (1885).

ings. As late as 1872 the average cost of a school was only $1,429. But by the seventies the log schoolhouse was disappearing. In 1865 there were 1,128 log buildings; by 1876 there were only 192.[31]

In the years after the war there began to be some interest in school architecture which took into account the comfort of the pupils, and more attention was paid to lighting and heat and ventilation. In the larger communities fairly large buildings of stone or brick were constructed. One of the most elaborate and expensive was the Evansville High School which cost $45,000 and contained twelve rooms. The Fort Wayne High School had eighteen rooms. Some elementary schools of eight or twelve rooms were built in the cities. The more elaborate buildings were three stories high and graced by towers and cupolas.[32]

The average length of the school term doubled in the fifteen years after the Civil War. In 1866 it was only 68 days; in 1879 it was 136 days. In 1861 the legislature had provided that all schools within the same township must be taught the same length of time, but there continued to be great variations from the average, sometimes even in the same county. In 1878 one school system had a term of 220 days, while one township had only 60 days. Within some counties there were great differences. For example, in Cass County in 1876 terms in different townships ranged from 200 days to 80 days, while in Ripley County they ranged from

---

[31] The following table shows the progress in school building:

Year	Stone	Brick	Frame	Log	Total
1865	65	440	5,770	1,128	7,403
1872	88	877	7,568	547	9,080
1876	81	1,418	7,743	192	9,434

Indiana State Superintendent of Public Instruction, *Twentieth Report* (1871-1872), 39-40; *Twenty-Fourth Report* (1875-1876), 53.

[32] See Indiana State Superintendent of Public Instruction, *Twenty-Eighth Report* (1879-1880), 255-327, for descriptions and pictures of some typical buildings.

200 days to 96.[33] In the same period enrollment increased sharply. Figures in the reports of the state superintendent of public instruction (never too reliable) show an increase from 273,459 in 1863, to 390,714 in 1866, to 450,282 in 1870, and 511,283 in 1880. In 1863 the number of persons of school age (from five to twenty-one years) enrolled was less than 50 per cent of the total. By 1880 more than 70 per cent were enrolled.[34]

The vast majority of those attending school went to rural township schools. In 1879 it was estimated that 72 per cent of school enrollment was in townships, 19 per cent in cities, and 9 per cent in towns.[35] With very few exceptions the rural schools were one-room, one-teacher affairs and were ungraded. In some places pupils ranging in age from six to twenty might be found in the same room. Attendance at these schools was likely to be irregular and the teaching inferior. One of the most serious problems was the constant turnover of teachers. For a teacher to teach two years in the same school was said to be the exception rather than the rule.[36]

In his report in 1856 Caleb Mills warned against the multiplication of small districts. He recommended fewer and better schools and deplored the organization of units which were too poor to employ competent teachers. "Small districts," he said, "ensure small and ill furnished structures, short terms, incompetent teachers and corresponding instruction. . . ." In his message to the legislature in 1852 Mills had also advocated graded schools. "It is a maxim of funda-

[33] Indiana State Superintendent of Public Instruction, *Sixteenth Report* (1867-1868), 30; *Twenty-Fourth Report* (1875-1876), 31-33; *Twenty-Sixth Report* (1877-1878), 49; *Twenty-Eighth Report* (1879-1880), 204; Indiana *Laws,* 1861, p. 71.

[34] Indiana State Superintendent of Public Instruction, *Eleventh Annual Report* (1863), 6; *Fourteenth Report* (1865-1866), 6; *Eighteenth Report* (1869-1870), 32; *Twenty-Eighth Report* (1879-1880), 196. These figures represent enrollment and not actual attendance, which was lower.

[35] *Ibid., Twenty-Eighth Report,* p. 190.

[36] *Ibid., Twenty-Sixth Report* (1877-1878), 290.

mental and admitted importance in all scientific and industrial pursuits," he said, "that division of labor is true economy. . . . Graded schools are nothing more than an application of this principle to the business of teaching. . . ." By graded schools he meant schools "classified and arranged according to the attainment of the pupils."[37] The 1852 school law permitted but did not require township schools to set up graded systems. But graded schools were an impossibility in small districts where only one teacher was employed. The school law of 1873 authorized trustees of two or more district schools to establish consolidated graded schools. An act of 1877 extended the authority to consolidate to trustees of adjacent townships and adjacent counties if the patrons petitioned for it. But school patrons were reluctant to consolidate small districts into larger ones because it meant less local control and necessitated traveling longer distances. In 1876 the state superintendent declared that the small country school was the paramount educational problem in the state. He pointed out that the only schooling which most children would ever receive was in rural schools which were vastly inferior to the schools in the cities. In order to equalize educational opportunities he urged consolidation and the introduction of the graded system in country schools as well as longer terms and better trained teachers. But relatively little progress had been made in carrying out these recommendations before 1880.[38]

While country schools made little progress, the quality of education improved substantially in the city schools. When the city school systems began to revive following the debacle created by the Supreme Court decision of 1858, most of them adopted graded systems. In Indianapolis a new era began in 1863 with the appointment of Abram C. Shortridge as super-

[37] Indiana State Superintendent of Public Instruction, *Fourth Annual Report* (1856), 18; Moores, *Caleb Mills*, p. 615.

[38] Boone, *Education in Indiana*, pp. 291-293; Indiana *Laws*, 1873, pp. 74-75; 1877, p. 125; Indiana State Superintendent of Public Instruction, *Twenty-Fourth Report* (1875-1876), 80.

intendent of the schools. Shortridge remained in this post until 1874, when he resigned to become president of Purdue University. Under his leadership the foundations were laid for the system which has continued to the present. A twelve-year program consisting of three departments—primary, intermediate, and high school—each of which was subdivided into four grades was established. In 1867 evening classes for adults were inaugurated.[39] In Evansville a similar twelve-year program was in operation. Evansville had graded schools as early as 1853. At first boys and girls were taught in separate classes, but this practice was abandoned in 1875.[40]

About 1865 James H. Smart came to Fort Wayne from Toledo to become superintendent of the schools, a post he held until 1876 when he became state superintendent of public instruction. Graded schools had been begun in Fort Wayne as early as 1857, but under Smart a twelve-year system was established. In New Albany public schools, which had been closed during the war, were reorganized and reopened in 1864, but for several years growth was slow. Several private schools where well-to-do parents sent their children continued to operate. As late as 1870 only 28 per cent of the children of the city attended public schools. After that date nearly all of the private schools except the Catholic ones were closed and most children began to attend public schools. In the neighboring town of Jeffersonville the record was similar. Until after the war public education was almost nonexistent. Parents who could afford to do so sent their children to private schools, and public schools were regarded as charity schools, but after 1865 this situation began to change. At first boys and girls were taught in separate classes, but in 1874 a system was set up under which all pupils were graded by age and advancement and without regard to sex. In Terre

39 Littell, "Development of the City School System," *Indiana Magazine of History*, XII, 199; Indianapolis *Daily Sentinel* (Centennial Issue), February 22, 1876; Indiana State Superintendent of Public Instruction, *Twenty-Second Report* (1873-1874), 49-50; *Twenty-Sixth Report* (1877-1878), 315-316.

40 *Ibid., Twenty-Sixth Report*, pp. 320-321.

Haute the public school system really had its beginning in 1860, and by 1870, when there were ten school buildings in operation, it was firmly established.[41]

Introduction of a graded system made it possible to teach more subjects, but reading, writing, and arithmetic continued to be the core of the curriculum in all schools. In the rural, ungraded schools little except these traditional subjects was taught. The school law of 1855 required that prospective teachers know orthography, reading, writing, geography, and English grammar, and for many years these subjects constituted the basic elementary school curriculum. But the 1855 law also permitted the residents of a school district to determine what subjects they wished taught. This meant that all these subjects were taught only if the school patrons wanted them. The law of 1861 permitted the teaching of additional subjects if the voters in a township indicated they wanted them. In 1865 United States history and physiology were added to the list of the subjects. The 1869 school law prescribed the teaching of orthography, reading, writing, arithmetic, geography, English grammar, physiology, the history of the United States, and "good behavior." It also provided that schools might teach such other branches of learning and such languages as the advancement of the pupils required. It expressly provided that German was to be taught if twenty-five or more parents desired it. In the schools in the larger communities such subjects as drawing, vocal music, and elocution were being taught by the 1870's.[42]

There was general agreement that the schools had a responsibility to inculcate good morals as well as teach academic subjects. Hence the introduction of a subject called "good

[41] Indiana State Superintendent of Public Instruction, *Twenty-Sixth Report*, pp. 325-326, 331, 346, 348. In some of the smaller cities the schools differed very little from the rural township schools. Some cities did not begin a graded system for several years after the Civil War. Littell, "Development of the City School System," *Indiana Magazine of History*, XII, 299-301.

[42] Indiana *Laws*, 1855, pp. 176, 181; 1861, pp. 76-77; 1865, p. 13; 1869, p. 40; Littell, "Development of the City School System," *Indiana Magazine of History*, XII, 311-312.

behavior." The law of 1865 had declared that the Bible should "not be excluded from the Public Schools of the State," and the Bible was read in the schools and used as a textbook in the course in good behavior. In 1870 the state superintendent insisted that the law regarding the use of the Bible did not in any way encroach upon freedom of conscience because it did not compel any teacher to read it. He admitted that it was desirable to distinguish between "*omni*-denominational and sectarian teaching." But, he said, teachers who were prepared "under a sense of their obligation as Christian teachers and patriots to impress upon the minds of the future citizens the precepts and commandments of the Divine Lawgiver, with a view to inducing in such a fear of God, and a regard for man, and thus securing obedience to law, not only for '*wrath* but *for conscience's sake,*' render the most important service to the State which the teacher can perform."[43]

The Bible was apparently read in most schools, but not in all. One teacher protested when she was tendered a position on the condition that she *refrain* from having devotional exercises. This caused one schoolman to comment that whether the Bible should be read and prayer offered in the public schools depended upon the opinions of the people in the school district and the opinion of the teachers, "and these two conditions must harmonize, if good results shall follow."[44]

Another development of the post Civil War period was the opening of public schools to Negroes. Before 1869 school laws had expressly stated that public schools were open to white children only, and the Indiana Supreme Court had ruled

[43] Indiana State Superintendent of Public Instruction, *Eighteenth Report* (1869-1870), 15. Another State Superintendent expressed the opinion that "Christianity should be made the basis of our popular education." *Twentieth Report* (1871-1872), 91. The Indiana State Teachers Association at their first meeting in 1854 adopted a resolution "to use their utmost efforts to have the Bible introduced as a Reader or Class Book into every school in the state." Warren F. Collins, A History of the Indiana State Teachers' Association (Unpublished Master's thesis in Education, Indiana University, 1926), p. 16.

[44] *The Educationist* (Indianapolis), I, No. 7 (October, 1873), 2.

that colored children could not attend public school with white children even if they paid their own tuition. In consequence such schooling as Negro children received was in private schools maintained through the efforts of Negroes themselves with the help of certain white religious groups, especially Quakers. After the Civil War the need for educational opportunities for Negroes was increased as many former slaves moved into Indiana from the South. Out of their meager resources Negroes tried to maintain schools for both children and adults.[45]

Governor Oliver P. Morton strongly urged legislation to provide public schooling for Negroes in his message to the special session of the legislature in 1865. He reiterated his plea in 1867, and his successor, Conrad Baker, echoed him in 1869. Both the Indiana State Teachers Association and the state superintendent of public instruction supported public schools for Negroes on the grounds that the welfare of the state demanded education for all children. These pleas were met by the traditional white supremacy arguments in the legislature, but finally the special session of 1869 passed an act which required school trustees to organize separate schools for colored children where their numbers were large enough to justify such a school. School districts might be consolidated for this purpose, but where there were not enough colored children to justify a separate school, trustees were permitted to "provide such other means of education for said children as shall use their proportion, according to numbers, of school revenue to the best advantage."[46]

During the next few years the communities where there were substantial numbers of Negroes proceeded to establish separate schools for them. By 1873 the state superintendent reported that he knew of no county where separate schools had not been provided where the number of colored children was large enough to support a school. In some places, where

---

[45] Thornbrough, *Negro in Indiana,* pp. 160-182, 317-320.

[46] *Ibid.,* pp. 320-323; Indiana *Laws,* special session, 1869, p. 41.

their numbers were smaller, colored children were admitted to the same schools as whites. But arrangements of this sort were upset by a decision of the Indiana Supreme Court in 1874. In a case involving Negro children who lived in a township in which there was no separate school for them, Judge Samuel H. Buskirk ruled that they could not attend the same school with white children, "because the legislature has not provided for the admission of colored children into the same school with white children, in any contingency." In the absence of express legislative action the courts were declared to have no authority to admit Negro children.[47]

As a consequence of this decision, the legislature amended the law in 1877 to provide that school authorities might still maintain separate school systems for white and colored pupils, but where there were no separate schools the "colored children shall be allowed to attend the public schools with white children." After the enactment of this measure, which permitted segregation but did not make it mandatory, communities with the largest numbers of Negroes continued to maintain separate schools. Counties in the southern part of the state maintained segregated schools even where the number of Negro children was very small, but in some parts of the state Negro children were admitted to the same schools with white children.[48]

In spite of the progress made in the postwar years toward a system of free schools for all children, Indiana continued to have a higher rate of illiteracy than other northern states. The 1870 census showed that 7½ per cent of the population could not read or write.[49] Most of the illiterates were adults,

---

[47] Thornbrough, *Negro in Indiana*, p. 325; Cory et al *v.* Carter, 48 Ind. 327-329 (1874).

[48] Indiana *Laws*, 1877, p. 124; Thornbrough, *Negro in Indiana*, pp. 329, 336.

[49] Indiana State Superintendent of Public Instruction, *Twentieth Report* (1871-1872), 95. In 1880 the census showed that 4.8 per cent of the population was unable to read, and 7.5 per cent unable to write. These percentages were higher in Indiana than in any other state in the Old Northwest but substantially lower than in Kentucky. United States Bureau of the Census, *Compendium of the Tenth Census* (1880), 1645.

but the persistence of illiteracy was advanced as a reason for strengthening the elementary schools and for making attendance compulsory. In 1872 State Superintendent Milton B. Hopkins called for a "judicious" compulsory attendance law. Its adoption, he claimed, would mark a new and better era in educational matters, and "erase from the Census Reports the figures that tell the disgraceful story of our illiteracy." Furthermore, such legislation, would be especially beneficial for orphans and other neglected children who were then denied an education because attendance was not compulsory.[50]

The proposal was premature. Public opinion was not ready for it. Hopkins was a Democrat, but the leading Democratic newspaper protested against compulsory schooling. It would mean, said the Indianapolis *Sentinel,* that the state would not only have to furnish schoolhouses, teachers, and books but would also have to furnish clothing and food for indigent pupils. The Terre Haute *Journal* indignantly protested that it wanted "no minions of Federal or State power to coerce the people in the matter of education or religion." On the other hand, the Indianapolis *Journal* consistently supported compulsory attendance. When Hopkins first made his proposal it declared: "Every child born in the United States is entitled to an education, and neither the poverty nor selfishness of its parents should be allowed to deprive it of this essential to good citizenship." The argument that compulsory schooling interfered with personal liberty the *Journal* rejected. Such legislation, it said, in reality sought to protect the individual from the consequences of ignorance and thereby protected his liberty. "It is a great folly," it said, "for the state to build school-houses and employ teachers and then

[50] Indiana State Superintendent of Public Instruction, *Twentieth Report* (1871-1872), 117. The Indianapolis *Daily Journal,* November 14, 1872, blamed the poor literacy record of Indiana on the country schools. It called for legislation to insure longer school terms.

allow those, above all others, who should be educated to remain in ignorance. . . ."[51]

Several bills for compulsory education were introduced in the legislature during the seventies, but none of them were adopted. A bill requiring children between the ages of eight and fourteen years to attend a school or be instructed at home at least fourteen weeks in each year was introduced in the Senate in 1877 and was recommended for passage by the committee on education. But it failed to pass for lack of a constitutional majority.[52]

§ § §

In the middle of the nineteenth century clear-cut distinctions between elementary and secondary education and between secondary and higher education had not yet developed, but until after the Civil War most of the work equivalent to modern secondary education was carried on in private academies. Nearly all of the colleges in the state also had preparatory departments in which the enrollment frequently exceeded the enrollment in the colleges themselves. The court decisions already mentioned which limited the power of local governments to tax for school purposes had the effect of retarding the growth of public secondary schools and gave an impetus to the establishment of private schools. After the Civil War public high schools, which had begun on a small scale in the 1850's, increased in number and gradually absorbed or replaced the private schools.

Academies were so numerous and so varied in character that it is difficult to generalize about them. The history of most of them was short, but a few remained in operation for many years, although not always continuously. It was not

[51] Indianapolis *Daily Sentinel,* January 2, 1872; Indianapolis *Daily Journal,* January 3, 1872, January 12, 1875; Terre Haute *Journal,* quoted *ibid.,* January 9, 1872.

[52] Indiana *Senate Journal,* 1877, p. 935. In his last report James H. Smart, Superintendent of Public Instruction, renewed his plea for a compulsory attendance law. Indiana State Superintendent of Public Instruction, *Twenty-Eighth Report* (1879-1880), 9. But Indiana failed to adopt such legislation until 1897.

uncommon for a school to be closed after a few years and later to reopen. Some of the academies were formerly county seminaries which were sold by the state as provided for in the 1852 school law and then operated as private institutions. Many academies were founded and directed by religious groups. Many of them were the outgrowth of earlier elementary schools, and most of them offered elementary as well as secondary programs. Some of them were boarding schools, some were day schools. Some were coeducational, some were not. Some academies were founded before 1850, but more seem to have been established in the fifties than during any other period. Among Protestant denominations Quakers and Presbyterians appear to have been most interested in education. By 1850 several schools operating under their direction were in operation. Methodists and Baptists, although more numerous in Indiana than other denominations, were slower to establish academies.

Among the institutions founded by the Society of Friends mention should be made of Spiceland Academy, the Friends' Academy at Carthage, Bloomingdale Academy in Parke County, Blue River Academy in Washington County, Farmers' Institute in Lafayette, and the Westfield Friends Academy. Two schools for the training of Negroes were founded by the Friends—Union Literary Institute in Randolph County and White's Indiana Manual Labor Institute near Wabash.[53]

Presbyterians were responsible for Delaney Academy in Newburgh, Waveland Academy in Montgomery County, Fort Wayne Academy, White Water Presbyterian Academy in Union County, and the excellent Hopewell Academy in Johnson County.[54] Methodist institutions included Brookville

---

[53] Sadie Bacon Hatcher, *A History of Spiceland Academy, 1826-1921* (Indiana Historical Society *Publications*, XI, No. 2, Indianapolis, 1934), pp. 62, 123, 128; Smart, *The Indiana Schools*, p. 161; Ethel Hittle McDaniel, *The Contribution of the Society of Friends to Education in Indiana* (Indiana Historical Society *Publications*, XIII, No. 2, Indianapolis, 1939), pp. 190-191, 196, 197-199, 200, 202-203; Thornbrough, *Negro in Indiana*, pp. 173-178; Boone, *Education in Indiana*, pp. 227-228.

[54] Darby and Jenkins, *Cumberland Presbyterianism in Southern Indiana,*

College, Stockwell Institute near Lafayette, the Battle Ground
Collegiate Institute, Wesley Academy in Montgomery County,
Thorntown Academy, and Rockport Academy.[55] The Baptists
operated Orland Academy near Angola. Eleutherian Institute
in Jefferson County was founded by a Baptist minister, the
Reverend Thomas Craven. A center of antislavery activity,
it was attended prodominantly by whites, but also by a few
Negroes, some from slave states.[56] Ladoga Academy was
founded by the Disciples of Christ as were Wayne County
Seminary at Centerville, Howard College at Kokomo, and
Fairview Academy in Fayette County.[57]

Most academies were coeducational, but a few were exclusively for girls. In Indianapolis there was the Indiana
Female College, in Greencastle the Asbury Female Institute,
and in Bloomington the Bloomington Female College and
Academy, all Methodist institutions. The Presbyterian
schools for girls included the Presbyterian Female College at
Salem and the Female College at Greencastle.[58] More typical

pp. 104-107; John Hardin Thomas, "The Academies of Indiana," *Indiana
Magazine of History*, X (1914), 350-356. For a more complete list see Albert
Mock, The Mid-Western Academy Movement: A Comprehensive Study of
Indiana Academies 1810-1900 (Mimeographed. Copyright, 1949, by the author),
p. 35.

[55] Herbert Heller, *Indiana Conference of the Methodist Church, 1836-1956*
(Greencastle, Ind., 1956), pp. 322, 326; Jack J. Detzler, *History of the North-
west Conference of the Methodist Church 1852-1951* (Nashville, Tenn., 1953),
pp. 55-58; George B. Manhart, *DePauw through the Years* (2 volumes,
Greencastle, Ind., 1962), I, 111; Thomas, "The Academies of Indiana," *Indiana
Magazine of History*, XI (1915), 17-20; Boone, *Education in Indiana*, p. 230.
See Mock, The Mid-Western Academy Movement, pp. 31-32, for a list of
Methodist academies founded between 1850 and 1860.

[56] Thomas, "The Academies of Indiana," *Indiana Magazine of History*,
XI, 23-24; Thornbrough, *Negro in Indiana*, pp. 178-180; William C. Thompson,
"Eleutherian Institute. A Sketch of a Unique Step in the Educational History
of Indiana," *Indiana Magazine of History*, XIX (1923), 107-131; Mock, The
Mid-Western Academy Movement, p. 37.

[57] Thomas, "The Academies of Indiana," *Indiana Magazine of History*,
XI, 26-28; Henry K. Shaw, "The Founding of Butler University, 1847-1855,"
ibid., LVIII (1962), 235.

[58] Heller, *Indiana Conference*, pp. 321-324; Manhart, *DePauw through the*

were academies for girls which were nonsectarian although sometimes conducted by clergymen. Outstanding was the Wolcottville Seminary, conducted by Miss Susan Griggs of Vermont, between 1852 and 1868.[59]

Most academies offered very much the same courses regardless of whether they were coeducational or not or whether they had a religious affiliation or not. The typical curriculum included academic subjects and also "normal subjects" for the preparation of teachers.[60] Usual academic courses were algebra, geometry, Latin, sometimes Greek and French, and some courses in science, perhaps "natural history" or "natural philosophy," or chemistry, geology, or botany. Courses in "Evidences of Christianity" and "moral philosophy" were required, while a practical course such as bookkeeping might be offered.[61] A few strictly business and commercial schools were opened, including the Indianapolis Business University, the Richmond Business College, the Terre Haute Commercial College, the Star City Business College of Lafayette, and Hall's Business College of Logansport. There were also some "Farmer's Academies" which stressed agriculture and industrial arts.[62]

In general the policy of Protestant churches was to support private schools only where there were no adequate public schools. By the 1870's most of the Protestant-sponsored

Years, I, 77; Thomas, "The Academies of Indiana," Indiana Magazine of History, XI, 20-21; First Annual Circular of the Presbyterian Female College, Salem, Washington Co., Ind. (New Albany, Ind., 1851); Female College, Greencastle, Annual Catalogue, 1870-1871, 1871-1872; Mock, Mid-Western Academy Movement, p. 35.

[59] Boone, Education in Indiana, pp. 222, 225.

[60] Terre Haute Female College, Fourth Annual Catalogue, 1862; Rockport Collegiate Institute, Annual Catalogue, 1866-1867; Brookville College, Eighth Annual Catalogue, 1858-1859.

[61] See, for example, Thomas, "The Academies of Indiana," Indiana Magazine of History, XI, 21, and passim; McDaniel, The Contribution of the Society of Friends to Education, pp. 186-88, 192, 198; catalogues of the academies.

[62] Boone, Education in Indiana, pp. 222-223, 226.

academies either had disappeared or been absorbed into the public school system. In contrast the number of schools established by the Roman Catholics continued to grow even after public schools, both elementary and secondary, were well established because they were regarded as important adjuncts of the Church in the teaching of religion. By midcentury it was estimated that one fourth of the parishes in Indiana had schools, and as the Catholic population increased in the fifties, the number of parochial schools increased. Some of them were taught by the parish priest, some by lay teachers, and others by members of the teaching orders. The Sisters of Providence were operating schools in Terre Haute, Madison, Jasper, and Fort Wayne, while the Sisters of St. Francis opened a village school in Oldenburg in 1851, and in 1855 began to establish schools in nearby communities. Protestant children sometimes attended these schools, perhaps paying a higher tuition than the Catholic pupils. In a few places Catholic schools were supported in part by public funds. A law passed by the Indiana legislature in 1849 provided that where schools had been established by "private liberality" it was lawful for township trustees to recognize them as public schools and to make such allowance for them as they considered "just and equitable." This law was interpreted as applying to Catholic parochial schools. As a result, in some of the counties where the percentage of Catholics was highest, as in Dubois and Franklin counties and part of Knox, parish schools were supported as public schools.[63]

Catholic boarding schools for girls were established in a number of towns mainly by the Sisters of Providence, though the Sisters of St. Francis and Sisters of the Holy Cross were

[63] Mary Carol Schroeder, *The Catholic Church in the Diocese of Vincennes, 1847-1877* (Washington, D. C., 1946), pp. 124, 126-129, 131-133; Sister Mary Borromeo Brown, *The History of the Sisters of Providence of Saint Mary-of-the-Woods* (New York, 1949); Indiana *General Laws,* 1848-1849, p. 130. For examples of schools founded by Catholics, see Charles Blanchard (ed. and comp.), *History of the Catholic Church in Indiana* (2 volumes, Logansport, Ind., 1898), I, 499-502, 504-505, 509-511, 514, 517-519.

responsible for a few. Brothers of the Holy Cross conducted a number of schools for boys, usually day schools.[64]

As the system of public education became firmly established some Catholic parents began to send their children to the public schools which they paid taxes to support, but the church authorities objected and insisted that parents had an obligation to give their children a truly religious education. Bishop de St. Palais of the Vincennes Diocese considered the question of such importance that he devoted his entire Lenten pastoral letter of 1872 to it. "We object to the public school," he said, "on account of the infidel source from which they originated. We object to these schools because the teacher of religion is excluded from them, and such exclusion will inevitably produce religious indifference, if not infidelity." The bishop also voiced objection to the "promiscuous assembling of both sexes" in the public schools at the secondary level, a practice which was avoided in the Catholic schools. Priests were instructed to refuse absolution to parents who had the means to send their children to Catholic schools but failed to do so out of "worldly motives."[65]

§ § § §

The public was slower to accept the obligation of paying taxes to support public secondary schools than to support elementary schools. During the 1850's several towns made a beginning of including high schools or high school departments in their graded systems, but most of these efforts were short-lived.

Madison opened a high school in 1852, New Albany opened one in 1854, Richmond in 1856. In 1855 or 1856 there was a high school in Evansville. This was one of the few established during the fifties which had a continuous

---

[64] Schroeder, *Catholic Church in the Diocese of Vincennes,* pp. 127, 188-90; Thomas "The Academies of Indiana," *Indiana Magazine of History,* XI, 31-34; Mock, Mid-Western Academy Movement, p. 28; Blanchard, *Catholic Church in Indiana,* I, 538, 577-578. See Boone, *Education in Indiana,* pp. 222-223, for the names of Catholic secondary schools founded in this period.

[65] Schroeder, *Catholic Church in the Diocese of Vincennes,* pp. 187-189.

existence. In Indianapolis a high school was opened in 1857, but was closed the following year as the result of the decision of the Supreme Court which denied cities and towns the power to levy taxes for school purposes. Most of the other infant high schools suffered a similar fate.[66]

During the sixties several schools which had closed were reopened while other cities opened high school departments for the first time. In 1864 the Indianapolis High School was reopened with a principal and one teacher but no regular building. By 1872 it had seven teachers, and by 1876 sixteen. At that date it had an enrollment of 485, the largest enrollment in the state. By the seventies all towns of any size had some sort of high school, and some townships had high school departments. Most of the high schools were small, with enrollments of less than one hundred, and a relatively small percentage of those who entered graduated. In spite of small enrollments in some places there were efforts at teaching boys and girls in separate classes. But after a short time these efforts were abandoned as being too costly, and coeducation became general. By 1874 there were reported to be seventy-eight high schools in the cities and incorporated towns of the state, but not all of these were separate schools. Some of them were merely departments.[67]

[66] Littell, "Development of the City School System," *Indiana Magazine of History,* XII, 303-307; Indiana State Superintendent of Public Instruction, *Twenty-Sixth Report* (1877-1878), 321, 344-345. In 1859 there were reported to be 73 high schools in the state; in 1863, 103 were reported. *Ibid., Eighth Annual Report* (1859), 5; *Eleventh Annual Report* (1863), 6. The meaning of these figures is not clear. Certainly there were not those numbers of separate high schools. The figures probably refer in some cases to "high school departments" in the graded schools.

[67] Littell, "Development of the City School System," *Indiana Magazine of History,* XII, 308; Oscar Findley, *Development of the High School in Indiana* (n.p., 1925), p. 48; Boone, *Education in Indiana,* pp. 302-303. See table, *ibid.,* p. 303, showing dates for founding of high schools which were established between 1850 and 1876. See Littell, *op. cit.,* p. 310, for figures showing the size of the enrollment in some typical high schools and the number of graduates. Knightstown and New Albany were among the towns in which classes were separated by sex for a time.

It is impossible to define with any precision just what a high school was in these early years. High schools owed their legal existence to the legislation which permitted graded schools, and they were simply a part of the graded system; the law made no separate provision for them. The school law of 1861 permitted cities and towns "to provide for admission into the higher departments of the graded schools of their township such pupils as are sufficiently advanced for such admission." In 1869 the state association of school superintendents agreed that only pupils who had passed examinations in all the branches of study which were included in the prescribed courses for the common schools should be counted as belonging to the high schools. In some places there appear to have been rigid entrance examinations; in others entrance appeared to depend mostly on age. In general the age level of those in attendance was higher than at present. Some early high school students were persons who already had experience as teachers.[68]

There was no general agreement as to the purpose and function of the high school. Some persons saw them as substitutes for colleges. For example, in 1856 the board of trustees of the Lafayette schools expressed the hope of establishing a high school "endowed with every faculty for an advanced or collegiate education, so that the children of our city may be kept under the influence of good examples and just restraints of home until prepared to take their parts in the active duties of life." But while some looked upon high schools as a substitute for colleges they were more widely regarded as being for the purpose of preparing students for college, and their curriculum was largely designed for this. In practice early high schools performed their most important function in preparing teachers and were thus in some respect like a normal school. Most of the early graduates of the Indianapolis High School became teachers.[69]

[68] Indiana *Laws,* 1861, pp. 70-71; Findley, *op. cit.,* p. 78; Littell, *op. cit.,* p. 310.

[69] Littell, *op. cit.,* p. 305; Indianapolis *Daily Sentinel* (Centennial Issue),

There was no uniform course of study. For example, the course of study in the New Albany High School was so different from that in the Indianapolis High School that it was almost impossible for a student to transfer from one school to the other. In most places subjects for teacher training were offered—arithmetic, reading, spelling, and theories of teaching. But the emphasis was upon academic subjects of the sort taught in the older academies and required for college entrance. During the late sixties and the early seventies there was a protracted discussion as to the relationship of the high school to the college, especially as to the extent to which the high school curriculum should be college preparatory. Much of the discussion centered on whether public high schools should spend money to teach pupils Greek, which the colleges required for admission. At a meeting of high school superintendents in 1873 it was agreed that high schools should not be expected to offer Greek, and it was recommended that the study of advanced mathematics be accepted by the colleges as an equivalent of Greek. As the result of this pressure from the public schools Indiana University dropped the requirement of Greek for admission, but the private institutions retained it.[70]

Greek was taught in only a few public high schools, but nearly all high schools emphasized Latin. German was also taught in the larger schools. English grammar, composition, literature, and rhetoric were usually taught, although at first some persons who wanted to emphasize the college preparatory subjects wanted to subordinate English to foreign languages. Algebra and plane geometry were taught in most schools, while the larger schools also offered trigonometry. There was relatively little emphasis on science, but "natural history," which was zoology, was widely taught. The Indi-

February 22, 1876. In 1876 more than half of the students in the Indianapolis High School were girls, a large percentage of whom were preparing to become teachers.

[70] *The Educationist,* I, No. 1 (April, 1873), 1; Findley, *Development of the High School,* pp. 58-62.

anapolis High School and a few others offered chemistry and botany. Little emphasis was placed on United States history because it was taught in the elementary schools, but courses in "general history" were widely offered. Courses in philosophy and "moral" philosophy were also taught. The usual high school course required four years, but in 1875, because relatively few pupils were able to complete the four-year course, the Indianapolis High School introduced a two-year course of study which included commercial arithmetic, bookkeeping, and commercial law and omitted foreign languages.[71]

During the seventies public high schools came under severe attack, partly because of the economic depression which caused protests against anything which might be regarded as "extravagance" and partly because there was no general agreement as to what function the high schools were performing or should perform. In 1875 the *Indiana School Journal,* organ of the Indiana State Teachers Association, noted that there was "rapidly growing sentiment among several different classes of society, of opposition to Free High Schools and Colleges as a part of the public school system." Some persons contended that the state was obligated to provide only so much education as was necessary to make good citizens, and that a common school education fulfilled this need. Because relatively few persons attended high school it was argued that all the people should not be taxed to support them.[72]

The Republican Indianapolis *Journal,* which staunchly supported the movement to make elementary schooling compulsory, questioned whether or not public money should be spent on some of the courses offered in the high schools. "It is hardly to be supposed," it said, "that the founders of the [public school] system ever imagined that the time would come when the dead languages and higher sciences would be

[71] Findley, *Development of the High School,* pp. 101, 113, 130, 136-139, 141-142; Littell, "Development of the City School System," *Indiana Magazine of History,* XII, 311-317.

[72] Findley, *op. cit.,* p. 42; Indiana State Superintendent of Public Instruction, *Twenty-Fourth Report* (1875-1876), 103.

taught in these schools and that academies and seminaries would be virtually superseded by them." The *Journal* felt that for the public schools to prepare pupils for college was "beyond the original plan and purpose of the system," which was established merely "to furnish the people with a simple, practical education in English. . . ." The Republican state platform in 1876 said that it was the duty of the state to provide a common school education, but no more. Instead of preparing pupils for college, it said, the public schools should be "what they were designed to be, the schools of the people." In their platform in 1876 the Democrats spoke in more general terms on education, avoiding committing themselves directly on the question of public high schools. They pledged continued support for common schools and denounced Republicans as being enemies of the public school system.[73]

In the 1879 session of the legislature one senator expressed the opinion that the spending of state money for high schools and state colleges was a violation of the constitution and proposed prohibiting the expenditure of public money for other than common schools. He declared that only three or four students out of fifty or sixty ever graduated from high school. Nearly all of those who did graduate then became teachers. The training of teachers he felt was not a function of the state. "In other words," he said, "the State is called upon to keep up schools for the manufacture of teachers. The State might as well educate lawyers, doctors, or blacksmiths."[74]

The state superintendent tried to defend the public high schools by insisting that they were an integral part of the

[73] Indianapolis *Daily Journal*, March 28, 1876, quoted in Carmichael, "Campaign of 1876 in Indiana," *Indiana Magazine of History*, IX, 278; *Indiana Republican Hand Book . . . 1876*, pp. 50, 54.

[74] *Brevier Legislative Reports*, XVII (1879), 76. Another senator insisted that the state had done its duty when it supplied a common school education. *Ibid.*, p. 77.

common school system and that they did not replace the colleges. Their purpose, he said, was "to lay the foundations of knowledge merely." But so great was the clamor against the high schools that school systems were forced to take cognizance of it. It was reported that in 1878 the school trustees in Fort Wayne "abolished the name of high school, as exciting opposition and carrying no strength." The schools were declared to be organized into "primary, intermediate and grammar grades." The change, it was said, "was not intended either to lower the standard or reduce the extent of the work." In Indianapolis the school board responded to charges that the high school was impractical and an extravagance by appointing a committee to consider whether or not the high school should be continued and whether or not its curriculum should be modified. The committee report said that it discountenanced the continuance of anything "having the appearance of extravagance," but it recommended the continuation of the high school as it existed. The high school was defended as the "poor man's college" and was declared to create a powerful incentive to the poor to progress. Moreover, said the report, a good high school caused the wealthier parents to send their children to public schools and this had the effect of strengthening public education. A minority of the committee recommended that German and the "dead" languages be dropped from the curriculum, and the entire committee recommended that these subjects be made purely elective.[75]

The attacks on the public high schools which began during the depression appear to have subsided with the return of more prosperous times. In 1885 the state superintendent of public instruction confidently asserted: "The high school argument has been made, the fight has been fought in this

---

[75] Indiana State Superintendent of Public Instruction, *Twenty-Fourth Report* (1875-1876), 107-108; *Twenty-Sixth Report* (1877-1878), 327; Indianapolis *Daily Journal*, May 4, 1878.

State, and the high school is accepted as an essential part of our common school system."[76]

§ § § § §

In his first address to the legislature in 1847 Caleb Mills made a plea for legislation which would lead to a force of teachers of "well trained minds and unblemished morals." He warned against the damage to future generations of placing children "under the instruction of those whose *incompetency* is as notorious as the paltry and contemptible sum they demand for their services." At the time that Mills wrote, incompetency and paltry pay and inadequate numbers were conspicuous characteristics of the teaching system in Indiana. In the years which followed Mills's message there were marked improvements in the training of teachers and some increase in the pay which they received for their services, especially in the schools in the cities and towns. But thirty years after Mills made his plea the competency and pay of teachers in the rural schools remained notoriously low. As late as 1876, according to the report of the state superintendent of public instruction, few country school teachers had ever attended high school and fewer still had had any professional training. They learned to teach, he said, "if at all, at the expense of the children." He deplored the "popular opinion that anybody can teach a country school," but it was an opinion which continued to be widely held to the detriment of the schools.[77]

The school law of 1852 provided that the state superintendent or his deputies (of whom there was to be one in each county) should examine all applicants for teachers' licenses. Licenses were to be valid for two years but could be revoked for incompetency. The law provided that no teacher was to be employed who was not of good moral character, but it

[76] Findley, *Development of the High School,* p. 45.

[77] Moores, *Caleb Mills,* pp. 454-455; Indiana State Superintendent of Public Instruction, *Twenty-Fourth Report* (1875-1876), 84-85.

did not prescribe the subject matter in which the prospective teacher was to be examined. The law of 1855 specified that common school teachers were to know orthography, reading, writing, arithmetic, geography, and English grammar. The 1861 law provided that prospective teachers should be examined in other subjects if the voters of the township wished additional subjects taught. As noted earlier, by the 1865 law elementary teachers were also required to be able to teach physiology and United States history.[78]

By the 1870's a more elaborate system of licensing had been developed under which there were different grades of licenses for persons who expected to teach in the higher grades, including high school. One type of license required examinations in English composition, natural philosophy, the Constitution of the United States, and morals. In addition to these subjects an applicant for a first-grade license was required to be examined in algebra, geometry, botany, general history, rhetoric, and zoology, but inasmuch as the vast majority of teachers continued to teach in ungraded rural schools few qualified for these licenses.[79]

Under the law of 1852 township trustees were authorized to employ teachers in township schools, but the law of 1855 gave the residents of a school district the right to designate the teacher whom they wished to be employed, and trustees were prohibited from hiring a teacher whom the residents did not want. This provision remained in effect until 1873. In cities and towns teachers were hired by school boards.[80]

A dearth of qualified teachers and the lack of facilities for training teachers were among the most serious obstacles to the establishment of adequate schools. There were few people who applied to take the examinations for teachers' licenses. In 1853 the state superintendent estimated that there were

78 Indiana *Revised Statutes,* 1852, I, 450-454; *Laws,* 1855, p. 181; 1861, pp. 76-77.

79 Indiana State Superintendent of Public Instruction, *Twenty-Second Report* (1873-1874), 52-53.

80 *Ibid.,* p. 42; Indiana *Laws,* 1855, p. 176.

not more than half enough qualified teachers available to fill the schools which were being opened. Among the better-trained teachers in this period were persons who had attended private academies. As already shown, many of these institutions included normal departments. In the years after the Civil War public high schools trained many teachers. Some cities also conducted special training classes in which prospective teachers received "in service" training.[81]

The most acute need was for a system of preparing teachers for the rural schools. In the address to the General Assembly in 1852 Caleb Mills recommended a system of teachers' institutes to fill this need. William C. Larrabee, the first state superintendent, echoed this plea, urging that institutes be held annually in each county. Institutes of the sort which Mills and Larrabee recommended had been introduced earlier in the eastern states. During the course of a few days or weeks intensive instruction was given in subject matter and methods of teaching. Mills also pleaded for normal schools established by the state. Governor Joseph A. Wright in his message to the legislature in 1857 urged that the state assume some responsibility for the training of teachers, pointing out that the state had never appropriated a single dollar for this purpose. Wright recommended both teachers' institutes and a normal school, but the legislature failed to take any action until after the Civil War.[82]

In the meantime, without the assistance of state funds, a number of county and regional teachers' institutes had been begun. An institute, modeled on those in the East, was held in Ontario, in La Grange County, in 1846. Beginning in 1849 a Northern Indiana Teachers Institute was held regularly for several years, drawing teachers from southern Michigan

---

[81] Indiana State Superintendent of Public Instruction, *Second Annual Report* (1853), 11-12; Littell, "Development of the City School System," *Indiana Magazine of History*, XII, 318-320.

[82] Moores, *Caleb Mills*, pp. 609-610; Indiana State Superintendent of Public Instruction, *First Annual Report* (1852), 33-34; *Second Annual Report* (1853), 14; Indiana *Senate Journal*, 1857, p. 59.

as well as Indiana. By 1852 sixteen sessions of two weeks each had been held with more than five hundred persons in attendance. In 1854 an institute was held in Wayne County, and the following year a six weeks' institute was held in Sullivan County. Beginning in 1858 a series of institutes were held in the towns along the Monon Railroad in Putnam and Montgomery counties. Teachers' associations, and especially the Indiana State Teachers Association, which was founded in 1854, gave an impetus to the institutes. In 1860 the State Teachers Association appointed a special committee in each congressional district for the purpose of establishing an institute in every county in the state. As a result the number of institutes increased.[83]

All of these early institutes were financed out of private funds, with teachers giving their services voluntarily. In 1865 the legislature passed a measure requiring that at least one institute be held in each county each year for which a small sum was to be appropriated by the county. The money expended was paltry—only $35.00 for an institute attended by twenty teachers, $50.00 when forty attended—but the legislation resulted in a rapid increase in the number of institutes. The state superintendent claimed these meetings, which were the only professional training which many teachers received, produced good results out of proportion to the small amount of money expended on them.[84]

In 1865 the legislature also finally provided for the establishment of a state normal school—a measure which had been urged for years by successive state superintendents and by the State Teachers Association. The law provided that the school should be located in the city which offered the largest donation, provided that at least $50,000 was offered. A committee from Terre Haute offered this amount of money plus real estate (the site of the old county seminary), and accordingly the school was located there. In 1867 the legislature

83 Smart, *The Indiana Schools,* pp. 120-122.
84 *Ibid.,* p. 122; Indiana *Laws,* 1865, pp. 35-36.

Indiana Cotton Mills, Cannelton
Designed by Thomas A. Tefft (1826-1859) of Rhode Island

A Country School. *By Winslow Homer*

Wise & Wilers, Drygoods Establishment, Lafayette, 1876

New Albany from the Kentucky and Indiana Bridge, 1880

appropriated $50,000 for construction and made an additional appropriation at the next session. The school was opened in 1870 with a two-year course of study which emphasized the subjects taught in the common schools. There were only thirty-nine students enrolled during the first term, and at first growth was slow. Enrollments varied, but by 1880 they averaged about three hundred per term. The largest class to graduate prior to 1880 included only twenty persons. In addition to the State Normal School several private normal schools were opened. Some of them also gave business and commercial courses. Among them were Northern Indiana Normal at Valparaiso, founded in 1873, and Central Indiana Normal School at Ladoga and Central Normal College and Commercial Institute at Danville, both of which were founded in 1876.[85]

Although opportunities for training had expanded somewhat, there remained a lack of qualified persons who were ready to make teaching their lifework. Miserable pay and short school terms and the greater financial rewards offered in other occupations caused many persons to regard teaching as a temporary vocation. Many young men taught for a year or two and then went into other work. The dearth of men teachers caused women to be hired in increasing numbers. When public schools were first opened nearly all of the teachers were men, some of whom were hired because of their physical prowess rather than their academic qualifications. In his first report, W. C. Larrabee, the first state superintendent, recommended the employment of women and tried to allay prejudice against them. He insisted that women were as capable as men of learning the subjects taught in the school and that by personality and temperament they were peculiarly suited to teach. "I have yet to learn that *intellect* is capable

85 Indiana *Laws*, special session 1865, pp. 140-142; Indiana State Superintendent of Public Instruction, *Twenty-Fourth Report* (1875-1876), 122, 124-128; William O. Lynch, *A History of Indiana State Teachers College [Indiana State Normal School 1870-1929]* (Terre Haute, 1946), pp. 1, 14, 15, 18, 30, 31, 40-41, 71, 91-92; Boone, *Education in Indiana*, pp. 434-437.

of sexual classifications and distinctions," he said. Women, he thought, were especially well adapted to teach in the graded schools—at both the primary and secondary levels.[86]

By 1859, 20 per cent of the teachers in the state were women. By 1864, as the result of manpower shortages created by the Civil War, 42 per cent were women. The necessity of hiring women was defended as a blessing in disguise by the wartime state superintendent. "We need not lament the necessity which is working this change," he said. "I think we should early encourage it, and draw largely upon the female portion of the community for a supply of teachers. With female teachers, their gentleness, patience, and kindness of their dispositions, their sympathies with the feelings, aspirations, foibles, playfulness and vagaries of children, well fit them to become their guides and instructors during the season of childhood." He also pointed out that women were more likely to remain permanently in the teaching occupation than were men.[87] During the years after the war there was a sharp increase in the number of both male and female teachers. There was probably a slight decline in the proportion of women, but during the seventies the percentage of women teachers continued to be about 40 per cent of the whole.[88]

[86] Indiana State Superintendent of Public Instruction, *First Annual Report* (1852), 19.

[87] Indiana State Superintendent of Public Instruction, *Thirteenth Report* (1863-1864), 30; *Eleventh Annual Report* (1861-1862), 14.

[88] The following table shows the increase in the number of teachers of both sexes.

Year	Total Men	Total Women	Total
1854	2,432	666	3,098
1866	5,330	4,163	9,493
1870	7,104	4,722	11,826
1880	7,802	5,776	13,578

Indiana State Superintendent of Public Instruction, *Third Annual Report* (1854), 29; *Sixteenth Report* (1867-1868), 30; *Eighteenth Report* (1869-1870), 32; *Twenty-Eighth Report* (1879-1880), 219.

As the public school system became more firmly established, pay for teachers increased somewhat, but teaching continued to be an occupation which was poorly paid and seasonal in character because of the shortness of the school term in many places. In his first address to the legislature Caleb Mills had made a plea for pay for teachers which would be commensurate with their services. He spoke of the "obvious incongruity between a proper appreciation of literary worth and moral excellence, and the pitiful compensation generally accorded to its services in this department of labor [teaching]."[89] But public opinion continued to sanction the incongruity, and little was done to make teaching, especially in rural schools, an occupation which would attract trained persons.

Nevertheless, the amount of money spent on teachers' salaries increased sharply. From such figures as are available it appears that total annual expenditures for this purpose rose from $239,924 in 1855 to $3,065,968 in 1878—more than a tenfold increase. In the same period the average annual pay per teacher rose from about $73.00 to $253.00. But such figures have little meaning. There were wide variations in the amount paid in various systems. In 1878 the state superintendent reported that many teachers were paid only about $144 per year and that few teachers were employed more than four months a year.[90] There were wide variations in the amount of pay in the different school systems. Teachers in the rural schools fared much worse than those in towns and cities. Their average daily pay was smaller and the length of the school term was shorter. In the 1870's it appeared that the average daily pay of men teachers in the

---

[89] Moores, *Caleb Mills*, p. 453.

[90] Indiana State Superintendent of Public Instruction, *Twenty-Sixth Report* (1877-1878), 12, 98. If the total number of teachers in 1878, which was 13,676, is divided into $3,065,968, the result is $224. The $144 which the State Superintendent reported as "average annual pay" must have applied to teachers in rural schools only. But even $224 represents annual pay less than that received by industrial workers. See Chapter X, pp. 441-442.

township schools was less than half the pay of men in the city schools.[91] High school teachers also generally were paid more than elementary school teachers.[92] The pay for women teachers was substantially lower than that of men, and one of the arguments used for employing women teachers was that it reduced costs and thereby made it possible to keep schools open for longer terms. There was a greater discrepancy between the pay of men and women in towns and cities than in rural schools, and between their pay in the high schools than in the rural schools. Pay remained so low that it was estimated that nearly 25 per cent of the experienced teachers left the occupation every year.[93]

Nevertheless, in spite of the lack of financial rewards, teaching was developing into a profession. The Indiana State Teachers Association, which was organized in 1854, played an important part in improving the quality of public education. At the first meeting representatives of thirty-three

[91] The following table, showing the average pay per day of men teachers in 1875 and 1878, shows the variations between rural and city school.

	1875	1878
Township schools	$2.03	$1.90
Town schools	3.24	3.09
City schools	4.49	4.06

Indiana State Superintendent of Public Instruction, *Twenty-Third Report* (1875), 7; *Twenty-Sixth Report* (1877-1878), 69.

[92] The following table shows the discrepancy between average pay for men high school teachers and the average pay for all men teachers.

	Average daily pay for all male teachers	Average daily pay for male high school teachers
1866	$1.83	$3.10
1870	1.85	3.96
1874	2.08	4.40

Ibid., Sixteenth Report (1867-1868), 31; *Eighteenth Report* (1869-1870), 32; *Twenty-Second Report* (1873-1874), 37-38.

[93] *Ibid., Thirteenth Report* (1863-1864), 32; *Twenty-Sixth Report* (1877-1878), 98.

The following figures show the differences in the pay of men and women teachers.

counties were present, and a constitution written by Caleb Mills was adopted. The Association soon embraced teachers throughout the state and became a vital force in the shaping of educational policies. It was influential in persuading the legislature to establish the State Normal School and to provide for county institutes and in the enactment of the legislation for the education of Negro children. It also worked for a compulsory attendance law.[94]

One of the important activities of the State Teachers Association was the publication of the *Indiana School Journal*, the first issue of which appeared in 1856. After languishing for a few years the *Journal* took on new life in the sixties under the management of George W. Hoss, who served as superintendent of the Indianapolis public schools and later as state superintendent. In 1869 William A. Bell became associated with the *Journal*, and after 1871 became the sole editor and publisher. Under his direction it became one of the leading educational journals in the county.[95]

	Average Pay per day of All Men and Women Teachers, 1875 and 1878	
1875	Men	Women
Townships	$2.03	$1.80
Towns	3.24	1.93
Cities	4.49	2.27
1878	Men	Women
Townships	$1.90	$1.70
Towns	3.09	1.81
Cities	4.06	2.29

Twenty-Third Report (1875), 7; *Twenty-Sixth Report* (1877-1878), 69. In 1874 the average pay per day of male high school teachers was $4.40, of women high school teachers, $2.72. *Twenty-Second Report* (1873-1874), 38.

94 Collins, Indiana State Teachers' Association, pp. 10-11, 13, 46, 47, 50, 53-56, 61-71. A number of county associations were formed prior to the organization of the state association. The Southern Indiana Teachers' Association was formed in 1876; the Northern Indiana Teachers' Association in 1880. Boone, *Education in Indiana*, p. 443.

95 Smart, *The Indiana Schools*, pp. 128-129. In 1852 Albert D. Wright began the publication of *The American Educational and Common School Journal* in Indianapolis. Apparently only three issues appeared. H. A. Ford began the

§ § § § § §

The Indiana Constitution of 1816 provided that it was the duty of the General Assembly to provide "as soon as circumstances will permit" for a "state university, wherein tuition shall be gratis and equally open to all." But at mid-century Indiana University was little more than a name. Under an act of the legislature a county seminary located at Bloomington was chartered in 1820. In 1827 the name of the seminary was changed to Indiana College, and degrees were conferred for the first time in 1831. In 1838 the name was changed to Indiana University, but for a number of years the school had to struggle for survival. In the Constitutional Convention of 1850-1851 proposals were made to abolish it entirely and to compel the legislature to sell its property and use the proceeds for common schools. Even Caleb Mills in his address to the convention expressed the view that higher education was best carried out by private enterprise. Proposals to abolish the state university were defeated, but the finished constitution made no mention of a university. In 1852 the Indiana House of Representatives went on record as being in favor of diverting the income from the property of Indiana University to the common school fund.[96]

Lack of popular support was but one of the obstacles, although the most important, to the growth and development of the school. In 1850 Bloomington was an isolated village of only a little more than one thousand residents. Even after the New Albany Railroad was partially completed in 1852 it still required twelve hours of travel from New Albany to Bloomington, but the completion of the railroad to the latter

publication of *The Northern Indiana Teacher, an Educational Monthly* in South Bend in 1874. It apparently survived only a year or two. *The Indiana Teacher*, which was published in Indianapolis for a few months in 1869, was merged with the *Indiana School Journal*, as was also *The Educationist*, which was published by A. C. Shortridge and George P. Brown in 1873 and 1874.

96 Kettleborough, *Constitution Making in Indiana*, I, 281-284; Indiana *House Journal*, 1851-1852, pp. 718-721.

town in 1853 made the school more easily accessible. At midcentury the total enrollment, including the preparatory department, was less than two hundred. In the class of 1852 there were seven graduating seniors, but the next year the class consisted of only two members—the smallest in the history of the institution. In 1854 the entire budget, including salaries and maintenance, was about $6,000.[97]

The darkest days of the university were probably during the early 1850's. After prolonged litigation, which eventually reached the United States Supreme Court, Vincennes University won a suit in which she claimed title to certain lands which had been sold by the legislators to endow Indiana University. It appeared for a time that the reimbursement of Vincennes would mean the financial ruin of Indiana University. On top of this, in 1854 the main building of the Bloomington school burned to the ground. The president of the board of trustees appealed to the legislature for funds to meet the crisis—otherwise suspension of the state university seemed inevitable. The lawmakers responded by an act which ended the possibility that funds of the university would be used to pay the claims in the Vincennes suit. Citizens of Bloomington and Monroe County rallied to raise $10,000 to replace the building destroyed by fire.[98]

The university survived the crises of the fifties but grew slowly. The Civil War led to another decline in enrollment. In 1863 there were only sixty-seven students. After the war the school entered upon an era of steady progress and expansion, but for many years enrollments remained very small. By 1878 there were one hundred seventy in the preparatory department. In 1867 the first woman student was admitted into the university and four years later there were thirty-two

[97] James Albert Woodburn, *History of Indiana University, Volume I, 1820-1902* (Bloomington, Ind., 1940), pp. 133, 149-150, 228.

[98] *Ibid.*, pp. 220-225, 226, 232-233, 235-236. Later another grant of land was made by Congress to replace the lands which were lost in the Vincennes University suit.

women in attendance. They were admitted on the same terms as men and were awarded the same degrees.[99]

In 1867 the legislature declared that it "should be the pride of every citizen of Indiana to place the State University in the highest condition of usefulness, and make it the crowning glory of our present great common school system. . . ." An act was passed providing for an annual appropriation of $8,000. With this appropriation, which supplemented income from a land endowment and fees, the legislature for the first time assumed some responsibility for operating expenses. In 1873 the annual appropriation was increased to $15,000. As finances improved, the size of the teaching staff increased and a wider variety of courses was offered. Although Indiana University was a state institution, the subjects taught were the same traditional ones taught in the denominational schools: Latin, Greek, mathematics, philosophy, and theology. Most of the professors were ministers. It was not until 1860 that a professorship of English language and literature was established. At the same time a department of modern languages and literature was begun. By the 1870's a trend toward specialization was apparent. The day of the professor who taught any and everything was passing, and science was receiving more attention. In 1873 a science building was erected, which it was claimed, included the most complete chemical laboratory in the West. Under the administration of Lemuel Moss, who became president in 1875, the curriculum was expanded somewhat and organized into three divisions: the ancient classics, leading to the Bachelor of Arts degree; the modern classics, leading to the Bachelor of Literature degree; and the scientific course, leading to the Bachelor of Science degree. History had been offered occasionally in earlier years, but it was not until 1879 that a professorship of history was established.[100]

[99] Woodburn, *Indiana University*, pp. 263, 287-289, 294.

[100] *Ibid.*, pp. 175, 290, 294, 324; Indiana *Laws*, 1867, p. 21; Boone, *Education in Indiana*, pp. 363-364.

In 1842 a law department was begun, with one professor who was expected "to furnish a complete course of legal education to gentlemen intended for the bar in any of the United States." The law department was separate from the scientific and classical departments, and the professors were usually men who had had judicial experience. The course of study and terms were irregular, but the enrollment was sometimes larger than in the other departments. In 1876 there was a graduating class of twenty, but the following year the legislature abolished the law department on the grounds that the expense of training men for the legal profession should not be borne by the public.[101] At the same time the legislature ended the affiliation of Indiana University with the Indiana Medical College. The latter institution, which was located in Indianapolis, had been made a part of the state university in 1871. During the 1850's there had been some talk of establishing an agricultural school at Bloomington and also a school of engineering, but these plans did not materialize. A normal school for teacher training was operated for a short time in 1852-1853 but was soon abandoned. Thus, at the end of the 1870's the course of study included only those subjects which today would be classified as belonging to the liberal arts. There were no professional schools. In a report to the university trustees in 1878 President Moss said that the courses were of "general, liberal discipline, and not of special or professional training."[102] It was not until the administration of his successor, David Starr Jordan, who assumed the presidency in 1885, that the course offerings were expanded and specialized to a point that the institution became worthy of the name university.

The lack of public support for the state university during its early years was not entirely due to indifference or hostility

101 Woodburn, *Indiana University*, pp. 179, 280-281; Leander J. Monks, *et al.* (eds.), *Courts and Lawyers of Indiana* (3 volumes, Indianapolis, 1916), II, 473-476. The law school was re-established in 1889.

102 Woodburn, *Indiana University*, pp. 118, 280, 324. The present school of medicine was organized in 1903.

to higher education. Many of the most enthusiastic champions of education felt that institutions of higher learning should be private. Every religious denomination attempted to maintain at least one college, and the supporters of these institutions were opposed to spending taxes for a state institution. The zeal for denominational schools led to the founding of more schools than the population and resources of the state could support. Numerous ephemeral institutions called "colleges" or "universities" were chartered only to disappear in a few years. Those which survived were almost without exception in chronic trouble financially. In spite of their titles and in spite of the fact that they offered degrees many of them were nothing more than secondary schools. Indeed it is almost impossible to make a clear-cut distinction between academies and institutions which today would be considered as offering work at the collegiate level because the name college was frequently given to academies. One historian has commented that the zeal of every religious denomination to found its own institution of higher learning was "a fruitful source of divided control in education, the occasion of weakling schools, dependent control, apologetic teaching, and pretentious plans." Religious control, he said, had given Indiana "almost a score of colleges or would-be colleges, all of whose students could at any time have been as well taught by one-half of their combined faculties."[103]

In 1850 in addition to Indiana University there were four degree-granting institutions in the state: Hanover College, Wabash College, Indiana Asbury University, and Franklin

[103] Boone, *Education in Indiana,* p. 406. A contemporary educational journal observed that there were too many "so-called" colleges in the state which were in reality little more than secondary schools. Most of them were established and controlled by religious denominations. "It is necessary," it commented, "that they be self-supporting, hence the other necessity, that pupils of a very low grade of advancement be admitted to the preparatory departments; and since the time for acquiring an education is limited, the tendency is to graduate them from the college at a very low standard of scholarship." *The Educationist,* I, No. 6 (September, 1873), 3.

College. Of these the oldest was Hanover, a Presbyterian institution located on the Ohio River, a short distance from Madison. It had originally been intended to be a manual labor type school modeled on the Pestalozzi schools in Germany and the Oneida Institute in New York. Incorporated as Hanover Academy in 1829, it became Hanover College in 1833 with a charter which permitted it to grant degrees in the liberal arts and sciences. Its ties with the Presbyterian church were strong. All of its presidents were Presbyterian ministers, and a majority of its graduates during the first half century of the college's existence became ministers.[104]

Like most colleges of the period Hanover had a precarious existence. The payment of the salaries of professors was constantly in arrears. In 1878 the finances were so depleted that a resolution was offered at a meeting of the board of trustees that the college "be suspended for an indefinite period until its financial condition shall have recuperated so that it may be opened as a first class institution upon a self-sustaining basis." The motion was defeated by one vote. A preparatory department which was maintained in connection with the college frequently had a larger enrollment than the college. In 1850 there were eighty-one students in the preparatory department, seventy-nine in the college. During the fifties enrollments rose in both departments and then declined in the Civil War period. During the prosperous years of the early 1870's enrollment in the college increased sharply, but fell again during the depression. In 1880 there were only fifty-seven students in the college and forty-five in the preparatory department.[105]

Meanwhile, another group of Presbyterians had founded Wabash College in Crawfordsville in 1833. During its early years the college was torn by a factional fight between "Old

---

104 William Alfred Millis, *The History of Hanover College from 1827 to 1927* (Hanover, Ind., 1927), pp. 86-87. In 1857 the seminary was moved to Chicago. It ultimately became McCormick Theological Seminary.

105 *Ibid.*, pp. 114-116, 224.

Light" and "New Light" Presbyterians, but it ultimately adhered to the New School.[106]

By the 1850's the college was firmly established, but like other institutions it had financial difficulties and frequently operated at a deficit even though its annual expenditures averaged only about $9,000. It received many gifts and gradually acquired an endowment, but most of the gifts were small. In 1872 the total endowment was only $134,000. The following year the financial condition of the college was greatly improved by a gift of $50,000 from Chauncey Rose, which was by far the largest single contribution to that date.[107]

At Wabash, as at Hanover, the preparatory department included a large part of the enrollment. The numbers in the college remained small. In 1862 there were only six members of the teaching staff for the entire school, and the number did not increase greatly. In 1876 there were a dozen members of the faculty and a little more than two hundred students. Twenty-four seniors received degrees that year.[108]

Methodists founded several institutions of higher learning before 1880, but few of them survived. The most enduring was Indiana Asbury University in Greencastle, which was chartered in 1837. It was founded under the patronage and control of the Indiana Conference of the Methodist Church, but its charter provided that it should be open to all young men. The first commencement was held in 1840. It was intended that the school should be financed principally out of endowments for both professorships and scholarships, and on the whole this plan was adhered to. Tuition paid by students covered only a minor part of the costs. Most of the funds were raised by agents who traveled about the country soliciting contributions. The endowment grew slowly, and

106 James I. Osborne and Theodore G. Gronert, *Wabash College, The First Hundred Years 1832-1932* (Crawfordsville, Ind., 1932), pp. 23, 37, 43, 49.

107 *Ibid.*, pp. 69, 137-138, 141-142.

108 *Ibid.*, p. 153; Smart, *The Indiana Schools*, p. 145.

for many years the school was subject to pecuniary embarrassments and chronic deficits. Frequently it was necessary to dip into endowment to pay for current expenses, even though operating costs in 1850 were estimated to be only about $3,600 a year. By 1855 the total resources of the university were less than $100,000. During the Civil War income from investments rose, and in the postwar period the endowment was increased by a number of substantial gifts. But the depression of the seventies caused a decline in income, and for several years the school operated once more at a deficit. It was rescued from its financial difficulties a few years later in large part through the generosity of Washington C. DePauw, the industrialist and financial magnate of New Albany, who had been a member of the board of trustees of Asbury since 1856. In 1884 the name of the school was changed to DePauw University in his honor.[109]

Before the Civil War a peak enrollment was reached in 1852-1853 when a total of ninety-two were enrolled in the college department. During the next few years enrollments declined as the result of difficulties between faculty and students over disciplinary matters. The most serious clashes occurred in 1856 over efforts of the faculty to regulate the activities of the student literary societies. A group of students withdrew from the school rather than sign a pledge to accept the regulations and discipline imposed by the college. These included all twenty-two members of the senior class, with the result that there was no graduation in 1857. The following year the number in the college classes dropped to forty-one, but the next year it increased, and it was possible to report to the Indiana Conference of the Methodist Church that "notwithstanding its temporary reverses" the prospects of Asbury "were never more flattering." During the war enrollments declined again but rose thereafter. By 1876 there were two hundred twenty-four students in the

109 Smart, *The Indiana Schools*, p. 147; Manhart, *DePauw through the Years*, I, 6-12, 19-20, 25, 119-122, 168-172.

college. In 1877 there were fifty-one members in the graduating class, the largest group up to that time. The number of students enrolled in the preparatory department was always larger than in the college, but the proportion in the college increased steadily. The faculty remained small. In the 1850's it usually consisted of the president and five others, and during the 1860's and 1870's of the president and six others. By 1876 the number of teachers had reached nine.[110]

In 1849 the Indiana Central Medical College was opened in Indianapolis under the supervision of the trustees of Indiana Asbury, but it was abandoned after three years, principally because of financial difficulties. In 1853 Asbury Law School was opened in Greencastle. It continued in operation until 1862 but usually had only one professor and a handful of students. It was abandoned in 1862 because of the war, but in 1871 a law department was revived for about three years.[111]

In 1874 the assets of the Indiana Female College at Indianapolis were given to Asbury. The college had been organized in 1850 and continued until 1868. It graduated a number of students, conferring upon them the degrees of Mistress of Liberal Arts and Mistress of English Literature. Efforts were made to consolidate DePauw Female College in New Albany, founded in 1852, with Asbury under a plan whereby the first part of the college course would be taken at New Albany and the latter part at Greencastle. These plans came to nothing, but after the New Albany school closed its assets were turned over to DePauw University in 1905.[112]

110 Manhart, *DePauw through the Years*, I, 52-56, 149; Smart, *The Indiana Schools*, p. 149.

111 Manhart, *DePauw through the Years*, I, 42-51; Monks, *et al.* (eds.), *Courts and Lawyers of Indiana;* II, 480-481; George B. Manhart, "The Indiana Central Medical College, 1849-1852," *Indiana Magazine of History*, LVI (1960), 105-122. The law school was revived briefly in 1881-1882. In 1884 it was reopened once more and continued to operate until 1894.

112 Manhart, *DePauw through the Years*, I, 111.

In 1854 the Moores Hill Male and Female Collegiate Institute was established under the auspices of the Southeast Indiana Conference of the Methodist Church. The school, usually known as Moores Hill College, was opened in 1856 in Dearborn County. It proved to be more enduring than many denominational colleges founded in the same period. During its entire existence it graduated only four hundred and eighty-seven persons, but it survived until 1917. In 1919 it was re-established as Evansville College.[113]

In 1855 Fort Wayne College was established as the result of the merging of two Methodist schools—Fort Wayne Female College, which had been opened in 1846, and Fort Wayne Collegiate Institute for young men, which had been opened in 1850. It offered both the A.B. and B.S. degrees and also included preparatory music and commercial departments. Few students enrolled in the courses leading to degrees. In 1870-1871 there were only four members of the senior class.[114]

In 1859 the Valparaiso Male and Female College was founded under the sponsorship of the Northwestern Indiana Conference of the Methodist Church. The venture was greeted with enthusiasm by the community. Local citizens donated money for the purchase of a site for the school. The school, like many institutions of the period, was intended to accommodate students from the elementary level through college. By 1860 it had an enrollment of more than three hundred, and its prospects looked bright. But the Civil War brought a decrease in enrollment, and efforts to revive the school after the war were unsuccessful. By 1869 there were only about one hundred students, and in 1871 the school was closed. This ended its existence as a Methodist institution, but in 1873 it was reopened as a nonsectarian school under

[113] John W. Winkley, *Moores Hill College. An Intimate History* (Evansville, Ind., 1954), pp. 13, 14, 68.

[114] Fort Wayne College, *Catalogue,* 1870-1871; Taylor University, Upland, Indiana, *Centennial Program: History and Events* (1946), p. 7. In 1890 Fort Wayne College became Taylor University.

the name of the Northern Indiana Normal School. The founder and principal was Henry Baker Brown, an enterprising and imaginative young man only twenty-six years old who had recently graduated from the National Normal School in Lebanon, Ohio. The school under his direction enjoyed a spectacular growth and constituted one of the most interesting educational experiments in the history of the state. Brown's guiding principles were to make it possible for young people to obtain a practical education at a minimum cost in minimum time. There were no formal entrance requirements, and students could advance as rapidly as they were able. The emphasis was on hard work, with little time for recreation or social activities. Tuition was $7.00 a term. Board and room were at first $3.00 a week but were later reduced to $2.00. The curriculum at first consisted of four courses of study: preparatory, music, teacher training, and scientific. Later other courses were added. In 1879 a law school was opened. By 1880 the school was firmly established and growing rapidly. It continued to expand and flourish until the era of World War I.[115]

Baptists although numerous showed less interest than did Presbyterians and Methodists in higher education. The sole Baptist institution of collegiate rank had been founded as a manual training institute but had been rechartered as Franklin College in 1845. Throughout the 1850's it struggled against financial difficulties, receiving little support from Baptist churches. In 1864 it was forced to close because of lack of

---

[115] Moore, *The Calumet Region*, pp. 453-460; John Strietelmeier, *Valparaiso's First Century: A Centennial History of Valparaiso University* (Valparaiso University, 1959), pp. 5-11 and *passim*. On the eve of World War I, 6,000 students (including persons enrolled from the kindergarten through the university) were reported to be enrolled at the institution which had by that time been named Valparaiso University. After the war the school entered upon a difficult period under the administration of a new president. Enrollments declined to a point that there were efforts to sell the buildings to the state. In 1925 a group associated with the Lutheran Church acquired the school.

funds and declining enrollments caused by the war. It reopened in 1869 but was suspended again in 1872. That same year it was reorganized and opened under the authority of the Franklin College Association, with pledges of support from the people of Johnson County. Since that time it has had a continuous existence. Enrollments were small. The largest graduating class during the first fifty years appears to have been the class of 1861, which consisted of six members. When the college reopened in 1872 it had a faculty of only three members.[116]

As already noted members of the Society of Friends established a number of excellent academies, but the only one of their schools to become a degree-granting institution was Earlham College in Richmond. The college had its inception as Friends Boarding School, which was opened in 1847 under the auspices of the Indiana Yearly Meeting. From the beginning some courses were taught which were of collegiate level, but at first no degrees or even diplomas were granted. Among western Friends in this period there was prejudice against the name of "college" and even stronger feeling against degrees, which were regarded as evidence of sinful pride and inconsistent with Quaker ideals. Not until 1857 were diplomas issued to show the completion of prescribed courses of study. In 1859 as the result of pressure from the teaching staff, the Indiana Yearly Meeting consented to adopt the name of Earlham College and to grant degrees, "excepting all unnecessary form and ceremonies which we do not approve."[117] The course of study was reorganized into primary, intermediate, and collegiate departments. In 1863 the primary and intermediate departments were abolished and a preparatory program established. The name of Earlham was taken from Earlham, the ancestral home of the

116 *Franklin College: First Half Century Jubilee Exercises* (Cincinnati, 1884), pp. 28-29, 37, 42, 44-45, 111-112.

117 Opal Thornburg, *Earlham. The Story of the College 1847-1962* (Richmond, Ind., 1963), pp. 44-79.

distinguished Quaker family of Gurney near Norwich, England. The first degrees were awarded in 1862.[118]

The aims of the institution were declared to be not so much "to make *brilliant scholars,* as to turn out well-instructed, serious and useful men and women. The acquisition of knowledge is chiefly to be prized as the *means* by which the cultivation of mental powers, and the formation of correct principles and habits are to be attained."[119]

Like other denominational colleges Earlham had few students and a precarious financial existence. In the 1860's total enrollments were only a little more than one hundred. Graduating classes ranged in size from a single member in 1863 to ten in 1865. By 1866 there were seventy-seven college students and one hundred and eighty in the preparatory department.[120]

North Western Christian University in Indianapolis was founded by members of the Disciples of Christ, sometimes known as Christians, one of the most rapidly growing denominations in the West. Among the group of men who took the lead in the movement to establish the school the most conspicuous was Ovid Butler, a prominent attorney and leader in the antislavery movement. The first college founded by the Disciples had been Bethany in Virginia, a slave state, and a principal reason for the founding of the school in Indianapolis, Butler said, was to establish an institution of higher learning in a free state, where "the youth of the Northwest might receive a liberal and Christian education, removed, as far as practicable, from the pernicious influences of slavery."[121]

The new school opened in a single building on a twenty-acre campus in northeastern Indianapolis on land which had been part of the Butler estate. It remained in this location

118 Thornburg, *Earlham,* p. 89.

119 *Ibid.,* pp. 88-89.

120 *Ibid.,* pp. 83-84, 91, 118.

121 Shaw, "The Founding of Butler University," *Indiana Magazine of History,* LVII, 255-259; Indianapolis *Daily Sentinel* (Centennial Issue), February 22, 1876.

for twenty years. In 1875 it moved to a new campus in Irvington, a suburban area at the east edge of Indianapolis. The move was made after the residents of Irvington offered a campus of twenty-five acres and a donation of $50,000. In 1877 the name was changed to Butler College in honor of the school's principal benefactor. Soon afterwards the institution was weakened by internal dissension. One faction, which had the backing of ministers of the Disciples of Christ, wanted the college to be purely a sectarian school and were opposed to the employment of professors who were not members of that denomination. Ovid Butler and the president of the board of trustees were not sympathetic with this view, but a majority of the board voted during the school year 1878-1879 to vacate three professorships which were held by persons who were not members of the Disciples Church. The action aroused much criticism, especially because the professors in question were among the most able and best loved on the staff. This sectarian policy, which was short-lived, had the effect of weakening support for the college among the people of Indianapolis for a number of years.[122]

Butler College was one of the few denominational institutions founded after 1850 to survive until the present. Another was Concordia College, a Lutheran institution founded to train persons preparing to enter the ministry, which opened in Fort Wayne in 1861. It had formerly been located in St. Louis.[123] Union Christian College, which was founded in 1859 in Merom in Sullivan County, remained in operation until 1924. It was founded by members of the "New Light" Christians—a group distinct from the Disciples of Christ. It offered a four-year course leading to the A.B. or B.S.

122 Indianapolis *Daily Sentinel* (Centennial Issue), February 22, 1876; Thomas Benton Fields, A History of Butler University (Unpublished Master's thesis in Education, Indiana University, 1928), pp. 28, 36; David Starr Jordan, *The Days of a Man, Being Memories of a Naturalist, Teacher and Minor Prophet of Democracy* (2 volumes, New York, 1922), I, 183-184.

123 Boone, *Education in Indiana,* pp. 418-419.

degree in addition to a preparatory course. In 1924 it was consolidated with Defiance Christian College in Defiance, Ohio.[124]

United Brethren founded Hartsville Academy in Bartholomew County in 1849. It was subsequently rechartered as Hartsville University and then in 1883 as Hartsville College. It offered a classical course leading to an A.B. degree and a scientific course leading to a B.S. degree. It also included a preparatory school and courses in commerce, pedagogy, and music. Most of the students enrolled in the preparatory or commercial departments. Very few students were found in the classical course and very few degrees were conferred.[125]

In 1872 Smithson College was opened in Logansport by members of the Universalist Church. It offered the usual classical course leading to an A.B. degree and also "academic" and "commercial" courses. It had no endowment and no income except from tuition and was in existence for only a few years.[126]

Although they were founded by different denominations, all of these small private colleges were much alike. No doubt some of them were superior to others in academic quality, but they all offered much the same course of study. The curriculum in all cases was at first narrowly classical. Emphasis was placed on Greek and Latin, mathematics, and theological and philosophical subjects such as "Mental and Moral Philosophy" and "Evidences of Christianity." The early professors were nearly always men with theological training and usually with some experience as ministers. They were not specialists but instead showed an amazing versatility

124 James W. Conlin, A History of Union Christian College (Unpublished Master's thesis in Education, Indiana University, 1931), *passim*.

125 Hartsville University, *Annual Catalogue*, 1867, 1872-1873, 1881-1882; Boone, *Education in Indiana*, pp. 423-424; Smart, *The Indiana Schools*, p. 162.

126 *Circular of Smithson College, Logansport, Ind. . . . 1872; Calendar of Smithson College* for 1873-74, Logansport, Ind.; Donald F. Carmony (ed.), "Smithson College Circular, 1871," *Indiana Magazine of History*, LIII (1957), 69-88.

in the scope and variety of courses which they taught. Beginning during the 1850's and increasingly after the Civil War scientific subjects began to receive some attention. Courses were more specialized, and there were efforts to introduce the laboratory method. Some professors were especially trained in science, and Darwinian theory was beginning to have an impact even in denominational colleges, although most Darwinists tried to reconcile the theory with religion. For example, Joseph Moore, who taught science at Earlham in the 1860's and was president of that college from 1868 to 1883, had been exposed to Darwinism while a student at Harvard, but as professor he reconciled Darwinism and theism. David Starr Jordan, an avowed evolutionist, taught at Butler College during the 1870's without encountering any strong opposition. But when he left the college, instead of appointing the successor whom he recommended, the board of trustees voted to appoint a young man "who had written articles on science for church papers, and who, it was thought, would be less pronouncedly an evolutionist," than Jordan or the man he recommended. After a time most colleges permitted students to elect French or German in place of Latin or Greek. English literature also began to take its place alongside the ancient classics. Many colleges offered both a classical and scientific course, the former leading to the Bachelor of Arts degree, the latter to the Bachelor of Science. The chief difference between the two usually was that Latin and Greek were not required for the science degree. In some cases only three instead of four years were required for the science degree.[127]

Women students were admitted to Earlham from the time it was organized as Friends Boarding School, and a young ladies department was organized at Franklin College in

[127] Millis, *Hanover College,* pp. 164-171; Manhart, *DePauw through the Years,* I, 21-22, 27, 39, 59-60, 89-93; Osborne and Gronert, *Wabash College,* pp. 72, 73, 85, 133, 147; Fields, Butler University, p. 49 and *passim;* Thornburg, *Earlham,* pp. 89, 97-99, 104, 154-157; Jordan, *Days of a Man,* I, 114, 184.

1842. At North Western Christian University sixteen women were enrolled during the first term, but they were not admitted to the regular course leading to the Bachelor of Arts degree. The curriculum for them was almost identical with that for men students, but they were awarded the degree of Mistress of Arts or Mistress of Science. In 1869 the special course for women was abolished, and thereafter men and women followed the same course and received the same degrees. As early as 1855 a committee was appointed to consider the establishment of a "Female Department" at Asbury University. Two years later a report was made which recommended admission of women on equal terms with men, but it was not until 1867 that women students actually enrolled. Five girls entered that year, four of whom remained to graduate. Their admission caused some grumbling among the male students, who liked to compare their college to eastern colleges such as Harvard and Yale which were exclusively for men. But after a few years coeducation was firmly established at Asbury. Women students were allowed to attend Hanover College for the first time in 1869, but at first they were not officially admitted. Their names were not published in the catalogue, and none of them applied for degrees. It was not until 1880 that the board of trustees voted to admit women with the same status as men. Among Protestant colleges in Indiana only Wabash remained all male. The other denominational colleges like Moores Hill, Union Christian College, and Hartsville were coeducational from the first.[128]

Discipline was stricter in some denominational colleges than others, but student life was much the same in all of them. By modern standards living conditions were austere and social

[128] *Franklin College: First Half Century Jubilee Exercises*, p. 35; Thornburg, *Earlham*, pp. 90-91; Fields, Butler University, p. 62; Manhart, *DePauw through the Years*, I, 75-87; Millis, *Hanover College*, pp. 183-184, 293. During the 1890's the question of making Wabash coeducational came before the board of trustees repeatedly, but in 1899 it was finally decided to keep Wabash all male.

life limited. But compulsory attendance at chapel and other religious requirements and restrictions of conduct did not prevent occasional outbursts of rowdyism and drunkenness. From the beginning extracurricular activities centered around literary and debating societies, which usually bore classical names such as Philomathean, Calliopaean, Platonian, and Theosophian. The chief activity of the societies was a weekly meeting at which members read papers or more frequently engaged in debates. Subjects might be literary, philosophical, religious, or political. Typical were such topics as: "Will the discovery of gold in California be beneficial to the United States?"; "Would the destruction of the Roman Catholic Church be beneficial to the world?"; "Which has the greater influence on human behavior, fear of punishment or hope of reward?" Sometimes intense feeling was generated over subjects like slavery and the impeachment of President Andrew Johnson.[129]

By the 1850's Greek letter fraternities had appeared on some campuses. At first there was opposition to them because of their secrecy, but their numbers grew and they played an increasingly important part in the social life at Hanover, Wabash, Asbury, North Western Christian, as well as at the state university. Organized sports began to develop after the Civil War. The first game in which there were intercollegiate contests was baseball. One of the earliest was a game between Wabash and Asbury in 1867. By the seventies a variety of football had been introduced, but there were not as yet intercollegiate games.[130]

[129] Osborne and Gronert, *Wabash College,* pp. 102-114; Manhart, *DePauw through the Years,* I, 128-133; Millis, *Hanover College,* pp. 232-235; Thornburg, *Earlham,* pp. 157-159.

[130] Osborne and Gronert, *Wabash College,* pp. 115-116, 167-168; Millis, *Hanover College,* p. 240; Manhart, *DePauw through the Years,* I, 133-137; Fields, *Butler University,* p. 84; Woodburn, *Indiana University,* I, 155-159; Indianapolis *Daily Sentinel,* December 9, 1870. At Purdue the question of Greek letter fraternities precipitated a genuine crisis. In 1877 the university adopted a rule prohibiting the secret organizations. This aroused intense protests from the students. In 1881 two students were expelled and two

Notre Dame University represented the only significant effort of Roman Catholics to establish an institution of higher learning in Indiana. Originally Notre Dame du Lac, it was founded in 1842 by members of the Congregation of the Holy Cross. The first president, Father Edward Frederick Sorin, was French as were most of the early members of the faculty and others associated with the school. The first pupils were admitted in 1843. The following year the school was chartered as a university with the power to confer degrees, but its growth was slow, and during the early years its survival sometimes seemed doubtful. It was located in the extreme north of the state in an area which was sparsely settled and still primitive. Between 1847 and 1855 it suffered from epidemics of malarial fever and cholera and a disastrous fire as well. In addition it was beset with the problems common to all small colleges—inadequate finances and small enrollments. Pupils of all levels were at first admitted, from elementary to university. During the early years most of the enrollment was in the preparatory school. In 1859 the total number of students was two hundred and eighteen. By 1865 this had reached more than five hundred, but in later years attendance declined. In 1879 the total was only three hundred and twenty-four. During the seventies the number of degrees awarded each year ranged from four to eleven. Before 1865 the only course of study was a strictly classical one in Arts and Letters. After that time a scientific course

others suspended for violating the ban. One of the students countered by a court action against the faculty. No decision was ever reached in the case, but in 1883 friends of the fraternities succeeded in having a rider attached to a legislative appropriation bill which was designed to prevent the payment of funds to the university unless the rule was rescinded. The result was a legislative imbroglio, and the session came to an end without the adoption of the appropriation. Emerson E. White, the president of Purdue, resigned during the crisis. Later the faculty modified, although it did not entirely rescind, the rule against fraternities. It was necessary for the university to borrow money to tide it over the financial crisis until the next session of the legislature. William M. Hepburn and Louis M. Sears, *Purdue University: Fifty Years of Progress* (Indianapolis, 1925), pp. 72, 73, 79-80.

was begun which did not include Latin and Greek. In 1865 a two-year commercial course was also instituted which attracted a larger enrollment than the academic courses. The law school, which was opened in 1869, also sometimes included more students than did the classical and scientific courses.[131]

While private colleges were multiplying, Indiana University remained the only state institution of higher learning until after the Civil War. In 1865, as already noted, the State Normal School at Terre Haute was chartered, but it did not at first give degrees. In 1869 the state legislature voted to establish a state agricultural college under the terms of the Morrill Land Grant Act passed by Congress in 1862. This action represented the culmination of a movement which had originated many years earlier. Governor Joseph A. Wright, always an advocate of scientific farming, had recommended the establishment of an agricultural school where experimental farming could be carried on. The State Board of Agriculture also supported the movement for an agricultural school or schools. In 1852 the state legislature passed an act providing for departments of agriculture and engineering at Indiana University, but neither department materialized because no funds were appropriated for them.[132]

During the late fifties proposals for Federal land grants to assist the states in establishing agricultural schools were considered in Congress but not adopted. Finally in 1862 the Morrill Land Grant Act was passed. It provided that aid in the form of public lands to the extent of thirty thousand

[131] Arthur J. Hope, C.S.J., *Notre Dame: One Hundred Years* (Notre Dame, Ind., 1943), pp. 54, 58, 82-84, 111, 141, 150, 167, 181, 191. In 1855 St. Mary's Academy for girls was chartered under the direction of the Sisters of the Holy Cross. It was located only one mile from Notre Dame and was under the same general control, but it did not become an institution of collegiate rank, granting degrees, until after 1880.

[132] Paul W. Gates, "Western Opposition to the Agricultural College Act," *Indiana Magazine of History*, XXXVII (1941), 126-127; Woodburn, *Indiana University*, pp. 177-179, 243, 246; Hepburn and Sears, *Purdue University*, pp. 13-14.

acres for each United States senator and representative be granted to the states for the purpose of fostering agricultural and technical education. States in which there was insufficient public land to fulfill the grant were to obtain from the Department of Interior land certificates or "scrip" which could be sold to purchasers who were allowed to select any public lands which were available outside the state. The land or scrip was to be sold and the proceeds invested and the interest therefrom "inviolably appropriated" for the endowment and support of at least one college in which the principal object would be the teaching of agriculture and mechanical arts. Ten per cent of the money realized from the sale might be used for the purchase of a site for the college, but none of the principal was to be used for operating expenses.[133]

Many of the most enthusiastic supporters of agricultural education in Congress were opposed to the Morrill Act. Some Westerners opposed it because it benefited populous eastern states more than those in the West since the amount of land granted depended upon the number of members in Congress. Another objection was that the law would benefit land speculators. By 1862 nearly all of the public lands in Indiana were already sold, but in the vote on the Morrill Act the state's delegation voted with the West against the act because it was felt that it was drawn too much in the interest of speculators. Joseph A. Wright, who was a member of the Senate, voted against the act as did representatives George W. Julian and William S. Holman, although all of these three were friends of agricultural education.[134]

The sale of the scrip allotted to Indiana after the state legislature voted in 1865 to accept the grant under the Morrill Act brought disappointingly small returns. States receiving the scrip dumped it upon the market in such quantities that prices fell. Indiana received 390,000 acres, which were sold in 1867 for about fifty-four cents an acre, yielding only $212,-

133 Hepburn and Sears, *op. cit.*, p. 25.
134 Gates, "Western Opposition to the Agricultural College Act," *Indiana Magazine of History*, XXXVII, 124-126.

238. About 98 per cent of the scrip was acquired by the agent of a syndicate of speculators from Detroit and Cleveland.[135] Differences over how the funds were to be spent delayed action in the establishment of the school until 1869. There were several proposals to divide the fund among existing colleges within the state, all of which were defeated. The issue narrowed to the choice of the location of a single college. Three sites finally received serious consideration although inducements were offered to the legislature in support of several others. Indiana University made a strong claim, and in 1865 a bill to locate the agricultural school in Bloomington actually passed the state senate. There was also considerable support for establishing the college in Indianapolis. Ovid Butler of North Western Christian University pleaded for that location, and the city offered grants of land and money. Tippecanoe County also had its supporters, and the site of Battle Ground Institute in that county was considered. The decision for the location finally came as the result of an offer from John Purdue to give one hundred thousand dollars in addition to other offers already made in behalf of Tippecanoe County on condition that his name be used in connection with the school.[136]

In 1872 Professor Richard Owen of Indiana University was named president of the new institution. The youngest

[135] *Ibid.*, p. 130; Hepburn and Sears, *Purdue University,* p. 34.

[136] *Ibid.*, pp. 25-31. John Purdue, a native of Pennsylvania, was an excellent example of the self-made man of the mid-nineteenth century. The only boy in a family of eight children, he was early compelled to help support the rest of his family and received little formal schooling. In 1839 he moved to Lafayette, where he opened a store and embarked upon a career as a merchant. In the fifties he started a commission house in New York City for the sale of western products. The great demand for western pork during the Civil War helped make Purdue a wealthy man, but in the postwar years he experienced some reverses as the result of bad investments. All of his obligations to Purdue University were met, but there was little left for his heirs except a mass of uncollectable accounts and notes.

Purdue showed a deep personal interest in the school which bore his name— to the point of interfering in academic affairs of which he had no real understanding. He died suddenly of a stroke of apoplexy in 1876 and was buried on the Purdue campus. *Ibid.*, pp. 46-50.

son of Robert Owen, founder of New Harmony, he was a noted scientist and a long-time advocate of an agricultural school. Owen, however, lacked administrative talents and resigned from the presidency before the school was opened. In 1874 Abram C. Shortridge, superintendent of the Indianapolis public schools, was named to the position. Classes opened in September of that year. Plans had been made for schools of agriculture, chemistry, civil engineering, physics, and mechanical engineering, but all of these courses did not materialize at once.[137]

There was at first a university academy for preparing persons in elementary scientific subjects. The College of General Science offered preparation for industrial pursuits and gave a Bachelor of Science degree. The curriculum included the natural and physical sciences, mathematics, Latin, German, and English. There were also more specialized offerings in schools of science and technology for students who had completed part of the general science course. The first student in civil engineering registered in 1876. There were no students in the schools of mechanical engineering or agriculture until 1879, and the full course in mechanical engineering was not taught until 1882. By the end of the first year there was a total enrollment of sixty-four of whom forty-nine were in the preparatory class. By 1880 the total enrollment was slightly more than one hundred, but the number at the college level remained small, and only a handful of students were found in the specialized schools. In 1875 the doors of Purdue were opened to women with "no distinctions in examinations, expense or classes." Nine women enrolled at once, but only one at the collegiate level.[138]

The endowment from the land grant along with the gift from John Purdue and other gifts assured the school of a steady, if small, income for operating expenses. This was

137 Hepburn and Sears, *Purdue University,* pp. 40-43, 51.

138 *Ibid.,* pp. 59, 63, 71; Indiana State Superintendent of Public Instruction, *Twenty-Fourth Report* (1875-1876), 130.

fortunate, for the state legislature was reluctant to appropriate money during the depression of the seventies. In 1879 it voted only nine thousand dollars for the ensuing biennium. There was little popular support for financing higher education out of taxpayers' money during this period. In the legislature the view was expressed that since the state could not give a college education to all persons, it should not give it to any. Even though its course of study was more practical than that of the traditional colleges, Purdue aroused criticism because it represented an innovation. One legislator scornfully remarked that at Purdue—"they educate people to be farmers—to learn how to plough and raise shanghai chickens." He asked: "Are we to misappropriate funds of the people in this way?" "Being a new departure in this section of the country," observed one newspaper, "it [Purdue] has aroused prejudice, being little understood; people consider themselves qualified to criticize, and belonging to the state, they feel it their duty to do so, and they have been very faithful in the performance of this duty."[139]

About the same time that Purdue opened, another technical school, the Terre Haute School of Industrial Science, which became Rose Polytechnic Institute, was launched. It was chartered in 1874 but did not actually open until 1883. It was founded through the beneficence of Chauncey Rose of the Indianapolis and Terre Haute Railroad, a man who had little formal education and who was interested in establishing a school which would offer a more practical course of study than the traditional classical one. Instruction was to be "based upon the practical mathematics, and the application of the physical sciences to the various arts and manufactures" and was to include "such training as would furnish the pupils with useful and practical knowledge of some art or occupation, and enable them to earn competent livings."[140]

139 Hepburn and Sears, *Purdue University*, p. 72; *Brevier Legislative Reports*, XVII (1879), 76-77; Indianapolis *Daily Sentinel* (Centennial Issue), February 22, 1876.

140 Boone, *Education in Indiana*, pp. 430-431.

The founding of Purdue University and Rose Polytechnic Institute was indicative of a trend away from the purely academic curriculum which had heretofore dominated higher education and the beginning of a trend toward studies designed to meet the needs of an industrialized society. Meanwhile, there were some efforts at establishing schools of medicine and law and formalizing the requirements for these professions. But many physicians and lawyers continued to practice who had not fulfilled formal requirements and who did not hold degrees. The traditional method of learning to practice medicine was to receive instruction from a preceptor who was already in practice. This procedure disappeared only gradually. At midcentury two medical schools were in operation in Indiana—at La Porte and Evansville. Between 1850 and 1880 nine more medical schools were chartered, but few survived for any length of time. For a thirteen-year period—from 1856 to 1869—there was no medical school of any kind in the state.[141]

The La Porte University School of Medicine (sometimes known as Indiana Medical College), organized in 1841, was one of the more successful schools of the period. It had an excellent faculty and continued in operation until 1856. In that year the building housing the school was destroyed by fire. The fire was partially responsible for the demise of the school but internal dissensions also played a part.[142] Meanwhile, the Indiana Central Medical College already mentioned above, which was to be the medical department of Asbury University, was opened in Indianapolis in 1849. In 1851 an affiliation was established between the new school and the one at La Porte. But the Indianapolis school closed the following year because of financial difficulties and factional disputes.[143]

141 Earlier there had been an attempt to establish a medical school in connection with Vincennes University in 1837-1838. Burton D. Myers, *History of Medical Education in Indiana* (Bloomington, Ind., 1956), pp. 2, 8.

142 *Ibid.,* pp. 18-25.

143 *Ibid.,* pp. 23-24, 25-28; George B. Manhart, "The Indiana Central Medical College, 1849-1852," *Indiana Magazine of History,* LVI (1960), 105-122.

In 1849 the Medical College of Evansville opened. It was suspended in 1854 and not reopened until 1871. After the closing of the La Porte school in 1856 no formal medical education was given in the state until after the Civil War. In 1869, largely as the result of the efforts of the Indianapolis Academy of Medicine, which by that time was a firmly established society, the Indiana Medical College was opened in Indianapolis. By that date Indianapolis had three hospitals and seemed to be a promising field for medical education. During 1871 the new school was affiliated with Indiana University, but the affiliation lasted only until 1876. In 1873 some members of the faculty of the Medical College withdrew to form the College of Physicians and Surgeons of Indiana, which operated from 1874 until 1878. Thus for four years there were two rival institutions in the capital city. In 1878 they were merged into the Medical College of Indiana. This institution had a longer life than any of its predecessors, lasting until 1905.[144]

In 1879 another successful school, the Central College of Physicians and Surgeons, was opened in Indianapolis. It also operated until 1905, when it and the Medical College of Indiana and the Fort Wayne College of Medicine merged to form the Indiana Medical School, which was a part of Purdue University.[145] Meanwhile, in 1873, the Physiomedical College of Indiana had opened in Indianapolis. The Physiomedics held theories regarding the causation and cure of disease which were somewhat at variance with other schools. In some respects they were forerunners of modern physical therapy. The Indianapolis school was more successful than most of its contemporaries, lasting until 1909.[146]

During the seventies, while these various efforts at medical education were being made in Indianapolis, two schools had opened in other parts of the state. The Medical College of

[144] Myers, *Medical Education in Indiana*, pp. 29-32, 47-53, 55-57.

[145] *Ibid.*, pp. 64-70.

[146] *Ibid.*, pp. 77-79; Indianapolis *Daily Sentinel* (Centennial Issue), February 22, 1876.

Evansville was revived in 1871 and operated until 1884 when it closed for the last time. In 1876 the Medical College of Fort Wayne was opened. It continued to operate until 1883, but in 1879 part of the faculty withdrew to form a rival school, the Fort Wayne College of Medicine. This institution proved to be more enduring, lasting until 1905, when, as already noted, it became a part of the Indiana Medical College of Purdue University.[147]

Except for the brief affiliation of the Indiana Medical College with Indiana University all of these early schools were entirely private. The only income which they had was from tuition fees. Financial problems were usually the reason that they were generally short-lived. Most of them included capable men on their faculties, but their standards were appallingly low in comparison with those of the present. Usually they had no formal entrance requirements. One of the reasons that President Lemuel Moss terminated the affiliation of Indiana University with the Indiana Medical College was his complaint that "persons who would fail in an examination for entrance into an ordinary grammar school" could enter medical school. Moss thought that a student seeking admission should have the equivalent of junior class standing in college. Although there were no fixed requirements for admission, most schools had similar graduation requirements. Candidates for the M.D. degree were usually required to be twenty-one years old, to be of good moral character, to have studied medicine for three years under a preceptor, and to have attended two courses of lectures in medical school. Before receiving the degree it was also necessary to pass examinations before the faculty and to present a thesis.[148]

147 Myers, *Medical Education in Indiana,* pp. 32-38, 73-76.

148 *Ibid.,* pp. 19, 31, 50-51, and *passim.* It was not until 1903 that two years of college were required for admission to the Indiana University School of Medicine. This requirement was not generally adopted throughout the United States until 1918. Standards in the medical schools in Indiana in the

Valparaiso Public Graded School

Evansville High School

Public School, Milton

North Western Christian (later Butler) University, Indianapolis

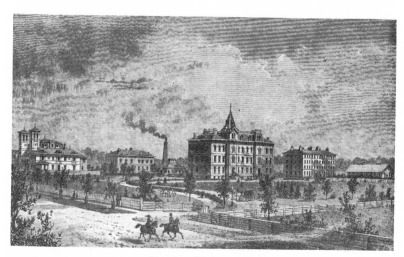

Purdue University

Part of the course of study was "didactic," part was "clinical" in nature. Some of the courses which are most important in present-day medical education were unknown because the part played by microorganisms in disease was as yet largely unknown. In courses in anatomy efforts were made to offer students opportunities at dissection, but lack of specimens made this difficult. Popular prejudice against dissection was a serious obstacle to scientific pursuits. State law made the removal of a body from a burial ground for the purpose of dissection a crime, and yet grave robbing was frequently the only way to obtain bodies. In 1879 the legislature finally passed "an act to promote the science of medicine and surgery, by providing methods whereby human subjects, for anatomical and scientific dissection and experiment, may be lawfully obtained. . . ." Bodies of inmates of prisons and public institutions which were not claimed by relatives and which were to be buried at public expense were made available with certain restrictions.[149]

A more serious obstacle to the development of a trained medical profession than the inadequacy of the medical schools was the laxity of requirements for the licensing of doctors. State laws offered no protection to the public against incompetency and quackery. "The profession which guards the threshold and all the ways of human life, from the cradle to the grave, is in Indiana an open highway, wherein every nostrum vending tramp may travel side by side with the wisest and best of the medical profession," declared a critic in 1879.[150] In 1825 the legislature had passed an act, which was amended slightly in 1829, giving the Indiana State Medical Association authority to license. But the law did not prescribe the qualifications for licensing nor provide penalties

nineteenth century were no lower than those found in most states. *Ibid.,* pp. 51-52.

149 Indiana *Laws,* 1879, p. 157.

150 *Address of Joseph K. Edgerton, President of the Board of Trustees of the Fort Wayne Medical College at the Annual Commencement,* at Fort Wayne, Ind., February 26th, 1879 (Fort Wayne, 1879), p. 10.

for practicing without a license. Efforts at securing legislation which provided adequate standards were unsuccessful.[151]

If standards for training doctors and admitting them to practice were low, standards for the legal profession were lower still. The Constitution of 1851 (Art. 7, sec. 21) declared that any person of good moral character who was a voter might practice law. This provision, which reflected the faith of the members of the convention in "democracy" and "the common man," was occasionally attacked. "Popularizing the legal profession in Indiana has increased its numbers," said one critic, "but not elevated its character, nor made public justice purer, surer and more effectual." But there were no serious efforts to change the constitutional provisions until the legislative session of 1885.[152]

Most lawyers obtained such knowledge as they possessed by reading a few law books and perhaps receiving instructions from men who were already practicing. A few attended law schools. As already noted law courses were offered from time to time by Indiana University, Asbury University, Notre Dame, and some of the other private colleges.[153]

At the close of the 1870's it could still be truly said that "Indiana has no schools of the highest order, in theology, in law or in medicine," and that a "university education of the highest order," must "still be sought beyond the borders of Indiana."[154] Nevertheless, by that time the foundations of the educational system of the state were firmly established. Indiana University had survived efforts of those who wanted

---

[151] Edgerton, *Address*, p. 10; Myers, *Medical Education in Indiana*, pp. 98-100. In 1885 the legislature provided that persons seeking to practice medicine must secure a license from the county clerk. Applicants were required to be graduates of a reputable medical school or to present evidence that they had successfully engaged in practice for ten years immediately prior to the adoption of the act. In 1897 legislation was adopted establishing the State Board of Medical Registration and Examination and specifying its duties. *Ibid.*, p. 100.

[152] Edgerton, *Address*, p. 8; Kettleborough, *Constitution Making in Indiana*, I, clv.

[153] See above, pp. 509, 514, 516, 525.

[154] Edgerton, *Address*, p. 7.

to abolish it completely. While it remained small and struggling, it had begun to receive regular appropriations from the legislature and in 1880 stood on the threshold of a period of significant growth. A second state-supported institution, Purdue, representing the trend toward more practical training, had been opened. Several private colleges had failed, but every major religious denomination in the state—Presbyterian, Methodist, Baptist, Quaker, Disciples of Christ, and Roman Catholic—had founded at least one college which has survived to the present. In all of these denominational colleges as well as the state university a movement had begun away from the narrowly traditional classical theological curriculum to a broader course of study which placed more emphasis upon science.

More significant than these beginnings in higher education was the acceptance of the responsibility of state and local governments to maintain tax-supported elementary schools open to all. Public schools of this sort, which had been in their infancy in 1850, were firmly established thirty years later. Most of the public schools were still one-room ungraded rural schools, but graded elementary schools and high schools were gaining wide acceptance in towns and cities. With the growth of tax-supported schools there was a corresponding decline in private schools. By 1880 the objective of the first state constitution of a system of education from township school to state university which was equally open to all without tuition had been in a large measure realized.

CHAPTER XII

POPULATION GROWTH AND SOCIAL CHANGE

BETWEEN 1850 AND 1880 the population of Indiana nearly doubled—from 988,416 at midcentury to 1,978,301 in 1880. The greatest increase occurred during the fifties. By 1860 United States census figures showed a total of 1,350,428, a net gain of 362,012 or more than 36 per cent. During the seventies the rate of growth declined somewhat, the net increase being 297,664 or 17.7 per cent.

During this period Indiana ranked higher in population relative to other states than at any other time in her history. In 1850 she was the seventh state in the United States in population. By 1860 she had attained sixth place, a rank which she retained in 1870 and 1880, after which her relative position declined. In 1850 Indiana was outranked by New York, Pennsylvania, Ohio, Virginia (which included West Virginia), Tennessee, and Massachusetts. During the next three decades New York, Pennsylvania, and Ohio retained their position as the most populous states, but during the fifties Illinois experienced a phenomenal growth which made her fourth in population, a position which she retained in 1870 and 1880. By 1860 Virginia was the fifth state, but Indiana had surpassed Massachusetts and Tennessee, becoming sixth in rank. By 1870 Missouri had moved into fifth place, a place she retained in 1880.[1]

Although Ohio, which was larger geographically than Indiana, continued to surpass Indiana in population, during the fifties and sixties, the rate of growth in Indiana was higher than that of her older eastern neighbor. But during the

1 The following tables show the population and rank of the most populous states in the decennial censuses.

seventies the rate of growth in Ohio was slightly higher than in Indiana, due, no doubt, to the fact that industry was growing more rapidly in Ohio. The rate of population growth in Illinois (101 per cent) in the fifties was almost three times that of Indiana, and during the sixties about twice as great (48.3 per cent). During the seventies the rate of growth in Illinois declined to 21 per cent but remained somewhat higher than that in Indiana.[2] By 1880

1850				1870		
1.	New York	3,097,394		1.	New York	4,382,759
2.	Pennsylvania	2,311,786		2.	Pennsylvania	3,521,951
3.	Ohio.	1,980,329		3.	Ohio	2,665,260
4.	Virginia	1,421,661		4.	Illinois	2,539,891
5.	Tennessee	1,002,717		5.	Missouri	1,721,295
6.	Massachusetts	994,514		6.	Indiana	1,680,637
7.	Indiana	988,416				

1860				1880		
1.	New York	3,880,735		1.	New York	5,082,871
2.	Pennsylvania	2,906,215		2.	Pennsylvania	4,282,891
3.	Ohio	2,339,511		3.	Ohio	3,198,062
4.	Illinois	1,711,951		4.	Illinois	3,077,871
5.	Virginia	1,596,318		5.	Missouri	2,168,380
6.	Indiana	1,350,428		6.	Indiana	1,978,301

The foregoing figures are compiled from United States Bureau of the Census, *Compendium of the Ninth Census* (1870), 8, and *Tenth Census* (1880), I, *Population*, p. 4.

2 The following tables show the rate of population growth in Indiana and the other states of the Old Northwest from 1850 to 1880.

Indiana			Michigan		
1850-1860	36.6 per cent		1850-1860	88.3 per cent	
1860-1870	24.4		1860-1870	58	
1870-1880	17.7		1870-1880	38.2	

Ohio			Wisconsin		
1850-1860	18.1 per cent		1850-1860	154 per cent	
1860-1870	13.9		1860-1870	35.9	
1870-1880	19.9		1870-1880	24.7	

Illinois		
1850-1860	101 per cent	
1860-1870	48.3	
1870-1880	21.1	

United States Bureau of the Census, *Tenth Census* (1880), I, 5.

Indiana had slightly less than two thirds the population of Illinois. As would be expected population increased at a more rapid rate in Michigan and Wisconsin, both newer and less-developed states, than in Indiana. During the fifties the population of Michigan increased by 88 per cent, while in Wisconsin it increased by 154 per cent. Between 1850 and 1880 the population in Michigan more than quadrupled— from 397,654 to 1,636,937. In Wisconsin the total increased from 305,391 in 1850 to 1,315,497 in 1880.[3]

In the period after 1850 the rate of population growth in the southern part of Indiana, the section which had been settled earliest, began to taper off, while the central and northern parts showed a more rapid increase. At midcentury the population of the southern third of the state was slightly greater than that in the central third, while the northern third of the state remained sparsely populated. During the fifties the relative position of the southern and central sections remained unchanged, each section increasing by about 25 per cent. But during the sixties the rate of growth in the central section was more rapid, with the result that by 1870 the population of the central third of the state exceeded that of the southern third. While the total population of the southern and central sections continued to increase, the population of some counties, especially in the

[3] The following table shows the total population of the other states of the Old Northwest from 1850 to 1880.

Ohio		Michigan	
1850	1,980,329	1850	397,654
1860	2,339,511	1860	749,113
1870	2,665,260	1870	1,184,059
1880	3,198,062	1880	1,636,937
Illinois		Wisconsin	
1850	851,470	1850	305,391
1860	1,711,951	1860	775,881
1870	2,539,891	1870	1,054,670
1880	3,077,871	1880	1,315,497

United States Bureau of the Census, *Compendium of the Ninth Census* (1870), 8, and *Tenth Census* (1880), I, 4.

southeast, remained almost static after midcentury and in some places showed a slight decline. For example, the population of Ohio, Jefferson, and Franklin counties was less in 1880 than it had been in 1870. Meanwhile, the northern third of the state, while lagging behind the central and southern parts in total numbers, grew at a more rapid rate. From 1850 to 1860 the counties in the north showed a growth of almost 60 per cent. From 1850 to 1880 the total population of that region increased more than 250 per cent.[4]

For the state as a whole a high birthrate among the native population was the most important factor in population growth. This is shown by the fact that the percentage of persons born in Indiana increased more rapidly than the rate of growth for the state as a whole. In 1850 a little more than half of the population consisted of persons born in the state. By 1880 more than 70 per cent were born in the state. The highest percentage of persons born in Indiana was found in the southern third, with almost as high a percentage in the central portion. In the newer counties in the north, as would be expected, the percentage of persons born in the state was smaller.[5]

[4] Barnhart and Carmony, *Indiana,* II, 11, 292; United States Bureau of the Census, *Tenth Census* (1880), I, 388-389. The following table shows the distribution of population in the three sections from 1850 to 1880.

Southern Indiana	Central Indiana	Northern Indiana
1850 418,373	404,743	165,300
1860 538,881	525,518	286,029
1870 644,735	651,316	384,586
1880 737,215	778,465	462,621

Barnhart and Carmony, *op. cit.,* II, 11, 292.

[5] In 1850 of a total population of 988,416 the number born in Indiana was 525,732. In 1880 the figure was 1,354,565 of a total population of 1,834,123. United States Bureau of the Census, *Seventh Census* (1850), xxxviii; *Tenth Census* (1880), I, 480. In almost all of the counties in the southern third of Indiana in 1870 three fourths or more of the American-born population was born in Indiana. The highest percentage of Indiana-born Americans was found in Ohio, Dubois, Washington, Orange, Pike, Harrison, Crawford, Jackson, Gibson, and Franklin counties. In the central third of the state slightly less than three fourths of the native Americans were born in Indiana; in the

The second largest element in the population was persons born in other parts of the United States who moved to Indiana. In 1850 about 40 per cent of the total was made up of persons born in other states. In 1880 this group constituted only about 25 per cent.[6] At midcentury no doubt a majority of Indiana residents were of southern extraction since persons from the upper South had constituted the most important element among early settlers. But by 1850 the percentage of Southerners among newcomers was already declining, and it continued to decline. In 1850 of persons who had migrated to Indiana from other parts of the Union 176,575 came from slave areas, while 213,738 came from free areas. Among persons born in other states, the largest group came from Ohio, while Kentucky ranked second, Pennsylvania third, Virginia fourth, North Carolina fifth, and New York sixth in the number of persons who moved to Indiana. Few persons from any of the states of the lower South except South Carolina were found in Indiana. Few persons came directly to Indiana from New England, although it is probable that many persons who came from Ohio, Pennsylvania, and New York were of New England ancestry. But the percentage of New Englanders was smaller in Indiana than in either Illinois or Michigan.[7]

After 1850 Ohio continued to send a larger number to Indiana than did any other state. In 1880 Kentucky remained in second place and Pennsylvania third, but Illinois was in fourth place, New York fifth, while Virginia and

northern third of the state less than three fifths. Stephen S. Visher, "Distribution of Birthplaces of Indianians in 1870," *Indiana Magazine of History,* XXVI (1930), 128, and map, 131.

6 In 1850 a total of 405,764 out of a population of 988,416 had been born in other states; in 1880 a total of 479,588 out of 1,834,123. United States Bureau of the Census, *Seventh Census* (1850), xxxviii; *Tenth Census* (1880), I, 472.

7 Barnhart and Carmony, *Indiana,* I, 414. The totals from the various states in 1850 were as follows: Ohio, 120,193; Kentucky, 68,651; Pennsylvania, 44,245; Virginia, 41,819; North Carolina, 33,175; New York, 24,310. There were 4,069 persons from South Carolina. *Ibid.*

North Carolina had dropped to sixth and seventh positions respectively.[8] Persons from Ohio were most numerous in the northeastern counties of Indiana. In twenty counties in that section they constituted from 20 to 30 per cent of the total population in 1870. Most persons coming from Kentucky settled in the counties along the Ohio River or along the routes of railroads running northward. Natives of Pennsylvania were most numerous in counties in the northern third of the state. The largest numbers were found in Elkhart and La Grange counties. The largest number of New Yorkers was found in the extreme north—in Steuben, La Porte, Porter, and Lake counties.[9]

Meanwhile, some persons born in Indiana were leaving the state and seeking homes elsewhere, although the immigration into the state remained much greater than the exodus from it. The United States census of 1860 showed 215,541 persons born in Indiana living in other states, while by 1880 the number had reached 436,551. At the latter date the largest number from Indiana were found in Illinois, the second largest number in Kansas, the third largest number in Missouri, and the fourth in Iowa.[10]

Among the native-born Americans who moved into Indiana were Negroes, nearly all of whom came from the South. The number of Negroes in the state more than trebled between 1850 and 1880, but the ratio of Negroes to the white population remained extremely small. In 1850 about 1 per cent of the population was Negro, in 1880 about 2 per cent. In 1850 there were 11,262 Negroes in the state. During the next decade, as the result of the operation of the Fugitive Slave Law of 1850, which caused some persons

[8] The distribution of persons from other states in 1880 was as follows: Ohio, 186,391; Kentucky, 73,928; Pennsylvania, 51,234; Illinois, 27,201; New York, 26,506; Virginia, 24,538; North Carolina, 20,884. United States Bureau of the Census, *Tenth Census* (1880), I, 480-483.

[9] Visher, "Distribution of Birthplaces of Indianians," *Indiana Magazine of History*, XXVI, 130, 133, 135, 137, 138.

[10] Barnhart and Carmony, *Indiana*, II, 300-301.

to move from Indiana to Canada, and the exclusion policy embodied in Indiana's new constitution, there was almost no increase in the total number of Negroes. In the period immediately after the Civil War there was a sharp increase in the Negro population as Negroes from former slave states moved northward. Between 1860 and 1870 the Negro population in the state more than doubled, from 11,428 to 24,560. By 1880 it had reached 39,228.[11]

In 1850 most of the Negro population was concentrated near the Ohio River, especially in Floyd and Clark counties, in Wayne and Randolph counties (where the presence of Quakers attracted Negroes), and in Vigo and Marion counties. Many of the Negroes who came into the state in the postwar period settled in the towns along the Ohio, but more of them moved northward to the central part of the state, especially Indianapolis. By 1880 the counties with the largest Negro population were Marion, Vanderburgh, Clark, Wayne, Floyd, Vigo, and Spencer, in that order.[12]

In the period before the Civil War the Negro population had been primarily rural, but many of the later settlers moved into the towns and cities. By 1880 more than six thousand Negroes lived in Indianapolis, making up more than 8 per cent of the total population. In Evansville the total number was smaller than in Indianapolis but the ratio was higher—more than 9 per cent. There were also high percentages of Negroes in such towns as Rockport, Mount Vernon, New Albany, and Jeffersonville in the extreme south, and in Terre Haute and Richmond.[13]

Most of the Negroes moving into Indiana before 1880 came from the states of the Upper South. By far the largest number came from Kentucky. In 1880 about sixteen thou-

11 Thornbrough, *Negro in Indiana*, pp. 44, 45, 53-54, 206.

12 *Ibid.*, pp. 45, 46; United States Bureau of the Census, *Tenth Census* (1880), I, 388-389. The Negro population in the counties was as follows: Marion, 8,038; Vanderburgh, 3,843; Clark, 2,536; Wayne, 1,710; Floyd, 1,552; Vigo, 1,506; Spencer, 1,492.

13 United States Bureau of the Census, *Tenth Census* (1880), I, 417-418.

sand of the Negro population had been born in Indiana and about thirteen thousand in Kentucky. Other states from which substantial numbers came were North Carolina, Virginia, Tennessee, and Ohio. Few came from the Lower South.[14]

Soon after the Civil War, as already shown, the Indiana Supreme Court had declared the exclusion provisions of the Indiana Constitution null and void. But although there was no legal impediment to their settlement after 1866, Negro arrivals frequently met with hostility, and in some communities there was a public policy which prevented Negroes from residing there. Washington County was an example of a place which became "off limits" to Negroes. Before the war a number of Negroes had come there in the company of white Quakers, but during the war years a number of acts of intimidation led to an exodus. By 1880 there were only three Negroes in the county. In Crawford County, just across the Ohio River from Kentucky, Negroes were discouraged from settling, and in 1880 only two were found in the county. In some other communities in the south, including Utica in Clark County, Aurora in Dearborn, and Scottsburg in Scott, Negroes dared not settle, and in many towns farther north a quasi-official policy kept them from residing or even remaining overnight.[15]

While Negro settlers were officially excluded before the Civil War and frequently greeted with hostility afterwards, European immigration was generally regarded as desirable. But Indiana failed to attract as many Europeans as did neighboring states. The reasons for this are not entirely clear, but two fundamental factors were that Indiana did not have as much desirable cheap land as did some of the newer states, nor did she develop large industrial centers

14 *Ibid.,* I, 488-491. The numbers born in the states were as follows: Indiana, 16,713; Kentucky, 12,965; North Carolina, 3,167; Virginia, 1,563; Tennessee, 1,390; Ohio, 1,091.

15 Thornbrough, *Negro in Indiana,* pp. 208-211, 225-226.

like Chicago and the large cities of Ohio. Another probable reason was that Indiana was less publicized in Europe as a place for immigration than were some other states, notably Wisconsin. In 1851 Governor Wright declared that there was less known abroad about Indiana "than any other state in the Union of her age and position." That same year a group of Fort Wayne citizens at a public meeting deplored the fact that Indiana was attracting fewer Germans than other states and voted to organize a committee to encourage immigration.[16] But except for the action of the Constitutional Convention granting the right to vote to aliens who had lived in the state for six months, the state failed to take any official action to encourage immigration during the fifties. Governor Morton urged the establishment of a state bureau of immigration, but the legislature failed to act. His successor, Baker, made a similar recommendation with no better success. On his own responsibility Morton had a booklet published entitled *Emigration to the United States of North America. Indiana as a Home for Emigrants.* It stressed the ease of acquiring citizenship and the right to vote, abundant job opportunities, high wages, low taxes, and numerous cheap schools as inducements for settling in Indiana. In 1866 on his own authority Baker designated John A. Wilstach of Lafayette, who planned a trip to Europe to attend the French Universal Exposition, as Indiana Commissioner of Emigration. Wilstach was instructed to point out the attractions which Indiana offered and to urge prospective emigrants to make it their home.[17]

16 Indiana State Board of Agriculture, *Annual Report,* 1851, p. 255; Richard Lyle Power, "Wet Lands and the Hoosier Stereotype," *Mississippi Valley Historical Review,* XXII (1934-1935), 34.

17 Maurice G. Baxter, "Encouragement of Immigration to the Middle West during the Era of the Civil War," *Indiana Magazine of History,* XLVI (1950), 34-35. The commission, dated January 8, 1866, is in the Governor Conrad Baker Papers, Indiana Historical Society Library. A printed brochure entitled *The Commissioner of Emigration to the Agriculturists, Manufacturers and Capitalists of Indiana, prepared by John A. Wilstach, Commissioner* (Indianapolis, 1866) is in the Governor Baker Papers in the Archives Division, Indiana State Library.

In spite of the failure of the state to carry out any organized program to attract settlers, foreign-born persons in Indiana increased from 54,426 in 1850 to 144,178 in 1880. During the fifties the number of foreign born more than doubled. During the sixties the rate of immigration remained high, but during the seventies it declined substantially. In 1850 foreign-born persons made up between 5 and 6 per cent of the population. By 1870 this had reached more than 9 per cent, but by 1880 it had dropped to 7.8.[18]

Before 1850 most immigrants—from the East, South, and from Europe—reached Indiana by a water route. Thereafter, they tended to settle in river towns and especially near urban railroad centers. The United States census for 1860, the first to show the distribution of the foreign born by counties, showed that more than half of them were in counties in the southern part of the state. Of the remainder the largest numbers were found in certain counties in the north. Except for Indianapolis the central part of the state attracted relatively few foreigners. In 1860 Vanderburgh County had by far the largest number of foreign born. Allen County in the north was second, Marion in the central section third, Dearborn in the southeast fourth, La Porte in the extreme north fifth, and Tippecanoe County in the north central part of the state sixth. In Vanderburgh County foreigners made up about 40 per cent of the whole, in Allen 23 per cent, in Marion 16 per cent, in Dearborn 24 per cent, in La Porte 22 per cent, and in Tippecanoe 22 per cent. In some of the less populous counties where the number of foreigners was not so large they constituted a larger percentage. In Dubois and Perry counties in the south foreigners made up 26 and 24 per cent of the whole respectively. In Lake and Porter counties in the newly settled area in the far north they made up 28 and 17 per cent.[19]

18 United States Bureau of the Census, *Tenth Census* (1880), I, 431, xxxix. The total number of foreign born in 1860 was 118,284.

19 United States Bureau of the Census, *Eighth Census* (1860), *Population,*

Twenty years later the pattern of distribution had changed somewhat. By that time the largest number of foreign born, 14,743, were found in Marion County, where they constituted 14 per cent of the whole. The second largest number, 9,187, was in Allen County, where they constituted 16 per cent of the whole. In Vanderburgh there were 8,528 or 20 per cent of the whole. The next largest number was in La Porte, 7,177, which was 23 per cent of the whole. In St. Joseph there were 5,518, which was 16 per cent of the whole; in Vigo County, 4,799, which was 10 per cent of the whole. In the state as a whole, as already noted, there was a decline in the ratio of foreign born to native population after 1860. In some places where foreigners had been most numerous there was a substantial decline. In Vanderburgh County the percentage of foreigners declined from about 40 per cent to 20 per cent, in Dubois County from 26 to 13 per per cent, in Perry County from 24 to 12 per cent.[20] The decline was due in part simply to the dying out of the first generation of immigrants. The percentage conceals the fact that there were in the population many persons whose parents were European but who were themselves born in the United States. In some places like Dubois County the decline was due to a movement of the rural population to the cities.

Of the larger cities in the state European immigration had the most important effect upon Evansville and Fort

pp. 128-129. The ten counties with the largest number of foreign born in 1860 were as follows:

	Foreign born	Total population
Vanderburgh County	8,374	20,552
Allen County	6,842	29,328
Marion County	6,395	39,855
Dearborn County	5,871	24,406
La Porte County	5,008	22,919
Tippecanoe County	4,126	25,726
Floyd County	3,836	20,183
Jefferson County	3,571	25,036
Ripley County	3,299	19,054
Franklin County	3,124	19,549

[20] United States Bureau of the Census, *Tenth Census* (1880), I, 431-432.

Wayne. In Evansville about 30 per cent of the population was foreign born in 1870, in Fort Wayne about 28 per cent. The total number of foreigners was greater in Indianapolis but the ratio was smaller—22 per cent in 1870. There were also large percentages of Europeans in the other Ohio River cities although not so large as in Evansville. In 1870 the percentage in Madison was 20, in Jeffersonville 17, in New Albany 13. Farther north by that date there was a higher percentage in some of the important transportation centers— 27 per cent in Lafayette, Logansport 21 per cent, and South Bend 18 per cent. In the far north at Michigan City and La Porte the percentages were 39 and 30 respectively.[21]

Germans constituted by far the largest element among European immigrants. Of the 54,426 persons of foreign birth resident in Indiana in 1850, according to the United States census, 29,324 or 53 per cent were natives of the German states. By 1860 the number had more than doubled— to 66,705 or 56 per cent of the whole. In 1870 the number was 78,060 or 55 per cent. Ten years later the total had grown but slightly, to 80,756 and the percentage remained the same. This represented 3.1 per cent of the total population.[22]

[21] *Ibid.,* I, 448-449. The number of foreign born in 1870 in relation to the total population in the leading cities is shown in the following table.

	Foreign born	Total population
Evansville	6,276	21,830
Fort Wayne	5,041	17,718
Indianapolis	10,657	48,244
Jeffersonville	1,297	7,254
Lafayette	3,639	13,506
La Porte	2,005	6,581
Logansport	1,956	8,950
Madison	2,194	10,709
Michigan City	1,585	3,985
New Albany	2,062	15,396
South Bend	1,365	7,206
Terre Haute	3,101	16,103

[22] *Ibid., Seventh Census* (1850), xxxvi; *Eighth Census* (1860), *Population,* p. 130; *Compendium of Ninth Census* (1870), 394-395; *Tenth Census* (1880), I, 465.

Germans were by no means an entirely homogeneous group, but wherever they settled they established German institutions and customs. They came from all parts of Germany. The United States census of 1870 shows that the largest group came from Prussia, the second largest from Bavaria, the third from Baden, the fourth from Würtemberg, the fifth from Hesse. Smaller groups came from Hanover, Mecklenburg, Hamburg, and Brunswick.[23]

Some of these immigrants settled in rural agricultural communities. Before 1850 a number of German families had established themselves in the extreme southwest of the state, especially in Dubois County, and in the Whitewater Valley in the southeast. These settlements grew during the 1850's as the result of new immigration. Villages like Jasper, Ferdinand, and Oldenburg were virtually replicas of the villages in Germany from which their residents had come. One visitor from Austria, who traveled northward from the Ohio River to Ferdinand in 1849, said that he traveled sixty to eighty miles through an area "inhabited . . . exclusively by Germans" and had not heard a word of English since he left the boat at Madison. Ferdinand he described as "a completely Catholic German village protected and governed by the church that crowns the hilltop." In the evening the men of the village came into the three bars which the tiny settlement boasted to drink and talk. The only ingredient of a true German village which the visitor found lacking was music.[24]

Some of the Germans who came before 1850 had settled in towns, especially along the Ohio, and a larger percentage

[23] The numbers from the various German states in 1870 were as follows: Prussia, 29,076; Bavaria, 11,500; Baden, 8,154; Würtemberg, 7,010; Hesse, 6,768; Hanover, 3,713; Mecklenburg, 2,454; Saxony, 1,472; Nassau, 707; Oldenburg, 664; Hamburg, 465; Brunswick, 208. Total, 78,060. *Compendium of Ninth Census* (1870), 394-395.

[24] Josephine Goldmark, *Pilgrims of '48. One Man's Part in the Austrian Revolution of 1848 and a Family Migration to America* (Yale University Press, 1930), p. 222.

of the later arrivals went to the cities. Most of the German settlers were poor folk. The failure of the potato crops in 1846 and 1847 and again in the period from 1852 to 1855 was an important reason for their emigration. Of the first Germans who settled in Indianapolis (and this was no doubt true also of those in Evansville, Fort Wayne, and the other towns) almost all were artisans or common laborers. In the census of 1850 most of them were classed simply as "laborers," while others were listed as carpenters, shoemakers, tailors, coopers, and blacksmiths. There were a few grocers and merchants. Among the "Forty-eighters" were some who came primarily for political reasons and who had been business and professional men of substance in Germany. After a few years others who had been poverty stricken when they arrived became prosperous businessmen. By 1880 Germans comprised over half of the brewers and maltsters, one third of the bakers, shoemakers, and cabinetmakers in Indianapolis. Many Germans became merchants. A large part of the downtown businesses in Indianapolis, including clothing, drygoods, boot and shoe, hardware, and furniture stores, were owned by German families. Germans were conspicuous in the ownership and operation of breweries and distilleries. They owned the beer gardens and many of the theaters. Other Germans became lawyers and doctors.[25]

In religion Bavarians and others from the Rhineland were nearly always Roman Catholic. They became the most important element in the Catholic church in Indiana. Prussians and those from the other north German states were Protestants—members of the Lutheran, German Evangelical, or Reformed churches. A few were "freethinkers" who rejected all orthodox religion. In communities where Germans

[25] George Theodore Probst, The Germans in Indianapolis 1850-1914 (Unpublished Master's thesis in History, Indiana University, 1951), pp. 66-70, 89, 91-92. See the table, ibid., pp. 68-70, for the German-owned businesses in downtown Indianapolis from 1865 to 1875. For a good contemporary picture of the impact of the Germans on the Middle West see F. F. Lalor, "The Germans in the West," Atlantic Monthly, XXXII (1873), 459-470.

were numerous, both Catholic and Protestant churches were established in which services were conducted in the German language.[26]

Schools in which the German language was used were conducted in connection with some of the churches, both Catholic and Protestant. In 1856 the Indianapolis City Council, in response to pressures from German residents, adopted a resolution that German pupils should be allowed to have instruction in their own language and that money should be appropriated to hire German teachers. But this was largely a meaningless gesture in view of the weak state of public education at the time. In 1859 a German-English Independent School was founded by German freethinkers who did not want their children to attend parochial schools but who wanted them to be taught the German language, literature, and music. The school was in operation from 1859 to 1882. In 1869 the state legislature provided that courses in German should be taught in any public school in which twenty-five parents requested them.[27]

In every community where Germans were numerous a German press developed.[28] Germans organized their turn-vereins and musical and dramatic groups, which greatly enriched the cultural life of Indiana cities.[29] Like all continental Europeans they enjoyed dancing and drinking beer and wine. These practices plus the fact that Germans failed to observe the Sabbath with the Puritanical strictness demanded by English Protestant groups brought bitter criticism from the older Protestant groups.[30] Most of the early German immigrants were Democrats in politics, and the emergence of the temperance issue in politics tended to

26 For a further account of religion see below Chapter XIII.

27 Probst, Germans in Indianapolis, pp. 40-43; Theodore Stein, *"Our Old School" Historical Sketch of the German English Independent School of Indianapolis* (Indianapolis, 1913), p. 7 and *passim;* above Chapter XI, page 480.

28 For a further discussion of the German press see below Chapter XIV, pages 686-688.

29 See Chapter XIV, page 693.

30 See Chapter XIII, pages 622-623.

strengthen their adherence to that party. On the other hand, as already seen, some Germans held antislavery views which took them into the Republican party in the 1850's. But many Germans never left the Democratic party, and it seems probable that some of them returned to it in the postwar years. Some of the "Forty-eighters" brought with them a revolutionary tradition. When Louis Kossuth visited Indiana in 1852, he was given an enthusiastic welcome by German groups. In the fifties in Indianapolis and other cities Germans formed antimonarchical societies to support European people who were struggling to establish free governments. The spirit of German nationalism remained high among many immigrants. In 1871 the Germans in Indianapolis held a celebration in observance of the victory over France in the Franco-Prussian War.[31]

Persons born in Ireland made up the second largest group of European immigrants. In 1850 there were 12,787 Irish-born in Indiana or 23 per cent of the total number of foreign born. During the fifties the number nearly doubled, reaching 24,495, but the rate of increase was not as great as among the Germans, with the result that in 1860 the Irish constituted only 20 per cent of the foreign born. During the sixties their numbers increased to 28,698, but during the next decade the number born in Ireland declined slightly to 25,741. At that date they made up about 17 per cent of the total number of persons of foreign birth and only about 1.3 per cent of the whole population.[32]

The story of these Irish immigrants is much more elusive than that of the Germans, partly, of course, because their numbers were fewer. Since information is fragmentary, a considerable amount of it must rest on inference. Most of the Irish were undoubtedly extremely poor, having left

[31] Probst, Germans in Indianapolis, pp. 26-27, 28-29; Indianapolis *Daily Journal,* March 15, 1871.

[32] United States Bureau of the Census, *Seventh Census* (1850), xxxvi; *Eighth Census* (1860), *Population,* p. xxix; *Compendium of the Ninth Census* (1870), 396; *Tenth Census* (1880), I, 465.

Ireland because of famine. The percentage of illiteracy among them was high, a factor which contributed to the paucity of records. It is probable that a substantial part of the Irish who settled in Indiana did not come there directly from Ireland. Many who landed at ports on the eastern seaboard such as New York or Boston worked as laborers in the East, sometimes for several years, before making their way westward. Some of them came into northern Indiana by way of Canada, where they had lived for several years.[33] By the time they reached Indiana they had lost some of the distinguishing marks of the foreigner.

Many Irish came into the state as laborers in the building of the Wabash and Erie Canal. In later years others came as construction workers on the railroads. Some of these were transients, but others took up permanent residence. In 1847 the Wabash and Erie Canal Company offered plots of land of from 40 to 160 acres to immigrants at reasonable prices. It is probable that some of the Irish workers acquired land in this way.[34] Groups of Irish were found along the routes of the canal, along railroad routes, and in all important transportation centers. Occasionally it is possible to identify an Irish settlement by a distinctive name like Cassidy's settlement in Perry County. Irish workers were found in large numbers in the cotton mills at Cannelton. Kingan's pork-packing plant in Indianapolis, which was owned by a family from Ulster, imported some workers directly from Ireland.[35]

Nearly all Irish were Roman Catholics, and the establishment of Roman Catholic churches in some communities is evidence of a sizeable Irish settlement.[36] Much of the social

[33] Elfrieda Lang, "Irishmen in Northern Indiana before 1850," *Mid-America*, XXXVI (New Series XXV, 1954), 195-196.

[34] *Ibid.*, p. 191.

[35] Schroeder, *Catholic Church in the Diocese of Vincennes*, pp. 65, 67-68; Kershner, Social and Cultural History of Indianapolis, p. 155.

[36] Churches which were founded primarily by Irish were frequently referred to as "Irish" to distinguish them from German Catholic churches. Schroeder, *Catholic Church in the Diocese of Vincennes*, p. 67, mentions four Catholic

life of the Irish centered around these churches. In addition several Irish fraternal and benevolent societies were formed. Perhaps the best known was the Ancient Order of Hibernians, a secret order with benevolent features. It attempted to pay benefits to members who were sick or disabled and to pay funeral expenses. It also had an employment committee to help members in securing work. In addition there were lodges of the United Irish Benevolent Society, the Emerald Beneficial Association, and the Knights of Father Mathew scattered over the state.[37]

The Irish were active in politics from the time of their arrival. A few of them went into the Republican party. During the sixties and seventies two Republicans of Irish ancestry, Dan Macauley and John Caven, were mayors of Indianapolis. But the Irish were for the most part identified with the Democratic party. Many also continued to retain their identification with Ireland. In the sixties about one hundred thirty men from Indianapolis took part in the Fenian invasion of Canada. St. Patrick's Day was always the occasion for important celebrations. In 1879, in observance of the day, delegates representing Irish societies from all over the state met in Indianapolis at an Irish Delegate Assembly. After a parade they heard an address by the Right Reverend Bishop Chatard on "The Social Mission of the Irish Race."[38]

No other national group exerted an influence comparable to the Germans and the Irish. In 1880 there were about fourteen thousand persons in the state who had been born in England, Scotland, or Wales and slightly less than six

parishes along the Madison and Indianapolis Railroad which were predominately Irish. See Rev. H. J. Alerding, *History of the Catholic Church in the Diocese of Vincennes* (Indianapolis, 1883) and H. J. Alerding, *The Diocese of Fort Wayne 1857-1907* (Fort Wayne, 1907), *passim*, for numerous examples.

[37] Blanchard (ed. and comp.), *Catholic Church in Indiana*, I, 623-624; Indianapolis *Daily Sentinel*, March 18, 1879.

[38] Kershner, *Social and Cultural History of Indianapolis*, p. 156; Indianapolis *Daily Sentinel*, March 18, 1879.

thousand who had been born in British America. There were slightly more than four thousand French, fewer than four thousand Scandinavians, a little more than three thousand Swiss, and about thirteen hundred from Holland. There were less than two hundred Italians in the entire state and only a few hundred persons from the countries of eastern Europe. In 1850 not a single Chinese was listed for Indiana in the census. In 1860 there were two and by 1880 twenty-nine. During the seventies about a dozen Chinese appeared in Indianapolis and opened laundries. In spite of the insignificance of their number they were treated with hostility.[39]

From all of the statistics on population one fact stands out —that Indiana was less affected by European immigration than almost any other northern state in spite of the considerable number of Europeans who settled in the state in the fifties and sixties. Indiana received a smaller proportion of immigrants during the great influx of the fifties than did any other state in the Old Northwest.[40] In 1880 Indiana ranked ninth among all the states in the Union in the number of German-born residents, fifteenth in the number of Irish, and thirteenth in the number of foreign born of all nationalities, although she stood in sixth place in total population.[41] With a total of 144,178 persons of foreign birth she stood far behind Illinois which had a total of 583,576, Wisconsin with 405,425, Ohio with 394,943, and Michigan with 388,508.[42]

The small ratio of foreign born in Indiana in relation to the whole population was even more striking. In no other northern state except Delaware was there such a small percentage of foreigners. Only in the states of the South was

[39] United States Bureau of the Census, *Tenth Census* (1880), I, 3, 465, 505-506, 539; Kershner, Social and Cultural History of Indianapolis, p. 158.

[40] Of the total foreign immigration to the Old Northwest in the fifties Indiana received only 9.7 per cent, while Illinois received 32.9 per cent, Wisconsin 25.8, Ohio 17, and Michigan 14.6 per cent. Schroeder, *Catholic Church in the Diocese of Vincennes*, p. 71.

[41] United States Bureau of the Census, *Tenth Census* (1880), I, 466.

[42] *Ibid.*, I, 426.

there a smaller percentage. In the states of the Old Northwest the population of Wisconsin was 44 per cent foreign born, that of Michigan 31 per cent, Illinois 23 per cent, Ohio 14 per cent, while in Indiana the percentage was only 7.8.[43]

§ §

As population increased and transportation facilities were built, town and city life began to develop. In 1850 only 4.5 per cent of the population of Indiana lived in towns of more than 2,500. By 1880 the percentage had increased to 19.5. At midcentury no town in the state had as many as ten thousand inhabitants. By 1880 Indianapolis, the state capital, had a population of seventy-five thousand. Three other cities —Evansville, Fort Wayne, and Terre Haute—had more than twenty-five thousand inhabitants, and five more had more than ten thousand. But in spite of the beginnings of urbanization Indiana remained predominantly rural, and most county seats were towns of only one or two thousand.[44]

At midcentury two Ohio River cities, New Albany and Madison, each with slightly more than eight thousand inhabitants, were close rivals for the distinction of being the most populous city. By 1850 Madison had reached its peak as a commercial and cultural center. Already an important river port in the pioneer period during the forties, growth was accelerated by being a terminus of the first railroad built in the state. As the Madison and Indianapolis line reached into the hinterlands the importance of Madison as an outlet for farm produce increased. Madison also led the state in manufacturing. But the competition of new railroads built

43 *Ibid.*, I, xxxix-xl.

44 Visher, "Population Changes in Indiana 1840-1940," *Indiana Academy of Science, Proceedings*, LI (1942), 188-189. The figures on the population of Indiana cities in this chapter are taken from the following: United States Bureau of the Census, *Seventh Census* (1850), 756-779; *Eighth Census* (1860), *Population*, pp. 113-128; *Ninth Census* (1870), *Statistics of Population*, pp. 122-130; *Tenth Census* (1880), I, 147-155. The figures for the 1860 census are unsatisfactory for some cities because the figures given are for the township in which the city was located rather than for the city alone.

during the fifties deprived her of her advantage. At first Madisonians adopted a defensive attitude. "Rival railroads cannot ruin the prospects of Madison," declared the Madison *Daily Courier* in 1853; "they must improve those prospects materially. . . . This city was never more prosperous." But between 1850 and 1860 the total population of the city increased by only about one hundred. During the war years of the sixties Madison enjoyed a slight boom, but during the seventies her population declined.[45]

In 1850 United States census figures showed New Albany as being slightly more populous than Madison, and with her neighbor, Jeffersonville, a town of slightly more than two thousand, she made up the most important urban center in the state. New Albany was already an important commercial center and also boasted a few small-scale manufacturing establishments. The building of the New Albany and Salem Railroad enhanced the prospects of the city. In 1857 the New Albany Board of Trade published a pamphlet entitled *The Commercial and Manufacturing Advantages of New Albany, Indiana* in an effort to attract investments and settlers. It emphasized "various communications with the South by railroads and river," which did indeed exist, but it also stressed such attractions as "paved and well lighted streets" and "superior free schools," which could scarcely be said to have become realities at that date. New Albany promoters claimed that their city possessed superior advantages to those of Pittsburgh as a potential center of industry. In 1860 there were claims that she led the cities of Indiana in manufacturing. During the fifties her population increased by 50 per cent—to more than twelve thousand. But thereafter the rate of growth declined. By 1880 New Albany had a population of only slightly more than sixteen thousand and was the fifth city in the state in size.[46]

[45] Madison *Daily Courier*, August 12, 1853, quoted in Daniels, *Village at the End of the Road*, p. 95. The population of Madison was 8,012 in 1850; 8,130 in 1860; 10,709 in 1870; 8,945 in 1880.

[46] Bogle, "New Albany: Mid-Nineteenth Century Economic Expansion,"

Farther down the Ohio River was Evansville, a town of only three thousand in 1850 but destined soon to outdistance both Madison and New Albany. At midcentury Evansville was already acquiring importance as a river port, and her prospects were greatly increased when the Wabash and Erie Canal was finally completed in 1853 and the railroad to Terre Haute was opened the following year. Evansville rapidly became an outlet for farm produce for points as far away as Lafayette. Her connections with points along the Ohio and Mississippi rivers were also important. Regular packet services operated to Paducah, Memphis, Cincinnati, and other river cities. Trade also developed with points on the Cumberland and Tennessee rivers. As already seen Evansville was the gateway to Indiana for European immigrants coming into the state by way of New Orleans. She received a larger share of these immigrants than any other city in the state. In 1856 she was made a United States port of entry. During the fifties the population of the infant city more than trebled. The Civil War stimulated further growth, and during the sixties population almost doubled again. By 1870 Evansville was the second city in the state.[47]

Until the late 1840's Indianapolis remained a small town, important only as the seat of the state government. She did not acquire the legal status of a city until 1847. The completion of the Madison and Indianapolis Railroad in October of that same year was the event which set Indianapolis on the road to becoming the leading city in the state. Until the coming of the railroad, business in the state capital had been almost entirely local. "It produced little, and it distributed little that it did not produce." When the railroad was first completed Madisonians spoke of Indianapolis pa-

Indiana Magazine of History, LIII, 139n, 142-143. The population of New Albany was 8,181 in 1850; 12,647 in 1860; 15,396 in 1870; 16,423 in 1880.

[47] Gilbert, *Evansville and Vanderburg County,* I, 47, 135; James E. Morlock, *The Evansville Story: A Cultural Interpretation* (Evansville, 1956), p. 67. The population of Evansville was 3,235 in 1850; 11,484 in 1860; 21,830 in 1870; 29,280 in 1880.

tronizingly as "the little town at the other end of the road,"
but the arrival of the railroad marked the beginning of an
era of expanding markets, the development of manufacturing, and population growth. In 1847 it was estimated that
the population of the city was about six thousand. By 1850
it had reached eight thousand. By 1853 it was reported that
every house in the city was occupied—some by two or three
families—that property values had risen several hundred per
cent, and that labor was in great demand. At that date other
railroads were under construction which radiated out from
the city in all directions. "Boston has heretofore been called
the Rail Road city. She will not long be entitled to the
honor," gloated the *Indiana State Journal* in 1850. "Indianapolis will take that laurel from her brow."[48]

At first there was skepticism that Indianapolis could become a leading city because she was not located on a major
water route. Richard Beste, the English traveler who visited
the city in the early fifties, predicted that the lack of water
transportation would hamper her growth. The New Albany
Ledger, which viewed the growth of a potential rival with
some misgivings, declared in 1857: "The examples of great
cities being built up off from regular water courses are so
extremely rare that we hardly believe she [Indianapolis]
will form an exception. No one can suppose that steamers will
ever be supplanted by railroads in carrying freight." But
Indianapolis enthusiasts insisted that her central location and
railroad facilities were "more valuable than three Ohio
rivers."[49] During the fifties the population of Indianapolis
more than doubled, from eight thousand to more than eighteen thousand persons. During the next decade an even more
spectacular growth occurred, the population reaching forty-

48 Holloway, *Indianapolis,* pp. 84-85; Daniels, *Village at the End of the
Road,* pp. 88, 92, 95; Indianapolis *Indiana State Journal,* August 3, 1850.

49 Beste, *The Wabash,* I, 268; New Albany *Ledger,* April 22, 1857, quoted
in Victor M. Bogle, "New Albany: Reaching for the Hinterland," *Indiana
Magazine of History,* L (1954), 166; Indianapolis *Daily Sentinel,* September
11, 1857.

eight thousand. The influx of troops into the city during the war and the demand for supplies for the military organization provided a powerful stimulus to growth. During the war years, one man who lived through the period observed, "everybody was in a fever of enterprise and nobody seemed to think that anything was impossible." The city, he said, "was actually burthened with population and trade." After the war the effects of demobilization were offset by the demands of a growing civilian population and the expansion of railroads. But the postwar period of intense activity and rapid growth came to a halt with the Panic of 1873. The depression which began that year was severe and prolonged. But in spite of economic stagnation the population of the city reached seventy-five thousand by 1880, a figure more than two and one half times that of Evansville, the second city in the state.[50]

West of Indianapolis on the National Road was Terre Haute, already in 1850 a center of commerce and pork packing of some importance as the result of her location on the Wabash River. During the winter of 1849-1850 the Wabash and Erie Canal reached the city from the north. "Terre Haute, the most beautifully situated town in the State, and perhaps in the whole West, will now go ahead rapidly," predicted the *Indiana State Sentinel*. Two years later the railroad connecting Indianapolis and Terre Haute was completed and shortly thereafter the line through Vincennes and Evansville. In 1856 connections with St. Louis were made with the completion of the Terre Haute and Alton Railroad. During the fifties the population of Terre Haute more than doubled, from four thousand to more than eight thousand. During the years following the Civil War the importance of the city increased as more railroads were built. During the sixties her population nearly doubled again. By 1870 she

50 Holloway, *Indianapolis*, p. 115; Kershner, Social and Cultural History of Indianapolis, pp. 53, 70-71, 76-77. The population of Indianapolis was 8;091 in 1850; 18,611 in 1860; 48,244 in 1870; 75,056 in 1880.

was the fourth city in the state.[51] Farther up the Wabash River in the heart of some of the richest farming country in the state was Lafayette. That city, a visitor remarked in 1853, "does more business in proportion to its population than any place with which we are acquainted. The amount of the produce shipped and of the goods sold there, is immense." The completion of the Wabash and Erie Canal across the northern part of the state in the forties had accelerated her growth, and by 1850 Lafayette was already a city of six thousand. Thereafter she became one of the important railroad centers in the state. She continued to show a steady growth, reaching almost fifteen thousand by 1880, when she ranked as the sixth city in the state.[52]

More spectacular was the growth of Fort Wayne on the Maumee River in the northeast. The building of the Wabash and Erie Canal was also an important factor of the growth of this settlement, which had been an Indian trading post, into a leading city. The growth of an agricultural population was also important, and, as already noticed, Fort Wayne received a large number of the Germans who came into the state. In the period after the Civil War Fort Wayne became increasingly important as a railroad center. By 1870 her population had reached more than seventeen thousand, making her the third city in the state.[53] In the extreme north, on the St. Joseph River, was South Bend, a village of 1,652 inhabitants in 1850. The Michigan Southern and Northern Indiana Railroad reached South Bend in 1851, and soon afterwards connections were made with Chicago. During

[51] Indianapolis *Indiana State Sentinel,* November 1, 1849, quoted in Daniels, *Village at the End of the Road,* p. 79; Bradsby, *Vigo County,* pp. 567-569. The population of Terre Haute was 4,051 in 1850; 8,594 in 1860; 16,103 in 1870; 26,042 in 1880.

[52] *Indiana State Journal,* September 19, 1853, quoted in Daniels, *Village at the End of the Road,* p. 87. The population of Lafayette was 6,129 in 1850; 9,387 in 1860; 13,506 in 1870; 14,860 in 1880.

[53] Accurate census figures for the population of Fort Wayne in 1850 and 1860 are not available. In 1870 the population was 17,718; in 1880 it was 26,880.

the next thirty years, like Fort Wayne, South Bend grew rapidly as the result of the movement of agricultural settlers into the north and especially as the result of railroad building. By 1880 she was also already on her way to becoming an important center for the manufacturing of wagons and farm implements. By that date she had a population of 13,280 and was the seventh city in the state.[54]

The eighth city in size in 1880 was Richmond in Wayne County on the National Road at the eastern edge of the state. The completion of the Whitewater Canal in 1848 increased her importance as a center of trade, but the building of railroads during the fifties was a more important stimulus. In 1853 the line westward between Richmond and Indianapolis was completed and also a line to the state border which made connections with lines running to the East. During the fifties the population of Richmond increased from 1,443 to 6,603. By 1860 the town was a center of small industries, especially the manufacture of farm implements. The completion of additional railroads northward and southward helped her maintain a steady growth. By 1880 she numbered more than twelve thousand.[55] The ninth city in size at that date was Logansport in Cass County. Her growth was due mainly to the building of railroads and the establishment of railroad shops. In tenth place was the old Ohio River town, Jeffersonville, which was a center of river trade, boat building, and the infant glass industry. Madison by 1880 was the eleventh city in the state.[56]

54 Stoll, *St. Joseph County*, p. 58. The population of South Bend was 1,652 in 1850; 3,832 in 1860; 7,206 in 1870; 13,280 in 1880.

55 *History of Wayne County* (1884), I, 456-459. The population of Richmond was 1,443 in 1850; 6,603 in 1860; 9,445 in 1870; 12,742 in 1880.

56 The ten most populous cities in 1880 were:

Indianapolis	75,056	Lafayette	14,860
Evansville	29,280	South Bend	13,280
Fort Wayne	26,880	Richmond	12,742
Terre Haute	26,042	Logansport	11,198
New Albany	16,423	Jeffersonville	9,357

As population increased infant cities faced new problems and were compelled to assume new responsibilities. Most of the older cities operated under special charters granted by the legislature, but in 1852 a comprehensive law was passed for the incorporation of communities of more than three thousand into cities. The act is evidence that the lawmakers anticipated some of the problems of urban growth although some of its provisions were not carried out for many years. Some features of the act have remained essentially unchanged to the present. An elected mayor and common council were to be the principal officers. The law also provided for a marshal as the chief law enforcement official, a street commissioner, a chief engineer of a fire department, and a board of health. It gave the common council authority to deal with such matters as public safety, sanitation, public health, and fire protection. An act adopted in 1867 replaced the 1852 law, but while containing some new provisions it reenacted most of the older law.[57]

Many provisions for public safety and public health which city charters required were largely ignored because of public indifference and unwillingness to pay taxes for public services. The entire cost of city government in Indianapolis for the year 1850 was only $7,554. Thereafter expenditures increased rapidly as the result of expanded activities, including the maintenance of a police force and fire protection and street improvements. By 1860 annual expenditures were $80,172. During the war years the amount of money spent increased sharply, but due principally to expenditures for soldiers' bounties rather than for municipal services. In 1865 the total reached $854,391. Thereafter it declined, but in 1870 it remained at $405,016.[58]

It was not until 1854 that the Indianapolis City Council voted to establish a regular police force. The following year the force was suspended, partly because of public oppo-

---

[57] Indiana *Revised Statutes, 1852,* I, 203-221; Indiana *Laws,* 1867, pp. 33-77.
[58] Holloway, *Indianapolis,* p. 138.

sition to the cost, partly because of dissatisfaction with the conduct of the police in attempting to enforce the state prohibition law against the Germans. During the next two years various efforts were made to re-establish the force. After 1857 the police system appears to have had a continuous existence, but appointments continued to be fraught with politics, the numbers of police small, and pay inadequate. A regular police system was not organized in Fort Wayne until 1863. By 1880 all of the larger cities of the state had police forces appointed by the city council or by boards made up of council members. At that date Indianapolis with a population of more than seventy-five thousand had a force of fifty-seven patrolmen. Evansville and Terre Haute, with twenty-seven and thirty patrolmen respectively, had larger forces proportionately. In all three cities the pay of a patrolman was $2.00 a day. Indianapolis paid the chief of police $1,200 a year, but Terre Haute paid only $900.[59]

Fire constituted a great hazard because of the highly inflammable character of wooden buildings which predominated in most cities. Once a wooden structure caught fire it was usually impossible to save it from total destruction. All that fire fighters could do was to prevent the fire from spreading. A visitor to Indianapolis in 1856 remarked that in that city "there seems to be hardly any cessation of fires. . . . We can scarcely attend a public service, either on the Sabbath or week-day, but during it we hear the fire-bell's loud and hurried clang, and the rattle of the fire-engines." In 1855 a fire in Evansville which started in a lumberyard almost destroyed the new courthouse which was then under construction. In New Albany fires in a lard factory in 1856 and a pork factory in 1860 were so destructive that fire companies were unable to control them. In 1852 a fire in Indianapolis destroyed a block of frame business buildings and

[59] *Ibid.,* pp. 101-102; Griswold, *Pictorial History of Fort Wayne,* I, 465; United States Bureau of the Census, *Tenth Census* (1880), XIX, *Social Statistics of Cities,* pp. 442, 454, 474.

the office of the city treasurer which contained the city records. In 1865 a spectacular fire occurred in the Kingan pork-packing plant which had been built the year before. The building, filled with pork and lard, became a holocaust which lighted up the countryside for miles. In 1870 a fire destroyed an opera house and adjoining buildings in the same city. In 1873 the Indianapolis fire chief was killed while fighting a fire in a building which housed a wheel-manufacturing establishment and was full of inflammable materials. In 1874 the most disastrous fire in the city to that time destroyed more than a city block in the downtown area.[60]

Because of the great threat of destruction by fire which was always present citizens generally appear to have been more concerned with fire protection than police protection. The 1852 law for the government of cities gave the common council authority to inspect for fire hazards, to regulate the construction of chimneys, fireplaces, stoves, and boilers and to prevent the erection of wooden buildings in parts of the city where they would constitute a hazard. It also authorized the appointment of a chief engineer for a fire department, the purchase of fire engines and fire-extinguishing apparatus, and the organization of hook and ladder companies.[61]

Prior to that date most cities had organized volunteer fire companies, but as late as 1850 Terre Haute had no fire-fighting organization, and South Bend had no organization until 1853. In other cities in earlier times membership in a fire company was said to have been "almost a badge of good citizenship for the able bodied. Everybody wanted to help." Fire companies were centers of good fellowship, in many respects like a lodge or fraternity, and also centers of political power. Great pride was taken in the procurement and

60 Jobson, *American Methodism*, p. 116; Holloway, *Indianapolis*, p. 97; Morlock, *The Evansville Story*, p. 69; Victor M. Bogle, "A View of New Albany Society at Mid-Nineteenth Century," *Indiana Magazine of History*, LIV (1958), 110; Dunn, *Greater Indianapolis*, I, 282-283.

61 Indiana *Revised Statutes*, 1852, I, 209, 211, 218.

maintenance of equipment and in wearing distinctive regalia. Volunteer companies took such names as "Invincibles" and "Rovers" and also gave picturesque names to their engines. Sometimes there was intense rivalry among companies.[62]

The volunteer groups originated as "bucket brigades," but as early as the 1830's in New Albany and Indianapolis they were using engines which were equipped with hand pumps. Purchase of this equipment was sometimes partly out of public funds, sometimes entirely from private donations. Fairs were sometimes held by women's groups to raise money to pay the cost of fire engines. But by the 1850's city governments had begun to organize fire companies and to assume most of the responsibility for equipping them although the members of the companies continued to be volunteers who served without pay. In 1847 the city of Evansville purchased a fire engine. By 1852 it owned five, but there was no regular paid force of firemen in Evansville until 1888. Prior to that time members of the police force assisted in operating the fire engines. In 1856 Fort Wayne organized a city fire department but fire companies continued to be manned by volunteers. In 1853 a fire chief was appointed in New Albany and in 1863 a city fire department was organized. In 1865 a steam fire engine was purchased for South Bend, but the city's fire companies continued on a volunteer basis until 1885 when a paid fire department was organized.[63]

In Indianapolis until about 1853 the cost of the volunteer system to the city was slight, and the various fire companies

[62] Dunn, *Greater Indianapolis*, I, 170; Bogle, "A View of New Albany Society at Mid-Nineteenth Century," *Indiana Magazine of History*, LIV, 109-110; Indianapolis *Indiana State Sentinel* (triweekly), December 10, 1850; *South Bend and the Men Who Have Made It* (South Bend, Ind., 1901), p. 42; Ernestine Bradford Rose, *The Circle* . . . (Indiana Historical Society *Publications*, XVIII, No. 4, Indianapolis, 1957), pp. 367-369.

[63] Dunn, *Greater Indianapolis*, I, 167; Bogle, "A View of New Albany Society at Mid-Nineteenth Century," *Indiana Magazine of History*, LIV, 107-108, 111; *History of Vanderburgh County* (1889), I, 189-190; South *Bend and the Men Who Have Made It*, p. 42.

operated almost independently. In 1853 they were brought under a common authority when the office of chief fire engineer was created and regular city appropriations for the companies were begun. In 1859 a city ordinance disbanded the volunteer companies and a paid fire department was established.[64]

Meanwhile, the old hand-pumped fire engines were being replaced by steam engines. Indianapolis acquired its first steam-operated engine in 1860. By 1880 it had six fire engines and supplementary equipment. New Albany acquired its first steam-operated equipment in 1863, Fort Wayne in 1861, Evansville in 1864, and South Bend in 1865. Other steps in fire fighting were also taken. In 1863 Indianapolis installed a central alarm bell. In 1868 this system was greatly improved by the installation of a telegraph system. By 1880 some of the engine houses were equipped with telephones. Other cities also installed telegraph systems.[65]

Need for an adequate supply of water to be used in fighting fires appears to have been the principal consideration in the establishment of municipal water systems. By the fifties city dwellers generally got their water from wells or cisterns capped with hand pumps rather than using the rope and bucket method which was still prevalent in the 1840's. There were some public pumps but city governments were slow to assume responsibilities for water. An act of the legislature in 1865 authorized city councils to organize companies to construct waterworks and gave cities the right to purchase the companies. Prior to that date there had been considerable discussion of a public water supply in Indianapolis but no company had actually begun operation. In 1860 a proposal was made to take water from the section of

[64] Holloway, *Indianapolis*, pp. 141-142.

[65] *Ibid.*, p. 143; Bogle, "A View of New Albany Society at Mid-Nineteenth Century," *Indiana Magazine of History*, LIV, 111; Robertson, *Allen County*, II, 302-303; *History of Vanderburgh County* (1889), I, 189; *South Bend and the Men Who Have Made It*, p. 42; United States Bureau of the Census, *Tenth Census* (1880), XIX, *Social Statistics of Cities*, p. 454.

the old Central Canal which ran through the city and pump it into a reservoir from which it would be distributed. In 1864 the owners of the canal proposed the formation of a company to pump water from the canal by means of the recently invented Holly process of direct pressure, but nothing came of it. In 1868 a similar proposal was again made but was rejected. In 1866 a charter had been actually granted to a company to supply water to the city with the stipulation that the water be taken from White River several miles above the city and that the city should have the option of purchasing the company at the end of twenty-five years. The company laid a few feet of pipe and then ceased operations. Finally in 1869 a charter was given to a company which constructed a system and began to supply water to consumers in 1871. The Holly system of pumping was used, and water was drawn in part from White River and in part from the canal. But the company had few customers in spite of efforts to convince the public that private wells were dangerous. People were suspicious of the water supplied by the company, and with good reason. A survey authorized by the City Council in 1880 showed that the water was not fit to drink. Lack of private patronage caused the company to fail, and it was sold by court order in 1881.[66]

Other cities were also slow to become concerned about the question of water, but by the seventies some sort of a public water system was established in every city of any size. In New Albany waterworks were operated by a private company. Waterworks were built in Evansville in 1871, in South Bend in 1873, and in Fort Wayne in 1879. Those in Evansville and Fort Wayne were owned by the city.[67]

[66] Bogle, "A View of New Albany Society at Mid-Nineteenth Century," *Indiana Magazine of History*, LIV, 99; Indiana *Revised Statutes*, 1876, I, 329-331; Dunn, *Greater Indianapolis*, I, 330-332, 334; Holloway, *Indianapolis*, pp. 112-113, 130; United States Bureau of the Census, *Tenth Census* (1880), XIX, *Social Statistics of Cities*, p. 451; Indiana State Medical Society, *Transactions*, 1880, pp. 200-201.

[67] *History of Vanderburgh County* (1889), I, 190; *South Bend and the Men*

City planning was almost nonexistent, the growth of most cities being haphazard or dictated by geographical factors. Indianapolis was exceptional in being laid out according to a plan. A description published in 1853 declared that it was "laid out with ingenuity and beauty. A circular street surrounds an open space, with the governor's mansion in the middle. From this diverge several streets, intersecting diagonally the others, which are rectangular."[68]

While the streets of Indianapolis were laid out according to a plan, like the streets of other cities of the period they were notoriously ill-kept and at times impassable. After a heavy rain they were so filled with water that a visitor remarked that it would have been possible to float along them in a canoe. "In any proper sense," a contemporary historian remarked, "we had no streets. They were merely openings which might be used or not, as the weather made them impassable mud or insufferable dust." Sometimes where the ground had not yet been trodden down planks were laid for vehicles to run on. In 1859 at the insistence of shopkeepers along Washington Street, in the principal business area, two blocks of hard surface pavement were installed, but the first pavements were of boulders, which made travel over them rough and noisy. In 1870 an experiment in paving with wooden blocks of pine was begun and hailed as a great advance. But experience proved that pine blocks soon went to pieces. After 1860 the city began to spend some money each year on street improvements, but the panic of 1873 brought a halt to this. In 1880 there were 211 miles of streets in Indianapolis, of which forty-five miles were paved with cobblestones, five miles with wood, while the remainder were either paved with boulders or were graveled or totally unimproved.[69]

Who Have Made It, p. 43; United States Bureau of the Census, *Tenth Census* (1880) XIX, *Social Statistics of Cities,* pp. 445-446, 461-462.

68 *Phelps' Description of 100 Cities and Large Towns of America* . . . (New York, Phelps, Fanning & Co., 1853), p. 69.

69 Jobson, *American Methodism,* pp. 109-110, 115; Holloway, *Indianapolis,*

In 1857 New Albany boasted twenty-two miles of macadamized streets—the greatest amount of pavement in the state, but as late as 1880 only twenty-seven miles were paved. In 1863 Fort Wayne began to plank some of the streets in the downtown area in an effort to prevent pedestrians and vehicles from being mired down in the mud. In 1880 of eighty-two miles of streets in Fort Wayne one mile was paved with broken stone, six miles were paved with wood, twelve were graveled, while the remainder were completely unimproved. In Evansville about three miles of streets were paved with cobblestones by 1880, six miles were graveled, and the rest unimproved in any way.[70]

Most streets remained unlighted as well as unpaved. But in the fifties a few gas street lamps began to appear. In 1851 Madison became the first city in the state to install street lights. The following year New Albany put gas lights in the business area, and within a few months most of the major streets were lighted. In 1851 the voters of Indianapolis rejected a proposal for a tax to pay for street lights. It was not until 1853 that the first lights were installed in the capital city, and these were paid for by the property owners in the two blocks which were illuminated. The following year the city government undertook to bear the expense. By 1860 there were lamps along eight and one half miles of the streets in the city and by 1880 at least forty miles of lighted streets. In 1857 the first gas street lights in Fort Wayne were authorized by the city government.[71]

p. 85; Kershner, Social and Cultural History of Indianapolis, p. 6; Dunn, Greater Indianapolis, I, 309; United States Bureau of the Census, Tenth Census (1880), XIX, Social Statistics of Cities, p. 451.

[70] Bogle, "A View of New Albany Society at Mid-Nineteenth Century," Indiana Magazine of History, LIV, 96-98; Griswold, Pictorial History of Fort Wayne, I, 445; United States Bureau of the Census, Tenth Census (1880), XIX, Social Statistics of Cities, pp. 440, 445, 461.

[71] Dunn, Greater Indianapolis, I, 322-323; Bogle, "A View of New Albany Society at Mid-Nineteenth Century," Indiana Magazine of History, LIV, 98-99; Holloway, Indianapolis, p. 93; Griswold, Pictorial History of Fort Wayne, I, 426.

In nearly all cases the gas used for street lights was supplied by privately owned corporations. A state law passed in 1857 authorized cities to establish their own gas works or to regulate those which were privately owned, but there appears to have been little interest in municipal ownership. Gas companies had already been chartered for Madison, New Albany, and Indianapolis in 1851 and the sale of stock begun. The Indianapolis Gas Light and Coke Company was given a monopoly for fifteen years by the City Council for lighting streets and houses, with the stipulation that the rates charged should not exceed the rates in Cincinnati. Progress in the laying of pipe was slow and private patrons few. The company did not prosper until the city government began to install street lights. When the franchise given by the city expired in 1866, a controversy developed over whether the company should continue to have a monopoly and, if so, what rates it should be permitted to charge. Opponents of the company claimed that its rates were excessive and that it was charging the city for the lighting of street lamps which were nonexistent. In 1867 a rival company was chartered which proposed to furnish the city with gas at lower rates. This caused the original company to propose to reduce its rates, and it received another franchise for another twenty years. The following year the city council appointed a gas inspector with the responsibility of protecting the interests of the city. Since the charter granted to the Indianapolis company was not exclusive, a second company, financed by a group of Philadelphia capitalists, was chartered. The appearance of the new company caused the old company to meet competition by offering to give discounts to customers on all streets where the new company built mains. But such benefits as the consumers enjoyed as the result of this competition were short-lived. The Indianapolis company secretly bought out its rival in 1877.[72]

[72] Indiana *Laws,* 1857, p. 56; Indianapolis *Indiana State Sentinel* (semi-weekly), March 5, 1851; Bogle, "A View of New Albany Society at Mid-

In 1852 a private company, the Evansville City Gas Works, was organized to supply that city. It continued to operate under a contract with the city which regulated the rates which it charged. The Fort Wayne Gas Company was chartered in 1855, the South Bend Fuel and Gas Company in 1868.[73]

The law for cities adopted in 1852 gave city governments broad authority to carry out sanitary measures and to protect public health. The duties of the city council included prevention of throwing "offal, dead animals, logs or rubbish" into streams and rivers and authority to fill up or drain grounds in which there was stagnant water. The council was also "to prevent the deposit of any unwholesome substance within the city limits, and punish persons guilty of the same, and to remove or destroy putrid animal or vegetable matter therein." It was authorized to compel the owner or occupant of any building which was "filthy or unwholesome, to cleanse and abate the same." The law provided for a board of health and gave the city council power to establish quarantine regulations and to remove persons having infectious or pestilential diseases. These provisions were supplemented by numerous municipal ordinances, but in actual practice requirements concerning sanitation and protection of public health appear to have been largely ignored.[74]

Not until 1875 did the city of Indianapolis take any action about the collection of garbage. That year provisions were made for collection by contractors at the expense of individual householders, but these arrangements lapsed because of unwillingness to bear the cost. The result was that garbage was disposed of in whatever manner the householder

Nineteenth Century," *Indiana Magazine of History,* LIV, 98; Holloway, *Indianapolis,* pp. 93-94; Dunn, *Greater Indianapolis,* I, 323-324.

73 *History of Vanderburgh County* (1889), I, 193; Griswold, *Pictorial History of Fort Wayne,* I, 424; *South Bend and the Men Who Have Made It,* p. 43; United States Bureau of the Census, *Tenth Census* (1880), XIX, *Social Statistics of Cities,* p. 438.

74 Indiana *Revised Statutes,* 1852, I, 209-211.

could arrange, the only restriction being that it was not to be left in the streets or allowed to become a public nuisance. In Evansville, on the other hand, garbage was removed by contractors who were paid by the city. But there were many complaints that the system was not efficient. In Terre Haute ashes as well as garbage were removed at public expense, but in Fort Wayne there was no public collection of any sort and disposal was the responsibility of the individual.[75]

By 1880 all major cities had constructed some sort of sewers, but sewers were at first regarded principally as means of carrying off surface water from rain, and only a small fraction of wastes was disposed of through them. During the late sixties some efforts at building small sewers in Indianapolis were made, but it was not until 1870 that a general plan for a system for the city was adopted. This provided for a trunk sewer into which smaller sewers emptied. The sewage was ultimately discharged into White River. But relatively little of either household or industrial wastes went into the sewers. In 1880 not more than 10 per cent of the private houses in Indianapolis had inside plumbing, and there were no effective controls for the disposal of wastes from manufacturing establishments. Pork-packing houses simply dumped their refuse into the river. Much the same situation existed in Evansville, Fort Wayne, and Terre Haute. In New Albany in 1880 there was only one sewer—about one half mile in length. Most of the drainage from the city continued to run off through the gutters of the street into Falling Run Creek and then into the Ohio River.[76]

All cities had boards of health, but their duties and authority were limited. In 1848 a smallpox epidemic led to the creation of the Indianapolis Board of Health. A city ordinance adopted in 1854 gave it broad powers over vaccination

[75] Kershner, Social and Cultural History of Indianapolis, p. 262; United States Bureau of the Census, Tenth Census (1880), XIX, Social Statistics of Cities, pp. 442, 447, 453.

[76] Holloway, Indianapolis, p. 130; United States Bureau of the Census, Tenth Census (1880), XIX, Social Statistics of Cities, pp. 442, 447, 452, 454, 463.

for smallpox, and in 1859 an ordinance was passed requiring a quarantine in the case of smallpox and "other contagious diseases." But the Board of Health complained that physicians were negligent about reporting diseases such as scarlet fever and that probably not more than half the cases were brought to its attention. In Evansville and New Albany there were requirements for compulsory vaccination against smallpox. In Fort Wayne vaccination was required only when specially ordered by the city council, while in Terre Haute there was no compulsory provision.[77]

As cities increased in size a need for public transportation developed. As early as 1860 there was talk of a street railway system in Indianapolis, and the sudden growth of the city during the war years stimulated interest. In 1863 two groups applied to the City Council for a charter. The franchise to operate the railways was finally given to the Citizens Company, which had been organized in New York and received its financial backing from that city. The company was given a perpetual charter under which it could lay track on any street or alley. It was required to use horse-drawn vehicles and to charge a fare of five cents only. The laying of track was soon under way, but progress was delayed because of wartime shortages of iron. High prices for iron and labor raised the cost of construction beyond that which had been anticipated. Costs were also increased because lines were extended into outlying areas which were as yet sparsely settled and where passengers were few. In consequence the company was soon in financial difficulties. The first horse-drawn streetcars began operation in Evansville in 1867 and in Fort Wayne in 1872. By 1880 street railways were also operating in New Albany and Richmond. In all cases they were owned by companies which received a franchise from the city council. In all places the fare was five cents. By

[77] Kershner, Social and Cultural History of Indianapolis, p. 33; United States Bureau of the Census, Tenth Census (1880), XIX, Social Statistics of Cities, pp. 442, 447, 463, 473.

1880 there were six miles of track in Evansville, five miles in New Albany, seven miles in Fort Wayne, and three miles in Richmond.[78]

As cities grew in size and wealth, larger and more ornate buildings—both public and private—were constructed. At midcentury the inspiration of the Classical Revival was still strong. The state capitol, completed in the 1830's and still the most imposing building in Indianapolis in 1850, was a good example. The Masonic Hall, which was completed in 1851 and which remained the most important public hall in that city until after the Civil War, was modeled after a Greek temple. Many courthouses built during the 1850's showed classical influences. The one at Madison, completed in 1854, was a good example of Greek Revival architecture. Frequently both Greek and Roman characteristics were seen in the same building. One of the more elaborate examples was the Vanderburgh County courthouse, which was completed in 1857. It was basically Greek in design but adorned with columns which were really Roman and was surmounted by a Roman dome.[79]

After 1850 new influences were rather suddenly introduced, and a trend toward eclectism and the mixing of various orders of architecture became pronounced. During the 1850's there was a strong Gothic revival, which was most evident in churches and schools. It was reflected in perpendicular lines and tall towers and spires. Other public buildings showed Romanesque influences—round arches, arcades, and flat towers. Italianate influences from the period of the Renaissance were also seen. During the seventies French in-

[78] Holloway, *Indianapolis*, pp. 127-128; Gilbert, *Evansville and Vanderburg County*, I, 152; Griswold, *Pictorial History of Fort Wayne*, I, 490; United States Bureau of the Census, *Tenth Census* (1880), XIX, *Social Statistics of Cities*, pp. 440, 445, 461, 466.

[79] Lee Burns, *Early Architects and Builders of Indiana* (Indiana Historical Society *Publications*, Indianapolis, 1935), pp. 196-198, 208; Howard E. Wooden, *Architectural Heritage of Evansville. An Interpretive Review of the Nineteenth Century* (Evansville, 1962), pp. 23-24.

fluences of the Second Empire were important. This borrow-
ing from European models was no doubt in part the result
of the fact that many of the successful architects after 1850
were men who were born and trained in Europe. Two early
examples of Gothic influence were North Western Christian
University and Christ Episcopal Church in Indianapolis. Both
were designed during the fifties by William Tinsley, a native
of Ireland. Dietrich A. Bohlen, a native of Germany who
settled in Indianapolis, was responsible for a number of
Gothic-type buildings, among them the convent and school
of St. Mary-of-the-Woods in Vigo County, the convent and
school at Oldenburg in Franklin County, and St. John's
Cathedral in Indianapolis. Second Presbyterian Church in
Indianapolis, begun in 1864 and designed by Joseph Curzon,
a native of England, was another good example of Gothic
influence. The most elaborate example of French architecture
of the Second Empire in Indiana was the Marion County
courthouse in Indianapolis. Designed by Isaac Hodgson, a
native of Ireland, and completed in 1876 at the enormous
cost of $1,400,000, it was for many years a showplace for
visitors to the city.[80]

In general, domestic architecture reflected the same trends
as public. During the fifties Greek influences remained strong
but many houses which reflected the Gothic revival began
to appear. Soon afterwards features adapted from Italian
architecture of different periods began to be incorporated into
Indiana houses, and in the seventies the influence of the Second
French Empire was apparent. Many houses belonged to no
particular architectural classification but showed characteristics drawn from a variety of sources.[81]

[80] Burns, *Early Architects and Builders,* pp. 195, 199-201; Holloway, *Indianapolis,* p. 209; Sulgrove, *Indianapolis,* pp. 249-250; J. D. Forbes, *Victorian
Architect: The Life and Work of William Tinsley* (Indiana University Press,
1953), pp. 66-67, 93, and *passim.*

[81] Wilbur D. Peat, *Indiana Houses of the Nineteenth Century* (Indiana
Historical Society, 1962), *passim.*

§ § §

Indianans in the middle of the nineteenth century were imbued with a political philosophy which said that the role of government should be limited, and in practice they were reluctant to pay taxes to support governmental services. But they were not devoid of humanitarianism, and as the rigors of the pioneer period passed and as population grew and society became somewhat more complex, they developed a greater sense of social responsibility. State and local governments and private benevolent societies began to show concern for the plight of unfortunates who in an earlier day had been shunted aside or treated as objects of individual charity.

During the pioneer era the county poor farm was the only public welfare institution. County commissioners were authorized to purchase land and build asylums for the poor and to "employ some humane and responsible person or persons" to take charge upon terms which the commissioners found "most advantageous for the interest of the county." If there was no poor farm the township trustees were authorized to let out contracts for the care of paupers to private individuals or to make payments directly to the paupers. The law also provided that "every idiot, lunatic, and insane person who is or shall become a pauper" was entitled to the benefit of the laws for relief of the poor.

In 1845 the legislature authorized the purchase of a site for a "State Lunatic Asylum." The following year it authorized the erection of buildings and made provisions for the administration of the institution, changing its name to the Indiana Hospital for the Insane. The site acquired was a large farm about two miles west of Indianapolis. The first patients were admitted in 1848.[82]

82 Indiana *Revised Statutes,* 1843, pp. 355-357, 859; 1852, I, 402-403, 406; Dunn, *Indiana and Indianans,* II, 993; Indiana *General Laws,* 1844-1845, p. 58; *Local Laws,* 1845-1846, pp. 220-222; Barbara Brandon, The State Care of the Insane in Indiana 1840-1890 (Unpublished Master's thesis, School of Social Service Administration, University of Chicago, 1938), pp. 13-22, 32. Indiana was said to be the first state to use the designation "hospital" in connection with a state institution for the insane.

The designation of "hospital" indicated that the institution was expected to serve a curative and not merely custodial function. In the admission of patients priority was given to cases in which some hope of recovery was indicated. This reflected the growing understanding by the medical profession that insanity was a disease and, in some instances at least, curable. For example, the president of the State Medical Association in 1852 mentioned as one of the evidences of the "scientific progress" of the age the fact that insanity was "generally, perhaps universally, regarded as a corporeal disorder." In consequence, he said, treatment had been modified and was more successful than formerly. But as yet there was no scientific method of diagnosis. Reports from the early years of the state hospital show that causes of insanity as given in the reports on the admission of patients included such diverse items as "Mexican War excitement," "Millerism," "epilepsy," and "puerperal fever." During the next twenty or thirty years there was a growing recognition that insanity was not a single disease entity, and there were efforts at classification. But no satisfactory system of classification of psychoses was as yet developed. At the same time it came to be recognized that there was no single method of cure. Bleeding as a method of treatment was abandoned as early as 1851 and the use of drugs instead was begun. There was also some recognition of the need for what later came to be called "psychiatric treatment" but was then called "moral." Reading, music, games, handicrafts, and sewing were introduced for their therapeutic values, and a religious program for patients was begun.

When the hospital opened, the superintendent and staff apparently believed that most cases of insanity were curable and that cures could be effected by good physical care, pleasant surroundings, and kind treatment. In 1865 the legislature authorized an additional building, which was finally completed in 1875, for the confinement of the incurably insane. But reports of the work of the hospital consistently emphasized the high percentage of cures. For example, in 1875 Governor Hendricks reported to the legislature: "Pure water, fresh and pure air, careful attention and eminent skill give the result of more than fifty per cent of cures." In 1877 it was reported that in the preceding year 696 patients had been discharged from the hospital of whom 516 were classified as "recovered," 50 as "improved," and 105 as "not improved." It appears probable that limited facilities made it necessary to discharge patients in order to admit others who were waiting and that the reports give a too optimistic picture of the percentage of cures.

The state hospital was generally defended as a humanitarian institution which was accomplishing much good. But the system of caring for the insane in one central hospital was not without its critics. In 1876 the president of the State Medical Society compared the hospital to a prison and urged abandonment of the practice of "massing of the entire insane population of the State" into one institution. He urged the establishment of numerous small hospitals throughout the state wherein patients could live in homelike cottages. But the most serious criticism of the state hospital was that it was totally inadequate in size and capable of caring for only a small fraction of the persons in need of care. The same president of the State Medical Society estimated that in 1876 there were at least two thousand insane persons in the state of whom less than five hundred were in the hospital. Of the remainder many were confined in jails or "still worse, within the walls of our loathsome county poor-houses." A survey made in 1880 showed that six hundred insane persons as well as three hundred and fifty persons classed as feeble-minded or idiots were confined in county poor farms. Nor had any provision as yet been made for the criminally insane who were simply confined with other prisoners.[83]

83 Indiana State Medical Society, *Proceedings,* 1852, p. 21, *Transactions,* 1876, pp. 2-4; Brandon, State Care of the Insane, pp. 83, 85, 93, 99-101; Indiana *Laws,* special session, 1865, pp. 199-200; Indiana *Senate Journal,* 1871, pp.

Even before the state legislature created the hospital for the insane it had taken steps to establish schools for deaf and dumb children. Legislation adopted in 1843 provided for a state tax to support a deaf and dumb asylum, and the following year legislation establishing the institution was adopted. The school, which was located in Indianapolis, was open without charge to all deaf mutes in the state between the ages of ten and thirty. By midcentury about one hundred pupils were in attendance. They received instruction in the same subjects which were taught in the public schools, and in addition some training in various trades. In 1847 the legislature voted to establish a state school for the blind, and a permanent building was opened in Indianapolis in 1851. In the school pupils were given board and tuition without charge and were taught academic subjects and also music and handicrafts.[84]

The state assumed no responsibility for the care of dependent children. The only provisions made in state law for such children were that they should be bound out as apprentices or should be cared for in the county poor farms. Township trustees or superintendents of poor farms were authorized to bind out minor children who were county charges or whose parents had abandoned or unreasonably neglected them. The revised law of 1852 stipulated that authorities who bound out the children should see that they were properly treated and should take legal steps to secure redress in case they were maltreated. A law passed in 1875 provided that orphans who were inmates of pauper asylums could be bound out "to some suitable person to have the custody and training of such child whenever the same can be done on such terms as will . . . secure to such child a proper maintenance

62-63; 1875, p. 29; 1877, p. 20; Indiana Yearly Meeting of Friends, *Minutes*, 1902, p. 127.

84 Indiana *General Laws*, 1842-1843, pp. 75-76; 1844-1845, pp. 58-59; 1846-1847, pp. 41-43; *Indiana Gazetteer*, 1850, pp. 139-140; Dunn, *Indiana and Indianans*, II, 1003.

and education." Children who were too young to bind out, both orphans and children of paupers, were found in poor farms as were older children who for some reason were not apprenticed. The law of 1852 provided that they should be sent to common schools, but otherwise there was no special provision in legislation for their care. They were usually simply mixed up indiscriminately with other inmates. An exception was in Marion County after the completion of new buildings for the county farm in 1870. There children were cared for in a separate nursery department. A survey made in 1880 showed that there were seven hundred children under sixteen years of age in county farms throughout the state. Not until 1897 was legislation enacted prohibiting the keeping of children on these farms.[85]

Earlier a number of private orphanages were established. Among the first was the Indianapolis Orphans' Home, which was chartered in 1850 through the efforts of the Indianapolis Benevolent Society. The first building was opened in 1855, and a large addition was built in 1869. In 1871 the Indianapolis Asylum for Friendless Colored Children was opened. It was organized through the efforts of the Western Yearly Meeting of Friends and was maintained in large part through the gifts of Quakers. In 1867 the German Protestant Orphans' Association was organized in the same city.[86] In a few other cities orphanages were established. They were usually founded by religious groups and most frequently by

[85] Indiana *Revised Statutes,* 1843, p. 615; *Revised Statutes,* 1852, I, 363, 406-407; *Laws,* 1875, p. 170; Holloway, *Indianapolis,* pp. 192-193; Indiana Yearly Meeting of Friends, *Minutes,* 1902, p. 127. The law on apprentices provided that apprentices could be bound out to the age of twenty-one if male, eighteen if female. Indiana *Revised Statutes,* 1843, p. 615. An act passed in 1897 gave county commissioners authority to establish orphanages and prohibited keeping children between the ages of three and seventeen in poor houses. Indiana *Laws,* 1897, pp. 45-48.

[86] Amos Butler, *A Century of Progress: A Study of the Development of Public Charities and Correction, 1790-1915* (Indiana Reformatory Printing Trade School, [1916]), p. 4; Thornbrough, *Negro in Indiana,* p. 378; Holloway, *Indianapolis,* p. 200.

Roman Catholics. As early as 1848 the Sisters of Providence operated an orphanage for girls at Vincennes. In 1876 this institution was moved to Terre Haute. St. Vincents' Orphanage for boys was opened in Vincennes in 1851. St. Joseph's Orphan Asylum, which was founded in 1866 near Rensselaer, was moved to Lafayette in 1876 as the result of a legacy. In 1886 the Sisters of the Holy Cross established an orphanage in Fort Wayne for children of all creeds. In 1875 the state legislature provided that county commissioners might subsidize private orphanages to the extent of twenty-five cents a day per child, but the law expressly prohibited any such donations for orphanages with any kind of religious affiliation.[87]

Hospitals either public or private were almost unknown. The only public assistance authorized by the state for the sick was by an act passed in 1852 which required county commissioners to contract with physicians to care for paupers in the county farms and prisoners in the county jails. This was amended in 1859 to give authority to township trustees to provide medical care for the poor who were under their care.[88] The general public equated the word "hospital" with "pest house." In 1852 when the Presbyterian Theological Seminary in New Albany offered to sell its buildings to the city for a hospital, the editor of one of the leading newspapers protested. A hospital, he said, would be a "manifest outrage" on citizens owning property in its vicinity since it would be "a receptacle for the victims of smallpox, ship fever, and other infectious diseases." The proposal for the hospital was rejected, and it was not until 1888 that the United Charities Hospital was established in New Albany.[89] During the Civil War military hospitals were operated in New Al-

---

[87] Blanchard (ed. and comp.), *Catholic Church in Indiana*, I, 607, 609, 614, 615; *The Catholic Church in Fort Wayne* (Allen County-Fort Wayne Historical Society, 1961), p. 50; Indiana *Laws*, 1875, pp. 169-170.

[88] Indiana *Revised Statutes*, 1852, I, 101; *Laws*, 1859, p. 35.

[89] Bogle, "A View of New Albany Society at Mid-Nineteenth Century," *Indiana Magazine of History*, LIV, 102.

bany, Evansville, Madison, and Indianapolis, but it was not until years after the war that hospitals in the present sense of the word were established in many cities.

The Indianapolis City Hospital appears to have been almost the only example of a publicly supported hospital. It was authorized by the city council in 1856, apparently as the result of a scare over a smallpox epidemic the previous year and was probably envisaged at the time principally as a pest house. A building was completed in 1859 but it was not actually put into use until the Civil War, when it served as a military hospital. After the war Dr. John M. Kitchen, who had given his services in the care of soldiers, urged the city to put the hospital building into use for residents of the city. The city council thereupon authorized renovating the building and equipping it to accommodate seventy-five patients. The hospital was opened in 1866 as a charity institution. During its early history it operated on an annual budget of a little more than six thousand dollars.[90]

In Evansville the old military hospital was purchased from the Federal government and converted into a private hospital, St. Mary's, which was operated by the Daughters of Charity. In 1869 St. Joseph's Hospital was opened in Fort Wayne in connection with the convent of the order of the Poor Handmaids of Jesus Christ. In 1868 there had been an attempt to open a city hospital in a private residence, but neighbors forced its removal by securing an injunction. In 1878 the City Hospital of Fort Wayne was opened. In spite of its name it received no tax support and was later renamed Hope Hospital. In 1872 the Little Sisters of the Poor opened Providence Hospital at Terre Haute, but it was not a success and was forced to close. In Lafayette the Sisters of St. Francis opened St. Elizabeth's Hospital in connection with their convent in 1876.[91]

[90] Holloway, *Indianapolis,* p. 195.

[91] Schroeder, *Catholic Church in the Diocese of Vincennes,* pp. 194-196; Blanchard (ed. and comp.), *Catholic Church in Indiana,* I, 605-606, 611; Griswold, *Pictorial History of Fort Wayne,* I, 481; Robertson, *Allen County,* I, 293.

With very few exceptions, such as the Home for the Aged Poor, which was established in Indianapolis by the Little Sisters of the Poor in 1873, institutional care of the poor continued to be limited to the poor farms. Poor farms, in the words of a contemporary writer, were usually "receptacles" into which were placed "that inconvenient class in the community, who being unable to help themselves, were thus stuck away out of sight and dismissed from public concern." The poor who were not inmates of poor farms were given public assistance by township trustees. In addition there were various private societies which gave assistance to the needy. One of the most important was the Indianapolis Benevolent Society, which was organized in 1835. Many prominent citizens of the young city were active in this philanthropy. Calvin Fletcher served as secretary of the society from its founding until his death in 1866. A principal activity of the society was the distribution of food and used clothing to the needy. As the city grew the society created a central depository where goods for distribution were collected, and the city was divided into districts which were canvassed by members of the society for contributions of money and goods. The society contracted with grocers to supply food to some families at the rate of $1.50 a week per family. As late as 1860 the annual expenditures of the society were not more than $548.[92]

As already seen the need to care for soldiers' families during the Civil War caused an expansion of private benevolence as well as some contributions from local government. But the depression of 1873, which brought unemployment and distress on an unprecedented scale, created greater demands, especially in Indianapolis. In 1870 there were about three hundred families in the city who were receiving assistance from the township trustees. During 1873 the number more than doubled, and by 1877 three thousand families were receiving aid. In addition the work of private charitable or-

92 Holloway, *Indianapolis*, pp. 192, 199.

ganizations increased greatly. This expansion of relief activity led to a movement to reform the existing system. Some persons were convinced that problems had been aggravated by a too generous policy of caring for all kinds of poor, including transients or "tramps," who came to the city to avail themselves of public charity. It was even charged that paupers were shipped into the city by trustees of other townships. As a result, the Indianapolis Charity Organization Society was formed in 1879 to serve as a clearing house for all charitable organizations and agencies. One of the leaders in the movement for founding the organization and its first president was Oscar McCulloch, minister of the Plymouth Congregational Church. The stated object of the new society was "to distinguish between poverty and pauperism, to relieve the one and to refuse the other." An office with a paid secretary and a staff of visitors was opened. Visitors were to investigate the cases of all applicants for assistance and to refer "worthy" cases to organizations which would help them. Visitors were also to give advice and counsel to the poor and to try to help them find employment.[93]

§ § § §

The Indiana Constitution of 1816 prohibited cruel and unusual punishments and made it the duty of the General Assembly "to form a penal Code, founded on the principles of reformation, and not of vindictive Justice" (Article I, section 15 and Article IX, section 4). By midcentury whipping as a form of punishment had long since disappeared. The only offenses which were punishable with death were treason and premeditated murder or killings which occurred in connection with the committing of rape, arson, or burglary. In all of these cases a jury had the discretion of substituting life imprisonment as a penalty. Before 1852 an occasional prisoner was executed at a public hanging, but the *Revised Statutes* of that year required that executions take place in

[93] *Indianapolis Year Book of Charities,* 1886, pp. 17-19; Jordan, *Days of A Man,* I, 132-133.

private. Unpremeditated murder was punished by imprisonment for life and manslaughter by imprisonment of from two
to twenty-one years in the state prison. Such major crimes
as burglary, arson, grand larceny, and forgery were also
punished by imprisonment in the state prison, but for lesser
crimes and misdemeanors the penalty was a fine or imprisonment in the county jail.[94]

County commissioners were required by law to maintain
a jail in every county; the sheriff was directly responsible
for the operation of the jail. The law required him to "provide proper meat, drink, and fuel for all prisoners, if they
have no other convenient way of supplying themselves." It
required that prisoners of different sexes be confined in different rooms. Inmates of county jails were persons who were
awaiting trial or persons convicted of minor offenses. Their
number was usually not large. In some places jails might at
times be completely empty, but in some instances they were
overcrowded. As population increased jails built in the
pioneer period were inadequate in the larger towns. Dorothea Dix, who made a survey of county jails, found widely
varying conditions. In a few places prisoners were lodged in
dungeons, in some places in blockhouses without light or air,
while in other places there were substantial brick buildings.[95]

As early as 1821 a state prison was built at Jeffersonville.
In 1861 a northern prison was authorized to be located at
Michigan City. From the beginning it was the practice to
lease the Jeffersonville prison to the highest bidder at three-
year intervals, thus leaving the prisoners to the mercy of a

[94] Indiana *Revised Statutes,* 1843, pp. 960 ff and 972 ff; 1852, II, 388-389,
396-397, 400-417, 424. In 1850 in New Albany several thousand people witnessed the hanging of a man convicted of murder. Gallows were constructed
on a vacant lot for the purpose. Bogle, "A View of New Albany Society at
Mid-Nineteenth Century," *Indiana Magazine of History,* LIV, 115.

[95] Indiana *Revised Statutes,* 1843, p. 1017; 1852, I, 345-346; Bogle, "A View
of New Albany Society at Mid-Nineteenth Century," *Indiana Magazine of
History,* LIV, 115-116; Helen Wilson, *The Treatment of the Misdemeanant in
Indiana, 1816-1936* (University of Chicago, *Social Service Monographs,* 1938),
pp. 85, 86-87, 101-103.

superintendent who was interested in getting as much personal gain from the contract as possible. To recompense the superintendent for feeding and clothing the inmates, he was permitted to hire them for work in the neighborhood or employ them at such industries as he was able to establish within the prison grounds, the products of which he then sold. By 1843 the crowded conditions in the original structure necessitated the erection of new buildings on a new site. A report of the prison for 1850-1851 shows that about thirty prisoners were employed in a brickyard or at cutting wood, while about twenty were employed in building the railroad depot at Jeffersonville. The remainder (about 140) were employed within the prison walls at such trades as coopering, carpentry, blacksmithing, and domestic labor.[96]

The policy of leasing the prison was acknowledged to be wrong by successive governors and by legislature after legislature, but no action was taken to modify it until 1846, when a partial change was made. By an act of that year the prison was to be leased for ten years for the annual sum of $8,000, to a superintendent elected by joint ballot of the General Assembly. In addition, a warden, who would have complete control of the internal police regulations of the prison, was to be elected for a three-year term with an annual salary of $600. Apparently this plan did not work; Governor Wright in his message to the legislature in 1853 described it as "radically wrong." In 1855 he reiterated a recommendation that the lease system be terminated. In the management of the prison, he said, "the idea of making it profitable, in a pecuniary way, should be outweighed by a higher consideration—the duty of adopting the best means for the reformation of the convicts within its walls."[97]

96 Dunn, *Indiana and Indianans,* II, 985, 987; Index to published *Messages and Letters* of governors from 1825 to 1843; Indiana State Prison, *Annual Report,* 1851, pp. 273, 274.

97 Indiana *General Laws,* 1845-1846, pp. 35-37; Indiana State Prison, *Annual Report,* 1856, pp. 213-214; Indiana *Senate Journal,* 1853, p. 23; 1855, p. 33.

The legislature responded with an act which provided that the prisoners "as far as may be consistent with their age, sex, health, and ability" were to be kept at hard labor and that the warden was to be in charge of the purchase of raw materials for manufacture of goods by the prisoners and in charge of the sale of such goods. The law thus apparently contemplated that convicts would be employed by the state, but it contained no appropriation to carry out this intent. When the contract of the lessee expired in 1856 there were no funds to purchase materials for manufactures. Consequently, the state attorney general ruled that from necessity a plan of hiring the prisoners out to contractors could be adopted. The warden thereupon entered into contracts with the highest bidders to lease the labor of the convicts. Under the system adopted the contractor was to have no control over the prisoners except to show them what work to do and how to do it. Guards were employed and paid by the state. These practices were regularized in an act adopted in 1857. Under it contracts for the use of prison labor were to be awarded to the highest bidders.[98]

Wright praised the new system as vastly superior to the old, as insuring better treatment for the prisoners and as being more advantageous financially to the state. But conditions arising from the panic of 1857 soon made it difficult to hire out the prisoners. In 1858 one hundred and eighty-five convicts were hired out at an average of fifty-three cents a day, but about one hundred and twenty-five were idle. Demand for labor increased somewhat during the next two years, but new problems arose when lessees failed to pay the state the amounts they had contracted to pay.[99] By 1861 the prison had lost eight or ten thousand dollars from such defaults and was operating at a deficit. Meanwhile the prison popula-

[98] Indiana *Laws,* 1855, pp. 197-198; 1857, p. 106; Indiana State Prison, *Annual Report,* 1856, pp. 209-210, 213.

[99] Indiana *Senate Journal,* 1857, pp. 64-65; Indiana State Prison, *Annual Report,* 1857, p. 225; 1858, p. 197.

tion was increasing so rapidly as to overtax existing facilities. By 1859 there were almost five hundred inmates, and conditions were so crowded that it was difficult to put the prisoners to work.[100] This situation was relieved temporarily by the opening of the second state prison at Michigan City.

During the Civil War demands for labor made it possible to contract for the labor of all prisoners, but at prices of only thirty-five to forty cents a day. A smallpox epidemic in 1864 meant a large scale loss of labor, and this plus the high cost of clothing and supplies caused the prison to operate at a deficit. In the postwar years nearly all of the convicts worked under contracts—86 per cent in 1869, for example—but the prison continued to fail to be self-sustaining. This was due in part to peculation on the part of the wardens and to lax financial practices which were revealed in various investigations.[101]   Another reason was the difficulty of finding satisfactory lessees. Small contractors frequently went bankrupt and failed to fulfill their contracts. Objections that convict labor created unfair competition also raised problems. During the early 1870's a contract was made with the Southwestern Car Company to employ most of the convicts at the rate of sixty cents a day. A rival company, the Ohio Falls Car and Locomotive Company, which had shops in Jeffersonville, objected as did other groups who claimed that the use of contract labor created unemployment in the community. But in spite of the advantages of cheap labor the Southwestern Company soon failed and went out of business, leaving a debt of over $22,000 of unpaid obligations to the state. Governor Hendricks meanwhile had urged that efforts be made to employ the prisoners in some way which would

100 Indiana *Senate Journal,* 1861, p. 20; special session, 1858, p. 20; 1859, p. 19.

101 Indiana State Prison South, *Annual Report,* 1863, p. 357; 1864, pp. 801-802; 1868, p. 3; *Report of the Committee on Prisons, together with the Evidence of the Officers and Others before the Committee at the Southern Prison* (Indianapolis, 1869), p. 6; *Testimony in the Southern Prison Investigation . . . March 6, 1875* (Indianapolis, 1875), pp. 4-8, 9.

not involve direct competition with free labor.[102] Because of conditions created by the depression it was difficult to find other contractors. After a time an arrangement was made to lease three hundred of the men at the rate of forty-five cents a day to a company which made shelf hardware, but about half of the prisoners remained unemployed, and the prison continued to operate at a deficit.[103]

At the northern prison at Michigan City, which was operated under the same general plan, income from convict labor appears consistently to have exceeded the cost of the maintenance of the prison. The first convicts were leased in 1863. Ten years later three hundred and twenty-five men were under contracts at rates of from fifty to sixty cents a day. With the onslaught of the depression the contractors insisted upon a reduction in rates, and contracts were modified to reduce costs to forty-five cents a day. Between four and five hundred men continued to be leased at these rates to contractors who were engaged in a variety of small-scale industries, including wagon making, cooperage, and cigar making. The prison regularly showed an income large enough that it was not dependent upon legislative appropriations for operating costs. In fact, in 1879 the directors of the prison recommended that it be enlarged so as to accommodate eight hundred convicts in order to increase revenues.[104]

The convict lease system seemed to be firmly entrenched although an occasional protest was raised against it. A

[102] Indiana State Prison South, *Annual Report,* 1868, p. 6; 1871, pp. 7-9; Indiana *Senate Journal,* 1875, p. 32; 1877, p. 26. Advertisements for the leasing of convict labor appeared regularly in the press. The following was in the Indianapolis *Daily Sentinel,* August 31, 1871:

PRISON LABOR FOR HIRE
CONVICTS OF THE INDIANA STATE
PRISON SOUTH

The advertisment stated that between 300 and 350 men were available for contract to the highest bidder for terms of five years or less.

[103] Indiana State Prison South, *Annual Report,* 1878, p. 4.

[104] Northern Indiana State Prison, *Annual Report,* 1862, p. 55; 1873, pp. 8-9; 1879, pp. 8-9, 12; Indiana *Senate Journal,* 1875, p. 30; 1877, p. 24.

minority of a legislative committee which reported on conditions at the Jeffersonville prison in 1867 branded the system a "relic of barbarism," which could not be justified. "To hire out our prisoners, as we would horses and mules," they declared, was "not only unkind to them, but unjust to ourselves and the people we represent." But the majority report recommended the continuation of the lease system as an economy measure. Governor Conrad Baker, who showed a considerable amount of interest in prison reform, spoke favorably of the operation of the contract system at the northern prison, asserting that the prison was a financial success without neglecting "the physical, moral or intellectual interests of the prisoners."[105]

The public as well as the lawmakers usually appeared to be indifferent to abuses in the penal system, although there was a general feeling that prisons should be centers of reform and rehabilitation as well as punishment. The laws regulating the prisons imposed some restrictions as to the administration of discipline and contained some minor provisions for the protection of the health and the promotion of the spiritual well being of the inmates. Laws enacted in 1846 and 1855 required that the services of a physician be employed at the Jeffersonville prison, and the 1855 law provided for the establishment of an infirmary. The 1846 law required the lessee to employ a chaplain and to provide a Sunday School library for the use of the convicts. In 1857 a provision was adopted which required the schooling of convicts who could not read or write. The 1855 law gave the directors of the state prison authority to establish rules and regulations concerning discipline and permitted the warden to order bodily punishment when he considered it necessary. The law of 1857 prohibited extreme and unusual punishments.[106] But in practice the requirements enacted by the lawmakers were not always observed.

---

[105] *Report of the Committee on State Prison South . . . 1866* (Indianapolis, 1867), pp. 5-6; Indiana *Senate Journal*, 1871, p. 62.

[106] Indiana *Local Laws*, 1845-1846, pp. 36-37; Indiana *Laws*, 1855, pp. 198,

In the years after the Civil War there was a flurry of interest in conditions at the Jeffersonville prison and some effort at correcting some of the more glaring abuses there. Members of the Society of Friends initiated the reform movement. In 1867 the Indiana Yearly Meeting appointed a committee to investigate prison conditions. The committee reported in 1869 that its investigations showed that "much corruption and wickedness existed in the State Prison at Jeffersonville," a statement which was more than corroborated by a legislative investigation which came about as the result of the preliminary investigation by the Quakers. With the co-operation of Governor Conrad Baker two members of the Friends committee, Charles F. Coffin and his wife Rhoda, visited the prison and talked to some of the inmates. The most sensational disclosures which resulted from their visit concerned the treatment of the women prisoners, of whom there were about twenty confined in the same building with the men prisoners. The legislative committee which investigated the following year confirmed charges that the officers and guards at the prison had engaged in sexual debaucheries and forced women prisoners into prostitution. There was also evidence of brutality in the discipline of prisoners although the committee denied that any convicts had actually died as the result of whippings.[107]

In his message to the next legislature Baker recommended a separate prison for women convicts and a reformatory institution for girls. He also recommended an intermediate institution to which younger and less hardened male of-

199, 201; 1857, pp. 107, 108-09, 110. In 1850 Governor Wright reported that on the advice of Miss Dorothea Dix he had purchased two hundred volumes of religious, historical, agricultural, and biographical works for the prison. Indiana *Senate Journal*, 1850-1851, p. 23.

107 Walter C. Woodward, *Timothy Nicholson, Master Quaker* (Richmond, Ind., 1927), pp. 84-89; Mary Coffin Johnson (ed.), *Rhoda M. Coffin, Her Reminiscences Addresses, Papers and Ancestry* (New York, 1910), pp. 150-152; *Report of the Committee on Prisons . . . before the Committee at the Southern Prison* (1869), pp. 6-7.

fenders could be sent. The recommendation for a separate female institution was followed, but otherwise no basic reforms in the operation of the two state prisons were adopted. The administration of the two institutions continued to be in the hands of persons who received their appointments as part of the system of political patronage. There were no more scandals comparable to those disclosed at Jeffersonville in 1869, but there were continued reports of financial mismanagement and occasionally of unduly harsh discipline. In a report made in 1878 the warden of the prison at Michigan City defended the methods which he used in dealing with refractory prisoners. These included the wearing of shackles and ball and chain, solitary confinement, and, when other methods failed, one to four stripes with "the four tailed cat" —a method which he said always brought the "most refractory convicts to submission." But there were also efforts at reform at Michigan City. The law establishing the prison provided for a "Moral Instructor," who was to attempt to inculcate religion. There was preaching every Sunday at the prison and also a Sunday school. In 1862 a series of revival meetings were held which resulted in the conversion of a number of prisoners. But such results were likely to be fleeting. A few years later a disillusioned Moral Instructor reported that experience had convinced him that "very few, after entering the Penitentiary, *try to learn how* to become honest members of society. And the difficulty of obtaining remunerative employment when discharged, added to the temptation by opportunity to return to old habits of vice, leave the impression on officers having charge of convicts that it is *impossible* to reform them." But although they might be indifferent to religious instruction some prisoners showed a thirst for other kinds of knowledge. At Michigan City there was a prison library of a few hundred volumes of books on history, science, religion, and a few textbooks. In 1879 it was reported that the books were "so much worn by reason of almost continual use, as to render much labor necessary to keep them in suitable condition for distribution."[108]

Physical conditions remained notoriously bad at the Jeffersonville prison. The buildings which were completed in 1847 were soon inadequate for the number of inmates. Cells were seven and one half feet long, four feet wide, and six and one half feet high with no ventilation or light except through the grated doors. Much of the time the prison was so crowded that there were two prisoners in a cell. Crowding and lack of sanitation helped cause a number of epidemics such as the smallpox epidemic of 1864 already mentioned. The death rate among inmates was extremely high. The prison was described by Joseph Coffin, the Quaker, as a place of "contamination and corruption" from which most convicts were released "much worse men than when they entered." As compared with conditions at Jeffersonville physical conditions at the Michigan City prison were good. Cells were better lighted and ventilated and the health of the prisoners was better.[109]

As already noticed, in 1869 the legislature voted to establish a separate prison for women. During the early years of the state prison very few women were sent there, a law of 1831 permitting women to be confined in county jails rather than in the prison. Until 1847 only four women had been sent to the Jeffersonville prison. Twenty years later there were about twenty women inmates. The act of 1869 provided for the establishment in Indianapolis of the Indiana Reformatory Institution for Women and Girls as a combination prison for adults and a reform school for girls. The objectives as described in the act were, as far as possible, to

[108] Indiana *Senate Journal,* 1869, pp. 44-45; Northern Indiana State Prison, *Annual Report,* 1861, pp. 515-516; 1862, p. 139; 1871, p. 19; 1878, pp. 18-21; 1879, pp. 24-25.

[109] Indiana *Senate Journal,* 1875, pp. 30-31; Charles F. Coffin, *Our Prisons: An Address delivered . . . before the Indiana Social Science Association at Indianapolis, June 9th, 1880* (n. p., n. d.), pp. 14-16. The prison at Jeffersonville was continued until 1897 when it was converted into a reformatory.

"reform the characters" of the inmates, to prepare them for employment, and "secure to them fixed habits of industry, morality and religion." A building was completed and the first inmates received in 1873. By 1875 there were thirty women in the penal department and ninety-three girls in the reformatory. The law creating the institution required that the officers be women. Sarah J. Smith, a Quaker, who had been interested in prison reform and active in securing the legislation of 1869, became the first superintendent. After 1877 all members of the governing board were women. Governor Williams described the women's prison as "the best managed institution in the state."[110]

Prior to 1867 juvenile offenders were sent to the state prison. A report of the warden of the Jeffersonville prison which was presented to the Constitutional Convention of 1850-1851 showed that more than one eighth of the persons committed to the institution since its opening had been minors —sometimes as young as eleven years. The new constitution contained a section which required the General Assembly to "provide houses of refuge, for the correction and reformation of juvenile offenders" (Article IX, section 2), but the legislature was slow to implement this provision. An 1852 law required that juvenile prisoners who were confined in county jails "be treated with humanity and in a manner calculated to promote their reformation," but juveniles continued to be sent to the state prison. In 1855 Governor Wright reported that of two hundred and sixty-seven men at the prison thirty-six were under twenty years of age and more than half of the prisoners were under twenty-five years. He recommended that all youthful offenders and all those convicted for the first time be placed in special institutions. The legislature in 1855 provided for the purchase of a tract of land for a house

110 Indiana State Prison, *Annual Report*, 1847, p. 131; Indiana *Senate Journal*, 1869, pp. 44-45; 1875, p. 33; Indiana *Laws*, 1869, pp. 61-63; Dunn, *Indiana and Indianans*, II, 1016-1017. A separate school for girls under eighteen years of age was authorized by the legislature in 1903, and in 1907 the Girls School at Clermont was opened.

of refuge but no further steps were taken until after the Civil War. In 1866 members of the Society of Friends took the initiative in reviving the question. The Western Yearly Meeting prepared a memorial to present to the next legislature on behalf of "Juvenile Criminals and Mendicant Children." "It is much better economy to prevent crime," it declared, "than first to neglect and then punish it. By timely aid, our youth who are spending time in idleness, vagrancy and crime, may be brought under a careful system of industrial and reformatory training that will fit them for orderly and useful citizenship." Quakers convinced Governor Morton of the desirability of establishing a reform school instead of a mere house of refuge, and he embodied their recommendations in his message to the next session of the legislature.[111]

The act which the General Assembly passed in 1867 creating a "House of Refuge for Juvenile Offenders" contained provisions which Quakers had recommended, and the first president of the board of trustees of the new institution was Charles F. Coffin. The law provided that at the discretion of the judge or jury any person under eighteen years of age who was liable to be confined in a state prison or county jail might be sent to the house of refuge. In addition inmates might be persons under eighteen whose "incorrigible or vicious conduct" rendered them beyond the control of parents or guardians, persons whose parents or guardians were unwilling to exercise proper control over them, or persons who were destitute of a proper home and who were in danger of being brought up to lead an "idle and immoral life." The law required that teachers be supplied for persons under sixteen years of age.[112]

The school was located on a large farm near Plainfield in Hendricks County. In establishing it the board of trustees

111 *Debates and Proceedings*, II, 1903; Indiana *Revised Statutes*, 1852, I, 347; Indiana *Senate Journal*, 1855, p. 33; Indiana *Laws*, 1855, p. 191; Western Yearly Meeting, *Minutes*, 1867, appendix, p. 2.

112 Woodward, *Timothy Nicholson*, p. 88; Indiana *Laws*, 1867, pp. 139-140, 145.

made a study of practices of other states where institutions for juveniles were in operation. They decided to adopt the "Family System," which was in use in Ohio. Under the plan the inmates were housed in groups of fifty with a house father in charge of each group. The boys went to school half a day and spent the remainder at work on the farm or at a trade. Within a short time there were two hundred or more inmates. Early reports concerning the institution were enthusiastic. Governor Baker said that it exceeded his most sanguine expectations. In 1875 it was claimed that reports showed the "reformation" of 60 per cent of the inmates.[113]

[113] Holloway, *Indianapolis*, pp. 190-192; Indiana *Senate Journal*, 1869, pp. 39-42; special session, 1872, p. 24; 1875, p. 34.

CHAPTER XIII
RELIGION

A BRITISH VISITOR TO INDIANAPOLIS in 1856 observed that there was "much public respect shown for religion." And certainly religion and the Bible were potent influences in shaping attitudes and mores. Nevertheless, there is reason to believe that religion and the churches were not as powerful as they sometimes have been assumed to have been. Certainly some of the statistics in United States census reports are misleading and must be used with caution. The census of 1850 did not attempt to show figures on actual church membership but instead listed the number of churches of various denominations and the "accommodations" in those churches —i.e. the number of persons who could be accommodated at church services. A careful student of the history of the Presbyterian Church in Indiana says that the figure given for the number of worshipers who could be accommodated was about ten times the number of actual church members.[1]

At midcentury conditions of pioneer society which had hampered the growth of churches still existed in many places— sparse and scattered population, difficult travel, and the lack of a trained clergy. Members were attracted for the most part by revivals and other extreme emotional appeals, and results were frequently short-lived. According to the *Indiana Gazetteer* published in 1850: "Great changes are constantly taking place by immigrations to and from the State, and by the fitful exertions more common, perhaps, in new countries than elsewhere, by which new members are induced to join

[1] Jobson, *American Methodism*, p. 112; L. C. Rudolph, *Hoosier Zion. The Presbyterians in Early Indiana* (Yale University Press, 1963), p. 191. The number of churches and the accommodations of the various denominations are given in United States Bureau of the Census, *Seventh Census* (1850), 799-807. See Chapter I, pages 11-12, 12-13, 15-16, 20-25, for a further discussion of religious attitudes.

(597)

the different churches, and for a time feel much interest in them; and then, sometimes, not a few of the new converts soon after resume their former habits and feelings." In some parts of the state, said the *Gazetteer,* "there is a very great indifference about religious instruction." Eastern church groups were concerned over the extent of "infidelity" in Indiana. "There *may be* fields in heathen lands less desirable than this, as places of comfortable labor," said the editor of the *Home Missionary* in 1849, "but they cannot be many. Nor do we know of any circumstances in which a missionary has a better right to regard himself as making a sacrifice for the sake of doing good."[2]

During the next three decades, as population grew, churches became more firmly established, and church membership increased, especially in the towns and cities. But there were those who doubted whether there had been any great increase in real spirituality. An idealistic Unitarian minister who came to Indianapolis from Brooklyn, New York, in 1868 became discouraged over the prospects for what he called "liberal Christianity" and returned East. "The West has not sufficient education or spirituality to receive liberal Christianity," he said. "It is dazed with its dreams of empire—of removing the national capital—of making the future presidents. It does not see Jesus, not even in the churches. It does not read the New Testament with any appreciation."[3]

Indiana was overwhelmingly Protestant in religion in 1850 and remained strongly Protestant although the number of Roman Catholics increased substantially. Protestantism was characterized by such a multiplicity of sects that it is impossible to deal with all denominations in a brief survey. But although United States census reports list about two dozen

2 *Indiana Gazetteer,* 1850, pp. 68-69; *Home Missionary,* XXII (Oct. 1849), 151, quoted in Power, *Planting Corn Belt Culture,* p. 83.

3 *The Presbyterian,* December 3, 1870, quoted in Indianapolis *Daily Sentinel,* December 7, 1870.

different denominations (some of which were subdivided into still more groupings), four denominations—Methodists, Baptists, Presbyterians, and Disciples of Christ—embraced a far larger membership than all other denominations combined.

Of these four the largest and most influential were the Methodists. The doctrines of Methodism, which were less rigid than those of the Calvinists, appealed to frontiersmen, and Methodists had an effective type of organization for proselyting and an emotional appeal which won many converts. In 1843 the Indiana Conference of the Methodist Church had been divided. The region south of the National Road, but including Indianapolis, retained the name Indiana Conference, while the remainder of the state became the North Indiana Conference. In 1852 these two conferences were further subdivided by the creation of the Southeastern Indiana Conference and the Northwest Indiana Conference. By 1850 the day of the circuit rider was passing, and a majority of the churches were served by resident ministers. At that date there were reported to be 223 "traveling preachers" in the state as compared with 548 who were classified as "local." Some of these preachers were men who received no fixed pay, whose work was supposed to be a labor of love, without financial reward. During the 1850's many Methodist ministers received only about one hundred dollars a year, but during the following years regular salaries became the custom. By 1863 the average salary in the Northwest Indiana Conference was $557 per year. By 1872 the average had reached $796, but during the depression it declined. Usually only part of the salary was paid in cash, with the remainder consisting of donations of food, clothing, and furniture.[4]

During the fifties many log churches were replaced by other structures, but most churches in rural areas remained wooden buildings. A typical new frame church could be erected at a cost of about $1,500. By the 1870's many more churches

[4] Heller, *Indiana Conference*, pp. 50, 52; *Indiana Gazetteer*, 1850, p. 69; Detzler, *Northwest Indiana Conference*, pp. 65, 67.

were located in towns and cities, and buildings had become larger and more elaborate. For example, in Kendallville, a small town in the northern part of the state, a substantial brick Gothic-type structure was built in 1875 at a cost of more than $23,000. In Indianapolis the Wesley Chapel (which took the name Meridian Street Church in 1870), the Roberts Park Church, and two mission churches were established prior to 1850. By 1870 there were ten Methodist churches in the city. The Meridian Street Church was in the process of building an elaborate Gothic-style structure at a cost of $100,000, while the Roberts Park Church was constructing a Renaissance-style building at a cost of $150,-000. City churches of this sort boasted organs and stained-glass windows and contained Sunday school rooms, libraries, and parlors as well as the main auditorium.[5]

Presbyterians, while less numerous than Methodists, were very influential. During the pioneer period the strength of the Presbyterian movement had been weakened somewhat by the schism between Old School and New School groups. Differences between the two groups are difficult to define, but New School men were charged with laxity as to discipline and doctrine. The New School adherents were also somewhat more imbued with abolitionism. In 1837 the General Assembly of the Presbyterian Church, which was under the control of the Old School group, instructed the synods in the West to "take order" as to the soundness of their churches and ministers on matters of doctrine and constitutional questions. At the same time four synods were exscinded. Following this action the New School General Assembly was organized in 1838. In Indiana the Old School group formed two synods—the Synod of Indiana and the Synod of Northern Indiana. The Indiana Synod of the New School group

5 Horace N. Herrick and William W. Sweet, *A History of the North Indiana Conference of the Methodist Episcopal Church From Its Organization in 1844 to the Present* (Indianapolis, 1917), p. 121; Holloway, *Indianapolis,* pp. 226-239.

included the whole state. In 1850 the Old School Presbyterians and the New School reported exactly the same number of ministers in Indiana. The New School group reported a small majority of churches, while the Old School reported a slight majority of members. Their combined membership was about ten thousand. During the early years there was much bitterness between the two groups, and many individual congregations were torn apart by strife, but by 1850 time had begun to heal the breach, and in some communities congregations reunited. Meanwhile, the Old School and New School synods had developed almost identical systems of administration and benevolent work. In 1870 the two schools were reunited.[6]

In addition to the above-mentioned Presbyterians there were some smaller groups, of whom the Cumberland Presbyterians were most numerous. They were the result of a schism in 1829 when the Cumberland Presbytery in Kentucky set itself up as an independent church. Most Cumberland Presbyterians were found in Kentucky, but a few congregations in southern Indiana were affiliated with them.[7]

Among Presbyterians the ratio of ministers per congregation was higher than among the Methodists and much higher than among the Baptists, and ministers were usually better trained. By 1850 a Presbyterian minister was expected to have graduated from college and from a theological sem-

[6] R. Carlyle Buley, *The Old Northwest. Pioneer Period, 1815-1840* (2 volumes, Indianapolis, 1950), II, 440-441; Rudolph, *Hoosier Zion,* pp. 121-133, 135; *Indiana Gazetteer,* 1850, p. 75; A. Y. Moore, *History of the Presbytery of Indianapolis* (Indianapolis, 1876), pp. 102-103, 112-113.

[7] Buley, *Old Northwest,* II, 424, 443-444; United States Bureau of the Census, *Eighth Census* (1860), *Mortality and Miscellaneous Statistics,* pp. 383, 387. Congregations of Cumberland Presbyterians were founded in Pike, Vanderburgh, Daviess, Dubois, and Spencer counties by families moving into Indiana from Kentucky. In 1859 there were seventeen churches, most of which were served by itinerant preachers. At the end of the Civil War it appeared that the denomination was dying out, but it revived somewhat during the postwar years. Darby and Jenkins, *Cumberland Presbyterianism in Southern Indiana,* pp. 18-20, 31, 35. For a list of the congregations in 1876 see *ibid.,* pp. 39-54.

inary. During the 1850's there were about one half as many ministers as there were congregations. In the larger towns full-time ministers were employed, but a single minister served more than one rural church. During the Civil War and the years following Presbyterianism grew in the towns but the rural churches declined.[8]

In the cities the older Presbyterian churches continued to grow and prosper and new churches were founded as offshoots from them. In 1850 there were two Presbyterian churches in Indianapolis, and by 1880 there were twelve. Some of the newer congregations were small and struggling, but the two oldest ones were strong and wealthy. The First Presbyterian Church had a membership of several hundred and occupied a large Gothic-type structure of stone. The Second Church, which was founded in 1838 by a group of New School Presbyterians who withdrew from the older church, had a membership at least as large and occupied a building of comparable size and elegance. In other cities there were large and wealthy congregations. One of the largest churches was the Walnut Street Presbyterian Church in Evansville, which was designed by a Philadelphia architect. It was built in what was described as Norman-style architecture, "characterized by great size, elevation, simplicity and strength, with the use of the semi-circular arch, massive columns, and a great variety of ornaments, and crowned with two spiral towers."[9]

Numerically Baptists were second only to Methodists, but accurate statistics on this denomination are impossible because of the many varieties of Baptists and the absence of any central authority to speak for all of them. Among Bap-

[8] Rudolph, *Hoosier Zion,* p. 191; Minutes of the Synod of Indiana of the Presbyterian Church (Old School) (Typewritten copy, Indiana Division, Indiana State Library), 1854-1856, p. 473; *ibid.,* 1857-1860, p. 557; *ibid.,* 1865-1867, pp. 188-189; *ibid.,* 1868-1869, p. 215; Minutes of the Indiana Synod North of the Presbyterian Church (Typewritten copy, Indiana Division, Indiana State Library), 1875-1877, p. 252.

[9] Holloway, *Indianapolis,* pp. 208-211, 214-215; Dunn, *Greater Indianapolis,* I, 582; *History of Vanderburgh County* (1889), I, 271.

tists there were many differences, especially as to the extent to which Calvinist doctrine was accepted, but all Baptists were alike in their belief in conversion as a condition for church membership, in immersion, in individual responsibility to God, in the congregational form of church government, and in separation of church and state. Many Baptists in Indiana were immigrants from the South, and their churches were closely akin to those in the South. But the influence of New England Baptist churches was strong in the northern part of the state. Large numbers of Indiana churches accepted the New Hampshire confession of faith, which partially rejected Calvinist doctrines on predestination. By 1850 most Baptists had begun to reject extreme predestinarianism.[10]

Each Baptist church was completely autonomous. Churches in a locality might join together in an association to further their mutual interests, but they were under no obligation to join and the association exercised no real authority over the member churches. Associations were joined together in a State Assembly, which in 1863 was replaced by the Baptist State Convention.[11]

At midcentury most Baptist churches were small rural congregations served by an itinerant minister, who was unlikely to have had any training and who was probably not paid for his services. A survey made in 1847 showed that there were six hundred and sixty-one churches in the state, but that most of them had only one service a month. In only twenty churches was there preaching every Sabbath, and a mere six churches employed the full-time services of a pastor. As a result of these revelations the State Assembly began a movement to promote the development of an educational program for prospective ministers and the raising of funds to pay their salaries. During the fifties the Home Missionary So-

10 Buley, *Old Northwest*, II, 463; John F. Cady, *The Origin and Development of the Missionary Baptist Church in Indiana* (Franklin College, 1942), pp. 77-78, 158-159.

11 Cady, *op. cit.*, pp. 143-144, 213.

ciety sent agents into the state to help in the promotion of these objectives. But the smallness of most Baptist congregations made it impossible to pay a minister adequately. During the 1850's monthly preaching, which was all that most churches enjoyed, cost from about $50 to $75 a year. A full-time minister was paid from $300 to $350 a year.[12] After 1850 some small rural churches disappeared while others consolidated, but the ratio of ministers to the number of churches remained small. In 1867 there were only 196 pastors serving the 438 churches affiliated with the State Baptist Convention, and less than 10 per cent of the churches had full-time preaching. In the period after the Civil War there was a trend for ministers to serve longer periods and to become more identified with the community in which they served. Baptists remained principally a rural denomination, but a few city churches developed. There was only one Baptist church in Indianapolis until 1859, when a mission was founded which became a church in 1869. Two more churches were founded in the city by 1880. By that date the First Baptist Church occupied an edifice large enough to seat more than a thousand persons and had a minister who held a divinity degree.[13]

Closely akin to the Baptists in their doctrines and form of church government and rivaling them in numbers by 1850 were the Disciples of Christ or the Christian Church. This denomination, which showed a remarkable growth, was founded early in the nineteenth century as the result of the fusion of two movements. One was led by Thomas and Alexander Campbell, father and son, both natives of North Ire-

[12] Cady, *Baptist Church in Indiana,* pp. 166-167, 176. James M. Smith, a Baptist minister, was invited in 1851 to preach once a month at a church near Kokomo, for the sum of one hundred dollars a year. "That was more than any one church had ever agreed to do for me," he recalled, "and they paid it all." James M. Smith, *A Work on Revivals. Sermons and Sketches* . . . (3d edition, Indianapolis, 1893), p. 69.

[13] Cady, *Baptist Church in Indiana,* p. 213; Indiana Baptist State Convention, *Minutes,* 1879, p. 21; Holloway, *Indianapolis,* p. 218; Dunn, *Greater Indianapolis,* I, 572.

land and originally Presbyterians educated at the University of Glasgow. The son settled in Virginia. The second movement was founded by Barton W. Stone, also a Presbyterian, but a native American. The basic articles of faith propounded by Alexander Campbell, whose leadership was responsible for the growth of the new denomination, were the unity of all Christians and the restoration of primitive Christianity. The New Testament was regarded as the perfect constitution for worship and church discipline. "Nothing ought to be an article of faith, a term of communion, or a rule for the constitution and management of the church," Campbell believed, "except what is expressly taught by Christ and his Apostles." Like the Baptists Campbell rejected infant baptism and upheld adult immersion, and like them he at first rejected the necessity for a trained clergy and a missionary system.[14]

The new denomination, which formally separated from the Baptists in 1832, grew rapidly in Indiana, partly as the result of the adherence of many persons who had formerly been Baptists. Disciples continued to place great emphasis upon the liberty of the Christian individual and the autonomy of the local congregation. They had no conferences or synods, but in 1839 a convention of Disciples in the state was held. Ten years later a leading Disciple warned that among the denomination there were many "small congregations formed by transient evangelists, without regular preaching or teaching." He insisted that some measures must be taken to help these infant churches or they would perish. As a result the Indiana Christian Home Missionary Society was formed, but for many years it accomplished little, partly because many Disciples continued to have doubts about the legitimacy of missionary societies.[15]

[14] Winfred Ernest Garrison, *An American Religious Movement: A Brief History of the Disciples of Christ* (St. Louis, 1945), pp. 11, 71. Stone preferred the name "Christian," Campbell, "Disciples of Christ." Sometimes members of the new sect were popularly known as Campbellites.

[15] *Ibid.*, p. 101; Winfred Ernest Garrison, *Religion Follows the Frontier:*

In spite of lack of organization and a trained clergy, membership in the denomination had grown to such a point that when Alexander Campbell visited the state in 1850 he reported: "Our Indiana brethren have much in their power. They are second only to the Methodists in number, wealth, and influence."[16] As with the Baptists the strength of the Disciples was principally in rural districts and small towns. For example, seven Christian churches were founded in Marion County before 1850, but only one in the city of Indianapolis. This was the Central Christian Church, which grew to be one of the largest churches of any denomination in the state. By 1880 there were six Christian churches in Indianapolis, but most of the others were small and struggling and frequently were without the services of a full-time minister. There was no systematic effort to organize a church of this denomination in Fort Wayne until 1870. In Evansville a church was started in 1868 but it was later abandoned and not revived until 1885.[17]

Although Congregationalists and Episcopalians engaged in some missionary activity in Indiana, neither of these denominations showed much strength. The American Home Missionary Society, which was active in the pioneer period, was supported by both Congregationalists and Presbyterians, and

A History of the Disciples of Christ (New York, 1931), p. 209. See H. Clay Trusty, "Formation of the Christian Church in Indiana," *Indiana Magazine of History,* VI (1910), 17-32, for an account of the founding of the earliest churches of the Disciples of Christ in Indiana.

16 Alexander Campbell, "Tour of Forty Days in the States of Ohio, Kentucky, and Indiana," *The Millenial Harbinger* (Bethany, Va.), 1851, p. 81. While in Indiana Campbell preached in many towns throughout the state and addressed the state Constitutional Convention which was then in session in Indianapolis. *Ibid.,* p. 16. It was estimated that in 1850 there were 150 congregations of Disciples in the state, 80 ministers, and as many as 30,000 members. *Indiana Gazetteer,* 1850, p. 72.

17 Perry Williams Swann, The History of the Christian Churches in Marion County, Indiana (Unpublished Master's thesis in Religion, Butler University, 1938), p. 82; Holloway, *Indianapolis,* pp. 222-224; Dunn, *Greater Indianapolis,* I, 607-608; Griswold, *Pictorial History of Fort Wayne,* I, 488; *History of Vanderburgh County* (1889), I, 303.

most of the ministers whom it sent into the field from the East were Congregationalists by previous training and affiliation. But almost without exception the churches which were founded through their efforts were Presbyterian in name and government. The only Congregational Church founded in Indiana through the efforts of the American Home Missionary Society which was entirely free of Presbyterian ties was at the little town of Ontario in the extreme north. In Terre Haute a Congregational Church was organized in 1834 which was not a mission and which became a strong church. By 1850 its membership reached four hundred and included many of the city's distinguished families. During the 1850's a few small Presbyterian churches "took the ground of independency" and assumed the Congregational form because they felt that the Presbyterian Church had not adopted a sufficiently strong stand against slavery. Under the leadership of the Reverend Isaac N. Taylor, a Yankee, churches in Jay and Adams counties formed the Upper Wabash Valley Association of Congregational churches. In the south, in Pike, Gibson, Posey, and Warrick counties, a group of churches which had been affiliated with the Cumberland Presbyterian Church seceded and became Congregational churches. In 1855 the Southern Indiana and Illinois Association was formed, but most of these churches languished and disappeared after a few years.[18]

In 1858 the Indiana Conference of Congregational Churches was formed, but Congregationalism did not flourish. In 1862 it was reported that the Indiana conference was the smallest of any in the United States. The largest congregation in the state continued to be the one in Terre Haute, which in 1879 reported a total of 347 members. In Indianapolis Plymouth Church attained a membership of about two

18 Buley, *Old Northwest,* II, 432; Nathaniel A. Hyde, *Congregationalism in Indiana* (Indianapolis, 1895), pp. 15-21, 28, 30, 32-34; Frederick Kuhns, "A Sketch of Congregationalism in Indiana to 1858," *Indiana Magazine of History,* XLII (1946), 348.

hundred. In 1870 a second church, the Mayflower Church was founded in that city. There were congregations numbering more than one hundred members in Michigan City and Kokomo, but the total number of church members for the entire state in 1879 was less than two thousand.[19]

Prior to 1850 Protestant Episcopal churches were established at Madison, Jeffersonville, New Albany, Lawrenceburg, Evansville, Vincennes, New Harmony, Indianapolis, Richmond, Logansport, Lafayette, Terre Haute, Crawfordsville, Delphi, Bristol, Fort Wayne, La Porte, Mishawaka, and Michigan City. Indianapolis was made the headquarters of the Diocese of Indiana in 1838. Although most of the mission churches founded in the pioneer period survived, few of them showed much vitality, and the number of new churches grew slowly after 1850. During the fifties churches were started at Cannelton, Connersville, Goshen, Hillsboro, Lima, and Worthington; during the sixties at Attica, Elkhart, and Warsaw; during the seventies at La Grange and South Bend. In a few of the cities Episcopalianism showed considerable strength. In Evansville a second church was founded in 1868, and in Fort Wayne in 1869. In 1868 a second church was founded in Lafayette, but it was abandoned after a few years, the members returning to St. John's, the original church.[20]

In Indianapolis the number of Episcopalians was larger than elsewhere. In 1859 Christ Church, the oldest church of the denomination in the city, moved into a new building of English Gothic style, which was designed by the architect William Tinsley. Meanwhile, in 1864 a few members from Christ Church had withdrawn to form Grace Church. In 1866 a third parish was organized, and in 1868 St. Paul's

[19] Kuhns, *op. cit.;* Hyde, *op. cit.,* pp. 35-37, 43-50; Holloway, *Indianapolis,* pp. 220-221; Dunn, *Greater Indianapolis,* I, 606; *Minutes of the General Association of Congregational Churches and Ministers of Indiana,* 1863, p. 7; *ibid.,* 1879, pp. 26, 27, 30.

[20] *Journal of the Annual Convention of the Protestant Episcopal Church in the Diocese of Indiana,* 1880, pp. 3-4; De Hart, *Tippecanoe County,* I, 255.

Church was completed. Like Christ Church it was Gothic in style, but larger in size. It was made the cathedral of the diocese. By 1880 there were thirty-nine parishes and six organized missions in the diocese, but few of them were growing. In fact some of them were not even supplied with clergymen. At the annual conventions of the diocese the bishop regularly complained of the lack of trained clergymen and the inability to fill posts. In 1866, for example, fourteen parishes and mission stations were unsupplied.[21]

More numerous and influential than Congregationalists or Episcopalians were members of the Society of Friends or Quakers. During the pioneer period large numbers of this denomination had moved into the Whitewater Valley in eastern Indiana. Smaller numbers were scattered over other parts of the state. Quakers were most numerous in Wayne, Henry, Randolph, Fayette, Rush, Hancock, Grant, Hamilton, Morgan, Hendricks, Washington, Jackson, Orange, Parke, Montgomery, Vermillion, and Tippecanoe counties. In 1850 there were reported to be eighty-nine churches of the society in the state, with a total membership of about fifteen thousand. At midcentury all of Indiana and a part of eastern Ohio were included in the Indiana Yearly Meeting, which had headquarters in Richmond. In 1858 the Western Yearly Meeting, with headquarters at Plainfield in Hendricks County, was organized.[22]

Friends placed little emphasis upon doctrine or creed. Their meetings were extremely simple, without the services of a "hireling ministry." Friends were expected to "maintain love towards each other," to educate their children "by

[21] Eli Lilly, *History of the Little Church on the Circle. Christ Church Parish Indianapolis 1837-1955* (Indianapolis, 1957), pp. 120, 132; Holloway, *Indianapolis*, pp. 204-205; *Journal of the Annual Convention of the Protestant Episcopal Church in the Diocese of Indiana*, 1866, p. 40; *ibid.*, 1871, p. 47; *ibid.*, 1880, p. 3.

[22] United States Bureau of the Census, *Seventh Census* (1850), 801; *Indiana Gazetteer*, 1850, pp. 72-73; Rudolph, *Hoosier Zion*, p. 191. In 1850 Indiana ranked fourth among all the states in the number of Friends' meetings.

precept and example" in "plainness of speech, deportment and apparel" and to encourage them to read the Scriptures. They were expected to give aid to the poor, to live within their incomes, and to refuse to take oaths or engage in military service.[23] Friends did not engage in evangelism nor did they use missionary activities to win converts. Partly for these reasons their numbers did not grow as did those of some other denominations. It appears that they had reached their greatest strength in Indiana by the fifties and that they probably declined slightly thereafter.[24] Friends exerted an influence in humanitarian movements out of proportion to their numbers. Their extremely important role in the antislavery movement has already been emphasized. They did more than any other religious group to improve the condition of Negro residents of Indiana, and they were also influential in the temperance movement and in efforts at prison reform.

All of the foregoing Protestant groups were made up primarily of persons of older native American stock, and they were relatively unaffected by later European immigration. But several other denominations owed their growth in large measure to the coming of the Germans. Among Protestant groups the Lutherans were the principal beneficiaries of German immigration. But, as one historian has observed, "the Lutheran Church has found more grounds for internal dissension than any other Protestant church—which is saying a great deal." Because of the many divisions it is almost impossible to trace the history of Lutheranism in Indiana. There were a few English-speaking Lutherans in Indiana before the arrival of the Germans. In Fort Wayne and Indianapolis, for

[23] The foregoing statement is based on answers to queries which were addressed to quarterly meetings prior to the yearly meeting. The answers were published in the minutes of the yearly meetings. See, for example, Indiana Yearly Meeting of Friends, *Minutes*, 1850, pp. 6-8.

[24] The United States census in 1850 showed 89 meetings in Indiana; in 1860 it showed 93 meetings; in 1870 only 81 meetings. United States Bureau of the Census, *Seventh Census* (1850), 801; *Eighth Census* (1860), *Mortality and Miscellaneous Statistics*, p. 386; *Compendium of the Ninth Census* (1870), 520.

example, they had formed churches. But the Germans usually
formed separate churches. In the period before 1850 German Lutherans in some places joined with members of the
German Reformed Church to establish congregations. In Indiana united churches of this sort were found in Evansville,
New Albany, Terre Haute, and in Posey and Knox counties.[25] But after 1850 Lutherans ceased from these co-operative efforts and in some places withdrew from the united
churches and formed separate churches. By 1850 there were
four distinct Lutheran organizations in Indiana, the largest
of which was the Synod of Indiana. In 1855 it was divided
and the Synod of Northern Indiana was formed. But in addition there were the German Synod of Indianapolis, the Synod
of Missouri, and a small group who called themselves the
Olive Branch Synod. In 1850 there were about sixty churches
in the state affiliated with one or another of these synods.
Twenty years later the number was almost two hundred. In
Evansville, where there was the largest concentration of
Germans, Lutherans were numerous. They established two
large churches—Trinity German Lutheran Church, the older
one, and St. Emmanuel's German Lutheran Church, which
was organized as the result of a schism in Trinity Church
and which was affiliated with the Missouri Synod. German
Lutherans were numerous in Fort Wayne, and in Indianapolis two of the three Lutheran churches were German
churches. In Terre Haute and Lafayette and other cities with
substantial numbers of Germans there were strong Lutheran
churches. In Lafayette a Swedish Evangelical Lutheran
Church was founded in 1870.[26]

---

[25] Dunn, *Greater Indianapolis*, I, 613; Holloway, *Indianapolis*, p. 243;
Robertson, *Allen County*, pp. 467-469; Carl E. Schneider, *The German Church
on the American Frontier. A Study in the Rise of Religion Among the Germans of the West* (St. Louis, Mo., 1939), pp. 185-189. In 1840 the Evangelical
Church Union of the West was formed by German members of the Lutheran
and Reformed churches. *Ibid.,* pp. 106-113.

[26] Abdel Ross Wentz, *A Basic History of Lutheranism in America* (Philadelphia, 1955), pp. 105-106; *Indiana Gazetteer*, 1850, pp. 74-75; William L.

German Reformed churches and German Evangelical churches were not so numerous as the Lutheran ones, but they were found in all of the cities where there were large German groups. There were also German Methodist churches in several cities in the state. The First German Methodist Church in Evansville was one of the largest in the United States.[27]

There were some other denominations which were derived from German pietist sects. The core of their membership was likely to be Americans of German ancestry rather than recent immigrants. Among these groups were German Baptists of pacifist leanings. Most of them affiliated with the Church of the Brethren (sometimes called Tunkers or Dunkards). Several of these churches were organized in Indiana independently of each other before 1850, and their numbers continued to increase slightly. They were groups of rural people who frequently had no regular church building but met in houses and barns to listen to itinerant preachers. They were most numerous in northern Indiana, especially in Elkhart County. During the fifties they began to hold annual meetings, which were large affairs at which public services of a revivalist nature were held and nonbelievers sometimes converted. By 1864 one hundred fifty churches in the state were represented.[28] Somewhat more numerous and somewhat more in-

Tedrow (ed.), *Our Church. A History of the Synod of Northern Indiana of the Evangelical Lutheran Church* (Ann Arbor, Mich., 1894), p. 5; Holloway, *Indianapolis*, pp. 243-245; *History of Vanderburgh County* (1889), pp. 299, 302; Robertson, *Allen County*, pp. 467-473; United States Bureau of the Census, *Seventh Census* (1850), 803; *Compendium of the Ninth Census* (1870), 521. The Missouri Synod was founded by a group of Lutherans of extremely conservative views who came from Saxony and settled in Missouri.

[27] Robertson, *Allen County*, pp. 480-481; *History of Vanderburgh County* (1889), p. 303; Holloway, *Indianapolis*, pp. 224-225; Morlock, *The Evansville Story*, p. 74; Bradsby, *Vigo County*, pp. 598-599; S. H. Baumgartner (comp.), *Historical Data and Life Sketches of the Deceased Ministers of the Indiana Conference of the Evangelical Association 1835 to 1915* (Cleveland, Ohio, 1915), pp. 21, 32-33, 72-95.

[28] Otho Winger, *History of the Church of the Brethren in Indiana* (Elgin, Ill., 1917), pp. 15-16, 169, 208, 210. See *ibid.*, pp. 172-175, 181-182, 190-191, for individual churches founded between 1850 and 1880.

stitutionalized were the churches of the United Brethren in Christ, a denomination organized in 1789. Among the charter members were ministers of the Reformed, Mennonite, and Moravian churches. The first societies of the United Brethren were established in Indiana in the territorial period. In 1830 the Indiana Conference was organized. The state was later divided. The White River Conference was created in 1845, embracing most of the northern half of the state. The St. Joseph Conference included the northernmost part of the state. The census of 1870 showed one hundred eighty-four congregations of United Brethren.

The first group of Mennonites and Amish to settle in the state came in 1838 directly from Switzerland, where they had originated in the sixteenth century; others came in the 1840's and 1850's from Pennsylvania and Ohio, where they had first settled. Adams and Elkhart counties received the largest number, while La Grange, De Kalb, Wells, Hamilton, Clay, and Owen had small settlements. They believed in conversion, a committed discipleship, in nonresistance, and in missionary work; while the two groups had similar beliefs, the Amish were more strict in some respects. Their meeting-houses were plain and unadorned, as was their dress. Their number increased from around four hundred in 1850 to two thousand in 1880.[29]

Quite distinct from other Protestants were Universalists, who attracted attention out of proportion to their small numbers. Universalists believed in individual religious freedom and the unity of all Christians as did some other denominations, but most Universalists also rejected the idea of future

29 A. W. Drury, *History of the Church of the United Brethren in Christ* (Dayton, Ohio, 1924), pp. 309-311, 383-386, 389, 722, 726; Donald F. Carmony, "Kingdom Church," *Indiana Magazine of History*, XXIX (1933), 104; Adam Byron Condo, *History of the Indiana Conference of the Church of the United Brethren in Christ* (Published by order of the Indiana Conference, [1927]), *passim;* Augustus Cleland Wilmore, *History of the White River Conference of the Church of the United Brethren in Christ* . . . (Dayton, Ohio, 1925), *passim;* John C. Wenger, *The Mennonites in Indiana and Michigan* (Scottsdale, Pa., 1961), pp. 1-55.

punishment, and some of them rejected the authenticity and authority of parts of the Scriptures. Their lack of orthodoxy caused them to be looked upon with suspicion by members of other groups. Even in the pioneer period there were a few Universalists in the state. In 1848 a State Convention, affiliated with the General Universalist Convention was formed. In 1850 it was estimated that there were perhaps as many as fifty-five Universalist societies in the state, but few of them had regular meetinghouses or even met regularly. By 1880 a total of more than one hundred had been formed, but many of them were short-lived and had either disappeared completely or had languished by that date.[30] Universalism placed too much emphasis upon the rational elements in religion to attract a large following, and many persons who accepted Universalist doctrines felt no need for an organized church. In Indianapolis a Universalist society was formed in 1844, then declined and then was revived as the First Universalist Church in 1853. The church did not acquire a permanent building and was without a regular minister after 1869. About 1860 part of the members withdrew to form another society but later disbanded. In other cities the record was similar.[31]

Unitarians were more of a rarity than were Universalists. Occasional Unitarian services were held in Evansville as early as 1851. In 1866 a Liberal Christian Church held services in that city for several months. In Indianapolis a Unitarian society was formed in 1868. The group adopted a Declaration of Belief in which they acknowledged "dependence on Almighty God, the One God and Father of us all" and in which they recognized Jesus of Nazareth as "the world's greatest Teacher and Example." The Reverend Henry Blanchard served as minister for the group until 1872.

30 Elmo Arnold Robinson, "Universalism in Indiana," *Indiana Magazine of History*, XIII (1917), 6, 8-12, 15-19, 157-158; *Indiana Gazetteer*, 1850, p. 75.

31 Holloway, *Indianapolis*, pp. 246-247; Bradsby, *Vigo County*, p. 599; Robertson, *Allen County*, pp. 490-491; De Hart, *Tippecanoe County*, I, 252-253; *History of the Ohio Falls Cities and Their Counties*, II, 209.

During these early years membership grew, but after Blanchard resigned to return East the organization languished and was served only intermittently by a minister. A few other churches of Unitarian persuasion were organized. In 1879 a state conference of Unitarian and Independent churches met. It included churches at Evansville, Vincennes, La Porte, Shelbyville, and Indianapolis.[32]

§ §

The slow growth of the minor Protestant denominations was due in part to their failure to proselytize as vigorously as the larger denominations. Methodists were especially active in the use of revivals to win converts. The winter of 1852-1853 was reported in the North Indiana Conference of the Methodist Church to have been "simply a long series of revivals." But revivals were not confined to the Methodists. Most converts to the Disciples Church were won by itinerant preachers who held services for several consecutive days.[33]

In many communities prolonged revivals were held at least once a year, and they were frequently interdenominational in character. For example, in February 1850, the press reported that revivals were being carried on simultaneously in Columbus, Madison, New Albany, Jeffersonville, Greencastle, Lafayette, Indianapolis, and several other towns. In some places businesses closed while revivals were in progress. In the winter of 1858 one circuit-riding minister of the Methodist Church reported: "Since last August we have held nine protracted meetings, and it has pleased the Lord to meet with us in every coming together, and the result is, 305 persons have been converted and made happy in the Saviour's love; 281 have joined the Methodist Episcopal Church, and others have joined the United Brethren and Evangelical

[32] *History of Vanderburgh County* (1889), p. 303; Holloway, *Indianapolis,* pp. 247-248; Indianapolis *Daily Sentinel,* April 24, 25, 1879.

[33] Herrick and Sweet, *North Indiana Conference,* p. 39; *Millenial Harbinger,* 1850, pp. 110-111; *ibid.,* 1861, p. 235. Practically every issue of the *Millenial Harbinger* contained accounts of group conversions at revivals at various points in Indiana.

Lutherans. . . . I think I can safely say that the fire of Divine Grace is burning all around the circuit." Revivals of this sort continued in the post Civil War years.[34] In 1866, 1867, and 1868 Methodists reported large numbers of conversions. In Indianapolis a revival was held in Roberts Chapel from December 1865 to March 1866 at which three hundred twenty-six persons were converted. Presbyterians also regularly held revivals. For example, during 1874 four Presbyterian churches in Indianapolis held revivals. The following year interdenominational revivals sponsored by the Y.M.C.A. were held at several places in the state. In the winter of 1881 the largest interdenominational revival to that time in Indianapolis was held at the Roberts Park Methodist Church. It was claimed that 1,525 persons were converted—1,025 Methodists, 389 Presbyterians, 102 Baptists, and 25 Congregationalists.[35]

Revivals resulted in spectacular numbers of converts, and they were sometimes followed by successful campaigns to raise money to build churches. But the results of these conversions were frequently not lasting. Methodist records show that revivals led to the acceptance of large numbers of probationers who were never received into full church membership. Although revivals appeared to increase in size and frequency by the 1870's, there appears to have been a decline in the extreme emotionalism which had characterized Methodist revivals in frontier days. Baptists also reported that there was a reaction against "sensational methods of preaching" and that "a more reverent and thoughtful manner is desired by ministry and people."[36]

34 Indianapolis *Locomotive,* February 9, 1850; Kershner, Social and Cultural History of Indianapolis, p. 214; *Western Christian Advocate,* February 17, 1858, quoted in Herrick and Sweet, *North Indiana Conference,* p. 67.

35 Herrick and Sweet, *op. cit.,* p. 103; J. C. Belman, *The Great Revival at Roberts Park M. E. Church and Other Churches* (Indianapolis, 1881), pp. 22, 295; Indianapolis *Daily Journal,* December 7, 1875.

36 Herrick and Sweet, *North Indiana Conference,* pp. 41, 47, 127; Detzler, *Northwest Indiana Conference,* p. 64; Indiana Baptist State Convention, *Minutes,* 1879, p. 21.

In the pioneer period many revivals had been conducted at camp meetings, but as towns developed and church buildings grew in size most revivals were held in churches. Camp meetings continued to be a part of religious life, especially among Methodists, but by the seventies their character had changed. They were no longer used primarily for the purpose of winning converts but for educating and strengthening the faith and morality of those who were already church members. Camps were no longer merely sites where tents were pitched. They had become permanent institutions in substantial buildings at points convenient to rail transportation. One of the larger camps was the one maintained by Methodists at Battle Ground, near Lafayette, on the site of the former Battle Ground Collegiate Institute.[37]

Less emotional in their appeal than revivals were religious debates by members of different denominations. Like the revivals these debates sometimes lasted for several days and attracted large crowds. Members of the Disciples of Christ, following a custom started by Alexander Campbell, were especially active in challenging members of other denominations to debate. They debated with members of such diverse faiths as Methodists, Baptists, Quakers, Universalists, and Spiritualists on a great variety of theological subjects, including baptism, eternal punishment, and universal salvation. At a debate between a Disciple and a Methodist on the subject of baptism at Cloverdale in 1866, sixty-nine persons were reported to have been converted to the Disciples' view and to have been immersed forthwith. Because of their unorthodox views Universalists, more than any group, were challenged to debate. The most sensational debates were those between Disciples and Universalists. One of the most notable occurred in Indianapolis in 1868 between the minister of the Central Christian Church and the Universalist minister. It was held at Morrison's Opera House and at-

37 Detzler, *Northwest Indiana Conference,* pp. 61-64; Herrick and Sweet, *North Indiana Conference,* pp. 126, 127.

tracted large crowds. In 1870 another famous debate was held at Union City between Universalist and Disciples ministers at the Christian Church. The subject was: "Do the Holy Scriptures teach that those who die in wilful disobedience of the Gospel of Jesus Christ will be ultimately holy and Happy?" The debate went on for four days from ten in the morning until noon and from seven until ten each night.[38]

The Sunday School was another institution important in winning and holding converts and inculcating doctrine. Indianapolis churches of all denominations were noted for their Sunday Schools. In 1850 it was estimated that two thirds of the children in the city attended Sunday School regularly. In 1856 there were reported to be twenty-seven Sunday Schools in the city, attended by adults as well as children. It was an annual custom for the children from all of the Sunday schools in the city to hold a parade on the Fourth of July. The weak state of public education made the role of the Sunday School especially important since it was the only school attended by many children.[39] During the Civil War years it appears that Sunday Schools declined, but after the war they were reinvigorated and became more institutionalized. Baptists claimed especially large enrollments. The Baptist State Convention hailed the Sunday School as "the most hopeful and promising field of Christian labor within the bounds of our state." Methodists and Presbyterians did not claim as large enrollments in their Sunday Schools, but both denominations spon-

[38] Wesley Cauble, *Disciples of Christ in Indiana: Achievements of A Century* (Indianapolis, 1930), pp. 145-147; Garrison, *Religion Follows the Frontier,* p. 209; Enos Everett Dowling, A Revival of the Christian Record (1867-1875) : A Study in Post-Bellum Religious Journalism in Indiana (Unpublished Master's Thesis, School of Religion, Butler University, 1943), p. 110; *The Destiny of Man: A Discussion, Held at Union City Indiana . . . between Rev. S. P. Carlton and Eld. W. D. Moore* (Cincinnati, 1870), p. 7. See Robinson, "Universalism in Indiana," *Indiana Magazine of History,* XIII, 177, for a list of debates in which Universalists were challenged by members of other denominations.

[39] *Indiana Gazetteer,* 1850, p. 256; Jobson, *American Methodism,* pp. 112, 114; Cady, *Baptist Church in Indiana,* pp. 167, 173; Lilly, *Christ Church,* p. 49.

sored Sunday School committees and conventions within their own organizations and also supported interdenominational Sunday School conventions. In 1872 a national meeting was held at the Second Presbyterian Church in Indianapolis to consider materials to be used in the teaching of Sunday School classes. Out of the deliberations of the meeting the International Series of Sunday School Lessons was developed and came into general use.[40]

Inculcation of sound morals among its members was, of course, a principal function of the church regardless of denomination. But within most congregations at one time or another debates arose over the morality or immorality of certain practices. One controversial issue was the use of instrumental music in churches. As larger and more elaborate churches were built organs were frequently installed, but this practice was sometimes condemned. The most spirited debate on the subject seems to have arisen in the Christian Church, where some members opposed the use of instrumental music because it was not expressly sanctioned in the New Testament. An editorial in the *Christian Record,* a journal published in Indiana, in 1868 recorded "determined opposition" to this modern innovation. "We regard the introduction of the organ, melodeon, or fiddle into Christian worship as a great evil, and fraught with danger to the spirituality of the divine worship," it declared. Among Methodists there was also discussion over the propriety of instrumental music. In Kokomo, where a new brick church was built, there was a serious feud over the introduction of an organ and music by a choir. More conservative elements also opposed the introduction of such activities as church socials and fairs, but these became more and more common, and opponents fought a losing battle. In 1875 the *Christian Record* reported that

40 Cady, *Baptist Church in Indiana,* p. 219; *The Second Presbyterian Church of Indianapolis; One Hundred Years 1838-1938* (Indianapolis, 1939), p. 233; Indiana State Baptist Convention, *Minutes,* 1878, p. 20; Indiana Conference of the Methodist Church, *Minutes,* 1865-1880 *passim;* Minutes of Indiana Synod North of the Presbyterian Church, 1870-1877 *passim.*

"nine tenths of the churches today are holding festivals, having Christmas trees, [and] paying money to have the privilege of saying who is the prettiest girl or the ugliest man."[41]

Churches also sought to regulate the conduct of their ministers and members outside the church. Such matters as the use of intoxicants, profanity, and types of entertainment received a great deal of attention in sermons and in the deliberations of church meetings. All Protestant denominations condemned the use of tobacco. At midcentury tobacco chewing was common, even among ministers. But by the late 1850's a crusade against tobacco had begun. Beginning in 1857 elders in the Methodist Church were asked to discontinue the use of it, and after 1875 all new ministers were required to take a pledge to abstain from its use. Disciples also frowned upon the use of tobacco. Such practices as dancing, card playing, horse racing, theater going, and even baseball and croquet playing were condemned at one time or another. A typical editorial in the *Christian Record* thus criticized dancing: "Shame then, on those Christians who advocate a cause by which many sons have become profligate, and many daughters ruined." Resolutions adopted by the North Indiana Conference of Methodists in 1879 condemned horse racing at fairs. In addition dancing, card playing, and baseball playing were proscribed as "injurious to sound piety" and because they tended to "lead to a disrelish of spiritual things, and alienate youth especially from the service of God."[42]

Participation in any of the above activities on Sunday was regarded as particularly objectionable. All Protestant organizations showed much concern over desecration of the

[41] *The Christian Record,* July, 1868, pp. 203-205, and October, 1875, p. 539, quoted in Dowling, Revival of the Christian Record, pp. 93, 137; Herrick and Sweet, *North Indiana Conference,* pp. 109-111.

[42] Herrick and Sweet, *op. cit.,* pp. 65, 130-131; Detzler, *Northwest Indiana Conference,* p. 71; Dowling, Revival of the Christian Record, pp. 137-138, 140; *Christian Record,* February 1867, p. 58, quoted *ibid.,* p. 136; Cady, *Baptist Church in Indiana,* pp. 240-241.

Sabbath, which was supposed to be observed with Puritan strictness. In every Methodist conference there was a committee on the Sabbath which reported annually, and regularly condemned secular activities on the Sabbath and regularly expressed discouragement over its failure to stop these activities. In 1860, for example, the Committee on the Sabbath of the Indiana Conference of Methodists expressed concern over "the common practice of visiting . . . neighbors on this holy day." Three years later it was resolved that ministers should discountenance "all species of Sabbath desecration," including pleasure excursions, social visiting, making contracts, and secular conversation.[43]

In 1854 Presbyterians prepared a memorial to the state legislature expressing regret that there was no law prohibiting desecration of the Sabbath. They appealed to the lawmakers "as patriots as philanthropists and as the representatives and lawmakers of a Christian people acting within your own proper sphere, to protect from licentious and wanton attacks the Christian morality of the people upon which rests the foundations of civil society and of the Social State." In response to this and similar appeals the legislature in 1855 passed an act for the protection of the Sabbath which imposed fines upon persons found rioting, quarreling, hunting, fishing, or engaging at common labor or their usual vocation on Sunday, "works of charity and necessity only excepted." In 1865 the sale of intoxicants on Sunday was expressly banned.[44]

After the adoption of the 1855 law a foreign visitor reported that Sunday in Indianapolis was observed with "Presbyterian strictness." But in later years a general relaxation occurred, partly as the result of the Civil War. As early as October, 1861, Indiana Presbyterians remarked on the "de-

---

[43] Heller, *Indiana Conference,* p. 97; Indiana Conference of the Methodist Church, *Minutes,* 1863-1864, p. 31.

[44] Minutes of the Synod of Indiana of the Presbyterian Church (Old School), 1854-1856, p. 431; Indiana *Laws,* 1855, p. 159; *ibid.,* special session, 1865, p. 197.

moralizing consequences of war" which were already "manifest in the unusual violation of the Sabbath day by our civil and military authorities and in the great increase of profanity intemperance and licentiousness especially among our youth who have given themselves to the service of their country." In the postwar years secular activities on Sunday continued to increase. In 1866 Methodists reported that "public works and private enterprises" were carried on "without apology on the holy Sabbath day," and that most alarming of all was the effrontery with which beer gardens and saloons were kept open.[45]

The Indianapolis *Herald* reported in 1866 that the Sabbath law was not generally observed. An editorial in the *Indiana Farmer* in 1878 said that violation of the law was notorious in all the cities and towns in the state. "The law allowing druggists to put up prescriptions on the Sabbath," it lamented, "has been so loosely interpreted by dealers as to include the right to sell cigars, fancy articles, candies, soda water and, too often, something much stronger." Proprietors of beer gardens and saloons received some of the blame for increased laxity, but so did the railroads. Methodists expressed alarm over violation of the Sabbath law by railroad excursions, while Presbyterians agreed that railroads had been "productive of untold mischief" in causing Sabbath breaking. "At the various Rail Road centers," said a report at the Indiana Synod North in 1876, "Sabbath breaking and Intemperance and false systems and fleeting pleasures obstruct the way of truth."[46]

European immigrants, especially the Germans, received most of the blame for the degeneration of Sunday into a

---

[45] Murray, *Letters from the United States*, p. 329; Minutes of the Synod of Indiana of the Presbyterian Church (Old School), 1861-1864, pp. 18-19; Herrick and Sweet, *North Indiana Conference*, p. 103; Heller, *Indiana Conference*, p. 110.

[46] Indianapolis *Daily Herald*, March 17, 1866; *Indiana Farmer* (Indianapolis), May 11, 1878; Minutes of Indiana Synod North of the Presbyterian Church, 1875-1877, p. 252.

mere day of pleasure. The Committee on the Sabbath of the Northern Indiana Conference of Methodists in 1868 complained that the foreign population, especially in cities, ignored the Sabbath laws. In 1877 the same conference deplored efforts to "Europeanize" the Sabbath. Some Americans, it declared, had been induced "to practically favor the emissaries of Rome and Rationalism, whose evil purpose is to repeal our Sunday laws, and virtually abolish this holy institution by its systematic desecration." And an Episcopalian minister in Indianapolis, in a sermon entitled "Dangers to the Republic," saw great dangers from transplanting the "continental Sabbath" to the United States. The Bible and the observance of the Sabbath, he said, were the strength of America. National ruin would follow converting Sunday into a day of "riotous recreation."[47]

§ § §

The churches also showed an interest in public questions which were less closely linked with religion than Sabbath laws and their enforcement. In earlier chapters it has already been seen that Protestant churches were a powerful force in securing the temperance legislation enacted during the 1850's and in the postwar period. The involvement of the churches in the slavery controversy during the fifties has also been seen.

The eruption of the slavery question into secession and Civil War posed new questions for religious groups. Opinions varied as to the effect of the war on the churches themselves. As already indicated the war was blamed for the increased desecration of the Sabbath, and in some places the call for troops led to a decline in church attendance, but in other places it was claimed that the war caused some churches to experience revivals. Early in the war one Methodist minister asserted that as the result of the war: "Elements which had

[47] Herrick and Sweet, *North Indiana Conference,* pp. 102-103; Indiana Conference of the Methodist Church, *Minutes,* 1877, pp. 232-233; Indianapolis *Daily Journal,* November 28, 1879.

long been dormant have been stirred up; the spell of indifference has been broken; and the spirit of worldliness quenched." But another Methodist minister said that while the war created "wild commotion in our hearts," it tended to "freeze our religious feelings." He expressed a fear "that we, as a church, have less interest in God's cause and less sympathy for suffering humanity than ever before." Another minister of the same denomination agreed that the church waned in spirituality and that religion was at a low ebb at the end of the war. Few attended prayer meetings during the war, and "the prayers were patriotic rather than strictly religious; they were dull and formal except when made for the country or the 'boys' in the army." Many Baptist churches closed during the war because of lack of attendance. "When the war finally dragged to a close," says one Baptist historian, "the Baptist churches were left with little spiritual vitality to combat the terrific moral let-down which ensued."[48]

Nearly all churches loudly proclaimed their support for the Union and the military effort to preserve it, and most of them saw in the sin of slavery the fundamental cause of the war. In October, 1862, the Presbyterian Synod of Indiana adopted resolutions which said that the war was the result of "the righteous judgment of God" upon the nation "for its complicity with and support of the system of slavery." Moreover it was not to be expected that God would turn away his judgment "until the nation shall have with sincere and godly repentance turned from the sins by which the judgment has been provoked." Indiana Baptists saw in the war a manifestation of divine providence in which God was "using the wrath of man for the accomplishment of grand designs." The 1864 State Baptist Convention declared: "The nation is . . . throw-

48 Minutes of the Synod of Indiana of the Presbyterian Church (Old School), 1861-1864, p. 10; *Western Christian Advocate,* May 15, 1861, p. 154, and September 25, 1861, p. 307, quoted in Estel Neace, A Study of Methodism in Indiana during the Civil War (Unpublished Master's thesis in Religion, Butler University, 1961), pp. 17-19; Heller, *Indiana Conference,* p. 108; Cady, *Baptist Church in Indiana,* pp. 208-209.

ing off a terrible incubus, as a strong man to run a race. She is wiping out, or God is wiping out for her in spite of herself, a foul stain upon her escutcheon."[49]

Among Baptists, as among other denominations, there were increasing expressions of bitterness against the Confederate cause as the war dragged on. In 1865 one Baptist association declared that the leaders of the rebellion deserved no more sympathy from civilized men than did Satan when he rebelled against Heaven. At the end of the war the Lutheran Synod of northern Indiana adopted a resolution which thanked divine providence for "crowning the efforts of the army and navy of the United States with success in crushing the slave-holders' rebellion and convincing the world that our Government has power to punish treason and quell insurrection at home. . . ."[50]

But it was Methodists who were most forthright in their denunciation of the southern cause and Southerners and in equating religion and patriotism, and they were especially bitter against their brethren in the South. The Indiana Conference expressed gratification that

the church of which we are humble ministers is so largely represented in the war. History will tell how, while the Methodist Episcopal Church South was treasonable to the very core, the great Methodist Episcopal Church, which knows no sectional landmarks, and will wear no sectional name, rose up in mass to give its united influence to the Government. . . . We rejoice with exceeding joy that we belong to a church of undivided and fervent Christian patriotism.

[49] Minutes of the Synod of Indiana of the Presbyterian Church (Old School), 1861-1864, p. 28; Cady, *Baptist Church in Indiana,* pp. 205-207. Resolutions adopted by the annual meeting of the Indiana General Association of Congregationalists declared that war became a "sacred duty" when peace could be purchased only "by a disgraceful betrayal of a Divine trust." The meeting endorsed a constitutional amendment abolishing slavery and endorsed the use of Negro troops, demanded the same protection for them as for white troops, and declared that it was a Christian duty to make provision for the physical, intellectual, and spiritual wants of the freedmen. *Minutes of the General Association of Congregational Churches,* 1864, p. 5.

[50] Cady, *Baptist Church in Indiana,* p. 205; Tedrow, *History of the Synod of Northern Indiana of the Evangelical Lutheran Church,* p. 72.

The other Methodist conferences adopted resolutions expressing similar sentiments. But some ministers felt that pressures from their congregations forced them to emphasize the war to the exclusion of the spiritual welfare of their flocks. "It would seem," one complained, "that many desire us, in almost every sermon to portray the abominations of slavery, descant upon our patriotic zeal, and look as though we would rather go to war than to heaven. . . ."[51]

Ministers from all denominations served as chaplains in the Union Army, but some Methodist ministers went further and actively helped recruit troops, and a few Methodist ministers enlisted for combat duty. In 1861 Governor Morton authorized the Reverend J. W. T. McMullen, a Richmond minister, and Reverend F. A. Hardin to raise a regiment. As the result of their efforts the Fifty-Seventh Indiana was organized at Camp Wayne and McMullen was commissioned a colonel. McMullen resigned after a few months, but two Methodist ministers remained in the regiment and took part in the fighting at Shiloh and elsewhere. Another Methodist minister attempted to recruit a regiment which was to become the Fifty-Fourth. The object was to raise a regiment in which religiously inclined young men could associate with other soldiers of similar character and be protected from contact with such vices as profanity and intemperance. But the required number of troops did not respond, and plans for the regiment had to be abandoned.[52]

A few religious voices were raised against the use of military force. At their annual meeting in 1864, the members of the Church of the Brethren, one of whose tenets was nonresistance, voted to exhort their members to remain true to

51 Indiana Conference of the Methodist Church, *Minutes,* 1862-1863, p. 20; *Western Christian Advocate,* June 20, 1861, p. 227, quoted in Neace, Methodism in Indiana during the Civil War, p. 44; Herrick and Sweet, *North Indiana Conference,* pp. 70-71; Southeastern Conference of the Methodist Church, *Minutes,* 1863, p. 23.

52 Herrick and Sweet, *North Indiana Conference,* pp. 73-74; Neace, Methodism in Indiana during the Civil War, pp. 21-22.

their principles and "to endure whatever sufferings and to make whatever sacrifice the maintaining of the principle may require, and not to encourage in any way the practice of war." At the same time they promised to pay their taxes and declared that the government had their sympathies and prayers and should have their aid "in any way that does not conflict with the Gospel of Christ."[53]

Members of the Society of Friends were unable to reconcile the use of military force with Christian principles. The Indiana Yearly Meeting in 1862 expressed sympathy for young men who were tempted to enlist out of love of country. "We love our country," they said, "and highly appreciate the excellent government under which we have enjoyed so large a share of liberty and security to person and property, and look with heartfelt sorrow upon the efforts to destroy it, but we . . . cannot believe that any cause is sufficient to . . . warrant us in violating what we believe to be the law of our Lord." The following year the Yearly Meeting advised parents "to watch over their children, and see that their minds are not filled with false views of military glory and achievements." In spite of the position taken by the yearly meetings some Quakers volunteered for military service. In 1865 the Western Yearly Meeting expressed "deep solicitude and Christian sympathy" for the many young men who, "notwithstanding the plain and clear language, both of prophecy and of the New Testament . . . have felt impelled, in the ardor of patriotism to take up arms in their country's defense."[54]

Although Quakers had scruples against bearing arms, like members of other denominations they gave support to the various benevolent activities connected with war, such as the work of the Sanitary Commission. And Quakers were especially active in behalf of the slaves who were emancipated as

53 Winger, *Church of the Brethren in Indiana*, p. 211.

54 Indiana Yearly Meeting of Friends, *Minutes*, 1862, pp. 14-15; *ibid.*, 1863, p. 19; Western Yearly Meeting of Friends, *Minutes*, 1865, pp. 15-16. See also *ibid.*, 1861, p. 6 and *ibid.*, 1862, p. 10.

the result of the war. In 1863 the Indiana Yearly Meeting adopted a recommendation that the Committee on the Concerns of the People of Color should undertake to relieve the physical needs of the freedmen and also should promote their advancement in knowledge and religion. During the remainder of the war and in the postwar period Friends contributed to the aid of freedmen by supporting schools and hospitals and helping to establish them as farmers. Other Protestant denominations also showed an interest in the welfare of the freedmen of the South although their interest in this problem appeared to be less intense than it had been over the sin of slavery before the war.[55] In 1863 Indiana Presbyterians pledged support to the Freedmen's Aid Society and support for missionary activity among the emancipated slaves to instruct them "in elements of learning and . . . those habits of industry which will render that liberty which God has given them a blessing and not a curse." In postwar years Presbyterians continued to support work among the freedmen.[56]

The 1863 meeting of the Indiana Conference of the Methodist Church voiced continued support for the work of colonization in Liberia as well as endorsement of the Emancipation Proclamation. At the same time it also expressed sympathy for the freedmen and urged support for agencies working in their behalf. During the war years Indiana Methodist churches collected money for freedmen's aid and in the postwar years gave support to the Freedman's Aid Society, which was founded by the Methodist Church. But Methodists did not intend that work in the South should be confined to aid for Negroes. They also contemplated missionary work among the whites of the South. The Northwest Indiana Conference declared that the Methodist Church should carry "tidings of

---

[55] Indiana Yearly Meeting of Friends, *Minutes*, 1863, p. 49; *ibid.*, 1864, pp. 17-21; *ibid.*, 1865, pp. 41-47; *ibid.*, 1866, pp. 32-36; *ibid.*, 1867, pp. 7-10; *ibid.*, 1868, pp. 41-42; *ibid.*, 1869, pp. 37-40; Western Yearly Meeting of Friends, *Minutes*, 1864, p. 22; *ibid.*, 1865, pp. 38-41.

[56] Minutes of the Synod of Indiana of the Presbyterian Church (Old School), 1861-1864, pp. 58, 79.

Marion County Courthouse, Indianapolis

Bates House, Indianapolis

Franklin County
Courthouse,
Brookville

Christ Church,
Indianapolis

free salvation to all classes" in the South. It called for work in the South "to check and eradicate that anti-Christian sectionalism which has so nearly wrought our ruin."[57]

During the period of Reconstruction Methodists continued to take a more outspoken stand on political issues than did other denominations. In the conflict between President Johnson and Congress they made it clear that their sympathies were with Congress. In 1866 the Indiana Conference expressed regret over "the present antagonism which exists between our Chief Magistrate and the Congress" and pledged their "undivided sympathies and earnest prayers" for Congress "in their great work of re-construction." The Northwest Conference forthrightly declared that they "deprecate[d] the course of the Chief Executive in his apparent determination to enforce his policy contrary to the clearly expressed wish of the people" and declared that they would sustain Congress in measures necessary to crush out a "spirit of rebellion."[58]

In the postwar years Quakers showed more solicitude for the southern Negroes who moved into Indiana than did any other religious group. They provided relief for destitute Negroes and helped them establish schools. Other Protestant denominations in a few instances helped establish mission churches for Negroes in which schools were sometimes held. In Indianapolis the Second Christian Church was founded in 1866 for Negroes. Students and faculty from North Western

[57] Indiana Conference of the Methodist Church, *Minutes*, 1862-1863, pp. 15, 20; Herrick and Sweet, *North Indiana Conference*, pp. 92-93; Northwest Indiana Conference of the Methodist Church, *Minutes*, 1865, pp. 39-40.

[58] Indiana Conference of the Methodist Church, *Minutes*, 1866, p. 22; Northwest Indiana Conference of the Methodist Church, *Minutes*, 1867, p. 35. The Southeastern Conference prayed that God might direct the President, "that he may not be led by the blind impulses of passion and appetite; that he may not be governed by the counsels of bad men." Southeastern Indiana Conference of the Methodist Church, *Minutes*, 1866, p. 25.

As early as 1865 the Whitewater Conference of the United Brethren passed a resolution in favor of Negro suffrage, the only such action by any Indiana religious group which this author has found. Wilmore, *History of the White Water Conference*, p. 162.

Christian University taught in the Sunday School in the early years of the church.[59]

Among Baptists and Methodists, the two denominations to which nearly all Negroes belonged, almost complete segregation prevailed after 1865, although in the period before the war there had been a few instances of Negro members in white churches. As the result of the migration from the South Baptists became the largest Negro group. In many places white persons helped Negroes to establish churches, but the Negro churches had no affiliation with the white churches. Several African Methodist Episcopal churches had been founded in the state before the war. After the war, with the increase in Negro population, these churches grew and others were established. A smaller number of Negroes were affiliated with the African Methodist Episcopal Zion Church.[60]

On the whole, except for Quakers who, as already seen, were interested in prison reform, Protestant churches showed little interest in any social question except temperance in the postwar period. For the most part churches ignored problems arising out of the beginnings of industrialization and urbanization. In their sermons ministers devoted themselves almost exclusively to theological subjects and exhortations to seek salvation. In 1871 at the Franklin College commencement, William Steele Holman, the long-time Democratic member of Congress, and a member of the Baptist Church, gave an address on the subject of "Capital and Labor." In it he reminded his listeners of the humble origins of the Baptist Church and expressed concern over the signs that increasing concentration of wealth in the hands of a few would lead to injustice. He called upon Baptists to throw their weight against such a development, but there is no evidence that his plea had any effect.[61]

Sermons on economic and social questions were rare, but there were occasional examples. In 1871 the Reverend Han-

59 Thornbrough, *Negro in Indiana*, pp. 211, 317-318, 372.
60 *Ibid.*, pp. 153, 368, 370-371.
61 Cady, *Baptist Church in Indiana*, p. 245.

ford A. Edson of the Second Presbyterian Church in Indianapolis delivered a sermon on the subject of business and commerce. It was a most remarkable performance in view of the membership of his congregation, which included such men as Thomas A. Morris, the railroad magnate, and other leading businessmen. In the sermon he emphasized the importance of business and industry in a young country such as the United States, but he found much that was "shockingly wrong" in the business world. Some of the leading railroads, he asserted, "openly purchase their legislation, and a man would pass for a simpleton, who thought the immense land grants of the Pacific roads were obtained by fair means." In addition he was critical of the "gold gamblers" of Wall Street and of the false labeling and adulteration of many articles which were sold in the stores.[62] In sharp contrast was a sermon which the Reverend William A. Bartlett delivered in the same church on the subject of capital and labor in 1877 at the time of acute labor unrest. Bartlett said that among the crowds of unemployed in Indianapolis were men who were unwilling to work and that a wrong was done small taxpayers "by giving away such vast sums of the public funds" for the relief of the unemployed. "It is simply wickedness," he said, "to pat on the back the miserable loafer who drags his miserable carcass from one kitchen to another. There isn't one reason why we should nurse a pauper class in this young city. . . . It is a crime against humanity to foster a generation of beggars."[63]

Apprehensions raised by the unrest of the depression years were more clearly enunciated in a sermon by the minister of St. Paul's Episcopal Church in Indianapolis in 1879. Speaking of "Dangers to the Republic," he warned against party

[62] Indianapolis *Daily Journal,* January 30, 1871; *Second Presbyterian Church of Indianapolis,* p. 64. In 1873 twenty-five members of the Second Presbyterian Church withdrew to form the Tenth Presbyterian Church and Edson resigned to become minister of the new congregation, but whether his social and economic views had anything to do with these developments is not clear. *Ibid.,* p. 71.

[63] Indianapolis *Daily Journal,* June 11, 1877. For a sketch of Bartlett, who came to Indianapolis in 1876, see *Second Presbyterian Church,* pp. 74-75.

strife and divisions between capital and labor. The latter, he said, was likely to lead to Communism. He also expressed doubts about the wisdom of universal suffrage, especially in view of the large number of European immigrants in the United States. "Fifty years ago," he said, "the emigrant was of a much better type." But now immigrants were arriving who could not read or write, and unless immigration was checked, "the day must come when atheists, communists, tramps, the slag and scurf of America and unenlightened foreigners will be able to outvote the decent people of the country."[64] Just two weeks later Oscar C. McCulloch, minister of the Plymouth Congregational Church, delivered a sermon in very different vein on the causes of poverty and crime. He pointed out that in an industrialized society in which machinery was replacing workers, men had difficulty in adjusting to new conditions. He urged his listeners to look at the poor as individuals, "each with his own peculiar personality," instead of "massing them into classes." Most of all he urged Christian *justice*. "Merely giving these people something," he said, "will not do much good, because they see that you give out of your abundance. They insist that they have rights and they demand that these rights shall be taken into consideration. It is no question of benevolence, but of justice."[65] The case of Gilbert De La Matyr, the Methodist minister who was elected to Congress in 1878, and his pleas for social justice have already been mentioned.[66] But men with the views of McCulloch and De La Matyr were exceptional.

Just as most ministers avoided disturbing social and economic issues, so in their sermons they also avoided disturbing theological issues raised by science and continued to cling to traditional and orthodox views. But by the seventies a few voices were being raised against traditional religion. In addition to Universalists and Unitarians there were a few avowed

---

[64] Indianapolis *Daily Journal*, November 28, 1879.

[65] *Ibid.*, December 15, 1879.

[66] See Chapter VII, p. 310.

freethinkers. In 1870 the German Association of Free-Thinkers was formed in Indianapolis. Its constitution emphasized its freedom from sectarian creed and ecclesiastical beliefs and declared that the members accepted as true only such conclusions as were "confirmed by the elucidations of science, and established by the light of reason." Members were completely materialistic in their views, rejecting the Christian view of creation and resurrection and embracing Darwinian views on evolution.[67]

In 1871 Parker Pillsbury delivered a sermon on Free Religion to a large audience in Indianapolis. In it he raised fundamental questions as to existing religious beliefs and sought to answer the question: "If you succeed in destroying faith in orthodoxy, what will you give the world instead?" In 1878 Robert G. Ingersoll gave an address in the same city in which he attacked traditional inherited religious beliefs. A few weeks later W. S. Bell of Boston addressed the German Free-Thinkers on the subject: "What has free thought to offer in place of Christianity?" In his remarks it was reported that he asserted that some of the teachings of the Bible were conducive to immorality.[68]

At the opposite end of the religious spectrum from the materialistic freethinkers, but also representing a rejection of orthodoxy, were the Spiritualists, who appear to have gained some following in the 1870's. They were sufficiently numerous and well organized to hold state conventions. In 1875 it was reported that Terre Haute was racked by a "spiritualist agitation." Spiritualists rejected the idea of an avenging God and declared that the doctrine of total depravity was a "monstrous lie." In resolutions adopted at their meeting in 1870 they declared that moral and spiritual sins were "diseases to be cured if possible" and that "wrong belief" was a "misfortune, not a crime." Spiritualists expressed a determination to "maintain

[67] Holloway, *Indianapolis,* p. 279; Indianapolis *Daily Journal,* February 10, 1874.

[68] *Ibid.,* March 13, 1871; May 2, June 12, 1878.

the blessed harmonial philosophy which promises life, love and immortality to the human race."[69]

§ § § §

In spite of the diversity of Protestant groups relations among the various denominations were usually amicable. Churches of the large, well-established denominations sometimes lent their buildings for the use of smaller denominations. Some activities of an interdenominational character, such as revivals, debates, and Sunday School conventions, were carried out. Doctrinal differences tended to become less sharp, and a large degree of toleration existed. Even unorthodox groups like Universalists and Unitarians and freethinkers aroused little opposition, perhaps because their numbers were so small. The same was apparently true of the attitude toward Jews, whose numbers were so small as to be almost negligible. Hebrew congregations were organized at Madison, Evansville, Indianapolis, Lafayette, and Fort Wayne during the 1850's and 1860's but they attracted little attention.[70]

In contrast, the attitude toward Roman Catholics, whose numbers grew rapidly after 1850, was far from tolerant. The dominant Protestant groups looked upon this growth with alarm. This was partly because anti-Catholic prejudice was a part of the heritage of all Protestant churches, but the fact that most Catholics were aliens who had recently arrived in the United States intensified this prejudice. The first Catholics in Indiana had, of course, been the French habitants. In the middle of the nineteenth century the Catholic priests who served in Indiana were almost entirely persons of European birth and training. Most of them were French, but by that time the French had ceased to be the important element among the laity. By 1850 most Catholics in Indiana were Germans.

[69] Indianapolis *Daily Sentinel,* June 6, 1870; Indianapolis *Daily Journal,* June 17, 1871, March 31, 1875.

[70] Holloway, *Indianapolis,* pp. 110, 242-243; *History of Vanderburgh County* (1889), p. 304; De Hart, *Tippecanoe County,* I, 260; Robertson, *Allen County,* pp. 506-507; "The History of Madison," *Indiana Magazine of History,* XVI (1920), 341-342.

As the church grew Germans continued to be the most important element in the membership with the Irish making up most of the remainder.[71]

At midcentury most Catholics were found in the larger towns along the Ohio and Wabash rivers and in two rural areas—one in Dubois County in the southwest, the other in the Whitewater Valley in the southeast. A few were also found around Fort Wayne and in the St. Joseph Valley. There were as yet few Catholics in the central part of the state. During the pioneer period several rural German settlements had been made in Dubois County at places like Jasper, Ferdinand, and Celeste. In the Whitewater area there were similar settlements. Before 1850 eleven Catholic churches had been founded in Dearborn, Franklin, and Ripley counties. One of the most important of these was at Oldenburg, where a convent and school were later founded.[72]

During the fifties the number of Catholics increased rapidly as the result of immigration. In that decade the total population of the state increased by 36 per cent, but the number of Catholics more than doubled. In 1850 all of Indiana was included in the diocese of Vincennes, and in only a small part of the state was there organized parish life. By 1860 many new churches had been founded, most of them in the areas where the largest numbers of Germans and Irish settled. In 1857 the diocese of Fort Wayne, including the forty-two counties in the northern part of the state, was created.[73]

Catholic churches had already been established in the Ohio River towns of Madison, New Albany, and Evansville before 1850. The arrival of large numbers of German immigrants during the next few years caused additional churches for

[71] Schroeder, *Catholic Church in the Diocese of Vincennes,* p. 1. In 1856 use of the English language supplanted the use of French at the Vincennes Cathedral. *Ibid.,* p. 202.

[72] *Ibid.,* pp. 21, 23-25; Emmett H. Rothan, *The German Catholic Immigrant in the United States (1830-1860)* (Washington, D. C., 1946), pp. 36-39.

[73] Schroeder, *Catholic Church in the Diocese of Vincennes,* p. 73; *The Catholic Church in Fort Wayne,* p. 40.

German-speaking members to be organized in all these towns. In Evansville, where the largest group of Germans settled, the first German church was Holy Trinity, founded in 1850. The edifice of the church was one of the largest in Indiana— evidence that the Germans in Evansville were substantial and prosperous citizens. The church was equipped with an organ and a bell tower taller than the one of the cathedral at Vincennes. An oil painting of the Assumption which hung over the main altar was the gift of King Ludwig of Bavaria. St. Mary's, a second German church, was opened in 1866, and a third, St. Boniface's, in 1878. In New Albany the Catholic population was about equally divided between Germans and Irish. Holy Trinity, the oldest church, remained primarily Irish when German members withdrew in 1854 to form St. Mary's (later known as the Church of the Annunciation). During the fifties four other Catholic churches were founded in the vicinity, including St. Augustine's in Jeffersonville. In 1876 a second church was founded in Jeffersonville. In the early 1850's a German church, St. Mary's, was founded in Madison, and at the same time St. Patrick's, made up principally of Irish members, was founded in North Madison.[74]

The number of Catholics in the smaller towns and in the rural areas of Spencer, Perry, and Dubois counties also increased rapidly during the fifties. In Cannelton there were both a German and an Irish church. In 1858 Tell City on the Ohio River was founded by German-speaking Swiss Catholics. In the same period the number of Catholics in the Whitewater Valley and other parts of the southeast increased. In 1860 St. Mary's, a German church, was founded in Richmond. In the western part of the state in Vigo County, St. Mary's Church and St. Joseph's Church in Terre Haute had been

[74] Blanchard, *Catholic Church in Indiana*, I, 261, 264, 265; Alerding, *Catholic Church in the Diocese of Vincennes*, pp. 278-279, 281-283, 334, 336, 338; Schroeder, *Catholic Church in the Diocese of Vincennes*, pp. 80, 92-93; *Ohio Falls Cities and Their Counties*, II, 210; "The History of Madison," *Indiana Magazine of History*, XVI, 34.

founded before 1850. In 1864 St. Benedict's, a German church, was founded in Terre Haute, and a third church, St. Ann's, in 1866.[75]

In the 1840's the Church of the Holy Cross was built to serve the few Catholic families in Indianapolis. In 1850 this was replaced by a larger building and renamed St. John's. In 1856 Germans decided to withdraw from this church and establish St. Mary's, which was completed in 1859. In 1875 a second German church, the Church of the Sacred Heart, was established in the southern part of the city. Meanwhile St. John's, the original church, had grown in membership and moved into new quarters which were large enough to accommodate two thousand worshipers. The new building was French Gothic in style, with two bell towers, a rose window, a baptismal chapel, and seven side chapels. In 1871 another church, St. Peter's, was dedicated in a parish which had been organized in 1864. In 1873 St. Joseph's parish was organized and a small church built. Thus by 1880 there were five Catholic parishes in the city. In 1878 the bishop of the diocese of Vincennes took up residence in Indianapolis.[76]

Farther north groups of Catholics had settled before 1850 in towns which were located on important routes of transportation such as Lafayette, Huntington, Fort Wayne, and South Bend. As the railroad network spread over the northern part of the state and immigrants poured in numerous mission churches were organized. At Lafayette, where there was already a substantial group of English-speaking Catholics, a second church for Germans, St. Boniface's, was organized in 1853. A third church, St. Ann's, was organized in 1871.[77]

[75] Alerding, *Catholic Church in the Diocese of Vincennes*, pp. 316-318, 444, 453, 458-459; Schroeder, *Catholic Church in the Diocese of Vincennes*, pp. 65, 67, 82-83; Rothan, *German Catholic Immigrant*, p. 41; Blanchard, *Catholic Church in Indiana*, I, 415.

[76] Holloway, *Indianapolis*, pp. 239-240; Blanchard, *Catholic Church in Indiana*, I, 305-306, 317; Schroeder, *Catholic Church in the Diocese of Vincennes*, pp. 101, 182-183; Dunn, *Greater Indianapolis*, I, 616-618.

[77] Schroeder, *Catholic Church in the Diocese of Vincennes*, pp. 109-110; Alerding, *Diocese of Fort Wayne*, p. 325.

At Fort Wayne a German church, St. Mary's, was organized in 1848. In 1857, when the diocese of Fort Wayne was created, the church was raised to the rank of a cathedral, and a German-born bishop, John Henry Luers, was appointed to the see. In 1859 construction of a lofty Gothic-type cathedral was begun. In 1864 a second German church, St. Paul's, was founded, and in 1871 St. Peter's. There were several other small Catholic churches in the Fort Wayne area, among them the German church at Hesse Cassel which was founded in 1851, and St. Louis at Besancon, founded in 1851, and St. Vincent, founded in 1856; the last two were largely French in membership.[78]

In South Bend the first Catholic church, St. Alexius' (later St. Joseph's), was founded in 1853 through the efforts of Father Sorin of Notre Dame. German Catholics settled in the South Bend area during the fifties, but they were outnumbered by the Irish, who came in large numbers as the result of railroad building. In 1859 St. Patrick's Church was founded. Enough Polish immigrants had settled in South Bend by 1877 to found St. Hedwig's. Irish Catholics were also numerous in Mishawaka, where St. Joseph's Church was organized in 1848. In 1868 St. Vincent's Church was founded at Elkhart.[79] At Michigan City a Catholic church was organized in 1849, and at La Porte, where large numbers of immigrants came, one was founded in 1853. In many other towns in the north such as Delphi, Attica, Plymouth, Marion, and Logansport, where Catholics came in the wake of railroad building, small churches were organized. In most instances they were principally Irish in membership.[80]

[78] Alerding, Diocese of Fort Wayne, pp. 30-33, 239, 241-242, 261, 330; Schroeder, Catholic Church in the Diocese of Vincennes, p. 111; Robertson, Allen County, pp. 415-416; Blanchard, Catholic Church in Indiana, I, 279.

[79] Alerding, Diocese of Fort Wayne, pp. 230-231, 277, 316, 351; Thomas T. McAvoy, History of the Catholic Church in the South Bend Area (South Bend, 1953), passim.

[80] Alerding, Diocese of Fort Wayne, pp. 234, 249, 283, 291, 295, 317, 320, 344 and passim.

By 1880, although there were still numerous rural parishes, like those in Dubois and Franklin counties, it was evident that the Catholic Church in Indiana was becoming increasingly an urban institution. Persons born in Germany or their descendants were the largest element in its membership, and the clergy was becoming increasingly of German stock. There were also many Irish clergymen, and some of the higher clergy continued to be French. Until 1877 the Bishop of Vincennes was St. Palais, who was born and trained in France. His successor was Bishop Chatard, a native of Baltimore. As already seen the Bishop of Fort Wayne was German-born but trained in America.[81]

The growing strength of the Catholic Church intensified anti-Catholicism among Protestant Christians. Protestant clergymen habitually denounced the Church of Rome and the large influx of German and Irish Catholics in the 1850's led to a powerful anti-Catholic, nativist outburst which culminated in the Know Nothing movement which has already been touched upon in connection with the history of politics. The visit of Father Allessandro Gavazzi, a defrocked Catholic priest, in 1853 fanned the anti-Catholic flames. He spoke on the power of the Church of Rome, the horrors of the Inquisition, and against Catholic schools. His visit was the forerunner of the formation of Know Nothing lodges in the state. It may also have been partly responsible for resolutions passed by Protestant churches expressing alarm over the spread of "Romanism." Typical was the warning issued by the General Baptist Association in 1853: "There is an immense foreign population drawn to our shores from all parts of the world by the hope of improving their conditions, trained often under institutions and influences averse to our views of civil and religious liberty. . . . From these sources, errorists of dangerous taint, subtle, crafty, designing, Papal, Infidel, Pantheistic, and

[81] Schroeder, *Catholic Church in the Diocese of Vincennes*, p. 202; Dunn, *Greater Indianapolis*, I, 616.

openly irreligious are spreading themselves."[82] As already seen, Protestants were aroused by the "Europeanization" of the Sabbath and by the association of Germans, mostly Catholics, with the liquor business. There was also apprehension over the political activities of the new immigrants. As early as 1852 the Whigs were talking about the "Catholic vote," while the Democratic press was denying its existence. The *Indiana State Sentinel* insisted that "Catholics like all other religious denominations, are divided in politics. The priests leave the members free and unrestrained." But it was frequently charged that because of their allegiance to the Pope Catholics were part of a movement which was disloyal to the United States and which was seeking to establish papal supremacy in this country. A typical editorial in the Vincennes *Gazette* during the local political campaign of 1855 warned: "If the native Catholics choose to combine with them [foreign Catholics] in trying to despoil our glorious Republic—if they prefer the Roman Pontiff as their civil head, to the President of the United States . . . they must meet the consequences that will surely be meted out to their allies."[83] During 1854 and 1855 in the towns where Catholics were most numerous they were subjected to various petty harassments, and there were some riots between nativists and Irish on election day in 1854.[84]

As already seen the Know Nothing movement died out as nativism was overshadowed by other issues. But in the years following the Civil War there were renewed outbursts of anti-Catholicism and nativism although they did not assume the political importance which they had in the fifties. Some of the anti-Catholicism appears to have been evoked by the

[82] Brand, "Know Nothing Party," *Indiana Magazine of History,* XVIII, 53; Cady, *Baptist Church in Indiana,* p. 190.

[83] *Indiana State Sentinel* (weekly), July 14, 1852; Vincennes *Gazette,* October 15, 1855, quoted in Schroeder, *Catholic Church in the Diocese of Vincennes,* p. 89.

[84] *Ibid.,* pp. 89, 91; Brand, "Know Nothing Party," *Indiana Magazine of History,* XVIII, 76-77.

Vatican Council of 1869-1870 at which the doctrine of papal infallibility was elevated to the rank of dogma.[85]

Closer home there was the question of parochial schools vs. public schools. Beginning about 1869 a campaign was begun by Catholics in several states to secure some public support for parochial schools and to eliminate the use of the King James version of the Bible in the public schools, which Catholics were taxed to support. In some places, especially in New York, the campaign enjoyed some success.[86] In Indiana, as already seen, a few Catholic schools already received some public support. There does not appear to have been any significant effort by Catholics in the state to secure additional aid or to prevent the use of the Protestant version of the Bible in the public schools, but pressures by Catholics in Cincinnati and elsewhere apparently aroused Indiana Protestants. For example, in 1869, after Cincinnati Catholics protested against the use of the Bible in public schools of that city, Protestants of all denominations met in Greensburg "to take into consideration the means necessary to prevent the perversion of the common school fund to sectarian uses." At the same time they vigorously defended the use of the King James Bible in the public schools. They adopted resolutions which said that an effort was being made in many parts of the country "to exclude not only the Christian teacher but the word of God" from the public schools. As "Protestant Christians" they condemned this "wicked movement" and called for united action by all Protestants to prevent the exclusion of the Bible from the public schools.[87]

During the 1870's the Indiana Conference of Methodists repeatedly expressed their support of public schools and opposition to Roman Catholic schools. In 1874 the conference passed a resolution asking that public financial assistance be

[85] *Christian Record*, March 7, 1870, p. 99, quoted in Dowling, Revival of the Christian Record, p. 114.

[86] John Higham, *Strangers in the Land. Patterns of American Nativism 1860-1925* (Rutgers University Press, 1955), p. 28.

[87] Indianapolis *Sentinel,* quoted in *Millenial Harbinger,* 1869, pp. 553-554.

denied private or sectarian schools and that a Bible be placed in every public school.[88] At the Baptist State Convention in 1879 the report of the Committee on the State of Religion called attention to "the growth of Romanism, with its priestly control, its policy of foreign dictation, its schools inviting protestant youth to inferior advantages and a corrupted faith.

"We think it wise," the report continued, "to recognize with hopeful patience and charity the influx of foreign population, with strange costumes, ideas and habits; some of them merely notional [sic] peculiarities but some of them alien to Christianity."[89]

Anti-Catholic sermons by Protestant ministers were common and were especially numerous in 1875. At a meeting of the Ministerial Union of Indianapolis, a Congregational minister addressed the other ministers on the subject: "Do the Encroachments of Romanism in This Country Threaten Any Peril to Our Free Institutions?" About the same time a visiting Protestant minister delivered a series of bitter anti-Catholic lectures in Shelbyville. After one of them local Catholics made threats against him, and the local priest attempted to answer some of the charges which he made.[90]

Anti-Catholicism had strong political overtones. This was especially evident in 1875 and 1876 when Republicans were looking for new issues to distract attention from the record of the Grant administration. While he was running for governor of Ohio in 1875 Rutherford B. Hayes attempted to stigmatize the Democratic party as being subservient to Catholic designs. Grant adopted a similar line in a speech which he made at a veterans' rally, and lesser politicians followed suit. The Indianapolis *Journal*, most influential Republican paper in Indiana, frequently took an anti-Catholic position on its editorial page. In 1875 it declared: "We are publishing no news in saying

88 Heller, *Indiana Conference,* pp. 116-117.

89 Indiana Baptist State Convention, *Minutes,* 1879, p. 21.

90 Indianapolis *Daily Journal,* May 25, June 8, 1875. Throughout 1875 the columns of the *Journal* frequently mentioned manifestations of anti-Catholicism.

that the Catholic Church of this country is Democratic wholly.
. . . There is not one Catholic in five hundred . . . who is
not a Democrat." During 1876, in defending the "purity" and
moral superiority of the Republican party in the face of
charges against the Grant administration, the *Journal* cited
the fact that the party embraced "almost the entire mass of
the Protestant clergymen of the Northern States" and that it
also embraced a "very large proportion" of the "Protestant
Christian element of society."[91]

[91] Higham, *Strangers in the Land,* pp. 28-29; Indianapolis *Daily Journal,*
June 9, 1875, April 14, 1876.

CHAPTER XIV
INTELLECTUAL, CULTURAL, AND SOCIAL LIFE

IN SPITE OF THE HIGH RATE of illiteracy in Indiana and the backwardness of the public school system, by the middle of the nineteenth century there was a reading public and an increasing interest in literature. By 1850 a few individuals were even writing books and poetry and many more were reading them. By that time a few of the more affluent had large private libraries, and there were bookstores where books published in the East and in Europe could be purchased. In 1851 the *Indiana State Journal* remarked, with satisfaction, that Indianapolis boasted four bookstores which would compare favorably with those in any city in the West, adding that the condition of a city's bookstores was "a sure index to the intelligence of its people." By the fifties a number of libraries of public or semipublic nature were available.[1]

In 1850 the oldest library of public character was the Indiana State Library, which had been established in 1825 by an act of the legislature from books already in the office of the secretary of state. The law provided that it might be increased through legislative appropriations or donations. In 1841 the library was placed under a state librarian who was elected every three years by the General Assembly. The library was originally intended for the use of state officials only but it was later opened to other groups, including teachers, clergymen, physicians, and newspaper editors. In 1867

---

[1] The most recently established bookstore at the time was owned by Samuel Merrill, former state treasurer and president of the State Bank of Indiana. The bookstore began to expand into publishing and eventually became the Bobbs-Merrill Publishing Company. Dunn, *Greater Indianapolis,* I, 508; Theodore F. Vonnegut, *Indianapolis Booksellers and Their Literary Background, 1822-1860* (Greenfield, Ind., 1926), pp. 21-23.

the law books in the library were removed and put into a library under the supervision of the Indiana Supreme Court. The collection in the State Library grew slowly because legislative appropriations were small. By 1880 it received an annual appropriation of $500 for books and binding. At that date it contained about seventeen thousand books of a miscellaneous character.[2]

The first State Constitution (Article IX, section 5) required the General Assembly to set aside 10 per cent of the proceeds from the sale of town lots in the county seat of every newly established county for a public library. This provision and legislation passed to implement it led to the establishment of libraries in a number of counties. A law of 1852 authorized county commissioners to appropriate a small additional sum of money for the purchase of books. Where county libraries were established they were usually housed in the courthouse and were open only one day a week. In Marion County a library was opened in 1844 which contained about two thousand books by 1870. A fee of $1.00 a year was required of persons using the books.[3] The school law of 1852 included a provision for township libraries. Under it a special tax was levied for two years. By 1854 about $147,000 had been spent on books, which were distributed among the townships on the basis of population. The average number of books per township was three hundred, but more populous townships received a larger number and more sparsely populated ones fewer. The number of books was small, and the system of allotment was not satisfactory, but these township libraries performed a valuable function. After 1855 they received no additional support from public funds. After the Civil War the legislature authorized a special tax once more,

2 LaVern Walther, Legal and Governmental Aspects of Public Library Development in Indiana, 1816-1953 (Unpublished Ph.D. thesis in Education, Indiana University, 1957), pp. 13-17; Dunn, *Greater Indianapolis*, I, 509.

3 Walther, *op. cit.*, pp. 36-39; Dunn, *Greater Indianapolis*, I, 511; Holloway, *Indianapolis*, p. 270.

but the money raised by it was diverted to the State Normal School.[4]

In the absence of support from public funds a number of libraries were founded by private groups of one sort or another. During the 1850's establishment of libraries was fostered by a bequest from William Maclure, who had been instrumental in the establishment of the Workingmen's Institute at New Harmony in 1838. In his will he directed that his executors should give $500 "to any club or society of laborers who may establish, in any part of the United States, a reading and lecture room with a library of at least one hundred volumes." The will defined laborers as "the working classes who labor with their hands and earn their living by the sweat of their brows." After Maclure's death in 1840 the will was contested by his heirs. Largely through the efforts of Alvin P. Hovey, then an attorney in Posey County, a case was taken to the Indiana Supreme Court which led to a decision permitting the distribution of the bequest to the libraries. In 1855 the distribution began. Records show that $500 was given to each of one hundred and forty-four associations (called variously workingmen's institutes, mechanics' associations, and literary societies) in eighty-nine of the ninety-two counties in the state. As a rule the libraries established under the terms of the Maclure will were short-lived. In many cases it appears that the original one hundred books were collected merely to enable a group to receive $500. But in a few places, including Evansville, Princeton, and La Porte, books from these workingmen's libraries eventually became a part of the collection of the public library.[5]

A number of libraries were started under the terms of acts of the legislature which authorized the formation of library associations. An act passed in 1852 permitted the incorpora-

[4] Jacob Piatt Dunn, *The Libraries of Indiana (Indiana World's Fair Monographs,* Indianapolis, 1893), pp. 15-19.

[5] *Ibid.,* pp. 13-15; Ella Lonn, "The History of an Unusual Library," *Indiana Magazine of History,* XIX (1923), 209-226; see below, p. 648.

tion of associations and the raising of money through the sale of stock.[6] Of the associations formed under this law one of the most successful and enduring was the one at Madison. The committee which launched this association declared that it was their purpose "to avoid all schemes which would restrict the benefits of the Association to a small number," but they felt that a system of annual subscriptions was too precarious. Accordingly a corporation was formed in which the members were persons who subscribed to stock at $30.00 a share. The use of the library was available to any person who paid an annual fee of $1.00. In 1854 the library was housed in a storeroom. It was open every day except Sunday from 8 A.M. until 10 P.M. In 1854 it had a collection of 1,500 volumes which had grown to 2,480 by the following year. The collection included fiction and works on fine arts, science, history, theology, travel, geography, and philosophy. A catalogue of the books and their authors indicates that the collection compared favorably with the best libraries in the United States at the time. The Madison library continued as a subscription library until 1888. At that time it was experiencing financial difficulties, and an arrangement was made under which the city gave it some financial support and the association made its books available to the public free of charge.[7]

---

[6] Dunn, *Libraries of Indiana*, p. 25.

[7] *Catalogue of the Books Belonging to the Madison Library Association* (Madison, 1856), pp. v-vii, 63, 65, 67, 107; Story of the Madison Library Association compiled from the Files of the Madison Courier and Other Data, at the request of the Board of Trustees (1928) of the Association by Miss E. M. Garber (Librarian 1888 to 1893) and William S. Garber (typewritten manuscript, Indiana Division, Indiana State Library). Among the authors whose works were catalogued were Jane Austen, Sir Edward Lytton Bulwer, Thomas Carlyle, Samuel Taylor Coleridge, James Fenimore Cooper, Daniel Defoe, Thomas DeQuincey, Charles Dickens, Ralph Waldo Emerson, Henry Fielding, Goethe, Francis Guizot, Alexander Von Humboldt, Washington Irving, Sir Charles Lyell, William H. Prescott, Friedrich Schiller, Sir Walter Scott, Jared Sparks, and William Makepeace Thackeray. There were also reference works, among them the *Encyclopædia Britannica* and the *Encyclopedia Americana*. A reading room contained such periodicals as *Blackwood's*

The Evansville Library Association was formed and began the sale of stock in 1855. By 1860 it had 239 stockholders and a library of 2,700 volumes. These included books purchased by the association and donations from the Mechanics' Library Association and other gifts. The association rented a room for the library and paid a librarian a salary of $400 a year. The library's reading room contained newspapers from the leading cities in the United States, the principal American periodicals, and some European journals. In spite of the initial success of the association interest lagged after a few years. In 1874 the library was donated to the city under the terms of a law passed in 1873 which permitted municipalities to establish public libraries and levy a small tax for their support. In 1876 Willard Carpenter gave property valued at $400,000 to the city. Part of the property was sold and the proceeds used to establish the Willard Library, which was opened to the public in 1883.[8]

In Indianapolis the movement for a city library developed slowly, perhaps because the Marion County Library was larger than most county libraries and the State Library served some parts of the population. In 1850 the *Locomotive,* a popular weekly paper, was asking: "Is there any person who would like to immortalize himself by founding a public library?" But it was not until after the Civil War that steps were taken which led to a city library. In 1869 an Indianapolis Library Association was formed which sold stock for $150 a share. It opened a library in a downtown storeroom where nonmembers might borrow books by paying an annual fee of $5.00. The association was formed with the intention of starting a collection of books with which to begin a public library. In 1871 the state legislature passed a measure which enabled the city to levy a tax for support of a library which

Edinburgh Magazine, the *North British Review,* and *Edinburgh Review, Putnam's Magazine, Harper's Monthly Magazine,* and the *Scientific American.*

    [8] *Annual Report of the President and Directors of the Evansville Library Association,* 1860, pp. 5, 7, 11; Dunn, *Libraries of Indiana,* p. 25; *History of Vanderburgh County* (1889), pp. 321-324.

would be under the administration of the school board. The Indianapolis Public Library opened its doors in 1873 with a collection of almost fourteen thousand books, of which 3,649 were the gift of the association. The remainder were purchased out of public funds. By 1879 the collection contained more than thirty-four thousand books and pamphlets. From the beginning the library was a great success and played a significant part in the cultural life of the city. Public interest exceeded expectations. One of the attractions of the library was a reading room which was open twelve hours a day every day in the year and where more than one hundred periodicals and newspapers were available.[9]

The Indianapolis library was established under an act of the legislature applying only to cities of more than thirty thousand population, a category to which only that city belonged at the time. In 1873 a law was passed which permitted any municipality to open a public library, but few cities took advantage of its provisions, probably because the tax provisions were inadequate. One of the few libraries founded under its provisions was the Muncie Public Library. In 1881 the legislature passed an act which permitted any city of more than ten thousand to establish a library under terms similar to those in the law for the Indianapolis library.[10]

Meanwhile, residents of Indiana were writing verses and novels which they no doubt hoped would be published and copies placed on library shelves. A surprisingly large number of would-be poets were composing verses by the 1850's. Original verses appeared frequently in newspapers and magazines. In 1860 William T. Coggeshall of Cincinnati published a fat volume entitled, *The Poets and Poetry of the West with*

---

9 *First Annual Report of the Indianapolis Public Library* (1873-1874), pp. 7-8, 14; Holloway, *Indianapolis*, pp. 269-270; Eva Draegert, "Cultural History of Indianapolis: Literature, 1875-1890," *Indiana Magazine of History*, LII (1956), 235-237; Indianapolis *Daily Journal*, March 22, April 9, 15, 1873; May 15, 1874.

10 Dunn, *Libraries of Indiana*, pp. 25-26; *First Annual Report of Department of Public Instruction City of Muncie, Indiana*, 1874-1875, pp. 17-21.

Biographical and Critical Notices (Columbus, Ohio, 1860). More than a dozen residents of Indiana were deemed worthy of notice in the book. The best known among them was Sarah T. Bolton, who was for years a kind of unofficial poetess laureate of the state. Her verses, which were usually sentimental or moralizing, were typical of those of other Hoosier poets of the period. Aspiring novelists were less numerous than persons who aspired to write poetry, but a few novels by Indiana authors were published in the fifties and sixties. Nearly all of them reflected the political turmoil and interest in reform which characterized those years and were little more than propaganda in the guise of fiction. Indiana produced no antislavery work like *Uncle Tom's Cabin,* but several novels were inspired by the temperance crusade. In *Beyond the Breakers. A Story of the Present Day,* Robert Dale Owen utilized the form of the novel to expound his views on woman's rights, prison reform, and other causes in which he was interested.[11]

All of these early propagandistic novels along with the poetry are all but forgotten, but during the seventies books by two novelists associated with Indiana were to attain lasting fame. The first of these was *The Hoosier School-Master* by Edward Eggleston which was first published in 1871. In this, his most enduring work, Eggleston made a significant contribution to the development of realism in American fiction.[12] In sharp contrast were the colorful and romantic works of Lew Wallace. His first novel, *The Fair God; or, The Last of the 'Tzins. A Tale of the Conquest of Mexico,* which was published in 1873, established Wallace as one of the most popular authors in the United States. *Ben-Hur. A Tale of the Christ,* first published in 1880, became one of the three most popular and long-lived novels in American literature.[13]

11 See Arthur W. Shumaker, *A History of Indiana Literature (Indiana Historical Collections,* XLII, Indianapolis, 1962), for the most comprehensive treatment of Indiana poets and novelists in the period 1850 to 1880.

12 *Ibid.,* pp. 261-266.

13 McKee, *"Ben-Hur" Wallace,* pp. 123-130, 164-188, Foreword, and *passim.*

As Indiana passed beyond the pioneer stage a few people began to be interested in preserving the records of the earlier era and in writing its history. As early as 1830, on the fourteenth anniversary of statehood, the Indiana Historical Society had been founded, but the society did not flourish even though some of the most distinguished men in the state were identified with it. It had no permanent quarters, and until 1886 it met infrequently and irregularly.[14]

At a meeting in 1859 it was recorded that the society had been "reorganized and placed on a permanent basis," but it continued to meet only at irregular intervals. In 1859 the legislature appropriated $500 to assist the society in the purchase of books, maps, and manuscripts "calculated to throw light upon the manners, customs, pursuits, and conditions of the pioneer settlers of the region now included within the boundaries of the state." Before this date John B. Dillon, the most active member in this period, had begun to collect documents and manuscripts for preservation by the society. These papers were at first deposited in the State Bank. In 1859 they were removed to the State House, where many were lost as the result of carelessness during the years of the Civil War. In 1873 Dillon proposed that the society begin the publication of a magazine, but this proposal did not bear fruit for many years.[15]

John B. Dillon deserves the title of "Father of Indiana History,"[16] and, indeed, he was the only person in the state in this period whose writings deserve to be called history by modern standards of historical scholarship. Like many of his contemporaries Dillon was largely self-educated, but his work shows the characteristics usually attributed to the trained historian. Dillon spent most of his life at meager pay in various

14 James A. Woodburn, "The Indiana Historical Society: A Hundred Years," in *Centennial Handbook Indiana Historical Society 1830-1930* (Indiana Historical Society *Publications*, X, No. 1, Indianapolis, 1930), pp. 5, 13.

15 *Ibid.*, pp. 12, 18, 19.

16 George S. Cottman, "John Brown Dillon, The Father of Indiana History," *Indiana Magazine of History*, I (1905), pp. 4-6.

government offices—as state librarian and secretary to the State Board of Agriculture in Indiana and as a clerk in the Department of the Interior in Washington. In his free time he devoted himself to his real love—historical research.[17] As early as 1843 he published *The History of Indiana from its Earliest Exploration by Europeans to the Close of the Territorial Government in 1816 with an Introduction Containing Historical Notes of the Discovery and Settlement of the Territory of the United States Northwest of the River Ohio* (Indianapolis, 1843). Apparently he intended this to be the first of two volumes covering the entire history of the state, but a second book which appeared in 1859 was merely a revision of the 1843 volume and covered the same period except for one chapter dealing with events after 1816.[18]

In a period when the question of the nature of the Union was of transcendent importance, Dillon showed an interest in constitutional history and a veneration for the United States Constitution and the Union. In 1860, as the secession crisis loomed, he published a pamphlet, *An Inquiry into the Nature and Uses of Political Sovereignty* (Indianapolis, 1860). In it he traced the history of political sovereignty under the Articles of Confederation and the Constitution and concluded

[17] Cottman, "John Brown Dillon," *Indiana Magazine of History;* John Coburn, *Life and Services of John B. Dillon, with a Sketch by Judge Horace P. Biddle* (Indiana Historical Society *Publications*, II, No. 2, 1886), pp. 50-52; John B. Dillon, *Oddities of Colonial Legislation in America as Applied to the Public Lands, Primitive Education, Religion, Morals, Indians, Etc. Etc.* (Indianapolis, 1879), Introduction, p. 3. Dillon was born in 1808 in what is now West Virginia and attended rural schools for a few terms in Ohio, where his family moved. His father died when he was nine and he was thrown entirely on his own resources. He was apprenticed to a printer and later moved to Cincinnati, where he followed the printer's trade. In 1834 he moved to Logansport, Indiana, where he read law and was admitted to the bar. He never actually practiced law, however, apparently because he found it dull and preferred work which gave him an opportunity to pursue historical research.

[18] *A History of Indiana from its Earliest Exploration by Europeans to the Close of the Territorial Government in 1816; Comprehending a History of the Discovery, Settlement, and Civil and Military Affairs of the Territory of the U. S. Northwest of the Ohio River and a General View of the Progress of Public Affairs in Indiana, from 1816 to 1856* (Indianapolis, 1859).

that under the Constitution the advocacy of secession was "of a treasonable nature."[19] In 1871 he published a book, *Notes on Historical Evidence in Reference to Adverse Theories of the Origin and Nature of the Government of the United States of America* (New York, 1871). This book was written in Washington where a mass of historical materials were easily available. Dillon consulted many government documents dealing with the framing, ratification, and interpretation of the Constitution, and the writings of John Adams, Madison, Marshall, Calhoun, Webster, and others. His research reinforced his nationalism. He decided that the evidence proved conclusively that the "Government of the United States did not originate in any alliance, confederation, or compact, formed by separate sovereign and independent States," and that "all political theories which are founded only on a presumption of the original sovereignty and independence of each of the thirteen revolutionary States of the Union, are errors."[20]

Dillon's last book, *Oddities of Colonial Legislation in America, As Applied to the Public Lands, Primitive Education, Religion, Morals, Indians, Etc., Etc.* (Indianapolis, 1879) was published posthumously. All of Dillon's writings show certain qualities which mark him as a "scientific" historian of the nineteenth century in spite of his lack of formal training. His critical use of documents and his objectivity are the most conspicuous characteristics of his work. In the preface to his first volume he made explicit his methods and his philosophy. For several years, he said, he had labored "with constant and careful perseverance, to find out and to perpetuate all the important facts which properly belong to an impartial history of Indiana." He had worked, he said, "with a sincere desire to cast from my mind those popular prejudices which have had their origins in ambitious contentions between distinguished individuals, or in national par-

19 Page 26.
20 Page 105.

tialities and antipathies, or in improbable narrative and fanciful conjectures, or in conflicting political systems, or in different creeds of religion."[21] In the preface to *Oddities of Colonial Legislation* he remarked that historical truths had often been "either overlooked or suppressed by different kinds of prejudices, or transformed into errors by the misleading brilliancy of the style of a historian."[22] Dillon wrote lucidly and well, but he carefully avoided what he referred to as "misleading brilliancy." Gen. John Coburn, who knew him well, said he frequently was critical of historians who moralized or "who embellished their works with comments upon events." He refrained, said Coburn, "from mingling his opinions, his sentiments, his praise or blame with the simple and severe narratve of the events."[23]

No other Indiana writer before 1880 deserved the appellation of historian in the same sense as Dillon, but there were others who showed an interest in past events and wrote accounts of them. In the fifties Oliver H. Smith wrote his *Early Indiana Trials: and Sketches. Reminiscences by Hon. O. H. Smith* (Cincinnati, 1858). Sandford C. Cox wrote a series of articles for the Lafayette *Courier* which were published in book form as *Recollections of the Early Settlement of the Wabash Valley* (Lafayette, 1860). The book was a collection of personal reminiscences and materials drawn from the files of old newspapers.

The Civil War increased interest in the preservation of historical records and especially the record of Indiana's contribution to military victory. In 1863 the General Assembly passed a resolution instructing the state librarian to collect and preserve the names of all soldiers who fell in battle together with the records of the battles in which they fell, and to place their names on a roll of honor. The librarian, David Stevenson, began the collection of materials which resulted

---

[21] Dillon, *History of Indiana from Its Earliest Exploration* (1843), Preface, p. iii.

[22] Dillon, *Oddities of Colonial Legislation*, p. 9.

[23] Coburn, *Life and Public Services of John B. Dillon*, p. 43.

in the publication of two large volumes entitled *Indiana's Roll of Honor*.[24] The work was a comprehensive military history, including histories of regiments, accounts of campaigns, and biographies of important officers. In the introduction to the second volume, which was written by Theodore T. Scribner, it was stated that the work was written with the purpose of making it acceptable "to all patriotic people." It was intended to be a popular history "for the people, and not alone for the dusty shelves of professional scholars." The two volumes give evidence of having been written in haste and are uncritical and overly laudatory, but they contain a tremendous amount of information.[25]

During the war a second military history, similar in scope to the *Roll of Honor,* was begun. The first volume of *The Soldier of Indiana in the War for the Union* appeared in 1866, the second in 1869. The publisher was Merrill and Company of Indianapolis. The volumes were published anonymously, and but a few persons knew that the author was a woman—Catharine Merrill, the daughter of the publisher, Samuel Merrill. Miss Merrill, who is best remembered as a teacher of literature, first in private girls' schools and later at North Western Christian University, was traveling and studying in Europe when the war began. She returned to Indianapolis in July, 1861, and was soon actively involved in war work, including a stint as a nurse in the field. The history which she wrote was planned as early as July, 1862, when a circular was mailed to the officers of every Indiana regiment asking for information to help in the preparation of a record. At that time it is not certain that it was expected that Miss Merrill would write the work, but she was persuaded to undertake the task as a patriotic duty and as a memorial to the men, including her brother-in-law, who had died for the Union cause. "With all my might," she wrote to a friend, "I have lifted up the names of our patriots (some

24 Indianapolis 1864 and 1866.
25 *Indiana's Roll of Honor,* II, xi.

small portion of the vast number) and dead or alive, but especially dead, have tried to do them honor."[26] In preparation of the book the author used letters from soldiers from all over the state, newspaper accounts, and materials from the office of the adjutant general. She also drew upon personal conversations with many participants in the war. The writing of the history, which she did without the help of a secretary, was a formidable task. It involved reading hundreds of letters, and, as she said, trying to glean regimental histories from inadequate records and "reconciling incongruous and deciding between contradictory statements." Apparently Miss Merrill was not satisfied with the work she had done and told few persons of her authorship.[27] Nevertheless, in spite of her limitations, she performed a difficult task creditably. She was no student of military strategy, and her work suffered from the same overly patriotic tone as the *Roll of Honor,* but her volumes were better and more carefully written than the other work. And it is a rather remarkable fact, in view of the great interest shown in the Civil War by both professional and amateur historians, that *Indiana's Roll of Honor* and Miss Merrill's work remain to this day the only comprehensive histories of the part played by Indiana's soldiers in the Civil War.

A different kind of work was the eight-volume *Report of the Adjutant General of the State of Indiana* (Indianapolis, 1869), which was compiled by William H. H. Terrell. The first volume was an account of Indiana's role in the war but not a history of military campaigns. Terrell dealt principally with the raising of troops and the measures taken to arm and supply them. He also gave some attention to internal political dissensions. The remaining seven volumes of the *Report* are principally statistical and include rosters of officers and enlisted men and brief regimental histories. Terrell, who

26 Katherine Merrill Graydon, *Catharine Merrill, Life and Letters* (Greenfield, Ind., 1934), pp. 302, 307, 323, 331.

27 *Ibid.,* pp. 323, 326; *Soldier of Indiana,* I, Preface, pp. v-vi.

served as military secretary to Governor Morton and as his financial secretary before being appointed adjutant general, treated political matters, especially the question of Democatic loyalty, in a somewhat partisan fashion, as was to be expected. But for the most part his work was factual and accurate. His style was clear and concise. In an introductory note he said: "This report does not aspire to the dignity of a history. It is but a compend of well authenticated facts, reliable official documents and accurate statistics." Possibly, he modestly said, his work might "furnish some material for history hereafter." The enduring value placed upon his work by historians is attested to by the reprinting of his first volume by the Indiana Historical Society in 1960.

In the period after the Civil War there was little historical writing except for local histories. In 1870 William R. Holloway, editor of the Indianapolis *Journal*, published *Indianapolis, A Historical and Statistical Sketch of the Railroad City, A Chronicle of Its Social, Municipal, Commercial and Manufacturing Progress*, a book of almost four hundred pages.[28] The first chapters gave a survey of the history of the city before the Civil War, while the remainder of the book was a detailed account of Indianapolis and its institutions in 1869. The approach of the centennial of the independence of the United States in 1876 gave a stimulus to the gathering of local history. In 1876 appeared *An Illustrated History of the State of Indiana: Being A Full and Authentic Civil and Political History of the State from Its First Exploration down to 1876* by De Witt C. Goodrich and Charles R. Tuttle.[29] The first part of the book dealt with a history of the state, the remainder included histories of several counties and biographical sketches of leading citizens. This volume was a forerunner of the many county histories which were to appear in the 1880's.

28 Indianapolis, 1870.
29 Indianapolis, 1876.

§ §

Some of the most significant developments in the history of science occurred in the years after 1850. In 1857 Louis Pasteur first stated the fundamental tenets of the germ theory. His subsequent discoveries, which revealed a whole world of microorganisms hitherto unknown, completely revolutionized medical science. The publication of Darwin's *Origin of the Species* in 1859 led to general acceptance in scientific circles of the theory of evolution although it created controversy among theologians and was completely rejected by some of them. Earlier geological studies had revealed an antiquity of the earth itself which had not been dreamed of and had thereby raised questions of the Biblical account of creation. These scientific developments were little heeded by most people in Indiana as elsewhere, but they fundamentally altered the thinking of the more educated part of the population as well as those engaged in strictly scientific pursuits.

In Indiana scientific inquiry was carried on by a number of private groups and individuals, among whom men of the medical profession were most prominent, and the state itself promoted geological studies out of an interest in learning about natural resources which would be important in the economic development of the state. Geological surveys, which were authorized by the legislature for utilitarian purposes, also contributed to enlargement of knowledge in some other fields of science. The most important figure in the early history of geology in Indiana was David Dale Owen of New Harmony, son of Robert Owen. In 1837 he conducted the first survey authorized by the legislature. His published reports laid the basis for most of the work in geology done subsequently. In New Harmony Owen maintained a laboratory and the museum founded by William Maclure which attracted other geologists to the town.[30] Some of the men who were as-

---

[30] Walter B. Hendrickson, *David Dale Owen, Pioneer Geologist of the Middle West (Indiana Historical Collections,* XXVII, Indianapolis, 1943), *passim.*

sociated with him as field workers and in his laboratory later made reputations for themselves as geologists.

A second geological survey of Indiana was authorized by the state legislature in 1851. Dr. Ryland T. Brown of Montgomery County, who had urged a survey of the mineralogy as well as the geology of the state was put in charge. With very limited facilities he attempted a survey of the building stone, coal fields, and possible iron deposits of the state.[31] In 1859 a third survey was authorized and an appropriation of $5,000 made for carrying it out. It was expected that David Dale Owen, who was then engaged in completing surveys in Kentucky and Arkansas, would direct it. But he died before he had finished the work in Indiana, and the survey was completed and the results published by his brother, Richard Owen, who was made state geologist. In the published report Richard Owen emphasized the utilitarian character of the survey and listed a number of practical purposes which it was intended to serve. Among its objects, he said, were a survey of the coal fields of the state and also a search for other mineral deposits, especially iron. He expected to examine the stone in the state to ascertain whether it was suitable for building purposes and to report on the clay deposits which would be suitable for pottery and brick making. The survey would serve the interests of farmers by providing an analysis of soil collected from different geological formations and by determining which types of soil were best adapted to different crops. It was also expected that a survey of swamplands would show the best methods of drainage. In addition the survey would show the distribution of varieties of timber, plants, and animals and the relation of their distribution to geological peculiarities.[32]

[31] R. T. Brown, "Geological Survey of the State of Indiana," in Indiana State Board of Agriculture, *Annual Report,* 1853, pp. 299-332; W. S. Blatchley, "A Century of Geology in Indiana," Indiana Academy of Science, *Proceedings,* 1916, p. 111.

[32] Richard Owen, *Report of a Geological Reconnoissance of Indiana made during the Years 1859 and 1860, under the direction of the late David Dale Owen, M.D., State Geologist* (Indianapolis, 1862), pp. vii-viii, x-xii.

The program which Owen envisaged was too ambitious for his limited budget and limited number of field workers. But during a survey of two years' duration much information was assembled. The published reports gave most attention to the coal fields, but they also contained material on the chemistry of soils in various parts of the state and on fossils and plant ecology. After the Civil War Richard Owen continued his scientific career as a professor at Indiana University. While he was there the geological museum which his brother had assembled at New Harmony was acquired by the University and a hall built to house it.[33]

In the period after the Civil War, when interest in coal mining was stimulated by hopes that Indiana might become an important center for the iron industry, the legislature provided for additional surveys. An act passed in 1869 required that the state geologist make a survey of the mineral resources of the state and also establish a laboratory to analyze ores. Edward T. Cox, who had been trained by David Owen and had been a field worker under him and his brother, served as state geologist for ten years. Under his direction a laboratory was built adjoining the State House and surveys of the state were conducted by a staff of field workers. In 1879 the legislature brought the office of geologist under a newly created department of statistics and geology and reduced the appropriation for geological surveys, probably because previous surveys had not resulted in the hoped-for economic development.[34]

The *Reports* which Cox published devoted much attention to the coal deposits, but some of them contained other geo-

[33] Victor Lincoln Albjerg, *Richard Owen (The Archives of Purdue,* Number 2, March, 1946), pp. 47-68; Hendrickson, *David Dale Owen,* pp. 136-137. Unfortunately in 1883 a fire destroyed the building at Indiana University and ruined most of the exhibits as well as destroying the catalogue of the contents of the collection.

[34] *First Annual Report of the Geological Survey of Indiana, Made during the Year 1869, by E. T. Cox, State Geologist* (Indianapolis, 1869), pp. 5-6; *Laws,* 1879, pp. 193-195. Reports of geological surveys will be cited hereafter as Indiana *Geological Report,* with the years.

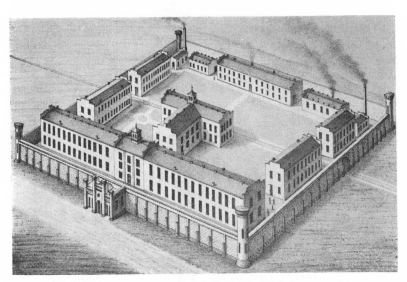

Northern Indiana State Prison, Michigan City, 1874

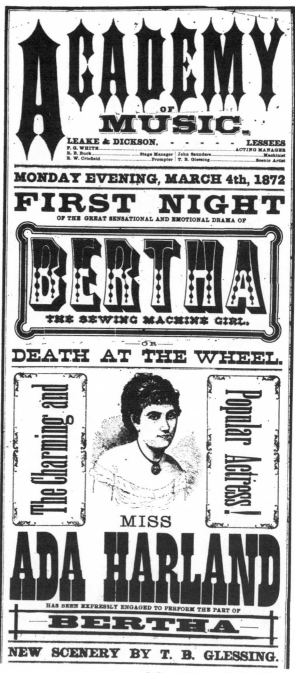

Advertisement, Academy of Music, Indianapolis

logical information, including catalogues of fossils found in different parts of the state.[35] In addition they included some articles on other fields of scientific knowledge. In the course of surveying the topography of the state a number of mounds attributed to prehistoric residents were found. These discoveries led to some primitive archaeological excavations and speculation concerning the persons who had produced the mounds and the artifacts discovered therein. The discovery of prehistoric stone walls in Clark County led to some excavations and a visit in 1874 by a party which included F. W. Putnam, editor of *The American Naturalist*. Other mounds were reported in Madison, Posey, and Dearborn counties. At mounds near Vincennes some exploratory excavations were made before 1880. In Greene County also there were some excavations which yielded pottery and other artifacts and some skeletons. The prehistoric inhabitants of these places were referred to as "mound builders," but there was speculation that archaeology might establish a chronology linking them with the Indians who still survived in the nineteenth century.[36]

The geological surveys also increased knowledge in the field of biological science. In the *Report of the Geological Survey* for 1869 Dr. Rufus Haymond, a medical practitioner of Brookville, published not only a geological survey of Franklin County, but also a survey of the timber of the county and lists of the mammals and birds found there.[37] Subsequent

[35] See for example S. A. Miller, "Catalogue of Fossils Found in Hudson River, Utica Slate and Trenton Groups as exposed in Southeast Part of Indiana, Southwest Part of Ohio, and Northern Part of Kentucky," Indiana *Geological Reports*, 1876-1878, pp. 22-56; "List of Fossils of the Carboniferous Formation found in ... Harrison County, Ind.," *ibid.*, pp. 313-340.

[36] F. W. Putnam, "Archaeological Researches in Kentucky and Indiana, 1874," Boston Society of Natural History, *Proceedings*, XVII (1875), pp. 314-322; "Antiquities," Indiana *Geological Report*, 1874, pp. 24-40; "Antiquities," *ibid.*, 1876-1878, pp. 121-137; "Archaeology," *ibid.*, 1879-1880, pp. 19-28.

[37] Indiana *Geological Report*, 1869, pp. 195-196, 203-235. For a further account of the work of Dr. Haymond see Will E. Edington, "There Were Giants in Those Days," Indiana Academy of Science, *Proceedings*, XLIV (1934), p. 27.

Reports contained a "Manual of the Botany of Jefferson County" by A. H. Young of Hanover College and a report of the fauna of Wyandotte Cave in Crawford County. In 1874 the *Report* contained a "Synopsis of the Genera of Fishes to be Looked for in Indiana," by David Starr Jordan. The same volume contained an article by another man who was to become an internationally known scientist—John Merle Coulter. Coulter, who had been educated at Hanover College and Indiana University, had just become professor of natural science at Hanover when he published "A Partial List of the Flora of Jefferson County." In 1875 a "Catalogue of the Flora of the Wabash Valley below the Mouth of White River and Observations Thereon" was published in the *Report*.[38]

Various scholarly societies fostered interest in science. The most vigorous and influential among them was the Indiana Medical Society, founded in 1849. Papers of interest to the medical profession were read at its annual meetings and subsequently published in the *Proceedings* and *Transactions* of the Society. In 1858 the Wabash Academy of Science was organized in Crawfordsville, ten years after the founding of the American Association for the Advancement of Science. The Wabash group took the initiative for the formation of the Indiana Association for the Advancement of Science. The first president of the Indiana Association was Dr. John S. Bobbs of Indianapolis. Although it was started with an ambitious program the academy did not last long. It died out during the Civil War while many of the members were in military service.[39]

[38] Indiana *Geological Report,* 1870, pp. 241-288; *ibid.,* 1871-1872, pp. 156-162; *ibid.,* 1874, pp. 197-228, 230-273; 1875, pp. 504-576. From Hanover College Coulter went to Wabash College in 1879. He taught there until 1891. Thereafter he served briefly as president of Indiana University before becoming head of the Botany Department at the University of Chicago. Andrew Denny Rogers, *John Merle Coulter, Missionary in Science* (Princeton, N. J., 1944), *passim.*

[39] Edington, "There Were Giants in Those Days," Indiana Academy of Science, *Proceedings,* XLIV (1934), pp. 25-26. Dr. John S. Bobbs is credited

After the war several local groups interested in scientific subjects were formed. Among the more important was the Indianapolis Academy of Science which was organized in 1870 with E. T. Cox, the state geologist, as its president. At its meetings members were expected to deliver papers on scientific subjects. During the winters of 1871-1872 and 1872-1873 the academy sponsored lecture series on scientific subjects for the general public.[40]

More vigorous and longer-lived was the State Medical Society. As has already been seen the legal requirements for the training and licensing of physicians were notoriously lax by present-day standards. But the Medical Society did much to maintain high professional standards and to keep members abreast of developments in medicine and surgery. At the 1852 meeting the presidential address dealt with recent progress in medicine. It emphasized anaesthesia as the greatest triumph in recent medical history and pointed out that the use of the stethoscope and the introduction of quinine in the treatment of malaria were also significant.[41] At every annual meeting reports were made on successful surgical operations and innovations in surgery. The society attempted to educate the general public as well as the medical profession in the subject of health and to exert pressure on government for health measures.

At the time the Medical Society was formed an epidemic of cholera was raging in parts of the state, and there continued to be outbreaks of the disease at various places during the fifties. A report of the epidemic made by George Sutton in the *Proceedings* of the society is of interest because of the light which it throws on the state of medical science and

with performing the first operation of cholecystectomy in 1867. He was a member of the faculty of the Indiana Asbury Medical College and of the Indiana Medical College. *Ibid.*, p. 26; Dunn, *Indiana and Indianans*, II, 851-853.

40 Minutes of the Indianapolis Academy of Science, 1870-1872, in Indiana Division, Indiana State Library.

41 Indiana State Medical Society, *Proceedings*, 1852, pp. 21-22.

science in general. Dr. Sutton carefully gathered such data as he could on the places where cholera appeared, the number of cases, and the conditions under which it appeared, and from this data he drew some conclusions as to possible causes of the disease. He observed that the disease spread from Europe to New Orleans and then up the Mississippi and Ohio rivers. At first it was confined mostly to cases on steamboats, but later it began to appear among residents of the towns along the rivers. In Aurora, on the Ohio River, where the disease was especially virulent there lived many traders who went regularly to New Orleans. During the epidemic in Aurora fires were burned at the street corners in the infected area of the town and cannons were fired every twenty-five minutes for a period of four or five hours. But these measures Dr. Sutton thought did more harm than good. "We had 14 deaths this day," he recorded, "and the disease was unusually malignant." Altogether 132 persons died of cholera in Aurora in 1849 and about 1,600 fled from the town. After they left the disease appeared in some of the places to which they fled.

Cholera appeared in many of the counties in the southern part of the state. In Floyd County eighty people died of the disease in 1849 and 1850. In Vanderburgh County about one hundred and fifty deaths occurred in each of those years. Farther north in Tippecanoe County over one hundred persons died, and in Allen County there was an epidemic. In most of these places there were large numbers of recently arrived immigrants, and Dr. Sutton observed that cholera appeared to be especially prevalent among the Germans and Irish. He reported that some persons attributed the outbreak of the disease to atmospheric conditions. In Aurora, when the epidemic began, the weather was warm and damp. Some persons believed that "an electrical condition of the atmosphere" helped to cause the disease to spread. In Jefferson County "the disease appeared to rise spontaneously," and "east winds, cold nights, and malarious localities favored its progress." In some places filth appeared to cause the disease, but some families living in well-kept homes also succumbed. Improper diet and intemperance were considered as possible causes for cholera in some places.[42]

Dr. Sutton made a conscientious effort to collect data and to interpret his findings, and if his report appears somewhat ludicrous to the present-day reader it is simply because he and his contemporaries had no inkling of the germ theory of disease. Until the discoveries of Pasteur revolutionized the methods of searching for causes of disease, causes were sought principally in geographical and climatic conditions. Numerous reports were made to the Medical Society of surveys of the incidence of various diseases along with descriptions of the conditions under which they occurred. In 1851 the society appointed a committee to prepare a study of "barometrical and thermometrical variations, the prevailing direction, and force of winds, prevalent forms of disease, their relative mortality, and other such analogous facts as may comprehend a general synopsis of Medical Statistics." In 1853 in a report on "Observations of the Topography, Climate, and Diseases of Eastern Indiana," the prevalence of epidemics of typhoid and scarlet fever was noted. It was thought that those diseases were most likely to occur near streams of water, especially stagnant water, and that "some peculiarity of season" was associated with their occurrence. "Many physicians," the report said, "maintain that these diseases are the legitimate effect of marsh miasma, a specific poison, generated by the decomposition of vegetable matter."[43]

42 George Sutton, M.D., "A Report to the Indiana State Medical Society on Asiatic Cholera, as It Prevailed in this State in 1849-50-51-52," Indiana State Medical Society, *Proceedings,* 1853, pp. 110, 114-117, 128-130, 132-134, 137-138, 140, 153-154, 157. For a vivid description of the effects of the cholera around Aurora see letter of William S. Holman to Allen Hamilton, July 6, 1849, in Hamilton Papers, Indiana Division, Indiana State Library. See also messages of Governors Dunning and Wright in Indiana *Senate Journal,* 1849-1850, p. 15; 1850-1851, p. 23. In Fort Wayne six hundred persons were reported to have died from cholera between 1849 and 1854. Griswold, *Pictorial History of Fort Wayne,* I, pp. 398-399.

43 Indiana State Medical Society, *Proceedings,* 1851, p. 11; *ibid.,* 1853, p. 30.

Dysentery frequently occurred in epidemic proportions. It was observed that it was most prevalent in the late summer and early autumn when sources of water from wells and springs were low. "It would be interesting to know," said one report on the subject, "how far this form of disease and the water of such situations bore the relations of cause and effect." The author speculated that calcareous matter in the water was the cause of the malady.[44] During the sixties and seventies numerous cases of a disease which was diagnosed as "spotted fever" or cerebrospinal meningitis were reported. It was thought that location had little to do with the incidence of this disease. It was observed that spotted fever was most prevalent and most likely to be fatal "amongst the poorer class of country people," who were most careless about personal cleanliness. It was reported that there was "not the slightest foundation for the belief that the disease is contagious." A report made in 1871 on diseases prevalent in the Seventh Congressional District said that consumption was very common. The disease was diagnosed as being of two kinds—hereditary, which was always fatal, and pneumonic, which was sometimes cured "by persistent use of iron, cod liver oil, and whisky." In the presidential address of the society in 1880 it was stated: "That consumption and scrofula are hereditary is universally admitted; therefore no facts need be offered to prove it."[45]

There continued to be cases of malarial fever, a disease which had plagued the pioneers. In 1873 a doctor in White County reported that the disease was most prevalent at certain times of the year when "a maximum quantity of malarial poison" was generated. The poison, he said, came from marshes and other places containing water, especially from "the evaporating margins around the water." But by the 1870's there was general agreement among doctors that cases of malaria were declining as the result of the draining of

[44] Indiana State Medical Society, *Proceedings*, 1853, p. 51.
[45] *Ibid., Transactions*, 1874, pp. 79-80; 1871, pp. 85-86; 1880, p. 20.

swamplands throughout the state. Other diseases of the pioneer period seemed to be disappearing. As early as 1850 it was reported that the chills and fevers which had prevailed during the period of first settlement in Indianapolis had grown less common as the surrounding country was brought under cultivation. Milk sickness, that mysterious disease of the pioneer period, seemed to disappear. In 1878 it was reported: "Forms of diseases which occupied our attention almost exclusively thirty to forty years ago, have almost disappeared. Other forms, generally of a milder and by far less fatal character, have appeared." The change was attributed to better drainage and the "absence of decomposing vegetable matter."[46] By the 1870's there was growing acceptance of the theory that many diseases were caused by "germs," although as yet there was little understanding of the causes of these microorganisms, and it was widely believed that they generated spontaneously.

In his presidential address in 1878 Dr. L. D. Waterman of Indianapolis told the members of the Medical Society that many devastating diseases arose from conditions as yet unknown, but which, when understood, would probably be avoidable. He said: "The further the microscope enables us to comprehend the number and variety of the otherwise invisible forms of living things—fungi and their countless spores everywhere swarming on the vegetable world that largely forms the food of man and of the animals that supply that food; and bacteria, those lowest microscopic organisms, the immense number of which, with their germs, infest the air we breathe, the food we eat, and the liquids we drink—the more we are impressed with the conviction that their investigation will reveal heretofore unknown causes of many diseases; and the study of these organisms enable man to avert diseases now fatal."[47] A questionnaire distributed by the State Medical

46 *Ibid., Transactions,* 1873, pp. 62, 77, 93; 1878, p. 74; Indianapolis *Indiana State Journal,* July 20, 1850.
47 Indiana State Medical Society, *Transactions,* 1878, p. 2.

Society to physicians throughout the state in 1878 showed that there was general acceptance among them that typhoid, malarial fever, and cholera were caused by germs.[48]

Recognition that many heretofore mysterious diseases were the result of microorganisms caused the medical profession to become interested as never before in preventive medicine and public health. Before this vaccination against smallpox was the only significant effort at preventing disease. By the middle of the century the importance of vaccination was generally recognized. Some communities adopted compulsory vaccination ordinances but not all, and there continued to be some devastating epidemics, but where vaccination was practiced fatalities were few.[49]

Although all cities had boards of health, effective public health measures except for requirements for vaccination against smallpox were almost nonexistent. At its first meeting in 1849 the State Medical Society appointed a committee to memoralize the legislature for a law requiring the registration of births, marriages, and deaths, but the legislature failed to act. In 1875 the society appointed a committee to draft a bill to create a State Board of Health which would work in cooperation with local boards in keeping records of vital statistics. Bills were introduced at the legislative sessions of 1875, 1877, and 1879, but no measure was adopted until 1881.[50] Meanwhile, the State Medical Society undertook a program of voluntary collection of vital statistics through its own members and began a program to educate the public on disease prevention.

In 1876 the president of the society said that half of the deaths in Indiana were caused by diseases which were preventable and that it was the duty of the medical profession to

[48] Indiana State Medical Society, *Transactions*, 1878, p. 73.

[49] *Ibid.*, 1873, pp. 63, 68.

[50] W. F. King, *One Hundred Years of Public Health in Indiana* (Indiana Historical Society *Publications*, VII, No. 6, Indianapolis, 1921), pp. 284, 286; Indiana State Medical Society, *Transactions*, 1875, pp. 65-72; Indiana *Senate Journal*, 1879, pp. 51-54.

teach the public the necessity for public health measures. In 1878 the president emphasized contaminated water, adulterated food, and air "impregnated with noxious gases or exhalations" as causes of disease. The society must not cease its efforts, he said, until the citizens of the state had "pure air to breathe, pure water to drink, unadulterated food and medicines, live in buildings that are not sources of infection to themselves or their neighbors, and have an intelligent body of agents to warn and protect them from preventable, indigenous, and importable causes of disease."[51] More than any other single item members of the medical profession attacked ignorance and apathy about the use of impure drinking water. A "Report on Public Hygiene" by Dr. Thad M. Stevens showed that wells were the principal source of drinking water and that they were prolific sources of disease. In another report Dr. Ben Newland of Bedford called attention to the "almost universal consumption of impure water in our cities." Every city in the state, almost without exception, he said, presented unsanitary conditions which invited epidemics.[52]

The general public does not appear to have shown any great interest in the germ theory of disease, nor was there any widespread opposition to its acceptance. Much more controversial than the discoveries of Pasteur were the theories of Darwin. By the 1870's catalogues of the public libraries in Indianapolis and Evansville show that the works of Darwin and such other books on evolution as Huxley's *Origin of Species* were available to readers.[53] There does not appear to have been much popular excitement over Darwinism, but among scientists and the clergy there were some lively debates over evolution. As already noticed some professors at Indiana colleges had accepted the Darwinian theory by the seventies. David Starr Jordan apparently did not encounter any strong opposition at

51 Indiana State Medical Society, *Transactions,* 1876, p. 2; 1878, pp. 2, 3.

52 *Ibid.,* 1878, p. 71; 1879, pp. 13-14; 1880, pp. 200-201.

53 Kershner, Social and Cultural History of Indianapolis, p. 212; *Catalogue of the Public Library of Evansville,* 1876, pp. 20, 44.

North Western Christian University because of his belief in evolution, but when he left that institution he was replaced by a man who was less of an avowed Darwinist.[54] On the other hand some academic men strongly opposed evolutionary theory. Among them was Joseph Tingley, professor of natural science at Indiana Asbury from 1849 to 1879. In 1874 it was reported in the *Asbury Review* that he had "demolished the theory of the Evolutionists, Darwin and the rest."[55]

Opposing points of view on evolution were given in the lecture series which the Indianapolis Academy of Science presented. In December, 1872, Professor B. Waterhouse Hawkins of London lectured on the subject, "The Gorillas and Other Monkeys Compared with Man." Hawkins took a strongly anti-Darwinian position, but a few weeks later Professor Edward S. Morse of Massachusetts presented a defense of Darwinism. Within the ranks of the medical profession there were sharp differences of opinion. Some doctors denounced Darwinism as atheistic. One Indianapolis physician labeled the conflict over Darwinism as "a struggle of atheism and infidelity for a foothold among the sciences." But by the seventies most men of the profession had accepted Darwinism.[56]

The German Free-Thinkers of Indianapolis were strongly pro-Darwinist, and Unitarians and other religious independents stressed the need for a church which could unite religion and science.[57] But for orthodox Christians Darwinism presented fundamental problems which at first appeared to be insoluble. Some ministers ignored evolutionary theory, others simply rejected it outright. In the *Western Christian Advocate* in 1878 one Methodist minister declared: "Dar-

[54] See above, Chapter XI, page 521.

[55] Truman G. Yuncker, "A Century of Botany and Botanists at DePauw University," Indiana Academy of Science *Proceedings*, LXXI (1961), p. 243.

[56] Indianapolis *Daily Journal*, December 2, 9, 10, 1872; February 4, 1873; Kershner, Social and Cultural History of Indianapolis, pp. 211-212.

[57] See, for example, Indianapolis *Daily Journal*, February 10, 1874; Indianapolis *Daily Sentinel*, April 24, 1879.

winism leads to, and in fact is materialism and hence is incompatible with religion. The two can harmonize no more than fire and water. Religion based upon Darwinism cannot prosper. It is based upon hopeless inconsistencies and contradictions. Its scientific impotency is supported by a dogmatism that is more fanatic than the fanaticism of the Mohammedans." But a few years later, in 1882, in the same journal another minister called for a reconciliation. "Let us reconcile the church with science," he pleaded, "and do away with this imaginary conflict; and let it be understood that Darwinism is neither anti-Christian nor Atheistic."[58]

Discoveries in the field of geology which appeared to conflict with the Biblical account of the creation of the earth did not generate as much emotion as did theories which conflicted with the Biblical account of the creation of man, but they presented problems. Some scientists sought to reconcile the Bible and geology. The efforts of William C. Larrabee, who taught science at Indiana Asbury University and served as the first state superintendent of public instruction, were especially notable. In 1853 he published *Lectures on the Scientific Evidences of Natural and Revealed Religion.* In the preface he declared that he presented "only well-authenticated facts and reasonable theories" and rejected "all new fangled systems and notions." One lecture was entitled: "On the Consistency between the Sacred History of the Creation, and the Science of Geology." In his lectures Larrabee claimed to present irrefutable evidence that the earth was created in six days and was six thousand years old.[59] Richard Owen, who taught geology at Indiana University, was also able to reconcile science and the Bible. Unlike his father, who had been a notorious freethinker, Owen was a devout Presbyterian. He frequently spoke before religious groups and

---

58 Herrick and Sweet, *North Indiana Conference,* pp. 129-130.

59 William C. Larrabee, *Lectures on the Scientific Evidences of Natural and Revealed Religion* (Cincinnati, 1853); Yuncker, "Century of Botany at DePauw University," Indiana Academy of Science, *Proceedings,* LXXI (1961), p. 243.

insisted that his study of science strengthened his belief in the Creator of the Universe. "I readily admit," he said, "that Omnipotence could create the world in seven days or in seven seconds." The word "day" as used in the Bible, he said, did not necessarily mean a period of twenty-four hours, and to buttress his argument he quoted the Scriptural passage: "One day with the Lord is as a thousand years and a thousand years as one day."[60] Some scientists of course dissented from such an interpretation. One of them was Frank H. Bradley, a Yale graduate, who was brought to Hanover College in the late 1860's to establish a paleontological museum and to teach natural history. He was discharged by the trustees of the college because he expressed disagreement with the Mosaic account of creation.[61]

§ § §

In 1850 about one hundred newspapers were being published in Indiana. Thirty years later the number was about four times as great. Precise figures are impossible because of the ephemeral character of the press of the period. It has been estimated that of the papers started in the pioneer period probably a majority lasted less than a year.[62] The mortality rate among those founded after 1850 continued to be high though not as high as in the earlier period. Some papers were proposed which did not materialize and which left no trace except a name and a prospectus. In 1850 the typical paper was a four-page weekly, which was likely to be published by an individual who was proprietor, editor, and printer combined. But in the larger towns there were well-established journals which were beginning to print daily editions. A printer sometimes tried to start a paper in one

[60] Albjerg, *Richard Owen*, pp. 62-63. In the Richard Owen Papers in the Lilly Library at Indiana University are notes for a lecture on "Genesis and Geology" for delivery at the Methodist Church, February 15, 1880.

[61] S. C. Adams, "A Century and a Quarter of Geology at Hanover College," Indiana Academy of Science, *Proceedings*, LXXII (1962), p. 244.

[62] Donald F. Carmony, "Highlights in Indiana Newspaper History," *Indiana Publisher*, February, 1945, p. 3.

town, and if that failed moved on to another town and tried again. Persons with no journalistic experience frequently launched their own newspapers, and occasionally they were successful. An example was Michael Garber of the Madison *Courier*. He was operating a general store in Rising Sun in 1849 when the publishers of the *Courier* decided they wanted to get rid of it—apparently because of the threat of cholera in Madison. Garber traded his store for the newspaper, which he made into one of the most successful in the state.[63]

Most papers were started with little or no capital beyond a hand printing press, and income was uncertain. In 1859 the proprietor of the *Marshall County Democrat* (whose paper appears to have survived longer than most) reported that his total receipts for a sixteen-month period had been about $1,600 and his expenditures about $1,200. He complained that his earnings were "barely sufficient to keep soul and body together" and were not even equivalent to the pay of a journeyman printer. Prior to the Civil War the average price of a subscription to a weekly paper was $1.50 to $2.00 a year if paid in advance, $2.00 to $3.00 if paid at the end of the period. Payments were not always in cash but were sometimes in miscellaneous goods.[64]

In 1850 news about state or national government and politics filled most of the average paper. There was little local news. There were as yet no services comparable to those of the Associated Press, but news from other cities was available through exchanges, and much material which appeared in newspapers was culled from these exchanges. Much space was devoted to such matters as reports of legislative debates, presidential messages, and political speeches. Frequently the entire text was printed. Many small papers were neutral politically and did not endorse any party or candidate, but the principal papers in the larger towns were likely

[63] Baker, "Michael C. Garber," *Indiana Magazine of History*, XLVIII, 398.
[64] Carmony, "Highlights in Indiana Newspaper History," *Indiana Publisher*, October, 1944, p. 3; November, 1944, p. 3.

to be partisan organs. Individual publishers frequently announced that theirs was a Whig or a Democratic publication. Partisan papers of this kind were sometimes indirectly subsidized by being awarded contracts for government printing. Politically loyal journalists were frequently rewarded by appointments to government jobs. Sometimes when there was no party organ in a town a group of politicians would combine to raise the necessary funds to start one. Some papers changed their political affiliations. This was especially true during the political upheaval of the fifties. A conspicuous example was the Madison *Courier*. When Garber began publication he announced his intention of making it a Democratic paper and a Democratic paper it continued to be until 1854. But, as already seen, during the Kansas-Nebraska controversy Garber was one of the first persons to call for a new political party. Thereafter the *Courier* became staunchly Republican.[65]

Most Whig papers became Republican, but a few embraced the Know Nothing cause first. An example was the New Albany *Tribune,* which had been a Whig paper, the *Gazette,* before it was purchased and renamed by Milton Gregg in 1852. In 1856 it supported Fillmore. With the decline of the Know Nothing movement the *Tribune* also declined and went out of business in the late 1850's. During the Civil War there was no Republican organ in New Albany. In 1864 a group of Republicans formed a company and the publication of the New Albany *Commercial* was begun. But in 1870 the *Commercial* was moved to Louisville and New Albany was again without a Republican paper. On the other hand the Democratic New Albany *Ledger,* which had been founded in 1836 as the *Argus,* survived numerous changes in ownership and had a long history.[66] In Evansville, in contrast with New Albany, no Democratic paper flourished.

[65] See above, Chapter II, p. 62.
[66] *History of the Ohio Falls Cities and Their Counties,* II, 181-183; Stoler, "Democratic Element in the New Republican Party," *Indiana Magazine of History,* XXXVI, 198.

The strongest paper in that city was the *Journal,* founded in 1839. It was Whig in politics so long as the party survived, then Know Nothing, and finally Republican. Its support of Lincoln in 1860 helped to carry Vanderburgh County for him, and as a reward James H. McNeely, one of the *Journal* proprietors, was made postmaster.[67] Meanwhile, in 1853, a group of Democrats had started to publish the Evansville *Daily Enquirer.* The *Enquirer* continued publication until 1861, when it was suspended because the publisher went into the Union army. In spite of the absence of a Democratic paper that party carried Vanderburgh County in the elections of 1862. After the election the Evansville *Times* was started by Democrats, but it soon went bankrupt. In 1865 it was revived as the Evansville *Daily and Weekly Courier,* which continued publication under a succession of owners.[68]

In Terre Haute in 1850 there were two strong papers, the *Wabash Courier* and the *Express,* both of which became Republican. In 1857 they were merged and published as the *Express.* In 1870 the *Daily Gazette* began publication as a Republican paper with Liberal Republican tendencies. In 1874 it was sold and became Democratic in politics.[69] In Lafayette the *Courier* was purchased in 1851 by William R. Ellis, who made it into a strong Democratic paper. But in 1854 Ellis renounced the Democracy, and the *Courier* was thereafter a Republican paper. The Lafayette *Journal,* which was the result of a merger in 1849 of the *Tippecanoe Journal* and the Lafayette *Free Press,* supported Fillmore in 1856 but thereafter became a Republican paper. In 1866 John Purdue, one of the wealthiest and most influential men in the area, bought a controlling interest in it in order to pro-

67 *History of Vanderburgh County* (1889), p. 560. Earlier McNeely had learned the printer's trade in a newspaper office in Lawrenceburg and had worked as a reporter on the Indianapolis *Journal. Ibid.,* p. 561.

68 *Ibid.,* pp. 562, 565-566.

69 Oakey, *Greater Terre Haute,* I, 316; Bradsby, *Vigo County,* pp. 634-636.

mote himself as a candidate for Congress. But he found that this was not as simple as he expected and that editors were not as amenable as he thought. When his campaign for Congress ended disastrously, he sold his interest in the paper. Lafayette was without a successful Democratic paper until 1869, when the *Daily Dispatch* was started. It continued publication for sixteen years although it was never a financial success.[70]

In Richmond, the *Palladium,* which began publication in 1831, was to have one of the longest histories of any paper in the state. It was Whig in politics and later Republican. Richmond was such a stronghold of Whiggery and Republicanism that Democrats had to struggle to maintain a paper. But the *Jeffersonian,* which was edited during its early years by Samuel E. Perkins, later chief justice of the Indiana Supreme Court, survived from 1836 to 1865. In near-by Centerville the *Indiana True Republican* was published by Isaac Julian, brother of George W. Julian. In 1865 it was moved to Richmond.[71]

In the northern part of the state the Fort Wayne *Times* was owned by John W. Dawson. Dawson was one of the founders of the Republican party in Indiana and a candidate of the People's party for secretary of state in 1854. After his affiliation with the new party the *Times,* formerly Whig, became Republican. After the election of Lincoln, Dawson was made governor of Utah Territory.[72] Around South Bend the most influential paper was the *St. Joseph Valley Register,* edited by Schuyler Colfax. In 1845 when Colfax was only twenty-three years old but already an experienced newspaper man he and Albert West bought the *Free Press* and renamed it. They announced that the *Register* would be "inflexibly Whig" in politics. During the political upheaval of 1854

70 De Hart, *Tippecanoe County,* I, 310-312, 314, 318, 324; Stoler, "Democratic Element," *Indiana Magazine of History,* XXXVI, 198.

71 *History of Wayne County* (1884), I, 527-529.

72 Griswold, *Pictorial History of Fort Wayne,* I, 426-427; *Representative Men of Indiana,* District Twelve, p. 21.

Colfax was elected to Congress by the People's party, and the paper became a Republican organ.[73] In 1853 a Democratic weekly, the *St. Joseph County Forum*, was started. In 1863 it was suspended by General Hascall for violating his General Order No. 9. It was later sold and reorganized under the name *National Union*. In the seventies it became the *Daily Herald*.[74]

By 1850 Indianapolis, the state capital, had become the most important center of journalism in the state. The two principal party organs, the Democratic *Indiana State Sentinel* and the Whig *Indiana State Journal*, which were published there, were no doubt the most influential papers in the state. The former, which was slightly the older of the two, was founded in 1822 as the Indianapolis *Gazette*. In 1841 it was sold to George A. and Jacob Page Chapman, who named it the *Sentinel* and made it into a true newspaper as well as a party organ. Under the Chapmans the *Sentinel* showed Free Soil tendencies, but this changed abruptly in 1850 when the paper was sold to William J. Brown, a member of the Bright faction of the Democratic party. Page Chapman became one of the founders of the Republican party while his former paper remained orthodoxly Democratic.[75] During the next fifteen years various changes occurred in the ownership of the *Sentinel*, but it continued to be the principal Democratic paper in the state throughout the vicissitudes which the party suffered during the fifties and the years of the Civil War. During most of this time it was edited by Joseph J. Bingham. During the war, as already seen, Bingham was arrested on charges of being involved in the Milligan conspiracy but was not brought to trial. In spite of efforts to stigmatize him with charges of disloyalty, Bingham appears to have been quite successful in steering the difficult course of supporting the Union cause without abandoning the right

[73] Smith, *Schuyler Colfax*, pp. 16-17, 45.

[74] *History of St. Joseph County* (1880), p. 575.

[75] Sulgrove, *Indianapolis*, pp. 232-233.

to criticize the Lincoln and Morton administrations. From 1865 to 1868 the name of the *Sentinel* was changed to the *Herald,* and the editorship of the paper was assumed by Samuel E. Perkins. In 1868 the *Herald* was bought by Richard G. Bright, son of Michael Bright of Madison, and Bingham returned to the editorship.[76]

The *Journal,* rival of the *Sentinel,* had its origin in 1823 as the *Western Censor and Emigrant's Guide,* which became the *Indiana Journal* in 1825. In 1845 the *Journal* was bought by John D. Defrees, who had just sold the South Bend *Free Press* to Schuyler Colfax. Defrees, like many of the journalists of the period, was without formal education and had been apprenticed as a printer. Through reading he acquired a broad education in history and literature. He was one of the most powerful members of the Whig party and one of the leaders of the fusion movement which resulted in the formation of the Republican party.[77] In 1854 he sold the *Journal* to a company of which Ovid Butler was a member and principal financier. Berry Sulgrove, an experienced newspaper man who had been associated with Defrees, was retained as editor. He purchased Butler's interest in the company in 1858 and continued as editor until 1863. Sulgrove was closely associated with Oliver P. Morton, and in 1864 the *Journal* was sold to William R. Holloway and Company. Holloway, who had been Morton's private secretary during the war and was also his brother-in-law, became editor of the paper. He later was appointed postmaster of Indianapolis but retained an interest in the *Journal.*[78]

76 Sulgrove, *Indianapolis,* p. 234. In 1872 Bright sold the paper to John Fishback and a group of associates who formed the Sentinel Company. In 1878 John C. Shoemaker, former state auditor, became sole owner.

77 *Ibid.,* pp. 234-235, 238-240.

78 *Ibid.,* pp. 241-242. In addition to papers of the kind described above which had political ties there were many ephemeral sheets, too numerous to mention, which were founded solely for political purposes and which seldom survived beyond a single political campaign. A few examples will suffice. In 1852 the *Daily Madisonian* was established by a group of Democrats, but it died after the Pierce campaign. In 1854 the *Democratic Platform* was published

During the 1850's important changes occurred in the newspapers published in the larger towns. About 1850 a number of daily papers made their appearance. Earlier there had been occasional daily publications, and both the Indianapolis *Sentinel* and *Journal* had regularly published a semi-weekly edition which became a triweekly when the legislature was in session. It is not clear which paper had the distinction of beginning the regular publication of a daily. Among the first were the New Albany *Daily Bulletin* (later the *Tribune*), the New Albany *Daily Ledger,* the Madison *Daily Banner,* the Evansville *Daily Journal,* and the Lafayette *Daily Journal.* During the Constitutional Convention in the winter of 1850 the Indiana *Journal* began a daily edition which continued to be published without interruption thereafter, and the following April the *Sentinel* began the permanent publication of a daily. During 1851 the Terre Haute *Express* and the *Wabash Courier* started daily publication, and by that time the Madison *Courier* also was publishing a daily. By 1860 there were about a dozen dailies out of approximately one hundred and eighty papers being published at that time.[79] In all cases the papers which published dailies also continued to publish a weekly edition. There were various

in Indianapolis, and a paper called *We The People* was published in the same city by the opposition party. During the 1860 campaign the Bright forces of the Democratic party published the *Old Line Guard* in support of Breckinridge. In 1868 *The Index,* a weekly Democratic paper, was published in Lafayette from July to November. Woollen, *Biographical and Historical Sketches,* p. 516; Sulgrove, *Indianapolis,* p. 243; De Hart, *Tippecanoe County,* I, 328.

79 Carmony, "Highlights in Indiana Newspaper History," *Indiana Publisher,* December, 1944, p. 3; *History of Ohio Falls Cities and Their Counties,* II, 183; Sulgrove, *Indianapolis,* pp. 233, 242; Schlicher, "Terre Haute in 1850," *Indiana Magazine of History,* XII, 267; *History of Vanderburgh County* (1889), p. 558. The following dailies were being published in 1860: in Evansville, the *Enquirer,* the *Journal,* and the *Volksbote;* in Fort Wayne, the *Times;* in Indianapolis, the *Journal* and the *Sentinel;* in Lafayette, the *Courier* and the *Journal;* in Madison, the *Courier;* in New Albany, the *Ledger* and the *Tribune;* in Terre Haute, the *Journal* and the *Wabash Express.* George W. Hawes, *Indiana State Gazetteer and Business Directory, 1860-1861* (Indianapolis, 1860), pp. xxxii-xxxvi.

reasons for the movement to the daily press. Increasing population in the towns made daily circulation possible. Competition also played a part. A daily edition was regarded as a means of attracting additional circulation, and once one paper in a town had started a daily the rival paper felt compelled to do the same. The coming of the telegraph was also certainly an important factor in the establishment of the daily press.

Telegraph lines reached Indiana in the late 1840's. In 1847 a Fort Wayne paper announced: "The telegraph is in operation at Vincennes, and the editors of the *Gazette* are amusing themselves by exchanging salutations with the editors in the neighboring cities." The Indianapolis *Sentinel* published the first news dispatch received by telegraph on May 24, 1848, and that same year the *St. Joseph Register* began to receive news by telegraph. On his visit to Indiana in 1851 the Englishman, Richard Beste, was impressed by the fact that as he traveled across the country telegraph wires accompanied him all along his route, bringing remote villages into contact with the outside world.[80]

At first there were several telegraph lines, just as there were different railroad lines. The first line across Indiana was known as the O'Reilly line from the name of its principal owner, Henry O'Reilly, who had acquired the right to build lines throughout much of the West from Samuel Morse, the inventor of the telegraph. The O'Reilly line, which ran from Dayton, Ohio, to Chicago, passed through Richmond, Indianapolis, and Lafayette. A branch ran from Lafayette southward along the Wabash River to Evansville. These lines were built before any railroad was constructed between these points and followed the regular highways. Later telegraph lines were built along the principal railroads. The Western Union Telegraph Company, which first built a line

[80] Carmony, "Highlights in Indiana Newspaper History," *Indiana Publisher,* November, 1944, p. 9; Holloway, *Indianapolis,* p. 89; Beste, *The Wabash,* II, 186.

in Indiana along the Indianapolis and Cincinnati Railroad in 1854, soon began to absorb the other lines in the state.[81]

But the development of the telegraph did not mean that most of the stories published in the press of the cities through which telegraph lines passed were gathered from that medium. In Indianapolis, for example, during the early fifties, telegraphed reports of news were cut from the Cincinnati papers which reached Indianapolis each evening and published in the local papers the following morning. It was not until the seige of Sevastopol during the Crimean War, which aroused great interest, that Indianapolis papers began to make regular use of telegraphic news. In 1856 the two major Indianapolis papers began receiving news through the services of the Associated Press. Use of this service reduced the cost of the transmission of telegraphic dispatches.[82]

About the same time that the larger newspapers began to receive accelerated and expanded coverage of national and international news through telegraphic dispatches they began to pay more attention to local news. As already mentioned, early papers had usually largely ignored what was happening in their own community. In Indianapolis a nonpolitical weekly called the *Locomotive,* which began publication in 1850, gained a large circulation by publishing local civic and church news and news about Indianapolis social events. In 1852 the Indianapolis *Journal* made history when it published an account of a local fire the morning after it occurred. Thereafter the *Journal* and *Sentinel* both began to cover more local events and to publish news of this sort immediately after it happened.[83]

81 Holloway, *Indianapolis,* p. 271.

82 *Ibid.,* pp. 158, 271; Sulgrove, *Indianapolis,* p. 240; "The Newspaper and Periodical Press," United States Bureau of the Census, *Tenth Census* (1880), VIII [Pt. 1], p. 107.

83 Sulgrove, *Indianapolis,* pp. 240, 243. The *Locomotive* had been published for a few weeks in 1845 and 1847 and then suspended. In 1861 it was combined with the *Sentinel.*

By 1880 the United States census reported that 467 newspapers and periodicals were being published in Indiana. A study of newspapers of the United States made in connection with the census of that year stated that "the remarkable localization" of the American press was the characteristic which distinguished it from the press of other countries and that the tendency was "constantly toward minuter localization." "Every hamlet," it said, "has its mouthpiece through the printing press, and every city is independent of every other city for its daily news supply." The effect of the extreme localization was to make papers self-reliant and "loyal to home and vicinity interest." In Indiana journalism reflected all of these characteristics in extreme form. In every one of the ninety-two counties of the state there was at least one newspaper. Of the 467 publications 422 were papers devoted primarily to news and politics. Of these 390 were weeklies, most of which had a circulation of only a few hundred. Fifty-five weeklies had a circulation of less than 500; 146 had a circulation of between 500 and 1,000; 146 had a circulation of between 1,000 and 5,000; while two weeklies (presumably the weekly editions of the Indianapolis *Journal* and *Sentinel*) had a circulation of more than 10,000.[84]

By 1880 there were forty daily papers in the state. A dozen towns had at least two dailies. Columbus in Bartholomew County and Seymour in Jackson County, each with a population of less than five thousand, had two daily newspapers. Five cities—Evansville, Indianapolis, Fort Wayne, Terre Haute, and Lafayette—had more than two daily papers apiece. Evansville, a city of less than thirty thousand,

---

[84] United States Bureau of the Census, *Tenth Census* (1880), VIII [Pt. 1], pp. 73, 170-171, 182, 183. See *ibid.*, pp. 231-237, for a list, arranged by counties, of the names of all newspapers and periodicals being published in Indiana in 1880. The list indicates whether the paper was daily, weekly, or monthly, the type of publication (i.e. newspaper, religious, railroad, etc.), date established, and the price of subscription per year. See Hawes, *Indiana State Gazetteer, 1860-1861,* pp. xxxii-xxxvi, for a complete list of all newspapers and periodicals being published in 1860 together with the names of their publishers.

boasted five daily papers—the *Journal,* the *Courier,* the *Evening Tribune,* the *Union,* and the *Demokrat,* a German paper. All of them published a weekly edition also. In Indianapolis there were four dailies—the *Journal,* the *Sentinel,* the *News* (all of which published a weekly edition), and the *Teaglicher Telegraph,* a German paper. Fort Wayne, with a population of twenty-six thousand, had four dailies—the *Sentinel,* the *Gazette,* the *News,* and a German daily, the *Indiana Staatszeitung.* In Terre Haute, a city about the same size, there were three dailies—the *Express,* the *Evening Gazette,* and the *Evening News.* Lafayette, with a population of less than fifteen thousand, had three dailies—the *Journal,* the *Courier,* and the *Dispatch.*[85]

In Indianapolis the total circulation of all four dailies was about thirty-five thousand for a population of seventy-five thousand—or one newspaper for every two persons. The aggregate circulation of the Indianapolis papers was almost as great as the combined circulation of all the other dailies in the state. Only one daily in the entire state had a circulation in excess of ten thousand, and only two others had more than five thousand. The circulation of nineteen dailies ranged from one thousand to five thousand, that of fourteen from five hundred to one thousand, while two dailies had a circulation of less than five hundred each.[86]

Among papers which were such small-scale enterprises it is not surprising that the mortality rate was high.[87] Many papers failed outright, others were bought up by stronger competitors, and quite frequently two papers consolidated and were published under a combined name. The papers which survived did so because they were able to attract advertisers as well as subscribers. By 1880 the daily papers in the state, and the weeklies which were connected with them, derived

[85] United States Bureau of the Census, *Tenth Census* (1880), VIII [Pt. 1], pp. 231-237.

[86] *Ibid.,* pp. 77, 174-177.

[87] See *ibid.,* p. 182, for some figures on the rate of survival.

about 53 per cent of their income from advertising and the remainder from subscriptions. For the other papers the ratio between income from advertising and from subscriptions was about equal.[88] Many of the smaller papers were started by printers, and a very large percentage of newspaper offices, large and small, did job printing as a means of supplementing income.

In the smaller towns the dailies differed little in size or form from the weeklies. Their newsgathering facilities were the same. They relied heavily on dispatches gleaned from other papers. Only thirteen papers in the state regularly received Associated Press dispatches.[89] But by the 1870's the papers in the larger cities were giving much more prompt and full coverage to national and international news than they had a few years before. The front pages of both the Indianapolis *Journal* and *Sentinel*, for example, daily carried a column on foreign affairs, in which latest developments were relayed by telegraphic dispatch. They also carried on the front page a column of dispatches of news from Washington, D.C., and other large cities in the United States. By the seventies advertising had almost, but not quite, disappeared from the front page. Headlines, by present-day standards, were restrained, but they appeared in larger and bolder type than in earlier years, and sometimes they were quite sensational. By the seventies the Indianapolis *Sentinel*, in particular, had become quite a lively sheet, with much space devoted to cases of murder, seduction, and marital infidelity. All of the larger papers gave some attention to social events such as receptions and balls, but there was as yet no woman's page or society page. Theatrical and musical performances were covered in some detail, and on Mondays lengthy coverage was given to sermons preached the previous

88 United States Bureau of the Census, *Tenth Census* (1880), VIII [Pt. 1], p. 179.

89 *Ibid.,* pp. 107, 170. The ratio of dailies in Indiana which were served by the Associated Press was about the same as that for the United States as a whole. In Indiana 13 dailies out of 40 received Associated Press dispatches. In the entire country about 30 per cent of daily papers had this service.

day. Little attention was given as yet to sports and athletic events.

The editorial page was an important part of the larger papers, and in general the quality of editorials, both in style and content, was high. By the 1870's the larger papers were frequently owned by companies or by an individual who was not actively concerned with the editorial page. Editorials were written by professional newspapermen, and the personal quality which had characterized the newspapers of the 1850's had largely disappeared. In the fifties the identity of writers of editorials, who were frequently the owners of the papers, was well known. Editors often indulged in personal feuds and name calling with their rivals, presumably to the delight of their readers.[90] But although competing newspapers of the seventies continued to feud with each other, the contests were more impersonal and carried on in more restrained language.

By 1880 the extreme political partisanship which had characterized the newspapers in the fifties and during the Civil War had abated somewhat. It was estimated that at that time two thirds of all newspapers in the United States were identified with a political party,[91] and certainly the percentage among the leading papers in Indiana was that high. But their partisanship was at times, at least, less blind and uncompromising than it had been. Writing in the early 1880's Berry Sulgrove, who had been associated with Indianapolis journalism for thirty years, commented on the "relaxation or disregard of party discipline," which had occurred in recent years.[92]

The establishment of a few avowedly "independent" papers was no doubt a factor in the softening of the extremism of the party press. The most significant example of an independent paper was the Indianapolis *News*, an afternoon

90 For some examples see Barnhart and Carmony, *Indiana,* I, 370-371.

91 United States Bureau of the Census, *Tenth Census* (1880), VIII [Pt. 1], p. 110.

92 Sulgrove, *Indianapolis,* p. 249.

daily, which first appeared in December, 1869. Under the able editorship of John H. Holliday the paper grew rapidly in circulation and influence.[93] The *News* was independent but far from neutral. In fact it expressed very strong opinions on political questions. Its strictures against Oliver P. Morton and its demands for the withdrawal of Will Cumback, the Republican gubernatorial candidate in 1876, which have already been noticed, are examples.

Another significant development in the press was the appearance of a substantial number of German-language newspapers as the result of the large immigration during the fifties. Many of these papers survived only a short time, but some of them continued publication until the first World War. In 1880 there were four daily German-language papers in the state and twenty-three weeklies.[94] The first successful German paper was the *Volksblatt*, founded in Indianapolis in 1848 by Julius Boetticher, a Prussian. After some early struggles it became firmly established as the German population in the city grew. The *Volksblatt* was Democratic in politics. In 1853 the *Freie Presse* was started by a group with Free Soil sympathies. *Der Taeglicher Telegraph*, a daily, began publication in 1864. The following year *Der Spottvogel*, a Sunday paper which featured comics, then a novelty, was founded. Between 1873 and 1877 a weekly Republican paper, *Die Deutsche Zeitung*, was published. In 1878 *Die Indiana Tribuene*, which was to be longer-lived, was launched.[95]

As might be expected, a large number of German papers were started in Evansville. In 1849 the *Union*, which was issued in both daily and weekly editions, began publication.

[93] Dunn, *Greater Indianapolis,* I, 399-401; Holloway, *Indianapolis,* pp. 159-160.

[94] United States Bureau of the Census, *Tenth Census* (1880), VIII [Pt. 1], p. 183.

[95] *Ibid.,* p. 234; Holloway, *Indianapolis,* pp. 160-161; Oscar L. Bockstahler, "The German Press in Indiana," *Indiana Magazine of History,* XLVIII (1952), 166.

In 1864 the *Demokrat,* which became one of the best and most successful German papers in the Middle West, was started. It was both a daily and a weekly and also printed a Sunday edition which was principally literary in character. In addition there was *Der Volksbote,* begun in 1851, *Die Reform,* published briefly in 1853, and *Die Indiana Post,* established in 1879 as the official organ of the Sangerbund. In Fort Wayne the *Indiana Staatszeitung* was founded as a Democratic weekly in 1857. In 1877 it began publishing a daily edition. In 1871 the *Indiana Volksfreund,* a Republican weekly, was started but apparently did not survive long. In 1876 a Republican paper, *Das Ft. Wayne Tageblatt,* was started but apparently it, too, was short-lived.[96]

In Lafayette the *Beobachter am Wabash* was founded in 1858. In 1868 its name was changed to the *Indiana Post.* In 1875 *Der Deutsche Amerikaner* was founded. It was the only German paper in the city which survived until 1880. In Terre Haute several German-language papers were founded during the sixties and seventies. The only one to survive for any length of time was *Das Banner,* which began publication in 1870. German papers which were started in New Albany in 1850 and 1861 failed, but *Die Deutsche Zeitung,* a weekly started in 1875, was more enduring. In South Bend a successful weekly, *Der Indiana Courier,* was founded in 1873. In Richmond there were three or four short-lived German papers and *Die Volkzeitung,* which was published from 1871 until 1906.[97]

German-language papers were started in many other smaller communities where Germans were numerous. Among the more important was the *Signal* of Huntingburg in Dubois County, which was published almost without interruption

96 Bockstahler, *op. cit.,* pp. 165-166; *History of Vanderburgh County* (1889), p. 567; United States Bureau of the Census, *Tenth Census* (1880), VIII [Pt. 1], p. 231.

97 *Tenth Census* (1880), VIII [Pt. 1], pp. 235, 237; De Hart, *Tippecanoe County,* I, 328; Bockstahler, "German Press in Indiana," *Indiana Magazine of History,* XLVIII, 167-168; Bradsby, *Vigo County,* p. 636.

from 1867 to 1914, when it began to appear as an English-language paper. German-language papers, most of which survived only briefly, were started before 1880 in Brookville, Crown Point, La Porte, Logansport, Michigan City, Mount Vernon, Rockport, Seymour, Tell City, and Vincennes. Most German newspapers, though not all, were identified with one of the major political parties. Democratic papers appear to have been more numerous and successful. Of twenty-five papers being published in 1876 which indicated a partisan affiliation eighteen were Democratic and seven were Republican.[98]

Newspapers devoted to the promotion of a particular group or interest appeared from time to time and usually survived only briefly. The Indianapolis *Sun* was published during the seventies in the interest of the Greenback cause. During the seventies a few short-lived labor papers appeared. Among them were the *Indianapolis Daily Union,* a paper strongly Democratic in tone, which announced that it was "published in the interests of the workingmen" and the *Workingmen's Map* also published in Indianapolis. Newspapers published in the interest of the antislavery movement and temperance have already been mentioned.

In addition to publications which were primarily newspapers, many weekly and monthly periodicals were also published. They were so numerous and so varied in content that only a few examples can be mentioned. Some of them were the organs of special groups—religious, educational, professional, or fraternal. Others were to promote some particular cause or to appeal to some particular interest. The following list of monthly periodicals which were being published in Indianapolis in 1870 gives an idea of their variety: *Masonic Advocate, Odd Fellows' Talisman, Western Journal of Medicine, North Western Farmer, Indiana*

[98] Bockstahler, *op. cit.,* pp. 164-168; United States Bureau of the Census, *Tenth Census* (1880), VIII [Pt. 1], pp. 231-237; Elfrieda Lang, "Germans of Dubois County, Their Newspapers, Their Politics, and Their Part in the Civil War," *Indiana Magazine of History,* XLII (1946), 231.

School Journal, Bentham's Musical Review, Willard's Musical Visitor, Christian Record, Phonic Advocate, Little Chief, Bee Journal, American Housewife, Ladies Own Magazine, and *Morning Match.*[99]

Numerous religious journals and publications with religious connections were issued, some of which have already been mentioned. In 1880 a total of thirteen periodicals classified as religious in the United States census were being published in Indiana,[100] but some contained material of interest to the general reader. Political and fraternal organizations also started journals which were principally devoted to literature or current affairs. Among the earliest of these was the *Western Odd Fellows Magazine,* which began publication in New Albany in 1852.[101] In 1854 a monthly, *The Western Democratic Review,* which announced its intention of being no mere party organ but rather a publication which would take its place with the "high toned American Press," made its appearance in Indianapolis. This was an ambitious project. Each number was almost one hundred pages in length and included articles on current political questions, international affairs, and literature as well as poetry. Apparently the journal did not attract enough subscribers to survive and ceased publication after a little more than a year.[102]

There were numerous efforts, mostly short-lived, to publish magazines which were not identified with any particular group or cause but which were intended to appeal to all members of the family. Among them was *The Western Fireside, A Magazine for Everybody,* which was launched in Indianapolis in 1868 but apparently was not a success. Another example was *The Western World: A Literary Journal for the*

---

[99] Holloway, *Indianapolis,* p. 162.

[100] United States Bureau of the Census, *Tenth Census* (1880), VIII [Pt. 1], p. 185.

[101] *Western Odd Fellows Magazine,* I, No. 1 (July, 1852), p. 23. This magazine continued to be published at New Albany until 1854, when it was moved to Centerville.

[102] *Western Democratic Review* (Indianapolis), January, 1854, pp. 14, 71.

Farm and Home, which was published in Indianapolis in the
seventies. There were several periodicals especially for
women. Among the more successful was *The Christian Monitor,* primarily for women of the Disciples of Christ Church,
which was first published in Cincinnati and then moved to
Indianapolis in 1863. It contained short stories, poetry, and
a juvenile department. In 1882 it was sold and moved to
St. Louis.[103] In 1869 *The Ladies Own Magazine,* edited by
Mrs. Cora Bland, began publication in Indianapolis and continued there until 1873 when it was moved to Chicago.[104]

Some of the religious and agricultural journals contained
departments for children, and at least two publications were
started especially for children. In 1865 the Reverend
William W. Dowling, who had been head of the preparatory
department of North Western Christian University, began
the publication of *The Little Sower* in Indianapolis. It was
the first Sunday School publication of the Disciples of Christ
and was quite successful. It started as a monthly and became
a weekly in 1869. It continued publication under its original
name until 1884, when it became *The Sunday School Evange-
list.* In 1868 Dowling and A. C. Shortridge started *The
Little Chief,* a monthly magazine for children in the public
schools.[105]

§ § § §

In his volume on Indianapolis, published in 1870, William
R. Holloway made some comments on the attitudes of the
residents of that city toward "entertainment" and "culture,"
which would, no doubt, have applied to the residents of Indiana generally. Attitudes toward the theater, music, and
public performances of all kinds, he said, were influenced by
a combination of Puritan traditions and backwoods culture
which caused certain forms of entertainment to be branded

103 Dunn, *Greater Indianapolis,* I, 405.

104 Extant copies of *The Ladies Own Magazine* and the other periodicals
mentioned in this chapter are in the Indiana Division of the Indiana State
Library.

105 Dunn, *Greater Indianapolis,* I, 406.

as "unclean." By 1870, he said, "moral antipathies" had been weakened as the result of the growth of population and decline in religious intensity, but they still existed. In the early history of the city concerts were regarded as "bearable," and even opera was not "altogether abominable," but a theatrical performance was "beyond moral toleration," and circuses were "devil's devices." But, said Holloway, it would be difficult to determine whether the moral opposition "injured the tabooed performances more than the additional allurement of doing a forbidden thing benefited them."[106]

Although most forms of music were acceptable on moral grounds, few persons had opportunities of cultivating musical tastes before 1850. Except for the music furnished by choirs in a few churches, a recital by an occasional teacher or pupil of music, the singing of a troupe in a minstrel show, or, perhaps, the performance of a brass band, few people, even among those living in towns, ever heard a musical performance. In the 1840's several brass bands were organized, and during the fifties conventions were held in Indianapolis at which bands from throughout the state participated.[107] Professional performers from the outside world also began to appear in the larger towns. In 1851 Indianapolis had its first concert of classical music when Madame Anna Bishop sang operatic selections. This performance, according to Berry Sulgrove, who was music and drama critic for two local newspapers at the time, "furnished the curious some idea of what music was that was neither hymn nor ballad, jig nor hornpipe."[108]

The musical event of the decade in Indianapolis was the appearance of the renowned Norwegian violinist, Ole Bull, who played there in 1853 on his first western tour. Even greater excitement was aroused by the appearance of Jenny

106 Holloway, *Indianapolis*, p. 145.

107 *Indiana Free Democrat*, December 1, 1853; Sulgrove, *Indianapolis*, p. 263.

108 Sulgrove, *Indianapolis*, p. 263; Dunn, *Greater Indianapolis*, I, 527-528.

Lind in Madison in 1851. Tickets sold at prices of five dollars and upwards, and forty persons from Indianapolis made the journey to hear the famed singer, who, unfortunately was forced to perform in a building which had originally been built as a pork house. In 1859 the first full-length opera was given by Cooper's English Opera Troupe when they gave Bellini's *La Somnambula* and Donizetti's *L'Elisir d'Amore* and *The Daughter of the Regiment*.[109]

In the sixties the number of musical performances increased, but during the seventies there appears to have been a decline as the result of the depression. Singers appeared more frequently and apparently drew better audiences than did instrumentalists. The programs of the Alleghenian Singers and the Swiss Bell Singers, who appeared during the sixties, had greater popular appeal than did operatic arias, but opera was patronized not only by music lovers but by the well-to-do without musical knowledge because it was considered fashionable. In 1863 the celebrated Adelina Patti gave two concerts in Indianapolis. She was reported to have sung like a bird and to have sent the musical critics into ecstasies, while "those who did not know whether the music was good or bad took their cue from those of cultivated taste and got extatic [*sic*] too."[110]

In 1872 Christine Nilsson appeared with the Italian Grand Opera Company in *Lucia di Lammermoor*. It was the first time that this opera had been performed in Indianapolis, and the *Journal* pronounced it the "greatest musical event" in the history of the city. Although the depression curtailed the appearances of traveling companies, in 1875 the Strakosch Italian Opera Company gave two performances in Indianapolis, and the Hess Opera Company also appeared during the seventies. In 1879 Carlotta Patti, sister of the more famous Adelina, sang in Indianapolis before an enthusiastic audience. In 1876 Hans von Bülow, the world famous pianist,

---

109 Sulgrove, *Indianapolis*, p. 264; Dunn, *Greater Indianapolis*, I, 530.
110 Indianapolis *Daily Sentinel*, January 26, 27, 1863.

gave a concert, but the auditorium was not full. During the seventies the Boston Philharmonic Club, which was regarded as one of the finest musical organizations in America, and the Mendelssohn Quintette Club of Boston also appeared in Indianapolis.[111]

Interest in musical performances by artists such as these was stimulated by the activities of local musical societies and private individuals. In 1851 in Indianapolis the Handel and Haydn Society, a choral group, was organized and gave a public concert which included part of Haydn's oratorio of *The Creation.* Music stores selling pianos and other musical instruments were opened as more people began to take music lessons. In 1856 a musical convention was held for four days in Indianapolis for the benefit of music teachers and choir directors.[112]

The greatest impetus to increased interest in music came from the arrival of large numbers of Germans during the fifties. Wherever a group of Germans settled they organized musical societies. In Evansville, for example, there were singing societies, the Liederkranz, the Germania Maennerchor, and the St. Cecilia Maennerchor, and such groups as Schrieber's Brass Band and Orchestra and Schmidt's Silver Band. In New Albany there were the Maennerchor and the Saengerbund, and in Terre Haute a Maennerchor. In 1854 the Indianapolis Maennerchor was organized, and in 1857 it was host to a state convention of all the German singing societies in the state. In 1867 it was host to a Saengerfest of all the North American Saengerbunds. In 1880 it celebrated its twenty-fifth anniversary in a three-day festival. Other German musical groups were organized in Indianapolis, among them the Liederkranz and the Lyra.[113]

111 Indianapolis *Daily Journal,* January 15, 1872; Eva Draegert, "Cultural History of Indianapolis: Music, 1875-1890," *Indiana Magazine of History,* LIII (1957), 272, 279, 281.

112 Dunn, *Greater Indianapolis,* I, 526, 530.

113 *Williams' Evansville City Directory,* 1880, p. 28; Morlock, *The Evansville Story,* p. 75; *Terre Haute Directory,* 1880-1881, p. 347; *Caron's New Albany*

Musical groups not so closely identified with the German community were also active. Among the most important was the Indianapolis Choral Union, which was founded in 1870. It presented a number of concerts which featured the singing of oratorios. Vocal music was generally more popular with both performers and audiences than instrumental, but several instrumental groups were formed. Among the more important was the Philharmonic Society of Indianapolis, which was organized in the seventies. In 1874 and 1875 the Choral Union and the Philharmonic Society joined together in musical festivals.[114]

Dramatic performances encountered greater prejudice than musical ones on the grounds of immorality. And considering the nature of some of the presentations this is not surprising. In the nineteenth century as at a later date, types of theatrical presentations varied greatly. There was always a limited audience for serious drama, while minstrel shows and farces and variety shows usually played to full houses.

During the fifties companies of actors would come to a town like Indianapolis or Terre Haute and remain for several weeks. One company which had presented a "side show" at the State Fair spent the winter of 1853 in Indianapolis. That same year another company gave the first performance in that city of *Uncle Tom's Cabin,* a drama which became a perennial attraction. There was nothing resembling a regular theater in Indianapolis until 1854 when a former distillery was remodeled into a theater and named the Atheneum. Here were presented numerous successful productions, which ranged from farces to *Romeo and Juliet.* Romeo was played by an actress, whose "exhibition in tights" was said to have

and Jeffersonville City Directory, 1882, pp. 36 and 551; Martha F. Bellinger, "Music in Indianapolis, 1821-1900," *Indiana Magazine of History,* XLI (1945), 351-352; Sulgrove, *Indianapolis,* pp. 264-265; Probst, Germans in Indianapolis, p. 71; Dunn, *Greater Indianapolis,* I, 531.

[114] Dunn, *Greater Indianapolis,* I, 531; Draegert, "Cultural History of Indianapolis: Music, 1875-1890," *Indiana Magazine of History,* LIII, 269; Bellinger, "Music in Indianapolis," *ibid.,* XLI, 349.

been especially attractive to the young men in the audience. In 1857 the managers of the Atheneum announced their intention "to elevate theatricals in the capital city by producing chaste and unobjectionable entertainments," but the character of the presentations does not seem to have changed greatly.[115]

In 1858 a rival to the Atheneum appeared in the Metropolitan Theater, the first building in the city which was actually designed for theatrical performances. It had a seating capacity of 1,200 and was probably as well equipped as any theater in the West. The quality of its offerings was as varied as those at the Atheneum. During its first season it presented the aforementioned Cooper English Opera Troupe, some Shakespeare, and Sallie St. Clair, known as a leader of the "naked school" of actresses, and another show of the "stripping" class. In spite of the variety of the attractions the first year of the Metropolitan was not a financial success. Part of the reason was that many respectable citizens still boycotted theatrical performances. In 1859 a bill was introduced into the legislature to inquire into the expediency of a law for the "suppression of theatrical representations, horse racing, and other things incompatible with true religion and good morals." The proposal was tabled, but antipathy to the theater continued. In an effort to conciliate some of the more influential citizens the manager of the Metropolitan offered a performance as a benefit for the Widows' and Orphans' Society, but the directors of the charity refused on moral grounds.[116]

During the war the theater in Indianapolis flourished, and the Metropolitan was reported to be the most profitable investment in the city. It was crowded regardless of the

[115] Holloway, *Indianapolis,* pp. 148-149; Indianapolis *Daily Sentinel,* October 16, 1857.

[116] Holloway, *Indianapolis,* p. 150; *Brevier Legislative Reports,* II (1859), 78. Some respectable organizations sponsored benefit theatrical performances in the 1850's. For example, the Union Fire Company of Indianapolis sponsored a performance of Mr. and Mrs. Harry Chapman in *A Glance at New York* at the Atheneum in 1857. Indianapolis *Daily Sentinel,* September 11, 1857.

type of program offered. Large audiences were due in part to the presence of large numbers of soldiers in the city, but opposition of the general public on moral grounds appears to have diminished during the war. A number of benefit performances for charitable causes were reported. Among them was a performance in 1863 of *The Duchess of Malfi* by a Mrs. Waller, who was said to be the best actress who had ever appeared in the city. In 1864 a performance of *Othello* was given for the benefit of the Sewing Women's Association. During the war years other plays which were presented included *She Stoops to Conquer, Richelieu,* and *The Octoroon.* The aforementioned Sallie St. Clair appeared in a "historical drama" about Lucretia Borgia and also something entitled *Cudjo's Cave* or *Battle Cry of Freedom.*[117]

In 1868 Valentine Butsch, the same man who had built and operated the Metropolitan, built a larger theater, the Academy of Music, which seated 2,500. In 1875 the Grand Opera House, an even more elaborate building, was completed. Among its many ornaments was a marble fountain which dispensed ice water to thirsty patrons. In 1879 the old Metropolitan was remodeled and renamed the Park.[118] All of these theaters presented much the same kind of fare— ranging from serious drama to burlesque shows. Among the most popular attractions in the postwar years was Joseph Jefferson's *Rip Van Winkle,* which was presented year after year and was always a sellout. Another favorite was Lotta Crabtree, who was billed simply as Lotta. Lawrence Barrett was always popular. He appeared most frequently in Shakespeare but his Richelieu was regarded as the best performance of that role on the American stage. In 1876 Agnes Booth and her husband, Junius Brutus Booth, Jr., the elder

117 Holloway, *Indianapolis,* p. 151; Indianapolis *Daily Sentinel,* January 23, February 13, 1863; May 7, 9, 1864; Indianapolis *Daily Journal,* July 28, 1864.

118 Holloway, *Indianapolis,* pp. 151-152; Eva Draegert, "The Theater in Indianapolis before 1880," *Indiana Magazine of History,* LI (1955), 126-127, 128-129.

brother of Edwin Booth, gave four performances—*As You Like It, King John, Femme de Feu,* and *Camille.* The same year Edward H. Sothern was well received in *Lord Dundreary.* Two Polish actresses, Fanny Janauschek and Helena Modjeska, appeared at different times. The latter played in *Camille, Frou Frou,* and *East Lynne.*[119]

Variety shows continued to be presented. During the depression of the seventies when the legitimate theater languished, theater managers tried to attract customers by various innovations. *The Black Crook,* which had started out as a comedy, added singing and a kicking chorus. This was shown at the Grand Opera House as was also something entitled Matt Morgan's Art Exhibition, which featured tableaux of beautiful women scantily attired before audiences in which men predominated. One performance which was given on Sunday was raided by police as being a violation of the Sabbath law, but when the case came to trial the actors were acquitted. The Indianapolis *News* complained that "the frequent admission of variety shows to the Grand Opera House has lowered the tone of the audience which is attracted." And it was undeniable that variety shows and the performances of a comedian named Jo Emmett, who specialized in German characterizations, and Haverly's Mastodon Minstrels attracted larger audiences than did serious drama.[120]

As the largest city in the state and a railroad center Indianapolis naturally attracted more theatrical companies than did the smaller cities. Traveling troupes of singers and actors which presented *Uncle Tom's Cabin,* minstrel shows, and like fare appeared in most towns of any size, but these usually constituted the extent of dramatic fare except for theatricals presented by local groups. Next to Indianapolis,

119 Draegert, "The Theater in Indianapolis before 1880," *Indiana Magazine of History,* LI, 130-134; Holloway, *Indianapolis,* p. 152; Indianapolis *Daily Sentinel,* February 28, 1879.

120 Draegert, "The Theater in Indianapolis before 1880," *loc. cit.,* LI, pp. 123-126, 132, 134, 135.

Terre Haute was probably the most important center of theatrical activity in the state. Dowling Hall, which was built about the end of the Civil War, was used for theatrical performances as well as lectures. In 1870 a group of Terre Haute businessmen put up the money to build Naylor's Opera House, which seated 1,400 persons and was reported to have cost $178,000. It was designed by a Belgian-born architect, Josse A. Vrydagh. The contract for the paintings which decorated it was given to Sir Robert Buckels of Oxford, England. The opening night was one of the grandest affairs in the history of the city. Seats were sold at auction—the best ones going for twenty-five dollars.[121] In Evansville Apollo Hall, the first theater, which was later called Mozart Hall, was opened in 1852. The 'first production presented there was *Lenora, the Bride of Death.* Few full companies of actors came to Evansville. Performers who appeared on the stage were for the most part local talent with only the leading roles being taken by professionals. In 1868 the Evansville Opera House, an elaborate and expensive building which seated 1,200, was opened. But the management which operated it was unable to attract large enough audiences to make it financially successful. "The complex nature of the city's population," said a county history written in the 1880's, "renders it extremely difficult to secure attractions interesting to all classes of citizens." But Evansville had a vaudeville theater which opened in 1872, and the Germans supported numerous beer gardens where entertainment was presented. In Fort Wayne the situation was probably about like that in Evansville. There was a theater, the Academy of Music, which seated 1,200, but it apparently was not often used. Beer gardens offered more popular entertainment.[122]

121 Oakey, *Greater Terre Haute,* I, 323-324.
122 Morlock, *The Evansville Story,* p. 73; *History of Vanderburgh County* (1889), p. 194; United States Bureau of the Census, *Tenth Census* (1880), XIX, 441.

Lectures on a great variety of subjects served both an educational and recreational function. In the 1840's lectures presented under the auspices of literary societies were begun and had become quite popular by the fifties. In 1850, in Terre Haute, a society called the Atlantian Litterate sponsored a course of lectures which ranged in subject matter from California to the siege of Troy and the history of epidemics. In Indianapolis that winter a series of lectures was given by men who were members of the Constitutional Convention. They started off with one by Robert Dale Owen on "An Evil Too Prevalent in Society—Ultraism." There were also lectures on more esoteric subjects. Phrenology was attracting much attention at midcentury, and lectures by phrenologists were common. In Madison it was announced that a lecturer would demonstrate the "science" by examining such heads as members of the audience might select. In Indianapolis a Professor Kelly gave a lecture on mesmerism in 1850.[123]

During the fifties there were several lectures by women prominent in the woman's rights movement, including a series of three in Indianapolis by Lucy Stone. In 1853 Horace Greeley spoke at the State Fair in Lafayette on agriculture and in Indianapolis on Henry Clay. In 1854 the Young Men's Christian Association of Indianapolis began a lecture series which was maintained for several years. Among the persons who appeared were ministers Henry Ward Beecher and Theodore Parker and statesmen Edward Everett, who lectured on Mount Vernon, and Governor Boutwell, who lectured on America prior to the discovery by Columbus. Horace Mann, the educator, who also gave a lecture, evidently offended some of the women in the audience because he touched on the subject of human physiology.[124] In Madison and Evans-

123 Schlicher, "Terre Haute in 1850," *Indiana Magazine of History,* XII, pp. 258-259; *Indiana State Sentinel* (semiweekly), May 18, December 10, 1850; Madison *Daily Courier,* May 23, 1850.

124 Sulgrove, *Indianapolis,* p. 262; Indianapolis *Daily Sentinel,* November 15, 21, 1857.

ville similar lecture series were sponsored by the library associations in the fifties.[125]

In later years famous literary figures who went on the lecture circuit made appearances in Indiana. Ralph Waldo Emerson came twice during the sixties, and in 1872, Mark Twain, who had not yet reached the peak of his fame, lectured in Indianapolis and Logansport. Indiana's own author, Lew Wallace, gave lectures on literary as well as political subjects.[126]

Lectures on scientific subjects sometimes attracted large audiences. During the fifties Professor O. M. Mitchell from the Cincinnati Observatory gave a series of lectures on astronomy in Indianapolis. In the winter of 1859-1860 a series on geology was given.[127] During the seventies, as noted elsewhere, the Indianapolis Academy of Science sponsored popular lectures on science. Lectures on theology, morals, and reform were too numerous to mention. Opponents of religious orthodoxy such as Robert G. Ingersoll attracted audiences and were given a respectful hearing. But a lecture by Victoria Claflin Woodhull in New Albany in 1873 on the subject of "Sexual Slavery" caused an uproar. In Louisville, where she had spoken earlier, it was reported that the newspapers had said that her lecture was too indecent for publication. Consequently when she came to New Albany many persons, "especially ladies of refinement," stayed away. Her audience, according to a dispatch in the Indianapolis *Journal*, was limited mostly to "spiritualists and infidels, many of whom brought their wives."[128]

Lectures appealed to relatively limited audiences. Circuses and menageries attracted much larger crowds. " 'Shows,' the generic Hoosier name for all sorts of exhibitions under can-

---

125 Story of the Madison Library Association, pp. 16-18; *Annual Report of the Evansville Library Association*, 1860, p. 12.

126 Paul Fatout, "Mark Twain Lectures in Indiana," *Indiana Magazine of History*, XLVI (1950), 363-365; Indianapolis *Daily Sentinel*, January 27, 1863; McKee, *"Ben-Hur" Wallace*, pp. 131-132.

127 Sulgrove, *Indianapolis*, p. 263.

128 Indianapolis *Daily Journal*, September 4, 1873.

vas," said Holloway, "may be considered the favorite weakness of the Capital." A circus, he said, would fill its seats "in spite of weather, mud or money," and a half dozen in close succession would play to large crowds, "as if people went to see how much better or worse one was than another." Religious groups frowned upon circuses. "Last week our city was cursed with the presence of one of those wandering nuisances," a correspondent to the Methodist *Western Christian Advocate* reported in 1851. "Large numbers attended it, mostly men and boys. We have known many who have attended circuses, and they can be classed as worthless and trifling." Secular papers like the *Locomotive* of Indianapolis and the Terre Haute *Journal* also deplored the habit of spending money on circuses. People allowed themselves to be "fleeced" by "travelling Harlequins," said the *Journal,* when their money would be better spent in libraries or railroad stock. In spite of such criticism enthusiasm for circuses remained undiminished. Various traveling companies visited the state. In the 1850's one of them was Sand's, Nathan's and Co. American Circus, which boasted acrobats, gymnasts, clowns, and trained animals, including performing elephants Victoria and Albert. During the sixties the G. F. Bailey and Co. Circus came, bringing not only an equestrian troupe, trapeze performers, clowns, and the usual animals, but also the only hippopotamus in the United States.[129]

Balloon ascensions created some excitement. In one of the early ones a Mr. Paullin went up to a height of ten thousand feet in a balloon called the Eclipse. He took off before a large crowd in Indianapolis and landed in Greenfield twenty miles away. Horse racing was popular although it was frowned upon by the better elements of society as was boxing.[130] There

129 Holloway, *Indianapolis,* p. 145; Herrick and Sweet, *North Indiana Conference,* pp. 31-32; Terre Haute *Journal,* quoted in *Locomotive,* June 8, 1850; Indianapolis *Daily Sentinel,* July 22, 1856; Indianapolis *Daily Journal,* August 6, 13, 1864.

130 *Indiana State Sentinel* (semiweekly), August 5, 1852; *Locomotive,* May 4, 1850.

were no other spectator sports before the Civil War. After the war baseball, which had started as a game for children, gained in popularity as a game for adults and gradually acquired a semiprofessional status. During the 1850's a college graduate from the East introduced baseball to Evansville, but it was not until 1866 that the first regular team was organized there, and not until 1882 did that city have a semiprofessional team. As early as 1862 a baseball team was formed at Fort Wayne, but it disbanded because most members left for military service. In Indianapolis in the late sixties there were two teams—the Military and the Great Western clubs. After the war a baseball association of Indiana teams was formed. In 1866 the Indianapolis Westerns won the state championship over Lafayette. But the Fort Wayne Kekiongas made a greater reputation. In 1870 they won the Indiana championship, and the following year became a member of the National League. It was not until 1876 that Indianapolis had a professional team—the Blue Legs.[131] After the war there were some efforts to develop interest in cricket in Indianapolis. The Indianapolis Cricket Club was formed which played matches with teams from Cincinnati and Louisville, but it apparently did not survive for long.[132]

Parades were as popular as circuses. Every political campaign was marked by torchlight processions. There were parades with floats and huge banners emblazoned with political slogans. During the fifties many volunteer military companies were organized. Their drills and parades were a popular diversion for their members and for the public. The Zouave company organized by Lew Wallace in Crawfordsville was one of the most colorful. When they paraded in Indianapolis on Washington's birthday in 1860 they caused a sensation. With the outbreak of hostilities these military companies

131 Gilbert, *Evansville and Vanderburg County*, I, 107-108; Griswold, *Pictorial History of Fort Wayne*, I, 468, 473-474; Kershner, Social and Cultural History of Indianapolis, pp. 227-228, 233; Indianapolis *Daily Herald*, November 7, 1865.

132 *Ibid.*, November 23, 1865; August 27, 1867.

went marching off to war to the huzzas of the populace. As the war wore on there were almost constant parades by newly organized regiments or by veteran troops who were home on recruiting furloughs. After the war every returning regiment paraded through Indianapolis and was greeted with appropriate ceremonies and oratory. In succeeding years reunions of veterans offered many occasions for parades. One of the largest reunions of all Indiana regiments was held in Indianapolis during October, 1875. It lasted for several days and was marked by several parades.[133]

The Fourth of July was regularly celebrated not only by patriotic speechmaking but also by fireworks and parades. As the centennial of Independence approached there were more and more celebrations which enlivened the gloom of the depression years. The climax came in Indianapolis on July 4, 1876. The whole city was gayly decorated, and half fares offered by the railroads attracted visitors from all over the state to witness a magnificent parade and fireworks. Three years later there was a gala celebration in connection with a visit to Indianapolis by President and Mrs. Hayes, who were accompanied by General Sherman and Richard Thompson, the Secretary of the Navy. The visit attracted the largest crowds which had ever assembled in the city. Again there were street decorations, a parade, and fireworks. Two months later General Grant made a triumphal tour through the state on a special train. In Indianapolis his visit was the occasion for many regimental reunions and a huge parade in which many veterans marched in honor of their old commander.[134]

133 Theodore G. Gronert, "The First National Pastime in the Middle West," *Indiana Magazine of History*, XXIX (1933), 171-186; McKee, *"Ben-Hur" Wallace*, p. 32; Indianapolis *Daily Journal*, October 12, 15, 1875.

134 Indianapolis *Daily Sentinel*, July 4, 1876; Indianapolis *Daily Journal*, October 3, December 9-10, 1879.

CONCLUSION

No doubt there were parts of Indiana, especially in the south, where conditions of life changed little between 1850 and 1880. But for the state as a whole this period brought significant developments. Population almost doubled, the state survived the crisis of the Civil War, enjoyed a period of prosperity resulting from the war boom, and suffered through a prolonged depression in the seventies. The physical face of Indiana underwent marked changes. As population increased and moved northward new land was brought under cultivation, virgin forests disappeared, towns sprang up, and a network of railroads spread across the state.

From 1850 to 1880 population increased from 988,416 to 1,978,301. In this period Indiana attained a higher rank in population relative to the rest of the states than at any other time in her history. In 1850 she was seventh among the states, and from 1860 to 1880 she was in sixth place. After 1850 the rate of population increase in the southern part of the state, where most of the early settlers had come, began to decline. By 1870 the number of persons in the central third of the state was greater than in the southern part. Meanwhile, the northern third was being peopled at a more rapid rate than any other section. A high birthrate among Indiana natives was the most important factor in population increase, with immigration of persons from the older states in the Union the second most important factor. The ratio of immigrants from the upper South, who had been the most important element in the population in the pioneer period, had already begun to decline by 1850 and continued to decline. After 1850 more persons settling in Indiana came from Ohio than any other state.

Immigration from Europe was the third factor in population growth. The influx of Europeans was greatest during the fifties and sixties. By 1870 more than 9 per cent of the population of the state was European born, but after 1870 the rate of increase from that source declined substantially. Germans constituted the largest element among the Europeans. Their numbers were large enough that they had a significant impact upon politics and religion, and most notably upon cultural life. The second largest group from Europe were the Irish, but they were fewer and more scattered and hence their influence was less evident. But Irish immigrants contributed to the growth of the Roman Catholic church and had an impact upon politics. The arrival of the Germans and the Irish, and especially the fact that both groups were predominantly Catholic in religion, led to an outburst of nativism during the fifties. Nevertheless, Indiana was less affected by European immigration than almost any northern state. She received a smaller percentage of the influx of the 1850's than any other state of the Old Northwest. In the years after the Civil War, when the rate of European immigration declined, there was a marked increase in the number of Negroes coming into the state, but as late as 1880 Negroes made up only 2 per cent of the total population.

In spite of rapid population growth Indiana remained primarily rural and agricultural. By the middle of the 1850's virtually all public lands had been disposed of, but in the swamplands of the north there continued to be vast tracts which were totally unimproved, and in other sections of the state, especially in some of the hilly parts of the south, there were areas which were almost uninhabited and unimproved. In 1850 slightly less than one fourth of the land in the state was under cultivation according to United States census reports, but by 1880 only one third to one half of the land remained unimproved.

Farming was the most important occupation and farm life the basis of society. As late as 1880 over half of all persons who were classified as having an occupation were engaged in agriculture and 80 per cent of the population was rural.

The typical farm was a relatively small one of about one hundred acres. There were some large farms and some farm tenancy but they were not common. Corn and hogs, the basis of pioneer agriculture, continued to be important, but wheat and cattle growing increased after 1850. The development of state and county fairs and agricultural societies in the 1850's reflected interest in improved farming methods. Increased demands for foodstuffs during the Civil War led to increased use of farm machinery. The opening of new lands and mechanization led to increased agricultural production. There was also much progress in the improvement of breeds of hogs and cattle, but the average farmer as yet showed little interest in soil conservation.

The building of a network of railroads which linked Indiana with the rest of the nation contributed more than any other single factor to the economic development of the state after 1850. Railroads brought many new settlers to the state. They helped to revolutionize the marketing of farm products and to break down rural isolation. They caused the growth of cities and stimulated mining and industry. In 1850, although many railroads had been projected, only one line of any importance had been completed—the Madison and Indianapolis. By 1880 there were more than 4,000 miles of railroads in the state, reaching eighty-five of the ninety-two counties. Scores of short lines were chartered and constructed, but by 1880 most of them were already consolidated into larger systems which were owned by eastern capitalists.

Building of the railroads accelerated the exploitation of natural resources and the beginnings of industrialization, although Indiana lagged behind neighboring states in manufacturing. A steady expansion of the lumber industry occurred as railroads reached into new areas. Development of the limestone quarries in the southern part of the state and of coal mining in the western counties was due in large part to the accessibility of rail transportation. Hopes that western Indiana would become an important center of steel and iron production failed to materialize. Many manufacturing establishments were founded, but they were nearly all small and were developed principally to utilize native timber and agricultural products and to serve the needs of an agricultural population. Among the leading industries were pork-packing houses, grist and flour mills, breweries, lumber mills, and small factories which made wood products and farm implements.

Absence of large-scale manufacturing was reflected in the absence of large cities. Nothing like the phenomenal growth of Chicago occurred in Indiana, nor was any Indiana city comparable in size to Cleveland or Cincinnati. Nevertheless a trend toward urbanization was beginning. In 1850 no city in the state had a population of ten thousand. By 1880 there were nine cities with more than that number of inhabitants. The most spectacular growth was that of Indianapolis—from a mere 8,000 in 1850 to more than 75,000 in 1880. Next to Indianapolis the three largest cities in 1880 were Evansville, Fort Wayne, and Terre Haute, the total population of which numbered more than 25,000 inhabitants. After the development of a national system of railroads the Ohio River communities of New Albany and Madison, which had been the principal centers of commerce and culture at midcentury, failed to keep pace with newer cities.

The political history of the period after 1850 was of unusual interest. Local and state issues were sometimes important—especially the temperance question in the fifties—but the focus of attention was usually on national issues. The decade of the fifties was a period of political upheaval and realignment. As a result the Democracy was toppled from its long-time dominance and the new Republican party emerged and swept the state in the election of 1860. The years of Civil War which followed were a period of agonizing crisis. The internal bitterness and strife engendered by the war were more intense in Indiana than in most states. The extent to which "disloyalty" existed will no doubt continue to be debated, but it appears that the number of "Confederate sympathizers" who actually wanted a Confederate victory and a permanent separation of the Union was negligible. In spite of internal feuding and charges of disloyalty the people of Indiana made an impressive contribution to military victory and the preservation of the Union. The bitterness of the war years carried over into the postwar period and strengthened the Republican party. For years the Democrats suffered from the stigma of "Copperheadism."

In spite of the intensity of feeling which politics aroused and the extreme partisanship of many Indianans there were not as profound differences in principle between the major political parties as might have been expected. On some issues there were sharper differences within parties than between parties. During the fifties, to the dismay of the abolitionists, the dominant element in the new Republican party took a cautious and moderate position on the slavery question, which, in fact, differed but little from the popular sovereignty which was advocated by their Democratic opponents. Sharp differences developed during the war years over the conduct of the war, and especially over the leadership of Lincoln and Morton, but there was general agreement over the necessity for a war to insure the military victory required for the preservation of the Union. There were also real differences between the parties over Reconstruction policy and the status of the Negro in the postwar period. The adoption of the Radical Reconstruction program for the South had the effect of settling the question of the legal and political status of Negroes in Indiana as well as in the South and thereby largely removed the race issue from state politics. Even in the years immediately after the war economic questions (especially monetary policy) began to distract attention from Reconstruction and the war record of the Democrats. During the depression of the seventies the money question came to overshadow all other issues, but most of the time differences between the two major parties in Indiana on the question were not clear-cut. The ambiguities and inconsistencies in the positions of Democrats and Republicans was an important factor in the rise of the Greenback party.

During most of the period from 1850 to 1880 the strength of the two major parties was fairly evenly balanced. In the 1850's many Democrats permanently defected to the Republican camp, and in 1864 many others undoubtedly left the party. But Union military victories and the identification of the Democrats with Copperheadism did not make Indiana into a one-party state. Republicans won substantial victories in 1860, 1864, and 1866, but in 1868 their margin of victory was narrow, and the Democratic candidate for the governorship failed of election by less than one thousand votes. In 1870 the Democrats regained control of the state legislature; in 1872 they won the governorship; and in 1876 they carried the state for Tilden as well as electing the governor. In the presidential elections Democrats won the electoral votes three times—in 1852, 1856, and 1876—while the Republicans were victorious four times. On the other hand, the Democrats won the governorship four times and the Republicans three. Control of the two houses of the legislature was sometimes divided between the two parties, and the outcome of statewide elections was often extremely close.

On the national scene Indiana received more attention and wielded more political power after 1850 than in the pioneer period. In 1868, Schuyler Colfax, who had already attained the post of Speaker of the United States House of Representatives, became the first Indianan to be elected Vice-President. As war governor Oliver P. Morton played a role of national importance in the preservation of the Union. As a member of the United States Senate in the postwar years he had a significant part in the shaping of Radical Reconstruction and exerted influence in the national councils of the Republican party. In 1876 he was an unsuccessful contender for the presidential nomination. Caleb B. Smith became the first Indianan appointed to a cabinet post when Lincoln made him Secretary of the Interior. His successor, John P. Usher, was also a resident of Indiana. Hugh McCulloch, who served as Comptroller General under Lincoln, was later elevated to the post of Secretary of the Treasury, a position he continued to hold under Johnson. Richard W. Thompson was the Secretary of the Navy under President Hayes.

Among Indiana Democrats Thomas A. Hendricks achieved greater national recognition than any other member of his party. After an undistinguished term in the United States Senate he attained national prestige by his election as governor of Indiana in 1872, at a time when the fortunes of Democrats generally were at a low ebb. Although his hopes for the presidential nomination in 1876 were thwarted, he was given second place on the ticket with Samuel Tilden. Earlier, in 1852, Jesse D. Bright, who was a powerful figure in the United States Senate, had received some consideration as a presidential nominee. Michael Kerr, although not a particularly influential figure, was elected Speaker of the United States House of Representatives after Democrats gained control of that body in 1874 for the first time since before the Civil War.

With the growth of population and beginnings of urbanization came a growing sense of social responsibility and an expansion of the role of government. As the rigors of pioneer life diminished, interest in education increased and something of a cultural awakening occurred. During the Civil War efforts at caring for soldiers, especially the sick and wounded, and for soldiers' families led to an expansion of private and public benevolence. The prolonged panic which began in 1873 caused a further expansion and institutionalization of private charity, especially in Indianapolis, but private efforts proved inadequate and city and township governments were compelled to accept unprecedented responsibilities in caring for the needy. Meanwhile, all cities of any size had begun such functions as providing police and fire protection, paving and lighting of streets, public water works and garbage and sewage disposal.

More significant was the growing acceptance of the responsibility of maintaining public, tax-supported schools. Although Indiana had been committed to the idea of free schools by the first state Constitution, they did not begin to become a reality until after 1850. The Constitution of 1851 made it mandatory for the General Assembly to provide for a uniform system of common schools open to all without charge. The school law adopted in 1852 laid the foundations for such a system and for the first time provided for state taxes for schools. But during the 1850's progress in public education was slowed by adverse court decisions and confusion over the respective financial responsibilities of state and local governments. In some places the Civil War disrupted schools. Consequently, it was not until after the war that the common school system was firmly established throughout the state. After the Civil War public high schools were opened in most cities and towns although there was reluctance in some quarters to paying taxes for the support of secondary education. In spite of progress in education, Indiana continued to show a higher rate of illiteracy than other northern states, and proposals for compulsory attendance laws were rejected by the state legislature.

Even some of the strongest advocates of tax-supported schools thought that higher education should be entirely private. Hence Indiana University had a precarious existence. Not until after the Civil War did the legislature begin to make regular appropriations for the support of the school. In 1880 it was still a small struggling liberal arts college, a university only in name. In 1869 the legislature voted to establish a second state institution, for the teaching of agriculture, under the terms of the Morrill Act. Purdue University opened in 1874, but the legislature was reluctant to appropriate funds for its operation and enrollments remained small. Consequently, such higher education as there was in the state remained largely in the hands of the numerous private denominational colleges, many of which offered courses which differed little from those offered in the academies and high schools.

As in the pioneer period, few legislative restraints were imposed upon individual conduct. Certain religious groups showed intense interest in temperance legislation and Sunday laws, but other groups, especially the Germans, exerted pressure to prevent the effective enforcement of such measures. There was relatively little interest in economic regulation of any kind. Although there were a few labor unions and some sporadic efforts at political activity by workingmen's groups, labor had little political influence. The growing importance of railroads and the power of railroad corporations led to numerous complaints as early as the legislative sessions of the Civil War years. Criticism of the railroads was greatly intensified by the Panic of 1873 and the rise of the Grange and the Greenback party. Numerous regulatory measures were proposed but no significant legislation was passed. During the seventies, when economic and political unrest was widespread, a number of moderate proposals for the protection of the interests of workers were introduced in the legislature, but few were adopted. The major political parties, the churches, and the people as a whole appeared to be indifferent to problems arising from the beginnings of industrialization. Even a prolonged depression did little to change the economic attitudes which had prevailed at midcentury.

BIBLIOGRAPHICAL ESSAY

BIBLIOGRAPHICAL ESSAY

This essay does not purport to be all inclusive. Instead, the author has attempted to list the most significant materials, published and unpublished, for the study of the history of Indiana for the period from 1850 to 1880. All items cited in the footnotes are not included. To have included them would have made a bibliography unmanageably long. Materials are included which are not cited in the footnotes but which should be useful to persons seeking to do more intensive research on some subjects than was possible within the limits of this volume.

An examination of the secondary works mentioned in this bibliography will show that much research has already been done by earlier writers on certain aspects of the period embraced in this volume but that other aspects have been neglected. Political history for the period before 1865 has been covered quite adequately by others, but little has been written on the period after the Civil War. With few exceptions economic developments have been neglected by earlier writers. A few good studies have been made on social and cultural subjects but much remains to be done.

The bibliography is organized partly on the basis of type of material, partly on the basis of subject matter.

UNPUBLISHED MATERIALS

MANUSCRIPTS

The most extensive collections of manuscripts on the history of Indiana are to be found in the Indiana Division of the Indiana State Library, the Indiana Historical Society Library, and the Lilly Library of Indiana University.

Indiana Division, Indiana State Library

There is an extensive card index of the manuscripts organized according to subject and also a useful chronological catalogue. Many of the larger collections are important principally for political history, but there are numerous smaller collections of letters and diaries and account books which throw light on virtually every aspect of the history of the period. There are materials on agriculture, business, church history, Civil War, education, land, medicine, plank roads, railroads, slavery, social conditions, temperance, and many other subjects.

Below are listed some of the more important collections which contain materials on the period from 1850 to 1880.

Joseph Beeler Papers. Letters, diaries, account books. Economic conditions.

Flavius C. Bellamy Papers, 1861-1864. 200 items. Diary and letters while in the Army of the Potomac.

Austin H. Brown Papers (Brown was publisher of *Indiana State Sentinel* and a prominent politician). Materials on politics, economic conditions, and social life.

George F. Chittenden Papers. Mostly Civil War letters of Chittenden, who was a surgeon with the 16th Regiment.

John Coburn Papers (Coburn was a lawyer, an officer in the Union Army, and a member of Congress). 125 items. Politics and Civil War.

Schuyler Colfax Papers. 300 items. Letters regarding personal matters and politics.

Adam Crosier Collection. 257 items. Medical practice, economic conditions, Civil War.

Elisha and Lucius C. Embree Papers. 3,700 items. Include papers of Lucius Embree who was a lawyer active in the Republican party. Legal matters, politics, and railroads.

W. G. and G. W. Ewing Papers. 30,000 items. Much of collection deals with earlier period, but there are materials on business and politics after 1850.

Allen Hamilton Papers (Hamilton was a Fort Wayne banker and political figure). 6,000 items. Letters on politics and banking.

William S. Holman Papers (Holman was a veteran Congressman from Aurora). 140 items. Political correspondence.

George W. Julian Papers. Letters on politics, slavery, Civil War; Julian's journals from 1869 to 1899.

James H. Luther Papers. 450 items. Letters written by Luther's four sons, who were members of the Union Army. Also other materials.

Samuel Merrill Papers. 218 items. Letters and diary of an officer in the Union Army.

Valette Miller Papers. Politics and Civil War.

Oliver P. Morton Papers. 750 items. Personal letters and speeches.

Daniel D. Pratt Collection (Pratt was a Logansport lawyer, member of the state legislature, and United States senator). 20,000 items. Politics, railroads, and legal matters.

James R. Slack Papers. 125 items. Civil War letters.

Richard W. Thompson Collection. 550 items. Political correspondence, including correspondence while Thompson was Secretary of the Navy, and Civil War correspondence.

Lew Wallace Papers. 600 items. Civil War letters and papers for the year 1862.

James T. Wilder Papers. 200 items. Letters of an officer in the Union Army.

Joseph A. Wright Papers. 600 items. Letters of Wright to members of his family and letters from political and business associates.

Indiana Historical Society Library

The greater part of the manuscripts in this library relate to the territorial and pioneer periods, but there are valuable materials on virtually every aspect of the history of the period from 1850 to 1880. There is a card index organized by subject matter which covers many but not all of the collections in the library.

Below are listed some of the more important collections which contain materials on the period from 1850 to 1880.

David Enoch Beem Papers. 199 Civil War letters. Also political and family matters.

Conrad Baker Papers. 24 letterbooks for the years 1866-1872, and several boxes of correspondence relating to the years when Baker was acting governor and governor.

John G. Davis Papers (Davis was a Democratic member of Congress from Vigo County 1851-1855 and 1857-1861). 1,812 items. Mostly political correspondence.

John Dowling Papers (Dowling was a Terre Haute newspaper editor and member of the state legislature). 587 items. Letters on politics and public affairs.

William H. English Papers. Political correspondence, especially for the 1850's. Includes letters from Jesse D. Bright and other prominent Democrats.

Calvin Fletcher Papers (Fletcher was a leading banker, reformer, and philanthropist, who was influential in politics). A large collection of letters which are mostly to and from members of the Fletcher family. Calvin Fletcher's diary, which covers the years 1817 to his death in 1864, contains almost daily entries during his later years. Much of the material is trivial, but there are significant observations on economic conditions, temperance, the slavery controversy, and politics.

Henry S. Lane Papers. 5 boxes of correspondence, principally for the years 1834 to 1865.

Caleb Mills Papers. Manuscripts of Mills's speeches and articles, pamphlets on education. Also letters to Mills, principally from Union soldiers, and letters from Mills to his son, Lieut. Benjamin M. Mills.

Robert H. Milroy Papers (Xerox) *ca.* 1840-1886. Civil War correspondence and reports, political and personal letters.

Lew Wallace Collection. 2,000 items. Includes a few items for the 1850's, substantial materials on Wallace's career during the Civil War, and some materials on postwar politics and Wallace's legal practice, including railroad matters.

Lilly Library, Indiana University

There is a good catalogue describing all of the collections, including detailed descriptions of some of the more significant items. The library contains a number of collections which are important for economic history as well as politics and the Civil War. Below are listed some of the larger collections which contain materials on the period from 1850 to 1880.

Baker, Hord, and Hendricks Papers. Papers of the law firm which included Conrad Baker and Thomas Hendricks.

Schuyler Colfax Papers. Letters to Colfax and a few letters written by Colfax, principally for the years 1855 to 1862.

James A. Cravens Papers. Mostly letters for the years 1861-1865 when Cravens was a member of Congress. National and state politics and Civil War.

William Cumback Papers. Letters on political questions and printed speeches.

Thomas Gaff Papers, 1857-1872 (Gaff was an Aurora merchant, banker, and distiller, who also furnished steamboats for the Union cause during the Civil War). Business records.

John Hanna Papers (Hanna was a politician and a Congressman from 1877 to 1879). Letters about election of 1860, Knights of Golden Circle, and other political matters.

Alvin P. Hovey Papers. Letters from Hovey to his wife during the Civil War and other correspondence on Civil War and politics.

Howard Shipyards and Dock Company Papers. Business records and letterbooks of the Jeffersonville company, which built steamboats and other craft.

Indiana Cotton Mills Papers. Indiana Cotton Mills, Inc., located at Cannelton. Business records including letterbooks, minutebooks, and letters received.

Nathan Kimball Papers. Letters relating to Kimball's Civil War career.

Henry S. Lane Papers. About half of collection belongs to years 1861-1867 when Lane was a member of United States Senate.

Hugh McCulloch Papers. 30 letter copybooks, 1864-1869, dealing with United States Treasury Department; also some personal letters.

Joseph E. McDonald Papers. 7 scrapbooks of newspaper clippings of McDonald's political speeches and other political materials, 1854-1891.

Joseph Barron Niles Papers (Niles was a lawyer of La Porte and a member of the Indiana senate). Letters on legal and personal matters; Minutes of Southern Plank Road Company, 1850-1854; Indiana Medical College Papers.

Oliver Papers. Materials relating to the Oliver Chilled Plow Works, mostly for period after 1880, but included are some printed materials beginning in 1860 and letters beginning in 1875.

Richard Owen Papers. Letters, including numerous Civil War letters, and notes for Owen's lectures on a wide variety of subjects.

Joseph Goodwin Rogers Papers (Rogers was a physician). Include materials on medical history. A casebook containing record of medical cases of Civil War soldiers and private patients, 1864-1878.

Hamilton Smith Papers (Smith was a lawyer and businessman of Louisville and Cannelton). Letters regarding American Cannel Coal Company, Cannelton, 1849-1860; letters on cotton manufacturing, 1848-1860, and on Cannelton Cotton Mills, 1849-1851; letters on proposed railroads in Middle West and West, 1848-1872.

ARCHIVES

Materials preserved in the Archives Division of the Indiana State Library constitute a rich but largely neglected source for historical research. Lack of detailed inventories and catalogues for all but a few of the collections has no doubt been a deterrent to their use by scholars. The following descriptions are by no means complete but are suggestive of the materials deposited there.

Governor

A large and valuable collection of papers pertaining to the administration of Oliver P. Morton has been preserved. It includes correspondence received; letterbooks of letters sent by Morton and his secretaries; dispatch books containing copies of telegrams sent and received; and miscellaneous materials. The Chicago-Morton Collection contains principally letters received by Morton while he was governor but also a few papers pertaining to the administrations of Governors Abram A. Hammond, Henry S. Lane, and Conrad Baker. Papers in this collection were taken to Chicago by William R. Holloway, Morton's secretary, but were later returned to the state as official records.

There are also collections of correspondence and other papers for the administrations of Governors Joseph A. Wright, Ashbel P. Willard, Conrad Baker, Thomas A. Hendricks, and James D. Williams. It was not customary in that period for governors to deposit the bulk of their correspondence with the state when they left office and these collections are small and fragmentary.

Adjutant General

The papers from this office contain extensive and valuable materials on the Civil War. They are well indexed. The following listing indicates the kinds of records but is by no means a complete inventory. Correspondence includes 11 volumes of letterbooks covering the terms of Adjutant Generals Lazarus Noble and W. H. H. Terrell; 14 drawers of correspondence on the history and records of Indiana troops, 1861-1866; correspondence on recruiting, re-enlistment, the draft, substitutes, and desertions; 4 volumes of letters from military agents. There are records of appointments, elections, and resignations of officers; 65 volumes on personnel of Indiana regiments, 1861-1865; rolls of sick and wounded soldiers; rolls of soldiers taken prisoner and paroled; registers of claims for bounties, back pay, and pensions; records of the quartermaster general and military agents, including accounts and abstracts of issues of supplies.

Attorney General

Letterbooks beginning in 1866 and files of correspondence and briefs and opinions in civil and criminal cases beginning in 1855.

Auditor of State

Records dealing with the following subjects are of greatest historical interest:

Banking. There are materials on the Indiana State Bank, the Bank of the State of Indiana, free banks, and state banks. These include correspondence, papers of incorporation, stocks and notes, and an index of state banks, 1873-1893.

Public Lands. There are extensive materials from the various land offices in Indiana. A large part of them relates to the earlier period but there are some for the years after 1850. There are records of transactions concerning the disposal of the swamplands in the 1850's.

Transportation. There are extensive records on the building and operation of the Wabash and Erie Canal and some materials on the Madison and Indianapolis and other railroads.

Superintendent of Public Instruction

Records preserved by this office include eight volumes of letterbooks covering the years 1865 to 1880; opinions and decisions rendered by the office; circulars sent to school officials; reports about township libraries, 1855-1859; two volumes of minutes of the Indiana State Teachers Association, 1854-1887; and miscellaneous materials.

Treasurer of State

Journal, ledgers, and letterbooks for the period covered by this volume and also two volumes of records of swampland sales for the years 1853 to 1860.

Indiana General Assembly

Reports of legislative committees for the period 1841 to 1861; original bills beginning in 1863; registers of bills beginning in 1851.

Indiana Supreme Court

Transcripts of records of cases in trial courts which were appealed to the Supreme Court and briefs filed in these cases.

The United States Census

The manuscript volumes of the following parts of the Seventh, Eighth, Ninth, and Tenth United States Censuses which pertain to Indiana are in the Indiana archives:

Seventh Census (1850). Agriculture, 8 volumes; Industry, 1 volume; Social Statistics, 1 volume.

Eighth Census (1860). Agriculture, 6 volumes; Industry, 1 volume; Social Statistics, 1 volume.

Ninth Census (1870). Agriculture, 6 volumes; Agricultural Production, 1 volume; Industry, 2 volumes; Social Statistics, 1 volume.

Tenth Census (1880). Agriculture, 16 volumes; Manufactures, 4 volumes; Defective, Dependent and Delinquent Classes, 3 volumes.

Unpublished Theses

Much important research is contained in unpublished doctoral and masters' theses in history and related subjects. The titles of individual theses are cited under the appropriate subject headings below.

PUBLISHED MATERIALS

DOCUMENTS—UNITED STATES

All of the decennial censuses for the period covered by this volume are useful, but especially the one for 1880, which was much more comprehensive and detailed than the earlier ones.

United States Bureau of Census, *Seventh Census: Statistics of the United States* (1850).

——————, *Compendium of the Seventh Census* (1850).

——————, *Eighth Census* (1860), 4 vols.

——————, *Ninth Census* (1870), 4 vols.

——————, *Compendium of the Ninth Census* (1870).

——————, *Tenth Census* (1880), 22 vols.

——————, *Compendium of the Tenth Census* (1880) 2 vols.

Other useful publications are:

United States Commissioner of Patents, *Reports: Agriculture,* 1850-1862.

United States Department of Agriculture, *Reports of the Commissioner,* 1863-1880.

United States Department of the Treasury, *Reports of the Secretary,* 1864-1866.

——————, *Reports of the Comptroller of the Currency,* 1867-1880.

GOVERNMENT DOCUMENTS—INDIANA

Adjutant General, see below, p. 727.

Auditor, *Reports,* 1861-1880.

General Assembly, *Brevier Legislative Reports,* compiled by Ariel and William Drapier, vols. 1-18 (1858-1879).

——————, *Documentary Journal,* 1850-1880. (Includes reports of state officials which were published separately, also reports of state institutions and special committee investigations not found elsewhere. An *Index* to the reports was published in 1900.)

——————, *House Journal,* 1850-1880.

——————, *Laws,* 1850-1880.

——————, *Senate Journal,* 1850-1880.

State Board of Agriculture, *Reports,* 1851-1880.

State Geologist, *Annual Reports of the Geological Survey of Indiana,* 1869-1880.

Superintendent of Public Instruction, *Reports,* 1852-1880.

Supreme Court, *Reports,* 1850-1880.

NEWSPAPERS

The Indiana State Library and the Indiana University Library contain the largest collections of Indiana newspapers. See Chapter XIV for an account of the leading newspapers.

Newspapers enrich and illuminate almost every aspect of the history of the period, and on some subjects they are almost the only source of information. Throughout the period 1850 to 1880 the two most important newspapers were the *Indiana State Journal,* which became the Indianapolis *Daily Journal,* and the *Indiana State Sentinel,* which became the Indianapolis *Daily Sentinel.* (The *Sentinel* became the Indianapolis *Daily Herald* from 1865 to 1868, when the name *Sentinel* was resumed.) The *Journal* was Whig and later Republican in politics, while the *Sentinel* was Democratic. Both papers gave coverage to events all over the state, and while both were partisan, a fairly balanced picture of politics is achieved by using both of them. Other papers from other parts of the state are, of course, useful in supplementing these two papers. On such subjects as the antislavery movement, temperance, and the Greenback movement the newspapers published in support of these particular causes contain important information.

GENERAL WORKS

Barnhart, John D., and Carmony, Donald F., *Indiana. From Frontier to Industrial Commonwealth* (5 vols. [vols. 3-5 biographical], New York, 1954).

Dunn, Jacob Piatt, *Indiana and Indianans. A History of Aboriginal and Territorial Indiana and the Century of Statehood* (5 vols. [vols. 3-5 biographical], Chicago and New York, 1919).

Esarey, Logan, *History of Indiana from Its Exploration to 1922* (2 vols., Fort Wayne, Ind., 1924).

Illustrated Historical Atlas of the State of Indiana (Bastin, Forster & Co., Chicago, 1876). Especially helpful for county maps.

Roll, Charles, *Indiana: One Hundred and Fifty Years of American Development* (5 vols. [vols. 3-5 biographical], Chicago, 1931).

Smith, William Henry, *The History of the State of Indiana from the Earliest Explorations by the French to the Present Time* (2 vols., Indianapolis, 1903).

The *Indiana Historical Collections,* published by the Indiana Historical Bureau, and the Indiana Historical Society *Publications* include a number of scholarly works on aspects of the period from 1850 to 1880.

The *Indiana Magazine of History,* a quarterly published by the Department of History of Indiana University in co-operation with the Indiana Historical Society, is the most important journal for the publication of scholarly articles on Indiana history. Research embodied in articles has been invaluable in the writing of this volume, and numerous articles published in the *Magazine* are cited. There are composite indexes covering Volumes 1-25 and 26-50, and indexes by Volume beginning with 51.

COUNTY AND CITY HISTORIES

Most Indiana counties boast at least one history, and for several of them there are two or three. The largest number of these county histories, along with histories of some of the larger cities, was published in the 1880's. They were valuable in the preparation of this volume because the dates of their publication were so nearly contemporary with the period covered by it. Several other county and city histories were published in the early years of the twentieth century. Many of these local histories are uncritical and overly laudatory, but they contain information not found elsewhere, especially on social, economic, and cultural developments. There are complete collections of these histories in the Indiana Division of the Indiana State Library and the Indiana Historical Society Library.

Gazetteers and Travel Accounts

Of the numerous gazetteers and business directories the most valuable is *The Indiana Gazetteer, or Topographical Dictionary of the State of Indiana* (Indianapolis, 1850). It contains descriptions of all of the towns of Indiana and information on such subjects as agriculture, land, churches, and state institutions.

There are not so many descriptions of Indiana in accounts of western travel by Europeans and Americans after 1850 as during the pioneer period, but the Hoosier state received attention in several books. Among the more valuable accounts are those by Richard J. Beste, John Candler, William Ferguson, Rev. Frederick Jobson, Amelia M. Murray, and Francis and Theresa Pulszky.

Biographical Materials

GENERAL. William W. Woollen, *Biographical and Historical Sketches of Early Indiana* (Indianapolis, 1883) contains valuable contemporary observations. Also helpful are *A Biographical History of Eminent and Self-Made Men of the State of Indiana* (2 vols., Cincinnati, 1880); *Encyclopedia of Biography of Indiana* (2 vols., Chicago, 1895 and 1899); John H. B. Nowland, *Sketches of Prominent Citizens of 1876* (Indianapolis, 1877). In the Indiana Division of the Indiana State Library is the Indiana Biographical Series, a compilation of newspaper clippings.

POLITICAL. A number of political leaders have been the subjects of book-length biographies, while there are articles covering the careers of others.

William Dudley Foulke, *Life of Oliver P. Morton, Including His Important Speeches* (2 vols., Indianapolis, 1899) contains much valuable material but it is overly laudatory and not well documented. Willard Smith, *Schuyler Colfax. The Changing Fortunes of a Political Idol* (Indianapolis, 1952) is a scholarly and judicious work. George W. Julian's *Political Recollections, 1840-1872* (Chicago, 1884), which views the Indiana scene through the eyes of a radical reformer, is valuable. The biography of Julian by his daughter, Grace Julian Clarke, *George W. Julian* (Indianapolis, 1923) is useful but not entirely satisfactory. More recent and more scholarly is Patrick W. Riddleberger, George W. Julian, Nineteenth Century Reformer as Politician (Unpublished Ph.D. thesis in History, University of California, 1953). Charles Roll, *Colonel Dick Thompson. The Persistent Whig* (Indianapolis, 1948), is a sympathetic and competent treatment. The two volumes by Harry J. Sievers, S. J., *Benjamin Harrison, Hoosier Warrier, 1833-1865* (Chicago, 1952) and *Benjamin Harrison, Hoosier Statesman, 1865-1888* (New York, 1959) contain useful material but are uncritical. There is no full-scale biography of Henry Smith Lane, but there is an article by James A. Woodburn in the *Indiana Magazine of History*, XXVII (1931), 279-287. Publications which treat the careers of lesser Republican figures are: Louis J. Bailey, "Caleb Blood Smith," *ibid.*, XXIX (1933), 213-239; Joseph E. Holliday, "Daniel D. Pratt," *ibid.*, LVII (1961), 99-126 and LVIII (1962), 17-51; Matilda Gresham, *The Life of Walter Quintin Gresham 1832-1895* (2 vols., Chicago, 1919); Hugh McCulloch, *Men and Measures of Half a Century: Sketches and Comments* (New York, 1888); Elmo R. Richardson and Alan W. Farley, *John Palmer Usher, Lincoln's Secretary of the Interior* (University of Kansas Press, 1960).

Biographical works on Democratic leaders are less numerous. The only book on Hendricks is John W. Holcombe and Hubert M. Skinner, *Life and Public Services of Thomas Hendricks with Selected Speeches and Writings* (Indianapolis, 1886) which is a mere compilation put together after his death. On Bright there are Charles B. Murphy, *The Political Career of Jesse D. Bright* (Indianapolis, 1931) and Wayne J. Van Der Weele, Jesse David Bright, Master Politician from the Old Northwest (Unpublished Ph.D. thesis in History, Indiana University, 1958). The latter represents more extensive use of sources and is the more scholarly work. Philip M. Crane, Onus with Honor: A Political History of Joseph A. Wright, 1809-1857 (Unpublished Ph.D. thesis in History, Indiana University, 1961) treats of Wright's gubernatorial career but does little to relate Wright to the period in which he lived. Voorhees, probably the most colorful Democratic leader of the period, is the subject of a book by Leonard Kenworthy, *The Tall Sycamore of the Wabash: Daniel W. Voorhees* (Boston, 1936), and two articles: Henry D. Jordan, "Daniel Wolsey Voorhees," *Mississippi Valley Historical Review*, VI (1919-20), 532-555; and Frank Smith Bogardus, "Daniel W. Voorhees," *Indiana Magazine of History*, XXVII (1931), 91-103. Another colorful figure is dealt with in Howard R. Burnett, "The Last Pioneer Governor of Indiana—'Blue Jeans' Williams," *ibid.*, XXII (1926), 101-130. The career of William S. Holman is covered in Israel George Blake, *The Holmans of Veraestau* (Oxford, Ohio, 1943). David Turpie has left his memoirs in *Sketches of My Own Times* (Indianapolis, 1903).

MISCELLANEOUS. Lew Wallace, who was an important military figure and influential in politics as well as being Indiana's most distinguished author, has left a somewhat romanticized account of his own life in *Lew Wallace. An Autobiography* (2 vols., New York, 1906). A good picture of Wallace's Indiana years is drawn in Irving McKee, *"Ben-Hur" Wallace. The Life of General Lew Wallace* (Berkeley, Calif., 1947). There is a good account of

Robert Dale Owen's career as a reformer and politician in Indiana in Richard W. Leopold, *Robert Dale Owen. A Biography* (Cambridge, Mass., 1940). Owen's two brothers, who are less famous, are treated in Victor L. Albjerg, *Richard Owen* (Purdue University, 1946) and Walter B. Hendrickson, *David Dale Owen* (Indianapolis, 1943). David Starr Jordan deals briefly with his early experiences in Indiana during the 1870's in his autobiography, *The Days of A Man, Being Memories of A Naturalist, Teacher and Minor Prophet of Democracy* (2 vols., New York, 1922). Katherine Merrill Graydon (comp.), *Catharine Merrill. Life and Letters* (Greenfield, Ind., 1934) is an account of a woman teacher who also wrote a history of Indiana's troops in the Civil War.

POLITICAL HISTORY

The following are useful as reference materials: *Appletons' Annual Cyclopædia and Register of Important Events;* W. E. Henry (comp.), *State Platforms of the Two Dominant Political Parties in Indiana 1850-1900* (Indianapolis, 1902); Charles Kettleborough (ed.), *Constitution Making in Indiana. A Source Book of Constitutional Documents with Historical Introduction and Critical Notes* (3 vols., Indianapolis, 1916-1930); Robert J. Pitchell, *Indiana Votes: Elections for Governor 1852-1956; Elections for United States Senator 1914-1958* (Bureau of Government Research, Indiana University, 1960).

Much of the biographical material listed above is principally concerned with political developments. The best single monograph on Indiana politics for the period covered by this book is Kenneth Stampp, *Indiana Politics during the Civil War* (Indianapolis, 1949). There is nothing comparable for the 1850's or the postwar years, but there are numerous useful articles and some good unpublished theses. The theses include those of Harvey L. Carter, A Decade of Hoosier History: Indiana, 1850-1860 (Unpublished Ph.D. thesis in History, University of Wisconsin, 1938); Mildred C. Stoler, Influence of the Democratic Element in the Republican Party of Illinois and Indiana, 1854-1860 (Unpublished Ph.D. thesis in History, Indiana University, 1938); and Roger Van Bolt, The Rise of the Republican Party in Indiana (Unpublished Ph.D. thesis in History, University of Chicago, 1950). Most of the Van Bolt thesis and the parts of the Stoler thesis pertaining to Indiana have been published in the *Indiana Magazine of History*. Other articles in the *Magazine* which have been useful for political history are those of A. Dale Beeler, Carl Fremont Brand, William G. Carleton, O. B. Carmichael, William S. Garber, Winfred A. Harbison, Reinhard H. Luthin, Charles Roll, J. Herman Schauinger, Willard H. Smith, Kenneth Stampp, Wendell Holmes Stephenson, Emma Lou Thornbrough, Charles Zimmerman, and William F. Zornow. See General Indexes for Vols. I-XXV and XXVI-L, and indexes in each volume beginning with LI. Also in the *Magazine* are Letters of Jesse D. Bright to William H. English, and Letters to John G. Davis.

The following articles in the *Mississippi Valley Historical Review* have been helpful: Walter R. Sharp, "Henry S. Lane and the Formation of the Republican Party in Indiana," Vol. VII, 93-112; Willard H. Smith, "Schuyler Colfax and the Political Upheaval of 1854-1855," Vol. XXVIII, 383-398; Kenneth

M. Stampp, "The Milligan Case and the Election of 1864 in Indiana," Vol. XXXI, 41-58.

On the subject of secret societies, Copperheads, disloyalty, and treason trials the following are useful: *Report and Evidence of the Committee on Arbitrary Arrests in the State of Indiana, authorized by Resolution of the House of Representatives* (Indianapolis, 1863); Samuel Klaus (ed.), *The Milligan Case (American Trials,* New York, 1929); Frank L. Klement, *The Copperheads in the Middle West* (University of Chicago Press, 1960); Gilbert R. Tredway, Indiana against the Administration 1861-1865 (Unpublished Ph.D. thesis in History, Indiana University, 1962); Mayo Fesler, "Secret Political Societies in the North," in *Indiana Magazine of History,* XIV (1918), 183-286; Frank L. Klement, "Middle Western Copperheadism and the Genesis of the Granger Movement," *Mississippi Valley Historical Review,* XXXVIII (1951-52), 679-694.

The best single work on the antislavery movement is Marion C. Miller, The Antislavery Movement in Indiana (Unpublished Ph.D. thesis in History, University of Michigan, 1938); on the Negro, Emma Lou Thornbrough, *The Negro in Indiana before 1900. A Study of a Minority* (Indianapolis, 1957). Also useful are: Robert Oldham Fife, Alexander Campbell and the Christian Church in the Slavery Controversy (Unpublished Ph.D. thesis in History, Indiana University, 1961); Thomas E. Drake, *Quakers and Slavery in America* (New Haven, Conn., 1950); Walter Edgerton, *A History of the Separation in the Yearly Meeting of Friends* . . .(Cincinnati, 1856); Etta Reeves French, "Stephen S. Harding: A Hoosier Abolitionist," *Indiana Magazine of History,* XXVII (1931), 207-229; Charles A. Money, "The Fugitive Slave Law of 1850 in Indiana," *ibid.,* XVII (1921), 159-198, 257-297; Patrick W. Riddleberger, "The Making of a Political Abolitionist: George W. Julian and the Free Soilers," *ibid.,* LI (1955), 221-236; William O. Lynch, "Anti-Slavery Tendencies of the Democratic Party in the Northwest, 1848-1850," *Mississippi Valley Historical Review,* XI (1924-25), 319-331; Ruth Ketring Nuermberger, *The Free Produce Movement. A Quaker Protest* (Duke University Press, 1942). The antislavery newspapers, Indianapolis *Free Democrat, The Free Labor Advocate and Anti-Slavery Chronicle* and *The Protectionist* (the last two published at New Garden in Wayne County), are all useful.

On Temperance, the most useful secondary accounts are Charles E. Canup, "Temperance Movements and Legislation in Indiana," *Indiana Magazine of History,* XVI (1920), 1-37, 112-151, and the chapter on Temperance in Dunn, *Indiana and Indianans.* Both of these draw on Thomas A. Goodwin, *Seventy Years Tussle with the Traffic* . . . (Indianapolis, 1883), an account by one who was active for many years in the fight against alcohol. The numerous temperance newspapers, most of which were short-lived, are useful. See Chapter I, n. 53. The *Proceedings* of the Grand Division of the Sons of Temperance also contain valuable material.

CIVIL WAR

It is somewhat surprising in view of the widespread popular interest in the subject and the attention focused on the Civil War by the observance of the centennial that there has been little scholarly writing on the military aspects of Indiana's part in the war. There are abundant source materials which have been largely neglected.

SOURCE MATERIALS. Many of the manuscript collections listed above contain materials on the Civil War. In addition to those listed there are numerous diaries and smaller collections of letters. In recent years, as a part of the observance of the centennial of the war, the Indiana Historical Society Library has acquired microfilms of numerous Civil War letters and diaries which are still privately owned but which were loaned for filming and are available for research.

The records of the Adjutant General contain an immense amount of material on the Civil War and are well indexed. See above, p. 719.

PRINTED SOURCES AND CONTEMPORARY ACCOUNTS. Most valuable is W. H. H. Terrell, *Report of the Adjutant General of Indiana* (8 vols., Indianapolis, 1869). Volume I is a narrative of Indiana's role in the war; Volumes II and III contain rosters of officers and brief regimental histories; Volumes IV-VIII contain rosters of enlisted men and statistics on such matters as prisoners of war and deserters. Terrell's narrative is somewhat partisan in its laudatory treatment of Morton and its emphasis upon alleged Democratic disloyalty, but his compilation is indispensable for military history. Volume I of the *Report* was reprinted in 1960 by the Indiana Historical Bureau and the Indiana Historical Society as *Indiana in the War of the Rebellion. Report of the Adjutant General.* A publication of the Federal government, *The War of the Rebellion: A Compilation of the Official Records of the Union and Confederate Armies* (4 series, 70 vols., Washington, D.C., 1880-1901) contains much on Indiana's military role. Statistical materials on enlistments, army organization, commanders, engagements, and losses for the Union army have been extracted from the *War of the Rebellion Records* in Frederick H. Dyer, *A Compendium of the War of the Rebellion* (With an introduction by Bell Irwin Wiley. 3 volumes, New York and London, 1959).

Printed Civil War diaries and letters are too numerous to list. Many of them have appeared in the *Indiana Magazine of History* and are cited in the index volumes of that publication. Of more than usual interest are: *The 1864 Diary of Lt. Col. Jefferson K. Scott, 59th Indiana Volunteer Infantry,* published jointly by the Monroe County Civil War Centennial Commission and Monroe County Historical Society, Bloomington, 1962; Albert T. Volwiler (ed.), "Letters from a Civil War Officer," *Mississippi Valley Historical Review,* XIV (1927-28), 508-529; Oscar O. Winther (ed.), *With Sherman to the Sea. The Civil War Letters, Diaries & Reminiscences of Theodore F. Upson* (Bloomington, Ind., 1958).

Two accounts of the military record of Indiana troops, written during the war and compiled principally from newspaper dispatches and letters, are: [Catharine Merrill] *The Soldier of Indiana in the War for the Union* (2 volumes, Indianapolis, 1866, 1869) and David Stevenson and Theodore T. Scribner, *Indiana's Roll of Honor* (2 volumes, Indianapolis, 1864, 1866). Although the authors were in no sense experts on military history these two works remain the most comprehensive accounts of the military engagements fought by Indiana troops.

The Indiana *Documentary Journals* contain a number of reports which are valuable for the picture they give of the work of the various state agencies which helped equip and care for Indiana troops. For a list of these see General Index to *Documentary Journal*. Also valuable is *Proceedings of the Indiana Sanitary Convention Held in Indianapolis Indiana, March 2, 1864* (Indianapolis, 1864).

SECONDARY WORKS

See above for works on the political history of the war years.

The following general works on military history are valuable: William J. Fox, *Regimental Losses in the American Civil War 1861-1865* (Albany, N. Y., 1893); Robert U. Johnson and Clarence C. Buel (eds.), *Battles and Leaders of the Civil War* (4 vols., New York, 1887); Kenneth P. Williams, *Lincoln Finds A General. A Military Study of the Civil War* (5 vols., New York, 1949-1959).

Regimental histories and memorial accounts of battles in which Indiana troops were engaged are too numerous to list. There is a large collection of these works in the Indiana State Library, but few of them are in any sense scholarly. A recent work, Alan T. Nolan, *The Iron Brigade. A Military History* (New York, 1961), contains an excellent account of the Indiana Nineteenth, but there is nothing comparable for other Indiana regiments. Accounts of Morgan's raid are found in: Basil W. Duke, *A History of Morgan's Cavalry (Civil War Centennial Series,* Indiana University Press, 1960); Allan Keller, *Morgan's Raid* (Indianapolis, 1961); William E. Wilson, "Thunderbolt of the Confederacy," *Indiana Magazine of History,* LIV (1958), 119-130.

Other aspects of the war are dealt with in John D. Barnhart, "The Impact of the Civil War on Indiana," *ibid.,* LVII (1961), 185-224; Charles Canup, "Conscription and Draft in Indiana," *ibid.,* X (1914), 70-83; Joseph A. Parsons, Jr., "Indiana and the Call for Volunteers, April, 1861," *ibid.,* LIV (1958), 1-24; Kenneth M. Stampp, "The Impact of the Civil War upon Hoosier Society," *ibid.,* XXXVIII (1942), 1-16; James O. Barnett, "The Bounty Jumpers of Indiana," *Civil War History,* IV (1958), 429-436; John H. Holliday, *Indianapolis and the Civil War* (Indianapolis, 1911); Olin D. Morrison, "Indiana's Care of Her Soldiers in the Field, 1861-1865," in *Studies in American History Inscribed to James Albert Woodburn* (Bloomington, 1926); Hattie Winslow and Joseph Moore, *Camp Morton 1861-1865* (Indianapolis, 1941).

ECONOMIC HISTORY

Except for a few special studies there is a dearth of scholarly research on economic subjects. There is no satisfactory general account of economic developments.

AGRICULTURE

SOURCE MATERIALS. Although not entirely reliable, the statistical reports on agriculture in the United States Censuses are indispensable. The *Reports of the Commissioner of Agriculture* of the United States Department of Agriculture are useful. The *Annual Reports* of the Indiana State Board of Agriculture contain information on methods of farming, farm products, machinery, fairs, agricultural societies, and other matters. The *Proceedings* of the Indiana State Grange are valuable as are also the agricultural journals mentioned in Chapter IX.

SECONDARY MATERIALS

I. Falconer, *History of Agriculture in the Northern United States, 1620-1860* (New York, 1941) ; Solon Buck, *The Granger Movement* (Harvard University Press, 1913) ; "Making a Farm on the Frontier: Diary of Mitchell Young Jackson, Wabash, Indiana, 1852," *Agricultural History*, IV (1930), 92-120; Harvey L. Carter, "Rural Indiana in Transition, 1850-1860," *ibid.*, XX (1946), 107-121; John Collett, *The State of Indiana* (Indianapolis, 1880) ; *Emigration to the United States of North America. Indiana as a Home for Emigrants* (Prepared and Published under the Direction and Authority of Oliver P. Morton, Governor of Indiana, Indianapolis, 1864) ; [Paul L. Farris and R. S. Euler], *Prices of Indiana Farm Products 1841-1955* (Agricultural Experiment Station, *Bulletin 644*, Purdue University, 1957) ; Richard S. Fisher, *Indiana: In Relation to Its Geography, Statistics, Institutions* (New York, 1852) ; *A General Description of Indiana . . . Compiled by the State Board of Agriculture for Information of Those Seeking Homes* (Indianapolis, 1877) ; Paul W. Gates, "Hoosier Cattle Kings," *Indiana Magazine of History*, XLIV (1948), 1-24; ———, "Land Policy and Tenancy in the Prairie Counties of Indiana," *ibid.*, XXXV (1939), 1-26; William Latta, *Outline History of Indiana Agriculture* (Lafayette, Ind., 1938) ; Edward Winslow Martin (pseud.), *History of the Granger Movement: Or, The Farmer's War Against Monopolies* (Chicago, 1873) ; Fred A. Shannon, *The Farmer's Last Frontier. Agriculture, 1860-1897 (The Economic History of the United States,* V, New York, 1945).

BANKING

SOURCE MATERIALS. *Journal of the Bank Investigating Committee: A Select Committee of the Indiana Senate, 1857* (Indianapolis, 1857) ; the Indiana Auditor's *Reports;* the *Reports of the Secretary of the Treasury* and the *Reports of the Comptroller of the Currency* of the United States Department of the Treasury.

SECONDARY MATERIALS. Logan Esarey, *State Banking in Indiana 1814-1873* (Indiana University *Studies* No. 15, Bloomington, 1912) deals with the Second State Bank, the Bank of the State of Indiana, and free banking, but there is no study which deals with the history of the National Banks in Indiana or the state banks of the period after the Civil War. The following supplement Esarey or deal with aspects of banking which he does not cover: Anderson, The National Banking System, 1865-1875: A Sectional Institution (Unpublished Ph.D. thesis in History, University of Illinois, 1933) ; George E. Barnett, *State Banks and Trust Companies since the Passage of the National*

Bank Act (National Monetary Commission Report, *Senate Documents,* 61 Congress, 3 Session, II, No. 659, Washington, 1911); Harold Knight Forsythe, "Growth of State and National Banks in Indiana," *The Hoosier Banker,* August, 1920 to February, 1921; Bray Hammond, *Banks and Politics in America from the Revolution to the Civil War* (Princeton, N.J., 1957); Leonard C. Helderman, *National and State Banks. A Study of Their Origins* (Boston, 1931).

MANUFACTURING, MINING, AND LABOR

SOURCE MATERIALS. The following volumes of the *Tenth Census of the United States* (1880) are especially valuable: II: *Report on the Manufactures of the United States* . . .; XV: *Report on the Mining Industries of the United States;* XX: *Report on the Statistics of Wages in Manufacturing Industries.* There is useful information in the Mine Inspector of Indiana, *Annual Report,* 1880-1881.

SECONDARY MATERIALS. Some of the best research is to be found in unpublished theses. The following contain important information: William Edward Bean, The Soft Coal Industry of Southern Indiana (Unpublished A.B. thesis in Economics, Indiana University, 1922); Victor Bogle, A Nineteenth Century River Town: New Albany (Unpublished Ph.D. thesis in History, Boston University, 1951); Frederick D. Kershner, A Social and Cultural History of Indianapolis, 1860-1914 (Unpublished Ph.D. thesis in History, University of Wisconsin, 1950); Osmond La Var Harline, Economics of the Indiana Coal Mining Industry (Unpublished Ph.D. thesis in Economics, Indiana University, 1958); Bernard A. Hewes, The Rise of the Pork Industry in Indiana (Unpublished Master's thesis in History, Indiana University, 1939); Douglas Laing Meikle, James Oliver and the Oliver Chilled Plow Works (Ph.D. thesis in History, Indiana University, 1958); Stephen G. Savage, James Howard of Jeffersonville, Master Builder of Steamboats (Unpublished Master's thesis in History, Indiana University, 1952).

The following published works are useful: Alden Cutshall, "Terre Haute Iron and Steel: A Declining Industry," *Indiana Magazine of History,* XXXVII (1941), 237-244; Joseph A. Batchelor, *An Economic History of the Indiana Oolitic Limestone Industry* (Indiana University *Studies in Business,* no. 27, Bloomington, 1944); Victor M. Bogle, "New Albany: Mid-Nineteenth Century Economic Expansion," *Indiana Magazine of History,* LIII (1957) 127-146; Albert Russell Erskine, *History of the Studebaker Corporation* (The Studebaker Corporation, 1924); Stephen Longstreet, *A Century on Wheels. The Story of Studebaker, 1852-1952* (New York, 1952); *Manufacturing and Mercantile Resources of Indianapolis, Indiana* (Pt. IV, *Resources and Industries of Indiana,* n.p., 1883); Edward Winslow Martin [pseud.], *History of the Great Riots* (Philadelphia, 1877); George W. Starr, *Industrial Development of Indiana* (Indiana University *Studies in Business,* no. 14, Bloomington, 1937).

RAILROADS AND TRANSPORTATION

SOURCE MATERIALS. For the early history of the railroads valuable information is found in the reports and promotional literature published by the various companies. The Indiana Division of the Indiana State Library contains a good collection, including annual reports of the Indianapolis and Bellefontaine, the Indianapolis and Cincinnati, the Jeffersonville, the Evansville, Indianapolis, and Cleveland, the Terre Haute and Indianapolis, the Lafayette and Indianapolis, and the Toledo and Wabash railroads.

The single most important source of information on railroads is Henry V. Poor (comp.), *Manual of the Railroads of the United States* (New York), which was first published in 1868 and appeared annually thereafter. Also valuable is the *Tenth Census of the United States* (1880), X: *Transportation*.

SECONDARY MATERIALS. Victor M. Bogle, "Railroad Building in Indiana, 1850-1855," *Indiana Magazine of History*, LVIII (1962), 211-232; Ared M. Murphy, "The Big Four Railroad in Indiana," *ibid.*, XXI (1925), 109-273; Wylie Daniels, *The Village at the End of the Road* (Indianapolis, 1938). Also useful are: Freda L. Bridenstine, The Madison and Indianapolis Railroad (Unpublished Master's thesis in History, Butler University, 1931); Harvey L. Carter, Decade of Hoosier History; Logan Esarey, *Internal Improvements in Early Indiana* (Indianapolis, 1912); Frank F. Hargrave, *A Pioneer Indiana Railroad. The Origin and Development of the Monon* (Indianapolis, 1932); Marie Johnston, "The Building of the Grand Rapids and Indiana Railroad," *Indiana Magazine of History*, XLI (1945), 152-166; "Matter Relating to the National Road in Indiana," *ibid.*, III (1907), 74-79; "Road Improvements in Indiana," *ibid.*, III, 81-83; Walter Nelles, "A Strike and Its Legal Consequences," *Yale Law Journal*, XL (1931), 507-554; Oran Perry (comp.), *History of Evansville and Indianapolis Railroad and Constituent Companies* (n.p., 1917); Frederic L. Paxson, "The Railroads of the 'Old Northwest' before the Civil War," *Transactions* of the Wisconsin Academy of Sciences, Arts and Letters, XVII, Pt. 1, pp. 243-274; Thomas C. Perring, "The New Albany-Salem Railroad," *Indiana Magazine of History*, XV (1919), 342-362; John Poucher, "Social Effects of the Monon Railway in Indiana," *ibid.*, XII (1916), 326-336; William Reser, "The Wabash and Erie Canal at Lafayette," *ibid.*, XXX (1934), 311-324; "The Roads and Road Materials of Indiana," Indiana Department of Geology and Natural Resources, *Annual Report*, 1905; Oliver H. Smith, "The Railroads of Indiana," Indiana State Board of Agriculture, *Annual Report*, 1856, pp. 477-490.

Population Changes

A number of studies have been made of elements in the population of Indiana but much remains to be done. Some work has been done on the German element, notably the articles by Elfrieda Lang on the Germans in Dubois County which are published in the *Indiana Magazine of History*, Vols. XLI-XLII, and which deal principally with the period before 1850. There are no scholarly studies of the German population for the state as a whole nor for the cities where German influence was most important. The Irish have been almost entirely ignored as have other ethnic groups, including Jewish immigrants.

SOURCE MATERIALS. Most important are the United States censuses. In addition to the volumes listed above, p. 721, the Genealogy Division of the Indiana State Library has microfilms of the original manuscript censuses of population in Indiana for 1850, 1860, 1870, and 1880.

SECONDARY WORKS. Vonneda Dunn Bailey, The Germans in Indiana, with Economic Emphasis (Unpublished Master's thesis in Economics, Indiana University, 1946); Fred J. Bartel, *The Institutional Influence of the German Element of the Population in Richmond, Indiana* (Wayne County Historical Society *Papers*, I, No. 2, Richmond, 1905); William A. Fritsch, *German Settlers and German Settlements in Indiana* (Evansville, 1915); Josephine Goldmark, *Pilgrims of '48* (Yale University Press, 1930); Theodore G. Probst, The Germans in Indianapolis 1850-1914 (Unpublished Master's thesis in History, Indiana University, 1951); Theodore Stein, *Our Old School: Historical Sketches of the German English Independent School of Indianapolis* (Indianapolis, 1913); articles by Maurice G. Baxter, Leon M. Gordon, Robert LaFollette, Elfrieda Lang, Chelsea Lawlis, and Stephen S. Visher in the *Indiana Magazine of History* (see Index volumes); Robert L. LaFollette, "Interstate Migration and Indiana Culture," *Mississippi Valley Historical Review*, XVI (1929-30), 347-358; Elfrieda Lang, "Irishmen in Northern Indiana before 1850," *Mid-America*, XXXVI (N.S. XXV, 1954), 190-198; F. F. Lalor, "The Germans in the West," *Atlantic Monthly*, XXXII (1873), 459-470.

URBANIZATION

Scholarly works on this subject are all too few. In addition to the statistics on population contained in the various United States census reports there is valuable information in United States Bureau of the Census, *Tenth Census* (1880), XIX, *Social Statistics of Cities*. City and county histories contain valuable information. More recent studies are Victor M. Bogle, "A View of New Albany Society at Mid-Nineteenth Century," *Indiana Magazine of History*, LIV (1958), 93-118; Daniels, *Village of the End of the Road;* Kershner, Social and Cultural History of Indianapolis; James E. Morlock, *The Evansville Story: A Cultural Interpretation* (Evansville, 1956).

BENEVOLENT AND PENAL INSTITUTIONS

SOURCE MATERIALS. Reports of various institutions in Indiana *Documentary Journal; Report of the Committee on Prisons, together with the Evidence of the Officers and Others before the Committee at the Southern Prison* (Indianapolis, 1869); *Testimony in the Southern Prison Investigation* (Indianapolis, 1875).

SECONDARY MATERIALS. Barbara Brandon, The State Care of the Insane in Indiana 1840-1890 (Unpublished Master's thesis, School of Social Service Administration, University of Chicago, 1938); Amos Butler, *A Century of Progress: A Study of the Development of Public Charities and Correction 1790-1895* [1916]; Charles F. Coffin, *Our Prisons* (Indianapolis, 1880); Mary Coffin Johnson (ed.), *Rhoda M. Coffin, Her Reminiscences Ad-*

dresses Papers and Ancestry (New York, 1910); Alice Shaffer, *et al., The Indiana Poor Law: Its Development and Administration with Special Reference to the Provision of State Care for the Sick Poor (Social Service Monographs,* University of Chicago, 1936); Helen Wilson, *The Treatment of the Misdemeanant in Indiana, 1816-1936 (Social Service Monographs,* University of Chicago, 1936); Walter C. Woodward, *Timothy Nicholson, Master Quaker* (Richmond, Ind., 1927).

EDUCATION

SOURCE MATERIALS. The *Reports* of the State Superintendent of Public Instruction are indispensable for a study of the development of the public school system and contain useful information on other aspects of education. An extensive collection of catalogues and bulletins of Indiana academies and colleges in the Indiana Division of the Indiana State Library contains much valuable information.

SECONDARY MATERIALS

PUBLIC SCHOOL SYSTEM. Richard G. Boone, *A History of Education in Indiana* (New York, 1892. Reprinted by Indiana Historical Bureau, Indianapolis, 1941), although old is still the best general account of the development of the public school system. The following are also useful: Warren F. Collins, A History of the Indiana State Teachers Association (Unpublished Master's thesis in Education, Indiana University, 1926); C. Ross Dean, The Development of State Control of Secondary Education in Indiana (Unpublished Ph.D. thesis in Education, Indiana University, 1947); Frances H. Ellis, "Historical Account of German Instruction in the Public Schools of Indianapolis, 1869-1919," *Indiana Magazine of History,* L (1954), 119-138, 251-276, 357-380; Oscar Findley, *Development of the High School in Indiana* (n.p., 1925); Everett E. Jarboe, The Development of the Public School System in Indiana from 1840 through 1870 (Unpublished Ph.D. thesis in Education, Indiana University, 1949); Harold Littell, "Development of the City School System of Indiana, 1851-1880," *Indiana Magazine of History,* XII (1916), 193-213, 299-325; Charles W. Moores, *Caleb Mills and the Indiana School System* (Indianapolis, 1905); Val Nolan, Jr., "Caleb Mills and the Indiana Free School Law," *Indiana Magazine of History,* XLIX (1953), 81-90; James H. Smart (ed.), *The Indiana Schools and the Men Who Have Worked in Them* (Cincinnati, 1876).

ACADEMIES. Sadie Bacon Hatcher, *A History of Spiceland Academy, 1826-1921* (Indianapolis, 1934); Ethel Hittle McDaniel, *The Contribution of the Society of Friends to Education in Indiana* (Indianapolis, 1939); Albert Mock, The Mid-Western Academy Movement: A Comprehensive Study of Indiana Academies 1810-1900 (Mimeographed. Copyright, 1949 by Albert Mock); John Hardin Thomas, "The Academies of Indiana," *Indiana Magazine of History,* X (1914), 332-358, and XI (1915), 8-35; William C. Thompson, "Eleutherian Institute," *ibid.,* XIX (1923), 109-131.

HIGHER EDUCATION. There is no general history of higher education in Indiana. All of the individual institutions have histories of some sort; most of them are principally chronicles which do little to relate the institution to the intellectual and social climate of the era. For the principal ones, see the citations to the accounts of these schools in Chapter XI.

RELIGION

Church history and the history of religious thought have been largely neglected by historians. There are many opportunities for research in these fields.

Records of the Baptist, Congregational, Episcopal, Friends, Methodist, and Presbyterian churches may be found in the Indiana Division of the State Library and are cited in the accounts of these denominations in Chapter XIII. DePauw University at Greencastle is the principal depository for Indiana Methodist material; Franklin College has Baptist material, and the University of Notre Dame has Catholic archives.

Secondary material is available for all the denominations studied in the period from 1850 to 1880. See the footnotes in Chapter XIII for the publications that have been most helpful.

CULTURAL AND INTELLECTUAL HISTORY

GENERAL ACCOUNTS

The histories of Indianapolis by Dunn, Holloway, and Sulgrove all contain excellent material on cultural history as does the thesis by Kershner on Social and Cultural Development of Indianapolis. Also useful is Eva Draegert, Indianapolis: The Culture of an Inland City (Unpublished Ph.D. thesis in History, Indiana University, 1952), parts of which were published in the *Indiana Magazine of History,* vols. L-LIII. Some of the county histories contain good material on the cultural development of other cities.

ARTS AND ARCHITECTURE

Wilbur D. Peat, *Pioneer Painters of Indiana* (Indianapolis, 1954) is a detailed and scholarly treatment. Also useful are Mary Q. Burnet, *Art and Artists of Indiana* (New York, 1921); Opal Thornburg, "Marcus Mote and His Pioneer School of Design," *Indiana Magazine of History,* LI (1955); Wilbur D. Peat, *Indiana Houses of the Nineteenth Century* (Indiana Historical Society, Indianapolis, 1962) is a distinguished book on domestic architecture. There is nothing comparable on public architecture, but the following are useful: Lee Burns, *Early Architects and Builders of Indiana* (Indianapolis, 1935); J. D. Forbes, *Victorian Architect. The Life and Works of William Tinsley* (Indiana University Press, 1953); Howard E. Wooden, *Architectural Heritage of Evansville. An Interpretive Review of the Nineteenth Century* (Evansville, 1962).

LIBRARIES, LITERATURE, AND HISTORY

On libraries and literary tastes the following are useful: Jacob Piatt Dunn, *The Libraries of Indiana* (Indianapolis, 1893); Ella Lonn, "The History of an Unusual Library," *Indiana Magazine of History,* XIX (1923), 209-226; Story of the Madison Library Association compiled by Miss E. M. Garber (Typewritten manuscript, 1928, Indiana Division, Indiana State Library); LaVern Walther, Legal and Governmental Aspects of Public Library Development in Indiana 1816-1953 (Unpublished Ph.D. thesis in Education, Indiana University, 1957); Theodore Vonnegut, *Indianapolis Booksellers and Their Literary Background* (Greenfield, Ind., 1926).

Arthur W. Shumaker, *A History of Indiana Literature (Indiana Historical Collections,* XLII, Indianapolis, 1962) is a detailed and comprehensive treatment which includes the writers of the period from 1850 to 1880. Other useful works on literary efforts are: Richard E. Banta (ed.) *Indiana Authors and Their Books 1816-1916* (Crawfordsville, Ind., 1949); William T. Coggeshall, *The Poets and Poetry of the West: With Biographical and Critical Notices* (Columbus, Ohio, 1860); Irving McKee, *"Ben-Hur" Wallace.* The following deal with early interest in Indiana history and historical writing: John Coburn, *Life and Services of John B. Dillon, with a Sketch by Judge Horace P. Biddle* (Indianapolis, 1886); George S. Cottman, "John Brown Dillon, The Father of Indiana History," *Indiana Magazine of History,* I (1905), 1-6; *Centennial Handbook Indiana Historical Society 1830-1930.*

JOURNALISM

The newspapers and journals themselves are the best sources. There is much valuable information in "The Newspaper and Periodical Press" United States Bureau of the Census, *Tenth Census* (1880), VIII. The following articles are also useful: Frank S. Baker, "Michael C. Garber, Sr., and the Early Years of the Madison, Indiana, *Daily Courier,"* *Indiana Magazine of History,* XLVIII (1952), 397-408; Oscar L. Bockstahler, "The German Press in Indiana," *ibid.,* 161-168; James Hanna Butler, "Indiana Newspapers 1829-1860," *ibid.,* XXII (1926), 297-334; Donald F. Carmony, "Highlights in Indiana Newspaper History," *Indiana Publisher,* October, 1944 to February, 1945.

MUSIC AND THE THEATER

Martha F. Bellinger, "Music in Indianapolis, 1821-1900," *Indiana Magazine of History,* XLI (1945), pp. 345-362; and Eva Draegert's articles on music and the theater in *ibid.,* LI, LIII.

SCIENCE AND MEDICINE

SOURCE MATERIALS. The following reports contain information on other scientific studies as well as geology: Richard Owen, *Report of a Geological Reconnoissance of Indiana made during the years 1859-1860* (Indianapolis, 1862); *Annual Reports* of the State Geologist, 1869-1880. The annual *Proceedings* and *Transactions* of the Indiana State Medical Society, 1851-1880, are extremely valuable for information not only on medicine but other aspects of scientific knowledge.

SECONDARY MATERIALS. The articles on the history of science in the Indiana Academy of Science *Proceedings* are valuable. Articles by S. C. Adams, W. S. Blatchley, Lawrence K. Boyce, Will E. Edington, Theodor Just, Clyde Malott, and Truman G. Yuncker touch on scientists and scientific studies in the period from 1850 to 1880. The biographies of Richard Owen and David Dale Owen contain material on scientific developments. Also useful are W. F. King, *One Hundred Years of Public Health in Indiana* (Indianapolis, 1921); G. W. H. Kemper, *A Medical History of the State of Indiana* (Chicago, 1911); Dorothy Russo (ed.), *One Hundred Years of Indiana Medicine* (n.p., 1949).

INDEX

Abolition of slavery, as political issue, 50, 75, 98, 103; denied as aim of war, 111-112; as military measure, 114. *See also* Emancipation.

Academies, 485-490, 510, 525n.

Adams, Charles Francis, 250.

Agricultural college, establishment of, 525-527. *See also* Purdue University.

Agricultural periodicals, 396-397.

Agricultural societies, 395-396.

Agriculture, percentage of population engaged in, 362-363, 423, 439; corn-hog basis of, 368-370, 381; size of farms, 369; farm tenancy, 368, 369; farm equipment and machinery, 374-380, 420; diversification and rotation of crops, 379-381; conservation and fertilization of soil, 379-381; prices, 393-394; investment in, and value of products, 394; effort at improvements in farming methods, 394-397; effect of secession on, 100; of depression on, 393; of railroads on, 336; impact of Grange on, 399; *crops:* clover, 380; corn, 368-369, 370-371, 377-378, 381, 390, 393; fruit, 374; hay, 373-374; oats, 372-373; tobacco, 373; wheat, 371-372, 378-379, 391; *livestock:* improvement of breeds, 382, 386-387, 388, 389; cattle, 368, 383-387; hogs, 381-382, 392-393n; horses, 387-388; oxen, 387; sheep, 388-389. *See also* Farmers, Farms.

Aliens, suffrage granted to, 39-40, 544.

American Antislavery Society, 18.

American Colonization Society, 16.

American Home Missionary Society, 606-607.

American Knights, 215.

American party, *see* Know Nothing movement.

American Woman's Suffrage Association, 261.

Amish, 613.

Andrews, John, 138.

Anti-Nebraska Democrats, 61-62.

Antislavery movement, 18-28; societies, 20; and churches, 13, 20-25, 98; and politics, 24-25, 28; publications, 20n, 24n; opposition to Fugitive Slave Law, 50. *See also* Abolition of slavery.

Appomattox, surrender at, 160.

Archaeology, 661.

Architecture, of churches, 600, 602, 637; homes, 575; public buildings, 574-575, 698; schoolhouses, 476.

Arsenal, state, 165-167, 189; attack on, feared, 202; United States, 166.

Asbury University, *see* Indiana Asbury University.

Associated Press, 681, 684.

Baker, Conrad, 282, 544; sketch, 252n; in Civil War, 129, 133, 146, 201; lieutenant governor, 210; *governor,* succeeds Morton as, 239; nomination and election, 240, 241; on woman suffrage, 261; proclamation against mobs, 271; on education of Negroes, 482; on prison reform, 590, 591-592, 596; letter from William Cumback, 241-242n.